Culture and Anarchy Arnold's most famous and widely read work—a masterpiece of political and social thought that is as relevant today as when first written 100 years ago. In this work Arnold developed such concepts as "Sweetness and light" and "Hebraism and Hellenism." His comments on middle-class Philistines and their relationship to English democracy have become guideposts for modern social criticism. *Culture and Anarchy* represents Arnold's peak both as a thinker and as a master of the English language.

This volume includes not only the complete *Culture and Anarchy* but also *Friendship's Garland,* a collection of letters Arnold wrote to the editor of the *Pall Mall Gazette,* and four shorter pieces—*Theodore Parker, A New History of Greece, Obermann,* and *Sainte-Beuve.* In all these works Arnold deals with the political, social, and literary issues of his day. His theme is a recurrent one: democracy without standards of perfection—regardless of its wealth, industry, and liberty—cannot survive. This volume provides further insight into the mind of the most trenchant critic of the 19th century, a man who foresaw much of what has come to pass and had the courage and intellect to prescribe a cure.

V

Culture and Anarchy
with
Friendship's Garland
and
Some Literary Essays

MATTHEW
ARNOLD

CULTURE
AND
ANARCHY

with

Friendship's Garland and Some Literary Essays

Edited by R. H. Super

ANN ARBOR   THE UNIVERSITY OF MICHIGAN PRESS

Second printing 1980
Copyright © by The University of Michigan 1965
All rights reserved
ISBN 0-472-11655-X
Library of Congress Catalog Card No. 60-5018
Published in the United States of America by
The University of Michigan Press and simultaneously
in Rexdale, Canada, by John Wiley & Sons Canada, Limited
Manufactured in the United States of America

Editor's Preface

When Arnold prepared an edition of his works for the American market in 1883, he brought together into a single volume his *Culture and Anarchy* and *Friendship's Garland*, the two principal works in the present volume. To these have been added here three letters from the *Friendship's Garland* series published in the *Pall Mall Gazette* but omitted when the *Garland* was assembled as a book (two of them are here republished for the first time), and four literary essays contemporary with them, all republished in 1960 by Fraser Neiman in *Essays, Letters and Reviews by Matthew Arnold* (Cambridge: Harvard University Press); these last are the five-part review of Curtius' *History of Greece*, "Theodore Parker," "Obermann," and "Sainte-Beuve." The basic text of *Culture and Anarchy* and *Friendship's Garland* is that of 1883, of the other works the version in the *Pall Mall Gazette* or the *Academy*. Where earlier editions differ in language from the 1883 text, the variants are recorded in the Textual Notes, as are the very few editorial corrections; variants in punctuation or spelling and obvious misprints are generally ignored. The footnotes at the bottom of the page in the text are all Arnold's, even those signed "Ed." (Arnold as "editor" of his correspondence with Arminius).

Though the present edition of Arnold's prose is committed to the chronological principle, the range in dates of works included in this volume is unusually great: "My Countrymen" (February, 1866) was published (though not written) before any of the lectures on Celtic literature that have already appeared in my third volume, and the last of the articles on Curtius' *History* was published in 1876, after *God and the Bible* and concurrently with some of the *Last Essays on Church and Religion* which will appear in my seventh volume. But Arnold himself (rightly) included "My Countrymen" in *Friendship's Garland*, and there seems no valid reason for keeping separate the various articles on Curtius' *History*.

No arrangement of the *Friendship's Garland* articles is entirely satisfactory, but the chronological order, by date of publication, seems to have fewer disadvantages than Arnold's arrangement in 1871. Arnold himself, of course, put the two earliest essays, "My Countrymen" and "A Courteous Explanation," at the end as a sort of Appendix to the Arminius correspondence which made up the substance of his book. Furthermore, the Arminius correspondence in the *Pall Mall Gazette* lapsed for two years (April, 1867, to June, 1869) and in that interval the whole of *Culture and Anarchy* was published. Arnold marked the break with his "editorial" note in *Friendship's Garland* but not with a formal division into "Part I" and "Part II"; in the present volume the letters are so divided, and *Culture and Anarchy* and the literary essays are placed between the two parts. A few reviewers have been puzzled by my printing some of Arnold's prefaces *after* the works they introduce, a practice I follow here with both *Friendship's Garland* and *Culture and Anarchy*. My reason is not that the prefaces were *written* after the rest of the work (prefaces usually are), but that all the other contents of the books had already been published in periodicals and Arnold's prefaces were likely to assume a prior familiarity with what followed. The beginning of the Preface to *Culture and Anarchy*, for example, must seem strange to a reader who has not read the rest of the work; moreover, the whole Preface is in fact a transition from the book it introduces to Arnold's next work, *St. Paul and Protestantism*, which Arnold began to publish only a few months later. Whenever a preface made its first appearance at the same time as the rest of the book (as in *The Popular Education of France, Schools and Universities on the Continent*, even *Literature and Dogma*) it will be found in its normal place in this edition. The reader may of course read the contents of this volume in whatever order he pleases, and I hope that my Notes have made Arnold's final order plain enough; nevertheless things will seem a good deal clearer if he follows the chronological order here adopted.

The Critical and Explanatory Notes aim at explaining Arnold's allusions, identifying his quotations, and giving the background of his essays. He had a way of re-using his sources, alluding to a politician's speech or a critic's essay over and over again; often these repeated handlings are given a cross-reference in the Notes, but if the reader in any instance does not find such a cross-reference, he may get the help he needs from the Index. When an allusion is not explained, the reason may be editorial oversight or a failure in the editor's judgment about the need for explanation, but most often it is that the editor has been unable to trace the source.

An editorial undertaking like the present must necessarily depend heavily on the scholarship of others, published or unpublished, and it is gratifying that for the very volume where the editor most needed assistance the researches of others have been most thoroughgoing. Professor John P. Kirby more than a quarter of a century ago made an excellent annotated edition of *Friendship's Garland* as a doctoral dissertation at Yale University (1937); it remains unpublished, and indeed such has been his modesty that although he uncovered no fewer than half a dozen unrecorded contributions of Arnold's to the *Pall Mall Gazette* he left it to other discoverers, working independently, to announce their existence (among these the present editor). His work has been a constant guide to Arnold's sources (though of course I have always confirmed these for myself), but there remains between its covers a great deal of substance that could not be indicated within the limits of the present edition, most notably his careful marshalling of the evidence respecting other writers who paralleled or followed Arnold's views. Mr. Peter Smith's master's thesis at the University of London on *Friendship's Garland* (1958) is more modest in scope, but deals more fully with reviews and comments on Arnold's work than Professor Kirby's. Professor Sidney M. B. Coulling's dissertation on *Matthew Arnold and His Critics* (University of North Carolina, 1957) is a fascinating study of the interplay between Arnold and the periodical press; fortunately much of it has become publicly available through scholarly articles. In the course of his research Professor Coulling found the sources of a good many of Arnold's allusions in *Culture and Anarchy*, and these he most kindly forwarded for my use. Mr. Satyaprasad SenGupta's University of London doctoral dissertation, *The Reception of Matthew Arnold as Poet and Critic (1849–1871)*, written (like Mr. Peter Smith's) under the direction of Professor Geoffrey Tillotson, is less sensitive to the interplay between Arnold and his critics but is the most exhaustive bibliography of reviews and comments yet to have been made; it was completed in 1961 and is unpublished. Mr. Ian Gregor edited *Culture and Anarchy* by way of doctoral dissertation at the University of Durham (King's College, Newcastle-on-Tyne) in 1954; his principle was to base his text on the original articles in the *Cornhill Magazine*, interpolate where appropriate the principal critiques of which Arnold took cognizance, and provide explanatory annotation. Wherever I have consciously depended upon this unpublished scholarship I have tried to append to my note the name of my informant, but I must acknowledge here a much wider general indebtedness to all. The published edition of *Culture and Anarchy* by Professor J. Dover Wilson (Cambridge, 1932) and such textbooks of the old school as Lewis E. Gates's *Selections from the Prose Writings of Matthew Arnold* (New York, 1897) and C. F. Harrold and W. D. Templeman's *Victorian Prose* (New York, 1938) have often saved a good deal of searching.

The list of scholars and friends to whom I am indebted for various kinds of assistance is a long one: as always, Arnold's grandson Professor Arnold Whitridge; Professors Warren D. Anderson, John Butt, Walter E. Houghton, Robert L. Lowe, Geoffrey Tillotson, and Basil Willey; Dr. Martha Salmon Vogeler; and my colleagues at the University of Michigan, Professors Warren E. Blake, Frank O. Copley, and G. B. Harrison, and Mr. Rolland C. Stewart. University Microfilms, Inc., have generously supplied me with photocopies of my texts. A grant from the Horace H. Rackham fund at the University of Michigan has met many of the expenses of my research, and the greater part of the work on this volume was done with the assistance of a fellowship from the John Simon Guggenheim Memorial Foundation. To all of these I should like publicly to express my gratitude.

Ann Arbor, Michigan.

Contents

Friendship's Garland

*Being the Conversations, Letters, and Opinions
of the Late*

Arminius, Baron von Thunder-ten-Tronckh.

*Collected and Edited,
with a Dedicatory Letter to Adolescens Leo, Esq.,
of "The Daily Telegraph"*

By Matthew Arnold

[Part I]

.... *manibus date lilia plenis.*

My Countrymen

(I have thought that the memorial raised to Arminius would not be complete without the following essay, in which, though his name is not actually mentioned, he will be at once recognised as the leading spirit of the foreigners whose conversation is quoted.

Much as I owe to his intellect, I cannot help sometimes regretting that the spirit of youthful paradox which led me originally to question the perfections of my countrymen, should have been, as it were, prevented from dying out by my meeting, six years ago, with Arminius. The *Saturday Review*, in an article called "Mr. Matthew Arnold and his Countrymen," had taken my correction in hand, and I was in a fair way of amendment, when the intervention of Arminius stopped the cure, and turned me, as has been often said, into a mere mouthpiece of this dogmatic young Prussian. It was not that I did not often dislike his spirit and boldly stand up to him; but, on the whole, my intellect was (there is no use denying it) overmatched by his. The following essay, which appeared at the beginning of 1866, was the first proof of this fatal predominance, which has in many ways cost me so dear.)—Ed.

About a year ago the *Saturday Review* published an article which gave me, as its articles often do give me, much food for reflection. The article was about the unjust estimate which, says the *Saturday Review*, I form of my countrymen, and about the indecency of talking of "British Philistines." It appears that I assume the truth of the transcendental system of

3

philosophy,[1] and then lecture my wiser countrymen because they will not join me in recognising as eternal truths a set of platitudes which may be proved to be false. "Now there is in England a school of philosophy which thoroughly understands, and, on theoretical grounds, deliberately rejects, the philosophical theory which Mr. Arnold accuses the English nation of neglecting; and the practical efforts of the English people, especially their practical efforts in the way of criticism, are for the most part strictly in accordance with the principles of that philosophy."

I do not quite know what to say about the transcendental system of philosophy, for I am a mere dabbler in these great matters, and to grasp and hold a system of philosophy is a feat much beyond my strength; but I certainly did talk about British Philistines, and to call people Philistines when they are doing just what the wisest men in the country have settled to be quite right, does seem unreasonable, not to say indecent. Being really the most teachable man alive, I could not help making, after I had read the article in the *Saturday Review*, a serious return, as the French say, upon myself; and I resolved never to call my countrymen Philistines again till I had thought more about it, and could be quite sure I was not committing an indecency.

I was very much fortified in this good resolution by something else which happened about the same time. Every one knows that the heart of the English nation is its middle class; there had been a good deal of talk, a year ago, about the education of this class, and I, among others, had imagined it was not good, and that the middle class suffered by its not being better. But Mr. Bazley,[2] the member for Manchester, who is a kind of representative of this class, made a speech last year at Manchester, the middle-class metropolis, which shook me a good deal. "During the last few months," said Mr. Bazley, "there had been a cry that middle-class education ought to receive more attention. He confessed himself very much surprised by the clamour that was raised. He did not think that class need excite the sympathy either of the legislature or the

---

[1] Philosophy has always been bringing me into trouble.—Ed.
[2] Now Sir Thomas Bazley, Bart.—Ed.

public." Much to the same effect spoke Mr. Miall, another middle-class leader, in the *Nonconformist:* "Middle-class education seems to be the favourite topic of the hour, and we must confess to a feeling of shame at the nonsense which is being uttered on the subject. It might be thought from what is said, that this section of the community, which has done everything else so well,—which has astonished the world by its energy, enterprise, and self-reliance, which is continually striking out new paths of industry and subduing the forces of nature,—cannot, from some mysterious reason, get their children properly educated." Still more strong were the words of the *Daily News* (I love to range all the evidence in black and white before me, though it tends to my own discomfiture) about the blunder some of us were making: "All the world knows that the great middle class of this country supplies the mind, the will, and the power for all the great and good things that have to be done, and it is not likely that that class should surrender its powers and privileges in the one case of the training of its own children. How the idea of such a scheme can have occurred to anybody, how it can have been imagined that parents and schoolmasters in the most independent, and active, and enlightened class of English society,[1] how it can have been supposed that the class which has done all the great things that have been done in all departments, will beg the Government to send inspectors through its schools, when it can itself command whatever advantages exist, might seem unintelligible but for two or three considerations." These considerations do not much matter just now; but it is clear how perfectly Mr. Bazley's stand was a stand such as it becomes a representative man like Mr. Bazley to make, and how well the *Daily Telegraph* might say of the speech: "It was at once grand, genial, national, and distinct;" and the *Morning Star* of the speaker: "He talked to his constituents as Manchester people like to be talked to, in the language of clear, manly intelligence, which

[1] How very fine and striking is this language! Eloquent as is the homage which our newspapers still pay in the same quarter, it seems as if, in 1866, their eulogy had a ring and fulness which it has since in some measure lost.—ED.

penetrates through sophisms, ignores commonplaces, and gives to conventional illusions their true value. His speech was thoroughly instinct with that earnest good sense which characterises Manchester, and which, indeed, may be fairly set down as the general characteristic of England and Englishmen everywhere."

Of course if Philistinism is characteristic of the British nation just now, it must in a special way be characteristic of the representative part of the British nation, the part by which the British nation is what it is, and does all its best things, the middle class. And the newspapers, who have so many more means than I of knowing the truth, and who have that trenchant authoritative style for communicating it which makes so great an impression, say that the British middle class is characterised, not by Philistinism, but by enlightenment; by a passion for penetrating through sophisms, ignoring commonplaces, and giving to conventional illusions their true value. Evidently it is nonsense, as the *Daily News* says, to think that this great middle class which supplies the mind, the will, and the power for all the great and good things that have to be done, should want its schools, the nurseries of its admirable intelligence, meddled with. It may easily be imagined that all this, coming on the top of the *Saturday Review*'s rebuke of me for indecency, was enough to set me meditating; and after a long and painful self-examination, I saw that I had been making a great mistake. Instead of confining myself to what alone I had any business with,—the slow and obscure work of trying to understand things, to see them as they are,—I had been meddling with practice, proposing this and that, saying how it might be if we established this or that. So I was suffering deservedly in being taunted with hawking about my nostrums of State schools for a class much too wise to want them, and of an Academy for people who have an inimitable style already. To be sure, I had said that schools ought to be things of local, not State, institution and management, and that we ought not to have an Academy; but that makes no difference. I saw what danger I had been running by thus intruding into a sphere where I have no business, and I resolved to offend in this way no more.

This I say as a sincere penitent; but I do not see that there is any harm in my still trying to know and understand things, if I keep humbly to that, and do not meddle with greater matters, which are out of my reach. So, having once got into my head this notion of British Philistinism and of the want of clear and large intelligence in our middle class, I do not consider myself bound at once to put away and crush such a notion, as people are told to do with their religious doubts; nor, when the *Saturday Review* tells me that no nation in the world is so logical as the English nation, and the *Morning Star,* that our grand national characteristic is a clear intelligence which penetrates through sophisms, ignores commonplaces, and gives to conventional illusions their true value, do I feel myself compelled to receive these propositions with absolute submission as articles of faith, transcending reason; indeed, this would be transcendentalism, which the *Saturday Review* condemns. Canvass them, then, as mere matters of speculation, I may; and having lately had occasion to travel on the Continent for many months, during which I was thrown in company with a great variety of people, I remembered what Burns says of the profitableness of trying to see ourselves as others see us, and I kept on the watch for anything to confirm or contradict my old notion, in which, without absolutely giving it up, I had begun certainly to be much shaken and staggered.

I must say that the foreign opinion about us is not at all like that of the *Saturday Review* and the *Morning Star.* I know how madly the foreigners envy us, and that this must warp their judgment; I know, too, that this test of foreign opinion can never be decisive; I only take it for what it is worth, and as a contribution to our study of the matter in question. But I do really think that the admirers of our great middle class, which has, as its friends and enemies both agree, risen into such preponderating importance of late years, and now returns the House of Commons, dictates the policy of Ministers, makes the newspapers speak with its voice, and in short governs the country,—I do think, I say, the admirers of this great class would be astounded if they could hear how cavalierly a foreigner treats this country of their making and managing. "It is

not so much that we dislike England," a Prussian official,[1] with
the graceful tact of his nation, said to me the other day, "as
that we think little of her." The *Cologne Gazette*, perhaps the
chief newspaper of Germany, published in the summer a series
of letters, much esteemed, I believe, by military men, on the
armies of the leading Continental powers. The writer was a
German officer, but not a Prussian. Speaking of the false military system followed by the Emperor Nicholas, whose great
aim was to turn his soldiers into perfectly drilled machines,
and contrasting this with the free play left to the individual
soldier in the French system: "In consequence of their purely
mechanical training," says this writer, "the Russians, in spite of
their splendid courage, were in the Crimean war constantly
beaten by the French, nay, decidedly beaten *even by the English and the Turks*." [2] Hardly a German newspaper can discuss
territorial changes in Europe but it will add, after its remarks
on the probable policy of France in this or that event: "England will probably make a fuss, but what England thinks is of
no importance." I believe the German newspapers must keep a
phrase of that kind stereotyped, they use it so often. France is
our very good friend just now, but at bottom our "clear intelligence penetrating through sophisms," and so on, is not held
in much more esteem there than in Germany. One of the
gravest and most moderate of French newspapers,—a newspaper, too, our very good friend, like France herself, into the
bargain,—broke out lately, when some jealousy of the proposed Cholera Commission in the East was shown on this side
the water, in terms which, though less rough than the "great
fool" of the *Saturday Review*, were still far from flattering.
"Let us speak to these English the only language they can
comprehend. England lives for her trade; Cholera interrupts
trade; therefore it is for England's interest to join in precau-
tions against Cholera." [3]

Compliments of this sort are displeasing to remember, dis-

[1] Not Arminius.—Ed.

[2] "Ja, selbst von den Engländern und Türken entschieden geschlagen."

[3] Poor France! As Mr. Bottles says, neither her favourable nor her
unfavourable criticisms are of much consequence just now.—Ed.

pleasing to repeat; but their abundance strikes the attention; and then the happy unconsciousness of those at whom they are aimed, their state of imperturbable self-satisfaction, strikes the attention too, and makes an inquisitive mind quite eager to see its way clearly in this apparent game of cross purposes. For never, surely, was there such a game of cross purposes played. It came to its height when Lord Palmerston died the other day. Lord Palmerston was England; "the best type of our age and country," the *Times* well called him; he was "a great representative man, emphatically the English Minister;" the interpreter of the wishes of that great middle class of this country which supplies the mind, the will, and the power requisite for all the great and good things that have to be done, and therefore "acknowledged by a whole people as their best impersonation." Monsieur Thiers says of Pitt, that though he used and abused the strength of England, she was the second country in the world at the time of his death, and the first eight years afterwards. That was after Waterloo and the triumphs of Wellington. And that era of primacy and triumphs, Lord Palmerston, say the English newspapers, has carried on to this hour. "What Wellington was as a soldier, that was Palmerston as a statesmen." When I read these words in some foreign city or other, I could not help rubbing my eyes and asking myself if I was dreaming. Why, taking Lord Palmerston's career from 1830 (when he first became Foreign Secretary) to his death, there cannot be a shadow of doubt, for any one with eyes and ears in his head, that he found England the first Power in the world's estimation, and that he leaves her the third, after France[1] and the United States. I am no politician; I mean no disparagement at all to Lord Palmerston, to whose talents and qualities I hope I can do justice; and indeed it is not Lord Palmerston's policy, or any minister's policy, that is in question here, it is the policy of all of us, it is the policy of England; for in a government such as ours is at present, it is only, as we are so often reminded, by interpreting public opinion, by being "the best type of his age and country," that a minister governs; and Lord Palmerston's greatness lay pre-

[1] Heu incredibiles humanarum rerum mutationes!—Ed.

cisely in our all "acknowledging him as our best impersonation." Well, then, to this our logic, our practical efforts in the
way of criticism, our clear manly intelligence penetrating
through sophisms and ignoring commonplaces, and above all,
5 our redoubtable phalanx possessing these advantages in the
highest degree, our great middle class, which makes Parliament, and which supplies the mind, the will, and the power
requisite for all the great and good things that have to be done,
have brought us; to the third place in the world's estimation,
10 instead of the first. He who disbelieves it, let him go round to
every embassy in Europe and ask if it is not true.

The foreigners, indeed, are in no doubt as to the real authors
of the policy of modern England; they know that ours is no
longer a policy of Pitts and aristocracies,[1] disposing of every
15 movement of the hoodwinked nation to whom they dictate it;
they know that our policy is now dictated by the strong middle part of England,—England happy, as Mr. Lowe, quoting
Aristotle, says, in having her middle part strong and her extremes weak; and that, though we are administered by one of
20 our weak extremes, the aristocracy, these managers administer
us, as a weak extreme naturally must, with a nervous attention
to the wishes of the strong middle part, whose agents they are.
It was not the aristocracy which made the Crimean war; it was
the strong middle part—the constituencies. It was the
25 strong middle part which showered abuse and threats on Germany for mishandling Denmark; and when Germany gruffly
answered, *Come and stop us,* slapped its pockets, and vowed that
it had never had the slightest notion of pushing matters as far as
this. It was the strong middle part which, by the voice of its
30 favourite newspapers, kept threatening Germany, after she had
snapped her fingers at us, with a future chastisement from
France, just as a smarting schoolboy threatens his bully with a
drubbing to come from some big boy in the background. It
was the strong middle part, speaking through the same news-
35 papers, which was full of coldness, slights, and sermons for the
American Federals during their late struggle; and as soon as
they had succeeded, discovered that it had always wished them

---

[1] Arminius; he says it over again in his last letter but one.—Ed.

well, and that nothing was so much to be desired as that the
United States, and we, should be the fastest friends possible.
Some people will say that the aristocracy was an equal
offender in this respect: very likely: but the behaviour of the
strong middle part makes more impression than the behaviour   5
of a weak extreme; and the more so, because from the middle
class, their fellows in numberless ways, the Americans expected sympathy, while from the aristocracy they expected
none. And, in general, the faults with which foreigners reproach us in the matters named,—rash engagement, intemper-   10
ate threatening, undignified retreat, ill-timed cordiality,—are
not the faults of an aristocracy, by nature in such concerns
prudent, reticent, dignified, sensitive on the point of honour;
they are rather the faults of a rich middle class,—testy, absolute, ill-acquainted with foreign matters, a little ignoble, very   15
dull to perceive when it is making itself ridiculous.

I know the answer one gets at home when one says that
England is not very highly considered just now on the Continent. There is first of all the envy to account for it,—that of
course; and then our clear intelligence is making a radical   20
change in our way of dealing with the Continent; the old, bad,
aristocratical policy of incessantly intermeddling with the
affairs of the Continent,—this it is getting rid of; it is leaving
the miserable foreigners to themselves, to their wars, despot-
isms, bureaucracy, and hatred of free, prosperous England. A   25
few inconveniences may arise before the transition from our
old policy to our new is fairly accomplished, and we quite
leave off the habit of meddling where our own interests are
not at stake. We may be exposed to a little mortification in the
passage, but our clear intelligence will discern any occasion   30
where our interests are really at stake. Then we shall come
forward and prove ourselves as strong as ever; and the foreigners, in spite of their envy, know it. But what strikes me so
much in all which these foreigners say is, that it is just this
clear intelligence of ours that they appear at the present mo-   35
ment to hold cheap. Englishmen are often heard complaining
of the little gratitude foreign nations show them for their sympathy, their good-will. The reason is, that the foreigners think

that an Englishman's good-will to a foreign cause, or dislike to
it, is never grounded in a perception of its real merits and
bearings, but in some chance circumstance. They say the
Englishman never, in these cases, really comprehends the situa-
5 tion, and so they can never feel him to be in living sympathy
with them. I have got into much trouble for calling my countrymen Philistines, and all through these remarks I am determined never to use that word; but I wonder if there can be
anything offensive in calling one's countryman a young man
10 from the country. I hope not; and if not, I should say, for the
benefit of those who have seen Mr. John Parry's amusing entertainment, that England and Englishmen, holding forth on
some great crisis in a foreign country,—Poland, say, or Italy,
—are apt to have on foreigners very much the effect of the
15 young man from the country who talks to the nursemaid after
she has upset the perambulator. There is a terrible crisis, and
the discourse of the young man from the country, excellent in
itself, is felt not to touch the crisis vitally. Nevertheless, on he
goes; the perambulator lies a wreck, the child screams, the
20 nursemaid wrings her hands, the old gentleman storms, the
policeman gesticulates, the crowd thickens; still, that astonishing young man talks on, serenely unconscious that he is not at
the centre of the situation.

Happening to be much thrown with certain foreigners, who
25 criticised England in this sort of way, I used often to think
what a short and ready way one of our hard-hitting English
newspapers would take with these scorners, if they fell into its
hands. But being myself a mere seeker for truth, with nothing
trenchant or authoritative about me, I could do no more than
30 look shocked and begin to ask questions. "What!" I said, "you
hold the England of to-day cheap, and declare that we do not
comprehend the situation; yet you rate the England of 1815 so
high, and call our fathers and grandfathers the foremost people
in Europe. Did they comprehend the situation better than
35 we?" "Yes," replied my foreign friends, "the situation as they
had it, a great deal better. Their time was a time for energy,
and they succeeded in it, perfectly. Our time is a time for
intelligence, and you are not succeeding in it at all."

Though I could not hear without a shudder this insult to the
earnest good sense which, as the *Morning Star* says, may be
fairly set down as the general characteristic of England and
Englishmen everywhere, yet I pricked up my ears when my
companions talked of energy, and England's success in a time   5
for energy, because I have always had a notion myself that
energy,—energy with honesty,—is England's great force; a
greater force to her, even, than her talent for penetrating
through sophisms and ignoring commonplaces; so I begged my
acquaintances to explain a little more fully to me what they   10
meant. "Nothing can be clearer," they answered. "Your *Times*
was telling you the other day, with the enlightenment it so
often shows at present, that instead of being proud of Waterloo and the great war which was closed by it, it really seemed
as if you ought rather to feel embarrassed at the recollection of 15
them, since the policy for which they were fought is grown
obsolete; the world has taken a turn which was not Lord Cas-
tlereagh's, and to look back on the great Tory war is to look
back upon an endless account of blood and treasure wasted.
Now, that is not so at all. What France had in her head,—from 20
the Convention, 'faithful to the principles of the sovereignty
of the people, which will not permit them to acknowledge
anywhere the institutions militating against it,' to Napoleon,
with his 'immense projects for assuring to France the empire
of the world,'—what she had in her head, along with many   25
better and sounder notions destined to happier fortune, was
supremacy. She had always a vision of a sort of federation of
the States of Europe under the primacy of France. Now to
this the world, whose progress no doubt lies in the direction of
more concert and common purpose among nations, but these   30
nations free, self-impelled, and living each its own life, was not
moving. Whoever knocks to pieces a scheme of this sort does
the world a service. In antiquity, Roman empire had a scheme
of this sort, and much more. The barbarians knocked it to
pieces;—honour to the barbarians. In the Middle Ages Freder-   35
ick the Second had a scheme of this sort. The Papacy knocked
it to pieces;—honour to the Papacy. In our own century,
France had a scheme of this sort. Your fathers knocked it to

pieces;—honour to your fathers. They were just the people to
do it. They had a vigorous lower class, a vigorous middle class,
and a vigorous aristocracy. The lower class worked and
fought, the middle class found the money, and the aristocracy
5 wielded the whole. This aristocracy was high-spirited, reticent, firm, despising frothy declamation. It had all the qualities
useful for its task and time; Lord Grenville's words, as early as
1793: 'England will never consent that France shall arrogate
the power of annulling at her pleasure, and under the pretence
10 of a pretended natural right, the political system of Europe,'—
these few words, with their lofty strength, contain, as one may
say, the prophecy of future success; you hear the very voice
of an aristocracy standing on sure ground, and with the stars
in its favour. Well, you succeeded, and in 1815, after Water-
15 loo, you were the first power in Europe. 'These people have a
secret,' we all said; 'they have discerned the way the world
was going, and therefore they have prevailed; while, on the
other hand, the "stars in their courses fought against Sisera." '
We held you in the greatest respect; we tried to copy your
20 constitutional government; we read your writers. 'After the
peace,' says George Sand, 'the literature of Great Britain
crossed the straits, and came to reign amongst us.' It reigned in
Byron and Scott, voices of the great aristocratical spirit which
had just won the victory: Scott expressing its robust, genial
25 conservatism, holding by a thousand roots to the past; Byron
its defiant force and indomitable pride.

"We believed in you for a good while; but gradually it
began to dawn upon us that the era for which you had had the
secret was over, and that a new era, for which you had not the
30 secret, was beginning. The work of the old era was to prevent
the formation of a second Roman empire, and to maintain a
store of free, rich, various national lives for the future to work
with and bring to harmony. This was a work of force, of
energy: it was a work for an aristocratical power, since, as you
35 yourself are always saying, aristocracies, poor in ideas, are rich
in energy. You were a great aristocratical power, and did it.
But then came an era with another work, a work of which it is
the great glory of the French Revolution (pardon us for say-

ing so, we know it makes some of your countrymen angry to hear it), passionately to have embraced the idea: the work of making human life, hampered by a past which it has outgrown, natural and rational. This is a work of intelligence, and in intelligence an aristocratic power, as you know, does not so much shine. Accordingly, since the world has been steadily moving this way, you seem to have lost your secret, and we are gradually ceasing to believe in you. You will say, perhaps, that England is no longer an aristocratical power, but a middle-class power, wielded by an industrial middle class, as the England of your fathers was wielded by a territorial aristocracy. This may be so; and indeed, as the style, carriage, and policy of England have of late years been by no means those of an aristocratical power, it probably is so. But whatever class dictates it, your course, allow us to say, has not of late years been intelligent; has not, at any rate, been successful. And depend upon it, a nation who has the secret of her era, who discerns which way the world is going, is successful, keeps rising. Can you yourselves, with all your powers of self-satisfaction, suppose that the Crimean war raised you, or that your Indian mutiny raised you, or that your attitude in the Italian war raised you, as your performances at the beginning of the century raised you? Surely you cannot. You held your own, if you will; you showed tenacity; you saved yourselves from disaster; but you did not raise yourselves, did not advance one jot. Can you, on the other hand, suppose that your attitude in the Danish business, in the American business, has not lowered you? You are losing the instinct which tells people how the world is going; you are beginning to make mistakes; you are falling out of the front rank. The era of aristocracies is over; nations must now stand or fall by the intelligence of their middle class and their people. The people with you is still an embryo; no one can yet quite say what it will come to. You lean, therefore, with your whole weight upon the intelligence of your middle class. And intelligence, in the true sense of the word, your middle class has absolutely none."

I was aghast. I thought of this great class, every morning and evening extolled for its clear, manly intelligence by a hundred

vigorous and influential writers; and though the fine enthusiasm of these writers had always seemed to me to be carrying
them a little too far, and I had even been guilty of the indecency of now and then calling my countrymen Philistines,
these foreign critics struck me as passing all bounds, and quite
out-Heroding Herod. Fortunately I had just received from
England a copy of Mr. Lowe's powerful and much-admired
speech against Reform. I took it out of my pocket. "Now,"
said I to my envious, carping foreigners, "just listen to me.
You say that the early years of this century were a time for
energy, and we did well in them; you say that the last thirty or
forty years have been a time for intelligence, and we have
done ill in them. Mr. Lowe shall answer you. Here is his reading of our last thirty or forty years' history, as made by our
middle-class Parliament, as he calls it; by a Parliament, therefore, filled by the mind and will of this great class whose rule
you disparage. Mr. Lowe says: 'The seven Houses of Commons that have sate since the Reform Bill have performed
exploits unrivalled, not merely in the six centuries during
which Parliament has existed, but in the whole history of representative assemblies.' He says: 'Look at the noble work, the
heroic work which the House of Commons has performed
within these thirty-five years. It has gone through and revised
every institution of the country; it has scanned our trade, our
colonies, our laws, and our municipal institutions; everything
that was complained of, everything that had grown distasteful,
has been touched with success and moderation by the amending
hand. And to such a point have these amendments been carried,
that when gentlemen come to argue this question, and do all in
their power to get up a practical grievance, they fail in suggesting even one.' There is what Mr. Lowe says. You see we have
nothing left to desire, absolutely nothing. As Mr. Lowe himself
goes on: 'With all this continued peace, contentment, happiness, and prosperity,—England in its present state of development and civilisation,—the mighty fabric of English prosperity,'
—what can we want more? Evidently nothing! therefore to
propose 'for England to make a step in the direction of democracy is the strangest and wildest proposition ever broached by

man.' People talk of America. 'In America the working classes are the masters; does anybody doubt that?' And compare, Mr. Lowe means, England, as the middle class is making her, with America, as the working classes are making her. How entirely must the comparison turn to the advantage of the English middle 5 class! Then, finally, as to the figure we cut in the eyes of the world, our grandeur and our future, here is a crowning sentence, worthy of Lord Macaulay himself, whose style Mr. Lowe enthusiastically admires: *'The destiny of England is in the great heart of England!'* " 10

Mr. Bright had not then made his famous speech about the misdeeds of the Tories, but, if he had, I should certainly have added that our middle class, by these unrivalled exploits of theirs, had not only raised their country to an unprecedented height of greatness, but had also saved our foolish and obstructive 15 aristocracy from being emptied into the Thames.

As it was, however, what I had urged, or rather what I had borrowed from Mr. Lowe, seemed to me exceedingly forcible, and I looked anxiously for its effect on my hearers. They did not appear so much disconcerted as I had hoped. "Undoubt- 20 edly," they said, "the coming of your middle class to power was a natural, salutary event, to be blessed, not anathematised. Aristocracies cannot deal with a time for intelligence; their sense is for facts, not ideas. The world of ideas is the possible, the future; the world of aristocracies is the established, the 25 past, which has made their fortune, and which they hope to prolong. No doubt, too, your middle class found a great deal of commercial and social business waiting to be done, which your aristocratic governments had left undone, and had no talents for doing. Their talents were for other times and tasks; 30 for curbing the power of the Crown when other classes were too inconsiderable to do it; for managing (if one compares them with other aristocracies) their affairs and their depend- ants with vigour, prudence, and moderation, during the feudal and patriarchal stage of society; for wielding the force of their 35 country against foreign powers with energy, firmness, and dignity. But then came the modern spirit, the modern time; the notion, as we say, of making human life more natural and

rational,—or, as your philosophers say, of getting the greatest
happiness for the greatest number. Have you succeeded, are
you succeeding, in this hour of the many, as your aristocracy
succeeded in the hour of the few? You say you are: you point
5 to 'the noble work, the heroic work which the House of Commons has performed within these last thirty-five years; everything that was complained of, everything that had grown distasteful, has been touched with success and moderation by the
amending hand.' Allow us to set clap-trap on one side; we are
10 not at one of your public meetings. What is the modern problem? to make human life, the life of society, all through, more
natural and rational; to have the greatest possible number of
one's nation happy. Here is the standard by which we are to
try ourselves and one another now, as national grandeur, in the
15 old regal and aristocratical conception of it, was the standard
formerly. Every nation must have wished to be England in
1815, tried by the old standard: must we all wish to be England, in 1865, tried by the new standard? Your aristocracy,
you say, is as splendid, as fortunate, as enviable as ever: very
20 likely; but all the world cannot be aristocracy. What do you
make of the mass of your society, of its vast middle and lower
portion? Are we to envy you your common people; is our
common people to wish to change places with yours; are we to
say that you, more than we, have the modern secret here?
25 Without insisting too much on the stories of misery and degradation which are perpetually reaching us, we will say that no
one can mix with a great crowd in your country, no one can
walk with his eyes and ears open through the poor quarters of
your large towns, and not feel that your common people, as it
30 meets one's eyes, is at present more raw, to say the very least,
less enviable-looking, further removed from civilised and humane life, than the common people almost anywhere. Well,
then, you are not a success, according to the modern standard,
with your common people. Are you a success with your mid-
35 dle class? They have the power now; what have they made of
themselves? what sort of a life is theirs? A life more natural,
more rational, fuller of happiness, more enviable, therefore,
than the life of the middle classes on the Continent? Yes, you

will say, because the English middle class is the most industrious and the richest. But it is just here that you go a great deal
too fast, and so deceive yourselves. What brings about, or
rather tends to bring about, a natural, rational life, satisfying
the modern spirit? This: the growth of a love of industry,   5
trade, and wealth; the growth of a love of the things of the
mind; and the growth of a love of beautiful things. There are
body, intelligence, and soul all taken care of. Of these three
factors of modern life, your middle class has no notion of any
but one, the first. Their love of industry, trade, and wealth, is   10
certainly prodigious; and their example has done us a great
deal of good; we, too, are beginning to get this love, and we
wanted it. But what notion have they of anything else? Do but
look at them, look at their lives. Some of us know your middle
class very well; a great deal better than your own upper class   15
in general knows them. Your middle class is educated, to begin
with, in the worst schools of your country, and our middle
class is educated in the best of ours. What becomes of them
after that? The fineness and capacity of a man's spirit is shown
by his enjoyments; your middle class has an enjoyment in its   20
business, we admit, and gets on well in business, and makes
money; but beyond that? Drugged with business, your middle
class seems to have its sense blunted for any stimulus besides,
except religion; it has a religion, narrow, unintelligent, repul-
sive. All sincere religion does something for the spirit, raises a   25
man out of the bondage of his merely bestial part, and saves
him; but the religion of your middle class is the very lowest
form of intelligential life which one can imagine as saving.
What other enjoyments have they? The newspapers, a sort of
eating and drinking which are not to our taste, a literature of   30
books almost entirely religious or semi-religious, books utterly
unreadable by an educated class anywhere, but which your
middle class consumes, they say, by the hundred thousand; and
in their evenings, for a great treat, a lecture on teetotalism or
nunneries. Can any life be imagined more hideous, more dis-   35
mal, more unenviable? Compare it with the life of our middle
class as you have seen it on the Rhine this summer, or at
Lausanne, or Zurich. The world of enjoyment, so liberalising

and civilising, belongs to the middle classes there, as well as the
world of business; the whole world is theirs, they possess life;
in England the highest class seems to have the monopoly of the
world of enjoyment, the middle class enjoys itself, as your
5   Shakspeare would say, in hugger-mugger, and possesses life
only by reading in the newspapers, which it does devoutly, the
doings of great people. Well, then, we do not at all want to be
as your middle class; we want to learn from it to do business
and to get rich, and this we are learning a great deal faster than
10   you think; but we do not, like your middle class, fix our consummation here: we have a notion of a whole world besides,
not dreamed of in your middle class's philosophy; so they, too,
like your common people, seem to us no success. They may be
the masters of the modern time with you, but they are not
15   solving its problem. They cannot see the way the world is
going, and the future does not belong to them. Talk of the
present state of development and civilisation of England,
meaning England as they represent it to us! Why, the capital,
pressing danger of England, is the barbarism of her middle
20   class; the civilisation of her middle class is England's capital,
pressing want."

"Well, but," said I, still catching at Mr. Lowe's powerful
help, "the Parliament of this class has performed exploits unrivalled not merely in the six centuries during which Parliament
25   has existed, but in the whole history of representative assemblies. The exploits are there; all the reforms we have made in
the last five-and-thirty years."

"Let us distinguish," replied the envious foreigners, "let us
distinguish. We named three powers,—did we not?—which go
30   to spread that rational humane life which is the aim of modern
society: the love of wealth, the love of intelligence, the love of
beauty. Your middle class, we agreed, has the first; its commercial legislation, accordingly, has been very good, and in
advance of that of foreign countries. Not that free-trade was
35   really brought about by your middle class: it was brought
about, as important reforms always are, by two or three great
men. However, let your middle class, which had the sense to
accept free trade, have the credit of it. But this only brings us

a certain way. The legislation of your middle class in all that goes to give human life more intelligence and beauty, is no better than was to be expected from its own want of both. It is nothing to say that its legislation in these respects is an improvement upon what you had before; that is not the question; you are holding up its achievements as absolutely admirable, as unrivalled, as a model to us. You may have done,—for you,— much for religious toleration, social improvement, public instruction, municipal reform, law reform; but the French Revolution and its consequences have done, upon the Continent, a great deal more. Such a spectacle as your Irish Church Establishment [1] you cannot find in France or Germany. Your Irish land-question you hardly dare to face [2]—Stein settled as threatening a land-question in Prussia. Of the schools for your middle class we have already spoken; while these schools are what they are, while the schools for your poor are maintained in the expensive, unjust, irrational way they are, England is full of endowments and foundations, capable by themselves, if properly applied, of putting your public education on a much better footing. In France and Germany all similar funds are thus employed, having been brought under public responsible management; in England they are left to private irresponsible management, and are, in nine cases out of ten, wasted. You talk of municipal reform; and cities and the manner of life in them have, for the modern business of promoting a more rational and humane life in the great body of the community, incalculable importance. Do you suppose we should tolerate in France, Germany, Switzerland, Italy, your London corporation and London vestries, and London as they make it? In your provincial towns you do better; but even there, do the municipalities show a tenth part either of the intelligence or the care for the ends, as we have laid them down, of modern society, that our municipalities show? Your middle-class man thinks it the highest pitch of development and civilisation when his letters are carried twelve times a day from Islington to Camberwell, and from Camberwell to Islington, and if railway-

---

[1] It is gone, thanks to Anti-State-Church-ism!—ED.
[2] We have faced it!—ED.

trains run to and fro between them every quarter of an hour.
He thinks it is nothing that the trains only carry him from an
illiberal, dismal life at Islington to an illiberal, dismal life at
Camberwell; and the letters only tell him that such is the life
there. A Swiss burgher takes heaven knows how many hours
to go up from Berne to Geneva, and his trains are very few;
this is an extreme on the other side; but compare the life the
Swiss burgher finds or leaves at Berne or Geneva with the life
of the middle class in your English towns. Or else you think to
cover everything by saying: 'We are free! we are free! Our
newspapers can say what they like!' Freedom, like Industry, is
a very good horse to ride;—but to ride somewhere. You seem
to think that you have only got to get on the back of your
horse Freedom, or your horse Industry, and to ride away as
hard as you can, to be sure of coming to the right destination.
If your newspapers can say what they like, you think you are
sure of being well advised. That comes of your inaptitude for
ideas, and aptitude for clap-trap; you can never see the two
sides of a question; never perceive that every human state of
things, even a good one, has its inconveniences. We can see the
conveniences of your state well enough; and the inconveniences
of ours, of newspapers not free, and prefects over-busy; and
there are plenty of us who proclaim them. You eagerly repeat
after us all we say that redounds to your honuor and glory; but
you never follow our example yourselves. You are full of acuteness to perceive the ill influence of our prefects on us; but if any
one says to you, in your turn: 'The English system of a great
landed aristocracy [1] keeps your lower class a lower class for
ever, and materialises and vulgarises your whole middle class,'
—you stare vacantly at the speaker, you cannot even take in
his ideas; you can only blurt forth, in reply, some clap-trap or

[1] What a contrast between this Jacobinism and the noble sentiments
of Barrow: "Men will never be heartily loyal and submissive to authority
till they become really good; nor will they ever be very good, till they
see their leaders such." I remember once quoting this passage to Arminius at the time when we were all full of the Mordaunt trial. "Yes,"
remarked Arminius, in his thoughtful manner, "that is what makes your
Lord Coles so inexpressibly precious!" But was this an answer? I say,
not.—ED.

other about a 'system of such tried and tested efficiency as no other country was ever happy enough to possess since the world was a world.' "

I have observed in my travels, that most young gentlemen of our highest class go through Europe, from Calais to Constantinople, with one sentence on their lips, and one idea in their minds, which suffices, apparently, to explain all that they see to them: *Foreigners don't wash*. No doubt, thought I to myself, my friends have fallen in with some distinguished young Britons of this sort, and had their feelings wounded by them; hence their rancour against our aristocracy. And as to our middle class, foreigners have no notion how much this class, with us, contains; how many shades and gradations in it there are, and how little what is said of one part of it will apply to another. Something of this sort I could not help urging aloud. "You do not know," I said, "that there is broken off, as one may say, from the top of our middle class, a large fragment, which receives the best education the country can give, the same education as our aristocracy; which is perfectly intelligent and which enjoys life perfectly. These men do the main part of our intellectual work, write all our best newspapers; and cleverer people, I assure you, are nowhere to be found."

"Clever enough," was the answer, "but they show not much intelligence, in the true sense of the word,—not much intelligence of the way the world is going. Whether it is that they must try to hit your current public opinion, which is not intelligent; whether it is that, having been, as you say, brought up with your aristocracy, they have been too much influenced by it, have taken, half insensibly, an aristocracy's material standard, and do not believe in ideas; certain it is that their intelligence has no ardour, no plan, leads them nowhere; it is ineffectual. Your intellect is at this moment, to an almost unexampled degree, without influence on the intellect of Europe."

While this was being said, I noticed an Italian,[1] who was one of our party, fumbling with his pocket-book, from whence he presently produced a number of gray newspaper slips, which I

[1] Little Pompeo Pococurante. Almost all the rest is Arminius.

could see were English. "Now just listen to me for a moment," he cried, "and I will show you what makes us say, on the Continent, that you English have no sense for logic, for ideas, and that your praise and blame, having no substantial founda-
5 tion, are worth very little. You remember the famous French pamphlet before our war began in 1859: *Napoleon the Third and Italy*. The pamphlet appealed, in the French way, to reason and first principles; the upshot of it was this: 'The treaties which bind governments would be invariable only if the world
10 was immovable. A power which should intrench itself behind treaties in order to resist modifications demanded by general feeling would have doubtless on her side an acquired right, but she would have against her moral right and universal conscience.' You English, on the other hand, took your stand on
15 things as they were: 'If treaties are made,' said your *Times*, 'they must be respected. Tear one, and all are waste paper.' Very well; this is a policy, at any rate, an aristocratical policy; much may be said for it. The *Times* was full of contempt for the French pamphlet, an essay, as it called it, 'conveying the
20 dreams of an agitator expressed in the language of an academician.' It said: 'No one accustomed to the pithy comments with which liberty notices passing history, can read such a production without complacency that he does not live in the country which produces it. To see the heavy apparatus of an essay
25 brought out to solve a question on which men have corresponded and talked and speculated in the funds, and acted in the most practical manner possible for a month past, is as strange as if we beheld some spectral review,' and so on. Still very well; there is the strong practical man despising theories
30 and reveries. 'The sentiment of race is just now threatening to be exceedingly troublesome. It is to a considerable extent in our days a literary revival.' That is all to the same effect. Then came a hitch in our affairs, and fortune seemed as if she was going to give, as she often does give, the anti-theorists a tri
35 umph. 'The Italian plot,' cried the *Times*, 'has failed. The Emperor and his familiars knew not the moral strength which is still left in the enlightened communities of Europe. To the unanimous and indignant reprobation of English opinion is due

the failure of the imperial plots. While silence and fear reign
everywhere abroad, the eyes and ears of the Continent are
turned continually to these Islands. English opinion has been
erected into a kind of Areopagus.' Our business went forward
again, and your English opinion grew very stern indeed. 'Sardinia,' said the *Times*, 'is told very plainly that she has deserted
the course by which alone she could hope either to be happy
or great, and abandoned herself to the guidance of fatal delusions, which are luring her on to destruction. By cultivating
the arts of peace she would have been solving, in the only
possible way, the difficult problem of Italian independence.
She has been taught by France to look instead to the acquisition of fresh territory by war and conquest. She has now been
told with perfect truth by the warning voice of the British
Parliament that she has not a moment to lose in retracing her
steps, if indeed her penitence be not too late.' Well, to make a
long story short, we did not retrace our steps; we went on, as
you know; we succeeded; and now let us make a jump from
the spring to the autumn. Here is your unanimous English
opinion, here is your Areopagus, here is your *Times*, in October: 'It is very irregular (Sardinia's course), it is contrary to
all diplomatic forms. Francis the Second can show a thousand
texts of international law against it. Yes; but there are extremi-
ties beyond all law, and there are laws which existed before
even society was formed. There are laws which are implanted
in our nature, and which form part of the human mind,' and so
on. Why, here you have entirely boxed the compass and come
round from the aristocratical programme to the programme of
the French pamphlet, 'the dreams of an agitator in the language of an academician!' And you approved not only our
present but our past, and kindly took off your ban of reprobation issued in February. 'How great a change has been effected
by the wisely courageous policy of Sardinia! The firmness and
boldness which have raised Italy from degradation form the
enduring character of a ten years' policy. King Victor Em-
manuel and his sagacious counsellor have achieved success by
remembering that fortune favours the bold.' There you may
see why the mind of France influences the Continent so much

and the mind of England so little. France has intelligence
enough to perceive the ideas that are moving, or are likely to
move, the world; she believes in them, sticks to them, and
shapes her course to suit them. You neither perceive them nor
5 believe in them, but you play with them like counters, taking
them up and laying them down at random, and following
really some turn of your imagination, some gust of liking or
disliking. When I heard some of your countrymen complaining of Italy and her ingratitude for English sympathy, I made,
10 to explain it, the collection of those extracts and of a good
many more. They are all at your service; I have some here
from the *Saturday Review*, which you will find exactly follow
suit with those from the *Times*." "No, thank you," I answered.
"The *Times* is enough. My relations with the *Saturday Re-*
15 *view* are rather tight-stretched, as you say here, already; make
me a party to none of your quarrels with them."

After this my original tormentor [1] once more took up his
parable. "You see now what I meant," he said, "by saying that
you did better in the old time, in the day of aristocracies. An
20 aristocracy has no ideas, but it has a policy,—to resist change.
In this policy it believes, it sticks to it; when it is beaten in it, it
holds its tongue. This is respectable, at any rate. But your
great middle class, as you call it, your present governing
power, having no policy, except that of doing a roaring trade,
25 does not know what to be at in great affairs,—blows hot and
cold by turns, makes itself ridiculous, in short. It was a good
aristocratical policy to have helped Austria in the Italian war;
it was a good aristocratical policy to have helped the South in
the American war. The days of aristocratical policy are over
30 for you; with your new middle-class public opinion you cut,
in Italy, the figure our friend here has just shown you; in
America you scold right and left, you get up a monster-mem-
orial to deprecate the further effusion of blood; you lament
over the abridgment of civil liberty by people engaged in a
35 struggle for life and death, and meaning to win: and when they
turn a deaf ear to you and win, you say, 'Oh, now let us be one
great united Anglo-Saxon family and astonish the world!' This

[1] Arminius, of course.

is just of a piece with your threatening Germany with the Emperor of the French. Do you not see that all these blunders dispose the Americans, who are very shrewd, and who have been succeeding as steadily as you have been failing, to answer: 'We have got the lead, no thanks to you, and we mean to astonish the world without you?' Unless you change, unless your middle class grows more intelligent, you will tell upon the world less and less, and end by being a second Holland. We do not hold you cheap for saying you will wash your hands of all concerns but your own, that you do not care a rush for influence in Europe; though this sentence of your Lord Bolingbroke is true: 'The opinion of mankind, which is fame after death, is superior strength and power in life.' We hold you cheap because you show so few signs, except in the one department of industry, of understanding your time and its tendencies, and of exhibiting a modern life which shall be a signal success. And the reaction is the stronger, because, after 1815, we believed in you as nowadays we are coming to believe in America. You had won the last game, and we thought you had your hand full of trumps, and were going to win the next. Now the game has begun to be played, and we have an inkling of what your cards are; we shrewdly suspect you have scarcely any trumps at all."

I am no arguer, as is well known, "and every puny whipster gets my sword." [1] So, instead of making bad worse by a lame answer, I held my tongue, consoling myself with the thought that these foreigners get from us, at any rate, plenty of Rolands for any stray Oliver they may have the luck to give us. I have since meditated a good deal on what was then said, but I cannot profess to be yet quite clear about it. However, all due deductions made for envy, exaggeration, and injustice, enough stuck by me of these remarks on our logic, criticism, and love of intelligence, to determine me to go on trying (taking care, of course, to steer clear of indecency) to keep my mind fixed on these, instead of singing hosannahs to our actual state of development and civilisation. The old recipe, to think a little

[1] And this is why it was peculiarly unlucky for me to be thrown so much with Arminius, who loved arguing.—Ed.

more and bustle a little less, seemed to me still the best recipe
to follow. So I take comfort when I find the *Guardian* reproaching me with having no influence; for I know what influence means,—a party, practical proposals, action; and I say to
5   myself: "Even suppose I could get some followers, and assemble them, brimming with affectionate enthusiasm, in a committee-room at some inn; what on earth should I say to them?
what resolutions could I propose? I could only propose the old
Socratic commonplace, *Know thyself;* and how blank they
10 would all look at that!" No; to inquire, perhaps too curiously,
what that present state of English development and civilisation
is, which according to Mr. Lowe is so perfect that to give
votes to the working class is stark madness; and, on the other
hand, to be less sanguine about the divine and saving effect of a
15 vote on its possessor than my friends in the committee-room at
the "Spotted Dog,"—that is my inevitable portion. To bring
things under the light of one's intelligence, to see how they
look there, to accustom oneself simply to regard the Marylebone Vestry, or the Educational Home, or the Irish Church
20 Establishment, or our railway management, or our Divorce
Court, or our gin-palaces open on Sunday and the Crystal
Palace shut, as absurdities,—that is, I am sure, invaluable exercise for us just at present. Let all persist in it who can, and
steadily set their desires on introducing, with time, a little
25 more soul and spirit into the too, too solid flesh of English
society.

I have a friend who is very sanguine, in spite of the dismal
croakings of these foreigners, about the turn things are even
now taking amongst us. "Mean and ignoble as our middle class
30 looks," he says, "it has this capital virtue, it has seriousness.
With frivolity, cultured or uncultured, you can do nothing;
but with seriousness there is always hope. Then, too, the present bent of the world towards amusing itself, so perilous to the
highest class, is curative and good for our middle class. A piano
35 in a Quaker's drawing-room is a step for him to more humane
life; nay, perhaps even the penny gaff of the poor East Lon-
doner is a step for him to more humane life; it is,—what example shall we choose? it is *Strathmore*, let us say,— it is the one-

pound-eleven-and-sixpenny gaff of the young gentlemen of
the clubs and the young ladies of Belgravia, that is for them
but a step in the primrose path to the everlasting bonfire.
Besides, say what you like of the idealessness of aristocracies,
the vulgarity of our middle class, the immaturity of our lower,
and the poor chance which a happy type of modern life has
between them, consider this: Of all that makes life liberal and
humane,—of light, of ideas, of culture,—every man in every
class of society who has a dash of genius in him is the born
friend. By his bringing up, by his habits, by his interest, he
may be their enemy; by the primitive, unalterable complexion
of his nature, he is their friend. Therefore, the movement of
the modern spirit will be more and more felt among us, it will
spread, it will prevail. Nay," this enthusiast often continues,
getting excited as he goes on, "the *Times* itself, which so stirs
some people's indignation,—what is the *Times* but a gigantic
Sancho Panza, to borrow a phrase of your friend Heine;—a
gigantic Sancho Panza, following by an attraction he cannot
resist that poor, mad, scorned, suffering, sublime enthusiast,
the modern spirit; following it, indeed, with constant grumbling, expostulation, and opposition, with airs of protection, of
compassionate superiority, with an incessant byplay of nods,
shrugs, and winks addressed to the spectators; following it, in
short, with all the incurable recalcitrancy of a lower nature,
but still following it?" When my friend talks thus, I always
shake my head, and say that this sounds very like the transcendentalism which has already brought me into so many
scrapes.

I have another friend again (and I am grown so cowed by all
the rebuke my original speculations have drawn upon me that
I find myself more and more filling the part of a mere lis-
tener), who calls himself Anglo-Saxon rather than English,[1]
and this is what he says: "We are a small country," he says,
"and our middle class has, as you say, not much gift for anything but making money. Our freedom and wealth have given
us a great start, our capital will give us for a long time an

[1] *Not* the talented author of *Greater Britain*, though the reader might
be inclined to suppose so.—ED.

advantage; but as other countries grow better governed and richer, we must necessarily sink to the position to which our size, and our want of any eminent gift for telling upon the world spiritually, doom us. But look at America; it is the
5 same race; whether we are first or they, Anglo-Saxonism triumphs. You used to say that they had all the Philistinism of the English middle class from which they spring, and a great many faults of their own besides. But you noticed, too, that, blindly as they seemed following in general the star of their god Bun-
10 combe, they showed, at the same time, a feeling for ideas, a vivacity and play of mind, which our middle class has not, and which comes to the Americans, probably, from their democratic life, with its ardent hope, its forward stride, its gaze fixed on the future. Well, since these great events have lately
15 come to purge and form them, how is this intelligence of theirs developing itself? Now they are manifesting a quick sense to see how the world is really going, and a sure faith, indispensable to all nations that are to be great, that greatness is only to be reached by going that way and no other? And then,
20 if you talk of culture, look at the culture their middle, and even their working class is getting, as compared with the culture ours are getting. The trash which circulates by the hundred thousand among our middle class has no readers in America; our rubbish is for home consumption; all our best books,
25 books which are read here only by the small educated class, are in America the books of the great reading public. So over there they will advance spiritually as well as materially; and if our race at last flowers to modern life there, and not here, does it so much matter?" So says my friend, who is, as I premised, a
30 devotee of Anglo-Saxonism; I, who share his pious frenzy but imperfectly, do not feel quite satisfied with these plans of vicarious greatness, and have a longing for this old and great country of ours to be always great in herself, not only in her progeny. So I keep looking at her, and thinking of her; and as
35 often as I consider how history is a series of waves, coming gradually to a head and then breaking, and that, as the successive waves come up, one nation is seen at the top of this wave, and then another of the next, I ask myself, counting all the

waves which have come up with England at the top of them: When the great wave which is now mounting has come up, will she be at the top of it? *Illa nihil, nec me quærentem vana moratur!*—

> "Yes, we arraign her; but she,   5
> The weary Titan, with deaf
> Ears, and labour-dimm'd eyes,
> Regarding neither to right
> Nor left, goes passively by,
> Staggering on to her goal;   10
> Bearing, on shoulders immense,
> Atlantéan, the load,
> Wellnigh not to be borne,
> Of the too vast orb of her fate."

(A Frenchman signing himself "Horace,"—not one of our 15 own set, but a person full of intellect,—wrote to the Editor of the *Pall Mall Gazette* a sort of electioneering letter from Paris in answer to the foregoing essay, saying what blessings our liberty and publicity were, and how miserable the French middle class was without them. I cannot do better than conclude 20 with the answer I made to him, from which it will appear, I hope, how courteous was always my moderation when I was left to myself, and had not Arminius at my elbow to make me say what he chose. I should premise that "My Countrymen" had been received with such a storm of obloquy, that for 25 several months after its appearance I was in hiding;—not, indeed, leaving Grub Street, but changing my lodgings there repeatedly.)—ED.

A Courteous Explanation

GRUB STREET, *March* 19, 1866.

SIR,—

Although I certainly am rather pained to find myself, after my long and arduous labours for the deliverance from Philistinism of this nation in general, and the civilisation and embellishment of our great middle class in particular, an object of aversion and mistrust to my countrymen, when I expected nothing from them but gratitude and love, still I have learnt to try and wrap myself on these occasions in my own virtue, knowing very well that the benefactors of mankind are seldom popular, and that your public favourite is generally some Barabbas. Meanwhile, for posterity's sake, I keep out of harm's way as much as I can; but as I sit shivering in my garret, listening nervously to the voices of indignant Philistines asking the way to Grub Street, a friend brings me the *Pall Mall Gazette* with "Horace's" two letters. Perhaps it would be my best way to keep perfectly still, and not to give any sign of life to my enemies; but such is my inveterate weakness (dear enough it has cost me, this weakness!) for the amiable nation to which "Horace" belongs, that I cannot find it in my heart to leave his letters without a word of acknowledgment. I write with a bit of coal on the lining of my hat, and in much perturbation of mind besides; so "Horace" will kindly excuse faults in my style, which indeed, as he has observed, even when I am at my best, is far from correct. But what is one to do? So few people know what it is to be born artless.

It is very kind of "Horace," and just like his generous nation, to come forward when he sees I am in trouble, to confirm what he thinks I said; only I did not say it, but the foreigners.

"Horace" says that with us mediocrity does make itself heard more loudly and more frequently than the thoughtful part of the nation, through the press and even in Parliament; he says that he is inclined to think the middle classes in Germany and Switzerland enjoy life more than the same classes in England; he says he is quite of opinion that the conduct of England in the affair of the Duchies lowered her considerably in the eyes of Europe, nor did she gain honour by the Crimean war, or by her attitude in Italian affairs. He adds, indeed, that it is probable some fifty years hence certain episodes of the Indian mutiny, and the heroism and charity displayed during the cotton famine, will be accepted as a set-off for many shortcomings; and I am sure I devoutly hope they may; but my foreign friends were only talking of the present.

It was the life of the middle class in Switzerland and Germany that my foreign friends said was more enjoyable than the life of the corresponding class in England, and "Horace" declares my foreign friends were right. But he goes on to draw a frightful picture of the middle class in his own country, France. This is what I so admire in these continental writers, and it is just what my foreign friends claimed for them: "We foreigners can see our own deficiencies well enough, and are not backward in proclaiming them; you English can see and say nothing but what redounds to your own honour and glory." It makes me blush to think how I winced under what the foreigners said of England, how I longed to be able to answer it, how I rejoiced at hearing from the English press that there was nothing at all in it, when I see the noble frankness with which these foreigners judge themselves. How "Horace" does give it to his poor countrymen when he thinks they deserve it! So did Monsieur de Tocqueville, so does Monsieur Renan. I lay up the example for my own edification, and I commend it to the editor of the *Morning Star* for his.

I have seen very little of the French middle class which "Horace" describes, and I dare say what he says of them is all true. But what makes me look at France and the French with such inexhaustible curiosity and indulgence is this,—their faults are not ours, so we are not likely to catch them; their merits are not ours, so we are not likely to become idle and self-sufficient from studying them. It is not that I so envy "Horace" his Paris as it is;—I no longer dance, nor look well when dressed up as the angel Gabriel, so what should I now do in Paris?—but I find such interest and instruction in considering a city so near London, and yet so unlike it! It is not that I so envy "Horace" his café-haunting, dominoes-playing *bourgeois*; but when I go through Saint Pancras, I like to compare our vestry-haunting, resolution-passing *bourgeois* with the Frenchman, and to say to myself: "This, then, is what comes of not frequenting cafés nor playing dominoes! My country-men here have got no cafés, and have never learnt dominoes, and see the mischief Satan has found for their idle hands to do!" Still, I do not wish them to be the café-haunting, dominoes-playing Frenchmen, but rather some third thing, neither the Frenchmen nor their present selves.

And this brings me to the one little point of difference (for there is just one) between "Horace" and me. Everything, as he himself says, depends on a man's point of view. Now, his point of view is French, mine English. He and his friends have, he says, one absorbing desire,—to diffuse in France the knowledge and love of true political liberty. For this purpose they are obliged to point to other countries, and England is, says "Horace," their "great stand-by." Now, those who speak evil of the English constituencies, of our great middle class, etc., etc., discredit, "Horace" says, English parliamentary government and the power of the press, and tend to damage the great stalking-horse behind which he and his friends are moving to the attack of the French Emperor, and so spoil their game for them.

"Horace" and his friends are evidently Orleanists, and I have always observed that the Orleanists are rather sly. They can put their tongue in their cheek as well as anybody at the expense of my dear country, but she is to be an angel of light as long as it serves their turn. So the *Morning Star* and I are to go on crying, "We are free! we are free! Our newspapers can say what they like," whether this cry does us good or no, because true political liberty is the one thing needful for

"Horace" and the French. The *Morning Star*, I must say, does its duty nobly, and "Horace" ought to be very grateful to it; but because I, thinking only of England, venture to go on a little farther, and to inquire what we do with ourselves when we are free to do just what we like, I give umbrage to "Horace;" he says I destroy his stalking-horse, and he accuses me of railing at parliamentary government and the power of the press. In short, he and his friends have lost their tails, and want to get them back again; and unless I talk of nothing but tails, and keep always saying that whoever has a tail is perfect, and whoever has not a tail is not worth twopence, "Horace" is vexed with me.

To prevent all such misunderstanding for the future, let me say, in the fullest, frankest, most unreserved manner, that I admit the French have lost their tails, and that I pity them for it. I rejoice that the English have kept theirs. I think our "true political liberty" a beautiful, bushy object, and whoever says I do not think so slanders me. But I do not see the slightest danger of our losing it. Well, then comes the question, whether, to oblige "Horace" and his friends, I am to talk of nothing but this beautiful tail of ours, and our good fortune in having it. I should not mind doing this if our human economy took in nothing but tails, if we were all tail; but our economy takes in other things as well,—hearts, for instance, and heads. In hearts we are (except when we find ourselves in India or Jamaica) very well off; but in heads there is always room for improvement. Now, I think it was after witnessing a great constitutional stand by the Saint Pancras Board of Guardians, —no, it was after reading the second or third of the *Daily Telegraph's* funeral orations on Lord Palmerston,—that it struck me there was a danger of our trading too extensively upon our tails, and, in fact, running to tail altogether. I determined to try and preach up the improvement and decoration of our heads. Our highest class, besides having of course true political liberty,—that regulation tail which every Briton of us is blessed with,—is altogether so beautiful and splendid [1] that for my part I hardly presume to inquire what it has or has not

[1] And above all, as Mr. Carlyle says, *polite*.—Ed.

in the way of heads. So I turn to my own class, the middle class, which, not being so beautiful and splendid, does not dazzle my eyes so much. And for this class I want to work out a deliverance from the horrid dilemma in which "Horace" and
5 others try to fix us;—liberty and Philistinism, or else culture and slavery.

After this candid explanation on our one point of difference (for the rest of his letters I heartily thank him), I trust that "Horace" will not in future think it his duty, whenever he
10 finds me preaching to my countrymen that with all our political liberty we are still, in many respects, unprofitable servants, —I trust, I say, that whenever he sees this, he will not now think it his duty to administer to me a sharp pinch and exclaim: "False one, what are you about? what have you done
15 with your tail? begin brandishing it in our tyrant's face again directly!" Let him and the French rather themselves get back their lost tails from their tyrant, who is generally supposed, too, to have had, when he talked of "crowning the edifice," this appendage in view.

20 I do hope, Sir, that the sentiments expressed in this letter may be the means of procuring for your excellent newspaper that free circulation in the French capital which is at present, I am told, denied you; and as my bit of coal is worn to a stump, I sign myself, your humble servant,

25   MATTHEW ARNOLD.

To the EDITOR *of the* PALL MALL GAZETTE.

———————

(In May of this year (1866) Arminius arrived in London; an event which I sometimes fancy future ages will parallel with the arrival of Augustine at Canterbury. In July, six weeks
30 later, began what, in talking to Arminius, I loved to call, half-playfully, half-seriously, "the preaching of *Geist*." In November, 1870, four short years afterwards, he lay buried under the Bougival poplar-tree! Shadows, indeed, as Mr. Sala says, we are, and shadows we pursue.

35 Farewell, Arminius!—Thou good soul, thou great intellect, farewell!)—ED.

Letter I

I Introduce Arminius and "Geist" to the British Public

(The acquaintance of the ever-to-be-lamented Arminius was made by the present Editor on the Continent in the year 1865. The early history of the noble family of Von Thunder-ten-Tronckh, to which Arminius belonged, their establishment in Westphalia, the sack of their castle in the middle of the last century by the Bulgarians, the fate of their principal dependents (among whom was the famous optimist philosopher, Dr. Pangloss), the adventures of Arminius's grandfather and his deportation to the Jesuits at Rome, are recorded in a well-known treatise of Voltaire. Additional information is supplied in several of the following letters.

Arminius came to England in 1866, and the correspondence now given in a collected form to the public commenced in the summer of that year, at the outbreak of the war between Prussia and Austria. Many will yet remember the thrill with which they originally received, through the unworthy ministry of the present Editor, the communication of the great doctrine of "Geist." What, then, must it have been to hear that doctrine in its first newness from the lips of Arminius himself! Yet it will, I hope, be admitted, that even in this position of exceptional privilege, the present Editor succeeded in preserving his coolness, his independent judgment, and his proper feelings as a Briton.)—Ed.

GRUB STREET, *July* 19, 1866.

SIR,—
A Prussian acquaintance of mine, one of the party of foreigners who so offensively criticised my countrymen to me when I was abroad last year, has been over here just now, and for the last week or so he has been favouring me with his remarks on all he hears us say about the present crisis in Germany. In confidence I will own to you that he makes himself intensely disagreeable. He has the harsh, arrogant, Prussian way of turn-

ing up his nose at things and laying down the law about them;
and though, as a lover of intellect, I admire him, and, as a
seeker of truth, I value his frankness, yet, as an Englishman,
and a member of what the *Daily Telegraph* calls "the Imperial
5 race," I feel so uncomfortable under it, that I want, through
your kindness, to call to my aid the great British public, which
never loses heart and has always a bold front and a rough word
ready for its assailants.

My Prussian friend got a little mortification at the beginning
10 of his visit, and as it is my belief this mortification set him
wrong from the first, I shall relate what it was. I took him with
me down to Reigate by the railroad, and in the carriage was
one of our representative industrial men (something in the
bottle way), a famous specimen of that great middle class
15 whose energy and self-reliance make England what it is, and
who give the tone to our Parliament and to our policy. News
had just come of the first bloodshed between the Austrians and
Prussians now at war together in Germany. "So they've begun
fighting," cried my countryman; "what fools they both are!"
20 And he handed us *Punch* with that masterly picture in it of
"Denmark avenged;" that scathing satire which represents the
King of Denmark sitting with his glass of grog and his cigar, to
gloat over the terrible retribution falling upon his great enemy
Prussia for her misdeeds towards him. My Prussian glared at
25 the striking moral lesson thus brought to his notice, but rage
and contempt made him speechless. I hastened, with a few
sentences taken from Mr. Gladstone's recent advice to the
Roumanians, to pay my homage to the great principles of
peaceful, industrial development which were invoked by my
30 countryman. "Yes; war," I said, "interrupts business, and
brings intolerable inconvenience with it; whereas people have
only to persist steadily in the manufacture of bottles, railways,
banks, and finance companies, and all good things will come to
them of their own accord." Before I had finished we reached
35 Reigate, and I got my still speechless Prussian quickly out of
the train.

But never shall I forget the flood when speech came at last:
"The dolt! the dunderhead! His ignorance of the situation, his

ignorance of Germany, his ignorance of what makes nations great, his ignorance of what makes life worth living, his ignorance of everything except bottles,—those infernal bottles!" I heard so much of all this that I am glad to forget it without going through it again with the British public. I only mention it to make the rudeness of expression in what follows less unaccountable.

The day before yesterday the *Daily News* published that powerful letter from Mr. Goldwin Smith, pronouncing in favour of the Prussian alliance. In great excitement I ran with it to my friend. "At last I have got something," I cried, "which will please you; a declaration by one of our best writers, in one of our best newspapers, for a united Germany under Prussian headship. She and we are thereupon to combine to curb France. Wherever I go, I hear people admiring the letter and approving the idea." A sardonic smile, such as Alexander von Humboldt used to have when he contemplated the late King of Prussia's missionary deaconesses, came over my Berliner's harsh countenance. "Good God!" said he, "the miracles that needle-gun is working! It is only a year ago you were threatening Prussia with France, and suggesting to that great and sagacious ruler, as you called him, the French Emperor, to take the Rhine Province from us; it is not six weeks since I saw him styled in this very newspaper, with the dignity usual in Englishmen at present, 'the arbiter of Europe.' He has done nothing in the meantime to injure you; he has done his best to keep well with you. How charmed he will be with his friends! But the declaration you are all so pleased at, who is it by?" "Mr. Goldwin Smith," I answered. "I know him," he said; "a good writer, but a fanatic." "Oh, no, no," said I; "a man of genius and virtue." Without answering, my Berliner took the newspaper and read the letter. "He should have served under Nelson," he said, as he finished it; "he hates a Frenchman as he does the devil. However, it is true that a preponderance in the world such as the French, thanks to your stupidity, were fast getting, is enough to make any human being, let alone a Frenchman, unbearable; and it is a good thing to have a great Germany in the world as well as a great France. It would be a good thing to have a great England too, if you would let us. But pray what is to unite Germany and England against France? What is to be the ground of sympathy between actual England and actual Germany?" "You are a strong Liberal," said I, "so I can easily answer you. You are drawn towards England because of her liberalism, and away from the French Emperor because of his despotism." "Liberalism and despotism!" cried the Prussian; "let us get beyond these forms and words. What unites and separates people now is *Geist*."

I had not the slightest idea what he meant, and my looks told my bewilderment. "I thought you had read Mr. Grant Duff's chapters on Germany," said he. "But Mr. Grant Duff knows what he writes about, so I suppose you have not. Your great Lord Palmerston used to call Germany 'that country of d——d professors;' and the English public, which supposes professors to be people who know something, and hates anybody who knows anything, has always kept its mind as clear of my unfortunate country as it could. But I advise you, for the sake of the events now passing, to read Mr. Grant Duff's book. There you will find that in Berlin we oppose 'Geist,'—*intelligence*, as you or the French might say,—to 'Ungeist.' The victory of 'Geist' over 'Ungeist' we think the great matter in the world. The same idea is at the bottom of democracy; the victory of reason and intelligence over blind custom and prejudice. So we German Liberals who believe in 'Geist' have a sympathy with France and its governors, so far as they are believers in democracy. We have no sympathy with English liberalism, whose centre is in the 'Ungeist' of such people as your wiseacre in the Reigate train."

"But then you play," cried I, "the game of the Tories; for listen to Mr. Goldwin Smith: 'The Tories in Europe, with the sure instinct of a party, recognise the great patron of reaction in the Emperor of the French.' You and we are to unite, in order to defeat the Tories and the Emperor of the French."

The Prussian answered: "Mr. Goldwin Smith blinds himself with the passions, as the Emperor of the French himself would say, of another age. The Tories of Europe have no real love for the Emperor of the French; they may admire and envy his

absolutism and strength, but they hate his fundamental principles: they can have no real sympathy with the Sovereign who
says boldly that he detests the actual public law of Europe, and
who tells the people that it is among the people he finds the
true genius of France, and breathes freely. Such a man works
for 'Geist' in his way; [1] not, perhaps, through a *Daily Telegraph*, or monster meetings in Trafalgar Square, or a Coles's
Truss Manufactory standing where it ought not, a glorious
monument of individualism and industrialism, to adorn the
'finest site in Europe;' but by making the common people feel
they are alive and have a human spirit in them. We North-
Germans have worked for 'Geist' in our way, by loving
knowledge, by having the best-educated middle and lower
class in the world. You see what this has just done for us.
France has 'Geist' in her democracy, and Prussia in her education. Where have you got it?—got it as a force, I mean, and
not only in a few scattered individuals. Your common people
is barbarous; in your middle class 'Ungeist' is rampant; and as
for your aristocracy, you know 'Geist' is forbidden by nature
to flourish in an aristocracy.

"So do not," he continued, "suffer yourself to be deceived
by parallels drawn from times before 'Geist.' What has won
this Austrian battle for Prussia is 'Geist;' 'Geist' has used the
King, and Bismarck, and the Junkers, and 'Ungeist in uniform,' all for its own ends; and 'Geist' will continue so to use
them till it has triumphed.[2] It will ally itself with 'Geist' where
it finds it, because there it has a ground for mutual respect and
understanding; and where there is no 'Geist,' it has none.

"And now," this odious man went on, "now, my dear
friend, I shall soon be leaving you, so one word more. You

[1] The indulgence of Arminius for this execrable and unsuccessful tyrant was unworthy of a member of our great Teutonic family. Probably,
after Sedan, he changed his opinion of him.—ED.

[2] I am unwilling to triumph over Arminius in his grave; but I cannot
help remarking that "Ungeist in uniform," as Mr. Bottles observes to me,
has just given a pretty good account of the "Geist" in French democracy;
and I have a shrewd suspicion it will give an equally good account of the
"Geist" of Arminius's educated and liberal friends in Prussia. Perhaps
Arminius was taken away from the evil to come!—ED.

have lately been writing about the Celts and the Germans, and in the course of your remarks on the Germans you have said, among many impertinences, one thing which is true. You have said that the strength of North Germany lay in this, that the idea of science governed every department of human activity there. You, my dear friend, live in a country where at present the idea of clap-trap governs every department of human activity. Great events are happening in the world, and Mr. Goldwin Smith tells you that 'England will be compelled to speak at last.' It would be truly sad if, when she does speak, she should talk nonsense. To prevent such a disaster, I will give you this piece of advice, with which I take my leave: *Get 'Geist.'* "

Thank God, this d——d professor (to speak as Lord Palmerston) is now gone back to his own *Intelligenz-Staat.* I half hope there may next come a smashing defeat of the Prussians before Vienna, and make my ghostly friend laugh on the wrong side of his mouth. Meanwhile, I shall take care that he hears whatever answers he gets. I know that they will be conclusive, and I hope that they will be speedy, and in this hope,

I am, Sir,

Your obedient servant,

MATTHEW ARNOLD.

To the EDITOR *of the* PALL MALL GAZETTE.

Letter II

Arminius Appears as His Own Interpreter

BERLIN, *July* 31, 1866.

Sir,—

An English friend of mine, Mr. Matthew Arnold, seems to have rushed into print with an idea or two he picked up from me when I was in England, and to have made rather a mess of it; at least, he sends me some newspapers which have answered him, and writes me a helpless sort of a letter at the same time, asking me how he is to parry this, and what he is to say in reply to that. Now, I have a regard for this Mr. Matthew Arnold, but I have taken his measure, and know him to be, as a disputant, rather a poor creature. Again and again I have seen him anxiously ruminating over what his adversary has happened to say against his ideas; and when I tell him (if the ideas were mine) that his adversary is a *dummkopf*, and that he must stand up to him firm and square, he begins to smile, and tells me that what is probably passing through his adversary's mind is so and so.[1]

I see your hideous truss manufactory in Trafalgar Square comes up in this controversy, and that very manufactory brings to my mind a ridiculous instance of my poor friend's weakness. I had been running over with him a few of the principal violations of æsthetic laws in London, illustrating the lesson by reference to the stucco palaces of my beautiful Berlin. After despatching the Duke of Wellington's statue and the black dome and gray pepper-boxes of your National Gallery, I came to Coles's manufactory. "Can anything be more atrocious?" I asked. "It is bad," answered my poor friend; "and

---

[1] A very ill-natured and exaggerated description of my (I hope) not unamiable candour.—ED.

yet," he went on, "and yet, Arminius, I have a tenderness for
that manufactory. That manufactory, with other things in
London like it, is one of my favourite arguments for the immortality of the soul." "What folly have you got in your head
now?" said I. "Remember," said he, "what is told us of the
statue of the Olympian Zeus by Phidias. It was life enough to
have seen it; felicity had then reached its consummation; the
spirit could grasp no more, and the man might end. And what
therefore, I ask, must not be in store for the British ratepayer,
who in his life has only seen the Duke of Wellington's statue
and Coles's truss manufactory? His felicity must surely be yet
to come. Somewhere, beyond the grave" . . . and for a good
twenty minutes my simple friend went on with stuff like this,
which I will not weary you with any more of.

I, Sir, as a true Prussian, have a passion for what is *wissenschaftlich* (I do not say "scientific," because then you English will think I mean I have an interest in the sea-bear, or in
the blue lights and smells of a chemical lecture). I am, I say,
wissenschaftlich; I love to proceed with the stringency of a
philosopher, and Mr. Matthew Arnold with his shillyshallying
spoils the ideas I confide to him. Therefore I write to you
myself, to tell you (since I like your nation for the sake of the
great men it has formerly produced, and of its brave-hearted,
industrious people) where the pinch of the matter for you
really lies.

It lies here—there is in you *"kein Ernst, der ins Ganze
geht."* You peck at the mere outside of problems; you have not
got your mind at work upon them; you fancy they will solve
themselves without mind, if only you keep making bottles, and
letting every one do what is right in his own eyes, and con-
gratulating yourselves at the top of your voices on your own
success. "Individualism and industrialism will in time replace
Coles by a worthier edifice," says one of your prophets. Not
without an *"Ernst der ins Ganze geht,"* I answer. Not without
"Geist" and faith in "Geist;" and this is just what your individualism and industrialism has not got. "A self-administering
community is surely an ideal."—That depends entirely on
what the self-administering community is like. If it has "Geist,"

and faith in "Geist," yes; if it has not, no. Then another of
your prophets asks: "Why should 'Geist' care about democracy? Democracy is government by the masses, by the light of
their own vulgar tastes."—Your democracy perhaps, but this is
just what makes your weakness; you have no *demos*, no peo-   5
ple, but "masses with vulgar tastes." The top part of them are
in training to be Philistines like your middle class; the lower
part is a rabble. Your democracy has not yet reached even the
idea of country; the friends of your northern workmen tell us
they read American newspapers, and care more for America   10
than for England. No wonder; they have never been quickened by an *"Ernst der ins Ganze geht,"* the only baptism that
makes masses into a people; they have never been in contact
with "Geist," only with clap-trap. To abate feudalism by providing that in one insignificant case out of one million land   15
shall not follow the feudal law of descent; to abolish English
church-rates because the English Dissenters are strong, and to
spare the Irish Church Establishment because the Irish Catholics are weak; [1] to give a man leave to marry his deceased
wife's sister; to give a man who lives in a particular kind of   20
house a vote for members of Parliament—that is the pabulum
by which the leaders of your people seek to develop "Geist" in
it, and to awaken an *"Ernst der ins Ganze geht."* If this is not
spiritual enough, as a final resource there is rioting in the
parks, and a despotism of your penny newspapers tempered by   25
the tears of your executive, to hasten the growth of English
democracy in dignity and intelligence.

The French are not solid enough for my taste; but, *Gott in
Himmel!* that people has had a fire baptism, and the democracy which is born of a fire baptism like theirs, "Geist" cannot   30
help caring about. They were unripe for the task they in '89
set themselves to do; and yet, by the strength of "Geist" and
their faith in "Geist," this "mere viper brood of canting egotists" did so much that they left their trace in half the beneficial reforms through Europe; and if you ask how, at Naples, a   35

[1] No doubt this remark of Arminius had some share in producing that
great measure which has since abolished the Irish Church by the power
of the English Dissenters' enmity to Church establishments.—ED.

convent became a school, or in Ticino an intolerable oligarchy
ceased to govern, or in Prussia Stein was able to carry his land-
reforms, you get one answer: *the French!* Till modern society
is finally formed, French democracy will still be a power in
5 Europe, and it will manage to have effective leaders at the
Tuileries, and not only in Cayenne. It will live, though the
classes above it may rot; because it has faith in "Geist," and
does not think that people can do without "Geist" by dint of
holding monster meetings, and having their *Star* [1] and *Tele-*
10 *graph* every morning, and paying no church-rates, and marrying their deceased wife's sister.

We Prussians, Sir, have, as a people, no great love for the
French, because we were blown into the air by the explosion
of their "Geist" some sixty years ago, and much quarrelling
15 and ill-blood followed. But we saw then what a power the
"Geist" in their democracy gave them; and we set to work to
make ourselves strong, not by a sort of wild fire-baptism of the
mass, but in our steady German way, by culture, by *forming*
our faculties of all kinds, by every man doing the very best he
20 could with himself, by trusting, with an *"Ernst der ins Ganze*
geht," to mind and not to clap-trap. Your "earnest Liberal" in
England thinks culture all moonshine; he is for the spiritual
development of your democracy by rioting in the parks, abolishing church-rates, and marrying a deceased wife's sister; and
25 for leaving your narrow and vulgar middle class (of which I
saw an incomparable specimen in a Reigate train when I was
over in England) just as it is. On the other hand, Mr. Matthew
Arnold writes me word that a club has just been formed
among you to do honour to the memory of that great man,
30 Richard Cobden; that this club has taken for its motto, "Peace,
Retrenchment, and Reform;" and that these words, by a special command from Mr. Cobden's ghost, are to bear the following interpretation:—"Peace to our nonsense, retrenchment
of our profligate expenditure of clap-trap, and reform of our-

35   [1] The *Star*, like Arminius himself, has passed from amongst us; but
may we not say that its work was done when it had once laid the basis of
that admirable and fruitful alliance between Mialism and Millism, which
the course of our politics is now every day consolidating?—ED.

selves." Whether this is true, or merely a stroke of my poor friend's so-called playfulness (Heaven save the mark!), I do not feel quite sure; I hope for your sakes it is true, as this is the very thing you want, and nothing else can save you from certain decline.

Do not be astonished at the aristocratic prefix to my name; I come of a family which has for three generations rubbed shoulders with philosophy.

Your humble servant,

VON THUNDER-TEN-TRONCKH.

To the EDITOR *of the* PALL MALL GAZETTE.

Letter III

I Expostulate with Arminius on His Revolutionary Sentiments

GRUB STREET, *August* 6, 1866.

SIR,—

I thought it was very odd I got no answer from Arminius von Thunder-ten-Tronckh (he was christened Hermann, but I call him Arminius, because it is more in the grand style), when I so particularly begged him to write soon, and save what rags he could of his tissue of nonsense about "Geist," after my countrymen had riddled it, as I knew they were sure to do. I supposed he had taken service, like the rest of the German Liberals, under Bismarck, and was too busy pillaging the poor Frankfort people to think of intellectual matters; but I now see he has been writing direct to you, and wants to leave me out in the cold altogether. I do not in the least care for his coarse Prussian sneers, but I must say it is rather good that he should not be above sponging on me week after week in Grub Street, swilling beer (none of your Bavarian wash, but sound English Bass) at my expense, filling my garret (for I don't smoke myself) with the smell of his execrable tobacco, getting the daily benefit of my *Star* and *Telegraph* (I take the *Star* for wisdom and charity, and the *Telegraph* for taste and style), and keeping me up yawning till two o'clock every morning to listen to his rubbishy transcendentalism, and yet be too fine a gentleman to make me the depositary of his ideas for transmission to the English public. But Arminius has the ridiculous pride of his grandfather, who, though the family estate had all gone to the dogs, and he was ruined and turned priest, chose to set his stiff German face against Candide's marriage with his sister. He got shipped off to the Jesuits at Rome, as every one

knows; but what is not so well known is,[1] that when the
French Revolution came, this precious priest, like Talleyrand,
married, and my Arminius is his grandson. Arminius came
over here to make acquaintance with Mr. Lowe, who he has
found out is in some odd way descended from the philosopher
Pangloss,[2] a great friend of the Von Thunder-ten-Tronckh
family; but ever since the sack of their château by the Bulgarians, the Von Thunder-ten-Tronckhs have not had a sixpence
in the world except what they could get by their "Geist," and
what Arminius gets by his is such beggar's allowance that he is
hardly presentable; well enough for Grub Street, but, as I told
him, not at all the sort of company Mr. Lowe keeps.

I don't think Arminius has gained much by being his own
expounder, for more vague declamatory trash than his letter I
never read. The truth is, he cannot rise to an Englishman's
conception of liberty, and understand how liberty, like virtue,
is its own reward. "We go for self-government," I am always
saying to him. "All right," he says, "if it is government by
your better self." "Fiddlesticks about our better self!" answer
I. "Who is to be the judge? No, the self every man chooses."
"And what is the self the mass of mankind will choose," cries
he, "when they are not told there is a better and a worse self,
and shown what the better is like?" "They will choose the
worse, very likely," say I, "but that is just liberty." "And what
is to bring good out of such liberty as that?" he asks. "The
glorious and sanative qualities of our matchless Constitution," I
reply; and that is always a stopper for him.

But what I grieve most to observe in Arminius's letter, and
what will lead to my breaking with him in the long run, in
spite of my love for intellect, is the bad revolutionary leaven
which I see works stronger and stronger in him, and which he

[1] It was necessarily unknown to Voltaire, who wrote the history of the
Von T. family.—ED.

[2] It is my firm belief that this relationship, which had become a fixed
idea with Arminius, never really existed. The optimism of Mr. Lowe's
estimate of the British middle class and its House of Commons, in his
celebrated speech on Reform, had, in my opinion, struck Arminius's
fancy, and made him imagine a kinship in the flesh where there was in
truth only a kinship in the spirit.—ED.

no doubt got from the worthless French company his grandfather kept.[1] I noticed an instance of it while he was over here,
and I have had another instance, besides his letter to you, since
he went away. The instance while he was over here was this. I
had taken him down to Wimbledon to see the shooting; and
there, walking up and down before the grand tent, was Lord
Elcho. Everybody knows Lord Elcho's appearance, and how
admirably he looks the part of our governing classes; to my
mind, indeed, the mere cock of his lordship's hat is one of the
finest and most aristocratic things we have. So of course I
pointed Lord Elcho out to Arminius. Arminius eyed him with
a jacobinical sort of a smile, and then: "Cedar of Lebanon
which God has not yet broken!" sneered he. I was pleased at
Arminius knowing his St. Augustine, for the Prussians are in
general thought to be much tainted with irreligion; but I felt
at the time, and I feel still, that this was not by any means the
proper way of speaking of a dashing nobleman like Lord
Elcho.

The other instance is worse still. Besides writing Arminius
long letters, I keep him regularly supplied with the *Star*, sending him my own copy after I have read it through twice. I
particularly begged him to study the number for last Wednesday week, in which there was the most beautiful account of
"An Aristocratic Reformer." The other papers had not got it.
It related how the Honourable Charles Clifford, a gentleman
of strikingly handsome appearance, addressed the crowd in
Hyde Park from the foot-board of a hansom. He told them he
cared nothing for the Walpoles or Pakingtons, who were for
putting down the voice of the people, for, said he, he was
higher in social position than they. He was the son of a peer,
his son-in-law was a peer, and all his family belonged to the
aristocratic classes. This announcement was received with enthusiastic applause by the street-Hampdens present. "May I
ask you, right honourable sir," cried one of them, "why, as
you are such a big man, you do not open the Park gates to us

---

[1] This partially explains, no doubt, though it cannot altogether excuse,
the weak indulgence always cropping out in Arminius for France and its
immoral people.—Ed.

poor people?" Mr. C. said he wished he had the keys of the Park in his pocket. But he delivered himself of the great principle that it is the duty of the aristocratic classes to protect and promote the interests of the working men, and then he drove off in his hansom amidst redoubled applause.

Now nothing, Sir, gives me such pride and pleasure as traits of this kind, which show that we have, as Lord Macaulay finely says, the most popular aristocracy and the most aristocratic people in the world. I thought it would do Arminius good to study the incident, and I wrote him word to that effect. Would you believe it, Sir? Mr. "Geist" cannot condescend to write me a letter, but he sends me back my *Star* with a vile sketch, or rather caricature, of this touching incident; and opposite Mr. C.'s gentlemanly figure he has written "Esel," and opposite the crowd "Lumpenpack," which a friend who knows German better than I do tells me are words of disrespect, and even contempt. This is a spirit which I hate and abhor, and I tell Arminius plainly through your columns (since he chooses to adopt this way of corresponding) that unless he can break himself of it all is ended between him and me, and when next he comes to England he will find the garret-door in Grub Street bolted against him.

Your obedient servant,
MATTHEW ARNOLD.

To the EDITOR *of the* PALL MALL GAZETTE.

Letter IV

Arminius Assails the British Press for Its Free and Independent Comments on Foreign Politics

BERLIN, *August* 11, 1866.

SIR,—

For Heaven's sake try and prevail upon your countrymen, who are so very anxious for peace for themselves, not to go on
5 biting first the French Emperor's tail and then ours, merely for the fun of the thing apparently, and to have the pleasure of at least seeing a fight between other people, if they cannot have one of their own. You know that Michelet, the French historian, all through his history, familiarly talks of your people as
10 *ce dogue;* "upon this, *ce dogue mordit* such a one;" "upon that *ce dogue déchira* such another." According to him, you must always be *mordre*-ing or *déchirer*-ing some one, at home or abroad, such is your instinct of savageness; and you have,—undoubtedly you have,—a strong share of pugnacity. When I
15 was over in England the other day, my poor friend Mr. Matthew Arnold insisted, with his usual blind adoration of everything English, on taking me down to admire one of your great public schools; precious institutions, where, as I tell him, for £250 sterling a year your boys learn gentlemanly deportment
20 and cricket. Well, down we went, and in the playing-fields (which with you are the school): "I declare," says Mr. Matthew Arnold, "if there isn't the son of that man you quarrelled with in the Reigate train! And there, close by him, is a son of one of our greatest families, a Plantagenet! It is only in Eng-
25 land, Arminius, that this beautiful salutary intermixture of classes takes place. Look at the bottle-merchant's son and the Plantagenet being brought up side by side; none of your absurd separations and seventy-two quarterings here. Very likely

52

young Bottles will end by being a lord himself." I was going to point out to Mr. Matthew Arnold that what a middle class wants is ideas, and ideas an aristocracy has nothing to do with; so that that vulgar dog, Bottles the father, in sending his son to learn only cricket and a gentlemanly deportment, like the aristocracy, had done quite the wrong thing with him. But just at this moment our attention was attracted by what was passing between the boys themselves. First, a boy goes up to Bottles, and says: "Bottles, Plantagenet says he could lick you with one hand; you are as big as he is,—you wouldn't take a licking from him, would you?" "No!" answered poor Bottles, rather hesitatingly. Upon this another boy rushes to Plantagenet. "Plantagenet," cries he, "that brute Bottles says he wouldn't take a licking from you." "Does he, the beast!" thunders Plantagenet, and, flying at Bottles, hits him full on the nose; and as Bottles's blood streamed out, and I turned away in disgust, I heard the exulting cries of your young "dogues" making the arrangements for a systematic encounter.

Now really, Sir, since I have been back in Germany your newspapers are perpetually bringing to my mind Michelet's "dogue" and what I saw in your playing-fields. First you go to the French Emperor, and say: "Ha, tyrant, we hope humble-pie agrees with you! We hope your tail between your legs is not productive of much inconvenience. Just as the intellectual Emperor was overmatched by an Italian statesman, he now finds himself outdone by a German statesman; a most agreeable thing for an intellectual Emperor—ha! ha! The intellectual Emperor distinctly intimated there must be no disturbing the European equilibrium, else he should interpose. Now the map has been altered enormously to the profit of Prussia, so what is the intellectual Emperor to do? Acknowledge himself outwitted by Count Bismarck, just as he was outwitted by Count Cavour?—ha, ha! Humble-pie! Humble-pie!"—With the greatest alacrity the malcontents in France, the old Constitutional party, take up your parable: "France is eating humble-pie!" they scream out; "the tyrant is making France eat humble-pie! France is humiliated! France is suffocating!" France is not difficult to stir up, and the French Emperor has already

had to ask for the frontier of 1814. If you go on at this rate I
expect he will have to ask for the Mark of Brandenburg next
week. Then you will come to Bismarck and say: "Bismarck,
the tyrant is stretching his greedy fist over German soil. Will
5   you let him have it? Think of the prodigious strength you
have just shown, of the glory you have just won. Think of
French insolence, think of 1813, think of German honour,
think of *sauer-kraut*, think of the moral support of England.
Not an inch of German soil for the French tyrant!" And so,
10 while you yourselves,—the new man in you, that is,—teach
the nations, as Lord Stanley says, how to live, by peacefully
developing your bottle-man in the Reigate train, your half-
naked starvelings selling matches in St. James's Park, your
truss manufactories in Trafalgar Square, and your *Daily Tele-*
15 *graph* saying in spite of all powers human and divine what it
likes, you at the same time want to throw a bone to the old
"dogue" in you, in the shape of a very pretty quarrel of your
getting up between other people.

Do, Sir, let other people also have a chance of teaching the
20 nations how to live, and emulating your bottle-man and your
Daily Telegraph. For my part, I have the greatest aversion,
and so have all the clearest-headed Germans of my acquaintance, to a quarrel with France. We, as genuine Liberals, know
that French democracy is our natural ally. You will observe it
25 is the Constitutionalists in France who are crying out so loudly
for more territory to make their strength keep pace with ours.
And then think of our poor delicate constitutionalism at home,
and of the cruelty of leaving it with its work to do in the face
of a war with France, and Bismarck made stronger than ever
30 by such a war! I know our German constitutionalism pretty
well. It comes up to the throne, "With fullest heart-devotion
we approach Prussia's King, reverently beseeching him to turn
away his unconstitutional ministers." Prussia's gracious King
gives a grunt, and administers a sound kick to his petitioner's
35 behind, who then departs, singing in fervent tones: "*Hoch* for
King and fatherland!"

No, Sir; peace, the growth of a republican spirit all through
Europe, and a mutual support between all those who share this

spirit, are what I wish for. The French are vain; they have
been spoilt; we have been going very fast; and you and the
Orleanists keep telling them they are humiliated if they do not
get something. No doubt people have a right to go to war for
the balance of power if they believe in it; you have gone to
war for it often enough when it suited your turn. So the
Emperor of the French, as you will not let him have a chance
of being wise and of seeing that here is a new spiritual force he
had not reckoned on, which yet he may perfectly make
friends of and live happily with, thinks he must do something
for the balance of power, must ask for some rectification or
other of frontier. I only hope he will ask for something moderate, and that we shall be moderate when he asks for it. Pray, Sir,
pray do not you play the "dogue" and make moderation
harder both for the Emperor and for us.

I assure you a war with France would be a curse to us which
even the blessing of your moral support would hardly compensate. And supposing (for certainly you do hate the French
pretty strongly) in a year or two you determined to give us
your active support,[1] and to send, with infinite crying out, an
expedition of fifteen thousand men to the coast of Gothland or
some such place, I am afraid, Sir, with the vast armaments and
rapid operations of modern warfare, even this active support
of yours would not do us any great good.

Your humble servant,

Von Thunder-ten-Tronckh.

To the Editor *of the* Pall Mall Gazette.

P.S.—By the way, I read poor Mr. Matthew Arnold's letter
to you the other day. You see just what he is; the discursive-

---

[1] This is puerile. War between France and Prussia has since happened.
We have not been able to give our undivided moral support to either
combatant; of our active support, therefore, there could be no question.
But it may be fearlessly asserted, that the well-balanced alternations of
our moral support, the wise and steady advice given by our newspapers,
and, in fact, our attitude generally in regard to this war, have raised
Great Britain to a height even more conspicuous than she has ever yet
occupied, in the esteem and admiration of foreign countries.—Ed.

ness, the incapacity for arguing, the artlessness, the not very
delicate allusions to my private circumstances and his own. It
is impossible to enter into any serious discussion with him. But
on one point of fact I will set him right. I saw Mr. Lowe and
found him very affable; even more like his ancestor Pangloss
than I should have thought possible. "The best of all possible
worlds" was always on his lips; "a system of such tried and
tested efficiency;" "what can we want more?" "the grumbler
fails to suggest even one grievance." I told him of that bottle
barbarian in the Reigate train, and he said that on men of this
kind rested "the mighty fabric of English prosperity." I could
not help saying that in my opinion no country could long
stand being ruled by the spirit (or rather matter) of men like
that; that a discontent with the present state of things was
growing up, and that to-morrow even, or next day, we might
see a change. Upon this, Mr. Lowe threw himself into a theatrical attitude, and with the most enthusiastic vehemence exclaimed:—

> "To-morrow?
> Oh, spare it, spare it!
> It ought not so to die." [1]

In a man like poor Mr. Matthew Arnold, this infatuation about
everything English is conceivable enough, but in a man of Mr.
Lowe's parts I own I cannot quite make it out, notwithstanding his descent from Pangloss.

VON T.

[1] As the sentiments here attributed to Mr. Lowe, together with this
very remarkable and splendid passage of poetry with which he concludes, are all taken from Mr. Lowe's printed speeches, and may have
been read by Arminius in the *Times*, I still retain my doubts whether his
interview with Mr. Lowe had ever any existence except in his own
fertile imagination.—ED.

Letter V

I Communicate a Valuable Exposition, by Arminius, of the System of Tenant-Right in Prussia

GRUB STREET, *November* 8, 1866.

SIR,—

My love for intellect has made me seek a reconciliation with Arminius, in spite of all I had to complain of in him, and any one who had looked in here to-night might have seen him puffing away at his pipe, and laying down the law just in his old style. He was so immensely tickled at the *Daily Telegraph* calling his poor friend,—artless and obscure garretteer that he knows him to be,—"a high priest of the kid-glove persuasion," [1] that he has been in a good humour ever since, and to-night he had been giving me some information which I do think, notwithstanding the horrid *animus* he betrays in delivering it, is highly curious and interesting, and therefore I hasten to communicate it to you.

It is about the Prussian land reforms, and this is how I got it out of him. "You made me look rather a fool, Arminius," I began, "by what you primed me with in Germany last year about Stein settling your land question." "I dare say you looked a fool," says my Prussian boor, "but what did I tell you?" "Why," says I, "you told me Stein had settled a land question like the Irish land question, and I said so in the *Cornhill Magazine,* and now the matter has come up again by Mr. Bright talking at Dublin of what Stein did, and it turns out he settled nothing like the Irish land question at all, but only a sort of tithe-commutation affair." "Who says that?" asked Arminius. "A very able writer in the *Times,*" I replied.

[1] Besides all I had to endure from Arminius himself, our leading newspapers persisted in holding me answerable for every paradox uttered by him.—ED.

I don't know that I have ever described Arminius's personal appearance. He has the true square Teutonic head, a blond and disorderly mass of tow-like hair, a podgy and sanguine countenance, shaven cheeks, and a whity-brown moustache. He wears a rough pilot-coat, and generally smokes away with his hands in the pockets of it, and his light blue eyes fixed on his interlocutor's face. When he takes his hands out of his pockets, his pipe out of his mouth, and his eyes off his friend's face, it is a sign that he is deeply moved. He did all this on the present occasion, and passing his short thick fingers two or three times through his blond hair: "That astonishing paper!" muttered he.

Then he began as solemn as if he was in a pulpit. "My dear friend," says he, "of the British species of the great genus Philistine there are three main varieties. There is the religious Philistine, the well-to-do Philistine, and the rowdy Philistine. The religious Philistine is represented by——" "Stop, Arminius," said I, "you will oblige me by letting religion alone!" "As you please," answered he; "well, then, the rowdy Philistine is represented by the *Daily Telegraph*, and the well-to-do Philistine by the *Times*. The well-to-do Philistine looks to get his own view of the British world,—that it is the best of all possible worlds as it is, because he has prospered in it,—preached back to him *ore rotundo* in the columns of the *Times*. There must be no uncertain sound in his oracle, no faltering, nothing to excite misgivings or doubts; like his own bosom, everything his oracle utters must be positive, pleasant, and comfortable. So of course about the great first article of his creed, the sacrosanctity of property, there must in the *Times* be no trifling. But what amuses me is that his oracle must not even admit, if these matters come to be talked of, that Stein trifled with it in another country. The ark is so sacred, the example so abominable, and the devotee so sensitive. And therefore Stein's reforms become in the *Times*, for the reassurance of the well-to-do British Philistine, a sort of tithe-commutation affair,—nothing in the world more! nothing in the world more!"

"Don't go on in that absurd way, Arminius," said I; "I don't tell you it was a tithe-commutation, but a commutation like

the tithe-commutation. It was simply, the *Times* says, the conversion of serf-tenures into produce-rents. I hope that gives
you a perfectly clear notion of what the whole thing was, for
it doesn't me. But I make out from the *Times* that the *leibeigener*——" "Rubbish about the *leibeigener*," cries Arminius, in   5
a rage, "and all this jargon to keep your stupid mind in a mist;
do you want to know what really happened?" "Yes, I do," said
I, quietly, my love for knowledge making me take no notice of
his impertinence. "Yes, I do, and particularly this: In the first
place, was the land, before Stein's reforms, the landlord's or   10
the tenant's?" "The landlord's," says Arminius. "You mean,"
said I, "that the landlord could and did really eject his tenant
from it if he chose." "Yes, I do," says Arminius. "Well, then,
what did Stein do?" asked I. "He did this," Arminius answered. "In these estates, where the landlord had his property-   15
right on the one hand, and the tenant his tenant-right on the
other, he made a compromise. In the first place he assigned,
say, two-fifths of the estate to the landlord in absolute property, without any further claim of tenant-right upon it thenceforth for ever. But the remaining three-fifths he compelled the   20
landlord to sell to the tenant at eighteen years' purchase, so
that this part should become the tenant's absolute property
thenceforth for ever. You will ask, where could the tenant find
money to buy? Stein opened rent-banks in all the provincial
chief towns, to lend the tenant the purchase-money required,   25
for which the State thus became his creditor, not the landlord.
He had to repay this loan in a certain number of years. To free
his land from this State mortgage on it and make it his own
clear property, he had every inducement to work hard, and he
did work hard; and this was the grand source of the frugality,   30
industry, and thrivingness of the Prussian peasant. It was the
grand source, too, of his attachment to the State." "It was
rotten bad political economy, though," exclaimed I. "Now I
see what the *Times* meant by saying in its leading article yesterday that Ireland is incomparably better governed than the   35
United States, France, Germany, or Italy, because the excellence of government consists in keeping obstacles out of the
way of individual energy, and you throw obstacles in the way

of your great proprietors' energy, and we throw none in the way of ours. Talk of a commutation like the tithe-commutation, indeed! Why it was downright spoliation; it was just what Lord Clanricarde says some people are driving at in Ire-
5 land, a system of confiscation." "Well," says Arminius, calmly, "that is exactly what the Prussian junkers called it. They did not call it commutation, they called it confiscation. They will tell you to this day that Stein confiscated their estates. But you will be shocked to hear that the Prussian Government had,
10 even before Stein's time, this sad habit of playing tricks with political economy. To prevent the absorption of small proprietors by a great landed aristocracy, the Prussian Government made a rule that a *bauer-gut*,—a peasant property,—could not, even if the owner sold it, be bought up by the Lord Clanri-
15 carde of the neighbourhood; it must remain a *bauer-gut* still. I believe you in England are for improving small proprietors off the face of the earth, but I assure you in Prussia we are very proud of ours, and think them the strength of the nation. Of late years the Hohenzollerns have taken up with the junkers,
20 but for a long time their policy was to uphold the *bauer* class against the *junker* class; and, if you want to know the secret of the hold which the house of Hohenzollern has upon the heart of the Prussian people, it is not in Frederick the Great's victories that you will find it, it is in this policy of their domestic
25 government." "My dear Arminius," said I, "you make me perfectly sick. Government here, government there! We English are for self-government. What business has any Mr. Stein to settle that this or that estate is too large for Lord Clanricarde's virtues to expand in? Let each class settle its own affairs, and
30 don't let us have Governments and Hohenzollerns pretending to be more enlightened than other people, and cutting and carving for what they call the general interest, and God knows what nonsense of that kind. If the landed class with us has got the magistracy and settled estates and game laws, has not the
35 middle class got the vestries, and business, and civil and religious liberty? I remember when the late Sir George Cornewall Lewis wanted to get some statistics about the religious denominations, your friend Bottles, who is now a millionaire and a

Churchman, was then a Particular Baptist. 'No,' says Bottles, 'here I put down my foot. No Government on earth shall ask me whether I am a Particular Baptist or a Muggletonian.' And Bottles beat the Government, because of the thorough understanding the upper and middle classes in this country have with one another that each is to go its own way, and Government is not to be thrusting its nose into the concerns of either. There is a cordial alliance between them on this basis." "Yes, yes, I know," Arminius sneeringly answered; "Herod and Pontius Pilate have shaken hands."

"But I will show you, Arminius," I pursued, "on plain grounds of political economy——" "Not to-night," interrupted Arminius, yawning; "I am going home to bed." And off he went, descending the garret stairs three at a time, and leaving me to burn the midnight oil in order to send you, Sir, what is really, I flatter myself, an interesting, and I may even say a valuable communication.

Your humble servant,
MATTHEW ARNOLD.

To the EDITOR *of the* PALL MALL GAZETTE.

Stein Plus Hardenberg

To the Editor *of the* Pall Mall Gazette.

Sir,—Like so many intellectual Germans at present in this metropolis, and indeed like so many famous professors of "Geist" in all ages, Arminius is often sadly short of ready money, and at
5   such times, when neither his fine old Westphalian family nor (which for my own part I value more) his many-sided culture can save him from the low intrusions of the British tradesman, and more particularly of his tobacconist, he is apt to be more or less what I may call in hiding, and very hard to get hold of.
10   I wanted to get hold of him because I was not at all satisfied, and I could see the British public was not at all satisfied, about the quality and condition of those Prussian tenants he made such capital out of; and his bold assertion that they were tenants whom the landlord could turn out struck, I found, some
15   of our best-informed public writers with astonishment as a regular thumper. So coming upon him by a lucky chance at the corner of Leicester-square to-day, I button-holed him at once; and, "Arminius," says I, "that was rather too cool of you about the Prussian tenants being people the landlord could
20   turn out, or people the least bit in the world like Irish tenants. Why, when the thing comes to be looked into, it appears they were regular copyholders, and could sell and bequeath their holdings." "Oh," says Arminius, with his disagreeable grin, "you have got as far as the *erb-pachter,* have you? It is some-
25   thing new for your great nation to attend to anything that concerns us wretched unwashed foreigners. Pursue your studies, my dear friend, *macte novâ virtute;* you will arrive at the *zeit-pachter* in time. Good morning, I am in an immense hurry." "Stop, Arminius," said I, firmly; "that respectable man

coming out of Messrs. Bickers and Bush's is *not* your tobacconist. Give me at least chapter and verse for the measure of Stein's which conferred possession on any tenant not a copyholder. And as I understand your noble but obscure language very imperfectly, be good enough to speak English." "In the first place," says Arminius, roughly, "when we Germans talk of Stein's reforms, we mean the whole batch of reforms from 1807 to 1811, because Stein was the originator of the whole movement; and this you, who have been in Germany, ought to have known. Stein led off by abolishing serfage, but Napoleon had Stein turned out in 1808, and our agrarian law, as we call it, dates from Hardenberg's Ministry in 1811. Hardenberg always said that this measure of his was concerted with Stein, and had Stein's approval; and, whether it was so or not, Stein gets the credit of it with the nation. By this measure a *zeit-pachter*, a tenant for a term of years, a tenant who could not leave his holding to his son, a tenant whom his landlord could turn out the moment his term expired, a tenant with a tenant-right as hard to define, as much reposing on sentiment and custom, as any Irish tenant's tenant-right, got half his holding in absolute property, free from all feudal services, in return for giving up at once the other half to his landlord." "It really sounds," I answered, "too shocking to be lightly believed. I shall look it up, Arminius, I assure you, and so will my countrymen." "Do so," says Arminius, sternly; "the longer you look at it the less you'll like it, I fancy. If you want the precise date of our agrarian law, it is the 14th of September, 1811. And now don't bore me any longer."

"Just one thing before you go, Arminius," I pleaded. "An Irish squire has been writing to me for information about his own position under legislation like Stein's applied to Ireland, and about Lord Clanricarde's position, and the position of a man called Tim Mullooly, and I don't know what all." "I remember," says Arminius, a grim smile breaking over his face; "that was not a bad joke about Tim Mullooly. If I recollect right, Tim Mullooly was an old *leibeigener* of your friend's or of Lord Clanricarde's, and now that the star of junkerdom is setting they want to make a junker of poor Tim, who had

emancipated himself and was beginning to hold up his head in the world. They should have thought of that sooner. Tell your squire," continued Arminius, his tone relaxing more and more as he went on, "tell that ex-proprietor of poor Tim Mullooly,
5   tell that bloodsucker, that his best plan now is to ponder night and day Hardenberg's 'Reflections on the Prussian Land Reforms,' and to exhort his brother squires round the bog of Allen to do the same. They will find them in a book called 'Mémoires tirés des Papiers d'un Homme d'État,' under the year
10   1810 or 1811. Hardenberg's papers are still locked up in the Berlin archives, but extracts from them are said to have been surreptitiously made, and to have got into this French book, and these reflections are among them." And so saying, Arminius darted up Rupert-street.
15   The Irish squire asked me so many questions to which I could make no answer that I thought the least I could do was to send him these reflections of Hardenberg's to serve instead. So to the British Museum I went, and, after rummaging in the "Mémoires" through 1810 and 1811, these were the only re-
20   flections I could find. They seem to me to be merely adding insult to injury; but I send them to you, Sir, for transmission to the Irish squire, because Arminius wished it. I send them in the original, because I suppose the squire can make them out with his dictionary as well as I:—

25   Quelques unes de ces réformes portaient atteinte au principe de la propriété; mais les circonstances où l'on se trouvait furent générale-ment senties. Aussi les riches subirent-ils leurs pertes avec résigna-tion, tandis qu'on satisfaisait le plus grand nombre des sujets prus-siens.

30   Your humble servant,
Grub-Street, Saturday Evening.   MATTHEW ARNOLD.

Letter VI

I Become Intrusted with the Views of Arminius on Compulsory Education

GRUB STREET, *April* 20, 1867.

SIR,—

It is a long while since you have heard anything of Arminius and me, though I do hope you have sometimes given a thought to us both. The truth is we have been in the country. You may imagine how horribly disagreeable Arminius made himself during the famous snow in London at the beginning of this year. About the state of the streets he was bad enough, but about the poor frozen-out working men who went singing without let or hindrance before our houses, he quite made my blood creep. "The dirge of a society *qui s'en va*," he used to call their pathetic songs. It is true I had always an answer for him— "Thank God, we are not Haussmannised yet!" and if that was not enough, and he wanted the philosophy of the thing, why I turned to a sort of constitutional common-place book, or true Englishman's *vade mecum*, which I have been these many years forming for my own use by potting extracts from the *Times*, and which I hope one day to give to the world, and I read him this golden aphorism: "Administrative, military, and clerical tyranny are unknown in this country, because the educated class discharges all the corresponding functions through committees of its own body." "Well, then," Arminius would answer, "show me your administrative committee for ridding us of these cursed frozen-out impostors." "My dear Arminius," was my quiet reply, "voluntary organisations are not to be dealt with in this peremptory manner. The administrative committee you ask for will develop itself in good time; its future members are probably now at nurse. In England we like our improvements to *grow*, not to be manufactured."

However the mental strain, day after day, of this line of high constitutional argument was so wearing, that I gladly acceded to a proposal made by Arminius in one of his fits of grumbling to go with him for a little while into the country. So into the country we went, and there, under his able guidance, I have been assiduously pursuing the study of German philosophy. As a rule, I attend to nothing else just now; but when we were taking one of our walks abroad the other morning, an incident happened which led us to discuss the subject of compulsory education, and, as this subject is beginning to awaken deep interest in the public mind, I think you may be glad to have an account of the incident, and of the valuable remarks on compulsory education which were drawn from Arminius by it.

We were going out the other morning on one of our walks, as I said, when we saw a crowd before the inn of the country town where we have been staying. It was the magistrates' day for sitting, and I was glad of an opportunity to show off our local self-government to a bureaucracy-ridden Prussian like Arminius. So I stopped in the crowd, and there we saw an old fellow in a smock-frock, with a white head, a low forehead, a red nose, and a foxy expression of countenance, being taken along to the justice-room. Seeing among the bystanders a contributor to the *Daily Telegraph*,[1] whom I formerly knew well enough,—for he had the drawing-room floor underneath me in Grub Street, but the magnificent circulation of that journal has long since carried him, like the course of empire, westward,—I asked him if he could tell me what the prisoner was charged with. I found it was a hardened old poacher, called Diggs,—Zephaniah Diggs,—and that he was had up for snaring a hare,—probably his ten-thousandth. The worst of the story, to my mind, was that the old rogue had a heap of young children by a second wife whom he had married late in life, and that not one of these children would he send to school, but persisted in letting them all run wild, and grow up in utter barbarism.

[1] Do you recognise yourself, Leo? Is it presumptuous in me, upon giving this volume to the world, to bid you too, my friend, say with the poet: *Non omnis moriar?*—Ed.

I hastened to tell Arminius that it was a poaching case; and I added that it was not always, perhaps, in poaching cases that our local self-government appeared to the best advantage. "In the present case, however, there is," said I, "no danger; for a representative of the *Daily Telegraph* is down here, to be on the look-out for justices' justice, and to prevent oppression." Immediately afterwards I was sorry I had said this, for there are unfortunately several things which operate on Arminius like scarlet on a bull, making him vicious the moment he comes across them; and the *Daily Telegraph* is one of these things. He declares it foments our worst faults; and he is fond of applying to it Dryden's dictum on Elkanah Settle, that its style is boisterous and its prose incorrigibly lewd. Though I do certainly think its prose a little full-bodied, yet I cannot bear to hear Arminius apply such a term to it as "incorrigibly lewd;" and I always remonstrate with him. "No, Arminius," I always say, "I hope not *incorrigibly;* I should be sorry to think that of a publication which is forming the imagination and taste of millions of Englishmen." "Pleasant news," was Arminius's answer, the last time I urged this to him, "pleasant news; the next batch of you, then, will be even more charming than the present!"

I trouble you with all this, Sir, to account for the acerbity of tone in some of Arminius's subsequent conversation; an acerbity he too often manifests, and which tends, as I tell him, to detract from the influence which his talents and acquirements would otherwise give him. On the present occasion he took no direct notice of my mention of the *Daily Telegraph*, but seemed quite taken up with scrutinising old Diggs. "Such a peasant as that wretched old creature," he said at last, "is peculiar, my dear friend, to your country. Only look at that countenance! Centuries of feudalism have effaced in it every gleam of humane life." ... "Centuries of fiddlesticks!" interrupted I (for I assure you, Sir, I can stand up to Arminius well enough on a proper occasion). "My dear Arminius, how can you allow yourself to talk such rubbish? Gleam of humane life, indeed! do but look at the twinkle in the old rogue's eye. He has plenty of life and wits about him, has old Diggs, I can assure

you; you just try and come round him about a pot of beer!"
"The mere cunning of an animal!" retorted Arminius. "For
my part," pursued I, "it is his children I think most about; I am
told not one of them has ever seen the inside of a school. Do
you know, Arminius, I begin to think, and many people in this
country begin to think, that the time has almost come for
taking a leaf out of your Prussian book, and applying, in the
education of children of this class, what the great Kant calls
the categorical imperative. The gap between them and our
educated and intelligent classes is really too frightful." "Your
educated and intelligent classes!" sneered Arminius, in his very
most offensive manner; "where are they? I should like to see
them."

I was not going to stand and hear our aristocracy and middle
class set down in this way; so, treating Arminius's ebullition of
spite as beneath my notice, I pushed my way through the crowd
to the inn-door. I asked the policeman there what magistrates
were on the bench to-day. "Viscount Lumpington," says the
man, "Reverend Esau Hittall, and Bottles, Esquire." "Good
heavens!" I exclaimed, turning round to Arminius, who had
followed me, and forgetting, in my excitement, my just cause
of offence with him,—"Good heavens, Arminius, if Bottles
hasn't got himself made a county magistrate! *Sic itur ad astra.*"
"Yes," says Arminius, with a smile, "one of your educated and
intelligent classes, I suppose. And I dare say the other two are
to match. Your magistrates are a sort of judges, I know; just
the people who are drawn from the educated and intelligent
classes. Now, what's sauce for the goose is sauce for the gan-
der; if you put a pressure on one class to make it train itself
properly, you must put a pressure on others to the same end.
That is what we do in Prussia, if you are going to take a leaf
out of our book. I want to hear what steps you take to put this
pressure on people above old Diggs there, and then I will talk
to you about putting it on old Diggs. Take his judges who are
going to try him to-day; how about them? What training
have you made them give themselves, and what are their qualifications?"

I luckily happen to know Lord Lumpington and Hittall pretty

well, having been at college with them in former days, when I
little thought the Philistines would have brought my gray hairs
to a garret in Grub Street; and I have made the acquaintance
of Mr. Bottles since, and know all about him. So I was able to
satisfy Arminius's curiosity, and I had great pleasure in making 5
him remark, as I did so, the rich diversity of our English life,
the healthy natural play of our free institutions, and the happy
blending of classes and characters which this promotes. "The
three magistrates in that inn," said I, "are not three Government functionaries all cut out of one block; they embody our 10
whole national life:—the land, religion, commerce, are all represented by them. Lord Lumpington is a peer of old family
and great estate; Esau Hittall is a clergyman; Mr. Bottles is one
of our self-made middle-class men. Their politics are not all of
one colour, and that colour the Government's. Lumpington is 15
a Constitutional Whig; Hittall is a benighted old Tory. As for
Mr. Bottles, he is a radical of the purest water; quite one of
the Manchester school. He was one of the earliest free-traders;
he has always gone as straight as an arrow about Reform; he is
an ardent voluntary in every possible line, opposed the Ten 20
Hours' Bill, was one of the leaders of the Dissenting opposition
out of Parliament which smashed up the education clauses of
Sir James Graham's Factory Act; and he paid the whole expenses of a most important church-rate contest out of his own
pocket. And, finally, he looks forward to marrying his de- 25
ceased wife's sister. Table, as my friend Mr. Grant Duff says,
the whole Liberal creed, and in not a single point of it will you
find Bottles tripping!"

"That is all very well as to their politics," said Arminius, "but
I want to hear about their education and intelligence." "There, 30
too, I can satisfy you," I answered. "Lumpington was at Eton.
Hittall was on the foundation at Charterhouse, placed there by
his uncle, a distinguished prelate, who was one of the trustees.
You know we English have no notion of your bureaucratic
tyranny of treating the appointments to these great founda- 35
tions as public patronage, and vesting them in a responsible
minister; we vest them in independent magnates, who relieve
the State of all work and responsibility, and never take a shil-

ling of salary for their trouble. Hittall was the last of six neph-
ews nominated to the Charterhouse by his uncle, this good
prelate, who had thoroughly learnt the divine lesson that charity begins at home." "But I want to know what his nephew
5   learnt," interrupted Arminius, "and what Lord Lumpington
learnt at Eton." "They followed," said I, "the grand, old, for-
tifying, classical curriculum." "Did they know anything when
they left?" asked Arminius. "I have seen some longs and shorts
of Hittall's," said I, "about the Calydonian Boar, which were
10 not bad. But you surely don't need me to tell you, Arminius,
that it is rather in training and bracing the mind for future
acquisition,—a course of mental gymnastics we call it,—than
in teaching any set thing, that the classical curriculum is so
valuable." "Were the minds of Lord Lumpington and Mr. Hit-
15 tall much braced by their mental gymnastics?" inquired Arminius. "Well," I answered, "during their three years at Oxford
they were so much occupied with Bullingdon and hunting that
there was no great opportunity to judge. But for my part I
have always thought that their both getting their degree at last
20 with flying colours, after three weeks of a famous coach for
fast men, four nights without going to bed, and an incredible
consumption of wet towels, strong cigars, and brandy-and-
water, was one of the most astonishing feats of mental gymnastics I ever heard of."

25   "That will do for the land and the Church," said Arminius.
"And now let us hear about commerce." "You mean how was
Bottles educated?" answered I. "Here we get into another line
altogether, but a very good line in its way, too. Mr. Bottles
was brought up at the Lycurgus House Academy, Peckham.
30 You are not to suppose from the name of Lycurgus that any
Latin and Greek was taught in the establishment; the name
only indicates the moral discipline, and the strenuous earnest
character, imparted there. As to the instruction, the thoughtful educator who was principal of the Lycurgus House Acad-
35 emy,—Archimedes Silverpump, Ph.D., you must have heard
of him in Germany?—had modern views. 'We must be men of
our age,' he used to say. 'Useful knowledge, living languages,
and the forming of the mind through observation and experi-

ment, these are the fundamental articles of my educational creed.' Or, as I have heard his pupil Bottles put it in his expansive moments after dinner (Bottles used to ask me to dinner till that affair of yours with him in the Reigate train): 'Original man, Silverpump! fine mind! fine system! None of your antiquated rubbish—all practical work—latest discoveries in science—mind constantly kept excited—lots of interesting experiments—lights of all colours—fizz! fizz! bang! bang! That's what I call forming a man.' "

"And pray," cried Arminius, impatiently, "what sort of man do you suppose this infernal quack really formed in your precious friend Mr. Bottles?" "Well," I replied, "I hardly know how to answer that question. Bottles has certainly made an immense fortune; but as to Silverpump's effect on his mind, whether it was from any fault in the Lycurgus House system, whether it was that with a sturdy self-reliance thoroughly English, Bottles, ever since he quitted Silverpump, left his mind wholly to itself, his daily newspaper, and the Particular Baptist minister under whom he sate, or from whatever cause it was, certainly his mind, *quâ* mind——" "You need not go on," interrupted Arminius, with a magnificent wave of his hand, "I know what that man's mind, *quâ* mind, is, well enough."

But, Sir, the midnight oil is beginning to run very low; I hope, therefore, you will permit me to postpone the rest of Arminius's discourse till to-morrow. And meanwhile, Sir, I am, with all respect,

Your humble servant,
MATTHEW ARNOLD.

To the EDITOR *of the* PALL MALL GAZETTE.

Letter VII

More about Compulsory Education

Grub Street, *April* 21, 1867.

Sir,—

I take up the thread of the interesting and important discussion
on compulsory education between Arminius and me where I
left it last night.

"But," continued Arminius, "you were talking of compulsory
education, and your common people's want of it. Now, my
dear friend, I want you to understand what this principle of
compulsory education really means. It means that to ensure, as
far as you can, every man's being fit for his business in life,
you put education as a bar, or condition, between him and
what he aims at. The principle is just as good for one class as
another, and it is only by applying it impartially that you save
its application from being insolent and invidious. Our Prussian
peasant stands our compelling him to instruct himself before
he may go about his calling, because he sees we believe in
instruction, and compel our own class, too, in a way to make it
really feel the pressure, to instruct itself before it may go
about its calling. Now, you propose to make old Diggs's boys
instruct themselves before they may go bird-scaring or sheep-
tending. I want to know what you do to make those three
worthies in that justice-room instruct themselves before they
may go acting as magistrates and judges." "Do?" said I; "why,
just look what they have done all of themselves. Lumpington
and Hittall have had a public-school and university education;
Bottles has had Dr. Silverpump's, and the practical training of
business. What on earth would you have us make them do
more?" "Qualify themselves for administrative or judicial
functions, if they exercise them," said Arminius. "That is what

really answers, in their case, to the compulsion you propose to apply to Diggs's boys. Sending Lord Lumpington and Mr. Hittall to school is nothing; the natural course of things takes them there. Don't suppose that, by doing this, you are applying the principle of compulsory education fairly, and as you apply it to Diggs's boys. You are not interposing, for the rich, education as a bar or condition between them and that which they aim at. But interpose it, as we do, between the rich and things they aim at, and I will say something to you. I should like to know what has made Lord Lumpington a magistrate?" "Made Lord Lumpington a magistrate?" said I; "why, the Lumpington estate, to be sure." "And the Reverend Esau Hittall?" continued Arminius. "Why, the Lumpington living, of course," said I. "And that man Bottles?" he went on. "His English energy and self-reliance," I answered very stiffly, for Arminius's incessant carping began to put me in a huff; "those same incomparable and truly British qualities which have just triumphed over every obstacle and given us the Atlantic telegraph!—and let me tell you, Von T., in my opinion it will be a long time before the 'Geist' of any pedant of a Prussian professor gives us anything half so valuable as that." "Pshaw!" replied Arminius, contemptuously; "that great rope, with a Philistine at each end of it talking inutilities!

"But in my country," he went on, "we should have begun to put a pressure on these future magistrates at school. Before we allowed Lord Lumpington and Mr. Hittall to go to the university at all, we should have examined them, and we should not have trusted the keepers of that absurd cockpit you took me down to see, to examine them as they chose, and send them jogging comfortably off to the university on their lame longs and shorts. No; there would have been some Mr. Grote as School Board Commissary, pitching into them questions about history, and some Mr. Lowe, as Crown Patronage Commissary, pitching into them questions about English literature; and these young men would have been kept from the university, as Diggs's boys are kept from their bird-scaring, till they instructed themselves. Then, if, after three years of their university, they wanted to be magistrates, another pressure!—a great

80785

Civil Service examination before a board of experts, an examination in English law, Roman law, English history, history of jurisprudence——" "A most abominable liberty to take with Lumpington and Hittall!" exclaimed I. "Then your compulsory education is a most abominable liberty to take with Diggs's boys," retorted Arminius. "But, good gracious! my dear Arminius," expostulated I, "do you really mean to maintain that a man can't put old Diggs in quod for snaring a hare without all this elaborate apparatus of Roman law and history of jurisprudence?" "And do you really mean to maintain," returned Arminius, "that a man can't go bird-scaring or sheep-tending without all this elaborate apparatus of a compulsory school?" "Oh, but," I answered, "to live at all, even at the lowest stage of human life, a man needs instruction." "Well," returned Arminius, "and to administer at all, even at the lowest stage of public administration, a man needs instruction." "We have never found it so," said I.

Arminius shrugged his shoulders and was silent. By this time the proceedings in the justice-room were drawn to an end, the majesty of the law had been vindicated against old Diggs, and the magistrates were coming out. I never saw a finer spectacle than my friend Arminius presented, as he stood by to gaze on the august trio as they passed. His pilot-coat was tightly buttoned round his stout form, his light blue eyes shone, his sanguine cheeks were ruddier than ever with the cold morning and the excitement of discourse, his fell of tow was blown about by the March wind, and volumes of tobacco-smoke issued from his lips. So in old days stood, I imagine, his great namesake by the banks of the Lippe, glaring on the Roman legions before their destruction.

Lord Lumpington was the first who came out. His lordship good-naturedly recognised me with a nod, and then eyeing Arminius with surprise and curiosity: "Whom on earth have you got there?" he whispered. "A very distinguished young Prussian *savant*," replied I; and then dropping my voice, in my most impressive undertones I added: "And a young man of very good family, besides, my lord." Lord Lumpington looked at Arminius again; smiled, shook his head, and then, turning

away, and half aloud: "Can't compliment you on your friend," says he.

As for that centaur Hittall, who thinks of nothing on earth but field-sports, and in the performance of his sacred duties never warms up except when he lights on some passage about hunt- ing or fowling, he always, whenever he meets me, remembers that in my unregenerate days, before Arminius inoculated me with a passion for intellect, I was rather fond of shooting, and not quite such a successful shot as Hittall himself. So, the moment he catches sight of me: "How d'ye do, old fellow?" he blurts out; "well, been shooting any straighter this year than you used to, eh?"

I turned from him in pity, and then I noticed Arminius, who had unluckily heard Lord Lumpington's unfavourable comment on him, absolutely purple with rage and blowing like a turkey- cock. "Never mind, Arminius," said I soothingly; "run after Lumpington, and ask him the square root of thirty-six." But now it was my turn to be a little annoyed, for at the same instant Mr. Bottles stepped into his brougham, which was wait- ing for him, and observing Arminius, his old enemy of the Reigate train, he took no notice whatever of me who stood there, with my hat in my hand, practising all the airs and graces I have learnt on the Continent; but, with that want of amenity I so often have to deplore in my countrymen, he pulled up the glass on our side with a grunt and a jerk, and drove off like the wind, leaving Arminius in a very bad temper indeed, and me, I confess, a good deal shocked and mortified.

However, both Arminius and I got over it, and have now re- turned to London, where I hope we shall before long have another good talk about educational matters. Whatever Ar- minius may say, I am still for going straight, with all our heart and soul, at compulsory education for the lower orders. Why, good heavens! Sir, with our present squeezable Ministry, we are evidently drifting fast to household suffrage, pure and sim- ple; and I observe, moreover, a Jacobinical spirit growing up in some quarters which gives me more alarm than even house- hold suffrage. My elevated position in Grub Street, Sir, where I sit commercing with the stars, commands a view of a certain spacious and secluded back yard; and in that back yard, Sir, I tell you confidentially that I saw the other day with my own eyes that powerful young publicist, Mr. Frederic Harrison, in full evening costume, furbishing up a guillotine. These things are very serious; and I say, if the masses are to have power, let them be instructed, and don't swamp with ignorance and unreason the education and intelligence which now bear rule amongst us. For my part, when I think of Lumpington's estate, family, and connections, when I think of Hittall's shooting, and of the energy and self-reliance of Bottles, and when I see the unexampled pitch of splendour and security to which these have conducted us, I am bent, I own, on trying to make the new elements of our political system worthy of the old; and I say kindly, but firmly, to the compound householder in the French poet's beautiful words,[1] slightly altered: "Be great, O working class, for the middle and upper class are great!"

I am, Sir,

Your humble servant,

MATTHEW ARNOLD.

To the EDITOR *of the* PALL MALL GAZETTE.

(From the autumn of this year (1867) dates one of the most painful memories of my life. I have mentioned in the last letter but one how in the spring I was commencing the study of German philosophy with Arminius. In the autumn of that year the celebrated young Comtist, Mr. Frederic Harrison, resenting some supposed irreverence of mine towards his master, permitted himself, in a squib, brilliant indeed, but unjustifiably severe, to make game of my inaptitude for philosophical pursuits. It was on this occasion he launched the damning sentence: "We seek vainly in Mr. A. a system of philosophy with principles coherent, interdependent, subordinate, and derivative." The blow came at an unlucky moment for me. I was studying, as I have said, German philosophy with Arminius; we were then engaged on Hegel's "Phenomenology of *Geist*,"

[1] "Et tâchez d'être grand, car le peuple grandit."

and it was my habit to develop to Arminius, at great length, my views of the meaning of his great but difficult countryman. One morning I had, perhaps, been a little fuller than usual over a very profound chapter. Arminius was suffering from dyspepsia (brought on, as I believe, by incessant smoking); his temper, always irritable, seemed suddenly to burst from all control,—he flung the *Phänomenologie* to the other end of the room, exclaiming: "That smart young fellow is quite right! it is impossible to make a silk purse out of a sow's ear!" This led to a rupture, in which I think I may fairly say that the chief blame was not on my side. But two invaluable years were thus lost; Arminius abandoned me for Mr. Frederic Harrison, who must certainly have many memoranda of his later conversations, but has never given them, as I always did mine of his earlier ones, to the world.)—ED.

Theodore Parker *

Hardly the barest record of Theodore Parker appears in any biographical dictionary of importance. The "Nouvelle Biographie Générale" devotes less than half a page to him, and thus sums up his history:—"Malgré le talent qu'il déploya, la variété de sa prédication et la nouveauté de ses idées, il ne réussit pas à attirer à lui beaucoup de partisans, et en fut toujours réduit à la bizarre position d'un novateur sans disciple, d'un prêtre sans église, et d'un politique sans parti."

Mr. Moncure Conway, an American preacher now resident in London, who has known personally almost all the chief contemporary writers and thinkers of New England, and whose accounts of them are always to be read with interest, has published in the last number of the *Fortnightly Review* a notice of Theodore Parker. His estimate of Parker's career is very different from the estimate of the French biographer. The young men who gathered round Parker formed, says Mr. Conway, "the largest and most important congregation that has ever existed in America." And yet the future which Mr. Conway prophesies for Parkerism, as he calls it, is so splendid as even to throw this bright beginning into the shade. "Theodore Parker has founded a many-gated temple, with a dome wide and lofty enough to include all earnest minds—a study, possibly, of the American Church."

These are strong words; but it is undoubtedly true that Theodore Parker's action, considerable in his lifetime, has greatly increased since his death in 1860, and that it bids fair to increase

* "Selections from Theodore Parker's Unpublished Sermons." (London: Trübner. 1865.)

yet more. A volume of selections from notes of his sermons, which was not long ago published in this country, with Miss Cobbe for its editor, affords to the English public the means of acquainting itself with the thoughts, and of determining for itself the position, of this remarkable man, whose name is daily   5
more and more claiming our attention.

It has often been remarked that American literature has no original individuality of its own, but draws its whole life from English literature. American authors are English authors of more or less merit, whose birth has happened to be in America,   10
but who are fed on English books, follow the literary move-
ment of England, and reproduce English thought. Germany and France, the most active centres, for these many years past, of intellectual life, act upon America only through England. This has been so, but it is ceasing to be so, and will soon be so   15
no longer. An American author will write, as an American citizen lives, under the influences of American life and opin-
ion. Parker wrote and preached so; he was not an English Unitarian writing and preaching in America but still governed by the religious thought and tradition of the mother country;   20
he was an American Unitarian moving with the movement of American life and determined by its influences. He is thus a new and original type. The basis of his nature is indeed still that of the Englishman's nature, the Englishman of the middle class, the English Puritan; but this basis is modified by the daily   25
pressure of American circumstance, and not hedged round, and kept in an artificial conformity with the Puritanism of the old country.

Theodore Parker's word has therefore the force, the exuber-
ant hope, the boldness, the expansiveness of America herself, and   30
here is its originality.

Man advances continually. No man is full-grown. Jesus will not be called good; his ideal haunts him and shames his actual. The cat and dog and ox kind are fast moored by Providence in the same harbour; the fleet of animals rides at anchor all their life; but mankind   35
looses from port and sails the sea with God, driven by every wind, voyaging to other shores and continents continually new. "Nothing venture, nothing have."

That is Puritanism in Boston, Massachusetts, instead of Boston, Lincolnshire, and Puritanism freely drinking in the inspiration of its new sphere. It has the hope of the new world in it, un-clogged by "the heavy and the weary weight" of the old. Again:—

The mind of New England runs through the schoolhouse, and then jumps over the ditch of poverty, where lie Spain, Italy, Portugal, Ireland, and many another country that never took its start by the run in the schoolhouse; and so failed to leap the ditch and there lies to perish.

I once knew a hard-working man, a farmer and mechanic, who in the winter nights rose a great while before day and out of the darkness coaxed him at least two hours of hard study; and then, when the morning peeped over the eastern hills, he yoked his oxen and went forth to his daily work, or in his shop he laboured all day long; and when the night came he read aloud some simple book to his family, but when they were snugly laid away in their sleep the great-minded mechanic took to his hard study anew; and so, year out and year in, he went on, neither rich nor much honoured, hardly entreated by daily work, and yet he probably had a happi-ness in his heart and mind which the whole county might have been proud to share.

Puritanism on our side the Atlantic, in presence of all our igno-rance, poverty, and misery, naturally deals in no such frank and cheerful spirit with our actual life, but busies itself with the life to come. It is Parker's merit that to a different social medium from ours he did not transfer our religious routine, but allowed the schooling, the plenty, the wholesome social condition of New England, to invigorate his preaching, and to drench it, in the happiest way, in matter.

Thus daring to be himself, to be open to the influences round him, and to touch life with courage and frankness, he often reaches a strain of genuine strength, genuine eloquence:—

In human action there is always more virtue of every kind than vice; more industry than idleness, more thrift than spendthrift, more temperance than intemperance, more wisdom than folly. Even the American politician does not tell so many lies as he tells truths. Sincerity is more common than hypocrisy; no nation is ever

affected; the mass of men are in real earnest. In all the world mankind never put up a single gravestone to evil, as such. No man will
ever write on his father's tomb, "He was an eminent slavetrader."
Mr. Mason's sons will not write on his tombstone, "Author of the
Fugitive Slave Bill." No miserable minister who for the meanest   5
fee shall stand in some pulpit and preach funeral eulogies on such
wicked men, will praise them for deeds of this kind; he will try to
varnish them over, and say they were mistakes.

Certainly, the Puritan preacher who, instead of the old story
about justification and hell-fire, gives us such new and lively   10
strokes as this, is an apparition of great interest and importance. Probably Mr. Conway is right in thinking that this apparition will greatly sway the development of religion in
America, and that Theodore Parker has founded "a study of
the American Church." The sincerity and nobleness of his life   15
and character, joined to the originality, insight, and eloquence
of his teaching, are well fitted to make of Parker such a
founder. But whether a Church with Theodore Parker for its
founder will be "a many-gated temple, with a dome wide
and lofty enough to include all earnest minds," is more doubt-   20
ful. Parker, born an American, is as a preacher and writer a
genuine American voice, not an echo of English pulpits and
books; that is much. In the same way, Mr. Walt Whitman,
born an American, is as a poet a genuine American voice, not
an echo of English poetry; that, too, is much. But the admirers   25
of Theodore Parker or of Mr. Walt Whitman easily make
more of it than it is worth. At this time of day it is not enough
to be an American voice, or an English voice, or a French
voice; for a real spiritual lead it is necessary to be a European
voice. When American intellect has not only broken, as it is   30
breaking, the leading strings of England, but has also learnt to
assimilate independently the intellect of France and Germany
and the ancient world as well as of England, then, and not till
then, may the spiritual construction of an American be "a
many-gated temple, with a dome wide and lofty enough to   35
include all earnest minds." That the spiritual construction
reared by Theodore Parker is not of this supreme order, its
very style quickly indicates to any one who has much tact for

these matters. Sureness of beauty the style has none; it is continually breaking into the flaws and weaknesses from which
the style of master-founders is free. "Blue-eyed Lyra is mine;
mine is the many coloured morning; and the ring which mar-
5   ries day and night, its beauty is my own,"—that is a sort of
dithyramb which may well fill us with misgiving. It is soon
matched by Parker's cry on a comet: "This hairy stranger is
far inferior to the mind that shall calculate its orbit;" or by his
homage to youth: "I love to look on these young faces, and see
10 the firstlings of the young man's beard;" or by his pleasures of
memory: "He is a blessed boy again, his early home lingering
in his venerable memory for all his mortal life, the glad remembrance of brother and sister, the beautiful affection of
uncles and aunts, who seemed a special providence of love
15 watching over him, and dropping their balmy offerings into
his expectant hand!"

These are outward and superficial indications of inadequacy
—not inadequacy in any disrespectful use of the word, but inadequacy in view of such eminence as Mr. Conway and others
20 of Parker's great admirers claim for him. A deeper indication is
his Theism:—

You know that all this change and disappointment was foreseen,
was provided for, is part of the heavenly mechanism of life; that
the Great Director of the world cast his parts wisely, knows how
25 it will turn out.... This is the first of all rights, our unalienable
right to the infinite providence of the perfect God.... God is perfect Cause of all, creating all from a perfect motive, for a perfect
purpose, as a perfect means. He has the perfect justice to will the
best, perfect wisdom to devise the best, and perfect power to
30 achieve the best.... The defeats of life, poverty, shame, sickness,
death—all that is little; the good God foreknew it, provided for it
all, and will round it all at last into a globe of infinite satisfaction.... The most obvious justice shows that if a man has suffered
wrongfully, he ought to have some compensation in the next life;
35 a deeper justice shows that if he has sinned he ought to have a
chance to retrieve his wrong.... Continually there are sorrows for
which the earth has no recompense. The compensation, the joy,
must come in the eternal world. I know not how; the fact I am
sure of. That one and one make two is not clearer to me. I am not
40 more certain of my own existence. It follows from God's infinity.

It was hardly worth while crying out so contemptuously against the "popular theology," to retain as the cardinal points of one's creed dogmas which have as little scientific substance as the dogmas of ordinary Calvinism. The man who would "found a many-gated temple to include all earnest minds" must henceforth build under the inevitable condition that he brings in nothing which the scientific intellect cannot accept. The idea that the world is in a course of development, of *becoming*, towards a perfection infinitely greater than we now can even conceive, the idea of a *tendance à l'ordre* present in the universe "groaning and travailing in pain together," this the scientific intellect may accept, and may willingly let the religious instincts and the language of religion gather around it. But the idea of a "Great Director," or "Wise Engineer," to use Parker's language, who has set this movement a-going on a foreknown plan, and who sits *outside* of it watching its operation, this the scientific intellect can at the present time no more admit than the idea of a God who turns himself into a sacrificial wafer or who foredooms a large proportion of the human race to hell.

Mr. Walt Whitman, who has been already mentioned above, relates that a wounded soldier whom he attended in hospital during the late war in America asked him "if he enjoyed religion." Mr. Walt Whitman answered, "Perhaps not, my dear, in the way you mean; and yet, maybe, it is the same thing." Miss Cobbe, a fervent disciple of Parker, believes that Pantheism and Positivism are threatening us with an "awful desolation," that Christianity is doomed, and that in Parker's Theism is our only hope. Let her be of good cheer. Man, according to Goethe's wise epigram, "calls the best he knows, *God;*" the God of the Pantheist, the Positivist, and the Theist is alike the best that each of them knows; and each of them, if the others ask him whether he enjoys religion, may well reply with Mr. Walt Whitman, "Perhaps not, my dear, in the way you mean; and yet, maybe, it is the same thing." The reply will have truth in it; but, nevertheless, the manner in which a man translates and expresses to us the best he knows must determine his claim to spiritual leadership of the highest order. Far as Theodore Parker had outgrown the popular, ghastly theology, as he

is fond of calling it, of Puritanism, his basis was Puritan; and
the defects of Puritanism—its want of full and harmonious
development, its excessive development on one special side
—are the defects of Parker, defects which inevitably exclude
5   him from the rank, which his disciples claim for him, of a
teacher of the first order.

Short of this claim, which is apt to be set up and allowed far
too easily, Theodore Parker has a right to our warm and un-
stinted respect and admiration. The questions which he says the
10 controlling men of the principal churches of Boston never ask
about a minister—"Is the man able? Has he talents large enough,
and genius for religion? Has he the morality to make us
better? Has he the piety to charm us in our sorrows, to beguile
us from our sins? Has he courage, justice, wisdom, love, and
15 religion enough to make us better men, the church better, the
city a better town, and the nation a better state?"—all these
questions, which the controlling men of the principal churches
anywhere, and not in Boston only, are not prompt to ask, are
to be answered, if asked about Theodore Parker, with a cordial
20 and admiring "Yes!"

Culture & Anarchy

*An Essay in
Political and Social Criticism*

Estote ergo vos perfecti!

Introduction

In one of his speeches a short time ago, that fine speaker and famous Liberal, Mr. Bright, took occasion to have a fling at the friends and preachers of culture. "People who talk about what they call *culture!*" said he, contemptuously; "by which they mean a smattering of the two dead languages of Greek and Latin." And he went on to remark, in a strain with which modern speakers and writers have made us very familiar, how poor a thing this culture is, how little good it can do to the world, and how absurd it is for its possessors to set much store by it. And the other day a younger Liberal than Mr. Bright, one of a school whose mission it is to bring into order and system that body of truth with which the earlier Liberals merely fumbled, a member of the University of Oxford, and a very clever writer, Mr. Frederic Harrison, developed, in the systematic and stringent manner of his school, the thesis which Mr. Bright had propounded in only general terms. "Perhaps the very silliest cant of the day," said Mr. Frederic Harrison, "is the cant about culture. Culture is a desirable quality in a critic of new books, and sits well on a professor of *belles-lettres;* but as applied to politics, it means simply a turn for small fault-finding, love of selfish ease, and indecision in action. The man of culture is in politics one of the poorest mortals alive. For simple pedantry and want of good sense no man is his equal. No assumption is too unreal, no end is too unpractical for him. But the active exercise of politics requires common sense, sympathy, trust, resolution, and enthusiasm, qualities which your man of culture has carefully rooted up, lest they damage the delicacy of his critical olfactories. Perhaps they are the only

class of responsible beings in the community who cannot with
safety be entrusted with power."

Now for my part I do not wish to see men of culture asking
to be entrusted with power; and, indeed, I have freely said, that
in my opinion the speech most proper, at present, for a man of
culture to make to a body of his fellow-countrymen who get him
into a committee-room, is Socrates's: *Know thyself!* and this is
not a speech to be made by men wanting to be entrusted with
power. For this very indifference to direct political action I
have been taken to task by the *Daily Telegraph*, coupled, by a
strange perversity of fate, with just that very one of the Hebrew prophets whose style I admire the least, and called "an
elegant Jeremiah." It is because I say (to use the words which
the *Daily Telegraph* puts in my mouth):—"You mustn't make
a fuss because you have no vote,—that is vulgarity; you
mustn't hold big meetings to agitate for reform bills and to
repeal corn laws,—that is the very height of vulgarity,"—it is
for this reason that I am called, sometimes an elegant Jeremiah,
sometimes a spurious Jeremiah, a Jeremiah about the reality of
whose mission the writer in the *Daily Telegraph* has his
doubts. It is evident, therefore, that I have so taken my line as
not to be exposed to the whole brunt of Mr. Frederic Harrison's censure. Still, I have often spoken in praise of culture, I
have striven to make all my works and ways serve the interests
of culture. I take culture to be something a great deal more
than what Mr. Frederic Harrison and others call it: "a desirable quality in a critic of new books." Nay, even though to a
certain extent I am disposed to agree with Mr. Frederic Harrison, that men of culture are just the class of responsible beings
in this community of ours who cannot properly, at present, be
entrusted with power, I am not sure that I do not think this
the fault of our community rather than of the men of culture.
In short, although, like Mr. Bright and Mr. Frederic Harrison,
and the editor of the *Daily Telegraph*, and a large body of
valued friends of mine, I am a Liberal, yet I am a Liberal
tempered by experience, reflection, and renouncement, and I
am, above all, a believer in culture. Therefore I propose now
to try and inquire, in the simple unsystematic way which best

suits both my taste and my powers, what culture really is, what good it can do, what is our own special need of it; and I shall seek to find some plain grounds on which a faith in culture, —both my own faith in it and the faith of others,—may rest securely.

Chapter I

Sweetness and Light

The disparagers of culture make its motive curiosity; sometimes, indeed, they make its motive mere exclusiveness and vanity. The culture which is supposed to plume itself on a smattering of Greek and Latin is a culture which is begotten by nothing
5 so intellectual as curiosity; it is valued either out of sheer vanity and ignorance or else as an engine of social and class distinction, separating its holder, like a badge or title, from other people who have not got it. No serious man would call this *culture*, or attach any value to it, as culture, at all. To find
10 the real ground for the very different estimate which serious people will set upon culture, we must find some motive for culture in the terms of which may lie a real ambiguity; and such a motive the word *curiosity* gives us.

I have before now pointed out that we English do not, like the
15 foreigners, use this word in a good sense as well as in a bad sense. With us the word is always used in a somewhat disapproving sense. A liberal and intelligent eagerness about the things of the mind may be meant by a foreigner when he speaks of curiosity, but with us the word always conveys a
20 certain notion of frivolous and unedifying activity. In the *Quarterly Review*, some little time ago, was an estimate of the celebrated French critic, M. Sainte-Beuve, and a very inadequate estimate it in my judgment was. And its inadequacy consisted chiefly in this: that in our English way it left out of
25 sight the double sense really involved in the word *curiosity*, thinking enough was said to stamp M. Sainte-Beuve with blame if it was said that he was impelled in his operations as a critic by curiosity, and omitting either to perceive that M. Sainte-Beuve himself, and many other people with him, would
30 consider that this was praiseworthy and not blameworthy, or

to point out why it ought really to be accounted worthy of blame and not of praise. For as there is a curiosity about intellectual matters which is futile, and merely a disease, so there is certainly a curiosity,—a desire after the things of the mind simply for their own sakes and for the pleasure of seeing them as they are,—which is, in an intelligent being, natural and laudable. Nay, and the very desire to see things as they are implies a balance and regulation of mind which is not often attained without fruitful effort, and which is the very opposite of the blind and diseased impulse of mind which is what we mean to blame when we blame curiosity. Montesquieu says: "The first motive which ought to impel us to study is the desire to augment the excellence of our nature, and to render an intelligent being yet more intelligent." This is the true ground to assign for the genuine scientific passion, however manifested, and for culture, viewed simply as a fruit of this passion; and it is a worthy ground, even though we let the term *curiosity* stand to describe it.

But there is of culture another view, in which not solely the scientific passion, the sheer desire to see things as they are, natural and proper in an intelligent being, appears as the ground of it. There is a view in which all the love of our neighbour, the impulses towards action, help, and beneficence, the desire for removing human error, clearing human confusion, and diminishing human misery, the noble aspiration to leave the world better and happier than we found it,—motives eminently such as are called social,—come in as part of the grounds of culture, and the main and pre-eminent part. Culture is then properly described not as having its origin in curiosity, but as having its origin in the love of perfection; it is *a study of perfection*. It moves by the force, not merely or primarily of the scientific passion for pure knowledge, but also of the moral and social passion for doing good. As, in the first view of it, we took for its worthy motto Montesquieu's words: "To render an intelligent being yet more intelligent!" so, in the second view of it, there is no better motto which it can have than these words of Bishop Wilson: "To make reason and the will of God prevail!"

Only, whereas the passion for doing good is apt to be over-hasty in determining what reason and the will of God say, be-cause its turn is for acting rather than thinking and it wants to be beginning to act; and whereas it is apt to take its own concep-
5 tions, which proceed from its own state of development and share in all the imperfections and immaturities of this, for a basis of action; what distinguishes culture is, that it is possessed by the scientific passion as well as by the passion of doing good; that it demands worthy notions of reason and the will of
10 God, and does not readily suffer its own crude conceptions to substitute themselves for them. And knowing that no action or institution can be salutary and stable which is not based on reason and the will of God, it is not so bent on acting and instituting, even with the great aim of diminishing human
15 error and misery ever before its thoughts, but that it can re-member that acting and instituting are of little use, unless we know how and what we ought to act and to institute.

This culture is more interesting and more far-reaching than that other, which is founded solely on the scientific passion for
20 knowing. But it needs times of faith and ardour, times when the intellectual horizon is opening and widening all round us, to flourish in. And is not the close and bounded intellectual horizon within which we have long lived and moved now lifting up, and are not new lights finding free passage to shine
25 in upon us? For a long time there was no passage for them to make their way in upon us, and then it was of no use to think of adapting the world's action to them. Where was the hope of making reason and the will of God prevail among people who had a routine which they had christened reason and the will of
30 God, in which they were inextricably bound, and beyond which they had no power of looking? But now the iron force of adhesion to the old routine,—social, political, religious,—has wonderfully yielded; the iron force of exclusion of all which is new has wonderfully yielded. The danger now is, not that
35 people should obstinately refuse to allow anything but their old routine to pass for reason and the will of God, but either that they should allow some novelty or other to pass for these too easily, or else that they should underrate the importance of

them altogether, and think it enough to follow action for its own sake, without troubling themselves to make reason and the will of God prevail therein. Now, then, is the moment for culture to be of service, culture which believes in making reason and the will of God prevail, believes in perfection, is the study and pursuit of perfection, and is no longer debarred, by a rigid invincible exclusion of whatever is new, from getting acceptance for its ideas, simply because they are new.

The moment this view of culture is seized, the moment it is regarded not solely as the endeavour to see things as they are, to draw towards a knowledge of the universal order which seems to be intended and aimed at in the world, and which it is a man's happiness to go along with or his misery to go counter to,—to learn, in short, the will of God,—the moment, I say, culture is considered not merely as the endeavour to *see* and *learn* this, but as the endeavour, also, to make it *prevail*, the moral, social, and beneficent character of culture becomes manifest. The mere endeavour to see and learn the truth for our own personal satisfaction is indeed a commencement for making it prevail, a preparing the way for this, which always serves this, and is wrongly, therefore, stamped with blame absolutely in itself and not only in its caricature and degeneration. But perhaps it has got stamped with blame, and disparaged with the dubious title of curiosity, because in comparison with this wider endeavour of such great and plain utility it looks selfish, petty, and unprofitable.

And religion, the greatest and most important of the efforts by which the human race has manifested its impulse to perfect itself,—religion, that voice of the deepest human experience,—does not only enjoin and sanction the aim which is the great aim of culture, the aim of setting ourselves to ascertain what perfection is and to make it prevail; but also, in determining generally in what human perfection consists, religion comes to a conclusion identical with that which culture,—culture seeking the determination of this question through *all* the voices of human experience which have been heard upon it, of art, science, poetry, philosophy, history, as well as of religion, in order to give a greater fulness and certainty to its solution,—

likewise reaches. Religion says: *The kingdom of God is within you;* and culture, in like manner, places human perfection in an *internal* condition, in the growth and predominance of our humanity proper, as distinguished from our animality. It places it in the ever-increasing efficacy and in the general harmonious expansion of those gifts of thought and feeling, which make the peculiar dignity, wealth, and happiness of human nature. As I have said on a former occasion: "It is in making endless additions to itself, in the endless expansion of its powers, in endless growth in wisdom and beauty, that the spirit of the human race finds its ideal. To reach this ideal, culture is an indispensable aid, and that is the true value of culture." Not a having and a resting, but a growing and a becoming, is the character of perfection as culture conceives it; and here, too, it coincides with religion.

And because men are all members of one great whole, and the sympathy which is in human nature will not allow one member to be indifferent to the rest or to have a perfect welfare independent of the rest, the expansion of our humanity, to suit the idea of perfection which culture forms, must be a *general* expansion. Perfection, as culture conceives it, is not possible while the individual remains isolated. The individual is required, under pain of being stunted and enfeebled in his own development if he disobeys, to carry others along with him in his march towards perfection, to be continually doing all he can to enlarge and increase the volume of the human stream sweeping thitherward. And here, once more, culture lays on us the same obligation as religion, which says, as Bishop Wilson has admirably put it, that "to promote the kingdom of God is to increase and hasten one's own happiness."

But, finally, perfection,—as culture from a thorough disinterested study of human nature and human experience learns to conceive it,—is a harmonious expansion of *all* the powers which make the beauty and worth of human nature, and is not consistent with the over-development of any one power at the expense of the rest. Here culture goes beyond religion, as religion is generally conceived by us.

If culture, then, is a study of perfection, and of harmonious perfection, general perfection, and perfection which consists in becoming something rather than in having something, in an inward condition of the mind and spirit, not in an outward set of circumstances,—it is clear that culture, instead of being the frivolous and useless thing which Mr. Bright, and Mr. Frederic Harrison, and many other Liberals are apt to call it, has a very important function to fulfil for mankind. And this function is particularly important in our modern world, of which the whole civilisation is, to a much greater degree than the civilisation of Greece and Rome, mechanical and external, and tends constantly to become more so. But above all in our own country has culture a weighty part to perform, because here that mechanical character, which civilisation tends to take everywhere, is shown in the most eminent degree. Indeed nearly all the characters of perfection, as culture teaches us to fix them, meet in this country with some powerful tendency which thwarts them and sets them at defiance. The idea of perfection as an *inward* condition of the mind and spirit is at variance with the mechanical and material civilisation in esteem with us, and nowhere, as I have said, so much in esteem as with us. The idea of perfection as a *general* expansion of the human family is at variance with our strong individualism, our hatred of all limits to the unrestrained swing of the individual's personality, our maxim of "every man for himself." Above all, the idea of perfection as a *harmonious* expansion of human nature is at variance with our want of flexibility, with our inaptitude for seeing more than one side of a thing, with our intense energetic absorption in the particular pursuit we happen to be following. So culture has a rough task to achieve in this country. Its preachers have, and are likely long to have, a hard time of it, and they will much oftener be regarded, for a great while to come, as elegant or spurious Jeremiahs than as friends and benefactors. That, however, will not prevent their doing in the end good service if they persevere. And, meanwhile, the mode of action they have to pursue, and the sort of habits they must fight against, ought to be made quite clear for every one to see, who may be willing to look at the matter attentively and dispassionately.

Faith in machinery is, I said, our besetting danger; often in machinery most absurdly disproportioned to the end which this
machinery, if it is to do any good at all, is to serve; but always
in machinery, as if it had a value in and for itself. What is
freedom but machinery? what is population but machinery?
what is coal but machinery? what are railroads but machinery?
what is wealth but machinery? what are, even, religious organisations but machinery? Now almost every voice in England is
accustomed to speak of these things as if they were precious
ends in themselves, and therefore had some of the characters
of perfection indissolubly joined to them. I have before now
noticed Mr. Roebuck's stock argument for proving the greatness and happiness of England as she is, and for quite stopping
the mouths of all gainsayers. Mr. Roebuck is never weary of
reiterating this argument of his, so I do not know why I
should be weary of noticing it. "May not every man in England say what he likes?"—Mr. Roebuck perpetually asks; and
that, he thinks, is quite sufficient, and when every man may
say what he likes, our aspirations ought to be satisfied. But the
aspirations of culture, which is the study of perfection, are not
satisfied, unless what men say, when they may say what they
like, is worth saying,—has good in it, and more good than bad.
In the same way the *Times*, replying to some foreign strictures
on the dress, looks, and behaviour of the English abroad, urges
that the English ideal is that every one should be free to do and
to look just as he likes. But culture indefatigably tries, not to
make what each raw person may like the rule by which he
fashions himself; but to draw ever nearer to a sense of what is
indeed beautiful, graceful, and becoming, and to get the raw
person to like that.

And in the same way with respect to railroads and coal. Every
one must have observed the strange language current during
the late discussions as to the possible failure of our supplies of
coal. Our coal, thousands of people were saying, is the real
basis of our national greatness; if our coal runs short, there is
an end of the greatness of England. But what *is* greatness?—
culture makes us ask. Greatness is a spiritual condition worthy
to excite love, interest, and admiration; and the outward proof

of possessing greatness is that we excite love, interest, and admiration. If England were swallowed up by the sea tomorrow, which of the two, a hundred years hence, would most excite the love, interest, and admiration of mankind,—would most, therefore, show the evidences of having possessed greatness,— the England of the last twenty years, or the England of Elizabeth, of a time of splendid spiritual effort, but when our coal, and our industrial operations depending on coal, were very little developed? Well, then, what an unsound habit of mind it must be which makes us talk of things like coal or iron as constituting the greatness of England, and how salutary a friend is culture, bent on seeing things as they are, and thus dissipating delusions of this kind and fixing standards of perfection that are real!

Wealth, again, that end to which our prodigious works for material advantage are directed,—the commonest of commonplaces tells us how men are always apt to regard wealth as a precious end in itself; and certainly they have never been so apt thus to regard it as they are in England at the present time. Never did people believe anything more firmly than nine Englishmen out of ten at the present day believe that our greatness and welfare are proved by our being so very rich. Now, the use of culture is that it helps us, by means of its spiritual standard of perfection, to regard wealth as but machinery, and not only to say as a matter of words that we regard wealth as but machinery, but really to perceive and feel that it is so. If it were not for this purging effect wrought upon our minds by culture, the whole world, the future as well as the present, would inevitably belong to the Philistines. The people who believe most that our greatness and welfare are proved by our being very rich, and who most give their lives and thoughts to becoming rich, are just the very people whom we call Philistines. Culture says: "Consider these people, then, their way of life, their habits, their manners, the very tones of their voice; look at them attentively; observe the literature they read, the things which give them pleasure, the words which come forth out of their mouths, the thoughts which make the furniture of their minds; would any amount of wealth be worth having with the condi-

tion that one was to become just like these people by having it?" And thus culture begets a dissatisfaction which is of the highest possible value in stemming the common tide of men's thoughts in a wealthy and industrial community, and which
5   saves the future, as one may hope, from being vulgarised, even if it cannot save the present.

   Population, again, and bodily health and vigour, are things which are nowhere treated in such an unintelligent, misleading, exaggerated way as in England. Both are really machinery; yet
10 how many people all around us do we see rest in them and fail to look beyond them! Why, one has heard people, fresh from reading certain articles of the *Times* on the Registrar-General's returns of marriages and births in this country, who would talk of our large English families in quite a solemn strain, as if
15 they had something in itself beautiful, elevating, and meritorious in them; as if the British Philistine would have only to present himself before the Great Judge with his twelve children, in order to be received among the sheep as a matter of right!

20 But bodily health and vigour, it may be said, are not to be classed with wealth and population as mere machinery; they have a more real and essential value. True; but only as they are more intimately connected with a perfect spiritual condition than wealth or population are. The moment we disjoin them
25 from the idea of a perfect spiritual condition, and pursue them, as we do pursue them, for their own sake and as ends in themselves, our worship of them becomes as mere worship of machinery, as our worship of wealth or population, and as unintelligent and vulgarising a worship as that is. Every one with
30 anything like an adequate idea of human perfection has distinctly marked this subordination to higher and spiritual ends of the cultivation of bodily vigour and activity. "Bodily exercise profiteth little; but godliness is profitable unto all things," says the author of the Epistle to Timothy. And the utilitarian
35 Franklin says just as explicitly:—"Eat and drink such an exact quantity as suits the constitution of thy body, *in reference to the services of the mind.*" But the point of view of culture, keeping the mark of human perfection simply and broadly in

view, and not assigning to this perfection, as religion or utili-
tarianism assigns to it, a special and limited character, this
point of view, I say, of culture is best given by these words of
Epictetus:—"It is a sign of ἀφυΐα," says he,—that is, of a
nature not finely tempered,—"to give yourselves up to things   5
which relate to the body; to make, for instance, a great fuss
about exercise, a great fuss about eating, a great fuss about
drinking, a great fuss about walking, a great fuss about riding.
All these things ought to be done merely by the way: the
formation of the spirit and character must be our real con-   10
cern." This is admirable; and, indeed, the Greek word εὐφυΐα,
a finely tempered nature, gives exactly the notion of perfection as culture brings us to conceive it: a harmonious perfection, a perfection in which the characters of beauty and intelligence are both present, which unites "the two noblest of   15
things,"—as Swift, who of one of the two, at any rate, had
himself all too little, most happily calls them in his *Battle of
the Books*,—"the two noblest of things, *sweetness and light*."
The εὐφυής is the man who tends towards sweetness and light;
the ἀφυής, on the other hand, is our Philistine. The immense   20
spiritual significance of the Greeks is due to their having been
inspired with this central and happy idea of the essential character of human perfection; and Mr. Bright's misconception of
culture, as a smattering of Greek and Latin, comes itself, after
all, from this wonderful significance of the Greeks having   25
affected the very machinery of our education, and is in itself a
kind of homage to it.

In thus making sweetness and light to be characters of perfection, culture is of like spirit with poetry, follows one law with
poetry. Far more than on our freedom, our population, and   30
our industrialism, many amongst us rely upon our religious
organisations to save us. I have called religion a yet more important manifestation of human nature than poetry, because it
has worked on a broader scale for perfection, and with greater
masses of men. But the idea of beauty and of a human nature   35
perfect on all its sides, which is the dominant idea of poetry, is
a true and invaluable idea, though it has not yet had the success
that the idea of conquering the obvious faults of our animality,

and of a human nature perfect on the moral side,—which is the
dominant idea of religion,—has been enabled to have; and it is
destined, adding to itself the religious idea of a devout energy,
to transform and govern the other.

5   The best art and poetry of the Greeks, in which religion and
poetry are one, in which the idea of beauty and of a human
nature perfect on all sides adds to itself a religious and devout
energy, and works in the strength of that, is on this account of
such surpassing interest and instructiveness for us, though it
10   was,—as, having regard to the human race in general, and,
indeed, having regard to the Greeks themselves, we must
own,—a premature attempt, an attempt which for success
needed the moral and religious fibre in humanity to be more
braced and developed than it had yet been. But Greece did not
15   err in having the idea of beauty, harmony, and complete human perfection, so present and paramount. It is impossible to
have this idea too present and paramount; only, the moral fibre
must be braced too. And we, because we have braced the
moral fibre, are not on that account in the right way, if at the
20   same time the idea of beauty, harmony, and complete human
perfection, is wanting or misapprehended amongst us; and evidently it *is* wanting or misapprehended at present. And when
we rely as we do on our religious organisations, which in
themselves do not and cannot give us this idea, and think we
25   have done enough if we make them spread and prevail, then, I
say, we fall into our common fault of overvaluing machinery.

Nothing is more common than for people to confound the inward peace and satisfaction which follows the subduing of the
obvious faults of our animality with what I may call absolute in-
30   ward peace and satisfaction,—the peace and satisfaction which
are reached as we draw near to complete spiritual perfection,
and not merely to moral perfection, or rather to relative moral
perfection. No people in the world have done more and strug-
gled more to attain this relative moral perfection than our
35   English race has. For no people in the world has the command
to *resist the devil*, to *overcome the wicked one*, in the nearest
and most obvious sense of those words, had such a pressing
force and reality. And we have had our reward, not only in

the great worldly prosperity which our obedience to this command has brought us, but also, and far more, in great inward
peace and satisfaction. But to me few things are more pathetic
than to see people, on the strength of the inward peace and
satisfaction which their rudimentary efforts towards perfection have brought them, employ, concerning their incomplete
perfection and the religious organisations within which they
have found it, language which properly applies only to complete perfection, and is a far-off echo of the human soul's
prophecy of it. Religion itself, I need hardly say, supplies them
in abundance with this grand language. And very freely do
they use it; yet it is really the severest possible criticism of
such an incomplete perfection as alone we have yet reached
through our religious organisations.

The impulse of the English race towards moral development
and self-conquest has nowhere so powerfully manifested itself as
in Puritanism. Nowhere has Puritanism found so adequate an expression as in the religious organisation of the Independents.
The modern Independents have a newspaper, the *Nonconformist*, written with great sincerity and ability. The motto,
the standard, the profession of faith which this organ of theirs
carries aloft, is: "The Dissidence of Dissent and the Protestantism of the Protestant religion." There is sweetness and light,
and an ideal of complete harmonious human perfection! One
need not go to culture and poetry to find language to judge it.
Religion, with its instinct for perfection, supplies language to
judge it, language, too, which is in our mouths every day.
"Finally, be of one mind, united in feeling," says St. Peter.
There is an ideal which judges the Puritan ideal: "The Dissidence of Dissent and the Protestantism of the Protestant religion!" And religious organisations like this are what people
believe in, rest in, would give their lives for! Such, I say, is the
wonderful virtue of even the beginnings of perfection, of having conquered even the plain faults of our animality, that the
religious organisation which has helped us to do it can seem to
us something precious, salutary, and to be propagated, even
when it wears such a brand of imperfection on its forehead as
this. And men have got such a habit of giving to the language

of religion a special application, of making it a mere jargon,
that for the condemnation which religion itself passes on the
shortcomings of their religious organisations they have no
ear; they are sure to cheat themselves and to explain this condemnation away. They can only be reached by the criticism
which culture, like poetry, speaking a language not to be so-
phisticated, and resolutely testing these organisations by the
ideal of a human perfection complete on all sides, applies to
them.

But men of culture and poetry, it will be said, are again and
again failing, and failing conspicuously, in the necessary first
stage to a harmonious perfection, in the subduing of the great obvious faults of our animality, which it is the glory of these religious organisations to have helped us to subdue. True, they do
often so fail. They have often been without the virtues as well as
the faults of the Puritan; it has been one of their dangers that they
so felt the Puritan's faults that they too much neglected the
practice of his virtues. I will not, however, exculpate them at
the Puritan's expense. They have often failed in morality, and
morality is indispensable. And they have been punished
for their failure, as the Puritan has been rewarded for his performance. They have been punished wherein they erred; but
their ideal of beauty, of sweetness and light, and a human nature
complete on all its sides, remains the true ideal of perfection
still; just as the Puritan's ideal of perfection remains narrow and
inadequate, although for what he did well he has been richly rewarded. Notwithstanding the mighty results of the Pilgrim
Fathers' voyage, they and their standard of perfection
are rightly judged when we figure to ourselves Shakspeare
or Virgil,—souls in whom sweetness and light, and all that
in human nature is most humane, were eminent,—accom-
panying them on their voyage, and think what intolerable
company Shakspeare and Virgil would have found them! In
the same way let us judge the religious organisations which we
see all around us. Do not let us deny the good and the happiness which they have accomplished; but do not let us fail to
see clearly that their idea of human perfection is narrow and
inadequate, and that the Dissidence of Dissent and the Protes-

tantism of the Protestant religion will never bring humanity to its true goal. As I said with regard to wealth: Let us look at the life of those who live in and for it,—so I say with regard to the religious organisations. Look at the life imaged in such a newspaper as the *Nonconformist*,—a life of jealousy of the Establishment, disputes, tea-meetings, openings of chapels, sermons; and then think of it as an ideal of a human life completing itself on all sides, and aspiring with all its organs after sweetness, light, and perfection!

Another newspaper, representing, like the *Nonconformist*, one of the religious organisations of this country, was a short time ago giving an account of the crowd at Epsom on the Derby day, and of all the vice and hideousness which was to be seen in that crowd; and then the writer turned suddenly round upon Professor Huxley, and asked him how he proposed to cure all this vice and hideousness without religion. I confess I felt disposed to ask the asker this question: And how do you propose to cure it with such a religion as yours? How is the ideal of a life so unlovely, so unattractive, so incomplete, so narrow, so far removed from a true and satisfying ideal of human perfection, as is the life of your religious organisation as you yourself reflect it, to conquer and transform all this vice and hideousness? Indeed, the strongest plea for the study of perfection as pursued by culture, the clearest proof of the actual inadequacy of the idea of perfection held by the religious organisations,—expressing, as I have said, the most widespread effort which the human race has yet made after perfection,—is to be found in the state of our life and society with these in possession of it, and having been in possession of it I know not how many hundred years. We are all of us included in some religious organisation or other; we all call ourselves, in the sublime and aspiring language of religion which I have before noticed, *children of God*. Children of God;—it is an immense pretension!—and how are we to justify it? By the works which we do, and the words which we speak. And the work which we collective children of God do, our grand centre of life, our *city* which we have builded for us to dwell in, is London! London, with its unutterable external hideousness, and with its internal

canker of *publicè egestas, privatim opulentia,*—to use the words
which Sallust puts into Cato's mouth about Rome,—unequalled in the world! The word, again, which we children of
God speak, the voice which most hits our collective thought,
the newspaper with the largest circulation in England, nay,
with the largest circulation in the whole world, is the *Daily
Telegraph!* I say that when our religious organisations,
—which I admit to express the most considerable effort after
perfection that our race has yet made,—land us in no better
result than this, it is high time to examine carefully their idea
of perfection, to see whether it does not leave out of account
sides and forces of human nature which we might turn to
great use; whether it would not be more operative if it were
more complete. And I say that the English reliance on our
religious organisations and on their ideas of human perfection
just as they stand, is like our reliance on freedom, on muscular
Christianity, on population, on coal, on wealth,—mere belief in
machinery, and unfruitful; and that it is wholesomely counter-
acted by culture, bent on seeing things as they are, and on
drawing the human race onwards to a more complete, a harmonious perfection.

Culture, however, shows its single-minded love of perfection,
its desire simply to make reason and the will of God prevail, its
freedom from fanaticism, by its attitude towards all this machinery, even while it insists that it *is* machinery. Fanatics,
seeing the mischief men do themselves by their blind belief in
some machinery or other,—whether it is wealth and industrialism, or whether it is the cultivation of bodily strength and
activity, or whether it is a political organisation, or whether
it is a religious organisation,—oppose with might and main the
tendency to this or that political and religious organisation, or
to games and athletic exercises, or to wealth and industrialism,
and try violently to stop it. But the flexibility which sweetness
and light give, and which is one of the rewards of culture
pursued in good faith, enables a man to see that a tendency
may be necessary, and even, as a preparation for something in
the future, salutary, and yet that the generations or individuals
who obey this tendency are sacrificed to it, that they fall short

of the hope of perfection by following it; and that its mis-
chiefs are to be criticised, lest it should take too firm a hold
and last after it has served its purpose.

Mr. Gladstone well .pointed out, in a speech at Paris,—and
others have pointed out the same thing,—how necessary is the
present great movement towards wealth and industrialism, in
order to lay broad foundations of material well-being for the society of the future. The worst of these justifications is, that they
are generally addressed to the very people engaged, body and
soul, in the movement in question; at all events, that they are always seized with the greatest avidity by these people, and taken
by them as quite justifying their life; and that thus they tend to
harden them in their sins. Now, culture admits the necessity of
the movement towards fortune-making and exaggerated industrialism, readily allows that the future may derive benefit from
it; but insists, at the same time, that the passing generations of
industrialists,—forming, for the most part, the stout main
body of Philistinism,—are sacrificed to it. In the same way, the
result of all the games and sports which occupy the passing
generation of boys and young men may be the establishment
of a better and sounder physical type for the future to work
with. Culture does not set itself against the games and sports; it
congratulates the future, and hopes it will make a good use of
its improved physical basis; but it points out that our passing
generation of boys and young men is, meantime, sacrificed.
Puritanism was perhaps necessary to develop the moral fibre of
the English race, Nonconformity to break the yoke of ecclesiastical domination over men's minds and to prepare the way
for freedom of thought in the distant future; still, culture
points out that the harmonious perfection of generations of
Puritans and Nonconformists have been, in consequence, sacrificed. Freedom of speech may be necessary for the society of
the future, but the young lions of the *Daily Telegraph* in the
meanwhile are sacrificed. A voice for every man in his country's government may be necessary for the society of the future, but meanwhile Mr. Beales and Mr. Bradlaugh are sacrificed.

Oxford, the Oxford of the past, has many faults; and she has

heavily paid for them in defeat, in isolation, in want of hold
upon the modern world. Yet we in Oxford, brought up amidst
the beauty and sweetness of that beautiful place, have not
failed to seize one truth,—the truth that beauty and sweetness
5 are essential characters of a complete human perfection. When
I insist on this, I am all in the faith and tradition of Oxford. I
say boldly that this our sentiment for beauty and sweetness, our
sentiment against hideousness and rawness, has been at the bottom of our attachment to so many beaten causes, of our oppo-
10 sition to so many triumphant movements. And the sentiment is
true, and has never been wholly defeated, and has shown its
power even in its defeat. We have not won our political bat-
tles, we have not carried our main points, we have not stopped
our adversaries' advance, we have not marched victoriously
15 with the modern world; but we have told silently upon the
mind of the country, we have prepared currents of feeling
which sap our adversaries' position when it seems gained, we
have kept up our own communications with the future. Look
at the course of the great movement which shook Oxford to
20 its centre some thirty years ago! It was directed, as any one
who reads Dr. Newman's *Apology* may see, against what in
one word may be called "Liberalism." Liberalism prevailed; it
was the appointed force to do the work of the hour; it was
necessary, it was inevitable that it should prevail. The Oxford
25 movement was broken, it failed; our wrecks are scattered on
every shore:—

Quæ regio in terris nostri non plena laboris?

But what was it, this liberalism, as Dr. Newman saw it, and as it
really broke the Oxford movement? It was the great middle-
30 class liberalism, which had for the cardinal points of its belief
the Reform Bill of 1832, and local self-government, in politics;
in the social sphere, free-trade, unrestricted competition, and
the making of large industrial fortunes; in the religious sphere,
the Dissidence of Dissent and the Protestantism of the Protes-
35 tant religion. I do not say that other and more intelligent
forces than this were not opposed to the Oxford movement:
but this was the force which really beat it; this was the force

which Dr. Newman felt himself fighting with; this was the
force which till only the other day seemed to be the paramount force in this country, and to be in possession of the
future; this was the force whose achievements fill Mr. Lowe
with such inexpressible admiration, and whose rule he was so   5
horror-struck to see threatened. And where is this great force
of Philistinism now? It is thrust into the second rank, it is
become a power of yesterday, it has lost the future. A new
power has suddenly appeared, a power which it is impossible
yet to judge fully, but which is certainly a wholly different   10
force from middle-class liberalism; different in its cardinal
points of belief, different in its tendencies in every sphere. It
loves and admires neither the legislation of middle-class Parlia-
ments, nor the local self-government of middle-class vestries,
nor the unrestricted competition of middle-class industrialists,   15
nor the dissidence of middle-class Dissent and the Protestantism of middle-class Protestant religion. I am not now praising
this new force, or saying that its own ideals are better; all I say
is, that they are wholly different. And who will estimate how
much the currents of feeling created by Dr. Newman's move-   20
ment, the keen desire for beauty and sweetness which it nourished, the deep aversion it manifested to the hardness and vulgarity of middle-class liberalism, the strong light it turned on
the hideous and grotesque illusions of middle-class Protestantism,—who will estimate how much all these contributed to   25
swell the tide of secret dissatisfaction which has mined the
ground under the self-confident liberalism of the last thirty
years, and has prepared the way for its sudden collapse and
supersession? It is in this manner that the sentiment of Oxford
for beauty and sweetness conquers, and in this manner long   30
may it continue to conquer!

In this manner it works to the same end as culture, and there
is plenty of work for it yet to do. I have said that the new and
more democratic force which is now superseding our old middle-class liberalism cannot yet be rightly judged. It has its main   35
tendencies still to form. We hear promises of its giving us
administrative reform, law reform, reform of education, and I
know not what; but those promises come rather from its advo-

cates, wishing to make a good plea for it and to justify it for
superseding middle-class liberalism, than from clear tendencies
which it has itself yet developed. But meanwhile it has plenty
of well-intentioned friends against whom culture may with
advantage continue to uphold steadily its ideal of human perfection; that this is *an inward spiritual activity, having for its
characters increased sweetness, increased light, increased life,
increased sympathy.* Mr. Bright, who has a foot in both
worlds, the world of middle-class liberalism and the world of
democracy, but who brings most of his ideas from the world
of middle-class liberalism in which he was bred, always inclines to inculcate that faith in machinery to which, as we have
seen, Englishmen are so prone, and which has been the bane of
middle-class liberalism. He complains with a sorrowful indignation of people who "appear to have no proper estimate of
the value of the franchise;" he leads his disciples to believe,—
what the Englishman is always too ready to believe,—that the
having a vote, like the having a large family, or a large business, or large muscles, has in itself some edifying and perfecting effect upon human nature. Or else he cries out to the
democracy,—"the men," as he calls them, "upon whose
shoulders the greatness of England rests,"—he cries out to
them: "See what you have done! I look over this country and
see the cities you have built, the railroads you have made, the
manufactures you have produced, the cargoes which freight
the ships of the greatest mercantile navy the world has ever
seen! I see that you have converted by your labours what was
once a wilderness, these islands, into a fruitful garden; I know
that you have created this wealth, and are a nation whose name
is a word of power throughout all the world." Why, this is just
the very style of laudation with which Mr. Roebuck or Mr.
Lowe debauches the minds of the middle classes, and makes
such Philistines of them. It is the same fashion of teaching a
man to value himself not on what he *is*, not on his progress in
sweetness and light, but on the number of the railroads he has
constructed, or the bigness of the tabernacle he has built. Only
the middle classes are told they have done it all with their
energy, self-reliance, and capital, and the democracy are told

they have done it all with their hands and sinews. But teaching
the democracy to put its trust in achievements of this kind is
merely training them to be Philistines to take the place of the
Philistines whom they are superseding; and they too, like the
middle class, will be encouraged to sit down at the banquet of 5
the future without having on a wedding garment, and nothing
excellent can then come from them. Those who know their
besetting faults, those who have watched them and listened to
them, or those who will read the instructive account recently
given of them by one of themselves, the *Journeyman Engi-* 10
neer, will agree that the idea which culture sets before us of
perfection,—an increased spiritual activity, having for its characters increased sweetness, increased light, increased life, increased sympathy,—is an idea which the new democracy needs
far more than the idea of the blessedness of the franchise, or 15
the wonderfulness of its own industrial performances.

Other well-meaning friends of this new power are for leading
it, not in the old ruts of middle-class Philistinism, but in ways
which are naturally alluring to the feet of democracy, though
in this country they are novel and untried ways. I may call 20
them the ways of Jacobinism. Violent indignation with the
past, abstract systems of renovation applied wholesale, a new
doctrine drawn up in black and white for elaborating down to
the very smallest details a rational society for the future,—
these are the ways of Jacobinism. Mr. Frederic Harrison and 25
other disciples of Comte,—one of them, Mr. Congreve, is an
old friend of mine, and I am glad to have an opportunity of
publicly expressing my respect for his talents and character,—
are among the friends of democracy who are for leading it in
paths of this kind. Mr. Frederic Harrison is very hostile to 30
culture, and from a natural enough motive; for culture is the
eternal opponent of the two things which are the signal marks
of Jacobinism,—its fierceness, and its addiction to an abstract
system. Culture is always assigning to system-makers and systems a smaller share in the bent of human destiny than their 35
friends like. A current in people's minds sets towards new
ideas; people are dissatisfied with their old narrow stock of
Philistine ideas, Anglo-Saxon ideas, or any other; and some

man, some Bentham or Comte, who has the real merit of having early and strongly felt and helped the new current, but
who brings plenty of narrowness and mistakes of his own into
his feeling and help of it, is credited with being the author of
5 the whole current, the fit person to be entrusted with its regulation and to guide the human race.

The excellent German historian of the mythology of Rome,
Preller, relating the introduction at Rome under the Tarquins of
the worship of Apollo, the god of light, healing, and reconcili-
10 ation, will have us observe that it was not so much the Tarquins who brought to Rome the new worship of Apollo, as a
current in the mind of the Roman people which set powerfully at that time towards a new worship of this kind, and
away from the old run of Latin and Sabine religious ideas. In a
15 similar way, culture directs our attention to the natural current there is in human affairs, and to its continual working, and
will not let us rivet our faith upon any one man and his doings.
It makes us see not only his good side, but also how much in
him was of necessity limited and transient; nay, it even feels a
20 pleasure, a sense of an increased freedom and of an ampler
future, in so doing.

I remember, when I was under the influence of a mind to
which I feel the greatest obligations, the mind of a man who was
the very incarnation of sanity and clear sense, a man the most
25 considerable, it seems to me, whom America has yet produced,
—Benjamin Franklin,—I remember the relief with which, after long feeling the sway of Franklin's imperturbable common-sense, I came upon a project of his for a new version of
the Book of Job, to replace the old version, the style of which,
30 says Franklin, has become obsolete, and thence less agreeable.
"I give," he continues, "a few verses, which may serve as a
sample of the kind of version I would recommend." We all
recollect the famous verse in our translation: "Then Satan
answered the Lord and said: 'Doth Job fear God for nought?' "
35 Franklin makes this: "Does your Majesty imagine that Job's
good conduct is the effect of mere personal attachment and
affection?" I well remember how, when first I read that, I
drew a deep breath of relief, and said to myself: "After all,

there is a stretch of humanity beyond Franklin's victorious good sense!" So, after hearing Bentham cried loudly up as the renovator of modern society, and Bentham's mind and ideas proposed as the rulers of our future, I open the *Deontology*. There I read: "While Xenophon was writing his history and Euclid teaching geometry, Socrates and Plato were talking nonsense under pretence of teaching wisdom and morality. This morality of theirs consisted in words; this wisdom of theirs was the denial of matters known to every man's experience." From the moment of reading that, I am delivered from the bondage of Bentham! the fanaticism of his adherents can touch me no longer. I feel the inadequacy of his mind and ideas for supplying the rule of human society, for perfection.

Culture tends always thus to deal with the men of a system, of disciples, of a school; with men like Comte, or the late Mr. Buckle, or Mr. Mill. However much it may find to admire in these personages, or in some of them, it nevertheless remembers the text: "Be not ye called Rabbi!" and it soon passes on from any Rabbi. But Jacobinism loves a Rabbi; it does not want to pass on from its Rabbi in pursuit of a future and still unreached perfection; it wants its Rabbi and his ideas to stand for perfection, that they may with the more authority recast the world; and for Jacobinism, therefore, culture,—eternally passing onwards and seeking,—is an impertinence and an offence. But culture, just because it resists this tendency of Jacobinism to impose on us a man with limitations and errors of his own along with the true ideas of which he is the organ, really does the world and Jacobinism itself a service.

So, too, Jacobinism, in its fierce hatred of the past and of those whom it makes liable for the sins of the past, cannot away with the inexhaustible indulgence proper to culture, the consideration of circumstances, the severe judgment of actions joined to the merciful judgment of persons. "The man of culture is in politics," cries Mr. Frederic Harrison, "one of the poorest mortals alive!" Mr. Frederic Harrison wants to be doing business, and he complains that the man of culture stops him with a "turn for small fault-finding, love of selfish ease, and indecision in action." Of what use is culture, he asks, except for "a

critic of new books or a professor of *belles-lettres?*" Why, it is
of use because, in presence of the fierce exasperation which
breathes, or rather, I may say, hisses through the whole production in which Mr. Frederic Harrison asks that question, it
5   reminds us that the perfection of human nature is sweetness
and light. It is of use because, like religion,—that other effort
after perfection,—it testifies that, where bitter envying and
strife are, there is confusion and every evil work.

The pursuit of perfection, then, is the pursuit of sweetness and
10 light. He who works for sweetness and light, works to make
reason and the will of God prevail. He who works for machinery, he who works for hatred, works only for confusion.
Culture looks beyond machinery, culture hates hatred; culture
has one great passion, the passion for sweetness and light. It has
15 one even yet greater!—the passion for making them *prevail*. It
is not satisfied till we *all* come to a perfect man; it knows that
the sweetness and light of the few must be imperfect until the
raw and unkindled masses of humanity are touched with
sweetness and light. If I have not shrunk from saying that we
20 must work for sweetness and light, so neither have I shrunk
from saying that we must have a broad basis, must have sweetness and light for as many as possible. Again and again I have
insisted how those are the happy moments of humanity, how
those are the marking epochs of a people's life, how those are
25 the flowering times for literature and art and all the creative
power of genius, when there is a *national* glow of life and
thought, when the whole of society is in the fullest measure
permeated by thought, sensible to beauty, intelligent and alive.
Only it must be *real* thought and *real* beauty; *real* sweetness
30 and *real* light. Plenty of people will try to give the masses, as
they call them, an intellectual food prepared and adapted in
the way they think proper for the actual condition of the
masses. The ordinary popular literature is an example of this
way of working on the masses. Plenty of people will try to
35 indoctrinate the masses with the set of ideas and judgments
constituting the creed of their own profession or party. Our
religious and political organisations give an example of this
way of working on the masses. I condemn neither way; but

culture works differently. It does not try to teach down to the level of inferior classes; it does not try to win them for this or that sect of its own, with ready-made judgments and watchwords. It seeks to do away with classes; to make the best that has been thought and known in the world current every- 5 where; to make all men live in an atmosphere of sweetness and light, where they may use ideas, as it uses them itself, freely,— nourished, and not bound by them.

This is the *social idea;* and the men of culture are the true apostles of equality. The great men of culture are those who have 10 had a passion for diffusing, for making prevail, for carrying from one end of society to the other, the best knowledge, the best ideas of their time; who have laboured to divest knowledge of all that was harsh, uncouth, difficult, abstract, professional, ex- clusive; to humanise it, to make it efficient outside the clique 15 of the cultivated and learned, yet still remaining the *best* knowledge and thought of the time, and a true source, there- fore, of sweetness and light. Such a man was Abelard in the Middle Ages, in spite of all his imperfections; and thence the boundless emotion and enthusiasm which Abelard excited. 20 Such were Lessing and Herder in Germany, at the end of the last century; and their services to Germany were in this way inestimably precious. Generations will pass, and literary monu- ments will accumulate, and works far more perfect than the works of Lessing and Herder will be produced in Germany; 25 and yet the names of these two men will fill a German with a reverence and enthusiasm such as the names of the most gifted masters will hardly awaken. And why? Because they *humanised* knowledge; because they broadened the basis of life and intel- ligence; because they worked powerfully to diffuse sweetness 30 and light, to make reason and the will of God prevail. With Saint Augustine they said: "Let us not leave thee alone to make in the secret of thy knowledge, as thou didst before the creation of the firmament, the division of light from darkness; let the children of thy spirit, placed in their firmament, make 35 their light shine upon the earth, mark the division of night and day, and announce the revolution of the times; for the old order is passed, and the new arises; the night is spent, the day

is come forth; and thou shalt crown the year with thy blessing,
when thou shalt send forth labourers into thy harvest sown by
other hands than theirs; when thou shalt send forth new
labourers to new seed-times, whereof the harvest shall be not
5   yet."

Chapter II

Doing as One Likes

I have been trying to show that culture is, or ought to be, the study and pursuit of perfection; and that of perfection as pursued by culture, beauty and intelligence, or, in other words, sweetness and light, are the main characters. But hitherto I have been insisting chiefly on beauty, or sweetness, as a character of perfection. To complete rightly my design, it evidently remains to speak also of intelligence, or light, as a character of perfection.

First, however, I ought perhaps to notice that, both here and on the other side of the Atlantic, all sorts of objections are raised against the "religion of culture," as the objectors mockingly call it, which I am supposed to be promulgating. It is said to be a religion proposing parmaceti, or some scented salve or other, as a cure for human miseries; a religion breathing a spirit of cultivated inaction, making its believer refuse to lend a hand at uprooting the definite evils on all sides of us, and filling him with antipathy against the reforms and reformers which try to extirpate them. In general, it is summed up as being not practical, or,—as some critics familiarly put it,—all moonshine. That Alcibiades, the editor of the *Morning Star*, taunts me, as its promulgator, with living out of the world and knowing nothing of life and men. That great austere toiler, the editor of the *Daily Telegraph*, upbraids me,—but kindly, and more in sorrow than in anger,—for trifling with æsthetics and poetical fancies, while he himself, in that arsenal of his in Fleet Street, is bearing the burden and heat of the day. An intelligent American newspaper, the *Nation*, says that it is very easy to sit in one's study and find fault with the course of modern society, but the thing is to propose practical improvements for it.

While, finally, Mr. Frederic Harrison, in a very good-tempered and witty satire, which makes me quite understand his having apparently achieved such a conquest of my young Prussian friend, Arminius, at last gets moved to an almost stern
5 moral impatience, to behold, as he says, "Death, sin, cruelty stalk among us, filling their maws with innocence and youth," and me, in the midst of the general tribulation, handing out my pouncet-box.

It is impossible that all these remonstrances and reproofs
10 should not affect me, and I shall try my very best, in completing my design and in speaking of light as one of the characters of perfection, and of culture as giving us light, to profit by the objections I have heard and read, and to drive at practice as much as I can, by showing the communications and passages
15 into practical life from the doctrine which I am inculcating.

It is said that a man with my theories of sweetness and light is full of antipathy against the rougher or coarser movements going on around him, that he will not lend a hand to the humble operation of uprooting evil by their means, and that therefore
20 the believers in action grow impatient with him. But what if rough and coarse action, ill-calculated action, action with insufficient light, is, and has for a long time been, our bane? What if our urgent want now is, not to act at any price, but rather to lay in a stock of light for our difficulties? In that case, to
25 refuse to lend a hand to the rougher and coarser movements going on round us, to make the primary need, both for oneself and others, to consist in enlightening ourselves and qualifying ourselves to act less at random, is surely the best and in real truth the most practical line our endeavours can take. So that
30 if I can show what my opponents call rough or coarse action, but what I would rather call random and ill-regulated action, —action with insufficient light, action pursued because we like to be doing something and doing it as we please, and do not like the trouble of thinking and the severe constraint of any
35 kind of rule,—if I can show this to be, at the present moment, a practical mischief and dangerous to us, then I have found a practical use for light in correcting this state of things, and

have only to exemplify how, in cases which fall under every-body's observation, it may deal with it.

When I began to speak of culture, I insisted on our bondage to machinery, on our proneness to value machinery as an end in itself, without looking beyond it to the end for which alone, in truth, it is valuable. Freedom, I said, was one of those things which we thus worshipped in itself, without enough regarding the ends for which freedom is to be desired. In our common notions and talk about freedom, we eminently show our idola-try of machinery. Our prevalent notion is,—and I quoted a number of instances to prove it,—that it is a most happy and important thing for a man merely to be able to do as he likes. On what he is to do when he is thus free to do as he likes, we do not lay so much stress. Our familiar praise of the British Constitution under which we live, is that it is a system of checks,—a system which stops and paralyses any power in interfering with the free action of individuals. To this effect Mr. Bright, who loves to walk in the old ways of the Constitu-tion, said forcibly in one of his great speeches, what many other people are every day saying less forcibly, that the central idea of English life and politics is *the assertion of personal liberty*. Evidently this is so; but evidently, also, as feudalism, which with its ideas and habits of subordination was for many centuries silently behind the British Constitution, dies out, and we are left with nothing but our system of checks, and our notion of its being the great right and happiness of an English-man to do as far as possible what he likes, we are in danger of drifting towards anarchy. We have not the notion, so familiar on the Continent and to antiquity, of *the State*,—the nation in its collective and corporate character, entrusted with stringent powers for the general advantage, and controlling individual wills in the name of an interest wider than that of individuals. We say, what is very true, that this notion is often made instrumental to tyranny; we say that a State is in reality made up of the individuals who compose it, and that every individ-ual is the best judge of his own interests. Our leading class is an aristocracy, and no aristocracy likes the notion of a State-au-

thority greater than itself, with a stringent administrative machinery superseding the decorative inutilities of lord-lieutenancy, deputy-lieutenancy, and the *posse comitatus*, which are
all in its own hands. Our middle class, the great representative
5   of trade and Dissent, with its maxims of every man for himself
in business, every man for himself in religion, dreads a powerful administration which might somehow interfere with it; and
besides, it has its own decorative inutilities of vestrymanship
and guardianship, which are to this class what lord-lieutenancy
10 and the county magistracy are to the aristocratic class, and a
stringent·administration might either take these functions out
of its hands, or prevent its exercising them in its own comfortable, independent manner, as at present.

Then as to our working class. This class, pressed constantly by
15 the hard daily compulsion of material wants, is naturally the
very centre and stronghold of our national idea, that it is man's
ideal right and felicity to do as he likes. I think I have somewhere related how M. Michelet said to me of the people of
France, that it was "a nation of barbarians civilised by the
20 conscription." He meant that through their military service
the idea of public duty and of discipline was brought to the
mind of these masses, in other respects so raw and uncultivated. Our masses are quite as raw and uncultivated as the
French; and so far from their having the idea of public duty
25 and of discipline, superior to the individual's self-will, brought
to their mind by a universal obligation of military service, such
as that of the conscription,—so far from their having this, the
very idea of a conscription is so at variance with our English
notion of the prime right and blessedness of doing as one likes,
30 that I remember the manager of the Clay Cross works in Der-
byshire told me during the Crimean war, when our want of
soldiers was much felt and some people were talking of a
conscription, that sooner than submit to a conscription the
population of that district would flee to the mines, and lead a
35 sort of Robin Hood life under ground.

For a long time, as I have said, the strong feudal habits of subordination and deference continued to tell upon the working
class. The modern spirit has now almost entirely dissolved those

habits, and the anarchical tendency of our worship of freedom
in and for itself, of our superstitious faith, as I say, in machinery, is becoming very manifest. More and more, because of
this our blind faith in machinery, because of our want of light
to enable us to look beyond machinery to the end for which   5
machinery is valuable, this and that man, and this and that
body of men, all over the country, are beginning to assert and
put in practice an Englishman's right to do what he likes; his
right to march where he likes, meet where he likes, enter
where he likes, hoot as he likes, threaten as he likes, smash as   10
he likes. All this, I say, tends to anarchy; and though a number
of excellent people, and particularly my friends of the Liberal
or progressive party, as they call themselves, are kind enough
to reassure us by saying that these are trifles, that a few transient outbreaks of rowdyism signify nothing, that our system   15
of liberty is one which itself cures all the evils which it works,
that the educated and intelligent classes stand in overwhelming
strength and majestic repose, ready, like our military force in
riots, to act at a moment's notice,—yet one finds that one's
Liberal friends generally say this because they have such faith   20
in themselves and their nostrums, when they shall return, as
the public welfare requires, to place and power. But this faith
of theirs one cannot exactly share, when one has so long had
them and their nostrums at work, and sees that they have not
prevented our coming to our present embarrassed condition.   25
And one finds, also, that the outbreaks of rowdyism tend to
become less and less of trifles, to become more frequent rather
than less frequent; and that meanwhile our educated and intelligent classes remain in their majestic repose, and somehow or
other, whatever happens, their overwhelming strength, like   30
our military force in riots, never does act.

How, indeed, *should* their overwhelming strength act, when
the man who gives an inflammatory lecture, or breaks down the
park railings, or invades a Secretary of State's office, is only
following an Englishman's impulse to do as he likes; and our   35
own conscience tells us that we ourselves have always regarded
this impulse as something primary and sacred? Mr. Murphy
lectures at Birmingham, and showers on the Catholic popula-

tion of that town "words," says the Home Secretary, "only fit to be addressed to thieves or murderers." What then? Mr. Murphy has his own reasons of several kinds. He suspects the Roman Catholic Church of designs upon Mrs. Murphy; and
5   he says if mayors and magistrates do not care for their wives and daughters, he does. But, above all, he is doing as he likes; or, in worthier language, asserting his personal liberty. "I will carry out my lectures if they walk over my body as a dead corpse; and I say to the Mayor of Birmingham that he is my servant
10 while I am in Birmingham, and as my servant he must do his duty and protect me." Touching and beautiful words, which find a sympathetic chord in every British bosom! The moment it is plainly put before us that a man is asserting his personal liberty, we are half disarmed; because we are believers in free-
15 dom, and not in some dream of a right reason to which the assertion of our freedom is to be subordinated. Accordingly, the Secretary of State had to say that although the lecturer's language was "only fit to be addressed to thieves or murder-ers," yet, "I do not think he is to be deprived, I do not think
20 that anything I have said could justify the inference that he is to be deprived, of the right of protection in a place built by him for the purpose of these lectures; because the language was not language which afforded grounds for a criminal prose-cution." No, nor to be silenced by Mayor, or Home Secretary,
25 or any administrative authority on earth, simply on their no-tion of what is discreet and reasonable! This is in perfect con-sonance with our public opinion, and with our national love for the assertion of personal liberty.

In quite another department of affairs, an experienced and dis-
30 tinguished Chancery Judge relates an incident which is just to the same effect as this of Mr. Murphy. A testator bequeathed £300 a year, to be for ever applied as a pension to some person who had been unsuccessful in literature, and whose duty should be to support and diffuse, by his writings, the testator's own
35 views, as enforced in the testator's publications. The views were not worth a straw, and the bequest was appealed against in the Court of Chancery on the ground of its absurdity; but, being only absurd, it was upheld, and the so-called charity was

established. Having, I say, at the bottom of our English hearts
a very strong belief in freedom, and a very weak belief in right
reason, we are soon silenced when a man pleads the prime
right to do as he likes, because this is the prime right for
ourselves too; and even if we attempt now and then to mumble 5
something about reason, yet we have ourselves thought so little
about this and so much about liberty, that we are in conscience
forced, when our brother Philistine with whom we are meddling turns boldly round upon us and asks: *Have you any
light?*—to shake our heads ruefully, and to let him go his own 10
way after all.

There are many things to be said on behalf of this exclusive
attention of ours to liberty, and of the relaxed habits of government which it has engendered. It is very easy to mistake or
to exaggerate the sort of anarchy from which we are in danger 15
through them. We are not in danger from Fenianism, fierce
and turbulent as it may show itself; for against this our conscience is free enough to let us act resolutely and put forth our
overwhelming strength the moment there is any real need for
it. In the first place, it never was any part of our creed that the 20
great right and blessedness of an Irishman, or, indeed, of anybody on earth except an Englishman, is to do as he likes; and
we can have no scruple at all about abridging, if necessary, a
non-Englishman's assertion of personal liberty. The British
Constitution, its checks, and its prime virtues, are for English- 25
men. We may extend them to others out of love and kindness;
but we find no real divine law written on our hearts constraining us so to extend them. And then the difference between an
Irish Fenian and an English rough is so immense, and the case,
in dealing with the Fenian, so much more clear! He is so 30
evidently desperate and dangerous, a man of a conquered race,
a Papist, with centuries of ill-usage to inflame him against us,
with an alien religion established in his country by us at his
expense, with no admiration of our institutions, no love of our
virtues, no talents for our business, no turn for our comfort! 35
Show him our symbolical Truss Manufactory on the finest site
in Europe, and tell him that British industrialism and individualism can bring a man to that, and he remains cold! Evidently,

if we deal tenderly with a sentimentalist like this, it is out of pure philanthropy.

But with the Hyde Park rioter how different! He is our own flesh and blood; he is a Protestant; he is framed by nature to do as we do, hate what we hate, love what we love; he is capable of feeling the symbolical force of the Truss Manufactory; the question of questions, for him, is a wages question. That beautiful sentence Sir Daniel Gooch quoted to the Swindon workmen, and which I treasure as Mrs. Gooch's Golden Rule, or the Divine Injunction "Be ye Perfect" done into British,—the sentence Sir Daniel Gooch's mother repeated to him every morning when he was a boy going to work:—*"Ever remember, my dear Dan, that you should look forward to being some day manager of that concern!"*—this fruitful maxim is perfectly fitted to shine forth in the heart of the Hyde Park rough also, and to be his guiding-star through life. He has no visionary schemes of revolution and transformation, though of course he would like his class to rule, as the aristocratic class like their class to rule, and the middle class theirs. But meanwhile our social machine is a little out of order; there are a good many people in our paradisiacal centres of industrialism and individualism taking the bread out of one another's mouths. The rough has not yet quite found his groove and settled down to his work, and so he is just asserting his personal liberty a little, going where he likes, assembling where he likes, bawling as he likes, hustling as he likes. Just as the rest of us,—as the country squires in the aristocratic class, as the political dissenters in the middle class,—he has no idea of a *State*, of the nation in its collective and corporate character controlling, as government, the free swing of this or that one of its members in the name of the higher reason of all of them, his own as well as that of others. He sees the rich, the aristocratic class, in occupation of the executive government, and so if he is stopped from making Hyde Park a bear-garden or the streets impassable, he says he is being butchered by the aristocracy.

His apparition is somewhat embarrassing, because too many cooks spoil the broth; because, while the aristocratic and middle classes have long been doing as they like with great vigour, he has been too undeveloped and submissive hitherto to join in the game; and now, when he does come, he comes in immense numbers, and is rather raw and rough. But he does not break many laws, or not many at one time; and, as our laws were made for very different circumstances from our present (but always with an eye to Englishmen doing as they like), and as the clear letter of the law must be against our Englishman who does as he likes and not only the spirit of the law and public policy, and as Government must neither have any discretionary power nor act resolutely on its own interpretation of the law if any one disputes it, it is evident our laws give our playful giant, in doing as he likes, considerable advantage. Besides, even if he can be clearly proved to commit an illegality in doing as he likes, there is always the resource of not putting the law in force, or of abolishing it. So he has his way, and if he has his way he is soon satisfied for the time. However, he falls into the habit of taking it oftener and oftener, and at last begins to create by his operations a confusion of which mischievous people can take advantage, and which, at any rate, by troubling the common course of business throughout the country, tends to cause distress, and so to increase the sort of anarchy and social disintegration which had previously commenced. And thus that profound sense of settled order and security, without which a society like ours cannot live and grow at all, sometimes seems to be beginning to threaten us with taking its departure.

Now, if culture, which simply means trying to perfect oneself, and one's mind as part of oneself, brings us light, and if light shows us that there is nothing so very blessed in merely doing as one likes, that the worship of the mere freedom to do as one likes is worship of machinery, that the really blessed thing is to like what right reason ordains, and to follow her authority, then we have got a practical benefit out of culture. We have got a much wanted principle, a principle of authority, to counteract the tendency to anarchy which seems to be threatening us.

But how to organise this authority, or to what hands to entrust the wielding of it? How to get your *State,* summing up the right reason of the community, and giving effect to it, as circumstances may require, with vigour? And here I think I see my enemies waiting for me with a hungry joy in their eyes. But I shall elude them.

5   The *State*, the power most representing the right reason of the nation, and most worthy, therefore, of ruling,—of exercising, when circumstances require it, authority over us all,—is for Mr. Carlyle the aristocracy. For Mr. Lowe, it is the middle class with its incomparable Parliament. For the Reform
10   League, it is the working class, the class with "the brightest powers of sympathy and readiest powers of action." Now culture, with its disinterested pursuit of perfection, culture, simply trying to see things as they are in order to seize on the best and to make it prevail, is surely well fitted to help us to
15   judge rightly, by all the aids of observing, reading, and thinking, the qualifications and titles to our confidence of these three candidates for authority, and can thus render us a practical service of no mean value.

So when Mr. Carlyle, a man of genius to whom we have all at
20   one time or other been indebted for refreshment and stimulus, says we should give rule to the aristocracy, mainly because of its dignity and politeness, surely culture is useful in reminding us, that in our idea of perfection the characters of beauty and intelligence are both of them present, and sweetness and light,
25   the two noblest of things, are united. Allowing, therefore, with Mr. Carlyle, the aristocratic class to possess sweetness, culture insists on the necessity of light also, and shows us that aristocracies, being by the very nature of things inaccessible to ideas, unapt to see how the world is going, must be somewhat
30   wanting in light, and must therefore be, at a moment when light is our great requisite, inadequate to our needs. Aristocracies, those children of the established fact, are for epochs of concentration. In epochs of expansion, epochs such as that in which we now live, epochs when always the warning voice is
35   again heard: *Now is the judgment of this world*,—in such epochs aristocracies with their natural clinging to the established fact, their want of sense for the flux of things, for the

inevitable transitoriness of all human institutions, are bewildered and helpless. Their serenity, their high spirit, their power of haughty resistance,—the great qualities of an aristocracy, and the secret of its distinguished manners and dignity,— these very qualities, in an epoch of expansion, turn against their possessors. Again and again I have said how the refinement of an aristocracy may be precious and educative to a raw nation as a kind of shadow of true refinement; how its serenity and dignified freedom from petty cares may serve as a useful foil to set off the vulgarity and hideousness of that type of life which a hard middle class tends to establish, and to help people to see this vulgarity and hideousness in their true colours. But the true grace and serenity is that of which Greece and Greek art suggest the admirable ideals of perfection,—a serenity which comes from having made order among ideas and harmonised them; whereas the serenity of aristocracies, at least the peculiar serenity of aristocracies of Teutonic origin, appears to come from their never having had any ideas to trouble them. And so, in a time of expansion like the present, a time for ideas, one gets perhaps, in regarding an aristocracy, even more than the idea of serenity, the idea of futility and sterility.

One has often wondered whether upon the whole earth there is anything so unintelligent, so unapt to perceive how the world is really going, as an ordinary young Englishman of our upper class. Ideas he has not, and neither has he that seriousness of our middle class which is, as I have often said, the great strength of this class, and may become its salvation. Why, a man may hear a young Dives of the aristocratic class, when the whim takes him to sing the praises of wealth and material comfort, sing them with a cynicism from which the conscience of the veriest Philistine of our industrial middle class would recoil in affright. And when, with the natural sympathy of aristocracies for firm dealing with the multitude, and his uneasiness at our feeble dealing with it at home, an unvarnished young Englishman of our aristocratic class applauds the absolute rulers on the Continent, he in general manages completely to miss the grounds of reason and intelligence which alone can give any colour of justification, any possibility of existence, to those rulers, and applauds them on grounds which it would make their own hair stand on end to listen to.

And all this time we are in an epoch of expansion; and the essence of an epoch of expansion is a movement of ideas, and the one salvation of an epoch of expansion is a harmony of ideas. The very principle of the authority which we are seeking as a defence against anarchy is right reason, ideas, light. The more, therefore, an aristocracy calls to its aid its innate forces,—its impenetrability, its high spirit, its power of haughty resistance, —to deal with an epoch of expansion, the graver is the danger, the greater the certainty of explosion, the surer the aristocracy's defeat; for it is trying to do violence to nature instead of working along with it. The best powers shown by the best men of an aristocracy at such an epoch are, it will be observed, non-aristocratical powers, powers of industry, powers of intelligence; and these powers thus exhibited, tend really not to strengthen the aristocracy, but to take their owners out of it, to expose them to the dissolving agencies of thought and change, to make them men of the modern spirit and of the future. If, as sometimes happens, they add to their non-aristocratical qualities of labour and thought, a strong dose of aristocratical qualities also,—of pride, defiance, turn for resistance, —this truly aristocratical side of them, so far from adding any strength to them, really neutralises their force and makes them impracticable and ineffective.

Knowing myself to be indeed sadly to seek, as one of my many critics says, in "a philosophy with coherent, interdependent, subordinate, and derivative principles," I continually have recourse to a plain man's expedient of trying to make what few simple notions I have, clearer and more intelligible to myself by means of example and illustration. And having been brought up at Oxford in the bad old times, when we were stuffed with Greek and Aristotle, and thought nothing of preparing ourselves by the study of modern languages,—as after Mr. Lowe's great speech at Edinburgh we shall do,—to fight the battle of life with the waiters in foreign hotels, my head is still full of a lumber of phrases we learnt at Oxford from

Aristotle, about virtue being in a mean, and about excess and defect, and so on. Once when I had had the advantage of listening to the Reform debates in the House of Commons, having heard a number of interesting speakers, and among them a well-known lord and a well-known baronet, I remember it struck me, applying Aristotle's machinery of the mean to my ideas about our aristocracy, that the lord was exactly the perfection, or happy mean, or virtue, of aristocracy, and the baronet the excess. And I fancied that by observing these two we might see both the inadequacy of aristocracy to supply the principle of authority needful for our present wants, and the danger of its trying to supply it when it was not really competent for the business. On the one hand, in the brilliant lord, showing plenty of high spirit, but remarkable, far above and beyond his gift of high spirit, for the fine tempering of his high spirit, for ease, serenity, politeness,—the great virtues, as Mr. Carlyle says, of aristocracy,—in this beautiful and virtuous mean, there seemed evidently some insufficiency of light; while, on the other hand, the worthy baronet, in whom the high spirit of aristocracy, its impenetrability, defiant courage, and pride of resistance, were developed even in excess, was manifestly capable, if he had his way given him, of causing us great danger, and, indeed, of throwing the whole commonwealth into confusion. Then I reverted to that old fundamental notion of mine about the grand merit of our race being really our honesty. And the very helplessness of our aristocratic or governing class in dealing with our perturbed social condition, their jealousy of entrusting too much power to the State as it now actually exists—that is to themselves—gave me a sort of pride and satisfaction; because I saw they were, as a whole, too honest to try and manage a business for which they did not feel themselves capable.

Surely, now, it is no inconsiderable boon which culture confers upon us, if in embarrassed times like the present it enables us to look at the ins and the outs of things in this way, without hatred and without partiality, and with a disposition to see the good in everybody all round. And I try to follow just the same course with our middle class as with our aristocracy. Mr.

Lowe talks to us of this strong middle part of the nation, of
the unrivalled deeds of our Liberal middle-class Parliament, of
the noble, the heroic work it has performed in the last thirty
years; and I begin to ask myself if we shall not, then, find in
our middle class the principle of authority we want, and if we
had not better take administration as well as legislation away
from the weak extreme which now administers for us, and
commit both to the strong middle part. I observe, too, that the
heroes of middle-class liberalism, such as we have hitherto
known it, speak with a kind of prophetic anticipation of the
great destiny which awaits them; and as if the future was
clearly theirs. The advanced party, the progressive party, the
party in alliance with the future, are the names they like to
give themselves. "The principles which will obtain recognition
in the future," says Mr. Miall, a personage of deserved eminence among the political Dissenters, as they are called, who
have been the backbone of middle-class liberalism,—"the principles which will obtain recognition in the future are the principles for which I have long and zealously laboured. I qualified
myself for joining in the work of harvest by doing to the best
of my ability the duties of seedtime." These duties, if one is to
gather them from the works of the great Liberal party in the
last thirty years, are, as I have elsewhere summed them up, the
advocacy of free trade, of Parliamentary reform, of abolition
of church-rates, of voluntaryism in religion and education, of
non-interference of the State between employers and employed, and of marriage with one's deceased wife's sister.

Now I know, when I object that all this is machinery, the
great Liberal middle class has by this time grown cunning
enough to answer that it always meant more by these things
than meets the eye; that it has had that within which passes show,
and that we are soon going to see, in a Free Church and all manner of good things, what it was. But I have learned from Bishop
Wilson (if Mr. Frederic Harrison will forgive my again quoting that poor old hierophant of a decayed superstition): "If
we would really know our heart let us impartially view our
actions;" and I cannot help thinking that if our Liberals had
had so much sweetness and light in their inner minds as they

allege, more of it must have come out in their sayings and doings.

An American friend of the English Liberals says, indeed, that their Dissidence of Dissent has been a mere instrument of the political Dissenters for making reason and the will of God prevail (and no doubt he would say the same of marriage with one's deceased wife's sister); and that the abolition of a State Church is merely the Dissenter's means to this end, just as culture is mine. Another American defender of theirs says just the same of their industrialism and free trade; indeed, this gentleman, taking the bull by the horns, proposes that we should for the future call industrialism culture, and the industrialists the men of culture, and then of course there can be no longer any misapprehension about their true character; and besides the pleasure of being wealthy and comfortable, they will have authentic recognition as vessels of sweetness and light.

All this is undoubtedly specious; but I must remark that the culture of which I talked was an endeavour to come at reason and the will of God by means of reading, observing, and thinking; and that whoever calls anything else culture, may, indeed, call it so if he likes, but then he talks of something quite different from what I talked of. And, again, as culture's way of working for reason and the will of God is by directly trying to know more about them, while the Dissidence of Dissent is evidently in itself no effort of this kind, nor is its Free Church, in fact, a church with worthier conceptions of God and the ordering of the world than the State Church professes, but with mainly the same conceptions of these as the State Church has, only that every man is to comport himself as he likes in professing them,—this being so, I cannot at once accept the Nonconformity any more than the industrialism and the other great works of our Liberal middle class as proof positive that this class is in possession of light, and that here is the true seat of authority for which we are in search; but I must try a little further, and seek for other indications which may enable me to make up my mind.

Why should we not do with the middle class as we have done

with the aristocratic class,—find in it some representative men who may stand for the virtuous mean of this class, for the perfection of its present qualities and mode of being, and also for the excess of them. Such men must clearly not be men of genius like Mr. Bright; for, as I have formerly said, so far as a man has genius he tends to take himself out of the category of class altogether, and to become simply a man. Some more ordinary man would be more to the purpose,—would sum up better in himself, without disturbing influences, the general liberal force of the middle class, the force by which it has done its great works of free trade, Parliamentary reform, voluntaryism, and so on, and the spirit in which it has done them. Now it happens that a typical middle-class man, the member for one of our chief industrial cities, has given us a famous sentence which bears directly on the resolution of our present question: whether there is light enough in our middle class to make it the proper seat of the authority we wish to establish. When there was a talk some little while ago about the state of middle-class education, our friend, as the representative of that class, spoke some memorable words:—"There had been a cry that middle-class education ought to receive more attention. He confessed himself very much surprised by the clamour that was raised. He did not think that class need excite the sympathy either of the legislature or the public." Now this satisfaction of our middle-class member of Parliament with the mental state of the middle class was truly representative, and makes good his claim to stand as the beautiful and virtuous mean of that class. But it is obviously at variance with our definition of culture, or the pursuit of light and perfection, which made light and perfection consist, not in resting and being, but in growing and becoming, in a perpetual advance in beauty and wisdom. So the middle class is by its essence, as one may say, by its incomparable self-satisfaction decisively expressed through its beautiful and virtuous mean, self-excluded from wielding an authority of which light is to be the very soul.

Clear as this is, it will be made clearer still if we take some representative man as the excess of the middle class, and remember that the middle class, in general, is to be conceived as a body

swaying between the qualities of its mean and of its excess, and
on the whole, of course, as human nature is constituted, inclining rather towards the excess than the mean. Of its excess no
better representative can possibly be imagined than a Dissenting minister from Walsall, who came before the public in 5
connection with the proceedings at Birmingham of Mr. Murphy, already mentioned. Speaking in the midst of an irritated
population of Catholics, this Walsall gentleman exclaimed: "I
say, then, away with the Mass! It is from the bottomless pit;
and in the bottomless pit shall all liars have their part, in the 10
lake that burneth with fire and brimstone." And again: "When
all the praties were black in Ireland, why didn't the priests say
the hocus-pocus over them, and make them all good again?"
He shared, too, Mr. Murphy's fears of some invasion of his
domestic happiness: "What I wish to say to you as Protestant 15
husbands is, *Take care of your wives!*" And finally, in the true
vein of an Englishman doing as he likes, a vein of which I have
at some length pointed out the present dangers, he recommended for imitation the example of some churchwardens at
Dublin, among whom, said he, "there was a Luther and also a 20
Melanchthon," who had made very short work with some
ritualist or other, hauled him down from his pulpit, and kicked
him out of church. Now it is manifest, as I said in the case of
our aristocratical baronet, that if we let this excess of the
sturdy English middle class, this conscientious Protestant Dis- 25
senter, so strong, so self-reliant, so fully persuaded in his own
mind, have his way, he would be capable, with his want of
light,—or, to use the language of the religious world, with his
zeal without knowledge,—of stirring up strife which neither
he nor any one else could easily compose. 30

And then comes in, as it did also with the aristocracy, the hon-
esty of our race, and by the voice of another middle-class man,
Alderman of the City of London and Colonel of the City of
London Militia, proclaims that it has twinges of conscience,
and that it will not attempt to cope with our social disorders, 35
and to deal with a business which it feels to be too high for it.
Every one remembers how this virtuous Alderman-Colonel, or
Colonel-Alderman, led his militia through the London streets;

how the bystanders gathered to see him pass; how the London roughs, asserting an Englishman's best and most blissful right of doing what he likes, robbed and beat the bystanders; and how the blameless warrior-magistrate refused to let his troops

5 interfere. "The crowd," he touchingly said afterwards, "was mostly composed of fine healthy strong men, bent on mischief; if he had allowed his soldiers to interfere they might have been overpowered, their rifles taken from them and used against them by the mob; a riot, in fact, might have ensued, and been

10 attended with bloodshed, compared with which the assaults and loss of property that actually occurred would have been as nothing." Honest and affecting testimony of the English middle class to its own inadequacy for the authoritative part one's admiration would sometimes incline one to assign to it! "Who

15 are we," they say by the voice of their Alderman-Colonel, "that we should not be overpowered if we attempt to cope with social anarchy, our rifles taken from us and used against us by the mob, and we, perhaps, robbed and beaten ourselves? Or what light have we, beyond a free-born Englishman's impulse

20 to do as he likes, which could justify us in preventing, at the cost of bloodshed, other free-born Englishmen from doing as they like, and robbing and beating us as much as they please?"

This distrust of themselves as an adequate centre of authority does not mark the working class, as was shown by their readi-

25 ness the other day in Hyde Park to take upon themselves all the functions of government. But this comes from the working class being, as I have often said, still an embryo, of which no one can yet quite foresee the final development; and from its not having the same experience and self-knowledge as the

30 aristocratic and middle classes. Honesty it no doubt has, just like the other classes of Englishmen, but honesty in an inchoate and untrained state; and meanwhile its powers of action, which are, as Mr. Frederic Harrison says, exceedingly ready, easily run away with it. That it cannot at present have a suffi-

35 ciency of light which comes by culture,—that is, by reading, observing, and thinking,—is clear from the very nature of its condition; and, indeed, we saw that Mr. Frederic Harrison, in

seeking to make a free stage for its bright powers of sympathy
and ready powers of action, had to begin by throwing over-
board culture, and flouting it as only fit for a professor of
belles-lettres. Still, to make it perfectly manifest that no more
in the working class than in the aristocratic and middle classes   5
can one find an adequate centre of authority,—that is, as culture teaches us to conceive our required authority, of light,
—let us again follow, with this class, the method we have
followed with the aristocratic and middle classes, and try to
bring before our minds representative men, who may figure to   10
us its virtue and its excess.

We must not take, of course, men like the chiefs of the Hyde
Park demonstration, Colonel Dickson or Mr. Beales; because
Colonel Dickson, by his martial profession and dashing exterior, seems to belong properly, like Julius Cæsar and Mirabeau   15
and other great popular leaders, to the aristocratic class, and to
be carried into the popular ranks only by his ambition or his
genius; while Mr. Beales belongs to our solid middle class, and,
perhaps, if he had not been a great popular leader, would have
been a Philistine. But Mr. Odger, whose speeches we have all   20
read, and of whom his friends relate, besides, much that is
favourable, may very well stand for the beautiful and virtuous
mean of our present working class; and I think everybody will
admit that in Mr. Odger there is manifestly, with all his good
points, some insufficiency of light. The excess of the working   25
class, in its present state of development, is perhaps best shown
in Mr. Bradlaugh, the iconoclast, who seems to be almost for
baptizing us all in blood and fire into his new social dispensa-
tion, and to whose reflections, now that I have once been set
going on Bishop Wilson's track, I cannot forbear commending   30
this maxim of the good old man: "Intemperance in talk makes
a dreadful havoc in the heart." Mr. Bradlaugh, like our types
of excess in the aristocratic and middle classes, is evidently
capable, if he had his head given him, of running us all into
great dangers and confusion. I conclude, therefore,—what in-   35
deed, few of those who do me the honour to read this disquisition are likely to dispute,—that we can as little find in the

working class as in the aristocratic or in the middle class our much-wanted source of authority, as culture suggests it to us.

Well, then, what if we tried to rise above the idea of class to the idea of the whole community, *the State*, and to find our centre of light and authority there? Every one of us has the idea of country, as a sentiment; hardly any one of us has the idea of *the State*, as a working power. And why? Because we habitually live in our ordinary selves, which do not carry us beyond the ideas and wishes of the class to which we happen to belong. And we are all afraid of giving to the State too much power, because we only conceive of the State as something equivalent to the class in occupation of the executive government, and are afraid of that class abusing power to its own purposes. If we strengthen the State with the aristocratic class in occupation of the executive government, we imagine we are delivering ourselves up captive to the ideas and wishes of our fierce aristocratical baronet; if with the middle class in occupation of the executive government, to those of our truculent middle-class Dissenting minister; if with the working class, to those of its notorious tribune, Mr. Bradlaugh. And with much justice; owing to the exaggerated notion which we English, as I have said, entertain of the right and blessedness of the mere doing as one likes, of the affirming oneself, and oneself just as it is. People of the aristocratic class want to affirm their ordinary selves, their likings and dislikings; people of the middle class the same, people of the working class the same. By our everyday selves, however, we are separate, personal, at war; we are only safe from one another's tyranny when no one has any power; and this safety, in its turn, cannot save us from anarchy. And when, therefore, anarchy presents itself as a danger to us, we know not where to turn.

But by our *best self* we are united, impersonal, at harmony. We are in no peril from giving authority to this, because it is the truest friend we all of us can have; and when anarchy is a danger to us, to this authority we may turn with sure trust. Well, and this is the very self which culture, or the study of perfection, seeks to develop in us; at the expense of our old untransformed self, taking pleasure only in doing what it likes or is used to do, and exposing us to the risk of clashing with every one else who is doing the same! So that our poor culture, which is flouted as so unpractical, leads us to the very ideas capable of meeting the great want of our present embarrassed times! We want an authority, and we find nothing but jealous classes, checks, and a dead-lock; culture suggests the idea of *the State*. We find no basis for a firm State-power in our ordinary selves; culture suggests one to us in our *best self.*

It cannot but acutely try a tender conscience to be accused, in a practical country like ours, of keeping aloof from the work and hope of a multitude of earnest-hearted men, and of merely toying with poetry and æsthetics. So it is with no little sense of relief that I find myself thus in the position of one who makes a contribution in aid of the practical necessities of our times. The great thing, it will be observed, is to find our *best* self, and to seek to affirm nothing but that; not,—as we English with our over-value for merely being free and busy have been so accustomed to do,—resting satisfied with a self which comes uppermost long before our best self, and affirming that with blind energy. In short,—to go back yet once more to Bishop Wilson,—of these two excellent rules of Bishop Wilson's for a man's guidance: "Firstly, never go against the best light you have; secondly, take care that your light be not darkness," we English have followed with praiseworthy zeal the first rule, but we have not given so much heed to the second. We have gone manfully according to the best light we have; but we have not taken enough care that this should be really the best light possible for us, that it should not be darkness. And, our honesty being very great, conscience has whispered to us that the light we were following, our ordinary self, was, indeed, perhaps, only an inferior self, only darkness; and that it would not do to impose this seriously on all the world.

But our best self inspires faith, and is capable of affording a serious principle of authority. For example. We are on our way to what the late Duke of Wellington, with his strong sagacity, foresaw and admirably described as "a revolution by due

course of law." This is undoubtedly,—if we are still to live and
grow, and this famous nation is not to stagnate and dwindle
away on the one hand, or, on the other, to perish miserably in
mere anarchy and confusion,—what we are on the way to.
5 Great changes there must be, for a revolution cannot accomplish itself without great changes; yet order there must be, for
without order a revolution cannot accomplish itself by due
course of law. So whatever brings risk of tumult and disorder,
multitudinous processions in the streets of our crowded towns,
10 multitudinous meetings in their public places and parks,—demonstrations perfectly unnecessary in the present course of our
affairs,—our best self, or right reason, plainly enjoins us to set
our faces against. It enjoins us to encourage and uphold the
occupants of the executive power, whoever they may be, in
15 firmly prohibiting them. But it does this clearly and resolutely,
and is thus a real principle of authority, because it does it with
a free conscience; because in thus provisionally strengthening
the executive power, it knows that it is not doing this merely
to enable our aristocratical baronet to affirm himself as against
20 our working-men's tribune, or our middle-class Dissenter to
affirm himself as against both. It knows that it is stablishing *the
State*, or organ of our collective best self, of our national right
reason. And it has the testimony of conscience that it is stablishing the State on behalf of whatever great changes are
25 needed, just as much as on behalf of order; stablishing it to
deal just as stringently, when the time comes, with our baronet's aristocratical prejudices, or with the fanaticism of our
middle-class Dissenter, as it deals with Mr. Bradlaugh's street-
processions.

Chapter III

Barbarians, Philistines, Populace

From a man without a philosophy no one can expect philosophical completeness. Therefore I may observe without shame, that in trying to get a distinct notion of our aristocratic, our middle, and our working class, with a view of testing the claims of each of these classes to become a centre of authority, I have omitted, I find, to complete the old-fashioned analysis which I had the fancy of applying, and have not shown in these classes, as well as the virtuous mean and the excess, the defect also. I do not know that the omission very much matters. Still, as clearness is the one merit which a plain, unsystematic writer, without a philosophy, can hope to have, and as our notion of the three great English classes may perhaps be made clearer if we see their distinctive qualities in the defect, as well as in the excess and in the mean, let us try, before proceeding further, to remedy this omission.

It is manifest, if the perfect and virtuous mean of that fine spirit which is the distinctive quality of aristocracies, is to be found in a high, chivalrous style, and its excess in a fierce turn for resistance, that its defect must lie in a spirit not bold and high enough, and in an excessive and pusillanimous unaptness for resistance. If, again, the perfect and virtuous mean of that force by which our middle class has done its great works, and of that self-reliance with which it contemplates itself and them, is to be seen in the performances and speeches of our commercial member of Parliament, and the excess of that force and of that self-reliance in the performances and speeches of our fanatical Dissenting minister, then it is manifest that their defect must lie in a helpless inaptitude for the great works of the middle class, and in a poor and despicable lack of its self-satisfaction.

To be chosen to exemplify the happy mean of a good quality, or set of good qualities, is evidently a praise to a man; nay, to be 5 chosen to exemplify even their excess, is a kind of praise. Therefore I could have no hesitation in taking actual personages to exemplify, respectively, the mean and the excess of aristocratic and middle-class qualities. But perhaps there might be a want of urbanity in singling out this or that personage as 10 the representative of defect. Therefore I shall leave the defect of aristocracy unillustrated by any representative man. But with oneself one may always, without impropriety, deal quite freely; and, indeed, this sort of plain-dealing with oneself has in it, as all the moralists tell us, something very wholesome. So I 15 will venture to humbly offer myself as an illustration of defect in those forces and qualities which make our middle class what it is. The too well-founded reproaches of my opponents declare how little I have lent a hand to the great works of the middle class; for it is evidently these works, and my slackness 20 at them, which are meant, when I am said to "refuse to lend a hand to the humble operation of uprooting certain definite evils" (such as church-rates and others), and that therefore "the believers in action grow impatient" with me. The line, again, of a still unsatisfied seeker which I have followed, the 25 idea of self-transformation, of growing towards some measure of sweetness and light not yet reached, is evidently at clean variance with the perfect self-satisfaction current in my class, the middle class, and may serve to indicate in me, therefore, the extreme defect of this feeling. But these confessions, though 30 salutary, are bitter and unpleasant.

To pass, then, to the working class. The defect of this class would be the falling short in what Mr. Frederic Harrison calls those "bright powers of sympathy and ready powers of action," of which we saw in Mr. Odger the virtuous mean, and in Mr. 35 Bradlaugh the excess. The working class is so fast growing and rising at the present time, that instances of this defect cannot well be now very common. Perhaps Canning's "Needy Knife-Grinder" (who is dead, and therefore cannot be pained at my taking him for an illustration) may serve to give us the notion of defect in the essential quality of a working class; or I might even cite (since, though he is alive in the flesh, he is dead to all heed of criticism) my poor old poaching friend, Zephaniah Diggs, who, between his hare-snaring and his gin-drinking, has 5 got his powers of sympathy quite dulled and his powers of action in any great movement of his class hopelessly impaired. But examples of this defect belong, as I have said, to a bygone age rather than to the present.

The same desire for clearness, which has led me thus to extend 10 a little my first analysis of the three great classes of English society, prompts me also to improve my nomenclature for them a little, with a view to making it thereby more manageable. It is awkward and tiresome to be always saying the aristocratic class, the middle class, the working class. For the middle 15 class, for that great body which, as we know, "has done all the great things that have been done in all departments," and which is to be conceived as moving between its two cardinal points of our commercial member of Parliament and our fanatical Protestant Dissenter,—for this class we have a designation 20 which now has become pretty well known, and which we may as well still keep for them, the designation of Philistines. What this term means I have so often explained that I need not repeat it here. For the aristocratic class, conceived mainly as a body moving between the two cardinal points of our chival- 25 rous lord and our defiant baronet, we have as yet got no special designation. Almost all my attention has naturally been concentrated on my own class, the middle class, with which I am in closest sympathy, and which has been, besides, the great power of our day, and has had its praises sung by all speakers 30 and newspapers.

Still the aristocratic class is so important in itself, and the weighty functions which Mr. Carlyle proposes at the present critical time to commit to it, must add so much to its importance, that it seems neglectful, and a strong instance of that want of 35 coherent philosophic method for which Mr. Frederic Harrison blames me, to leave the aristocratic class so much without notice and denomination. It may be thought that the charac-

teristic which I have occasionally mentioned as proper to aristocracies,—their natural inaccessibility, as children of the established fact, to ideas,—points to our extending to this class
also the designation of Philistines; the Philistine being, ·as is
5 well known, the enemy of the children of light or servants of
the idea. Nevertheless, there seems to be an inconvenience in
thus giving one and the same designation to two very different
classes; and besides, if we look into the thing closely, we shall
find that the term Philistine conveys a sense which makes it
10 more peculiarly appropriate to our middle class than to our
aristocratic. For *Philistine* gives the notion of something particularly stiff-necked and perverse in the resistance to light and
its children; and therein it specially suits our middle class, who
not only do not pursue sweetness and light, but who even
15 prefer to them that sort of machinery of business, chapels, tea-
meetings, and addresses from Mr. Murphy, which makes up
the dismal and illiberal life on which I have so often touched.
But the aristocratic class has actually, as we have seen, in its
well-known politeness, a kind of image or shadow of sweet-
20 ness; and as for light, if it does not pursue light, it is not that it
perversely cherishes some dismal and illiberal existence in preference to light, but it is lured off from following light by those
mighty and eternal seducers of our race which weave for this
class their most irresistible charms,—by worldly splendour,
25 security, power, and pleasure. These seducers are exterior
goods, but in a way they are goods; and he who is hindered by
them from caring for light and ideas, is not so much doing
what is perverse as what is too natural.

Keeping this in view, I have in my own mind often indulged
30 myself with the fancy of employing, in order to designate our
aristocratic class, the name of *the Barbarians*. The Barbarians,
to whom we all owe so much, and who reinvigorated and
renewed our worn-out Europe, had, as is well known, eminent
merits; and in this country, where we are for the most part
35 sprung from the Barbarians, we have never had the prejudice
against them which prevails among the races of Latin origin.
The Barbarians brought with them that staunch individualism,
as the modern phrase is, and that passion for doing as one likes,

for the assertion of personal liberty, which appears to Mr. Bright the central idea of English life, and of which we have, at any rate, a very rich supply. The stronghold and natural seat of this passion was in the nobles of whom our aristocratic class are the inheritors; and this class, accordingly, have signally manifested it, and have done much by their example to recommend it to the body of the nation, who already, indeed, had it in their blood. The Barbarians, again, had the passion for field-sports; and they have handed it on to our aristocratic class, who of this passion too, as of the passion for asserting one's personal liberty, are the great natural stronghold. The care of the Barbarians for the body, and for all manly exercises; the vigour, good looks, and fine complexion which they acquired and perpetuated in their families by these means,—all this may be observed still in our aristocratic class. The chivalry of the Barbarians, with its characteristics of high spirit, choice manners, and distinguished bearing,—what is this but the attractive commencement of the politeness of our aristocratic class? In some Barbarian noble, no doubt, one would have admired, if one could have been then alive to see it, the rudiments of our politest peer. Only, all this culture (to call it by that name) of the Barbarians was an exterior culture mainly. It consisted principally in outward gifts and graces, in looks, manners, accomplishments, prowess. The chief inward gifts which had part in it were the most exterior, so to speak, of inward gifts, those which come nearest to outward ones; they were courage, a high spirit, self-confidence. Far within, and unawakened, lay a whole range of powers of thought and feeling, to which these interesting productions of nature had, from the circumstances of their life, no access. Making allowances for the difference of the times, surely we can observe precisely the same thing now in our aristocratic class. In general its culture is exterior chiefly; all the exterior graces and accomplishments, and the more external of the inward virtues, seem to be principally its portion. It now, of course, cannot but be often in contact with those studies by which, from the world of thought and feeling, true culture teaches us to fetch sweetness and light; but its hold upon these very studies appears remarkably external, and unable to exert any deep power upon its spirit. Therefore the one insufficiency which we noted in the perfect mean of this class was an insufficiency of light. And owing to the same causes, does not a subtle criticism lead us to make, even on the good looks and politeness of our aristocratic class, and of even the most fascinating half of that class, the feminine half, the one qualifying remark, that in these charming gifts there should perhaps be, for ideal perfection, a shade more *soul?*

I often, therefore, when I want to distinguish clearly the aristocratic class from the Philistines proper, or middle class, name the former, in my own mind, *the Barbarians.* And when I go through the country, and see this and that beautiful and imposing seat of theirs crowning the landscape, "There," I say to myself, "is a great fortified post of the Barbarians."

It is obvious that that part of the working class which, working diligently by the light of Mrs. Gooch's Golden Rule, looks forward to the happy day when it will sit on thrones with commercial members of Parliament and other middle-class potentates, to survey, as Mr. Bright beautifully says, "the cities it has built, the railroads it has made, the manufactures it has produced, the cargoes which freight the ships of the greatest mercantile navy the world has ever seen,"—it is obvious, I say, that this part of the working class is, or is in a fair way to be, one in spirit with the industrial middle class. It is notorious that our middle-class Liberals have long looked forward to this consummation, when the working class shall join forces with them, aid them heartily to carry forward their great works, go in a body to their tea-meetings, and, in short, enable them to bring about their millennium. That part of the working class, therefore, which does really seem to lend itself to these great aims, may, with propriety, be numbered by us among the Philistines. That part of it, again, which so much occupies the attention of philanthropists at present,—the part which gives all its energies to organising itself, through trades' unions and other means, so as to constitute, first, a great working-class power independent of the middle and aristocratic classes, and then, by dint of numbers, give the law to them and itself reign absolutely,—this lively and promising part must also, according to our definition, go with the Philistines; because it is its class and its class instinct which it seeks to affirm—its ordinary self, not its best self; and it is a machinery, an industrial machinery, and power and pre-eminence and other external goods, which fill its thoughts, and not an inward perfection. It is wholly occupied, according to Plato's subtle expression, with the things of itself and not its real self, with the things of the State and not the real State. But that vast portion, lastly, of the working class which, raw and half-developed, has long lain half-hidden amidst its poverty and squalor, and is now issuing from its hiding-place to assert an Englishman's heaven-born privilege of doing as he likes, and is beginning to perplex us by marching where it likes, meeting where it likes, bawling what it likes, breaking what it likes,—to this vast residuum we may with great propriety give the name of *Populace*.

Thus we have got three distinct terms, *Barbarians, Philistines, Populace*, to denote roughly the three great classes into which our society is divided; and though this humble attempt at a scientific nomenclature falls, no doubt, very far short in precision of what might be required from a writer equipped with a complete and coherent philosophy, yet, from a notoriously unsystematic and unpretending writer, it will, I trust, be accepted as sufficient.

But in using this new, and, I hope, convenient division of English society, two things are to be borne in mind. The first is, that since, under all our class divisions, there is a common basis of human nature, therefore, in every one of us, whether we be properly Barbarians, Philistines, or Populace, there exist, sometimes only in germ and potentially, sometimes more or less developed, the same tendencies and passions which have made our fellow-citizens of other classes what they are. This consideration is very important, because it has great influence in begetting that spirit of indulgence which is a necessary part of sweetness, and which, indeed, when our culture is complete, is, as I have said, inexhaustible. Thus, an English Barbarian who examines himself will, in general, find himself to be not so entirely a Barbarian but that he has in him, also, something of the Philistine, and even something of the Populace as well. And the same with Englishmen of the two other classes.

This is an experience which we may all verify every day. For instance, I myself (I again take myself as a sort of *corpus vile* to serve for illustration in a matter where serving for illustration may not by every one be thought agreeable), I myself am properly a Philistine,—Mr. Swinburne would add, the son of a Philistine. And although, through circumstances which will perhaps one day be known if ever the affecting history of my conversion comes to be written, I have, for the most part, broken with the ideas and the tea-meetings of my own class, yet I have not, on that account, been brought much the nearer to the ideas and works of the Barbarians or of the Populace. Nevertheless, I never take a gun or a fishing-rod in my hands without feeling that I have in the ground of my nature the self-same seeds which, fostered by circumstances, do so much to make the Barbarian; and that, with the Barbarian's advantages, I might have rivalled him. Place me in one of his great fortified posts, with these seeds of a love for field-sports sown in my nature, with all the means of developing them, with all pleasures at my command, with most whom I met deferring to me, every one I met smiling on me, and with every appearance of permanence and security before me and behind me,—then I too might have grown, I feel, into a very passable child of the established fact, of commendable spirit and politeness, and, at the same time, a little inaccessible to ideas and light; not, of course, with either the eminent fine spirit of our type of aristocratic perfection, or the eminent turn for resistance of our type of aristocratic excess, but, according to the measure of the common run of mankind, something between the two. And as to the Populace, who, whether he be Barbarian or Philistine, can look at them without sympathy, when he remembers how often,—every time that we snatch up a vehement opinion in ignorance and passion, every time that we long to crush an adversary by sheer violence, every time that we are envious, every time that we are brutal, every time that we adore mere power or success, every time

that we add our voice to swell a blind clamour against some
unpopular personage, every time that we trample savagely on
the fallen,—he has found in his own bosom the eternal spirit of
the Populace, and that there needs only a little help from
circumstances to make it triumph in him untamably.   5

The second thing to be borne in mind I have indicated several
times already. It is this. All of us, so far as we are Barbarians,
Philistines, or Populace, imagine happiness to consist in doing
what one's ordinary self likes. What one's ordinary self likes
differs according to the class to which one belongs, and   10
has its severer and its lighter side; always, however, remaining machinery, and nothing more. The graver self of the
Barbarian likes honours and consideration; his more relaxed self, field-sports and pleasure. The graver self of one
kind of Philistine likes fanaticism, business, and money-   15
making; his more relaxed self, comfort and tea-meetings. Of
another kind of Philistine, the graver self likes rattening;
the relaxed self, deputations, or hearing Mr. Odger speak.
The sterner self of the Populace likes bawling, hustling, and
smashing; the lighter self, beer. But in each class there are   20
born a certain number of natures with a curiosity about their
best self, with a bent for seeing things as they are, for disen-
tangling themselves from machinery, for simply concerning
themselves with reason and the will of God, and doing their
best to make these prevail;—for the pursuit, in a word, of   25
perfection. To certain manifestations of this love for perfection mankind have accustomed themselves to give the name of
genius; implying, by this name, something original and heaven-
bestowed in the passion. But the passion is to be found far
beyond those manifestations of it to which the world usually   30
gives the name of genius, and in which there is, for the most
part, a *talent* of some kind or other, a special and striking faculty of execution, informed by the heaven-bestowed ardour,
or genius. It is to be found in many manifestations besides
these, and may best be called, as we have called it, the love and   35
pursuit of perfection; culture being the true nurse of the
pursuing love, and sweetness and light the true character of
the pursued perfection. Natures with this bent emerge in all

classes,—among the Barbarians, among the Philistines, among the Populace. And this bent always tends to take them out of their class, and to make their distinguishing characteristic not their Barbarianism or their Philistinism, but their *humanity*.
They have, in general, a rough time of it in their lives; but they are sown more abundantly than one might think, they appear where and when one least expects it, they set up a fire which enfilades, so to speak, the class with which they are ranked; and, in general, by the extrication of their best self as the self to develop, and by the simplicity of the ends fixed by them as paramount, they hinder the unchecked predominance of that class-life which is the affirmation of our ordinary self, and seasonably disconcert mankind in their worship of machinery.

Therefore, when we speak of ourselves as divided into Barbarians, Philistines, and Populace, we must be understood always to imply that within each of these classes there are a certain number of *aliens*, if we may so call them,—persons who are mainly led, not by their class spirit, but by a general *humane* spirit, by the love of human perfection; and that this number is capable of being diminished or augmented. I mean, the number of those who will succeed in developing this happy instinct will be greater or smaller, in proportion both to the force of the original instinct within them, and to the hindrance or encouragement which it meets with from without. In almost all who have it, it is mixed with some infusion of the spirit of an ordinary self, some quantity of class-instinct, and even, as has been shown, of more than one class-instinct at the same time; so that, in general, the extrication of the best self, the predominance of the *humane* instinct, will very much depend upon its meeting, or not, with what is fitted to help and elicit it. At a moment, therefore, when it is agreed that we want a source of authority, and when it seems probable that the right source is our best self, it becomes of vast importance to see whether or not the things around us are, in general, such as to help and elicit our best self, and if they are not, to see why they are not, and the most promising way of mending them.

Now, it is clear that the very absence of any powerful author-

ity amongst us, and the prevalent doctrine of the duty and happiness of doing as one likes, and asserting our personal liberty,
must tend to prevent the erection of any very strict standard
of excellence, the belief in any very paramount authority of
right reason, the recognition of our best self as anything very   5
recondite and hard to come at. It may be, as I have said, a
proof of our honesty that we do not attempt to give to our
ordinary self, as we have it in action, predominant authority,
and to impose its rule upon other people. But it is evident, also,
that it is not easy, with our style of proceeding, to get beyond   10
the notion of an ordinary self at all, or to get the paramount
authority of a commanding best self, or right reason, recognised. The learned Martinus Scriblerus well says:—"The taste
of the bathos is implanted by nature itself in the soul of man;
till, perverted by custom or example, he is taught, or rather   15
compelled, to relish the sublime." But with us everything
seems directed to prevent any such perversion of us by custom
or example as might compel us to relish the sublime; by all
means we are encouraged to keep our natural taste for the
bathos unimpaired.   20

I have formerly pointed out how in literature the absence of
any authoritative centre, like an Academy, tends to do this. Each
section of the public has its own literary organ, and the mass
of the public is without any suspicion that the value of these
organs is relative to their being nearer a certain ideal centre of   25
correct information, taste, and intelligence, or farther away
from it. I have said that within certain limits, which any one
who is likely to read this will have no difficulty in drawing for
himself, my old adversary, the *Saturday Review,* may, on matters of literature and taste, be fairly enough regarded, rela-   30
tively to the mass of newspapers which treat these matters, as a
kind of organ of reason. But I remember once conversing with
a company of Nonconformist admirers of some lecturer who
had let off a great firework, which the *Saturday Review* said
was all noise and false lights, and feeling my way as tenderly as   35
I could about the effect of this unfavourable judgment upon
those with whom I was conversing. "Oh," said one who was
their spokesman, with the most tranquil air of conviction, "it is

true the *Saturday Review* abuses the lecture, but the *British Banner*" (I am not quite sure it was the *British Banner*, but it was some newspaper of that stamp) "says that the *Saturday Review* is quite wrong." The speaker had evidently no notion
5 that there was a scale of value for judgments on these topics, and that the judgments of the *Saturday Review* ranked high on this scale, and those of the *British Banner* low; the taste of the bathos implanted by nature in the literary judgments of man had never, in my friend's case, encountered any let or
10 hindrance.

Just the same in religion as in literature. We have most of us little idea of a high standard to choose our guides by, of a great and profound spirit which is an authority while inferior spirits are none. It is enough to give importance to things that this or
15 that person says them decisively, and has a large following of some strong kind when he says them. This habit of ours is very well shown in that able and interesting work of Mr. Hepworth Dixon's, which we were all reading lately, *The Mormons, by One of Themselves*. Here, again, I am not quite sure that my
20 memory serves me as to the exact title, but I mean the well-known book in which Mr. Hepworth Dixon described the Mormons, and other similar religious bodies in America, with so much detail and such warm sympathy. In this work it seems enough for Mr. Dixon that this or that doctrine has its Rabbi,
25 who talks big to him, has a staunch body of disciples, and, above all, has plenty of rifles. That there are any further stricter tests to be applied to a doctrine, before it is pronounced important, never seems to occur to him. "It is easy to say," he writes of the Mormons, "that these saints are dupes
30 and fanatics, to laugh at Joe Smith and his church, but what then? *The great facts remain*. Young and his people are at Utah; a church of 200,000 souls; an army of 20,000 rifles." But if the followers of a doctrine are really dupes, or worse, and its promulgators are really fanatics, or worse, it gives the doctrine
35 no seriousness or authority the more that there should be found 200,000 souls,—200,000 of the innumerable multitude with a natural taste for the bathos,—to hold it, and 20,000 rifles to defend it. And again, of another religious organisation in

America: "A fair and open field is not to be refused when hosts
so mighty throw down wager of battle on behalf of what they
hold to be true, however strange their faith may seem." A fair
and open field is not to be refused to any speaker; but this
solemn way of heralding him is quite out of place, unless he   5
has, for the best reason and spirit of man, some significance.
"Well, but," says Mr. Hepworth Dixon, "a theory which has
been accepted by men like Judge Edmonds, Dr. Hare, Elder
Frederick, and Professor Bush!" And again: "Such are, in
brief, the bases of what Newman Weeks, Sarah Horton, Deb-   10
orah Butler, and the associated brethren, proclaimed in Pratt's
Hall as the new covenant!" If he was summing up an account
of the doctrine of Plato, or of St. Paul, and of its followers,
Mr. Hepworth Dixon could not be more earnestly reverential.
But the question is, Have personages like Judge Edmonds, and   15
Newman Weeks, and Elderess Polly, and Elderess Antoinette,
and the rest of Mr. Hepworth Dixon's heroes and heroines,
anything of the weight and significance for the best reason and
spirit of man that Plato and St. Paul have? Evidently they, at
present, have not; and a very small taste of them and their   20
doctrines ought to have convinced Mr. Hepworth Dixon that
they never could have. "But," says he, "the magnetic power
which Shakerism is exercising on American thought would of
itself compel us,"—and so on. Now, so far as real thought is
concerned,—thought which affects the best reason and spirit   25
of man, the scientific or the imaginative thought of the world,
the only thought which deserves speaking of in this solemn
way,—America has up to the present time been hardly more
than a province of England, and even now would not herself
claim to be more than abreast of England; and of this only real   30
human thought, English thought itself is not just now, as we
must all admit, the most significant factor. Neither, then, can
American thought be; and the magnetic power which Shakerism exercises on American thought is about as important, for
the best reason and spirit of man, as the magnetic power which   35
Mr. Murphy exercises on Birmingham Protestantism. And as
we shall never get rid of our natural taste for the bathos in
religion,—never get access to a best self and right reason

which may stand as a serious authority,—by treating Mr.
Murphy as his own disciples treat him, seriously, and as if he
was as much an authority as any one else: so we shall never get
rid of it while our able and popular writers treat their Joe
Smiths and Deborah Butlers, with their so many thousand
souls and so many thousand rifles, in the like exaggerated and
misleading manner, and so do their best to confirm us in a bad
mental habit to which we are already too prone.

If our habits make it hard for us to come at the idea of a high
best self, of a paramount authority, in literature or religion,
how much more do they make this hard in the sphere of
politics! In other countries the governors, not depending so
immediately on the favour of the governed, have everything
to urge them, if they know anything of right reason (and it is
at least supposed that governors should know more of this than
the mass of the governed), to set it authoritatively before the
community. But our whole scheme of government being representative, every one of our governors has all possible temptation, instead of setting up before the governed who elect him,
and on whose favour he depends, a high standard of right
reason, to accommodate himself as much as possible to their
natural taste for the bathos; and even if he tries to go counter
to it, to proceed in this with so much flattering and coaxing,
that they shall not suspect their ignorance and prejudices to be
anything very unlike right reason, or their natural taste for the
bathos to differ much from a relish for the sublime. Every one
is thus in every possible way encouraged to trust in his own
heart; but, "He that trusteth in his own heart," says the Wise
Man, "is a fool;" and at any rate this, which Bishop Wilson
says, is undeniably true: "The number of those who need to
be awakened is far greater than that of those who need comfort."

But in our political system everybody is comforted. Our
guides and governors who have to be elected by the influence of
the Barbarians, and who depend on their favour, sing the praises
of the Barbarians, and say all the smooth things that can be said
of them. With Mr. Tennyson, they celebrate "the great broad-
shouldered genial Englishman," with his "sense of duty," his

"reverence for the laws," and his "patient force," who saves us from the "revolts, republics, revolutions, most no graver than a schoolboy's barring out," which upset other and less broad-shouldered nations. Our guides who are chosen by the Philistines and who have to look to their favour, tell the Philistines how "all the world knows that the great middle class of this country supplies the mind, the will, and the power requisite for all the great and good things that have to be done," and congratulate them on their "earnest good sense, which penetrates through sophisms, ignores commonplaces, and gives to conventional illusions their true value." Our guides who look to the favour of the Populace, tell them that "theirs are the brightest powers of sympathy, and the readiest powers of action."

Harsh things are said too, no doubt, against all the great classes of the community; but these things so evidently come from a hostile class, and are so manifestly dictated by the passions and prepossessions of a hostile class, and not by right reason, that they make no serious impression on those at whom they are launched, but slide easily off their minds. For instance, when the Reform League orators inveigh against our cruel and bloated aristocracy, these invectives so evidently show the passions and point of view of the Populace, that they do not sink into the minds of those at whom they are addressed, or awaken any thought or self-examination in them. Again, when our aristocratical baronet describes the Philistines and the Populace as influenced with a kind of hideous mania for emasculating the aristocracy, that reproach so clearly comes from the wrath and excited imagination of the Barbarians, that it does not much set the Philistines and the Populace thinking. Or when Mr. Lowe calls the Populace drunken and venal, he so evidently calls them this in an agony of apprehension for his Philistine or middle-class Parliament, which has done so many great and heroic works, and is now threatened with mixture and debasement, that the Populace do not lay his words seriously to heart.

So the voice which makes a permanent impression on each of our classes is the voice of its friends, and this is from the nature of things, as I have said, a comforting voice. The Barbarians remain in the belief that the great broad-shouldered genial Englishman may be well satisfied with himself; the Philistines remain in the belief that the great middle class of this country,

5   with its earnest common-sense penetrating through sophisms and ignoring commonplaces, may be well satisfied with itself; the Populace, that the working man with his bright powers of sympathy and ready powers of action, may be well satisfied with himself. What hope, at this rate, of extinguishing the

10   taste of the bathos implanted by nature itself in the soul of man, or of inculcating the belief that excellence dwells among high and steep rocks, and can only be reached by those who sweat blood to reach her?

But it will be said, perhaps, that candidates for political influ-

15   ence and leadership, who thus caress the self-love of those whose suffrages they desire, know quite well that they are not saying the sheer truth as reason sees it, but that they are using a sort of conventional language, or what we call clap-trap, which is essential to the working of representative institutions.

20   And therefore, I suppose, we ought rather to say with Figaro: *Qui est-ce qu'on trompe ici?* Now, I admit that often, but not always, when our governors say smooth things to the self-love of the class whose political support they want, they know very well that they are overstepping, by a long stride, the bounds

25   of truth and soberness; and while they talk, they in a manner, no doubt, put their tongue in their cheek. Not always; because, when a Barbarian appeals to his own class to make him their representative and give him political power, he, when he pleases their self-love by extolling broad-shouldered genial

30   Englishmen with their sense of duty, reverence for the laws, and patient force, pleases his own self-love and extols himself, and is, therefore, himself ensnared by his own smooth words. And so, too, when a Philistine wants to be sent to Parliament by his brother Philistines, and extols the earnest good sense

35   which characterises Manchester and supplies the mind, the will, and the power, as the *Daily News* eloquently says, requisite for all the great and good things that have to be done, he

intoxicates and deludes himself as well as his brother Philistines who hear him.

But it is true that a Barbarian often wants the political support of the Philistines; and he unquestionably, when he flatters the self-love of Philistinism, and extols, in the approved fashion, its energy, enterprise, and self-reliance, knows that he is talking clap-trap, and so to say, puts his tongue in his cheek. On all matters where Noncomformity and its catchwords are concerned, this insincerity of Barbarians needing Nonconformist support, and, therefore, flattering the self-love of Nonconformity and repeating its catchwords without the least real belief in them, is very noticeable. When the Nonconformists, in a transport of blind zeal, threw out Sir James Graham's useful Education Clauses in 1843, one-half of their Parliamentary advocates, no doubt, who cried aloud against "trampling on the religious liberty of the Dissenters by taking the money of Dissenters to teach the tenets of the Church of England," put their tongue in their cheek while they so cried out. And perhaps there is even a sort of motion of Mr. Frederic Harrison's tongue towards his cheek when he talks of "the shriek of superstition," and tells the working class that "theirs are the brightest powers of sympathy and the readiest powers of action." But the point on which I would insist is, that this involuntary tribute to truth and soberness on the part of certain of our governors and guides never reaches at all the mass of us governed, to serve as a lesson to us, to abate our self-love, and to awaken in us a suspicion that our favourite prejudices may be, to a higher reason, all nonsense. Whatever by-play goes on among the more intelligent of our leaders, we do not see it; and we are left to believe that, not only in our own eyes, but in the eyes of our representative and ruling men, there is nothing more admirable than our ordinary self, whatever our ordinary self happens to be, Barbarian, Philistine, or Populace.

Thus everything in our political life tends to hide from us that there is anything wiser than our ordinary selves, and to prevent our getting the notion of a paramount right reason. Royalty itself, in its idea the expression of the collective nation, and a sort of constituted witness to its best mind, we try to turn into a kind of grand advertising van, meant to give publicity and credit to the inventions, sound or unsound, of the ordinary self of individuals.

5   I remember, when I was in North Germany, having this very strongly brought to my mind in the matter of schools and their institution. In Prussia, the best schools are Crown patronage schools, as they are called: schools which have been established and endowed (and new ones are to this day being estab-
10   lished and endowed) by the Sovereign himself out of his own revenues, to be under the direct control and management of him or of those representing him, and to serve as types of what schools should be. The Sovereign, as his position raises him above many prejudices and littlenesses, and as he can always
15   have at his disposal the best advice, has evident advantages over private founders in well planning and directing a school; while at the same time his great means and his great influence secure, to a well-planned school of his, credit and authority. This is what, in North Germany, the governors do in the matter of
20   education for the governed; and one may say that they thus give the governed a lesson, and draw out in them the idea of a right reason higher than the suggestions of an ordinary man's ordinary self.

But in England how different is the part which in this matter
25   our governors are accustomed to play! The Licensed Victuallers or the Commercial Travellers propose to make a school for their children; and I suppose, in the matter of schools, one may call the Licensed Victuallers or the Commercial Travellers ordinary men, with their natural taste for the bathos still strong;
30   and a Sovereign with the advice of men like Wilhelm von Humboldt or Schleiermacher may, in this matter, be a better judge, and nearer to right reason. And it will be allowed, probably, that right reason would suggest that, to have a sheer school of Licensed Victuallers' children, or a sheer school of
35   Commercial Travellers' children, and to bring them all up, not only at home but at school too, in a kind of odour of licensed victualism or of bagmanism, is not a wise training to give to these children. And in Germany, I have said, the action of the

national guides or governors is to suggest and provide a better.
But, in England, the action of the national guides or governors
is, for a Royal Prince or a great Minister to go down to the
opening of the Licensed Victuallers' or of the Commercial
Travellers' school, to take the chair, to extol the energy and 5
self-reliance of the Licensed Victuallers or the Commercial
Travellers, to be all of their way of thinking, to predict full
success to their schools, and never so much as to hint to them
that they are probably doing a very foolish thing, and that the
right way to go to work with their children's education is 10
quite different. And it is the same in almost every department
of affairs. While, on the Continent, the idea prevails that it is
the business of the heads and representatives of the nation, by
virtue of their superior means, power, and information, to set
an example and to provide suggestions of right reason, among 15
us the idea is that the business of the heads and representatives
of the nation is to do nothing of the kind, but to applaud the
natural taste for the bathos showing itself vigorously in any
part of the community, and to encourage its works.

Now I do not say that the political system of foreign coun- 20
tries has not inconveniences which may outweigh the inconveniences of our own political system; nor am I the least proposing to get rid of our own political system and to adopt theirs.
But a sound centre of authority being what, in this disquisition, we have been led to seek, and right reason, or our best 25
self, appearing alone to offer such a sound centre of authority,
it is necessary to take note of the chief impediments which
hinder, in this country, the extrication or recognition of this
right reason as a paramount authority, with a view to afterwards trying in what way they can best be removed. 30

This being borne in mind, I proceed to remark how not only
do we get no suggestions of right reason, and no rebukes of our
ordinary self, from our governors, but a kind of philosophical
theory is widely spread among us to the effect that there is no
such thing at all as a best self and a right reason having claim to 35
paramount authority, or, at any rate, no such thing ascertain-
able and capable of being made use of; and that there is nothing but an infinite number of ideas and works of our ordinary

selves, and suggestions of our natural taste for the bathos, pretty nearly equal in value, which are doomed either to an irreconcilable conflict, or else to a perpetual give and take; and that wisdom consists in choosing the give and take rather than
5   the conflict, and in sticking to our choice with patience and good humour.

And, on the other hand, we have another philosophical theory rife among us, to the effect that without the labour of perverting ourselves by custom or example to relish right reason, but
10   by continuing all of us to follow freely our natural taste for the bathos, we shall, by the mercy of Providence, and by a kind of natural tendency of things, come in due time to relish and follow right reason.

The great promoters of these philosophical theories are our
15   newspapers, which, no less than our Parliamentary representatives, may be said to act the part of guides and governors to us; and these favourite doctrines of theirs I call,—or should call, if the doctrines were not preached by authorities I so much respect, —the first, a peculiarly British form of Atheism, the second, a
20   peculiarly British form of Quietism. The first-named melancholy doctrine is preached in the *Times* with great clearness and force of style; indeed, it is well known, from the example of the poet Lucretius and others, what great masters of style the atheistic doctrine has always counted among its promulga-
25   tors. "It is of no use," says the *Times*, "for us to attempt to force upon our neighbours our several likings and dislikings. We must take things as they are. Everybody has his own little vision of religious or civil perfection. Under the evident impossibility of satisfying everybody, we agree to take our
30   stand on equal laws and on a system as open and liberal as is possible. The result is that everybody has more liberty of action and of speaking here than anywhere else in the Old World." We come again here upon Mr. Roebuck's celebrated definition of happiness, on which I have so often commented:
35   "I look around me and ask what is the state of England? Is not every man able to say what he likes? I ask you whether the world over, or in past history, there is anything like it? Nothing. I pray that our unrivalled happiness may last." This is the

old story of our system of checks and every Englishman doing as he likes, which we have already seen to have been convenient enough so long as there were only the Barbarians and the Philistines to do what they liked, but to be getting inconvenient, and productive of anarchy, now that the Populace wants to do what it likes too.

But for all that, I will not at once dismiss this famous doctrine, but will first quote another passage from the *Times,* applying the doctrine to a matter of which we have just been speaking, —education. "The difficulty here" (in providing a national system of education), says the *Times,* "does not reside in any removable arrangements. It is inherent and native in the actual and inveterate state of things in this country. All these powers and personages, all these conflicting influences and varieties of character, exist, and have long existed among us; they are fighting it out, and will long continue to fight it out, without coming to that happy consummation when some one element of the British character is to destroy or to absorb all the rest." There it is! the various promptings of the natural taste for the bathos in this man and that amongst us are fighting it out; and the day will never come (and, indeed, why should we wish it to come?) when one man's particular sort of taste for the bathos shall tyrannise over another man's; nor when right reason (if that may be called an element of the British character) shall absorb and rule them all. "The whole system of this country, like the constitution we boast to inherit, and are glad to uphold, is made up of established facts, prescriptive authorities, existing usages, powers that be, persons in possession, and communities or classes that have won dominion for themselves, and will hold it against all comers." Every force in the world, evidently, except the one reconciling force, right reason! Barbarian here, Philistine there, Mr. Bradlaugh and Populace striking in!—pull devil, pull baker! Really, presented with the mastery of style of our leading journal, the sad picture, as one gazes upon it, assumes the iron and inexorable solemnity of tragic Destiny.

After this, the milder doctrine of our other philosophical teacher, the *Daily News,* has, at first, something very attractive and assuaging. The *Daily News* begins, indeed, in appearance, to weave the iron web of necessity round us like the *Times*. "The alternative is between a man's doing what he likes and his doing what some one else, probably not one whit wiser than himself, likes." This points to the tacit compact, mentioned in my last paper, between the Barbarians and the Philistines, and into which it is hoped that the Populace will one day enter; the compact, so creditable to English honesty, that since each class has only the ideas and aims of its ordinary self to give effect to, none of them shall, if it exercise power, treat its ordinary self too seriously, or attempt to impose it on others; but shall let these others,—the fanatical Protestant, for instance, in his Papist-baiting, and the popular tribune in his Hyde Park anarchy-mongering,—have their fling. But then the *Daily News* suddenly lights up the gloom of necessitarianism with bright beams of hope. "No doubt," it says, "the common reason of society ought to check the aberrations of individual eccentricity." This common reason of society looks very like our best self or right reason, to which we want to give authority, by making the action of the *State*, or nation in its collective character, the expression of it. But of this project of ours, the *Daily News*, with its subtle dialectics, makes havoc. "Make the State the organ of the common reason?"—it says. "You may make it the organ of something or other, but how can you be certain that reason will be the quality which will be embodied in it?" You cannot be certain of it, undoubtedly, if you never try to bring the thing about; but the question is, the action of the State being the action of the collective nation, and the action of the collective nation carrying naturally great publicity, weight, and force of example with it, whether we should not try to put into the action of the State as much as possible of right reason or our best self, which may, in this manner, come back to us with new force and authority; may have visibility, form, and influence; and help to confirm us, in the many moments when we are tempted to be our ordinary selves merely, in resisting our natural taste of the bathos rather than in giving way to it?

But no! says our teacher: "It is better there should be an infinite variety of experiments in human action; the common reason of society will in the main check the aberrations of individual eccentricity well enough, if left to its natural operation." This is what I call the specially British form of Quietism, or a devout, but excessive, reliance on an over-ruling Providence. Providence, as the moralists are careful to tell us, generally works in human affairs by human means; so, when we want to make right reason act on individual inclination, our best self on our ordinary self, we seek to give it more power of doing so by giving it public recognition and authority, and embodying it, so far as we can, in the State. It seems too much to ask of Providence, that while we, on our part, leave our congenital taste for the bathos to its natural operation and its infinite variety of experiments, Providence should mysteriously guide it into the true track, and compel it to relish the sublime. At any rate, great men and great institutions have hitherto seemed necessary for producing any considerable effect of this kind. No doubt we have an infinite variety of experiments and an ever-multiplying multitude of explorers. Even in these few chapters I have enumerated many: the *British Banner*, Judge Edmonds, Newman Weeks, Deborah Butler, Elderess Polly, Brother Noyes, Mr. Murphy, the Licensed Victuallers, the Commercial Travellers, and I know not how many more; and the numbers of the noble army are swelling every day. But what a depth of Quietism, or rather, what an over-bold call on the direct interposition of Providence, to believe that these interesting explorers will discover the true track, or at any rate, "will do so in the main well enough" (whatever that may mean) if left to their natural operation; that is, by going on as they are! Philosophers say, indeed, that we learn virtue by performing acts of virtue; but to say that we shall learn virtue by performing any acts to which our natural taste for the bathos carries us, that the fanatical Protestant comes at his best self by Papist-baiting, or Newman Weeks and Deborah Butler at right reason by following their noses, this certainly does appear over-sanguine.

It is true, what we want is to make right reason act on individual reason, the reason of individuals; all our search for authority has that for its end and aim. The *Daily News* says, I observe,

that all my argument for authority "has a non-intellectual root;" and from what I know of my own mind and its poverty I think this so probable, that I should be inclined easily to admit it, if it were not that, in the first place, nothing of this
5   kind, perhaps, should be admitted without examination; and, in the second, a way of accounting for the charge being made, in this particular instance, without good grounds, appears to present itself. What seems to me to account here, perhaps, for the charge, is the want of flexibility of our race, on which I
10 have so often remarked. I mean, it being admitted that the conformity of the individual reason of the fanatical Protestant or the popular rioter with right reason is our true object, and not the mere restraining them, by the strong arm of the State, from Papist-baiting, or railing-breaking,—admitting this, we
15 English have so little flexibility that we cannot readily perceive that the State's restraining them from these indulgences may yet fix clearly in their minds that, to the collective nation, these indulgences appear irrational and unallowable, may make them pause and reflect, and may contribute to bringing, with
20 time, their individual reason into harmony with right reason. But in no country, owing to the want of intellectual flexibility above mentioned, is the leaning which is our natural one, and, therefore, needs no recommending to us, so sedulously recommended, and the leaning which is not our natural one, and,
25 therefore, does not need dispraising to us, so sedulously dispraised, as in ours. To rely on the individual being, with us, the natural leaning, we will hear of nothing but the good of relying on the individual; to act through the collective nation on the individual being not our natural leaning, we will hear
30 nothing in recommendation of it. But the wise know that we often need to hear most of that to which we are least inclined, and even to learn to employ, in certain circumstances, that which is capable, if employed amiss, of being a danger to us.

      Elsewhere this is certainly better understood than here. In a
35 recent number of the *Westminster Review*, an able writer, but with precisely our national want of flexibility of which I have been speaking, has unearthed, I see, for our present needs, an English translation, published some years ago, of Wilhelm

von Humboldt's book, *The Sphere and Duties of Government.* Humboldt's object in this book is to show that the operation of government ought to be severely limited to what directly and immediately relates to the security of person and property. Wilhelm von Humboldt, one of the most beautiful souls that have ever existed, used to say that one's business in life was first to perfect one's self by all the means in one's power, and secondly, to try and create in the world around one an aristocracy, the most numerous that one possibly could, of talents and characters. He saw, of course, that, in the end, everything comes to this,—that the individual must act for himself, and must be perfect in himself; and he lived in a country, Germany, where people were disposed to act too little for themselves, and to rely too much on the Government. But even thus, such was his flexibility, so little was he in bondage to a mere abstract maxim, that he saw very well that for his purpose itself, of enabling the individual to stand perfect on his own foundations and to do without the State, the action of the State would for long, long years be necessary. And soon after he wrote his book on *The Sphere and Duties of Government,* Wilhelm von Humboldt became Minister of Education in Prussia; and from his ministry all the great reforms which give the control of Prussian education to the State,—the transference of the management of public schools from their old boards of trustees to the State, the obligatory State-examination for schoolmasters, and the foundation of the great State-University of Berlin,—take their origin. This his English reviewer says not a word of. But, writing for a people whose dangers lie, as we have seen, on the side of their unchecked and unguided individual action, whose dangers none of them lie on the side of an over-reliance on the State, he quotes just so much of Wilhelm von Humboldt's example as can flatter them in their propensities, and do them no good; and just what might make them think, and be of use to them, he leaves on one side. This precisely recalls the manner, it will be observed, in which we have seen that our royal and noble personages proceed with the Licensed Victuallers.

In France the action of the State on individuals is yet more preponderant than in Germany; and the need which friends of human perfection feel for what may enable the individual to stand perfect on his own foundations is all the stronger. But what says one of the staunchest of these friends, M. Renan, on State action; and even State action in that very sphere where in France it is most excessive, the sphere of education? Here are his words:—"A Liberal believes in liberty, and liberty signifies the non-intervention of the State. *But such an ideal is still a long way off from us, and the very means to remove it to an indefinite distance would be precisely the State's withdrawing its action too soon.*" And this, he adds, is even truer of education than of any other department of public affairs.

We see, then, how indispensable to that human perfection which we seek is, in the opinion of good judges, some public recognition and establishment of our best self, or right reason. We see how our habits and practice oppose themselves to such a recognition, and the many inconveniences which we therefore suffer. But now let us try to go a little deeper, and to find, beneath our actual habits and practice, the very ground and cause out of which they spring.

Chapter IV

Hebraism and Hellenism

This fundamental ground is our preference of doing to thinking. Now this preference is a main element in our nature, and as
we study it we find ourselves opening up a number of large
questions on every side.

Let me go back for a moment to Bishop Wilson, who says: 5
"First, never go against the best light you have; secondly, take
care that your light be not darkness." We show, as a nation, laudable energy and persistence in walking according to the best
light we have, but are not quite careful enough, perhaps, to see
that our light be not darkness. This is only another version of   10
the old story that energy is our strong point and favourable
characteristic, rather than intelligence. But we may give to this
idea a more general form still, in which it will have a yet larger
range of application. We may regard this energy driving at
practice, this paramount sense of the obligation of duty, self-   15
control, and work, this earnestness in going manfully with the
best light we have, as one force. And we may regard the
intelligence driving at those ideas which are, after all, the basis
of right practice, the ardent sense for all the new and changing
combinations of them which man's development brings with   20
it, the indomitable impulse to know and adjust them perfectly,
as another force. And these two forces we may regard as in
some sense rivals,—rivals not by the necessity of their own
nature, but as exhibited in man and his history,—and rivals
dividing the empire of the world between them. And to give   25
these forces names from the two races of men who have supplied the most signal and splendid manifestations of them, we
may call them respectively the forces of Hebraism and Hellenism. Hebraism and Hellenism,—between these two points of

influence moves our world. At one time it feels more powerfully the attraction of one of them, at another time of the other; and it ought to be, though it never is, evenly and happily balanced between them.

5 The final aim of both Hellenism and Hebraism, as of all great spiritual disciplines, is no doubt the same: man's perfection or salvation. The very language which they both of them use in schooling us to reach this aim is often identical. Even when their language indicates by variation,—sometimes a broad vari
10 ation, often a but slight and subtle variation,—the different courses of thought which are uppermost in each discipline, even then the unity of the final end and aim is still apparent. To employ the actual words of that discipline with which we ourselves are all of us most familiar, and the words of which,
15 therefore, come most home to us, that final end and aim is "that we might be partakers of the divine nature." These are the words of a Hebrew apostle, but of Hellenism and Hebraism alike this is, I say, the aim. When the two are confronted, as they very often are confronted, it is nearly always with
20 what I may call a rhetorical purpose; the speaker's whole design is to exalt and enthrone one of the two, and he uses the other only as a foil and to enable him the better to give effect to his purpose. Obviously, with us, it is usually Hellenism which is thus reduced to minister to the triumph of Hebraism.
25 There is a sermon on Greece and the Greek spirit by a man never to be mentioned without interest and respect, Frederick Robertson, in which this rhetorical use of Greece and the Greek spirit, and the inadequate exhibition of them necessarily consequent upon this, is almost ludicrous, and would be cen
30 surable if it were not to be explained by the exigencies of a sermon. On the other hand, Heinrich Heine, and other writers of his sort, give us the spectacle of the tables completely turned, and of Hebraism brought in just as a foil and contrast to Hellenism, and to make the superiority of Hellenism more
35 manifest. In both these cases there is injustice and misrepresentation. The aim and end of both Hebraism and Hellenism is, as I have said, one and the same, and this aim and end is august and admirable.

Still, they pursue this aim by very different courses. The uppermost idea with Hellenism is to see things as they really are; the uppermost idea with Hebraism is conduct and obedience. Nothing can do away with this ineffaceable difference. The Greek quarrel with the body and its desires is, that they hinder right thinking; the Hebrew quarrel with them is, that they hinder right acting. "He that keepeth the law, happy is he;" "Blessed is the man that feareth the Eternal, that delighteth greatly in his commandments;"—that is the Hebrew notion of felicity; and, pursued with passion and tenacity, this notion would not let the Hebrew rest till, as is well known, he had at last got out of the law a network of prescriptions to enwrap his whole life, to govern every moment of it, every impulse, every action. The Greek notion of felicity, on the other hand, is perfectly conveyed in these words of a great French moralist: *"C'est le bonheur des hommes,"*—when? when they abhor that which is evil?—no; when they exercise themselves in the law of the Lord day and night?—no; when they die daily?—no; when they walk about the New Jerusalem with palms in their hands?—no; but when they think aright, when their thought hits: *"quand ils pensent juste."* At the bottom of both the Greek and the Hebrew notion is the desire, native in man, for reason and the will of God, the feeling after the universal order,—in a word, the love of God. But, while Hebraism seizes upon certain plain, capital intimations of the universal order, and rivets itself, one may say, with unequalled grandeur of earnestness and intensity on the study and observance of them, the bent of Hellenism is to follow, with flexible activity, the whole play of the universal order, to be apprehensive of missing any part of it, of sacrificing one part to another, to slip away from resting in this or that intimation of it, however capital. An unclouded clearness of mind, an unimpeded play of thought, is what this bent drives at. The governing idea of Hellenism is *spontaneity of consciousness;* that of Hebraism, *strictness of conscience.*

Christianity changed nothing in this essential bent of Hebraism to set doing above knowing. Self-conquest, self-devotion, the following not our own individual will, but the will of God, *obed-*

ience, is the fundamental idea of this form, also, of the discipline to which we have attached the general name of Hebraism. Only, as the old law and the network of prescriptions with which it enveloped human life were evidently a motive-power not driving and searching enough to produce the result aimed at,—patient continuance in well-doing, self-conquest, —Christianity substituted for them boundless devotion to that inspiring and affecting pattern of self-conquest offered by Jesus Christ; and by the new motive-power, of which the essence was this, though the love and admiration of Christian churches have for centuries been employed in varying, amplifying, and adorning the plain description of it, Christianity, as St. Paul truly says, "establishes the law," and in the strength of the ampler power which she has thus supplied to fulfil it, has accomplished the miracles, which we all see, of her history.

So long as we do not forget that both Hellenism and Hebraism are profound and admirable manifestations of man's life, tendencies, and powers, and that both of them aim at a like final result, we can hardly insist too strongly on the divergence of line and of operation with which they proceed. It is a divergence so great that it most truly, as the prophet Zechariah says, "has raised up thy sons, O Zion, against thy sons, O Greece!" The difference whether it is by doing or by knowing that we set most store, and the practical consequences which follow from this difference, leave their mark on all the history of our race and of its development. Language may be abundantly quoted from both Hellenism and Hebraism to make it seem that one follows the same current as the other towards the same goal. They are, truly, borne towards the same goal; but the currents which bear them are infinitely different. It is true, Solomon will praise knowing: "Understanding is a well-spring of life unto him that hath it." And in the New Testament, again, Jesus Christ is a "light," and "truth makes us free." It is true, Aristotle will undervalue knowing: "In what concerns virtue," says he, "three things are necessary —knowledge, deliberate will, and perseverance; but, whereas the two last are all-important, the first is a matter of little importance." It is true that with the same impatience with which St. James enjoins a man to be not a forgetful hearer, but a *doer of the word*, Epictetus exhorts us to *do* what we have demonstrated to ourselves we ought to do; or he taunts us with futility, for being armed at all points to prove that lying is wrong, yet all the time continuing to lie. It is true, Plato, in words which are almost the words of the New Testament or the Imitation, calls life a learning to die. But underneath the superficial agreement the fundamental divergence still subsists. The understanding of Solomon is "the walking in the way of the commandments;" this is "the way of peace," and it is of this that blessedness comes. In the New Testament, the truth which gives us the peace of God and makes us free, is the love of Christ constraining us to crucify, as he did, and with a like purpose of moral regeneration, the flesh with its affections and lusts, and thus establishing, as we have seen, the law. The moral virtues, on the other hand, are with Aristotle but the porch and access to the intellectual, and with these last is blessedness. That partaking of the divine life, which both Hellenism and Hebraism, as we have said, fix as their crowning aim, Plato expressly denies to the man of practical virtue merely, of self-conquest with any other motive than that of perfect intellectual vision. He reserves it for the lover of pure knowledge, of seeing things as they really are,—the φιλομαθής.

Both Hellenism and Hebraism arise out of the wants of human nature, and address themselves to satisfying those wants. But their methods are so different, they lay stress on such different points, and call into being by their respective disciplines such different activities, that the face which human nature presents when it passes from the hands of one of them to those of the other, is no longer the same. To get rid of one's ignorance, to see things as they are, and by seeing them as they are to see them in their beauty, is the simple and attractive ideal which Hellenism holds out before human nature; and from the simplicity and charm of this ideal, Hellenism, and human life in the hands of Hellenism, is invested with a kind of aërial ease, clearness, and radiancy; they are full of what we call sweetness and light. Difficulties are kept out of view, and the beauty and rationalness of the ideal have all our thoughts. "The best man

is he who most tries to perfect himself, and the happiest man is
he who most feels that he *is* perfecting himself,"—this account
of the matter by Socrates, the true Socrates of the *Memorabilia*, has something so simple, spontaneous, and unsophisti-
cated about it, that it seems to fill us with clearness and hope
when we hear it. But there is a saying which I have heard
attributed to Mr. Carlyle about Socrates,—a very happy saying, whether it is really Mr. Carlyle's or not,—which excellently marks the essential point in which Hebraism differs
from Hellenism. "Socrates," this saying goes, "is terribly *at
ease in Zion*." Hebraism,—and here is the source of its wonderful strength,—has always been severely preoccupied with
an awful sense of the impossibility of being at ease in Zion; of
the difficulties which oppose themselves to man's pursuit or
attainment of that perfection of which Socrates talks so hopefully, and, as from this point of view one might almost say, so
glibly. It is all very well to talk of getting rid of one's ignorance, of seeing things in their reality, seeing them in their
beauty; but how is this to be done when there is something
which thwarts and spoils all our efforts?

This something is *sin*; and the space which sin fills in Hebraism,
as compared with Hellenism, is indeed prodigious. This obstacle
to perfection fills the whole scene, and perfection appears remote and rising away from earth, in the background. Under
the name of sin, the difficulties of knowing oneself and conquering oneself which impede man's passage to perfection, become, for Hebraism, a positive, active entity hostile to man, a
mysterious power which I heard Dr. Pusey the other day, in
one of his impressive sermons, compare to a hideous hunch-
back seated on our shoulders, and which it is the main business
of our lives to hate and oppose. The discipline of the Old
Testament may be summed up as a discipline teaching us to
abhor and flee from sin; the discipline of the New Testament,
as a discipline teaching us to die to it. As Hellenism speaks of
thinking clearly, seeing things in their essence and beauty, as a
grand and precious feat for man to achieve, so Hebraism
speaks of becoming conscious of sin, of awakening to a sense
of sin, as a feat of this kind. It is obvious to what wide diver-

gence these differing tendencies, actively followed, must lead. As one passes and repasses from Hellenism to Hebraism, from Plato to St. Paul, one feels inclined to rub one's eyes and ask oneself whether man is indeed a gentle and simple being, showing the traces of a noble and divine nature; or an unhappy chained captive, labouring with groanings that cannot be uttered to free himself from the body of this death.

Apparently it was the Hellenic conception of human nature which was unsound, for the world could not live by it. Absolutely to call it unsound, however, is to fall into the common error of its Hebraising enemies; but it was unsound at that particular moment of man's development, it was premature. The indispensable basis of conduct and self-control, the platform upon which alone the perfection aimed at by Greece can come into bloom, was not to be reached by our race so easily; centuries of probation and discipline were needed to bring us to it. Therefore the bright promise of Hellenism faded, and Hebraism ruled the world. Then was seen that astonishing spectacle, so well marked by the often-quoted words of the prophet Zechariah, when men of all languages of the nations took hold of the skirt of him that was a Jew, saying:—"*We will go with you, for we have heard that God is with you.*" And the Hebraism which thus received and ruled a world all gone out of the way and altogether become unprofitable, was, and could not but be, the later, the more spiritual, the more attractive development of Hebraism. It was Christianity; that is to say, Hebraism aiming at self-conquest and rescue from the thrall of vile affections, not by obedience to the letter of a law, but by conformity to the image of a self-sacrificing example. To a world stricken with moral enervation Christianity offered its spectacle of an inspired self-sacrifice; to men who refused themselves nothing, it showed one who refused himself everything;—"*my Saviour banished joy!*" says George Herbert. When the *alma Venus*, the life-giving and joy-giving power of nature, so fondly cherished by the Pagan world, could not save her followers from self-dissatisfaction and ennui, the severe words of the apostle came bracingly and refreshingly: "Let no man deceive you with vain words, for because of these things

cometh the wrath of God upon the children of disobedience."
Through age after age and generation after generation, our
race, or all that part of our race which was most living and
progressive, was *baptized into a death;* and endeavoured, by
suffering in the flesh, to cease from sin. Of this endeavour, the
animating labours and afflictions of early Christianity, the
touching asceticism of mediæval Christianity, are the great
historical manifestations. Literary monuments of it, each in its
own way incomparable, remain in the Epistles of St. Paul, in St.
Augustine's Confessions, and in the two original and simplest
books of the Imitation.[1]

Of two disciplines laying their main stress, the one, on clear
intelligence, the other, on firm obedience; the one, on compre-
hensively knowing the grounds of one's duty, the other, on diligently practising it; the one, on taking all possible care (to use
Bishop Wilson's words again) that the light we have be not
darkness, the other, that according to the best light we have
we diligently walk,—the priority naturally belongs to that discipline which braces all man's moral powers, and founds for
him an indispensable basis of character. And, therefore, it is
justly said of the Jewish people, who were charged with setting powerfully forth that side of the divine order to which
the words *conscience* and *self-conquest* point, that they were
"entrusted with the oracles of God;" as it is justly said of
Christianity, which followed Judaism and which set forth this
side with a much deeper effectiveness and a much wider influence, that the wisdom of the old Pagan world was foolishness
compared to it. No words of devotion and admiration can be
too strong to render thanks to these beneficent forces which
have so borne forward humanity in its appointed work of
coming to the knowledge and possession of itself; above all, in
those great moments when their action was the wholesomest
and the most necessary.

But the evolution of these forces, separately and in themselves,
is not the whole evolution of humanity,—their single history is
not the whole history of man; whereas their admirers are always apt to make it stand for the whole history. Hebraism and

[1] The two first books.

Hellenism are, neither of them, the *law* of human development, as their admirers are prone to make them; they are, each of them, *contributions* to human development,—august contributions, invaluable contributions; and each showing itself to us more august, more invaluable, more preponderant over the other, according to the moment in which we take them, and the relation in which we stand to them. The nations of our modern world, children of that immense and salutary movement which broke up the Pagan world, inevitably stand to Hellenism in a relation which dwarfs it, and to Hebraism in a relation which magnifies it. They are inevitably prone to take Hebraism as the law of human development, and not as simply a contribution to it, however precious. And yet the lesson must perforce be learned, that the human spirit is wider than the most priceless of the forces which bear it onward, and that to the whole development of man Hebraism itself is, like Hellenism, but a contribution.

Perhaps we may help ourselves to see this clearer by an illustration drawn from the treatment of a single great idea which has profoundly engaged the human spirit, and has given it eminent opportunities for showing its nobleness and energy. It surely must be perceived that the idea of immortality, as this idea rises in its generality before the human spirit, is something grander, truer, and more satisfying, than it is in the particular forms by which St. Paul, in the famous fifteenth chapter of the Epistle to the Corinthians, and Plato, in the *Phædo*, endeavour to develop and establish it. Surely we cannot but feel, that the argumentation with which the Hebrew apostle goes about to expound this great idea is, after all, confused and inconclusive; and that the reasoning, drawn from analogies of likeness and equality, which is employed upon it by the Greek philosopher, is over-subtle and sterile. Above and beyond the inadequate solutions which Hebraism and Hellenism here attempt, extends the immense and august problem itself, and the human spirit which gave birth to it. And this single illustration may suggest to us how the same thing happens in other cases also.

But meanwhile, by alternations of Hebraism and Hellenism, of a man's intellectual and moral impulses, of the effort to see things as they really are, and the effort to win peace by self-conquest, the human spirit proceeds; and each of these two forces has its appointed hours of culmination and seasons of rule. As the great movement of Christianity was a triumph of Hebraism and man's moral impulses, so the great movement which goes by the name of the Renascence [1] was an uprising and re-instatement of man's intellectual impulses and of Hellenism. We in England, the devoted children of Protestantism, chiefly know the Renascence by its subordinate and secondary side of the Reformation. The Reformation has been often called a Hebraising revival, a return to the ardour and sincereness of primitive Christianity. No one, however, can study the development of Protestantism and of Protestant churches without feeling that into the Reformation too,—Hebraising child of the Renascence and offspring of its fervour, rather than its intelligence, as it undoubtedly was,—the subtle Hellenic leaven of the Renascence found its way, and that the exact respective parts, in the Reformation, of Hebraism and of Hellenism, are not easy to separate. But what we may with truth say is, that all which Protestantism was to itself clearly conscious of, all which it succeeded in clearly setting forth in words, had the characters of Hebraism rather than of Hellenism. The Reformation was strong, in that it was an earnest return to the Bible and to doing from the heart the will of God as there written. It was weak, in that it never consciously grasped or applied the central idea of the Renascence,—the Hellenic idea of pursuing, in all lines of activity, the law and science, to use Plato's words, of things as they really are. Whatever direct superiority, therefore, Protestantism had over Catholicism was a moral superiority, a superiority arising out of its greater sincerity and earnestness,—at the moment of its apparition at any rate,—in dealing with the heart and conscience. Its pretensions to an intellectual superiority are in general quite illusory. For Hellenism, for the thinking side in man

[1] I have ventured to give to the foreign word *Renaissance*,—destined to become of more common use amongst us as the movement which it denotes comes, as it will come, increasingly to interest us,—an English form.

as distinguished from the acting side, the attitude of mind of Protestantism towards the Bible in no respect differs from the attitude of mind of Catholicism towards the Church. The mental habit of him who imagines that Balaam's ass spoke, in no respect differs from the mental habit of him who imagines that a Madonna of wood or stone winked; and the one, who says that God's Church makes him believe what he believes, and the other, who says that God's Word makes him believe what he believes, are for the philosopher perfectly alike in not really and truly knowing, when they say *God's Church* and *God's Word,* what it is they say, or whereof they affirm.

In the sixteenth century, therefore, Hellenism re-entered the world, and again stood in presence of Hebraism,—a Hebraism renewed and purged. Now, it has not been enough observed, how, in the seventeenth century, a fate befell Hellenism in some respects analogous to that which befell it at the commencement of our era. The Renascence, that great re-awakening of Hellenism, that irresistible return of humanity to·nature and to seeing things as they are, which in art, in literature, and in physics, produced such splendid fruits, had, like the anterior Hellenism of the Pagan world, a side of moral weakness and of relaxation or insensibility of the moral fibre, which in Italy showed itself with the most startling plainness, but which in France, England, and other countries was very apparent too. Again this loss of spiritual balance, this exclusive preponderance given to man's perceiving and knowing side, this unnatural defect of his feeling and acting side, provoked a reaction. Let us trace that reaction where it most nearly concerns us.

Science has now made visible to everybody the great and pregnant elements of difference which lie in race, and in how signal a manner they make the genius and history of an Indo-European people vary from those of a Semitic people. Hellenism is of Indo-European growth, Hebraism is of Semitic growth; and we English, a nation of Indo-European stock, seem to belong naturally to the movement of Hellenism. But nothing more strongly marks the essential unity of man, than the affinities we can perceive, in this point or that, between members of one family of peoples and members of another. And no affinity of

this kind is more strongly marked than that likeness in the strength and prominence of the moral fibre, which, notwithstanding immense elements of difference, knits in some special sort the genius and history of us English, and our American
5 descendants across the Atlantic, to the genius and history of the Hebrew people. Puritanism, which has been so great a power in the English nation, and in the strongest part of the English nation, was originally the reaction in the seventeenth century of the conscience and moral sense of our race,
10 against the moral indifference and lax rule of conduct which in the sixteenth century came in with the Renascence. It was a reaction of Hebraism against Hellenism; and it powerfully manifested itself, as was natural, in a people with much of what we call a Hebraising turn, with a signal affinity for the
15 bent which was the master-bent of Hebrew life. Eminently Indo-European by its *humour*, by the power it shows, through this gift, of imaginatively acknowledging the multiform aspects of the problem of life, and of thus getting itself unfixed from its own over-certainty, of smiling at its own over-tenac-
20 ity, our race has yet (and a great part of its strength lies here), in matters of practical life and moral conduct, a strong share of the assuredness, the tenacity, the intensity of the Hebrews. This turn manifested itself in Puritanism, and has had a great part in shaping our history for the last two hundred years.
25 Undoubtedly it checked and changed amongst us that movement of the Renascence which we see producing in the reign of Elizabeth such wonderful fruits. Undoubtedly it stopped the prominent rule and direct development of that order of ideas which we call by the name of Hellenism, and gave the
30 first rank to a different order of ideas. Apparently, too, as we said of the former defeat of Hellenism, if Hellenism was defeated, this shows that Hellenism was imperfect, and that its ascendency at that moment would not have been for the world's good.
35   Yet there is a very important difference between the defeat inflicted on Hellenism by Christianity eighteen hundred years ago, and the check given to the Renascence by Puritanism. The greatness of the difference is well measured by the differ-

ence in force, beauty, significance, and usefulness, between
primitive Christianity and Protestantism. Eighteen hundred
years ago it was altogether the hour of Hebraism. Primitive
Christianity was legitimately and truly the ascendant force in
the world at that time, and the way of mankind's progress lay
through its full development. Another hour in man's development began in the fifteenth century, and the main road of his
progress then lay for a time through Hellenism. Puritanism
was no longer the central current of the world's progress, it
was a side stream crossing the central current and checking it.
The cross and the check may have been necessary and salutary, but that does not do away with the essential difference
between the main stream of man's advance and a cross or side
stream. For more than two hundred years the main stream of
man's advance has moved towards knowing himself and the
world, seeing things as they are, spontaneity of consciousness;
the main impulse of a great part, and that the strongest part, of
our nation has been towards strictness of conscience. They
have made the secondary the principal at the wrong moment,
and the principal they have at the wrong moment treated as
secondary. This contravention of the natural order has produced, as such contravention always must produce, a certain
confusion and false movement, of which we are now beginning to feel, in almost every direction, the inconvenience. In
all directions our habitual courses of action seem to be losing
efficaciousness, credit, and control, both with others and even
with ourselves. Everywhere we see the beginnings of confusion, and we want a clue to some sound order and authority.
This we can only get by going back upon the actual instincts
and forces which rule our life, seeing them as they really are,
connecting them with other instincts and forces, and enlarging
our whole view and rule of life.

Chapter V

Porro Unum Est Necessarium

The matter here opened is so large, and the trains of thought to which it gives rise are so manifold, that we must be careful to limit ourselves scrupulously to what has a direct bearing upon our actual discussion. We have found that at the bottom of our present unsettled state, so full of the seeds of trouble, lies the notion of its being the prime right and happiness, for each of us, to affirm himself, and his ordinary self; to be doing, and to be doing freely and as he likes. We have found at the bottom of it the disbelief in right reason as a lawful authority. It was easy to show from our practice and current history that this is so; but it was impossible to show why it is so without taking a somewhat wider sweep and going into things a little more deeply. Why, in fact, should good, well-meaning, energetic, sensible people, like the bulk of our countrymen, come to have such light belief in right reason, and such an exaggerated value for their own independent doing, however crude? The answer is: because of an exclusive and excessive development in them, without due allowance for time, place, and circumstance, of that side of human nature, and that group of human forces, to which we have given the general name of Hebraism. Because they have thought their real and only important homage was owed to a power concerned with their obedience rather than with their intelligence, a power interested in the moral side of their nature almost exclusively. Thus they have been led to regard in themselves, as the one thing needful, *strictness of conscience*, the staunch adherence to some fixed law of doing we have got already, instead of *spontaneity of consciousness*, which tends continually to enlarge our whole law of doing. They have fancied themselves to have in their

176

religion a sufficient basis for the whole of their life fixed and certain for ever, a full law of conduct and a full law of thought, so far as thought is needed, as well; whereas what they really have is a law of conduct, a law of unexampled power for enabling them to war against the law of sin in their members and not to serve it in the lusts thereof. The book which contains this invaluable law they call the Word of God, and attribute to it, as I have said, and as, indeed, is perfectly well known, a reach and sufficiency co-extensive with all the wants of human nature.

This might, no doubt, be so, if humanity were not the composite thing it is, if it had only, or in quite overpowering eminence, a moral side, and the group of instincts and powers which we call moral. But it has besides, and in notable eminence, an intellectual side, and the group of instincts and powers which we call intellectual. No doubt, mankind makes in general its progress in a fashion which gives at one time full swing to one of these groups of instincts, at another time to the other; and man's faculties are so intertwined, that when his moral side, and the current of force which we call Hebraism, is uppermost, this side will manage somehow to provide, or appear to provide, satisfaction for his intellectual needs; and when his intellectual side, and the current of force which we call Hellenism, is uppermost, this again will provide, or appear to provide, satisfaction for men's moral needs. But sooner or later it becomes manifest that when the two sides of humanity proceed in this fashion of alternate preponderance, and not of mutual understanding and balance, the side which is uppermost does not really provide in a satisfactory manner for the needs of the side which is undermost, and a state of confusion is, sooner or later, the result. The Hellenic half of our nature, bearing rule, makes a sort of provision for the Hebrew half, but it turns out to be an inadequate provision; and again the Hebrew half of our nature, bearing rule, makes a sort of provision for the Hellenic half, but this, too, turns out to be an inadequate provision. The true and smooth order of humanity's development is not reached in either way. And therefore, while we willingly admit with the Christian apostle that the

world by wisdom,—that is, by the isolated preponderance of
its intellectual impulses,—knew not God, or the true order of
things, it is yet necessary, also, to set up a sort of converse to
this proposition, and to say likewise (what is equally true) that
5 the world by Puritanism knew not God. And it is on this
converse of the apostle's proposition that it is particularly needful to insist in our own country just at present.

Here, indeed, is the answer to many criticisms which have
been addressed to all that we have said in praise of sweetness and
10 light. Sweetness and light evidently have to do with the bent
or side in humanity which we call Hellenic. Greek intelligence
has obviously for its essence the instinct for what Plato calls
the true, firm, intelligible law of things; the law of light, of
seeing things as they are. Even in the natural sciences, where
15 the Greeks had not time and means adequately to apply this
instinct, and where we have gone a great deal further than
they did, it is this instinct which is the root of the whole
matter and the ground of all our success; and this instinct the
world has mainly learnt of the Greeks, inasmuch as they are
20 humanity's most signal manifestation of it. Greek art, again,
Greek beauty, have their root in the same impulse to see things
as they really are, inasmuch as Greek art and beauty rest on
fidelity to nature,—the *best* nature,—and on a delicate discrim-
ination of what this best nature is. To say we work for sweet-
25 ness and light, then, is only another way of saying that we
work for Hellenism. But, oh! cry many people, sweetness and
light are not enough; you must put strength or energy along
with them, and make a kind of trinity of strength, sweetness
and light, and then, perhaps, you may do some good. That is to
30 say, we are to join Hebraism, strictness of the moral conscience, and manful walking by the best light we have, together with Hellenism, inculcate both, and rehearse the
praises of both.

Or, rather, we may praise both in conjunction, but we must
35 be careful to praise Hebraism most. "Culture," says an acute,
though somewhat rigid critic, Mr. Sidgwick, "diffuses sweetness and light. I do not undervalue these blessings, but religion
gives fire and strength, and the world wants fire and strength

even more than sweetness and light." By religion, let me explain, Mr. Sidgwick here means particularly that Puritanism on the insufficiency of which I have been commenting and to which he says I am unfair. Now, no doubt, it is possible to be a fanatical partisan of light and the instincts which push us to it, a fanatical enemy of strictness of moral conscience and the instincts which push us to it. A fanaticism of this sort deforms and vulgarises the well-known work, in some respects so remarkable, of the late Mr. Buckle. Such a fanaticism carries its own mark with it, in lacking sweetness; and its own penalty, in that, lacking sweetness, it comes in the end to lack light too. And the Greeks,—the great exponents of humanity's bent for sweetness and light united, of its perception that the truth of things must be at the same time beauty,—singularly escaped the fanaticism which we moderns, whether we Hellenise or whether we Hebraise, are so apt to show. They arrived,— though failing, as has been said, to give adequate practical satisfaction to the claims of man's moral side,—at the idea of a comprehensive adjustment of the claims of both the sides in man, the moral as well as the intellectual, of a full estimate of both, and of a reconciliation of both; an idea which is philosophically of the greatest value, and the best of lessons for us moderns. So we ought to have no difficulty in conceding to Mr. Sidgwick that manful walking by the best light one has,— fire and strength as he calls it,—has its high value as well as culture, the endeavour to see things in their truth and beauty, the pursuit of sweetness and light. But whether at this or that time, and to this or that set of persons, one ought to insist most on the praises of fire and strength, or on the praises of sweetness and light, must depend, one would think, on the circumstances and needs of that particular time and those particular persons. And all that we have been saying, and indeed any glance at the world around us shows that with us, with the most respectable and strongest part of us, the ruling force is now, and long has been, a Puritan force,—the care for fire and strength, strictness of conscience, Hebraism, rather than the care for sweetness and light, spontaneity of consciousness, Hellenism.

Well, then, what is the good of our now rehearsing the praises of fire and strength to ourselves, who dwell too exclusively on them already? When Mr. Sidgwick says so broadly, that the world wants fire and strength even more than sweetness and
5 light, is he not carried away by a turn for broad generalisation? does he not forget that the world is not all of one piece, and every piece with the same needs at the same time? It may be true that the Roman world at the beginning of our era, or Leo the Tenth's Court at the time of the Reformation, or
10 French society in the eighteenth century, needed fire and strength even more than sweetness and light. But can it be said that the Barbarians who overran the empire needed fire and strength even more than sweetness and light; or that the Puritans needed them more; or that Mr. Murphy, the Birmingham
15 lecturer, and his friends, need them more?

The Puritan's great danger is that he imagines himself in possession of a rule telling him the *unum necessarium*, or one thing needful, and that he then remains satisfied with a very crude conception of what this rule really is and what it tells him,
20 thinks he has now knowledge and henceforth needs only to act, and, in this dangerous state of assurance and self-satisfaction, proceeds to give full swing to a number of the instincts of his ordinary self. Some of the instincts of his ordinary self he has, by the help of his rule of life, conquered; but
25 others which he has not conquered by this help he is so far from perceiving to need subjugation, and to be instincts of an inferior self, that he even fancies it to be his right and duty, in virtue of having conquered a limited part of himself, to give unchecked swing to the remainder. He is, I
30 say, a victim of Hebraism, of the tendency to cultivate strictness of conscience rather than spontaneity of consciousness. And what he wants is a larger conception of human nature, showing him the number of other points at which his nature must come to its best, besides the points which he himself
35 knows and thinks of. There is no *unum necessarium*, or one thing needful, which can free human nature from the obligation of trying to come to its best at all these points. The real *unum necessarium* for us is to come to our best at all points.

Instead of our "one thing needful," justifying in us vulgarity, hideousness, ignorance, violence,—our vulgarity, hideousness, ignorance, violence, are really so many touchstones which try our one thing needful, and which prove that in the state, at any rate, in which we ourselves have it, it is not all we want. And as the force which encourages us to stand staunch and fast by the rule and ground we have is Hebraism, so the force which encourages us to go back upon this rule, and to try the very ground on which we appear to stand, is Hellenism,—a turn for giving our consciousness free play and enlarging its range. And what I say is, not that Hellenism is always for everybody more wanted than Hebraism, but that for Mr. Murphy at this particular moment, and for the great majority of us his fellow-countrymen, it is more wanted.

Nothing is more striking than to observe in how many ways a limited conception of human nature, the notion of a one thing needful, a one side in us to be made uppermost, the disregard of a full and harmonious development of ourselves, tells injuriously on our thinking and acting. In the first place, our hold upon the rule or standard, to which we look for our one thing needful, tends to become less and less near and vital, our conception of it more and more mechanical, and more and more unlike the thing itself as it was conceived in the mind where it originated. The dealings of Puritanism with the writings of St. Paul afford a noteworthy illustration of this. Nowhere so much as in the writings of St. Paul, and in that great apostle's greatest work, the Epistle to the Romans, has Puritanism found what seemed to furnish it with the one thing needful, and to give it canons of truth absolute and final. Now all writings, as has been already said, even the most precious writings and the most fruitful, must inevitably, from the very nature of things, be but contributions to human thought and human development, which extend wider than they do. Indeed, St. Paul, in the very Epistle of which we are speaking, shows, when he asks, "Who hath known the mind of the Lord?"—who hath known, that is, the true and divine order of things in its entirety,—that he himself acknowledges this fully. And we have already pointed out in another Epistle of St. Paul

a great and vital idea of the human spirit,—the idea of immortality,—transcending and overlapping, so to speak, the exposi-
tor's power to give it adequate definition and expression.

But quite distinct from the question whether St. Paul's expression, or any man's expression, can be a perfect and final expression of truth, comes the question whether we rightly seize and
understand his expression as it exists. Now, perfectly to seize
another man's meaning, as it stood in his own mind, is not
easy; especially when the man is separated from us by such
differences of race, training, time, and circumstances as St.
Paul. But there are degrees of nearness in getting at a man's
meaning; and though we cannot arrive quite at what St. Paul
had in his mind, yet we may come near it. And who, that comes
thus near it, must not feel how terms which St. Paul employs,
in trying to follow with his analysis of such profound power
and originality some of the most delicate, intricate, obscure,
and contradictory workings and states of the human spirit, are
detached and employed by Puritanism, not in the connected
and fluid way in which St. Paul employs them, and for which
alone words are really meant, but in an isolated, fixed, mechanical way, as if they were talismans; and how all trace and sense
of St. Paul's true movement of ideas, and sustained masterly
analysis, is thus lost? Who, I say, that has watched Puritanism,
—the force which so strongly Hebraises, which so takes St.
Paul's writings as something absolute and final, containing the
one thing needful,—handle such terms as *grace, faith, election,
righteousness*, but must feel, not only that these terms have for
the mind of Puritanism a sense false and misleading, but also
that this sense is the most monstrous and grotesque caricature
of the sense of St. Paul, and that his true meaning is by these
worshippers of his words altogether lost?

Or to take another eminent example, in which not Puritanism
only, but, one may say, the whole religious world, by their
mechanical use of St. Paul's writings, can be shown to miss or
change his real meaning. The whole religious world, one may
say, use now the word *resurrection*,—a word which is so often
in their thoughts and on their lips, and which they find so
often in St. Paul's writings,—in one sense only. They use it to

mean a rising again after the physical death of the body. Now it is quite true that St. Paul speaks of resurrection in this sense, that he tries to describe and explain it, and that he condemns those who doubt and deny it. But it is true, also, that in nine cases out of ten when St. Paul thinks and speaks of resurrection, he thinks and speaks of it in a sense different from this;—in the sense of a rising to a new life before the physical death of the body, and not after it. The idea on which we have already touched, the profound idea of being baptized into the death of the great exemplar of self-devotion and self-annulment, of repeating in our own person, by virtue of identification with our exemplar, his course of self-devotion and self-annulment, and of thus coming, within the limits of our present life, to a new life, in which, as in the death going before it, we are identified with our exemplar,—this is the fruitful and original conception of being *risen with Christ* which possesses the mind of St. Paul, and this is the central point round which, with such incomparable emotion and eloquence, all his teaching moves. For him, the life after our physical death is really in the main but a consequence and continuation of the inexhaustible energy of the new life thus originated on this side the grave. This grand Pauline idea of Christian resurrection is worthily rehearsed in one of the noblest collects of the Prayer-Book, and is destined, no doubt, to fill a more and more important place in the Christianity of the future. But meanwhile, almost as signal as the essentialness of this characteristic idea in St. Paul's teaching, is the completeness with which the worshippers of St. Paul's words as an absolute final expression of saving truth have lost it, and have substituted for the apostle's living and near conception of a resurrection now, their mechanical and remote conception of a resurrection hereafter.

In short, so fatal is the notion of possessing, even in the most precious words or standards, the one thing needful, of having in them, once for all, a full and sufficient measure of light to guide us, and of there being no duty left for us except to make our practice square exactly with them,—so fatal, I say, is this notion to the right knowledge and comprehension of the very words or standards we thus adopt, and to such strange distortions and perversions of them does it inevitably lead, that whenever we hear that commonplace which Hebraism, if we venture to inquire what a man knows, is so apt to bring out against us, in disparagement of what we call culture, and in praise of a man's sticking to the one thing needful,—*he knows*, says Hebraism, *his Bible!*—whenever we hear this said, we may, without any elaborate defence of culture, content ourselves with answering simply: "No man, who knows nothing else, knows even his Bible."

Now the force which we have so much neglected, Hellenism, may be liable to fail in moral strength and earnestness, but by the law of its nature,—the very same law which makes it sometimes deficient in intensity when intensity is required,—it opposes itself to the notion of cutting our being in two, of attributing to one part the dignity of dealing with the one thing needful, and leaving the other part to take its chance, which is the bane of Hebraism. Essential in Hellenism is the impulse to the development of the whole man, to connecting and harmonising all parts of him, perfecting all, leaving none to take their chance.

The characteristic bent of Hellenism, as has been said, is to find the intelligible law of things, to see them in their true nature and as they really are. But many things are not seen in their true nature and as they really are, unless they are seen as beautiful. Behaviour is not intelligible, does not account for itself to the mind and show the reason for its existing, unless it is beautiful. The same with discourse, the same with song, the same with worship, all of them modes in which man pours his activity and expresses himself. To think that when one produces in these what is mean, or vulgar, or hideous, one can be permitted to plead that one has that within which passes show; to suppose that the possession of what benefits and satisfies one part of our being can make allowable either discourse like Mr. Murphy's, or poetry like the hymns we all hear, or places of worship like the chapels we all see,—this it is abhorrent to the nature of Hellenism to concede. And to be, like our honoured and justly honoured Faraday, a great natural philosopher with one side of his being and a Sandemanian with the other, would to Archimedes have been impossible.

It is evident to what a many-sided perfecting of man's powers
and activities this demand of Hellenism for satisfaction to be
given to the mind by everything which we do, is calculated to
impel our race. It has its dangers, as has been fully granted. The
notion of this sort of equipollency in man's modes of activity   5
may lead to moral relaxation; what we do not make our one
thing needful, we may come to treat not enough as if it were
needful, though it is indeed very needful and at the same time
very hard. Still, what side in us has not its dangers, and which of
our impulses can be a talisman to give us perfection outright,   10
and not merely a help to bring us towards it? Has not Hebraism, as we have shown, its dangers as well as Hellenism? or
have we used so excessively the tendencies in ourselves to
which Hellenism makes appeal, that we are now suffering
from it? Are we not, on the contrary, now suffering because   15
we have not enough used these tendencies as a help towards
perfection?

For we see whither it has brought us, the long exclusive predominance of Hebraism,—the insisting on perfection in one part
of our nature and not in all; the singling out the moral side, the   20
side of obedience and action, for such intent regard; making
strictness of the moral conscience so far the principal thing,
and putting off for hereafter and for another world the care
for being complete at all points, the full and harmonious development of our humanity. Instead of watching and following   25
on its ways the desire which, as Plato says, "for ever through
all the universe tends towards that which is lovely," we think
that the world has settled its accounts with this desire, knows
what this desire wants of it, and that all the impulses of our
ordinary self which do not conflict with the terms of this   30
settlement, in our narrow view of it, we may follow unre-
strainedly, under the sanction of some such text as "Not sloth-
ful in business," or, "Whatsoever thy hand findeth to do, do it
with all thy might," or something else of the same kind. And
to any of these impulses we soon come to give that same   35
character of a mechanical, absolute law, which we give to our
religion; we regard it, as we do our religion, as an object for
strictness of conscience, not for spontaneity of consciousness;

for unremitting adherence on its own account, not for going
back upon, viewing in its connection with other things, and
adjusting to a number of changing circumstances. We treat it,
in short, just as we treat our religion,—as machinery. It is in
this way that the Barbarians treat their bodily exercises, the
Philistines their business, Mr. Spurgeon his voluntaryism, Mr.
Bright the assertion of personal liberty, Mr. Beales the right of
meeting in Hyde Park. In all those cases what is needed is a
freer play of consciousness upon the object of pursuit;
and in all of them Hebraism, the valuing staunchness and
earnestness more than this free play, the entire subordination
of thinking to doing, has led to a mistaken and misleading
treatment of things.

The newspapers a short time ago contained an account of the
suicide of a Mr. Smith, secretary to some insurance company,
who, it was said, "laboured under the apprehension that he
would come to poverty, and that he was eternally lost." And
when I read these words, it occurred to me that the poor man
who came to such a mournful end was, in truth, a kind of
type,—by the selection of his two grand objects of concern,
by their isolation from everything else, and their juxtaposition
to one another,—of all the strongest, most respectable, and
most representative part of our nation. "He laboured under
the apprehension that he would come to poverty, and that he
was eternally lost." The whole middle class have a conception
of things,—a conception which makes us call them Philistines,
—just like that of this poor man; though we are seldom,
of course, shocked by seeing it take the distressing, violently
morbid, and fatal turn, which it took with him. But how generally, with how many of us, are the main concerns of life
limited to these two: the concern for making money, and the
concern for saving our souls! And how entirely does the narrow and mechanical conception of our secular business proceed from a narrow and mechanical conception of our religious business! What havoc do the united conceptions make of
our lives! It is because the second-named of these two master-
concerns presents to us the one thing needful in so fixed, narrow, and mechanical a way, that so ignoble a fellow master-

concern to it as the first-named becomes possible; and, having been once admitted, takes the same rigid and absolute character as the other.

Poor Mr. Smith had sincerely the nobler master-concern as well as the meaner,—the concern for saving his soul (according to the narrow and mechanical conception which Puritanism has of what the salvation of the soul is), as well as the concern for making money. But let us remark how many people there are, especially outside the limits of the serious and conscientious middle class to which Mr. Smith belonged, who take up with a meaner master-concern,—whether it be pleasure, or field-sports, or bodily exercises, or business, or popular agitation, —who take up with one of these exclusively, and neglect Mr. Smith's nobler master-concern, because of the mechanical form which Hebraism has given to this noble master-concern. Hebraism makes it stand, as we have said, as something talis-manic, isolated, and all-sufficient, justifying our giving our ordinary selves free play in bodily exercises, or business, or popular agitation, if we have made our accounts square with this master-concern; and, if we have not, rendering other things indifferent, and our ordinary self all we have to follow, and to follow with all the energy that is in us, till we do. Whereas the idea of perfection at all points, the encouraging in ourselves spontaneity of consciousness, and letting a free play of thought live and flow around all our activity, the indisposition to allow one side of our activity to stand as so all-important and all-sufficing that it makes other sides indifferent,—this bent of mind in us may not only check us in following unreservedly a mean master-concern of any kind, but may even, also, bring new life and movement into that side of us with which alone Hebraism concerns itself, and awaken a healthier and less mechanical activity there. Hellenism may thus actually serve to further the designs of Hebraism.

Undoubtedly it thus served in the first days of Christianity. Christianity, as has been said, occupied itself, like Hebraism, with the moral side of man exclusively, with his moral affections and moral conduct; and so far it was but a continuation of Hebraism. But it transformed and renewed Hebraism by

criticising a fixed rule, which had become mechanical, and had thus lost its vital motive power; by letting the thought play freely around this old rule, and perceive its inadequacy; by developing a new motive power, which men's moral con-
5   sciousness could take living hold of, and could move in sympathy with. What was this but an importation of Hellenism, as we have defined it, into Hebraism? St. Paul used the contradiction between the Jew's profession and practice, his shortcomings on that very side of moral affection and moral conduct
10 which the Jew and St. Paul, both of them, regarded as all in all ("Thou that sayest a man should not steal, dost thou steal? thou that sayest a man should not commit adultery, dost thou commit adultery?"), for a proof of the inadequacy of the old rule of life in the Jew's mechanical conception of it; and tried
15 to rescue him by making his consciousness play freely around this rule,—that is, by a so far Hellenic treatment of it. Even so we, too, when we hear so much said of the growth of commercial immorality in our serious middle class, of the melting away of habits of strict probity before the temptation to get
20 quickly rich and to cut a figure in the world; when we see, at any rate, so much confusion of thought and of practice in this great representative class of our nation,—may we not be disposed to say, that this confusion shows that his new motive-power of grace and imputed righteousness has become to the
25 Puritan as mechanical, and with as ineffective a hold upon his practice, as the old motive-power of the law was to the Jew? and that the remedy is the same as that which St. Paul employed,—an importation of what we have called Hellenism into his Hebraism, a making his consciousness flow freely
30 round his petrified rule of life and renew it? Only with this difference: that whereas St. Paul imported Hellenism within the limits of our moral part only, this part being still treated by him as all in all; and whereas he well-nigh exhausted, one may say, and used to the very uttermost, the possibilities of
35 fruitfully importing it on that side exclusively; we ought to try and import it,—guiding ourselves by the ideal of a human nature harmoniously perfect in all points,—into all the lines of our activity. Only by so doing can we rightly quicken, re-

fresh, and renew those very instincts, now so much baffled, to which Hebraism makes appeal.

But if we will not be warned by the confusion visible enough at present in our thinking and acting, that we are on a false line in having developed our Hebrew side so exclusively, and our Hellenic side so feebly and at random, in loving fixed rules of action so much more than the intelligible law of things, let us listen to a remarkable testimony which the opinion of the world around us offers. All the world now sets great and increasing value on three objects which have long been very dear to us, and pursues them in its own way, or tries to pursue them. These three objects are industrial enterprise, bodily exercises, and freedom. Certainly we have, before and beyond our neighbours, given ourselves to these three things with ardent passion and with high success. And this our neighbours cannot but acknowledge; and they must needs, when they themselves turn to these things, have an eye to our example, and take something of our practice.

Now, generally, when people are interested in an object of pursuit, they cannot help feeling an enthusiasm for those who have already laboured successfully at it, and for their success. Not only do they study them, they also love and admire them. In this way a man who is interested in the art of war not only acquaints himself with the performance of great generals, but he has an admiration and enthusiasm for them. So, too, one who wants to be a painter or a poet cannot help loving and admiring the great painters or poets who have gone before him and shown him the way.

But it is strange with how little of love, admiration, or enthusiasm, the world regards us and our freedom, our bodily exercises, and our industrial prowess, much as these things themselves are beginning to interest it. And is not the reason because we follow each of these things in a mechanical manner, as an end in and for itself, and not in reference to a general end of human perfection; and this makes our pursuit of them uninteresting to humanity, and not what the world truly wants? It seems to them mere machinery that we can, knowingly, teach them to worship,—a mere fetish. British freedom,

British industry, British muscularity, we work for each of these three things blindly, with no notion of giving each its due proportion and prominence, because we have no ideal of harmonious human perfection before our minds, to set our work

5   in motion, and to guide it. So the rest of the world, desiring industry, or freedom, or bodily strength, yet desiring these not, as we do, absolutely, but as means to something else, imitate, indeed, of our practice what seems useful for them, but us, whose practice they imitate, they seem to entertain

10   neither love nor admiration for.

Let us observe, on the other hand, the love and enthusiasm excited by others who have laboured for these very things. Perhaps of what we call industrial enterprise it is not easy to find examples in former times; but let us consider how Greek freedom and

15   Greek gymnastics have attracted the love and praise of mankind, who give so little love and praise to ours. And what can be the reason of this difference? Surely because the Greeks pursued freedom and pursued gymnastics not mechanically, but with constant reference to some ideal of complete human per-

20   fection and happiness. And therefore, in spite of faults and failures, they interest and delight by their pursuit of them all the rest of mankind, who instinctively feel that only as things are pursued with reference to this ideal are they valuable.

Here again, therefore, as in the confusion into which the

25   thought and action of even the steadiest class amongst us is beginning to fall, we seem to have an admonition that we have fostered our Hebraising instincts, our preference of earnestness of doing to delicacy and flexibility of thinking, too exclusively, and have been landed by them in a mechanical and unfruitful rou-

30   tine. And again we seem taught that the development of our Hellenising instincts, seeking ardently the intelligible law of things, and making a stream of fresh thought play freely about our stock notions and habits, is what is most wanted by us at present.

35   Well, then, from all sides, the more we go into the matter, the currents seem to converge, and together to bear us along towards culture. If we look at the world outside us we find a disquieting absence of sure authority. We discover that only

in right reason can we get a source of sure authority; and culture brings us towards right reason. If we look at our own inner world, we find all manner of confusion arising out of the habits of unintelligent routine and one-sided growth, to which a too exclusive worship of fire, strength, earnestness, and action, has brought us. What we want is a fuller harmonious development of our humanity, a free play of thought upon our routine notions, spontaneity of consciousness, sweetness and light; and these are just what culture generates and fosters. We will not stickle for a name, and the name of culture one might easily give up, if only those who decry the frivolous and pedantic sort of culture, but wish at bottom for the same things as we do, would be careful on their part, not, in disparaging and discrediting the false culture, to unwittingly disparage and discredit, among a people with little natural reverence for it, the true also. But what we are concerned for is the thing, not the name; and the thing, call it by what name we will, is simply the enabling ourselves, by getting to know, whether through reading, observing, or thinking, the best that can at present be known in the world, to come as near as we can to the firm intelligible law of things, and thus to get a basis for a less confused action and a more complete perfection than we have at present.

And now, therefore, when we are accused of preaching up a spirit of cultivated inaction, of provoking the earnest lovers of action, of refusing to lend a hand at uprooting certain definite evils, of despairing to find any lasting truth to minister to the diseased spirit of our time, we shall not be so much confounded and embarrassed what to answer for ourselves. We shall say boldly that we do not at all despair of finding some lasting truth to minister to the diseased spirit of our time; but that we have discovered the best way of finding this to be not so much by lending a hand to our friends and countrymen in their actual operations for the removal of certain definite evils, but rather in getting our friends and countrymen to seek culture, to let their consciousness play freely round their present operations and the stock notions on which they are founded, show what these are like, and how related to the intelligible law of things, and auxiliary to true human perfection.

Chapter VI

Our Liberal Practitioners

But an unpretending writer, without a philosophy based on inter-dependent, subordinate, and coherent principles, must not presume to indulge himself too much in generalities. He must keep close to the level ground of common fact, the only safe ground for understandings without a scientific equipment. Therefore, since I have spoken so slightingly of the practical operations in which my friends and countrymen are at this moment engaged for the removal of certain definite evils, I am bound to take, before concluding, some of those operations, and to make them, if I can, show the truth of what I have advanced.

Probably I could hardly give a greater proof of my confessed inexpertness in reasoning and arguing, than by taking, for my first example of an operation of this kind, the proceedings for the disestablishment of the Irish Church, which we are now witnessing.[1] It seems so clear that this is surely one of those operations for the uprooting of a certain definite evil in which one's Liberal friends engage, and have a right to complain, and to get impatient, and to reproach one with delicate Conservative scepticism and cultivated inaction, if one does not lend a hand to help them. This does, indeed, seem evident; and yet this operation comes so prominently before us at this moment,[2] —it so challenges everybody's regard,—that one seems cowardly in blinking it. So let us venture to try and see whether this conspicuous operation is one of those round which we need to let our consciousness play freely and reveal what manner of spirit we are of in doing it; or whether it is one which

[1] Written in 1868.   [2] 1868.

by no means admits the application of this doctrine of ours, and one to which we ought to lend a hand immediately.

I

Now it seems plain that the present Church-establishment in Ireland is contrary to reason and justice, in so far as the Church of a very small minority of the people there takes for itself all the Church-property of the Irish people. And one would think, that property, assigned for the purpose of providing for a people's religious worship when that worship was one, the State should, when that worship is split into several forms, apportion between those several forms. But the apportionment should be made with due regard to circumstances, taking account only of great differences, which are likely to be lasting, and of considerable communions, which are likely to represent profound and widespread religious characteristics. It should overlook petty differences, which have no serious reason for lasting, and inconsiderable communions, which can hardly be taken to express any broad and necessary religious lineaments of our common nature. This is just in accordance with that maxim about the State which we have more than once used: *The State is of the religion of all its citizens, without the fanaticism of any of them.* Those who deny this, either think so poorly of the State that they do not like to see religion condescend to touch the State, or they think so poorly of religion that they do not like to see the State condescend to touch religion. But no good statesman will easily think thus unworthily either of the State or of religion.

Our statesmen of both parties were inclined, one may say, to follow the natural line of the State's duty, and to make in Ireland some fair apportionment of Church-property between large and radically divided religious communions in that country. But then it was discovered that in Great Britain the national mind, as it is called, is grown averse to endowments for religion and will make no new ones; and though this in itself looks general and solemn enough, yet there were found politi-

cal philosophers to give it a look of more generality and more
solemnity still, and to elevate, by their dexterous command of
powerful and beautiful language, this supposed edict of the
British national mind into a sort of formula for expressing a
great law of religious transition and progress for all the world.

But we, who, having no coherent philosophy, must not let
ourselves philosophise, only see that the English and Scotch
Nonconformists have a great horror of establishments and endowments for religion, which, they assert, were forbidden by
Jesus Christ when he said: "My kingdom is not of this world;"
and that·the Nonconformists will be.delighted to aid statesmen in
disestablishing any church, but will suffer none to be established or endowed if they can help it. Then we see that the
Nonconformists make the strength of the Liberal Majority in
the House of Commons; and that, therefore, the leading Liberal statesmen, to get the support of the Nonconformists, forsake the notion of fairly apportioning Church-property in Ireland among the chief religious communions, declare that the
national mind has decided against new endowments, and propose simply to disestablish and disendow the present establishment in Ireland without establishing or endowing any other.
The actual power, in short, by virtue of which the Liberal
party in the House of Commons is now trying to disestablish
the Irish Church, is not the power of reason and justice, it is
the power of the Nonconformists' antipathy to Church establishments.

Clearly it is this; because Liberal statesmen, relying on the
power of reason and justice to help them, proposed something
quite different from what they now propose; and they proposed
what they now propose, and talked of the decision of the
national mind, because they had to rely on the English and
Scotch Nonconformists. And clearly the Nonconformists are
actuated by antipathy to establishments, not by antipathy to
the injustice and irrationality of the present appropriation of
Church-property in Ireland; because Mr. Spurgeon, in his eloquent and memorable letter, expressly avowed that he would
sooner leave things as they are in Ireland, that is, he would
sooner let the injustice and irrationality of the present appro-

priation continue, than do anything to set up the Roman image,—that is, than give the Catholics their fair and reasonable share of Church-property. Most indisputably, therefore, we may affirm that the real moving power by which the Liberal party are now operating the overthrow of the Irish establishment is the antipathy of the Nonconformists to Church-establishments, and not the sense of reason or justice, except so far as reason and justice may be contained in this antipathy. And thus the matter stands at present.

Now surely we must all see many inconveniences in performing the operation of uprooting this evil, the Irish Church-establishment, in this particular way. As was said about industry and freedom and gymnastics, we shall never awaken love and gratitude by this mode of operation; for it is pursued, not in view of reason and justice and human perfection and all that enkindles the enthusiasm of men, but it is pursued in view of a certain stock notion, or fetish, of the Nonconformists, which proscribes Church-establishments. And yet, evidently, one of the main benefits to be got by operating on the Irish Church is to win the affections of the Irish people. Besides this, an operation performed in virtue of a mechanical rule, or fetish, like the supposed decision of the English national mind against new endowments, does not easily inspire respect in its adversaries, and make their opposition feeble and hardly to be persisted in, as an operation evidently done in virtue of reason and justice might. For reason and justice have in them something persuasive and irresistible; but a fetish or mechanical maxim, like this of the Nonconformists, has in it nothing at all to conciliate either the affections or the understanding. Nay, it provokes the counter-employment of other fetishes or mechanical maxims on the opposite side, by which the confusion and hostility already prevalent are heightened. Only in this way can be explained the apparition of such fetishes as are beginning to be set up on the Conservative side against the fetish of the Nonconformists:—*The Constitution in danger! The bulwark of British freedom menaced! The lamp of the Reformation put out! No Popery!*—and so on. To elevate these against an operation relying on reason and justice to back it, is not so easy, or

so tempting to human infirmity, as to elevate them against an
operation relying on the Nonconformists' antipathy to Church-
establishments to back it. For after all, *No Popery!* is a rallying
cry which touches the human spirit quite as vitally as *No*
5   *Church-establishments!*—that is to say, neither the one nor the
other, in themselves, touch the human spirit vitally at all.

Ought the believers in action, then, to be so impatient with us,
if we say, that even for the sake of this operation of theirs itself
and its satisfactory accomplishment, it is more important to
10   make our consciousness play freely round the stock notion or
habit on which their operation relies for aid, than to lend a
hand to it straight away? Clearly they ought not; because
nothing is so effectual for operating as reason and justice, and a
free play of thought will either disengage the reason and jus-
15   tice lying hid in the Nonconformist fetish, and make them
effectual, or else it will help to get this fetish out of the way,
and to let statesmen go freely where reason and justice take
them.

So, suppose we take this absolute rule, this mechanical maxim
20   of Mr. Spurgeon and the Nonconformists, that Church-establishments are bad things because Jesus Christ said: "My kingdom
is not of this world." Suppose we try and make our consciousness bathe and float this piece of petrifaction,—for such it now
is,—and bring it within the stream of the vital movement of
25   our thought, and into relation with the whole intelligible law
of things. An enemy and a disputant might probably say that
much of the machinery which Nonconformists themselves
employ,—the Liberation Society which exists already, and the
Nonconformist Union which Mr. Spurgeon desires to see ex-
30   isting,—come within the scope of Christ's words as well as
Church-establishments. This, however, is merely a negative
and contentious way of dealing with the Nonconformist
maxim; whereas what we desire is to bring this maxim within
the positive and vital movement of our thought. We say,
35   therefore, that Jesus Christ's words mean that his religion is a
force of inward persuasion acting on the soul, and not a force
of outward constraint acting on the body; and if the Nonconformist maxim against Church-establishments and Church-en-

dowments has warrant given to it from what Christ thus meant, then their maxim is good, even though their own practice in the matter of the Liberation Society may be at variance with it.

And here we cannot but remember what we have formerly said about religion, Miss Cobbe, and the British College of Health in the New Road. In religion there are two parts, the part of thought and speculation, and the part of worship and devotion. Jesus Christ certainly meant his religion, as a force of inward persuasion acting on the soul, to employ both parts as perfectly as possible. Now thought and speculation is eminently an individual matter, and worship and devotion is eminently a collective matter. It does not help me to think a thing more clearly that thousands of other people are thinking the same; but it does help me to worship with more emotion that thousands of other people are worshipping with me. The consecration of common consent, antiquity, public establishment, long-used rites, national edifices, is everything for religious worship. "Just what makes worship impressive," says Joubert, "is its publicity, its external manifestation, its sound, its splendour, its observance universally and visibly holding its way through all the details both of our outward and of our inward life." Worship, therefore, should have in it as little as possible of what divides us, and should be as much as possible a common and public act; as Joubert says again: "The best prayers are those which have nothing distinct about them, and which are thus of the nature of simple adoration." For, "the same devotion," as he says in another place, "unites men far more than the same thought and knowledge." Thought and knowledge, as we have said before, is eminently something individual, and of our own; the more we possess it as strictly of our own, the more power it has on us. Man worships best, therefore, with the community; he philosophises best alone.

So it seems that whoever would truly give effect to Jesus Christ's declaration that his religion is a force of inward persuasion acting on the soul, would leave our thought on the intellectual aspects of Christianity as individual as possible, but would make Christian worship as collective as possible. Worship,

then, appears to be eminently a matter for public and national establishment; for even Mr. Bright, who, when he stands in Mr. Spurgeon's great Tabernacle, is so ravished with admiration, will hardly say that the great Tabernacle and its worship
5 are in themselves, as a temple and service of religion, so impressive and affecting as the public and national Westminster Abbey, or Notre Dame, with their worship. And when, immediately after the great Tabernacle, one comes plump down to the mass of private and individual establishments of religious
10 worship, establishments falling, like the British College of Health in the New Road, conspicuously short of what a public and national establishment might be, then one cannot but feel that Jesus Christ's command to make his religion a force of persuasion to the soul, is, so far as one main source of persua-
15 sion is concerned, altogether set at nought.

But perhaps the Nonconformists worship so unimpressively because they philosophise so keenly; and one part of religion, the part of public national worship, they have subordinated to the other part, the part of individual thought and knowledge?
20 This, however, their organisation in congregations forbids us to admit. They are members of congregations, not isolated thinkers; and a free play of individual thought is at least as much impeded by membership of a small congregation as by membership of a great Church. Thinking by batches of fifties is to
25 the full as fatal to free thought as thinking by batches of thousands. Accordingly, we have had occasion already to notice that Nonconformity does not at all differ from the Established Church by having worthier or more philosophical ideas about God, and the ordering of the world, than the Estab-
30 lished Church has. It has very much the same ideas about these as the Established Church has, but it differs from the Established Church in that its worship is a much less collective and national affair.

So Mr. Spurgeon and the Nonconformists seem to have mis-
35 apprehended the true meaning of Christ's words, *My kingdom is not of this world*. Because, by these words, Christ meant that his religion was to work on the soul. And of the two parts of the soul on which religion works,—the thinking and speculative

part, and the feeling and imaginative part,—Nonconformity satisfies the first no better than the Established Churches, which Christ by these words is supposed to have condemned, satisfy it; and the second part it satisfies even worse than the Established Churches. And thus the balance of advantage 5 seems to rest with the Established Churches; and they seem to have apprehended and applied Christ's words, if not with perfect adequacy, at least less inadequately than the Nonconformists.

Might it not, then, be urged with great force that the way to 10 do good, in presence of this operation for uprooting the Church-establishment in Ireland by the power of the Nonconformists' antipathy to publicly establishing or endowing religious worship, is not by lending a hand straight away to the operation, and Hebraising,—that is, in this case, taking an uncritical inter- 15 pretation of certain Bible words as our absolute rule of conduct,—with the Nonconformists? It may be very well for born Hebraisers, like Mr. Spurgeon, to Hebraise; but for Liberal statesmen to Hebraise is surely unsafe, and to see poor old Liberal hacks Hebraising, whose real self belongs to a kind of 20 negative Hellenism,—a state of moral indifferency without intellectual ardour,—is even painful. And when, by our Hebraising, we neither do what the better mind of statesmen prompted them to do, nor win the affections of the people we want to conciliate, nor yet reduce the opposition of our adver- 25 saries but rather heighten it, surely it may not be unreasonable to Hellenise a little, to let our thought and consciousness play freely about our proposed operation and its motives, dissolve these motives if they are unsound,—which certainly they have some appearance, at any rate, of being,—and create in their 30 stead, if they are, a set of sounder and more persuasive motives conducting to a more solid operation. May not the man who promotes this be giving the best help towards finding some lasting truth to minister to the diseased spirit of his time, and does he really deserve that the believers in action should grow 35 impatient with him?

II

But now to take another operation which does not at this moment so excite people's feelings as the disestablishment of the Irish Church, but which, I suppose, would also be called exactly one of those operations of simple, practical, common-sense re-
5 form, aiming at the removal of some particular abuse, and rigidly restricted to that object, to which a Liberal ought to lend a hand, and deserves that other Liberals should grow impatient with him if he does not. This operation I had the great advantage of with my own ears hearing discussed in the House of
10 Commons, and recommended by a powerful speech from that famous speaker, Mr. Bright. So that the effeminate horror which, it is alleged, I have of practical reforms of this kind, was put to a searching test; and if it survived, it must have, one would think, some reason or other to support it, and can
15 hardly quite merit the stigma of its present name.

The operation I mean was that which the Real Estate Intestacy Bill aimed at accomplishing, and the discussion on this bill I heard in the House of Commons. The bill proposed, as every one knows, to prevent the land of a man who dies intestate
20 from going, as it goes now, to his eldest son, and was thought, by its friends and by its enemies, to be a step towards abating the now almost exclusive possession of the land of this country by the people whom we call the Barbarians. Mr. Bright, and other speakers on his side, seemed to hold that there is a
25 kind of natural law or fitness of things which assigns to all a man's children a right to equal shares in the enjoyment of his property after his death; and that if, without depriving a man of an Englishman's prime privilege of doing what he likes by making what will he chooses, you provide that when he makes
30 none his land shall be divided among his family, then you give the sanction of the law to the natural fitness of things, and inflict a sort of check on the present violation of this by the Barbarians.

It occurred to me, when I saw Mr. Bright and his friends proceeding in this way, to ask myself a question. If the almost exclusive possession of the land of this country by the Barbarians is a bad thing, is this practical operation of the Liberals, and the stock notion, on which it seems to rest, about the natural right 5 of children to share equally in the enjoyment of their father's property after his death, the best and most effective means of dealing with it? Or is it best dealt with by letting one's thought and consciousness play freely and naturally upon the Barbarians, this Liberal operation, and the stock notion at the 10 bottom of it, and trying to get as near as we can to the intelligible law of things as to each of them?

Now does any one, if he simply and naturally reads his consciousness, discover that he has any rights at all? For my part, the deeper I go in my own consciousness, and the more simply I 15 abandon myself to it, the more it seems to tell me that I have no rights at all, only duties; and that men get this notion of rights from a process of abstract reasoning, inferring that the obligations they are conscious of towards others, others must be conscious of towards them, and not from any direct witness 20 of consciousness at all. But it is obvious that the notion of a right, arrived at in this way, is likely to stand as a formal and petrified thing, deceiving and misleading us; and that the notions got directly from our consciousness ought to be brought to bear upon it, and to control it. So it is unsafe and misleading 25 to say that our children have rights against us; what is true and safe to say is, that we have duties towards our children. But who will find among these natural duties, set forth to us by our consciousness, the obligation to leave to all our children an equal share in the enjoyment of our property? Or, though 30 consciousness tells us we ought to provide for our children's welfare, whose consciousness tells him that the enjoyment of property is in itself welfare? Whether our children's welfare is best served by their all sharing equally in our property, depends on circumstances and on the state of the community in 35 which we live. With this equal sharing, society could not, for example, have organised itself afresh out of the chaos left by the fall of the Roman Empire; and to have an organised society to live in is more for a child's welfare than to have an equal share of his father's property.

So we see how little convincing force the stock notion on which the Real Estate Intestacy Bill was based,—the notion that in the nature and fitness of things all a man's children have a right to an equal share in the enjoyment of what he leaves,—really has; and how powerless, therefore, it must of necessity be to persuade and win any one who has habits and interests which disincline him to it. On the other hand, the practical operation proposed relies entirely, if it is to be effectual in altering the present practice of the Barbarians, on the power of truth and persuasiveness in the notion which it seeks to consecrate; for it leaves to the Barbarians full liberty to continue their present practice, to which all their habits and interests incline them, unless the promulgation of a notion, which we have seen to have no vital efficacy and hold upon our consciousness, shall hinder them.

Are we really to adorn an operation of this kind, merely because it proposes to *do* something, with all the favourable epithets of simple, practical, common-sense, definite; to enlist on its side all the zeal of the believers in action, and to call indifference to it an effeminate horror of useful reforms? It seems to me quite easy to show that a free disinterested play of thought on the Barbarians and their land-holding is a thousand times more really practical, a thousand times more likely to lead to some effective result, than an operation such as that of which we have been now speaking. For if, casting aside the impediments of stock notions and mechanical action, we try to find the intelligible law of things respecting a great land-owning class such as we have in this country, does not our consciousness readily tell us that whether the perpetuation of such a class is for its own real good and for the real good of the community, depends on the actual circumstances of this class and of the community? Does it not readily tell us that wealth, power, and consideration are,—and above all when inherited and not earned,—in themselves trying and dangerous things? as Bishop Wilson excellently says: "Riches are almost always abused without a very extraordinary grace." But this extraordinary grace was in great measure supplied by the circumstances of the feudal epoch, out of which our land-holding class, with its rules of inheritance, sprang. The labour and contentions of a rude, nascent, and struggling society supplied it. These perpetually were trying, chastising, and forming the class whose predominance was then needed by society to give it points of cohesion, and was not so harmful to themselves because they were thus sharply tried and exercised. But in a luxurious, settled and easy society, where wealth offers the means of enjoyment a thousand times more, and the temptation to abuse them is thus made a thousand times greater, the exercising discipline is at the same time taken away, and the feudal class is left exposed to the full operation of the natural law well put by the French moralist: *Pouvoir sans savoir est fort dangereux.* And, for my part, when I regard the young people of this class, it is above all by the trial and shipwreck made of their own welfare by the circumstances in which they live that I am struck. How far better it would have been for nine out of every ten among them, if they had had their own way to make in the world, and not been tried by a condition for which they had not the extraordinary grace requisite!

This, I say, seems to be what a man's consciousness, simply consulted, would tell him about the actual welfare of our Barbarians themselves. Then, as to the effect upon the welfare of the community, how can that be salutary, if a class which, by the very possession of wealth, power and consideration, becomes a kind of ideal or standard for the rest of the community, is tried by ease and pleasure more than it can well bear, and almost irresistibly carried away from excellence and strenuous virtue? This must certainly be what Solomon meant when he said: "As he who putteth a stone in a sling, so is he that giveth honour to a fool."

For any one can perceive how this honouring of a false ideal, not of intelligence and strenuous virtue, but of wealth and station, pleasure and ease, is as a stone from a sling to kill in our great middle class, in us who are called Philistines, the desire before spoken of, which by nature for ever carries all men towards

that which is lovely; and to leave instead of it only a blind
deteriorating pursuit, for ourselves also, of the false ideal. And
in those among us Philistines whom the desire does not wholly
abandon, yet, having no excellent ideal set forth to nourish and
5   to steady it, it meets with that natural bent for the bathos
which together with this desire itself is implanted at birth in
the breast of man, and is by that force twisted awry, and
borne at random hither and thither, and at last flung upon
those grotesque and hideous forms of popular religion which
10   the more respectable part among us Philistines mistake for the
true goal of man's desire after all that is lovely. And for the
Populace this false idea is a stone which kills the desire before
it can even arise; so impossible and unattainable for them do
the conditions of that which is lovely appear according to this
15   ideal to be made, so necessary to the reaching of them by the
few seems the falling short of them by the many. So that,
perhaps, of the actual vulgarity of our Philistines and brutality
of our Populace, the Barbarians and their feudal habits of succession, enduring out of their due time and place, are involun-
20   tarily the cause in a great degree; and they hurt the welfare of
the rest of the community at the same time that, as we have
seen, they hurt their own.

But must not, now, the working in our minds of considerations like these, to which culture, that is, the disinterested and
25   active use of reading, reflection, and observation, in the endeavour to know the best that can be known, carries us, be really
much more effectual to the dissolution of feudal habits and rules
of succession in land than an operation like the Real Estate Intestacy Bill, and a stock notion like that of the natural right of all
30   a man's children to an equal share in the enjoyment of his
property; since we have seen that this mechanical maxim is
unsound, and that, if it is unsound, the operation relying upon
it cannot possibly be effective? If truth and reason have, as we
believe, any natural, irresistible effect on the mind of man, it
35   must. These considerations, when culture has called them
forth and given them free course in our minds, will live and
work. They will work gradually, no doubt, and will not bring
us ourselves to the front to sit in high place and put them into

effect; but so they will be all the more beneficial. Everything teaches us how gradually nature would have all profound changes brought about; and we can even see, too, where the absolute abrupt stoppage of feudal habits has worked harm. And appealing to the sense of truth and reason, these consider- 5 ations will, without doubt, touch and move all those of even the Barbarians themselves, who are (as are some of us Philistines also, and some of the Populace) beyond their fellows quick of feeling for truth and reason. For indeed this is just one of the advantages of sweetness and light over fire and 10 strength, that sweetness and light make a feudal class quietly and gradually drop its feudal habits because it sees them at variance with truth and reason, while fire and strength are for tearing them passionately off, because this class applauded Mr. Lowe when he called, or was supposed to call, the working 15 class drunken and venal.

III

But when once we have begun to recount the practical operations by which our Liberal friends work for the removal of definite evils, and in which if we do not join them they are apt to grow impatient with us, how can we pass over that very interest- 20 ing operation,—the attempt to enable a man to marry his deceased wife's sister? This operation, too, like that for abating the feudal customs of succession in land, I have had the advantage of myself seeing and hearing my Liberal friends labour at.

I was lucky enough to be present when Mr. Chambers brought 25 forward in the House of Commons his bill for enabling a man to marry his deceased wife's sister, and I heard the speech which Mr. Chambers then made in support of his bill. His first point was that God's law,—the name he always gave to the Book of Leviticus,—did not really forbid a man to marry his 30 deceased wife's sister. God's law not forbidding it, the Liberal maxim, that a man's prime right and happiness is to do as he likes, ought at once to come into force, and to annul any such check upon the assertion of personal liberty as the prohibition

to marry one's deceased wife's sister. A distinguished Liberal
supporter of Mr. Chambers, in the debate which followed the
introduction of the bill, produced a formula of much beauty
and neatness for conveying in brief the Liberal notions on this
5   head: "Liberty," said he, "is the law of human life." And,
therefore, the moment it is ascertained that God's law, the
Book of Leviticus, does not stop the way, man's law, the law
of liberty, asserts its right, and makes us free to marry our
deceased wife's sister.

10   And this exactly falls in with what Mr. Hepworth Dixon, who
may almost be called the Colenso of love and marriage,—such a
revolution does he make in our ideas on these matters, just as
Dr. Colenso does in our ideas on religion,—tells us of the notions and proceedings of our kinsmen in America. With that
15   affinity of genius to the Hebrew genius which we have already
noticed, and with the strong belief of our race that liberty is
the law of human life, so far as that fixed, perfect, and paramount rule of conscience, the Bible, does not expressly control
it, our American kinsmen go again, Mr. Hepworth Dixon tells
20   us, to their Bible, the Mormons to the patriarchs and the Old
Testament, Brother Noyes to St. Paul and the New, and having never before read anything else but their Bible, they now
read their Bible over again, and make all manner of great discoveries there. All these discoveries are favourable to liberty,
25   and in this way is satisfied that double craving so characteristic
of our Philistine, and so eminently exemplified in that crowned
Philistine, Henry the Eighth,—the craving for forbidden fruit
and the craving for legality.

Mr. Hepworth Dixon's eloquent writings give currency, over
30   here, to these important discoveries; so that now, as regards
love and marriage, we seem to be entering, with all our sails
spread, upon what Mr. Hepworth Dixon, its apostle and evangelist, calls a Gothic Revival, but what one of the many newspapers that so greatly admire Mr. Hepworth Dixon's lithe and
35   sinewy style and form their own style upon it, calls, by a yet
bolder and more striking figure, "a great sexual insurrection of
our Anglo-Teutonic race." For this end we have to avert our
eyes from everything Hellenic and fanciful, and to keep them

steadily fixed upon the two cardinal points of the Bible and liberty. And one of those practical operations in which the Liberal party engage, and in which we are summoned to join them, directs itself entirely, as we have seen, to these cardinal points, and may almost be regarded, perhaps, as a kind of first instalment, or public and parliamentary pledge, of the great sexual insurrection of our Anglo-Teutonic race.

But here, as elsewhere, what we seek is the Philistine's perfection, the development of his best self, not mere liberty for his ordinary self. And we no more allow absolute validity to his stock maxim, *Liberty is the law of human life*, than we allow it to the opposite maxim, which is just as true, *Renouncement is the law of human life*. For we know that the only perfect freedom is, as our religion says, a service; not a service to any stock maxim, but an elevation of our best self, and a harmonising in subordination to this, and to the idea of a perfected humanity, all the multitudinous, turbulent, and blind impulses of our ordinary selves. Now, the Philistine's great defect being a defect in delicacy of perception, to cultivate in him this delicacy, to render it independent of external and mechanical rule, and a law to itself, is what seems to make most for his perfection, his true humanity. And his true humanity, and therefore his happiness, appears to lie much more, so far as the relations of love and marriage are concerned, in becoming alive to the finer shades of feeling which arise within these relations, in being able to enter with tact and sympathy into the subtle instinctive propensions and repugnances of the person with whose life his own life is bound up, to make them his own, to direct and govern in harmony with them the arbitrary range of his personal action, and thus to enlarge his spiritual and intellectual life and liberty, than in remaining insensible to these finer shades of feeling and this delicate sympathy, in giving unchecked range, so far as he can, to his mere personal action, in allowing no limits or government to this except such as a mechanical external law imposes, and in thus really narrowing, for the satisfaction of his ordinary self, his spiritual and intellectual life and liberty.

Still more must this be so when his fixed eternal rule, his God's

law, is supplied to him from a source which is less fit, perhaps, to supply final and absolute instructions on this particular topic of love and marriage than on any other relation of human life. Bishop Wilson, who is full of examples of that
5 fruitful Hellenising within the limits of Hebraism itself, of that renewing of the stiff and stark notions of Hebraism by turning upon them a stream of fresh thought and consciousness, which we have already noticed in St. Paul,—Bishop Wilson gives an admirable lesson to rigid Hebraisers, like Mr. Cham-
10 bers, asking themselves: Does God's law (that is, the Book of Leviticus) forbid us to marry our wife's sister?—Does God's law (that is, again, the Book of Leviticus) allow us to marry our wife's sister?—when he says: "Christian duties are founded on reason, not on the sovereign authority of God com-
15 manding what He pleases; God cannot command us what is not fit to be believed or done, all his commands being founded in the necessities of our nature." And, immense as is our debt to the Hebrew race and its genius, incomparable as is its authority on certain profoundly important sides of our hu-
20 man nature, worthy as it is to be described as having uttered, for those sides, the voice of the deepest necessities of our nature, the statutes of the divine and eternal order of things, the law of God,—who, that is not manacled and hoodwinked by his Hebraism, can believe that, as to love and marriage, our
25 reason and the necessities of our humanity have their true, sufficient, and divine law expressed for them by the voice of any Oriental and polygamous nation like the Hebrews? Who, I say, will believe, when he really considers the matter, that where the feminine nature, the feminine ideal, and our rela-
30 tions to them, are brought into question, the delicate and apprehensive genius of the Indo-European race, the race which invented the Muses, and chivalry, and the Madonna, is to find its last word on this question in the institutions of a Semitic people, whose wisest king had seven hundred wives and three
35 hundred concubines?

IV

If here again, therefore, we minister better to the diseased spirit of our time by leading it to think about the operation our Liberal friends have in hand, than by lending a hand to this operation ourselves, let us see, before we dismiss from our view the practical operations of our Liberal friends, whether the same thing does not hold good as to their celebrated industrial and economical labours also. Their great work of this kind is, of course, their free-trade policy. This policy, as having enabled the poor man to eat untaxed bread, and as having wonderfully augmented trade, we are accustomed to speak of with a kind of thankful solemnity. It is chiefly on their having been our leaders in this policy that Mr. Bright founds for himself and his friends the claim, so often asserted by him, to be considered guides of the blind, teachers of the ignorant, benefactors slowly and laboriously developing in the Conservative party and in the country that which Mr. Bright is fond of calling *the growth of intelligence,*—the object, as is well known, of all the friends of culture also, and the great end and aim of the culture that we preach.

Now, having first saluted free-trade and its doctors with all respect, let us see whether even here, too, our Liberal friends do not pursue their operations in a mechanical way, without reference to any firm intelligible law of things, to human life as a whole, and human happiness; and whether it is not more for our good, at this particular moment at any rate, if, instead of worshipping free-trade with them Hebraistically, as a kind of fetish, and helping them to pursue it as an end in and for itself, we turn the free stream of our thought upon their treatment of it, and see how this is related to the intelligible law of human life, and to national well-being and happiness. In short, suppose we Hellenise a little with free-trade, as we Hellenised with the Real Estate Intestacy Bill, and with the disestablishment of the Irish Church by the power of the Nonconform-

ists' antipathy to religious establishments, and see whether
what our reprovers beautifully call ministering to the diseased
spirit of our time is best done by the Hellenising method of
proceeding, or by the other.

5   But first let us understand how the policy of free-trade really
shapes itself for our Liberal friends, and how they practically
employ it as an instrument of national happiness and salvation.
For as we said that it seemed clearly right to prevent the
Church-property of Ireland from being all taken for the bene-
10   fit of the Church of a small minority, so it seems clearly right
that the poor man should eat untaxed bread, and, generally,
that restrictions and regulations which, for the supposed benefit of some particular person or class of persons, make the price
of things artificially high here, or artificially low there, and
15   interfere with the natural flow of trade and commerce, should
be done away with. But in the policy of our Liberal friends
free-trade means more than this, and is specially valued as a
stimulant to the production of wealth, as they call it, and to
the increase of the trade, business, and population of the coun-
20   try. We have already seen how these things,—trade, business,
and population,—are mechanically pursued by us as ends precious in themselves, and are worshipped as what we call fetishes; and Mr. Bright, I have already said, when he wishes to
give the working class a true sense of what makes glory and
25   greatness, tells it to look at the cities it has built, the railroads it
has made, the manufactures it has produced. So to this idea of
glory and greatness the free-trade which our Liberal friends
extol so solemnly and devoutly, has served,—to the increase of
trade, business, and population; and for this it is prized. There-
30   fore, the untaxing of the poor man's bread has, with this view of
national happiness, been used not so much to make the existing
poor man's bread cheaper or more abundant, but rather to create more poor men to eat it; so that we cannot precisely say
that we have fewer poor men than we had before free-trade,
35   but we can say with truth that we have many more centres of
industry, as they are called, and much more business, population, and manufactures. And if we are sometimes a little troubled by our multitude of poor men, yet we know the increase

of manufactures and population to be such a salutary thing in itself, and our free-trade policy begets such an admirable movement, creating fresh centres of industry and fresh poor men here, while we were thinking about our poor men there, that we are quite dazzled and borne away, and more and more industrial movement is called for, and our social progress seems to become one triumphant and enjoyable course of what is sometimes called, vulgarly, outrunning the constable.

If, however, taking some other criterion of man's well-being than the cities he has built and the manufactures he has produced, we persist in thinking that our social progress would be happier if there were not so many of us so very poor, and in busying ourselves with notions of in some way or other adjusting the poor man and business one to the other, and not multiplying the one and the other mechanically and blindly, then our Liberal friends, the appointed doctors of free-trade, take us up very sharply. "Art is long," says the *Times*, "and life is short; for the most part we settle things first and understand them afterwards. Let us have as few theories as possible; what is wanted is not the light of speculation. If nothing worked well of which the theory was not perfectly understood, we should be in sad confusion. The relations of labour and capital, we are told, are not understood, yet trade and commerce, on the whole, work satisfactorily." I quote from the *Times* of only the other day.[1] But thoughts like these, as I have often pointed out, are thoroughly British thoughts, and we have been familiar with them for years.

Or, if we want more of a philosophy of the matter than this, our free-trade friends have two axioms for us, axioms laid down by their justly esteemed doctors, which they think ought to satisfy us entirely. One is, that, other things being equal, the more population increases, the more does production increase to keep pace with it; because men by their numbers and contact call forth all manner of activities and resources in one another and in nature, which, when men are few and sparse, are never developed. The other is, that, although population

[1] Written in 1868.

always tends to equal the means of subsistence, yet people's
notions of what subsistence is enlarge as civilisation advances,
and take in a number of things beyond the bare necessaries of
life; and thus, therefore, is supplied whatever check on popula-
5   tion is needed. But the error of our friends is precisely, perhaps, that they apply axioms of this sort as if they were self-
acting laws which will put themselves into operation without
trouble or planning on our part, if we will only pursue free-
trade, business, and population zealously and staunchly.
10 Whereas the real truth is, that, however the case might be
under other circumstances, yet in fact, as we now manage the
matter, the enlarged conception of what is included in *subsistence* does not operate to prevent the bringing into the world
of numbers of people who but just attain to the barest neces-
15 saries of life or who even fail to attain to them; while, again,
though production may increase as population increases, yet it
seems that the production may be of such a kind, and so related, or rather non-related, to population, that the population
may be little the better for it.
20   For instance, with the increase of population since Queen
Elizabeth's time the production of silk-stockings has wonderfully increased, and silk-stockings have become much cheaper,
and procurable in greater abundance by many more people, and
tend perhaps, as population and manufactures increase, to get
25 cheaper and cheaper, and at last to become, according to Bastiat's favourite image, a common free property of the human
race, like light and air. But bread and bacon have not become
much cheaper with the increase of population since Queen
Elizabeth's time, nor procurable in much greater abundance by
30 many more people; neither do they seem at all to promise to
become, like light and air, a common free property of the
human race. And if bread and bacon have not kept pace with
our population, and we have many more people in want of
them now than in Queen Elizabeth's time, it seems vain to tell
35 us that silk-stockings have kept pace with our population, or
even more than kept pace with it, and that we are to get our
comfort out of that.

    In short, it turns out that our pursuit of free-trade, as of so many other things, has been too mechanical. We fix upon some object, which in this case is the production of wealth, and the increase of manufactures, population, and commerce through free-trade, as a kind of one thing needful, or end in itself; and then we pursue it staunchly and mechanically, and say that it is our duty to pursue it staunchly and mechanically, not to see how it is related to the whole intelligible law of things and to full human perfection, or to treat it as the piece of machinery, of varying value as its relations to the intelligible law of things vary, which it really is.

So it is of no use to say to the *Times*, and to our Liberal friends rejoicing in the possession of their talisman of free-trade, that about one in nineteen of our population is a pauper,[1] and that, this being so, trade and commerce can hardly be said to prove by their satisfactory working that it matters nothing whether the relations between labour and capital are understood or not; nay, that we can hardly be said not to be in sad confusion. For here our faith in the staunch mechanical pursuit of a fixed object comes in, and covers itself with that imposing and colossal necessitarianism of the *Times* which we have before noticed. And this necessitarianism, taking for granted that an increase in trade and population is a good in itself, one of the chiefest of goods, tells us that disturbances of human happiness caused by ebbs and flows in the tide of trade and business, which, on the whole, steadily mounts, are inevitable and not to be quarrelled with. This firm philosophy I seek to call to mind when I am in the East of London, whither my avocations often lead me; and, indeed, to fortify myself against the depressing sights which on these occasions assail us, I have transcribed from the *Times* one strain of this kind, full of the finest economical doctrine, and always carry it about with me. The passage is this:—

"The East End is the most commercial, the most industrial, the most fluctuating region of the metropolis. It is always the first to suffer; for it is the creature of prosperity, and falls to the ground the instant there is no wind to bear it up. The whole of that region is covered with huge docks, shipyards, manufacto-

[1] This was in 1868.

ries, and a wilderness of small houses, all full of life and happiness in brisk times, but in dull times withered and lifeless, like the deserts we read of in the East. Now their brief spring is over. There is no one to blame for this; it is the result of
5   Nature's simplest laws!" We must all agree that it is impossible that anything can be firmer than this, or show a surer faith in the working of free-trade, as our Liberal friends understand and employ it.

But, if we still at all doubt whether the indefinite multiplica-
10 tion of manufactories and small houses can be such an absolute good in itself as to counterbalance the indefinite multiplication of poor people, we shall learn that this multiplication of poor people, too, is an absolute good in itself, and the result of divine and beautiful laws. This is indeed a favourite thesis with
15 our Philistine friends, and I have already noticed the pride and gratitude with which they receive certain articles in the *Times,* dilating in thankful and solemn language on the majestic growth of our population. But I prefer to quote now, on this topic, the words of an ingenious young Scotch writer, Mr.
20 Robert Buchanan, because he invests with so much imagination and poetry this current idea of the blessed and even divine character which the multiplying of population is supposed in itself to have. "We move to multiplicity," says Mr. Robert Buchanan. "If there is one quality which seems God's, and his
25 exclusively, it seems that divine philoprogenitiveness, that passionate love of distribution and expansion into living forms. Every animal added seems a new ecstasy to the Maker; every life added, a new embodiment of his love. He would *swarm* the earth with beings. There are never enough. Life, life, life,—
30 faces gleaming, hearts beating, must fill every cranny. Not a corner is suffered to remain empty. The whole earth breeds, and God glories."

It is a little unjust, perhaps, to attribute to the Divinity exclusively this philoprogenitiveness, which the British Philistine,
35 and the poorer class of Irish, may certainly claim to share with him; yet how inspiriting is here the whole strain of thought! and these beautiful words, too, I carry about with me in the East of London, and often read them there. They are quite in

agreement with the popular language one is accustomed to hear about children and large families, which describes children as *sent*. And a line of poetry, which Mr. Robert Buchanan throws in presently after the poetical prose I have quoted,— 5

"'Tis the old story of the fig-leaf time"—

this fine line, too, naturally connects itself, when one is in the East of London, with the idea of God's desire to *swarm* the earth with beings; because the swarming of the earth with beings does indeed, in the East of London, so seem to revive *the old* 10 *story of the fig-leaf time*, such a number of the people one meets there having hardly a rag to cover them; and the more the swarming goes on, the more it promises to revive this old story. And when the story is perfectly revived, the swarming quite completed, and every cranny choke-full, then, too, no 15 doubt, the faces in the East of London will be gleaming faces, which Mr. Robert Buchanan says it is God's desire they should be, and which every one must perceive they are not at present, but, on the contrary, very miserable.

But to prevent all this philosophy and poetry from quite run- 20 ning away with us, and making us think with the *Times*, and our practical Liberal free-traders, and the British Philistines generally, that the increase of houses and manufactories, or the increase of population, are absolute goods in themselves, to be mechanically pursued, and to be worshipped like fetishes,—to 25 prevent this, we have got that notion of ours immovably fixed, of which I have long ago spoken, the notion that culture, or the study of perfection, leads us to conceive of no perfection as being real which is not a *general* perfection, embracing all our fellow-men with whom we have to do. Such is the sympa- 30 thy which binds humanity together, that we are indeed, as our religion says, members of one body, and if one member suffer, all the members suffer with it. Individual perfection is impossible so long as the rest of mankind are not perfected along with us. "The *multitude* of the wise is the welfare of the world," 35 says the wise man. And to this effect that excellent and often-quoted guide of ours, Bishop Wilson, has some striking words:

—"It is not," says he, "so much our neighbour's interest as our own that we love him." And again he says: "Our salvation does in some measure depend upon that of others." And the author of the *Imitation* puts the same thing admirably when he says:
—"*Obscurior etiam via ad cœlum videbatur quando tam pauci regnum cœlorum quærere curabant;* the fewer there are who follow the way to perfection, the harder that way is to find." So all our fellow-men, in the East of London and elsewhere, we must take along with us in the progress towards perfection, if we ourselves really, as we profess, want to be perfect; and we must not let the worship of any fetish, any machinery, such as manufactures or population,—which are not, like perfection, absolute goods in themselves, though we think them so,—create for us such a multitude of miserable, sunken, and ignorant human beings, that to carry them all along with us is impossible, and perforce they must for the most part be left by us in their degradation and wretchedness. But evidently the conception of free-trade, on which our Liberal friends vaunt themselves, and in which they think they have found the secret of national prosperity,—evidently, I say, the mere unfettered pursuit of the production of wealth, and the mere mechanical multiplying, for this end, of manufactures and population, threatens to create for us, if it has not created already, those vast, miserable, unmanageable masses of sunken people, to the existence of which we are, as we have seen, absolutely forbidden to reconcile ourselves, in spite of all that the philosophy of the *Times* and the poetry of Mr. Robert Buchanan may say to persuade us.

Hebraism in general seems powerless, almost as powerless as our free-trading Liberal friends, to deal efficaciously with our ever-accumulating masses of pauperism, and to prevent their accumulating still more. Hebraism builds churches, indeed, for these masses, and sends missionaries among them; above all, it sets itself against the social necessitarianism of the *Times,* and refuses to accept their degradation as inevitable. But with regard to their ever-increasing accumulation, it seems to be led to the very same conclusions, though from a point of view of its own, as our free-trading Liberal friends. Hebraism, with that mechanical and misleading use of the letter of Scripture on which we have already commented, is governed by such texts as: *Be fruitful and multiply*, the edict of God's law, as Mr. Chambers would say; or by the declaration of what he would call God's word in the Psalms, that the man who has a great number of children is thereby made happy. And in conjunction with such texts as these, Hebraism is apt to place another text: *The poor shall never cease out of the land.* Thus Hebraism is conducted to nearly the same notion as the popular mind and as Mr. Robert Buchanan, that children are *sent*, and that the divine nature takes a delight in swarming the East End of London with paupers. Only, when they are perishing in their helplessness and wretchedness, it asserts the Christian duty of succouring them, instead of saying, like the *Times:* "Now their brief spring is over; there is nobody to blame for this; it is the result of Nature's simplest laws!" But, like the *Times*, Hebraism despairs of any help from knowledge and says that "what is wanted is not the light of speculation."

I remember, only the other day, a good man looking with me upon a multitude of children who were gathered before us in one of the most miserable regions of London,—children eaten up with disease, half-sized, half-fed, half-clothed, neglected by their parents, without health, without home, without hope,— said to me: "The one thing really needful is to teach these little ones to succour one another, if only with a cup of cold water; but now, from one end of the country to the other, one hears nothing but the cry for knowledge, knowledge, knowledge!" And yet surely, so long as these children are there in these festering masses, without health, without home, without hope, and so long as their multitude is perpetually swelling, charged with misery they must still be for themselves, charged with misery they must still be for us, whether they help one another with a cup of cold water or no; and the knowledge how to prevent their accumulating is necessary, even to give their moral life and growth a fair chance!

May we not, therefore, say, that neither the true Hebraism of this good man, willing to spend and be spent for these sunken multitudes, nor what I may call the spurious Hebraism of our

free-trading Liberal friends,—mechanically worshipping their
fetish of the production of wealth and of the increase of manufactures and population, and looking neither to the right nor
left so long as this increase goes on,—avail us much here; and
5   that here, again, what we want is Hellenism, the letting our
consciousness play freely and simply upon the facts before us,
and listening to what it tells us of the intelligible law of things
as concerns them? And surely what it tells us is, that a man's
children are not really *sent,* any more than the pictures upon
10 his wall, or the horses in his stable are *sent;* and that to bring
people into the world, when one cannot afford to keep them
and oneself decently and not too precariously, or to bring
more of them into the world than one can afford to keep thus,
is, whatever the *Times* and Mr. Robert Buchanan may say, by
15 no means an accomplishment of the divine will or a fulfilment
of Nature's simplest laws, but is just as wrong, just as contrary
to reason and the will of God, as for a man to have horses, or
carriages, or pictures, when he cannot afford them, or to have
more of them than he can afford; and that, in the one case as in
20 the other, the larger the scale on which the violation of reason's
law is practised, and the longer it is persisted in, the greater
must be the confusion and final trouble. Surely no laudations
of free-trade, no meetings of bishops and clergy in the East
End of London, no reading of papers and reports, can tell us
25 anything about our social condition which it more concerns us
to know than that! and not only to know, but habitually to
have the knowledge present, and to act upon it as one acts
upon the knowledge that water wets and fire burns! And not
only the sunken populace of our great cities are concerned to
30 know it, and the pauper twentieth of our population; we Philistines of the middle class, too, are concerned to know it, and
all who have to set themselves to make progress in perfection.
      But we all know it already! some one will say; it is the simplest
law of prudence. But how little reality must there be in our
35 knowledge of it; how little can we be putting it in practice;
how little is it likely to penetrate among the poor and struggling masses of our population, and to better our condition, so
long as an unintelligent Hebraism of one sort keeps repeating

as an absolute eternal word of God the psalm-verse which says that the man who has a great many children is happy; or an unintelligent Hebraism of another sort,—that is to say, a blind following of certain stock notions as infallible,—keeps assigning as an absolute proof of national prosperity the multiplying 5 of manufactures and population! Surely, the one set of Hebraisers have to learn that their psalm-verse was composed at the resettlement of Jerusalem after the Captivity, when the Jews of Jerusalem were a handful, an undermanned garrison, and every child was a blessing; and that the word of God, or the 10 voice of the divine order of things, declares the possession of a great many children to be a blessing only when it really is so! And the other set of Hebraisers, have they not to learn that if they call their private acquaintances imprudent or unlucky, when, with no means of support for them or with precarious 15 means, they have a large family of children, then they ought not to call the State well managed and prosperous merely because its manufactures and its citizens multiply, if the manufactures, which bring new citizens into existence just as much as if they had actually begotten them, bring more of them into 20 existence than they can maintain, or are too precarious to go on maintaining those whom for a while they maintained?

Hellenism, surely, or the habit of fixing our mind upon the intelligible law of things, is most salutary if it makes us see that the only absolute good, the only absolute and eternal object pre- 25 scribed to us by God's law, or the divine order of things, is the progress towards perfection,—our own progress towards it and the progress of humanity. And therefore, for every individual man, and for every society of men, the possession and multiplication of children, like the possession and multiplica- 30 tion of horses and pictures, is to be accounted good or bad, not in itself, but with reference to this object and the progress towards it. And as no man is to be excused in having horses or pictures, if his having them hinders his own or others' progress towards perfection and makes them lead a servile and ignoble 35 life, so is no man to be excused for having children if his having them makes him or others lead this. Plain thoughts of this kind are surely the spontaneous product of our conscious-

ness, when it is allowed to play freely and disinterestedly upon the actual facts of our social condition, and upon our stock notions and stock habits in respect to it. Firmly grasped and simply uttered, they are more likely, one cannot but think, to
5 better that condition, than is the mechanical pursuit of free-trade by our Liberal friends.

V

So that, here as elsewhere, the practical operations of our Liberal friends, by which they set so much store, and in which they invite us to join them and to show what Mr. Bright calls a
10 commendable interest, do not seem to us so practical for real good as they think; and our Liberal friends seem to us themselves to need to Hellenise, as we say, a little,—that is, to examine into the nature of real good, and to listen to what their consciousness tells them about it,—rather than to pursue
15 with such heat and confidence their present practical operations. And it is clear that they have no just cause, so far as regards several operations of theirs which we have canvassed, to reproach us with delicate Conservative scepticism. For often by Hellenising we seem to subvert stock Conservative notions
20 and usages more effectually than they subvert them by Hebraising. But, in truth, the free spontaneous play of consciousness with which culture tries to float our stock habits of thinking and acting, is by its very nature, as has been said, disinterested. Sometimes the result of floating them may be agreeable to this
25 party, sometimes to that; now it may be unwelcome to our so-called Liberals, now to our so-called Conservatives; but what culture seeks is, above all, to *float* them, to prevent their being stiff and stark pieces of petrifaction any longer. It is mere Hebraising, if we stop short, and refuse to let our conscious-
30 ness play freely, whenever we or our friends do not happen to like what it discovers to us. This is to make the Liberal party, or the Conservative party, our one thing needful, instead of human perfection; and we have seen what mischief arises from making an even greater thing than the Liberal or the Conserva-

tive party,—the predominance of the moral side in man,—our one thing needful. But wherever the free play of our consciousness leads us, we shall follow; believing that in this way we shall tend to make good at all points what is wanting to us, and so shall be brought nearer to our complete human perfection. 5

Everything, in short, confirms us in the doctrine, so unpalatable to the believers in action, that our main business at the present moment is not so much to work away at certain crude reforms of which we have already the scheme in our own mind, as 10 to create, through the help of that culture which at the very outset we began by praising and recommending, a frame of mind out of which the schemes of really fruitful reforms may with time grow. At any rate, we ourselves must put up with our friends' impatience, and with their reproaches against cul- 15 tivated inaction, and must still decline to lend a hand to their practical operations, until we, for our own part at least, have grown a little clearer about the nature of real good, and have arrived nearer to a condition of mind out of which really fruitful and solid operations may spring. 20

In the meanwhile, since our Liberal friends keep loudly and resolutely assuring us that their actual operations at present are fruitful and solid, let us in each case keep testing these operations in the simple way we have indicated, by letting the natural stream of our consciousness flow over them freely; and if 25 they stand this test successfully, then let us give them our interest, but not else.

Conclusion

And so we bring to an end what we had to say in praise of culture, and in evidence of its special utility for the circumstances
in which we find ourselves, and the confusion which environs us.
Through culture seems to lie our way, not only to perfection,
but even to safety. Resolutely refusing to lend a hand to the
imperfect operations of our Liberal friends, disregarding their
impatience, taunts, and reproaches, firmly bent on trying to
find in the intelligible laws of things a firmer and sounder basis
for future practice than any which we have at present, and
believing this search and discovery to be, for our generation
and circumstances, of yet more vital and pressing importance
than practice itself, we nevertheless may do more, perhaps, we
poor disparaged followers of culture, to make the actual present, and the frame of society in which we live, solid and
seaworthy, than all which our bustling politicians can do.

For we have seen how much of our disorders and perplexities
is due to the disbelief, among the classes and combinations of
men, Barbarian or Philistine, which have hitherto governed
our society, in right reason, in a paramount best self; to the
inevitable decay and break-up of the organisations by which,
asserting and expressing in these organisations their ordinary
self only, they have so long ruled us; and to their irresolution,
when the society, which their conscience tells them they have
made and still manage not with right reason but with their
ordinary self, is rudely shaken, in offering resistance to its
subverters. But for us,—who believe in right reason, in the
duty and possibility of extricating and elevating our best self,
in the progress of humanity towards perfection,—for us the
framework of society, that theatre on which this august drama

has to unroll itself, is sacred; and whoever administers it, and however we may seek to remove them from their tenure of administration, yet, while they administer, we steadily and with undivided heart support them in repressing anarchy and disorder; because without order there can be no society, and without society there can be no human perfection.

And this opinion of the intolerableness of anarchy we can never forsake, however our Liberal friends may think a little rioting, and what they call popular demonstrations, useful sometimes to their own interests and to the interests of the valuable practical operations they have in hand, and however they may preach the right of an Englishman to be left to do as far as possible what he likes, and the duty of his government to indulge him and connive as much as possible and abstain from all harshness of repression. And even when they artfully show us operations which are undoubtedly precious, such as the abolition of the slave-trade, and ask us if, for their sake, foolish and obstinate governments may not wholesomely be frightened by a little disturbance, the good design in view and the difficulty of overcoming opposition to it being considered,—still we say no, and that monster-processions in the streets and forcible irruptions into the parks, even in professed support of this good design, ought to be unflinchingly forbidden and repressed; and that far more is lost than is gained by permitting them. Because a State in which law is authoritative and sovereign, a firm and settled course of public order, is requisite if man is to bring to maturity anything precious and lasting now, or to found anything precious and lasting for the future.

Thus, in our eyes, the very framework and exterior order of the State, whoever may administer the State, is sacred; and culture is the most resolute enemy of anarchy, because of the great hopes and designs for the State which culture teaches us to nourish. But as, believing in right reason, and having faith in the progress of humanity towards perfection, and ever labouring for this end, we grow to have clearer sight of the ideas of right reason, and of the elements and helps of perfection, and come gradually to fill the framework of the State with them, to fashion its internal composition and all its laws and institutions conformably to them, and to make the State more and more the expression, as we say, of our best self, which is not manifold, and vulgar, and unstable, and contentious, and ever-varying, but one, and noble, and secure, and peaceful, and the same for all mankind,—with what aversion shall we not *then* regard anarchy, with what firmness shall we not check it, when there is so much that is so precious which it will endanger!

So that, for the sake of the present, but far more for the sake of the future, the lovers of culture are unswervingly and with a good conscience the opposers of anarchy. And not as the Barbarians and Philistines, whose honesty and whose sense of humour make them shrink, as we have seen, from treating the State as too serious a thing, and from giving it too much power;—for indeed the only State they know of, and think they administer, is the expression of their ordinary self. And though the headstrong and violent extreme among them might gladly arm this with full authority, yet their virtuous mean is, as we have said, pricked in conscience at doing this; and so our Barbarian Secretaries of State let the Park railings be broken down, and our Philistine Alderman-Colonels let the London roughs rob and beat the bystanders. But we, beholding in the State no expression of our ordinary self, but even already, as it were, the appointed frame and prepared vessel of our best self, and, for the future, our best self's powerful, beneficent, and sacred expression and organ,—we are willing and resolved, even now, to strengthen against anarchy the trembling hands of our Barbarian Home Secretaries, and the feeble knees of our Philistine Alderman-Colonels; and to tell them, that it is not really in behalf of their own ordinary self that they are called to protect the Park railings, and to suppress the London roughs, but in behalf of the best self both of themselves and of all of us in the future.

Nevertheless, though for resisting anarchy the lovers of culture may prize and employ fire and strength, yet they must, at the same time, bear constantly in mind that it is not at this moment true, what the majority of people tell us, that the world wants fire and strength more than sweetness and light, and that things are for the most part to be settled first and understood afterwards. We have seen how much of our present perplexities and confusion this untrue notion of the majority of people amongst us has caused, and tends to perpetuate. Therefore the true business of the friends of culture now is, to dissipate this false notion, to spread the belief in right reason and in a firm intelligible law of things, and to get men to try, in preference to staunchly acting with imperfect knowledge, to obtain some sounder basis of knowledge on which to act. This is what the friends and lovers of culture have to do, however the believers in action may grow impatient with us for saying so, and may insist on our lending a hand to their practical operations and showing a commendable interest in them.

To this insistence we must indeed turn a deaf ear. But neither, on the other hand, must the friends of culture expect to take the believers in action by storm, or to be visibly and speedily important, and to rule and cut a figure in the world. Aristotle says that those for whom alone ideas and the pursuit of the intelligible law of things can, in general, have much attraction, are principally the young, filled with generous spirit and with a passion for perfection; but the mass of mankind, he says, follow seeming goods for real, bestowing hardly a thought upon true sweetness and light;—"and to *their* lives," he adds mournfully, "who can give another and a better rhythm?" But, although those chiefly attracted by sweetness and light will probably always be the young and enthusiastic, and culture must not hope to take the mass of mankind by storm, yet we will not therefore, for our own day and for our own people, admit and rest in the desponding sentence of Aristotle. For is not this the right crown of the long discipline of Hebraism, and the due fruit of mankind's centuries of painful schooling in self-conquest, and the just reward, above all, of the strenuous energy of our own nation and kindred in dealing honestly with itself and walking steadfastly according to the best light it knows,—that when in the fulness of time it has reason and beauty offered to it, and the law of things as they really are, it should at last walk by this true light with the same staunchness and zeal with which it formerly walked by its

imperfect light? And thus man's two great natural forces, Hebraism and Hellenism, will no longer be dissociated and rival, but will be a joint force of right thinking and strong doing to carry him on towards perfection. This is what the lovers of
5   culture may perhaps dare to augur for such a nation as ours.

Therefore, however great the changes to be accomplished, and however dense the array of Barbarians, Philistines, and Populace, we will neither despair on the one hand, nor, on the other, threaten violent revolution and change. But we will look
10 forward cheerfully and hopefully to "a revolution," as the Duke of Wellington said, "by due course of law;" though not exactly such laws as our Liberal friends are now, with their actual lights, fond of offering to us.

But if despondency and violence are both of them forbidden
15 to the believer in culture, yet neither, on the other hand, is public life and direct political action much permitted to him. For it is his business, as we have seen, to get the present believers in action, and lovers of political talking and doing, to make a return upon their own minds, scrutinise their stock notions
20 and habits much more, value their present talking and doing much less; in order that, by learning to think more clearly, they may come at last to act less confusedly. But how shall we persuade our Barbarian to hold lightly to his feudal usages; how shall we persuade our Nonconformist that his time spent
25 in agitating for the abolition of church-establishments would have been better spent in getting worthier ideas of God and the ordering of the world, or his time spent in battling for voluntaryism in education better spent in learning to value and found a public and national culture; how shall we persuade,
30 finally, our Alderman-Colonel not to be content with sitting in the hall of judgment or marching at the head of his men of war, without some knowledge how to perform judgment and how to direct men of war,—how, I say, shall we persuade all these of this, if our Alderman-Colonel sees that we want to get
35 his leading-staff and his scales of justice for our own hands; or the Nonconformist, that we want for ourselves his platform; or the Barbarian, that we want for ourselves his pre-eminency and function? Certainly they will be less slow to believe, as we

want them to believe, that the intelligible law of things has in itself something desirable and precious, and that all place, function, and bustle are hollow goods without it, if they see that we ourselves can content ourselves with this law, and find in it our satisfaction, without making it an instrument to give 5 us for ourselves place, function, and bustle.

And although Mr. Sidgwick says that social usefulness really means "losing oneself in a mass of disagreeable, hard, mechanical details," and though all the believers in action are fond of asserting the same thing, yet, as to lose ourselves is not what 10 we want, but to find ourselves through finding the intelligible law of things, this assertion too we shall not blindly accept, but shall sift and try it a little first. And if we see that because the believers in action, forgetting Goethe's maxim, "to act is easy, to think is hard," imagine there is some wonderful virtue 15 in losing oneself in a mass of mechanical details, therefore they excuse themselves from much thought about the clear ideas which ought to govern these details, then we shall give our chief care and pains to seeking out those ideas and to setting them forth; being persuaded that if we have the ideas firm and 20 clear, the mechanical details for their execution will come a great deal more simply and easily than we now suppose.

At this exciting juncture, then, while so many of the lovers of new ideas, somewhat weary, as we too are, of the stock performances of our Liberal friends upon the political stage, are 25 disposed to rush valiantly upon this public stage themselves, we cannot at all think that for a wise lover of new ideas this stage is the right one. Plenty of people there will be without us,—country gentlemen in search of a club, demagogues in search of a tub, lawyers in search of a place, industrialists in 30 search of gentility,—who will come from the east and from the west, and will sit down at that Thyestean banquet of claptrap which English public life for these many years past has been. And, so long as those old organisations, of which we have seen the insufficiency,—those expressions of our ordinary 35 self, Barbarian or Philistine,—have force anywhere, they will have force in Parliament. There, the man whom the Barbarians send, cannot but be impelled to please the Barbarians' ordinary

self, and their natural taste for the bathos; and the man whom
the Philistines send, cannot but be impelled to please those of
the Philistines. Parliamentary Conservatism will and must long
mean there, that the Barbarians should keep their heritage; and
Parliamentary Liberalism, that the Barbarians should pass
away, as they will pass away, and that into their heritage the
Philistines should enter. This seems, indeed, to be the true and
authentic promise of which our Liberal friends and Mr. Bright
believe themselves the heirs, and the goal of that great man's
labours. Presently, perhaps, Mr. Odger and Mr. Bradlaugh will
be there with their mission to oust both Barbarians and Philistines, and to get the heritage for the Populace.

We, on the other hand, are for giving the heritage neither to
the Barbarians nor to the Philistines, nor yet to the Populace; but
we are for the transformation of each and all of these according to the law of perfection. Through the length and breadth
of our nation a sense,—vague and obscure as yet,—of weariness with the old organisations, of desire for this transformation, works and grows. In the House of Commons the old
organisations must inevitably be most enduring and strongest,
the transformation must inevitably be longest in showing
itself; and it may truly be averred, therefore, that at the present juncture the centre of movement is not in the House of
Commons. It is in the fermenting mind of the nation; and his is
for the next twenty years the real influence who can address
himself to this.

Pericles was perhaps the most perfect public speaker who ever
lived, for he was the man who most perfectly combined
thought and wisdom with feeling and eloquence. Yet Plato
brings in Alcibiades declaring, that men went away from the
oratory of Pericles, saying it was very fine, it was very good,
and afterwards thinking no more about it; but they went away
from hearing Socrates talk, he says, with the point of what he
had said sticking fast in their minds, and they could not get rid
of it. Socrates has drunk his hemlock and is dead; but in his
own breast does not every man carry about with him a possible Socrates, in that power of a disinterested play of consciousness upon his stock notions and habits, of which this wise

and admirable man gave all through his lifetime the great example, and which was the secret of his incomparable influence? And he who leads men to call forth and exercise in themselves this power, and who busily calls it forth and exercises it in himself, is at the present moment, perhaps, as Socrates was in his time, more in concert with the vital working of men's minds, and more effectually significant, than any House of Commons' orator, or practical operator in politics.

Every one is now boasting of what he has done to educate men's minds and to give things the course they are taking. Mr. Disraeli educates, Mr. Bright educates, Mr. Beales educates. We, indeed, pretend to educate no one, for we are still engaged in trying to clear and educate ourselves. But we are sure that the endeavour to reach, through culture, the firm intelligible law of things, we are sure that the detaching ourselves from our stock notions and habits, that a more free play of consciousness, an increased desire for sweetness and light, and all the bent which we call Hellenising, is the master-impulse even now of the life of our nation and of humanity,—somewhat obscurely perhaps for this actual moment, but decisively and certainly for the immediate future; and that those who work for this are the sovereign educators.

Docile echoes of the eternal voice, pliant organs of the infinite will, such workers are going along with the essential movement of the world; and this is their strength, and their happy and divine fortune. For if the believers in action, who are so impatient with us and call us effeminate, had had the same good fortune, they would, no doubt, have surpassed us in this sphere of vital influence by all the superiority of their genius and energy over ours. But now we go the way the human race is going, while they abolish the Irish Church by the power of the Nonconformists' antipathy to establishments, or they enable a man to marry his deceased wife's sister.

Preface

(1869)

My foremost design in writing this Preface is to address a word of exhortation to the Society for Promoting Christian Knowledge. In the essay which follows, the reader will often find Bishop Wilson quoted. To me and to the members of the Society for Promoting Christian Knowledge his name and writings are still, no doubt, familiar. But the world is fast going away from old-fashioned people of his sort, and I learnt with consternation lately from a brilliant and distinguished votary of the natural sciences, that he had never so much as heard of Bishop Wilson, and that he imagined me to have invented him. At a moment when the Courts of Law have just taken off the embargo from the recreative religion furnished on Sundays by my gifted acquaintance and others, and when St. Martin's Hall and the Alhambra will soon be beginning again to resound with their pulpit-eloquence, it distresses one to think that the new lights should not only have, in general, a very low opinion of the preachers of the old religion, but that they should have it without knowing the best that these preachers can do. And that they are in this case is owing in part, certainly, to the negligence of the Christian Knowledge Society. In the old times they used to print and spread abroad Bishop Wilson's *Maxims of Piety and Christianity*. The copy of this work which I use is one of their publications, bearing their imprint, and bound in the well-known brown calf which they made familiar to our childhood; but the date of my copy is 1812. I know of no copy besides, and I believe the work is no longer one of those printed and circulated by the Society.[1]

[1] The Christian Knowledge Society has, since 1869, republished the *Maxims* of Bishop Wilson.

Hence the error, flattering, I own, to me personally, yet in itself to be regretted, of the distinguished physicist already mentioned.

But Bishop Wilson's *Maxims* deserve to be circulated as a religious book, not only by comparison with the cartloads of rubbish circulated at present under this designation, but for their own sake, and even by comparison with the other works of the same author. Over the far better known *Sacra Privata* they have this advantage, that they were prepared by him for his own private use, while the *Sacra Privata* were prepared by him for the use of the public. The *Maxims* were never meant to be printed, and have on that account, like a work of, doubtless, far deeper emotion and power, the *Meditations* of Marcus Aurelius, something peculiarly sincere and first-hand about them. Some of the best things from the *Maxims* have passed into the *Sacra Privata*. Still, in the *Maxims*, we have them as they first arose; and whereas, too, in the *Sacra Privata* the writer speaks very often as one of the clergy, and as addressing the clergy, in the *Maxims* he almost always speaks solely as a man. I am not saying a word against the *Sacra Privata*, for which I have the highest respect; only the *Maxims* seem to me a better and more edifying book still. They should be read, as Joubert says Nicole should be read, with a direct aim at practice. The reader will leave on one side things which, from the change of time and from the changed point of view which the change of time inevitably brings with it, no longer suit him; enough will remain to serve as a sample of the very best, perhaps, which our nation and race can do in the way of religious writing. M. Michelet makes it a reproach to us that, in all the doubt as to the real author of the *Imitation*, no one has ever dreamed of ascribing that work to an Englishman. It is true, the *Imitation* could not well have been written by an Englishman; the religious delicacy and the profound asceticism of that admirable book are hardly in our nature. This would be more of a reproach to us if in poetry, which requires, no less than religion, a true delicacy of spiritual perception, our race had not done great things; and if the *Imitation*, exquisite as it is, did not, as I have elsewhere remarked, belong to a class of works in which the perfect balance of human nature is lost, and which have therefore, as spiritual productions, in their contents something excessive and morbid, in their form something not thoroughly sound. On a lower range than the *Imitation*, and awakening in our nature chords less poetical and delicate, the *Maxims* of 5 Bishop Wilson are, as a religious work, far more solid. To the most sincere ardour and unction, Bishop Wilson unites, in these *Maxims*, that downright honesty and plain good sense which our English race has so powerfully applied to the divine impossibilities of religion; by which it has brought religion so 10 much into practical life, and has done its allotted part in promoting upon earth the kingdom of God.

With ardour and unction religion, as we all know, may still be fanatical; with honesty and good sense, it may still be prosaic; and the fruit of honesty and good sense united with ardour 15 and unction is often only a prosaic religion held fanatically. Bishop Wilson's excellence lies in a balance of the four qualities, and in a fulness and perfection of them, which makes this untoward result impossible. His unction is so perfect, and in such happy alliance with his good sense, that it becomes ten- 20 derness and fervent charity. His good sense is so perfect, and in such happy alliance with his unction, that it becomes moderation and insight. While, therefore, the type of religion exhibited in his *Maxims* is English, it is yet a type of a far higher kind than is in general reached by Bishop Wilson's country- 25 men; and yet, being English, it is possible and attainable for them. And so I conclude as I began, by saying that a work of this sort is one which the Society for Promoting Christian Knowledge should not suffer to remain out of print and out of currency. 30

And now to pass to the matters canvassed in the following [i.e., preceding] essay. The whole scope of the essay is to recommend culture as the great help out of our present difficulties; culture being a pursuit of our total perfection by means of getting to know, on all the matters which most concern us, the 35 best which has been thought and said in the world; and through this knowledge, turning a stream of fresh and free thought upon our stock notions and habits, which we now follow staunchly but mechanically, vainly imagining that there is a virtue in following them staunchly which makes up for the mischief of following them mechanically. This, and this alone, is the scope of the following [i.e., preceding] essay. And the culture we recommend is, above all, an inward operation.

But we are often supposed, when we criticise by the help of culture some imperfect doing or other, to have in our eye some well-known rival plan of doing, which we want to serve and recommend. Thus, for instance, because we have freely pointed out the dangers and inconveniences to which our literature is exposed in the absence of any centre of taste and authority like the French Academy, it is constantly said that we want to introduce here in England an institution like the French Academy. We have, indeed, expressly declared that we wanted no such thing; but let us notice how it is just our worship of machinery, and of external doing, which leads to this charge being brought; and how the inwardness of culture makes us seize, for watching and cure, the faults to which our want of an Academy inclines us, and yet prevents us from trusting to an arm of flesh, as the Puritans say,—from blindly flying to this outward machinery of an Academy, in order to help ourselves. For the very same culture and free inward play of thought which shows how the Corinthian style, or the whimsies about the One Primeval Language, are generated and strengthened in the absence of an Academy, shows us, too, how little any Academy, such as we should be likely to get, would cure them. Every one who knows the characteristics of our national life, and the tendencies so fully discussed in the following [i.e., preceding] pages, knows exactly what an English Academy would be like. One can see the happy family in one's mind's eye as distinctly as if it were already constituted. Lord Stanhope, the Dean of St. Paul's,[1] the Bishop of Oxford,[2] Mr. Gladstone, the Dean of Westminster, Mr. Froude, Mr. Henry Reeve,—everything which is influential, accomplished, and distinguished; and then, some fine morning, a dissatisfaction of the public mind with this brilliant and select coterie, a flight of Corinthian leading articles, and an irruption of Mr. G. A.

[1] The late Dean Milman.   [2] The late Bishop Wilberforce.

Sala. Clearly, this is not what will do us good. The very same faults,—the want of sensitiveness of intellectual conscience, the disbelief in right reason, the dislike of authority,—which have hindered our having an Academy and have worked injuriously in our literature, would also hinder us from making our Academy, if we established it, one which would really correct them. And culture, which shows us truly the faults to be corrected, shows us this also just as truly.

Natural, as we have said, the sort of misunderstanding just noticed is; yet our usefulness depends upon our being able to clear it away, and to convince those who mechanically serve some stock notion or operation, and thereby go astray, that it is not culture's work or aim to give the victory to some rival fetish, but simply to turn a free and fresh stream of thought upon the whole matter in question. In a thing of more immediate interest, just now, than any question of an Academy, the like misunderstanding prevails; and until it is dissipated, culture can do no good work in the matter. When we criticise the present operation of disestablishing the Irish Church, not by the power of reason and justice, but by the power of the antipathy of the Protestant Nonconformists, English and Scotch, to establishments, we are called enemies of the Nonconformists, blind partisans of the Anglican Establishment, possessed with the one desire to help the clergy and to harm the Dissenters. More than a few words we must give to showing how erroneous are these charges; because if they were true, we should be actually subverting our own design, and playing false to that culture which it is our very purpose to recommend.

Certainly we are no enemies of the Nonconformists; for, on the contrary, what we aim at is their perfection. But culture, which is the study of perfection, leads us, as we in the following [i.e., preceding] pages have shown, to conceive of true human perfection as a *harmonious* perfection, developing all sides of our humanity; and as a *general* perfection, developing all parts of our society. For if one member suffer, the other members must suffer with it; and the fewer there are that follow the true way of salvation, the harder that way is to find. And while the Nonconformists, the successors and representatives of the

Puritans, and like them staunchly walking by the best light they have, make a large part of what is strongest and most serious in this nation, and therefore attract our respect and interest, yet all which, in what follows [i.e., precedes], is said about
5 Hebraism and Hellenism, has for its main result to show how our Puritans, ancient and modern, have not enough added to their care for walking staunchly by the best light they have, a care that that light be not darkness; how they have developed one side of their humanity at the expense of all others, and have
10 become incomplete and mutilated men in consequence. Thus falling short of harmonious perfection, they fail to follow the true way of salvation. Therefore that way is made the harder for others to find, general perfection is put further off out of our reach, and the confusion and perplexity in which our so-
15 ciety now labours is increased by the Nonconformists rather than diminished by them. So, while we praise and esteem the zeal of the Nonconformists in walking staunchly by the best light they have, and desire to take no whit from it, we seek to add to this what we call sweetness and light, and to develop
20 their full humanity more perfectly. To seek this is certainly not to be the enemy of the Nonconformists.

But now, with these ideas in our head, we come upon the operation for disestablishing the Irish Church by the power of the Nonconformists' antipathy to religious establishments and
25 endowments. And we see Liberal statesmen, for whose purpose this antipathy happens to be convenient, flattering it all they can; saying that though they have no intention of laying hands on an Establishment which is efficient and popular, like the Anglican Establishment here in England, yet it is in the ab-
30 stract a fine and good thing that religion should be left to the voluntary support of its promoters, and should thus gain in energy and independence; and Mr. Gladstone has no words strong enough to express his admiration of the refusal of State-aid by the Irish Roman Catholics, who have never yet been
35 seriously asked to accept it, but who would a good deal embarrass him if they demanded it. And we see philosophical politicians with a turn for swimming with the stream, and philosophical divines with the same turn, seeking to give a sort of

grand stamp of generality and solemnity to this antipathy of
the Nonconformists, and to dress it out as a law of human
progress in the future. Now, nothing can be pleasanter than
swimming with the stream; and we might gladly, if we could,
try in our unsystematic way to take part in labours at once so 5
philosophical and so popular. But we have got fixed in our
minds that a more full and harmonious development of their
humanity is what the Nonconformists most want, that narrowness, one-sidedness, and incompleteness is what they most
suffer from; in a word, that in what we call *provinciality* they 10
abound, but in what we may call *totality* they fall short.

And they fall short more than the members of Establishments.
The great works by which, not only in literature, art, and
science generally, but in religion itself, the human spirit has
manifested its approaches to totality and to a full, harmonious 15
perfection, and by which it stimulates and helps forward the
world's general perfection, come, not from Nonconformists,
but from men who either belong to Establishments or have
been trained in them. A Nonconformist minister, the Rev.
Edward White, who has written a temperate and well-rea- 20
soned pamphlet against Church Establishments, says that "the
unendowed and unestablished communities of England exert
full as much moral and ennobling influence upon the conduct of
statesmen as that Church which is both established and endowed." That depends upon what one means by moral and 25
ennobling influence. The believer in machinery may think that
to get a Government to abolish Church-rates or to legalise
marriage with a deceased wife's sister is to exert a moral and
ennobling influence upon Government. But a lover of perfection, who looks to inward ripeness for the true springs of 30
conduct, will surely think that as Shakspeare has done more
for the inward ripeness of our statesmen than Dr. Watts, and
has, therefore, done more to moralise and ennoble them, so an
Establishment which has produced Hooker, Barrow, Butler,
has done more to moralise and ennoble English statesmen and 35
their conduct than communities which have produced the
Nonconformist divines. The fruitful men of English Puritanism and Nonconformity are men who were trained within the

pale of the Establishment,—Milton, Baxter, Wesley. A generation or two outside the Establishment, and Puritanism produces men of national mark no more. With the same doctrine
and discipline, men of national mark are produced in Scotland;
but in an Establishment. With the same doctrine and discipline, men of national and even European mark are produced
in Germany, Switzerland, France; but in Establishments. Only
two religious disciplines seem exempted, or comparatively exempted, from the operation of the law which appears to forbid
the rearing, outside of national Churches, of men of the highest
spiritual significance. These two are the Roman Catholic and
the Jewish. And these, both of them, rest on Establishments,
which, though not indeed national, are cosmopolitan; and perhaps here, what the individual man does not lose by these
conditions of his rearing, the citizen, and the State of which he
is a citizen, loses.

What, now, can be the reason of this undeniable provincialism
of the English Puritans and Protestant Nonconformists? Men of
genius and character are born and reared in this medium as in
any other. From the faults of the mass such men will always be
comparatively free, and they will always excite our interest;
yet in this medium they seem to have a special difficulty in
breaking through what bounds them, and in developing their
totality. Surely the reason is, that the Nonconformist is not in
contact with the main current of national life, like the member of an Establishment. In a matter of such deep and vital
concern as religion, this separation from the main current of
the national life has peculiar importance. In the following
[i.e., preceding] essay we have discussed at length the tendency in us to *Hebraise*, as we call it; that is, to sacrifice all
other sides of our being to the religious side. This tendency
has its cause in the divine beauty and grandeur of religion, and
bears affecting testimony to them. But we have seen that it has
dangers for us, we have seen that it leads to a narrow and
twisted growth of our religious side itself, and to a failure in
perfection. But if we tend to Hebraise even in an Establishment, with the main current of national life flowing round us,
and reminding us in all ways of the variety and fulness of

human existence,—by a Church which is historical as the State itself is historical, and whose order, ceremonies, and monuments reach, like those of the State, far beyond any fancies and devisings of ours; and by institutions such as the Universities, formed to defend and advance that very culture and many-sided development which it is the danger of Hebraising to make us neglect,—how much more must we tend to Hebraise when we lack these preventives. One may say that to be reared a member of a national Church is in itself a lesson of religious moderation, and a help towards culture and harmonious perfection. Instead of battling for his own private forms for expressing the inexpressible and defining the undefinable, a man takes those which have commended themselves most to the religious life of his nation; and while he may be sure that within those forms the religious side of his own nature may find its satisfaction, he has leisure and composure to satisfy other sides of his nature as well.

But with the member of a Nonconforming or self-made religious community, how different! The sectary's *eigene grosse Erfindungen*, as Goethe calls them,—the precious discoveries of himself and his friends for expressing the inexpressible and defining the undefinable in peculiar forms of their own, cannot but, as he has voluntarily chosen them, and is personally responsible for them, fill his whole mind. He is zealous to do battle for them and affirm them; for in affirming them he affirms himself, and that is what we all like. Other sides of his being are thus neglected, because the religious side, always tending in every serious man to predominance over our other spiritual sides, is in him made quite absorbing and tyrannous by the condition of self-assertion and challenge which he has chosen for himself. And just what is not essential in religion he comes to mistake for essential, and a thousand times the more readily because he has chosen it of himself; and religious activity he fancies to consist in battling for it. All this leaves him little leisure or inclination for culture; to which, besides, he has no great institutions not of his own making, like the Universities connected with the national Church to invite him; but only such institutions as, like the order and discipline of his

religion, he may have invented for himself, and invented under the sway of the narrow and tyrannous notions of religion fostered in him as we have seen. Thus, while a national establishment of religion favours totality, *hole-and-corner* forms of
5   religion (to use an expressive popular word) inevitably favour provincialism.

But the Nonconformists, and many of our Liberal friends along with them, have a plausible plan for getting rid of this provincialism, if, as they can hardly quite deny, it exists. "Let us
10 all be in the same boat," they cry; "open the Universities to everybody, and let there be no establishment of religion at all!" Open the Universities by all means; but, as to the second point about establishment, let us sift the proposal a little. It does seem at first a little like that proposal of the fox, who had lost
15 his own tail, to put all the other foxes in the same case by a general cutting off of tails; and we know that moralists have decided that the right course here was, not to adopt this plausible suggestion, and cut off tails all round, but rather that the other foxes should keep their tails, and that the fox without a
20 tail should get one. And so we might be inclined to urge, that, to cure the evil of the Nonconformists' provincialism, the right way can hardly be to provincialise us all round.

However, perhaps we shall not be provincialised. For Mr. White says that probably, "when all good men alike are placed
25 in a condition of religious equality, and the whole complicated iniquity of Government Church patronage is swept away, more of moral and ennobling influence than ever will be brought to bear upon the action of statesmen."

We already have an example of religious equality in our colo-
30 nies. "In the colonies," says *The Times*, "we see religious communities unfettered by State-control, and the State relieved from one of the most troublesome and irritating responsibilities." But America is the great example alleged by those who are against establishments for religion. Our topic at this moment is
35 the influence of religious establishments on culture; and it is remarkable that Mr. Bright, who has taken lately to representing himself as, above all, a promoter of reason and of the simple natural truth of things, and his policy as a fostering of

the growth of intelligence,—just the aims, as is well known, of culture also,—Mr. Bright, in a speech at Birmingham about education, seized on the very point which seems to concern our topic, when he said: "I believe the people of the United States have offered to the world more valuable information during the last forty years, than all Europe put together." So America, without religious establishments, seems to get ahead of us all, even in light and the things of the mind.

On the other hand, another friend of reason and the simple natural truth of things, M. Renan, says of America, in a book he has recently published, what seems to conflict violently with what Mr. Bright says. Mr. Bright avers that not only have the United States thus informed Europe, but they have done it without a great apparatus of higher and scientific instruction, and by dint of all classes in America being "sufficiently educated to be able to read, and to comprehend, and to think; and that, I maintain, is the foundation of all subsequent progress." And then comes M. Renan, and says: "The sound instruction of the people is an effect of the high culture of certain classes. *The countries which, like the United States, have created a considerable popular instruction without any serious higher instruction, will long have to expiate this fault by their intellectual mediocrity, their vulgarity of manners, their superficial spirit, their lack of general intelligence.*" [1]

Now, which of these two friends of light are we to believe? M. Renan seems more to have in view what we ourselves mean by culture; because Mr. Bright always has in his eye what he calls "a commendable interest" in politics and in political agitations. As he said only the other day at Birmingham: "At this moment,—in fact, I may say at every moment in the history of a free country,—there is nothing that is so much worth discussing as politics." And he keeps repeating, with all the powers of his noble oratory, the old story, how to the thoughtfulness

[1] "Les pays qui, comme les États-Unis, ont créé un enseignement populaire considérable sans instruction supérieure sérieuse, expieront longtemps encore cette faute par leur médiocrité intellectuelle, leur grossièreté de mœurs, leur esprit superficiel, leur manque d'intelligence générale."

and intelligence of the people of great towns we owe all our improvements in the last thirty years, and how these improvements have hitherto consisted in Parliamentary reform, and free trade, and abolition of Church rates, and so on; and how they are now about to consist in getting rid of minority-members, and in introducing a free breakfast-table, and in abolishing the Irish Church by the power of the Nonconformists' antipathy to establishments, and much more of the same kind. And though our pauperism and ignorance, and all the questions which are called social, seem now to be forcing themselves upon his mind, yet he still goes on with his glorifying of the great towns, and the Liberals, and their operations for the last thirty years. It never seems to occur to him that the present troubled state of our social life has anything to do with the thirty years' blind worship of their nostrums by himself and our Liberal friends, or that it throws any doubts upon the sufficiency of this worship. But he thinks that what is still amiss is due to the stupidity of the Tories, and will be cured by the thoughtfulness and intelligence of the great towns, and by the Liberals going on gloriously with their political operations as before; or that it will cure itself. So we see what Mr. Bright means by thoughtfulness and intelligence, and in what manner, according to him, we are to grow in them. And, no doubt, in America all classes read their newspaper, and take a commendable interest in politics, more than here or anywhere else in Europe.

But in the following [i.e., preceding] essay we have been led to doubt the sufficiency of all this political operating, pursued mechanically as our race pursues it; and we found that *general intelligence*, as M. Renan calls it, or, as we say, attention to the reason of things, was just what we were without, and that we were without it because we worshipped our machinery so devoutly. Therefore, we conclude that M. Renan, more than Mr. Bright, means by reason and intelligence the same thing as we do. And when M. Renan says that America, that chosen home of newspapers and politics, is without general intelligence, we think it likely, from the circumstances of the case, that this is so; and that in the things of the mind, and in culture and totality, America, instead of surpassing us all, falls short.

And,—to keep to our point of the influence of religious establishments upon culture and a high development of our humanity,—we can surely see reasons why, with all her energy and fine gifts, America does not show more of this development, or more promise of this. In the following [i.e., preceding] essay it will be seen how our society distributes itself into Barbarians, Philistines, and Populace; and America is just ourselves, with the Barbarians quite left out, and the Populace nearly. This leaves the Philistines for the great bulk of the nation;—a livelier sort of Philistine than ours, and with the pressure and false ideal of our Barbarians taken away, but left all the more to himself and to have his full swing. And as we have found that the strongest and most vital part of English Philistinism was the Puritan and Hebraising middle class, and that its Hebraising keeps it from culture and totality, so it is notorious that the people of the United States issues from this class, and reproduces its tendencies,—its narrow conception of man's spiritual range and of his one thing needful. From Maine to Florida, and back again, all America Hebraises. Difficult as it is to speak of a people merely from what one reads, yet that, I think, one may without much fear of contradiction say. I mean, when in the United States any spiritual side in man is wakened to activity, it is generally the religious side, and the religious side in a narrow way. Social reformers go to Moses or St. Paul for their doctrines, and have no notion there is anywhere else to go to; earnest young men at schools and universities, instead of conceiving salvation as a harmonious perfection only to be won by unreservedly cultivating many sides in us, conceive of it in the old Puritan fashion, and fling themselves ardently upon it in the old, false ways of this fashion, which we know so well, and such as Mr. Hammond, the American revivalist, has lately at Mr. Spurgeon's Tabernacle been refreshing our memory with.

Now, if America thus Hebraises more than either England or Germany, will any one deny that the absence of religious establishments has much to do with it? We have seen how establishments tend to give us a sense of a historical life of the human spirit, outside and beyond our own fancies and feelings; how

they thus tend to suggest new sides and sympathies in us to cultivate; how, further, by saving us from having to invent and fight for our own forms of religion, they give us leisure and calm to steady our view of religion itself,—the most over-
5   powering of objects, as it is the grandest,—and to enlarge our first crude notions of the one thing needful. But, in a serious people, where every one has to choose and strive for his own order and discipline of religion, the contention about these non-essentials occupies his mind. His first crude notions about the
10 one thing needful do not get purged, and they invade the whole spiritual man in him, and then, making a solitude, they call it heavenly peace.

I remember a Nonconformist manufacturer, in a town of the Midland counties, telling me that when he first came there,
15 some years ago, the place had no Dissenters; but he had opened an Independent chapel in it, and now Church and Dissent were pretty equally divided, with sharp contests between them. I said that this seemed a pity. "A pity?" cried he; "not at all! Only think of all the zeal and activity which the collision calls
20 forth!" "Ah, but, my dear friend," I answered, "only think of all the nonsense which you now hold quite firmly, which you would never have held if you had not been contradicting your adversary in it all these years!" The more serious the people, and the more prominent the religious side in it, the greater is
25 the danger of this side, if set to choose out forms for itself and fight for existence, swelling and spreading till it swallows all other spiritual sides up, intercepts and absorbs all nutriment which should have gone to them, and leaves Hebraism rampant in us and Hellenism stamped out.
30 Culture, and the harmonious perfection of our whole being, and what we call totality, then become quite secondary matters. And even the institutions, which should develop these, take the same narrow and partial view of humanity and its wants as the free religious communities take. Just as the free churches of
35 Mr. Beecher or Brother Noyes, with their provincialism and want of centrality, make mere Hebraisers in religion, and not perfect men, so the university of Mr. Ezra Cornell, a really noble monument of his munificence, yet seems to rest on a

misconception of what culture truly is, and to be calculated to produce miners, or engineers, or architects, not sweetness and light.

And, therefore, when Mr. White asks the same kind of question about America that he has asked about England, and wants to know whether, without religious establishments, as much is not done in America for the higher national life as is done for that life here, we answer in the same way as we did before, that as much is not done. Because to enable and stir up people to read their Bible and the newspapers, and to get a practical knowledge of their business, does not serve to the higher spiritual life of a nation so much as culture, truly conceived, serves; and a true conception of culture is, as M. Renan's words show, just what America fails in.

To the many who think that spirituality, and sweetness, and light, are all moonshine, this will not appear to matter much; but with us, who value them, and who think that we have traced much of our present discomfort to the want of them, it weighs a great deal. So not only do we say that the Nonconformists have got provincialism and lost totality by the want of a religious establishment, but we say that the very example which they bring forward to help their case makes against them; and that when they triumphantly show us America without religious establishments, they only show us a whole nation touched, amidst all its greatness and promise, with that provincialism which it is our aim to extirpate in the English Nonconformists.

But now to evince the disinterestedness which culture teaches us. We have seen the narrowness generated in Puritanism by its hole-and-corner organisation, and we propose to cure it by bringing Puritanism more into contact with the main current of national life. Here we are fully at one with the Dean of Westminster; and, indeed, he and we were trained in the same school to mark the narrowness of Puritanism, and to wish to cure it. But he and others seem disposed simply to give to the present Anglican Establishment a character the most latitudinarian, as it is called, possible; availing themselves for this purpose of the diversity of tendencies and doctrines which

does undoubtedly exist already in the Anglican formularies;
and then they would say to the Puritans: "Come all of you
into this liberally conceived Anglican Establishment." But to
say this is hardly, perhaps, to take sufficient account of the
5   course of history, or of the strength of men's feelings in what
concerns religion, or of the gravity which may have come to
attach to points of religious order and discipline merely. When
Mr. White talks of "sweeping away the whole complicated
iniquity of Government Church patronage," he uses language
10 which has been forced upon him by his position, but which is
devoid of all real solidity. But when he talks of the religious
communities "which have for three hundred years contended
for the power of the congregation in the management of their
own affairs," then he talks history; and his language has behind
15 it, in my opinion, facts which make the latitudinarianism of
our Broad Churchmen quite illusory.

Certainly, culture will never make us think it an essential of
religion whether we have in our Church discipline "a popular authority of elders," as Hooker calls it, or whether we have
20 Episcopal jurisdiction. Certainly, Hooker himself did not think
it an essential; for in the dedication of his *Ecclesiastical Polity*,
speaking of these questions of church-discipline which gave
occasion to his great work, he says they are "in truth, for the
greatest part, such silly things, that very easiness doth make
25 them hard to be disputed of in serious manner." Hooker's
great work against the impugners of the order and discipline
of the Church of England was written (and this is too indistinctly seized by many who read it), not because Episcopalianism is essential, but because its impugners maintained that
30 Presbyterianism is essential, and that Episcopalianism is sinful.
Neither the one nor the other is either essential or sinful, and
much may be said on behalf of both. But what is important to
be remarked is, *that both were in the Church of England at the
Reformation*, and that Presbyterianism was only extruded
35 gradually. We have mentioned Hooker, and nothing better
illustrates what has just been asserted than the following incident in Hooker's own career, which every one has read, for it

is related in Isaac Walton's *Life of Hooker,* but of which, probably, the significance has been fully grasped by very few of those who have read it.

Hooker was through the influence of Archbishop Whitgift appointed, in 1585, Master of the Temple; but a great effort had first been made to obtain the place for a Mr. Walter Travers, well known in that day, though now it is Hooker's name which alone preserves his. This Travers was then afternoon-lecturer at the Temple. The Master whose death made the vacancy, Alvey, recommended on his deathbed Travers for his successor. The Society was favourable to Travers, and he had the support of the Lord Treasurer Burghley. Although Hooker was appointed to the Mastership, Travers remained afternoon-lecturer, and combated in the afternoons the doctrine which Hooker preached in the mornings. Now, this Travers, originally a Fellow of Trinity College, Cambridge, afterwards afternoon-lecturer at the Temple, recommended for the Mastership by the foregoing Master whose opinions, it is said, agreed with his, favoured by the Society of the Temple and supported by the Prime Minister,—this Travers was not an Episcopally ordained clergyman at all. He was a Presbyterian, a partisan of the Geneva church-discipline, as it was then called, and "had taken orders," says Walton, "by the Presbyters in Antwerp." In another place Walton speaks of his orders yet more fully:—"He had disowned," he says, "the English Established Church and Episcopacy, and went to Geneva, and afterwards to Antwerp, to be ordained minister, as he was by Villers and Cartwright and others the heads of a congregation there; and so came back again more confirmed for the discipline." Villers and Cartwright are in like manner examples of Presbyterianism within the Church of England, which was common enough at that time. But perhaps nothing can better give us a lively sense of its presence there than this history of Travers, which is as if Mr. Binney were now [1] afternoon-reader at Lincoln's Inn or the Temple; were to be a candidate, favoured by the Benchers and by the Prime Minister, for the

[1] 1869.

Mastership; and were only kept out of the post by the accident of the Archbishop of Canterbury's influence with the Queen carrying a rival candidate.

Presbyterianism, with its popular principle of the power of
5   the congregation in the management of their own affairs, was extruded from the Church of England, and men like Travers can no longer appear in her pulpits. Perhaps if a government like that of Elizabeth, with secular statesmen like the Cecils, and ecclesiastical statesmen like Whitgift, could have been pro-
10 longed, Presbyterianism might, by a wise mixture of concession and firmness, have been absorbed in the Establishment. Lord Bolingbroke, on a matter of this kind a very clear-judging and impartial witness, says, in a work far too little read, his *Remarks on English History*:—"The measures pursued and
15 the temper observed in Queen Elizabeth's time tended to diminish the religious opposition by a slow, a gentle, and for that very reason an effectual progression. There was even room to hope that when the first fire of the Dissenters' zeal was passed, reasonable terms of union with the Established Church might
20 be accepted by such of them as were not intoxicated with fanaticism. These were friends to order, though they disputed about it. If these friends of Calvin's discipline had been once incorporated with the Established Church, the remaining sectaries would have been of little moment, either for numbers or
25 reputation; and the very means which were proper to gain these friends were likewise the most effectual to hinder the increase of them, and of the other sectaries in the meantime." The temper and ill judgment of the Stuarts made shipwreck of all policy of this kind. Yet speaking even of the time of the
30 Stuarts, but their early time, Clarendon says that if Bishop Andrewes had succeeded Bancroft at Canterbury, the disaffection of separatists might have been stayed and healed. This, however, was not to be; and Presbyterianism, after exercising for some years the law of the strongest, itself in Charles the
35 Second's reign suffered under this law, and was finally cast out from the Church of England.

Now the points of church-discipline at issue between Presbyterianism and Episcopalianism are, as has been said, not essential.

They might probably once have been settled in a sense altogether favourable to Episcopalianism. Hooker may have been right in thinking that there were in his time circumstances which made it essential that they should be settled in this sense, though the points in themselves were not essential. But by the very fact of the settlement not having then been effected, of the breach having gone on and widened, of the Nonconformists not having been amicably incorporated with the Establishment but violently cast out from it, the circumstances are now altogether altered. Isaac Walton, a fervent Churchman, complains that "the principles of the Nonconformists grew at last to such a height and were vented so daringly, that, beside the loss of life and limbs, the Church and State were both forced to use such other severities as will not admit of an excuse, if it had not been to prevent confusion and the perilous consequences of it." But those very severities have of themselves made union on an Episcopalian footing impossible. Besides, Presbyterianism, the popular authority of elders, the power of the congregation in the management of their own affairs, has that warrant given to it by Scripture and by the proceedings of the early Christian Churches, it is so consonant with the spirit of Protestantism which made the Reformation and which has great strength in this country, it is so predominant in the practice of other Reformed Churches, it was so strong in the original Reformed Church of England, that one cannot help doubting whether any settlement which suppressed it could have been really permanent, and whether it would not have kept appearing again and again, and causing dissension.

Well, then, if culture is the disinterested endeavour after man's perfection, will it not make us wish to cure the provincialism of the Nonconformists, not by rendering Churchmen provincial along with them, but by letting their popular church-discipline, formerly present in the national Church and still present in the affections and practice of a good part of the nation, appear in the national Church once more; and thus to bring Nonconformists into contact again, as their greater fathers were, with the main stream of national life? Why should not a Presbyterian Church, based on this considerable and important, though not essential principle, of the congregation's share in the church-management, be established,—with equal rank for its chiefs with the chiefs of Episcopacy, and with admissibility of its ministers, under a revised system of patronage and prefer-

5   ment, to benefices,—side by side with the Episcopal Church, as the Calvinist and Lutheran Churches are established side by side in France and Germany? Such a Presbyterian Church would unite the main bodies of Protestants who are now separatists; and separation would cease to be the law of their religious

10   order. And thus,—through this concession on a really considerable point of difference,—that endless splitting into hole-and-corner churches on quite inconsiderable points of difference, which must prevail so long as separatism is the first law of a Nonconformist's religious existence, would be checked. Cul-

15   ture would then find a place among English followers of the popular authority of Elders, as it has long found it among the followers of Episcopal jurisdiction. And this we should gain by merely recognising, regularising, and restoring an element which appeared once in the reformed national Church, and

20   which is considerable and national enough to have a sound claim to appear there still.

So far, then, is culture from making us unjust to the Nonconformists because it forbids us to worship their fetishes, that it even leads us to propose to do more for them than they them-

25   selves venture to claim. It leads us, also, to respect what is solid and respectable in their convictions. Not that the forms in which the human spirit tries to express the inexpressible, or the forms by which man tries to worship, have or can have, as has been said, for the follower of perfection, anything necessary

30   or eternal. If the New Testament and the practice of the primitive Christians sanctioned the popular form of church-government a thousand times more expressly than they do, if the Church since Constantine were a thousand times more of a departure from the scheme of primitive Christianity than it

35   can be shown to be, that does not at all make, as is supposed by men in bondage to the letter, the popular form of church-government alone and always sacred and binding, or the work of Constantine a thing to be regretted.

What is alone and always sacred and binding for man is the making progress towards his total perfection; and the machinery by which he does this varies in value according as it helps him to do it. The planters of Christianity had their roots in deep and rich grounds of human life and achievement, both Jewish and also Greek; and had thus a comparatively firm and wide basis amidst all the vehement inspiration of their mighty movement and change. By their strong inspiration they carried men off the old basis of life and culture, whether Jewish or Greek, and generations arose who had their roots in neither world, and were in contact therefore with no full and great stream of human life. If it had not been for some such change as that of the fourth century, Christianity might have lost itself in a multitude of hole-and-corner churches like the churches of English Nonconformity after its founders departed; churches without great men, and without furtherance for the higher life of humanity. At a critical moment came Constantine, and placed Christianity,—or let us rather say, placed the human spirit, whose totality was endangered,—in contact with the main current of human life. And his work was justified by its fruits, in men like Augustine and Dante, and indeed in all the great men of Christianity, Catholics or Protestants, ever since.

And one may go beyond this. M. Albert Réville, whose religious writings are always interesting, says that the conception which cultivated and philosophical Jews now entertain of Christianity and its Founder, is probably destined to become the conception which Christians themselves will entertain. Socinians are fond of saying the same thing about the Socinian conception of Christianity. Now, even if this were true, it would still have been better for a man, during the last eighteen hundred years, to have been a Christian and a member of one of the great Christian communions, than to have been a Jew or a Socinian; because the being in contact with the main stream of human life is of more moment for a man's total spiritual growth, and for his bringing to perfection the gifts committed to him, which is his business on earth, than any speculative opinion which he may hold or think he holds. Luther,—whom we have called a Philistine of genius, and who, because he was

a Philistine, had a coarseness and lack of spiritual delicacy which have harmed his disciples, but who, because he was a genius, had splendid flashes of spiritual insight,—Luther says admirably in his Commentary on the Book of Daniel: "A God
5 is simply *that* whereon the human heart rests with trust, faith, hope, and love. If the resting is right, then the God too is right; if the resting is wrong, then the God too is illusory." In other words, the worth of what a man thinks about God and the objects of religion depends on what the man *is;* and what
10 the man *is,* depends upon his having more or less reached the measure of a perfect and total man.

Culture, disinterestedly seeking in its aim at perfection to see things as they really are, shows us how worthy and divine a thing is the religious side in man, though it is not the whole of
15 man. But while recognising the grandeur of the religious side in man, culture yet makes us also eschew an inadequate conception of man's totality. Therefore to the worth and grandeur of the religious side in man, culture is rejoiced and willing to pay any tribute, except the tribute of man's totality.
20 Unless it is proved that contact with the main current of national life is of no value (and we have shown that it is of the greatest value), we cannot safely, even to please the Nonconformists in a matter where we would please them as much as possible, admit their doctrines of disestablishment and sep-
25 aration.

Culture, again, can be disinterested enough to perceive and avow, that for Ireland the ends of human perfection might be best served by establishing,—that is, by bringing into contact with the main current of the national life,—the Roman Catholic
30 and the Presbyterian Churches along with the Anglican Church. It can perceive and avow that we should really, in this way, be working to make reason and the will of God prevail; because we should be making Roman Catholics better citizens, and both Protestants and Roman Catholics larger-minded and more
35 complete men. Undoubtedly there are great difficulties in such a plan as this; and the plan is not one which looks very likely to be adopted. The Churchman must rise above his ordinary self in order to favour it. And the Nonconformist has wor-

shipped his fetish of separatism so long that he is likely to wish
to remain, like Ephraim, "a wild ass alone by himself." It is a
plan more for a time of creative statesmen, like the time of
Elizabeth, than for a time of instrumental statesmen like the
present. The centre of power being where it is, our statesmen   5
have every temptation, when they must act, to go along as
they do with the ordinary self of those on whose favour they
depend, to adopt as their own its desires, and to serve them
with fidelity, and even, if possible, with ardour. This is the
more easy for them, because there are not wanting,—and there   10
never will be wanting,—thinkers to call the desires of the ordinary self of any great section of the community edicts of the
national mind and laws of human progress, and to give them a
general, a philosophic, and imposing expression. Therefore a
plan such as that which we have indicated does not seem a plan   15
so likely to find favour as a plan for abolishing the Irish
Church by the power of the Nonconformists' antipathy to
establishments.

But although culture makes us fond stickers to no machinery,
not even our own, and therefore we are willing to grant that per- 20
fection can be reached without it,—with free churches as with
established churches, and with instrumental statesmen as with
creative statesmen,—yet perfection can never be reached
without seeing things as they really are; and it is to this, therefore, and to no machinery in the world, that we stick. We   25
insist that men should not mistake, as they are prone to mistake, their natural taste for the bathos for a relish for the
sublime. And if statesmen, either with their tongue in their
cheek or with a fine impulsiveness, tell people that their natural taste for the bathos is a relish for the sublime, there is the   30
more need to tell them the contrary.

It is delusion on this point which is fatal, and against delusion
on this point culture works. It is not fatal to our Liberal friends
to labour for free trade, extension of the suffrage, and abolition
of church-rates, instead of graver social ends; but it is fatal to   35
them to be told by their flatterers, and to believe, with our social
condition what it is, that they have performed a great, a heroic
work, by occupying themselves exclusively, for the last thirty

years, with these Liberal nostrums, and that the right and good course for them now is to go on occupying themselves with the like for the future. It is not fatal to Americans to have no religious establishments and no effective centres of high cul-
5 ture; but it is fatal to them to be told by their flatterers, and to believe, that they are the most intelligent people in the whole world, when of intelligence, in the true and fruitful sense of the word, they even singularly, as we have seen, come short. It is not fatal to the Nonconformists to remain with their sepa-
10 rated churches; but it is fatal to them to be told by their flatterers, and to believe, that theirs is the one true way of worshipping God, that provincialism and loss of totality have not come to them from following it, or that provincialism and loss of totality are not evils. It is not fatal to the English nation
15 to abolish the Irish Church by the power of the Nonconform-ists' antipathy to establishments; but it is fatal to it to be told by its flatterers, and to believe, that it is abolishing it through reason and justice, when it is really abolishing it through this power: or to expect the fruits of reason and justice from any-
20 thing but the spirit of reason and justice themselves.

Now culture, because of its keen sense of what is really fatal, is all the more disposed to be rather indifferent about what is not fatal. And because machinery is the one concern of our actual politics, and an inward working, and not machinery, is what
25 we most want, we keep advising our ardent young Liberal friends to think less of machinery, to stand more aloof from the arena of politics at present, and rather to try and promote, with us, an inward working. They do not listen to us, and they rush into the arena of politics, where their merits, indeed, seem
30 to be little appreciated as yet; and then they complain of the reformed constituencies, and call the new Parliament a Philis-tine Parliament. As if a nation, nourished and reared as ours has been, could give us, just yet, anything but a Philistine Parliament!—and would a Barbarian Parliament be even so
35 good, or a Populace Parliament? For our part, we rejoice to see our dear old friends, the Hebraising Philistines, gathered in force in the Valley of Jehoshaphat previous to their final con-version, which will certainly come. But, to attain this conver-

sion, we must not try to oust them from their places and to contend for machinery with them, but we must work on them inwardly and cure their spirit. Ousted they will not be, but transformed. Ousted they do not deserve to be, and will not be.

For *the days of Israel are innumerable;* and in its blame of Hebraising too, and in its praise of Hellenising, culture must not fail to keep its flexibility, and to give to its judgments that passing and provisional character which we have seen it impose on its preferences and rejections of machinery. Now, and for us, it is a time to Hellenise, and to praise knowing; for we have Hebraised too much, and have over-valued doing. But the habits and discipline received from Hebraism remain for our race an eternal possession; and, as humanity is constituted, one must never assign to them the second rank to-day, without being prepared to restore to them the first rank to-morrow. Let us conclude by marking this distinctly.

To walk staunchly by the best light one has, to be strict and sincere with oneself, not to be of the number of those who say and do not, to be in earnest,—this is the discipline by which alone man is enabled to rescue his life from thraldom to the passing moment and to his bodily senses, to ennoble it, and to make it eternal. And this discipline has been nowhere so effectively taught as in the school of Hebraism. The intense and convinced energy with which the Hebrew, both of the Old and of the New Testament, threw himself upon his ideal of righteousness, and which inspired the incomparable definition of the great Christian virtue, faith,—*the substance of things hoped for, the evidence of things not seen,*—this energy of devotion to its ideal has belonged to Hebraism alone. As our idea of perfection widens beyond the narrow limits to which the over-rigour of Hebraising has tended to confine it, we shall yet come again to Hebraism for that devout energy in embracing our ideal, which alone can give to man the happiness of doing what he knows. "If ye know these things, happy are ye if ye do them!"—the last word for infirm humanity will always be that. For this word, reiterated with a power now sublime, now affecting, but always admirable, our race will, as

long as the world lasts, return to Hebraism; and the Bible, which preaches this word, will for ever remain, as Goethe called it, not only a national book, but the Book of the Nations. Again and again, after what seemed breaches and separa-
5   tions, the prophetic promise to Jerusalem will still be true:—
*Lo, thy sons come, whom thou sentest away; they come gath-
ered from the west unto the east by the word of the Holy
One, rejoicing in the remembrance of God.*

A New History of Greece*

It is now forty years since Goethe, who was not apt to flatter his countrymen, remarked how high was the rank of modern Germany among the nations of Europe in every department of science and learning. A foreigner might then have been tempted to reply that it was unlucky the Germans could do everything but write. Full of science and learning they undoubtedly were, but they seemed unable to communicate their acquisitions in a readable way. But the grounds for this reproach are now disappearing. Book after book now appears in Germany, which is not only full of information, but also eminently well written. Above all is this the case with the recent productions of Germans in the department of Greek and Roman history. It was necessary, no doubt, to work for a long time among the materials of the science of classical antiquity before it became possible to get a firm grasp upon them, to combine them for a general result such as the composition of history, and to use them towards this result with facility and power. It is because Germany has with such indefatigable industry and interest mastered the multifarious materials, supplied not only by Greece and Rome, but by the cognate and parent East also, out of which the history of the Greeks and Romans has to be made up—it is because of the number of good heads busying themselves, in Germany, with these matters, and the medium of clear ideas and sound information thus created there for those who write on them, that productions such as the histories of Dr. Mommsen and Dr. Curtius have now become possible. These two historians write so firmly and

* "The History of Greece." By Professor Dr. Ernst Curtius. Translated by Adolphus William Ward, M.A. (London: Richard Bentley. 1868.)

257

currently because of the near and full relation in which they
stand with their subject-matter, a nearness and fulness which
Englishmen generally reserve for their relations with topics of
the day, such as election prospects, the Abergele accident, or
the progress of Ritualism. While, therefore, the valuable History of Dr. Thirlwall seems to move in an atmosphere somewhat far off and shadowy, and while round the monumental
work of Mr. Grote there seems to hang a certain air of the
isolated scholar's study, an air of tentative labour and still continuing research, Dr. Mommsen and Dr. Curtius write Greek
or Roman history with the same confidence and animation
with which the *Times* discusses the Wesleyan Conference or
Mdme. Rachel's trial. In revenge, the German newspapers are
apt to treat topics of the day with a want of briskness and of
all living sense of reality which nearly equals what most Englishmen feel in touching the philological and historical sciences.

Dr. Mommsen's history smacks even a little too much, perhaps,
of the leading article; it is somewhat too pamphleteering, too
trenchant, too charged with likes and dislikes. The soberness
of history is better maintained in the history of Dr. Curtius,
which is now before us. But with the soberness there is a living
hold upon his subject-matter, which communicates itself to the
reader, and makes the reading of the history in the highest
degree fruitful and impressive. To enable the student to *ori-
enter* himself, as the French say—to find his bearings—in the
region of history with which he busies himself, is the most real
service which a historical work can render him. Particularly
this is so in the history of the Greek and Roman world; of the
Greek world above all, where the single facts have each and all
been the objects of such voluminous research, and where yet
to see them in their connection and to comprehend the general
result from them is so important.

There can be no thorough knowledge of the Greek people
without knowing the original works which they have left. He
who has read again and again what is left to us of Pindar will have
a more living sense of the Greek world as it was in the first fifty
years of the fifth century before Christ than he who has read

the most voluminous modern history of that period. But he
who has read Dr. Curtius will learn a thousand times more from
his Pindar, and will read, as the Germans say, *between the
lines*. A work on the scale of Mr. Grote's, on the other hand, is,
from its very fulness, of much less service as a readily grasped
presentation of the development of the Greek world in its vital
characteristics and essential connection, and as a clue to the
student seeking to know this development, where alone it can
really be known, in the original documents. Much more does a
work like Mr. Grote's History of Greece, or a work like Sismondi's History of France, seem to afford the means of dis-
pensing with the study of the original documents, and to supply enough of them to give the reader an adequate notion of
what they all come to. Yet this history cannot, as has been said,
really do; and the semblance of its doing so is, and must be, in
real truth, illusory. Sometimes, however, the region of history
to be surveyed is such that, the length of human life and the
compass of human faculties being what they are, the partial
and inadequate knowledge to be gathered from a modern historian is all that it is worth our while to try for. It is the felicity
of Gibbon that his immortal work has for its field a region of
this nature. Gibbon is a classic, not because the later Empire
can be really or adequately known from his History, but because with admirable learning and skill he gives account of a
period which we do not most of us care to study in its original
documents, or to know more of than he gives us.

But there are other portions of the life of humanity which deserve studying in quite another fashion; and Greek history is
emphatically one of them. For these periods the student can
hardly wish for anything better in the shape of a modern
history than a history on the scale and with the character of
that of Dr. Curtius, to serve as a guide and centre of reference
in that large study of the original documents which he will
still feel impelled to make. Mr. Ward has as yet published but
the first volume of his translation, and that volume is not quite
coextensive with the first volume of Dr. Curtius; but we hope
that he will impose it as a strict rule on himself and his publisher not to let the whole work swell beyond four volumes,

the number fixed, we believe, by Dr. Curtius, and wisely fixed, as his utmost limit.

Taking the one volume which has been made accessible to English readers, we shall, perhaps, best give a notion of its merits if we select three or four of the main points of interest to the student of the Greek world and its development—points which have afforded matter for infinite disquisition, which meet the student perpetually in reading the Greek authors, and on which it is of the greatest importance to him to have clear ideas—and see how Dr. Curtius deals with them. "The science of origins," as the French call it, we have most of us had occasion in the course of our training to employ in regard to ancient Greece and its people. The contact of the Greeks with the Phœnicians, the relations of Asiatic with European Greece, the Dorian migration, the question who were the Pelasgians, the Minyans, the Achæans, the Ionians; these are points of historical research which every schoolboy is constantly finding himself invited to elucidate. Clear conceptions about them are very needful for a right understanding of the most commonly read Greek authors; yet how few of us who have had recourse, we will not say to our common books of reference only, but even to authorities of the most eminent merit and learning, such as, for example, Mr. Fynes Clinton and his essays, printed in the first volume of the "Fasti Hellenici," have come away with conceptions which can with any truth at all be called clear? Let us see how the case stands with us after having recourse to Dr. Curtius.

First, then, as to the Phœnicians, and the origin of the traditions of Greek contact with them. We shall use Dr. Curtius's own words, though we must perforce abridge and condense:—

Pressed in a narrow strip of land between mountains and water, it was by sea alone that the Phœnicians could extend themselves. Their ships went forth to bring home gain of every kind; above all, to import the materials for the manufactories flourishing in their populous towns—Byblus, Sidon, Tyre. The discoveries made by individuals on a lucky voyage were used by mercantile societies in possession of means sufficient to organize settlements, and to secure to the business thus commenced a lasting importance. Whilst in civilized countries the right of settlement had to be purchased dearly and under oppressive conditions, the rocks on the Greek coasts, hitherto a place of rest only for swarms of quails, were to be had for nothing, and yet yielded manifold profits. Sea and 5 shore thus came into the hands of the strangers, who on the one hand terrified the natives by craft and force, and again ever continued to attract them anew to commercial intercourse. The myth of Helen contains reminiscences of a time when the island of Cranæ, with its sanctuary of Aphrodite, lay like a foreign territory 10 close by the coast of Laconia, a Phœnician emporium, where the foreigners safely stowed away the women and the rest of the gain and loot carried off by them. So close and so constantly extending a contact with the foreign traders could not remain without its effect on the natives. At the market-fairs held on the shore, they 15 had to come to an agreement with them about the objects of trade; about numbers, weights, and measures. Thus a series of the most important inventions, which had been gradually matured in the East, came, as rearranged by the practical Phœnicians, to the knowledge of the natives, who wondered, observed, and learnt; 20 their slumbering powers were awakened, and the spell unbound which had kept men fettered in their monotonous conditions of life. The motion of the mind begins, and with it Greek history draws its first breath.

The Phœnicians were, as time went on, pushed out by a branch 25 of the more gifted and energetic Greek people, whom they left in possession of their civilization. And what branch of this people first and chiefly received the fruitful boon and communicated it to the rest? The Ionians, says Dr. Curtius, of the coast of Asia Minor—Ionians who were the original possessors 30 of this widespread name, as well as of the characteristics which have become for us the distinguishing characteristics of the Greek genius and people:—

Among all the Greeks, the inhabitants of this thickly peopled coast, by virtue of their special natural endowment and of the ex- 35 ceedingly happy conditions of their land and climate, were the first to secure for themselves the civilization of the Phœnicians. Sagaciously they contrived to learn their arts from them, while the Pelasgian people remained inert. Thus they became known to the nations of the East before any of the rest of the Greeks. The common name of Greeks in the whole East was no other than that which this maritime race of Greek descent gave to itself—that of the Iaones or Ionians, a name subsequently domesticated by the Phœnicians in various dialectic forms, such as Javan with the Hebrews, Iuna or Iauna with the Persians, Uinim with the Egyptians. After the Ionians had learnt navigation and become the masters of their own sea, they sailed in the track of the Phœnicians, as Thucydides so aptly expresses it in reference to Sicily. Especially they settled at the mouths of the streams, where these were of a kind to afford their vessels a safe entrance and a voyage a short way into the interior of the land. The routes of the island sea were opened, and now, in a more and more rapid succession of landings, the Greeks of the East came to the Greeks of the west. From their original habitations, as well as from other regions where they had taken up their abode, an innate impulse of kinmanship led them on across the passage to European Hellas. Here land and air must have met them with the pleasantest of greetings; here they were eager to domesticate themselves, to introduce all the arts and inventions which they had gradually appropriated during a lively intercourse with other nations, and to awaken the natives to a higher phase of life.

That important contact of Hellas with the East, accordingly, of which, in the traditions about the Greek gods, and about personages like Cadmus and Ægyptus, we have such indelible traces, was properly a contact with a *Greek* East, and with Ionic Greeks, who, having absorbed and transformed Phœnician or Egyptian civilization, and coming to Hellas from the other side of the sea, not from the coast of Asia Minor only, but from many a settlement in non-Hellenic lands to which their adventurous genius had led them, "easily came to be called Phœnicians and Egyptians."

And as Cadmus and Ægyptus were not Phœnicians and Egyptians, but Greeks, Greeks awakened and transformed by contact with older civilizations, so Pelasgus and the primitive dwellers on the soil of Hellas were Greeks too, but Greeks not yet fully born, not yet awakened.

There exist no Pelasgian myths, no Pelasgian gods, to be contrasted with the Greek. The first genuine Hellene known to us, the Ho-

meric Achilles, prays to the Pelasgian Zeus; and Dodona, at all times considered the primitive seat of the Pelasgi, was also the most ancient Hellas in Europe. But for all this Pelasgi and Hellenes are by no means identical or merely different names for one idea. Such a view is proved untenable by the manifest fact that from the Hel-   5
lenes sprang entirely new currents of life. The Pelasgian times lie in the background—a vast period of monotony; impulse and mo-tion are first communicated by Hellen and his sons, and with their arrival history commences. Accordingly, we must interpret them to signify tribes which, endowed with special gifts, and animated   10
by special powers of action, issue forth from the mass of a great people.

The action of one brilliant branch of Hellen's descendants, the maritime Ionians, we have already noticed. This first breaks the monotony of the Pelasgian age; "everywhere with the   15
combination of Pelasgians and Ionians commenced, as by an electric contact, the current of historic life." But in contrast with the action of the mobile Ionians arises presently that of other descendants of Hellen, the firm and stedfast mountain-eers of northern Greece. This action develops itself from the   20
land, as that of the Ionians develops itself from the sea. The Minyans, so famous in Greek poetry, the first dwellers in northern Greece, "with whom a perceptible movement of the Pelasgian tribes beyond the sea—in other words, a Greek his-tory in Europe—begins," are in communication with Asiatic   25
Ionia, and with Ionian settlements in Greece itself, and receive their impulse from thence. The same influence appears in the Achæans. "Achæans are everywhere settled on the coast, and are always regarded as particularly near relations of the Io-nians." The Achæans, however, in Phthiotis develop much of   30
the strong spirit and tenacity which was the secret, afterwards, of the success of the Dorian mountaineers; "they called forth a more independent development in European Greece than the older tribes had succeeded in producing," and Dr. Curtius therefore styles the Achæan Achilles "the first Hellene". But   35
the true centre of an independent development for European Greece was in the Dorian highlanders, who came down from the roots of Olympus to the district between Parnassus and

Œta. Their subsequent history may almost be described as the history of Greece without Attica; but the traits which gave them this splendid fortune are thus marked by Dr. Curtius:—

Above all other Greek tribes the Dorians possessed an innate tend-
5 ency towards the establishment, preservation, and spread of fixed systems. While the maritime Greeks in their continual voyages made a home of every coast, the tribes participating in the Thessalian Amphictyony, of which the Dorians were the representatives, were the first who learnt to regard a territory within fixed
10 limits as their common country, and to love, honour, and defend it as their fatherland. With the wandering of the Dorians, the strength of the highland tribes came forth from the North to assert its claim to take part in the national history. They had been outstripped by centuries by the tribes of the coasts and islands, but
15 now made their appearance among the latter with a doubly impressive vigour of healthy nature. Their wishes and powers turned towards practical life, towards the performance of fixed tasks, towards serious and purposed action. The changes and new formations arising from their expeditions of conquest endured through
20 the whole course of Greek history. And for this reason the ancient historical writers began the historic times, in contradistinction to the Heroic pre-historic age, with the first deeds of the Dorians.

We hope that by these extracts the reader may gain some notion of what we mean, when we praise Dr. Curtius for having
25 laid firm hold on the main points in the development of the Greek people, and treated them with living clearness and freshness. This seems to us the essential merit for a history of Greece to possess. There are, no doubt, several points where the conclusions reached by Dr. Curtius may be open to dispute. But, in
30 our view of the matter, a reader of Greek history suffers no great loss in having to regard his author's conclusions, on certain points, as provisional; his great loss is in having the essential points indistinctly marked for him, and discussed without living force and freshness.
35 Mr. Ward's translation has some roughnesses and some misprints, but on the whole it seems to us a production eminently *kernhaft,* as the Germans say, and thus to suit its original, of

which it reproduces the mingled freshness and solidity. Clearness, solidity, method, firm and orderly progression—it is of these qualities that the book of Dr. Curtius gives us a sense; and this sense is by Mr. Ward's translation retained, whereas many a more elegant English version of such an original would in all   5
probability have clean lost it.

Curtius's "History of Greece"* [II]

We are in arrear with Mr. Ward's translation of this important History of Greece by Dr. Curtius. Since we called attention to the first volume, not only has the second volume appeared, but the third also. The work, however, is one which from the   10
permanent interest of its subject can afford to wait, and from the solidity and thoughtfulness of its execution gains by being well considered. We will not even now attempt to review the second and third volumes together, but will confine ourselves to the second volume, allowing the third, which certainly re-   15
quires a separate notice, to wait for this yet a little longer.

As to the translation, it has the merit of keeping, in a remarkable degree, the solidity and fulness of significance of the work itself. It is not carefully printed, and the list of errata at the end of the volume needs to be lengthened considerably. The   20
translation is not particularly elegant, and sometimes its English is not only inelegant but inaccurate. "The naval force of the enemy was nothing less than annihilated" (p. 293) means the very contrary of what Mr. Ward intends it to mean. It is not allowable to say in English "the dynasty which *was be-*   25
friended with the Lydians," or to say that Herodotus was not "blind *against* the praiseworthy characteristics of the enemy." The word *frostig* has its own rights in German, but an English writer who says that in Æschylus certain "allusions were not the result of impure and frosty secondary designs obscuring   30

* "The History of Greece." By Professor Dr. Ernst Curtius. Translated by Adolphus William Ward, M.A. Vol. II. (London: Bentley and Son. 1871.)

the pure effect of poetry," expresses himself neither perspicu-
ously nor gracefully. These are blemishes which Mr. Ward
would do well to remove; but in general his rendering, though
it wants grace, has the great merit of retaining the substantial-
5   ness, the fulness of meaning, and the serious forward stride of
the style of his author.

His author sometimes, in matters where a delicate touch is required, has too much of the hardness of the schoolman, and
makes us desire the tact of the man of imagination or even of
10 the man of the world. Yet the impression he leaves is on the
whole scarcely less agreeable than it is satisfying, from his
thorough command over the rich abundance of materials
which, with German honesty, he has collected from every side
for his work, and from the natural unostentatious way in
15 which he uses them. How simple and yet how instructive, how
unlike the vagueness and coldness with which in the old histories of Greece Greek topography is presented to us, is this
mention of Paros and Naxos, the two chief and closely connected islands of the Cyclades:—

20 Paros may be distinguished even in the distance by her mountains,
which rise in forms of such grandeur that they seemingly intend
to announce the costly treasure they contain—an inexhaustible supply of the fairest marble. Paros is, moreover, of great importance
for navigation, on account of the abundance of springs on her
25 shores and the deep bays of her harbours. In this respect she forms
the natural complement of the larger contiguous island. For Naxos
rises out of the sea, rounded off on all sides without deeper inlets;
and her wide circumference and strong position mark her out as
the chief among the neighbouring islands, while at the same time
30 nature has blessed her with manifold products, so that the ancients
were at times wont to call her the Lesser Sicily. From the broad
summit of the Naxian mountains more than twenty islands are visible, lying at their feet, and to the east the view extends as far as
the massive ranges of Asia.

35   In connection with the populousness of ancient Hellas and the
importance of her islands now so insignificant, here, again, is
information just of the kind to be useful and to stand clear in
the memory. The birthplace of the poet Simonides, the island

of Ceos, off the southern promontory of Attica, contained at the time of the Persian war, says Dr. Curtius,—

On an entirely mountainous area of about nine square miles four towns, every one of which possessed a harbour, a legislation, and a coinage of its own. To this, the most flourishing period of Greek 5
population, belongs the careful system of building at all possible points, the vestiges of which astonish the traveller to this day, when he beholds how once upon a time every little spot was put to its particular use, every difficulty of settlement and intercourse overcome, and every part of the country pervaded by human life and 10
activity. On rocky crags, whence in the present day lonely herds of goats derive a scanty sustenance, are found the remains of towns, surrounded by strong walls, and supplied with cisterns and aqueducts, while the surrounding heights are gradated off in artificial terraces up to their summit, for the purpose of obtaining space for 15
the culture of corn and fruit trees.

The same definiteness marks the statements of Dr. Curtius on that most important and interesting point in the life of Hellenic communities—slavery:—

By the side of the civic society existed a slave population of very 20
considerable numbers in mercantile and manufacturing cities such as Corinth and Ægina. Here its numbers must have amounted to as many as ten times those of the free inhabitants. Even in Attica they must be assumed to have preponderated over the freemen in a proportion of at least four to one. 25

Dr. Curtius points out very well how it was that, in general, the multitude of slaves constituted no political danger for a Greek State, but in recollection of Mr. Lucraft's confession to his colleagues of the School Board, that he often found it difficult to make both ends meet, there is an especial interest for us in 30
the following:—

Without the slaves the Attic democracy would have been an impossibility, for they alone enabled the poor, as well as the rich, to take a daily part in public affairs. For only a very small minority were poor enough to have to get through life without the help of 35
slaves; and we find Attic families complaining of being forced to the most painful retrenchment if they were not able to keep more than seven slaves.

Easily may it have been, therefore, that "the contrast between rich and poor was altogether neither excessive nor irremovable." The seven slaves would just make all the difference to Mr. Lucraft; with them, the contast between him and Lord West-
5   minster need not, perhaps, be excessive and irremovable; without them, it can hardly help being so.

Thus far we have tried to illustrate the fulness and yet definiteness of our author's way of writing history; its strenuousness and seriousness are not less praiseworthy. Take this sum-
10   ming up of the career of the Spartan Cleomenes, that "remarkable man, whose naturally grand character had degenerated into criminal selfishness and indomitable ferocity:"—

We find Cleomenes recalled and reinstated in all his honours; but as what manner of man does he return home? Brutalized by his
15   restless wanderings, distracted by evil passions and the torments of an unsatisfied ambition, burdened with the load of his guilt, and spiritually and physically ruined by sensual excesses. This state of mind ended in raving madness. It was necessary to bind the Spartan king and set his own helots as guards over him, till at last he died
20   the most awful of deaths from his own hand.

But the crowning merit of Dr. Curtius as an historian of Greece lies, according to our judgment, in his power of exhibiting Greek history in its essential connection and vital development. Here he seems to us superior to Mr. Grote; although in
25   describing the course and incidents of political struggles, he is inferior to the English politician, and as a narrator of military actions he shows no special talent for lively and picturesque writing. But an historian who makes us see the tying of the thread which a people's life and fortunes follow does more
30   than any one else to make us really apprehend history, and retain it in our minds as a lasting possession. A merit of this kind signalizes Dr. Curtius in his second volume no less than in his first, and what space we have yet left shall be employed in showing it.

35   As the contact with Asia quickened into life the old Pelasgian world, and made it Hellenic, so the formative impulse to this Hellenic world after it had come into being was given by Delphi. Hardy and serious tribes from the mountains of north-

western Greece crossed Pindus, and at the foot of Olympus formed a first federation, or Amphictyony, of which the sanctuary of Tempe was the centre, and the Apolline worship the sanction. Moving thence southward to the foot of Parnassus, they there established a second federation, under the guardianship of the same religion, with the already founded Delphi for its sanctuary. Moving again southward, and conquering Peloponnesus, they established there no new sanctuary; but Delphi, its priesthood, and its religion, retained their hold upon them. The combinations which grew out of the Dorian conquest of Peloponnesus were all drawn towards Delphi as an Amphictyonic sanctuary, the one common centre of national Hellenic life. Thither turned the Ionic Athenians, no less than the Doric Spartans. The Apolline worship had come over the sea from Asia, and the Apolline priesthoods, whose strength was now concentrated at Delphi, owed their original ascendency over the rude tribes of Hellas to the possession of an older and higher culture. To retain and secure their ascendency as guides and arbitrators among the tribes of Hellas as they grew in civilization, the Delphian priesthood kept up and extended in every possible way its own communication with places and priesthoods beyond the sea, and the friendly meetings of the Hellenic communities at religious and festive solemnities. To the Apolline religion and to Delphi were due, therefore, the Hellenic festivals with their Amphictyonic and national character; to these festivals were due road-making and bridge-making, safe conducts and peace, interchange of ideas between the communities of Hellas, and commerce. To the same religion and its priesthood were due the introduction of chronology, records, writing, and history; from the practice of depositing treasures in the sanctuary for safe-keeping and management by the priesthood came finance-institutions and banking; from the priesthood's carefully maintained communications with the outer world came mapping and geography, colonization and missions, foreign culture and its religious ideas. Finally, from the religious action of Delphi there proceeded a most powerful influence on Hellenic poetry, architecture, and the plastic arts.

Hellenic development, as such, was therefore a result of the influence of Delphi. At Delphi, Dorians and Ionians, Spartans and Athenians, were Hellenes. Delphic, Doric, and Ionic often occur as interchangeable terms, because the grave differences of race were comparatively merged in the common character impressed from Delphi. At the time of the Persian wars, when the brilliant historic period of Hellas begins, the living influence of Delphi had ceased. Federation under the religious shadow of its temple had disappeared; first, Sparta had become preponderant, and had wrapped herself up in her Peloponnesian interests; then Athens had arisen as a great State to balance Sparta; Delphi had had to trim between them, bribes had discredited its sanctity, seriousness and vital power had left it. Delphi had come to be little more than a name, and what continued to exist there was merely a number of forms. But European Greece had grown into existence, and grown into existence under Delphi's influence; Athens, Sparta, Corinth had taken their bent; what they were to become they in the main were, and they owed it to Delphi.

An Apolline character belongs, as Dr. Curtius points out, to every prophecy resulting from a state of illumination and elevation of the human soul, and Apollo is thus the great awakener and sustainer of genius and intellect. Why was the destiny of Sparta so superior to that of the tribes of grave and sturdy mountaineers left behind in north-western Greece—tribes with much the same original basis of mind, soul, and character as the Spartans? Because Sparta had been in contact with the inspiring and mind-awakening influence of Delphi, so that there were moments when the intellectual development of Hellas seemed bidding fair to find for itself a centre in a Dorian State; and to this quickening of the Doric genius by Delphi the Dorism of Greek lyric poetry is an abiding witness.

But the Hellas of Hellas is Athens, and it is for enabling us to see the nature and consequences of Delphian influence upon Athens that Dr. Curtius so deserves our gratitude. Athens was Ionian: why was she not like Asiatic Ionia, which could found nothing, which had not character and energy enough to bal-

ance the love of change and the love of pleasure? In Ionia no
city engaged in the enduring and heroic pursuit of great aims
existed. Why was Athens so engaged? Why did it drop the
Ionic love of ornament and sumptuousness for Dorian simplicity? why was marriage treated seriously there when in Ionia it   5
was treated with laxity? why does the Asiatic Ionia raise the
idea of what is luxuriant and overflowing in taste and language,
while Attica raises the idea of neatness, measure, and the pur-
gation of superfluities? Why had Athens politicians and leaders
of the people like Aristides and Pericles—men with a strong   10
admixture of Dorian severity in their character, while in Ionia
men of this seriousness occur only as recluse students and
thinkers?

It was because Athens had felt the Delphic discipline. For
Apollo was not only the nourisher of genius, he was also the au-   15
thor of every higher moral effort; he was the prophet of his
father Zeus, in the highest view of Zeus, as the source of the ideas
of moral order and of right. These ideas are in human nature, but
they had "especially been a treasure in the possession of the
less gay and more solitary tribes in the mountains of northern   20
Greece." These tribes were Delphi's first pupils, and Delphi
did its best to develop those ideas which gave it a hold upon
them. Thus the graver view of life, and the thoughts which
deepen man's consciousness, became connected with Delphi;
and there the Athenians imbibed influences of character and   25
Halt which for a long time balanced in the happiest way
their native vivacity and mobility, and blended with it.

The main element in our nature conquers at last; the steady,
according to Aristotle's profound remark, becomes stupid, and
the brilliant becomes non-sane. Dorian Sparta died in the end   30
of dulness; Ionian Athens perished in the end for want of bal-
last. But their history is in their resistance to the natural excess of
their own tendencies, and it is the signal merit of the volume
of which we have been treating that it makes manifest the
source from which this power of resistance proceeded.   35

Curtius's "History of Greece"* [III]

We return to this interesting history, which grows faster than
we can follow it. The fourth volume of Mr. Ward's translation
has appeared, and we are only at the third. Nay, in some sort
we are still only at the second; for the last chapter of the
5   second volume belongs to the history of Greece after the Persian War, and our last notice stopped at the Persian War. For
after the Persian War begins a new period, having its unity in
the mounting and declining fortunes of Athens; and with this
period, which at the end of the third volume comes to its close
10 in the conclusion of the Peloponnesian War and the surrender
of Athens to Lysander, we desire to deal to-day.

Dr. Curtius himself says of Herodotus, that he sought "a general view of the varied multiplicity of human affairs which might
enable him to *recognize the invisible connection pervading the*
15 *course of their development.*" This quest betokens the genuine
historian, and in one of our preceding notices we pointed it
out as characterizing Dr. Curtius. In the history of Greece he
seeks for the essential connection, the vital development; and
his work thus gains a seriousness and unity which more than
20 make amends for certain sides of talent which are wanting. A
more picturesque narrative, a more masterly handling of military matters, a more vivacious and sympathetic following of
political struggles, it would be easy to find in other historians.
But while some of these historians leave in the mind a mere
25 hubbub of pictures and words, and others leave a distinct impression of but parts and moments in the subject of their history, Dr. Curtius leaves, and it is his signal merit, the impression of a whole. His translator, though his English is still blem-
ished by such expressions as "*surexcited*," and "states of *second-*
30 *ary and tertiary* rank," well maintains in his serious and solid
translation this impression of a whole. And that whole, in the

* "The History of Greece." By Professor Dr. Ernst Curtius. Translated
by Adolphus William Ward, M.A. Vol. III. (London: Richard Bentley
and Son. 1872.)

present case, is the course and meaning of the most important period in the life of the most important factor in the world's intellectual history—Athens. We shall try to exhibit these after Dr. Curtius, and in his own words. If we do not always quite agree with him, yet it is his grouping and handling of the facts that we have to thank for the light which makes us see them differently.

We start with B.C. 479, the days that follow Salamis and Platæa. "The victory over the Persians was at the same time a victory of democracy over aristocracy—a victory of Athens, whose constitution had fully proved itself a victory-giving power." We end with B.C. 405, the days that precede the surrender of Athens to Lysander:—

Such was the state of matters within the walls of the unhappy city. On the one side, the impetuosity of a savage demagogue, whose senseless obstinacy cut off all remaining means of preservation; on the other, the crafty leaders of the Lacedæmonian party who looked with heartless satisfaction upon the troubles rising to a height around them; while those citizens who loved their native city and her laws constituted too decided a minority for their patriotism to prove of any use. The great multitude was under the absolute influence of terror and want, and lay as an instrument, with no will of its own, in the hands of discordant and raging partisans.

As we look on this picture and on that we cannot but inquire with keen interest for the causes which in less than three-quarters of a century led the "victory-giving power" of democracy from that height of triumph to this depth of ruin; more especially when we have the same "victory-giving power" at work all round us, in various stages of success, in the politics of our own day. To convince ourselves of the likeness of situation we have only to read in Dr. Curtius a passage such as the following:—

The splendour of the rise of the young Athenian State necessarily became a stumbling block for all those who considered the welfare of States to be founded upon the cautious conduct of affairs by the members of ancient families, and who hated nothing more deeply than a political revolution which brought the multi-

tude into power and which allowed the latter in tumultuous meetings in the market-place to decide the destinies of States. The new
generation which was unfolding its forces with incredible activity
would no longer have anything to do with privileged classes, but
5   demanded that all things should be within the reach of all men.
Meanwhile, in the midst of this free competition of all forces, the
ancient families saw their whole authority endangered; and their
fall was regarded by the adherents of the old times as the ruin of
Hellenic polity and of a higher system of manners and morals.

10   In fact, as we have already seen in the earlier part of Dr. Curtius's work, what differentiates Ionian Athens from Asiatic Ionia,
is the gravity, the steadiness, the centripetal influence tending to
a common Hellenism, to religious fixity, and to conservative
habits, which Athens imbibed from the discipline of Delphi.
15 This steadiness, or *Halt*, as Goethe calls it, for a long time
balanced in the Athenians their native vivacity and mobility.
But this conservative period ends with the Persian War, and
the pure democratic development of Athens then begins;
though Cimon still represented the old spirit in politics, and on
20 domestic life and ways of thinking it still had a strong hold. "It
would indeed be a natural conclusion," says Dr. Curtius, "that
the mobility and love of change innate in the Attic people
offered only a slight pledge for the preservation of ancient
usage; but the attachment which the families of worthy citi-
25 zens felt towards everything handed down to them by their
fathers, and the quiet power of tradition, supported by religion and by various remnants of primitive institutions, were
strong enough to hold fast the people on the given foundations." Yes, but the question is *how long;* and, once you are
30 fairly launched on the democratic incline, does the check
offered by "the quiet power of tradition, supported by religion and by various remnants of primitive institutions" long
endure; if it fails, where do you find a check and what is it; or
can you do without one? There is much to be said for launch-
35 ing frankly on the democratic incline, as Athens did; Pericles
felt this and Dr. Curtius feels it:—

Pericles recognized in democracy the only constitution which
could count on a lasting life at Athens; it constituted her real

strength, which, considering the smallness of the State and the difficulty of the tasks incumbent upon it, *lay in the free and independent participation of all in the affairs of the commonwealth,
which may count upon the readiness of all to make sacrifices on its
behalf, because to all is opened, by means of it, the path to equal*   5
honours and equal influence.

There cannot be a better statement of the democratic theory,
and nothing can sound more promising; every individual is developed, stimulated, improved to the uttermost, because every
individual feels that he is alive, that he *counts;* masses are not   10
sacrificed, as they are apt to be when government is what
M. Renan calls "an aristocratic work." How then was "the
party of progress," to use the words of Dr. Curtius, "to proceed, in order to call the democracy, in the full sense of the
word, into life?"—   15

The primary motive (of the party of reform) was the necessity of
breaking the power of wealth, in order to make possible the free
development of the constitution; for the liberality practised by
wealthy citizens brought the poor into a condition of dependence,
and served as a support for the efforts of the aristocratic party, at   20
the same time confusing the political consciousness of the nation.
To free the citizens from the operation of influences of this kind,
the State moneys were employed to enable the poor to procure
sources of enjoyment, without on that account feeling themselves
under an obligation to single individuals among their fellow-cit-   25
izens.

In short:—

The power of the party of movement was based upon the multitude of the poorer citizens, and it was desired that the lower classes
should be prevented neither by timidity nor by poverty from tak-   30
ing part in public affairs.

And well may Dr. Curtius say that "the means employed for
this end were of an extremely effective character!"—

The public treasury continued more and more to be used for the
purpose of freeing the poorer citizens from the influence which   35
might be exercised upon them by the munificence of the rich; of
gaining their favour by means of presents and distributions of corn;
and by compensation in money inducing them more and more

generally to take part in public affairs. For upon the multitude of the poorer citizens was based the power of the party of reform.

And this policy, Dr. Curtius thinks, was but fair:—

5   Since in all States the power of the ruler is surrounded by a certain splendour of life which also redounds to the credit of the entire State, in a democracy the Demos is, as a matter of fairness, entitled to share in this privilege of rulers.

Not only was it fair in itself, but the condition of things which it redressed was unjust:—

10   Harsh contrasts in social life are an evil in the case of any and every State; but in a democracy, which is based on the joyous participation of all its citizens in the commonwealth, such contrasts are most keenly felt and amount to dissonances contravening the spirit of the constitution. In a democratic State, no class of men
15   ought to be treated as inferior to the rest, or to feel itself hurt by the social position of the rich; no fermenting matter ought to be left in the State, and the peace of public life ought to be endangered by no feelings of envy, jealousy, and distrust between the different classes of the citizens.

20   Thus democracy was "completely established;" and we hardly require to be told further that the Athenians, thus democratized, were "a difficult people to govern; for every man wished to inquire and judge for himself, democracy being in general disinclined to have anything to do with men who lay claim to
25   obedience." Pericles, however, and the party of reform, had made their Frankenstein; what was to be done with him? Singularly enough, the greatness of Pericles seems to consist in his having provided the democracy with a dictator:—

The sovereign power belonged to the Demos. But no man could be
30   more fully persuaded than Pericles of the incapacity of the multitude to govern by itself. Every popular body must be governed, its steps guided, and its interests pointed out to it, unless the well-being of the State is to be given up to accident and unreason.

Pericles, however, having destroyed the permanent conserva-
35   tive influences of the Athenian State, the influences of family, property, and office, did undoubtedly substitute for them, in his own personality, a governing influence even stronger,

while it lasted. By the force of his personality he was permanent Commander-in-Chief, Minister of Finance, Minister of
Public Works:—

No official class existed to oppose him, because all officials on the
expiration of their term of office returned immediately into private   5
life. Pericles alone, invested with a continuous official authority
which commanded all the various branches of public life, stood in
solitary grandeur firm and calm above the surging State.

But what, then, becomes of the essential idea of democracy—*the
free and independent participation of all in the affairs of the*   10
commonwealth? Dr. Curtius himself tells us, in describing the
government of Pericles:—

Thus a consistent and firm Government was made possible,
such as all reasonable citizens must have desired to live under
in times of danger; *though, on the other hand, it is true that*   15
all the principles of democracy were virtually abolished—viz. the
constant change and distribution of official power, and even the
responsibility attaching to it, and forming the strongest guarantee
of the sovereignity of the people.

The idea in the mind of Pericles, therefore, was "a combina-   20
tion of democracy and monocracy;" and in order to realize this
idea, "Pericles became a party man, and combined with Ephial-
tes and the other leaders of the party of progress" to democratize
Athens as we have seen. But then the anchor-chains by which
the ship of State held—the anchor-chains of the influence of   25
family and property, and of the old institutions which made
government "an aristocratic work"—were cut, not in order
that the people by free development and by the practical
school of public life might become a set of individuals able
each to think and act wisely for himself, but "in order that the   30
people *might unconditionally give itself up to the guidance of*
the orator in possession of its confidence." This is much less
than the other; but Pericles, it seems, was "fully persuaded of
the incapacity of the multitude to govern by itself," and that it
should be taught and enabled "to give its confidence to the   35
right man," instead of to the often blind superiorities of
family, property, and office, was something. Dr. Curtius says:

"The Attic Demos was beyond a doubt superior to all other civic communities in this respect, that its happy natural gifts supplied it with a sure tact and correct judgment in the choice of its leaders, and that it knew how to follow these leaders
5   when chosen, if they with superior intelligence indicated to it its true interests." No doubt it redounds to the credit of the Athenian people that it followed Pericles. But how long did it follow him? Fifteen years, and at the end of that time very imperfectly. And afterwards it followed Cleon and Cleophon.
10 Something must have interfered, then, with the natural effects of the beneficent revolution wrought by the party of progress. Dr. Curtius finds this interference mainly in two disturbing causes: the plague and the clubs. Of the plague he says:—

During the whole course of the war no more fatal event happened
15 than the Attic pestilence . . . for, although the position of Athens towards foreign States remained for a time the same, yet the city had at home undergone essential changes. The flower of the citizens had perished; many families in which ancient discipline and usage had maintained themselves had died out, and thus the living
20 connection with the age of Aristides and Cimon had come to an end.

That is to say, as long as some remains were left of that non-democratic order which the party of progress was for eradicating, the Athenian State had still something to hold it together,
25 had elements of permanence and stability; when they were gone and democracy was left to itself, the pulverizing and dissolving forces in it worked fully. It is to exaggerate the effect of the plague to say that it *caused* this: it only quickened a little the disappearance of checks which were already condemned and
30 failing. The true check had been the personality of Pericles, the dictatorship of Pericles; this could not outlast his life, and even before he died it had been manifest how things were tending:—

The moral change which had befallen the Attic community had, it
35 is true, even during the lifetime of Pericles, manifested itself by means of sufficiently clear premonitory signs; but Pericles had, notwithstanding, up to the days of his last illness, remained the centre of the State; the people had again and again returned to him, and

by subordinating themselves to the personal authority of Pericles had succeeded in recovering the demeanour which befitted them. But now the voice was hushed which had been able to sway the unruly citizens even against their will. *No other authority was in existence*—no aristocracy, no official class, no board of experienced statesmen—nothing, in fact, to which the citizens might have looked for guidance and control. *The multitude had recovered absolute independence.*

And now, as men of the stamp of Pericles are rare, it got another sort of leaders:—

Pericles stood *above* the multitude. He ruled by arousing the noble and active impulses in the minds of the citizens, who by the earnestness marking his treatment of them, and by the moral demands which he made upon them, *were raised above their own level;* they were ashamed to give voice in his hearing to their weaknesses and low cravings. *His successors were obliged to adopt other means;* in order to acquire influence they took advantage not so much of the strong as of the weak points in the character of the citizens, and achieved popularity by flattering their inclinations and endeavouring to satisfy the cravings of their baser nature. Thus the demagogues, who had formerly been the leaders and solemn counsellors of the people, now became its servants and flatterers.

And thus, also, accordingly:—

In a short space of time the civic community of Athens became an unsteady multitude which allowed itself to be swayed by uncertain feelings, a multitude which vacillated between arrogance and cowardice, between infidelity and superstitious excitement.

The other main cause which spoiled the fair experiment of democracy at Athens was, according to Dr. Curtius, the clubs:—

These clubs differed in all respects from the political associations of earlier times. They were for the most part composed of members of ancient families with innate oligarchical tendencies—passionate and excited young men of loose habits of life, who found no sphere for their ambition in the Athens of the day, who had received a sophistic education and were full of unintelligible political theories, which obscured in them the plain perception of law and sense of duty; who were accordingly vain and devoid of conscientiousness, contemners of law and usage, and scorners of the multitude and its rule. In proportion as the foreign policy of the State became democratic, the aristocratic clubs grew into associations of anti-patriotic conspirators.

5   It is well to remember what one of the great men of the Renaissance, Gemistus, says to the philosopher: that he should always suppose there is some fault in himself when he cannot bring people to his way of thinking. Surely it is of the very essence of *country*, of *constitution*, if they are worth anything, to be attaching; to inspire respect and affection. Then they are not threatened by intriguers; or, if they are threatened, they easily get the better of them. But what blame to the young Barbarians of Athens if they were "scorners of the multitude and its rule," when this multitude "vacillated between arrogance and cowardice, between infidelity and superstitious excitement"? They felt that this multitude had no right to be in power, that it had upset an old state of things which was better than its own rule; they intrigued against it, and their intrigues produced confusion because what they intrigued against had too little worth and dignity to be a firm rallying-point. So we are brought to the end of the period with which we to-day deal, to the crowning defeat of Ægos-potami and to the spectacle presented by the Athenians there:—

Opposed to a well-trained and well-supplied force, which unconditionally obeyed the will of a commander as sagacious as he was enterprising, this the last fleet which Athens was able to send out was *discordant in itself and split up into parties; its strangely mixed crews lacking all discipline, coherence, and moral bearing, and being commanded by six generals who severally pursued utterly different aims.*

To this end has come the great work of the party of progress— "to call the democracy, in the full sense of the word, into life." Dr. Curtius, like modern Liberals generally, considers this work a good and wise one; like them, he is disposed to throw the blame of its not succeeding anywhere rather than on the work itself. We have let him show, in his own words, the nature and history of the work; they are so interesting that one is tempted, in defiance of Mr. Cobden, to think that "all the works of Thucydides" may be nearly as good reading as the *Times,* at any rate in the Whitsuntide recess. For us, the moral we draw is not that the aim of the party of progress was bad, but that it was inadequate. To give to a whole people entire freedom and the practical school of public life is well; but entire freedom and the practical school of public life are not enough; even joined, as at Athens, to high natural intelligence they are not enough; they are not self-acting for a people's salvation; by themselves, they even bring it not to salvation but to ruin. What Athens lived upon, in her brilliant Periclean period, was the stores of *Halt* and character accumulated through less seen and less heard generations, these stores being moved and used by the new, vigorous force of democracy, by a whole gifted people with the fresh sense of being alive and astir. They were used, and used up, and then came the end; here is our moral. It may be said, indeed, that nothing lasts, and that we may well be satisfied with a nation if it has produced a Periclean period, and done no more. Something of this sort Dr. Curtius urges on behalf of Pericles, as head of the party of reform: "He was aware that the true greatness of an epoch is not dependent on the time of its endurance; he knew that the realization of the loftiest ideal of a Hellenic community in Athens would be a possession for ever. Accordingly, notwithstanding the sadness of his own end, the work of his life was crowned with immortal success." This is nobly said, but it does not quite satisfy the aspirations of a good citizen, who demands of the builders of his State to make it stand permanently, not in spirit only, but in palpable body. And though to permanence of this kind human things can but approximate, yet these aspirations of a good citizen are, we cannot but think, natural and just; the true builder of a State should and will procure for them satisfaction.

Curtius's "History of Greece"* [IV]

We have got into the ungracious habit of remarking on the spots
which blemish Mr. Ward's solid and sensible translation of this
useful history, and to be faithful to that habit we will begin by
saying that in the volume now before us we find "a city *be-*
5   *fallen by* its great calamity," and "that all those *were pried on*
who had stood in any relations with the oligarchs." But in
general the translator seems to us to show in this volume a
style much improved by increasing practice; the English is
more easy and idiomatic than in his earlier volumes, and some-
10   times, as in the account of Socrates, or in the final estimate of
Epaminondas, rises into real impressiveness and power.

The volume now before us continues the history of Greece
from the surrender of Athens down to the battle of Mantinea, a
period of about forty years. This period exhibits the reign of
15   Sparta and her mistakes, the partial recovery by Athens of her
old position, the rise of Thebes to be a great Power. That the
narrow and stationary policy of Sparta could not work out the
salvation of Hellas we need not say, for Dr. Curtius is never
weary of saying it. We prefer to continue to point out, from
20   Dr. Curtius's own history, the insufficiency of the anti-Spartan
policy—the democratic policy, the policy of movement—to
found anything. We think that Dr. Curtius is too much inclined to stamp this policy as right, whereas events prove it
wrong, or at least inadequate. Absolute freedom, the inde-
25   pendent participation of all in the affairs of the commonwealth, the abolition of the permanent conservative influences
in the State, influences of family, property, and office—this,
we have seen, was the democratic programme. Those who
praise it say that it makes *all* live and *all* count, and rescues the
30   masses from being sacrificed; those who blame it call it, with
Æschylus, merely "an unblest escape from all restraint." We

* "The History of Greece." By Professor Dr. Ernst Curtius. Translated
by Adolphus William Ward, M.A. Vol. IV. (London: Richard Bentley
and Son. 1872.)

prefer to neither praise nor blame it, but to call it *inadequate*. Unlimited freedom and the practical school of public life are not enough by themselves, are not self-acting for a people's salvation—this is what we say, and what Greek history, and all history, seems to us to prove. The power to respect, the power to obey, are at least as needful for man as unlimited freedom and the practical school of public life; give him these last alone, teach him to rely on these last alone, and you give him forces which but wear out both him and themselves. When first they appear they find present a store of habits of respect and obedience accumulated from old times of discipline, old institutions; the new forces are highly stimulative, undoubtedly, and they create a new life; instead of accepting its chief as hereditary, a Hippias or Hipparchus, the people now choose him as the best, a Pericles. For it has still the *habit* to respect and obey, but its one *doctrine* now is to be free and independent, and the doctrine is at variance with the habit and beats it, and the people will soon have a Cleon who does not make them respect and obey, but lets them feel free and independent; and so a society goes to pieces. And even when circumstances give it a chance to recover itself it cannot; it has no *Halt*, nothing to bind and brace it.

The faults of Sparta, the necessities of Persia, the successes of Conon, gave Athens a chance again after her crushing defeat by Lysander; her walls were rebuilt, her maritime influence revived, Greek States looked to her to lead, she seemed likely to become once more a great Power with a great policy. She could not; national virtue was gone out of her, she could produce henceforth only great individuals, not a great people. Dr. Curtius shall show us that this was so; shall show us how great a change both within and without had come over the Athens of Aristides and Pericles. First for the change within:—

Poetic art at Athens maintained itself for a season at its full height even after the symmetry of public life had been destroyed; but only in the works of Sophocles, who continued to live in the spirit of the Periclean age. After his death poetry, like music, was *seized by the same current which dissolved the foundations of the people's life*, and which swept away the soil wherein the emotions of the classical period had been rooted. Accordingly, in these times of general oscillation, poetry was unable to supply a moral anchorage; the old perished, but the modern age, with all its readiness in thought and speech, was incapable of creating a new art as a support to its children. In the same way the faith of former generations had been cast aside like antiquated household gear, but without any other assurance of morality, without any other impulse towards the virtues indispensable for the life of the community having been obtained in its stead. The need of a regeneration was acknowledged; serious endeavours were made to introduce improvements and order; but political reforms could not heal such wounds as these, or furnish a new basis for the commonweal.

And now for the change without, the political incapacity which must always accompany such inward disease:—

The appearance of Conon suddenly changed everything for the better. But neither was the influence of Conon enduring. His task could only be that of freeing Athens from the ban under which she had lain, of restoring to her freedom of movement, obtaining for her allies, and, as it were, opening the portal for a new era in her history. The rest depended on the conduct of the Athenians themselves; it was imperative that they should in a spirit of self-sacrifice recover their manly vigour, and by their own exertions continue the construction of the edifice on the basis offered to them. *But no such sustained onward effort ensued.*

And therefore see what happened at the peace of Antalcidas:—

Thus it came to pass that, in spite of the various particular successes obtained by Athens in this war, she upon the whole lost more in it than she gained. At its close she was more thoroughly disintegrated than before; she had lost all her allies, had found her best men untrustworthy, and had anew recognized the insufficiency of her own resources; and was in the end forced under the pressure of necessity to conclude a peace which deeply injured the honour of the city and by no means corresponded to the original purposes of the war.

So it was, too, after the successes of Timotheus ten years later:—

Athens herself was no longer what she had been of old. The citizens were no longer joyously ready to make all necessary sacrifices, no longer energetically determined to stake everything upon the restoration of their power. The most splendid successes of Timotheus failed to call forth any lasting ardour.

So it was, again, when Leuctra had given to Athens another splendid chance, and she actually summoned the Peloponnesian States to send deputies to Athens, and made as though she were assuming the leadership which they, on their part, were willing and eager to confer on her. "*It soon, however, became manifest that the Athenians were incapable of taking the direction of Peloponnesian affairs into their hands.*"

Therefore the lead came to Thebes, whose guiding spirit, Epaminondas, is brought before us by Dr. Curtius with much feeling and power. There at last had come at Thebes the same change which at Athens we have seen come earlier; the old traditional institutions, the aristocratical organization of the State, broke up; a democratic development prevailed. As at Athens, the new force working with what the old force bequeathed to it produced a time of high energy and a great man to wield that energy. The analogy between Epaminondas and Pericles is striking; "indeed it would be difficult to find in the entire course of Greek history any two great statesmen who in spite of differences of character and of outward conditions of life resembled one another so greatly and were as men so truly the peers of one another as Pericles and Epaminondas." The nature of the Bœotian race was grosser than that of the Athenian, the Theban aristocracy during its rule had been more brutal than the Athenian, the democracy was less spiritually gifted; the action of Epaminondas upon his people was more moral, less intellectual, than that of Pericles. The Christian world resorts to Greece for mental stimulus, not moral; our gaze, therefore, is fixed on Pericles rather than Epaminondas. With the Pagan world, whose sources of moral inspiration were more scanty, it was different; to them Epaminondas was a figure of incomparable interest, and his character has indeed a rare beauty, and with him the acceptance of the programme of the "party of movement" shows many more reserves, much more resolution not to be forced beyond what he thought right, to act, when necessary, against the mechanical policy of his party, than with Pericles. He certainly, as he showed in Achaia, "had a loftier end in view than a democratic propaganda, and desired not to excite party passions but to appease them." The propaganda, however, remained, and was the one idea of the many, the one policy the party of movement in general thought saving; that in all cases where a democratic power got the upper hand, "the entire political system of the community should be radically changed, the ancient families driven into exile, their possessions confiscated, legal proceedings instituted against all the members of the wealthier classes as pretended friends of Sparta, property belonging to the temples seized, and a multitude of new citizens admitted into the civic body." While Epaminondas lived he in great measure imposed his own will on the Theban democracy; like Pericles, he was a dictator; but "no sooner had his influence been impaired than they fell back into their old faults; and to such intervals belong those actions which brought shame and failure to the Thebans." Therefore, his work upon Thebes ended with his own life; "like Pericles, Epaminondas left no successor behind him, and his death also was the close of a historical epoch which could never again return." When he was dying on the field of Mantinea, when his policy was victorious at all points, when the fruit for which he had toiled waited only to be gathered, he felt that there was no one to gather it; before he drew out the spear, he recommended his country *to make peace.* "He lived to acknowledge that the goal for which he had striven had not been reached and could not be reached." How indeed could it be, by the virtue of no better forces than were contained in the democratic programme: *Unlimited freedom, absolute independence, strict extirpation of all institutions with an aristocratic taint, constant participation of every citizen in the management of public affairs?* It could not; and after Mantinea, no less than after Leuctra, the political situation is truly summed up in these words:—"In spite of these successes the result was small. The old system had been destroyed, the overbearing power of Sparta had been annihilated; but instead of a new and fixed order of relations, there was perceptible among the Hellenic tribes nothing but an increase of agitation and confusion."

Accordingly Socrates, who assuredly was no mere conservative, who introduced a stream of thought so fresh, bold, and transforming that it frightened "respectable" people and was the cause of his death, Socrates was never weary of recalling the Hellenic mind to the old-fashioned maxims of righteousness, temperance, and self-knowledge engraved on the temple at Delphi. The democratic programme and the teaching of the Sophists possessed the thoughts and affections of the most living communities in the Hellenic family; and the gospel of both these liberalisms came pretty much to the same thing—*freedom and movement.* Where you move to, and how you use your freedom, are left out of the account; and the ground-idea of the working of Socrates and Plato may really be said to be this: *the insufficiency of the liberal programme for salvation.* Modern Liberals do not enough consider that although then, as now, Liberalism could point to its continual advance and its victories of the day and hour, yet the long run, the full development of things, proved Socrates and Plato right.

Of Socrates Dr. Curtius treats in his chapter on "Athens after her Restoration;" and the whole of this chapter, with its account of the change in religion, poetry, music, and thought in general, is most interesting, and shows to great advantage the author's fulness of knowledge and powers of criticism. Particularly we recommend the pages on Euripides, that "lifelong sufferer from the unsolved conflict between speculation and art," who yet was able by the force and versatility of his genius to make good his place by the side of "Æschylus the soldier of Marathon, and Sophocles the witness of the Periclean age." It is not difficult to do justice to Euripides in respect of "all his natural gifts and all the acquisitions of his experience and culture; the quick sensibility of his disposition; his brilliant gift of finding the right word for every phase of feeling; his accurate knowledge of all the impulses moving his generation; and his sophistic training, which enabled him incisively to illustrate and account for all standpoints of human opinion." But in general the critic is wont to satisfy himself with passing from this praise to an unfavourable verdict on Euripides, as lacking the "inner contentment, the inner illumination of mind, which mark out the born poet." He did lack them; but the critic, to be complete, should add, like Dr. Curtius, this commentary:—

Euripides, as a poet not less than as a man, was a true martyr to Sophistry. It possessed without satisfying him; he employed it in order to bestow a new interest upon art; he contended for the right of every individual to approach in inquiring meditation all things human and divine; *but at the same time he was not blind to the dangers of this tendency. He openly declared them, uttered warnings and pronounced invectives against it, and at last wrote an entire tragedy* ("The Bacchæ") *with no other object than that of representing the miserable end of·a man who opposes his reason to the system of the gods.*

The author of "Archelaus" reminds us of Macedon. We hear that Dr. Curtius intends to give us but one volume more: to bring us to the establishment of the Macedonian supremacy by "that dishonest victory" of Chæronea, and there to leave us. We hope he will be induced to reconsider his intention. We can ill spare the account of Alexander and his Asiatic conquests; and we shall be glad to persuade Dr. Curtius that there is at any rate enough which is Hellenic in Macedon to make it right that the political history of ancient Greece should end with the fall of the Macedonian power, not its rise; with the last Philip and his son, not the first.

Curtius's "History of Greece" * [V]

With real regret we say to ourselves, on closing the volume now before us, that here we have the last instalment of Mr. Ward's sound and substantial translation of this excellent history. As we read the volume, however, we become convinced that Dr. Curtius has done right in ending here, and in not carrying on the history—as in our review of his fourth volume we expressed our wish to see him carry it—to the death of Alexander. The characteristic political life of the Hellenic people

* "The History of Greece." By Professor Dr. Ernst Curtius. Translated by Adolphus William Ward, M.A. Vol. V. (London: Richard Bentley and Son.)

ceased, as Dr. Curtius clearly shows, with the battle of Chæronea and the supremacy of Philip of Macedon; and a history of
ancient Greece fitly ends with the extinction of the characteristic political life of the Hellenic people. Macedonia had
many Hellenic elements, but its political life and system were   5
in no wise those of a true Greek State. Its conquests, therefore,
though they spread wide the Greek language and culture, and
made them cosmopolitan, did nothing to spread the type of a
genuine Greek State, like the States where this culture had had
its rise. And, this type disappearing, it was no longer Greece   10
itself which was charged with the continued development of
Greek culture, but the world.

The present volume affords to Dr. Curtius, before he parts
with us, the opportunity of once more showing his strength in
all the points where he is strong. His vivid account of the moun- 15
tain and river system of Macedonia recalls the admirable geo-
graphical touch which charmed us in the former volumes.
The moral and philosophical interest arising from the development of national character, and from the growth, sure and
fatal, of its faults, reappear strikingly in the continuation and   20
close of the life of independent Athens. Finally, the personal
and dramatic interest, which Dr. Curtius has so often aroused
by his mode of treating his personages, returns with all its
force in his presentation of Demosthenes.

But Dr. Curtius shall himself show us his quality as a geog-   25
rapher, as a philosophical moralist, and as a delineator of men.
What can be more delightful than this sketch of Ægæ or Edessa,
the primitive capital of the royal race of the founders of Macedonia, the Argive Temenidæ:—

In all Macedonia there is no more excellent situation. As the travel-   30
ler coming from Salonica ascends the gradually narrowing plain,
his attention is already from afar enchained by the glittering silver
streak which reaches vertically down into the valley from the rim
of the mountain side nearest to the front. It announces the waterfalls of Vódena, which lies on the site of ancient Ægæ, on a well-   35
wooded declivity turned straight to the east, while in the background rises in solemn grandeur the lofty mountain range. The
waterfalls, which at this day mark out the place and give to it a

striking resemblance to Tibur, were not in existence in ancient times. Only gradually, by means of a progressive formation of tufa, the waters have managed to stop up the passages in the rocks, through which they formerly found a subterraneous outlet. But at all times Ægæ must have been a spot of exceeding beauty and salubrity, the portal of the highlands and the dominant castle of the plain in the rear of which it lies, like Mycenæ or Ilium. The view from the castle extends over the gulf to the hills of the Chalcidice, and at its feet unite all the main rivers of the country. Ægæ was the natural capital of the land. With its foundation the history of Macedonia had its beginning; Ægæ is the germ out of which the Macedonian Empire grew.

The present volume exhibits the ultimate development of political character in Athens and the other Greek republics. In what condition did Philip find them all? What had they to oppose to his ambitious projects and to his great material force—great, but not greater than what Greece had already repelled at the Persian invasion?

The position of affairs could not have been more promising (for Philip). Thebes had sunk back into her former impotence, and, after the death of Epaminondas, Athens was the solitary State in which the idea of a national policy survived, but it was merely a dreamy reminiscence of the past which her citizens would not bear to renounce, while at the same time they felt themselves possessed of no vital powers for making the idea a reality.... When Philip took into consideration this condition of things; when with his keen glance he perceived how the petty States had degenerated, how the still existing forces of population were uselessly consuming themselves in party discord, in war, and in a lawless life of mercenary service, how among the best citizens many were longing for a vigorous leadership without finding the right men for the purpose in their own people; when Philip could convince himself how in the same measure in which the faith in the vitality of the small republics had sunk, the reputation of royal power had risen in the eyes of many of the most intelligent Hellenes; he naturally and necessarily arrived at the conviction that the objects of his personal ambition were also that which was historically necessary and alone rational, and must thus in the end be also acknowledged by the Greeks, in spite of their obstinate local patriotism and of their contempt for the Macedonian people. The national history of the

Greeks had lived its life to an end in the orbit of their native country, in the more limited sense of the term, and under the form of Republican Constitutions.

And why this loss of faith among the Greeks themselves in the vitality of their small republics? Take Athens, the chief of them. "The great difference between the new and the old Athens lay in this, that it was now no longer the entire civic community which of one accord desired progress, and that the efforts made had no endurance. Athens betrayed her exhaustion, and when she had made a vigorous advance she soon sank back into an attitude of fatigue, and craved for nothing but a tranquil enjoyment of life, and undisturbed comfort within the limited sphere of her civic life." The aristocratic and the democratic classes were alike enfeebled. "On the one side a wealthy intellectual life, floating in ideal elevation, from the standpoint of which the Attic civic State was regarded as a thing without value; on the other, an indolent existence, swayed by selfishness, lazily sunk in obedience to daily habit, and unwilling to allow its ease to be disturbed by any exertion. It was thus that the Athens of Eubulus drifted on, like a ship without a helmsman, with the current of the age."

The sixteen years of the administration of Eubulus (B.C. 354–338) mark, therefore, a critical time in Athenian history. Eubulus was generally acceptable. He pleased the poor by making the distribution of the festival-moneys, formerly occasional, a regular law-ordained practice, and by doubling and trebling the amount distributed. He pleased the rich by "a peace-policy, which kept at a distance the terror of the property-tax." Eubulus, in short, "knew how to strike chords which found a ready response on all sides; he based his policy upon the low and vulgar inclinations of humanity, and by satisfying these estranged his fellow-citizens from all more serious endeavours. The grandeur and loftiness of Athenian democracy had vanished, while all the germs of perniciousness contained in it were fully developed." Eubulus was able for sixteen years to conduct on these lines the Athens of Pericles, and one can well understand that the deterioration worked by such a leading was fatal. What one asks oneself is, why the

faultier side in the Athenian character, the side which made
the reign of Eubulus possible, should have finally prevailed
rather than the nobler side, the side which made possible the
reign of Pericles? One asks oneself whether it is inevitable,
then, that the faultier side of a national character should be always the one to prevail finally; and whether, therefore, since
every national character has its faultier side, the greatness of no
great nation can be permanent. And the answer probably is
that the greatness cannot be permanent of any nation which is
not great by its mere material numbers as well as by its qualities. Great qualities are balanced by faults, and in any community there will be more individuals with the faults of their
nation than with its great qualities. Now, in a small community like Athens, a community counting its members by thousands instead of by millions, there is not a sufficient recruiting-
ground from whence to draw ever-fresh supplies of men of
the better type, capable of maintaining their country's greatness at a high level permanently, or of bringing it back there
after it has for a time retrograded owing to faults or misfortunes.

However, in no State, great or small, is it the business of a good
citizen to believe that the decline and fall of his country are
inevitable, and to resign himself to that belief. The grandeur of
Demosthenes, and his civic superiority to a man, even, so fascinating as Plato, consists in his having refused to allow himself
to entertain such a belief, in his having worked as if the restoration of the true Athens were possible, in his having accomplished something towards that restoration, and in his having
thus, though he could not save Athens, contributed in no mean
degree to save the ideal of national greatness and of true political effort among mankind. Dr. Curtius shall characterize for us
both him and Plato—the divine Plato, who indeed "passes far
beyond that which was comprehended in the moral consciousness of his nation," and who therefore "stands like a prophet
above his times and his people." But, "In proportion as Plato in
his ideal demands rose above the data of the circumstances and
principles around him, it became impossible to expect that he
would exercise a transforming influence upon the great body

of the people. He was by his whole nature far more aristocratic than Socrates, the simple man of the people; and his teachings and aims could only become the possession of a circle of elect."

Dear, therefore, as Athens was to Plato, he found himself by nature unable to look for her recovery or to strive for it. Demosthenes, on the contrary, amidst "the dark experiences of his early life, yet acquired confidence in the sound and honest spirit which lived in the better part of the civic community—a confidence which never afterwards deserted him." Towards the followers of Plato, who constituted an intellectual power at Athens, Demosthenes stood in an attitude of direct opposition. For "he could not but be averse from any philosophy which estranged man from his civic duties, and removed him from the sphere of practical efficiency into the realms of ideas." On the other hand, "He closely studied the ideas of Solon, in whose sayings and laws he found the moral mission of the Attic State most perfectly expressed; he drew strength from recalling the great past of his native city, and already for this reason loved Thucydides more than any other author; to him he felt inwardly akin; the work of Thucydides was to him, so to speak, the canonical book of the Attic spirit; he is said to have copied it out eight times with his own hand, and to have known the greater part of it by heart." Demosthenes was in vital sympathy, therefore, with the Athenian democracy; nevertheless,

His talents had not easily and lightly developed themselves by following the prevailing tendencies of the age; on the contrary, he was opposed to all the tendencies of the present, to rhetoric, to sophistry and philosophy, and similarly to the great world and to the political sentiments which ruled the citizens in the times of Eubulus. It was in solitary struggles that he laboured and strove to form himself, and it was thus that he impressed upon his development the perfect stamp of his own individuality. The weight of the seriousness of his life is impressed upon his eloquence; hence his aversion from all phrase-making and from rhetorical verbiage. His style is short and condensed; he adheres strictly to the subject, seeking to seize it in the most thorough possible way from every

side, and to cut off by anticipation all possible objections. With this mastery over the dialectical art are combined a force of moral conviction and a passionate hatred of all that is base, an inflexible courage, and a fervent love for his native city; so that thus the art
5   of the orator becomes the expression of the entire man.

Demosthenes did not succeed, and with the defeat of Chæronea ends the genuine existence of the Greek republics and of Athens, the pearl of them. We regret to part with Dr. Curtius; but he has convinced us, we repeat, that he does right in ending his history
10   here. In its close, as also throughout its entire course, his history remains faithful to those moral ideas which, however they may be sometimes obscured or denied, are yet in the natural order of things the master-light for men of the Germanic race, for both Germans and Englishmen. And in our common, instinc-
15   tive appreciation of those ideas lies the true, the indestructible ground of sympathy between Germany and England.

Obermann

Obermann.—Par De Senancour. Nouvelle édition, revue et corrigée avec une Préface, par George Sand. Charpentier, Paris, 1863.

The most recent edition of *Obermann* lies before me, the date on its title-page being 1863. It is, I believe, the fourth edition which has been published; the book made its first appearance in 1804; three editions, and not large editions, have sufficed for the demand of sixty years. Yet the book has lived, though with but this obscure life, and is not likely to die. Madame George Sand and Monsieur Sainte-Beuve have spoken in prose much and excellently of the book and its author. It may be in the recollection of some who read this that I have spoken of *Obermann* in verse, if not well, at least abundantly. It is to be wished, however, that Obermann should also speak to English readers for himself; and my present design is to take those two or three points where he is most significant and interesting, and to present some of his deliverances on those points in his own words.

It may be convenient, however, that first I should repeat here the short sketch which I have already given elsewhere of the uneventful life of the personage whom we call Obermann. His real name is Senancour. In the book which occupies us,—a volume of letters of which the writer, calling himself Obermann, and writing chiefly from Switzerland, delivers his thoughts about God, nature, and the human soul,—it is Senancour himself who speaks under Obermann's name. Étienne Pivert de Senancour, a Frenchman, although having in his nature much that we are accustomed to consider as by no means French, was born in 1770, was trained for the priesthood, and passed some time in the seminary of St. Sulpice, broke away from his training and country to live some years in Switzerland, where he married, came back to France in middle life, and followed thenceforward the career of a man of letters, but

with hardly any fame or success. His marriage was not a
happy one. He died an old man in 1846, desiring that on his
grave might be placed these words only: "*Éternité, deviens
mon asile.*"

5   Of the letters of Obermann, the writer's profound inwardness,
his austere and sad sincerity, and his delicate feeling for nature,
are, as I have elsewhere remarked, the distinguishing characteristics. His constant inwardness, his unremitting occupation
with that question which haunted St. Bernard—*Bernarde, ad*
10   *quid venisti?*—distinguish him from Goethe and Wordsworth,
whose study of this question is relieved by the thousand dis-
tractions of a poetic interest in nature and in man. His severe
sincerity distinguishes him from Rousseau, Chateaubriand, or
Byron, who in their dealing with this question are so often
15   attitudinising and thinking of the effect of what they say on
the public. His exquisite feeling for nature, though always
dominated by his inward self-converse and by his melancholy,
yet distinguishes him from the men simply absorbed in philosophical or religious concerns, and places him in the rank of
20   men of poetry and imagination. Let me try to show these three
main characteristics of Senancour from his own words.
     A Frenchman, coming immediately after the eighteenth cen-
tury and the French Revolution, too clear-headed and austere
for any such sentimental Catholic reaction as that with which
25   Chateaubriand cheated himself, and yet, from the very pro-
foundness and meditativeness of his nature, religious, Senancour
felt to the uttermost the bare and bleak spiritual atmosphere into
which he was born. Neither to a German nor to an Englishman, perhaps, would such a sense of absolute religious denuda-
30   tion have then been possible, or such a plainness and even
crudity, therefore, in their way of speaking of it. Only to a
Frenchman were these possible; but amid wars, bustle, and the
glory of the *grande nation* few Frenchmen had meditativeness
and seriousness enough for them. Senancour was of a character
35   to feel his spiritual position, to feel it without dream or illusion, and to feel, also, that in the absence of any real inward
basis life was weariness and vanity, and the ordinary considerations so confidently urged to induce a man to master himself
and to be busy in it, quite hollow.

"People keep talking," says he, "of doing with energy that which ought to be done; but, amidst all this parade of firmness, *tell me, then, what it is that ought to be done.* For my part I do not know; and I venture to suspect that a good many others are in the same state of ignorance." 5

He was born with a passion for order and harmony, and a belief in them; his being so utterly divested of all conventional beliefs, makes this single elementary belief of his the more weighty and impressive.

"May we not say that the tendency to order forms an essential 10 part of our propensities, our *instinct,* just like the tendency to self-preservation, or to the reproduction of the species? Is it nothing, to live with the calm and the security of the just?"

And therefore, he concludes, "inasmuch as man had this feeling of order planted in him, inasmuch as it was in his nature, the 15 right course would have been to try and make every individual man sensible of it and obedient to it." But what has been done? Since the beginning of the world, instead of having recourse to this innate feeling, the guides of mankind have uniformly sought to control human conduct by means of supernatural 20 hopes, supernatural terrors, thus misleading man's intelligence, and debasing his soul. *"Depuis trente siècles, les résultats sont dignes de la sagesse des moyens."* What are called *the virtues,* "are laws of nature as necessary to man as the laws of his bodily senses." Instead of teaching men to feel this, instead of 25 developing in them that sentiment of order and that consciousness of the divine which are the native possession of our race, Paganism and Christianity alike have tampered with man's mind and heart, and wrought confusion in them.

"Conquerors, slaves, poets, pagan priests, and nurses, succeeded in 30 disfiguring the traditions of primitive wisdom by dint of mixing races, destroying memorials, explaining allegories and making nonsense of them, abandoning the profound and true meaning in order to discover in them absurd ideas which might inspire wonder and awe, and personifying abstract beings in order to have plenty of 35 objects of worship. The principle of life—that which was intelligence, light, the eternal—became nothing more than the husband

of Juno; harmony, fruitfulness, the bond of all living things, became nothing more than the mistress of Adonis; imperishable wisdom came to be distinguished only through her owl; the great
ideas of immortality and retribution consisted in the fear of turn-
5   ing a wheel, and the hope of strolling in a green wood. The in-
divisible divinity was parcelled into a hierarchical multitude torn
by miserable passions; the fruit of the genius of primitive mankind, the emblems of the laws of the universe, had degenerated into
superstitious usages which the children in great cities turned into
10   ridicule."

Paul at Athens might have set forth, in words not unlike these,
the degradation of the Unknown God; now for the religion of
which Paul was a minister:—

"A moral belief was wanted, because pure morality was gone out
15   of men's knowledge; dogmas were wanted, which should be profound and perhaps unfathomable, but not by any means dogmas
which should be absurd, because intelligence was spreading more
and more. All religions being sunk into degradation, there was
needed a religion of majesty, and answering to man's effort to ele-
20   vate his soul by the idea of a God of all things. There were needed
religious rites which should be imposing, not too common, objects
of desire, mysterious yet simple; rites which seemed to belong to
a higher world, and which yet a man's reason should accept as
naturally as his heart. There was needed, in short, what only a
25   great genius could institute, and what I can only catch glimpses of.
"But you have fabricated, patched, experimented, altered; renewed I know not what incoherent multitude of trivial ceremonies
and dogmas, more fitted to scandalize the weak than to edify them.
This dubious mixture you have joined to a morality sometimes
30   false, often exceedingly noble, and almost always austere; the one
single point in which you have shown sagacity. You pass some
hundreds of years in arranging all this by inspiration; and your
slowly built work, industriously repaired, but with a radical fault
in plan, is so made as to last hardly longer than the time during
35   which you have been accomplishing it."

There is a passage to be meditated by the new Œcumenical
Council! Not that Senancour has a trace of the Voltairian bitterness against Christianity, or against Catholicism which to him
represented Christianity:—

"So far am I from having any prejudice against Christianity, that I deplore, I may say, what the majority of its zealous adherents never themselves think of deploring. I could willingly join them in lamenting the loss of Christianity; but there is this difference be- tween us, that they regret it in the form into which it settled, nay, 5 in the form, even, which it wore a century ago; whereas I cannot consider such a Christianity as that was to be much worthy of re- gret."

He owns that religion has done much; but, "si la religion a fait des grands choses, *c'est avec des moyens immenses.*" Dispos- 10 ing of such means, it ought to have done much more. Remark, he says, that for the educated class religion is one of the weakest of the motive-powers they live by; and then ask yourself whether it is not absurd that there should be only a tenth part of our race educated. That religion should be of use as some 15 restraint to the ignorant and brutal mass of mankind, shows, he thinks, not so much the beneficence of religion as the state of utter confusion and misery into which mankind has, in spite of religion, drifted:—

"I admit that the laws of civil society prove to be not restraint 20 enough for this multitude to which we give no training, about which we never trouble our heads, which we bring into the world and then leave to the chance of ignorant passions and of habits of low debauchery. This only proves that there is mere wretchedness and confusion under the apparent calm of vast states; that the 25 science of politics, in the true sense of the term, is a stranger to our world, where diplomacy and financial administration produce prosperity to be sung in poems, and win victories to figure in gazettes."

This concern for the state and prospects of what are called the 30 masses is perpetually recurring with Senancour; it came to him from his singular lucidity and plain-dealing, for it was no com- monplace with his time and contemporaries, as it is with ours. "There are men," he says, and he was one of them, "who cannot be happy except among men who are contented; who 35 feel in their own persons all the enjoyment and suffering they witness, and who cannot be satisfied with themselves except they contribute to the order of the world and to man's welfare." "Arrange one's life how one will," he says in another place, "who can answer for its being any happier, so long as it is and must be *sans accord avec les choses, et passée au milieu des peuples souffrans*"? This feeling returns again and again:—

5   "Inequality is in the nature of things; but you have increased it out of all measure, when you ought, on the contary, to have studied to reduce it. The prodigies of your industry must surely be a baneful work of superfluity, if you have neither time nor faculties for doing so many things which are indispensable. The mass of mankind
10 is brutal, foolish, given over to its passions; *all your ills come from this cause*. Either do not bring men into existence, or, if you do, give them an existence which is human."

But as deep as his sense that the time was out of joint, was the feeling of this Hamlet that he had no power to set it right.
15 *Vos douleurs ont flétri mon âme*, he says:—

"Your miseries have worn out my soul; they are intolerable, because they are objectless. Your pleasures are illusory, fugitive; a day suffices for knowing them and abandoning them. I enquired of myself for happiness, but with my eyes open; I saw that it was
20 not made for the man who was isolated: I proposed it to those who stood round me; they had not leisure to concern themselves with it. I asked the multitude in its wear and tear of misery, and the great of earth under their load of ennui; they answered me: We are wretched to-day, but we shall enjoy ourselves to-morrow. For
25 my part, I know that the day which is coming will only tread in the footsteps of the day which is gone before."

But a root of failure, powerlessness, and ennui, there certainly was in the constitution of Senancour's own nature; so that, unfavourable as may have been his time, we should err in attributing
30 to any outward circumstances the whole of the discouragement by which he is pervaded. He himself knew this well, and he never seeks to hide it from us. "Il y a dans moi un dérangement," says he; "*c'est le désordre des ennuis*."

"I was born to be not happy. You know those dark days, bordering
35 on the frosts of winter, when mists hang heavily about the very dawn, and day begins only by threatening lines of a lurid light upon the masses of cloud. That glooming veil, those stormy squalls,

those uncertain gleams, that whistling of the wind through trees which bend and shiver, those prolonged throes like funeral groans—you see in them the morning of life; at noon, cooler storms and more steadily persistent; at evening, thicker darkness still, and the day of man is brought to an end." 5

No representation of Senancour can, however, be complete without some of the gleams which relieved this discouragement. Besides the inwardness, besides the sincerity, besides the renouncement, there was the poetic emotion and the deep feeling for nature. 10

"And I, too, I have my moments of forgetfulness, of strength, of grandeur; I have desires and yearnings that know no limit. But I behold the monuments of effaced generations; I see the flint wrought by the hand of man, and which will subsist a hundred centuries after him. I renounce the care for that which passes away, 15 and the thought of a present which is already gone. I stand still, and marvel; I listen to what subsists yet, I would fain hear what will go on subsisting; in the movement of the forest, in the murmur of the pines, I seek to catch some of the accents of the eternal tongue." 20

Nature, and the emotion caused by nature, inspire so many beautiful passages in Obermann's letters that one is embarrassed to make a choice among them. The following, with which we will end our extracts, is a morning and night-piece from the north end of the Lake of Neufchâtel, where the river Thiele 25 enters the lake from Bienne, between Saint Blaise and Morat:—

"My window had remained open all night, as is my habit. Towards four o'clock in the morning I was awakened by the dawn, and by the scent of the hay which they had been cutting in the 30 cool early hours by the light of the moon. I expected an ordinary view; but I had a moment of perfect astonishment. The midsummer rains had kept up the waters which the melting snow in the Jura had previously swollen. The space between the lake and the Thiele was almost entirely flooded; the highest spots formed islands 35 of pasture amidst the expanse of waters ruffled with the fresh breeze of morning. The waves of the lake could be made out in the distance, driven by the wind against the half-flooded bank. Some goats and cows, with their herdsman, who made a rustic music with a horn, were passing at the moment over a tongue of land left dry between the flooded plain and the Thiele. Stones set in the parts where it was worst going supported this natural causeway or filled up gaps in it; the pasture to which the docile animals were proceeding was not in sight, and to see their slow and irresolute advance, one would have said they were about to get out into the lake and be lost there. The heights of Anet and the thick woods of Julemont rose out of the waters like a desert island without an inhabitant. The hilly chain of Vuilly edged the lake on the horizon. To the south, this chain stretched away behind the slopes of Montmirail; and farther on than all these objects, sixty leagues of eternal snows stamped the whole country with the inimitable majesty of those bold lines of nature which give to places sublimity."

He dines at the toll-house by the river-bank, and after passing the afternoon there, goes out again late in the evening:—

"The moon had not yet risen; my path lay beside the green waters of the Thiele. I had taken the key of my lodging that I might come in when I liked without being tied to a particular hour. But feeling inclined to muse, and finding the night so warm that there was no hardship in being all night out of doors, I took the road to Saint Blaise. I left it at a little village called Marin, which has the lake to the south of it. I descended a steep bank, and got upon the shore of the lake where its ripple came up and expired. The air was calm; not a sail was to be seen on the lake. Every one was at rest; some in the forgetfulness of their toils, others in the forgetfulness of their sorrows. The moon rose; I remained there hours. Towards morning, the moon shed over earth and waters the ineffable melancholy of her last gleams. Nature seems unspeakably grand, when, plunged in a long reverie, one hears the washing of the waves upon a solitary strand, in the calm of a night still enkindled and luminous with the setting moon.

"Sensibility which no words can express, charm and torment of our vain years! vast consciousness of a nature everywhere greater than we are, and everywhere inpenetrable! all-embracing passion, ripened wisdom, delicious self-abandonment,—everything that a mortal heart can contain of life-weariness and yearning, I felt it all, I experienced it all, in this memorable night. I have made an ominous step towards the age of decline; I have swallowed up ten years of life at once. Happy the simple, whose heart is always young!"

There, in one of the hours which were at once the inspiration and the enervation of Senancour's life, we leave him. It is possible that an age, breaking with the past, and inclined to tell it the most naked truths, may take more pleasure than its predecessors in Obermann's bleak frankness, and may even give him a kind of celebrity. Nevertheless it may be predicted with certainty that his very celebrity, if he gets it, will have, like his life, something maimed, incomplete, and unsuccessful about it; and that his intimate friends will still be but a few, as they have hitherto been. These few will never fail him.

Sainte-Beuve

This is neither the time nor the place to attempt any complete account of the remarkable man whose pen, busy to the end,
and to the end charming and instructing us, has within the last
few weeks dropped from his hand for ever. A few words are
all that the occasion allows, and it is hard not to make them
words of mere regret and eulogy. Most of what is at this
moment written about him is in this strain, and very naturally;
the world has some arrears to make up to him, and now, if
ever, it feels this. Late, and as it were by accident, he came to
his due estimation in France; here in England it is only within
the last ten years that he can be said to have been publicly
known at all. We who write these lines knew him long and
owed him much; something of that debt we will endeavour to
pay, not, as we ourselves might be most inclined, by following
the impulse of the hour and simply praising him, but, as he
himself would have preferred, by recalling what in sum he
chiefly was, and what is the essential scope of his effort and
working.

Shortly before Sainte-Beuve's death appeared a new edition
of his *Portraits Contemporains,* one of his earlier works, of which
the contents date from 1832 and 1833, before his method and
manner of criticism were finally formed. But the new edition
is enriched with notes and retouches added as the volumes
were going through the press, and which bring our communications with him down to these very latest months of his life.
Among them is a comment on a letter of Madame George
Sand, in which she had spoken of the admiration excited by
one of his articles. "I leave this as it stands," says he, "because
the sense and the connection of the passage require it; but,

personne ne sait mieux que moi à quoi s'en tenir sur le mé-
rite absolu de ces articles qui sont tout au plus, et même lors-
qu'ils réussissent le mieux, des choses sensées dans un genre
médiocre. Ce qu'ils ont eu d'alerte et d'à-propos à leur mo-
ment suffit à peine à expliquer ces exagérations de l'amitié. 5
Réservons l'admiration pour les oeuvres de poésie et d'art, pour
les compositions élevées; la plus grande gloire du critique est
dans l'approbation et dans l'estime des bons esprits."

This comment, which extends to his whole work as a critic,
has all the good breeding and delicacy by which Sainte-Beuve's 10
writing was distinguished, and it expresses, too, what was to a
great extent, no doubt, his sincere conviction. Like so many who
have tried their hand at *oeuvres de poésie et d'art*, his preference, his dream, his ideal, was there; the rest was comparatively journeyman-work, to be done well and estimably rather 15
than ill and discreditably, and with precious rewards of its
own, besides, in exercising the faculties and in keeping off
ennui; but still work of an inferior order. Yet when one looks
at the names on the title-page [i.e., contents page] of the *Por-*
traits Contemporains: Chateaubriand, Béranger, Lamennais, 20
Lamartine, Victor Hugo, George Sand,—names representing,
in our judgment, very different degrees of eminence, but
none of which we have the least inclination to disparage,—is it
certain that the works of poetry and art to which these names
are attached eclipse the work done by Sainte-Beuve? Could 25
Sainte-Beuve have had what was no doubt his will, and in the
line of the *Consolations* and *Volupté* have produced works
with the power and vogue of Lamartine's works, or Chateaubriand's, or Hugo's, would he have been more interesting to us
to-day,—would he have stood permanently higher? We ven- 30
ture to doubt it. Works of poetry and art like Molière's and
Milton's eclipse no doubt all productions of the order of the
Causeries du Lundi, and the highest language of admiration
may very properly be reserved for such works alone. Inferior
works in the same kind have their moment of vogue when 35
their admirers apply to them this language; there is a moment
when a drama of Hugo's finds a public to speak of it as if it
were Molière's, and a poem of Lamartine's finds a public to

speak of it as if it were Milton's. At no moment will a public
be found to speak of work like Sainte-Beuve's *Causeries* in
such fashion; and if this alone were regarded, one might allow
oneself to leave to his work the humbler rank which he assigns
5   to it. But the esteem inspired by his work remains and grows,
while the vogue of all works of poetry and art but the best,
and the high-pitched admiration which goes with vogue, diminish and disappear; and this redresses the balance. Five-and-
twenty years ago it would have seemed absurd, in France, to
10   place Sainte-Beuve, as a French author, on a level with Lamartine. Lamartine had at that time still his vogue, and though
assuredly no Molière or Milton, had for the time of his vogue
the halo which surrounds properly none but great poets like
these. To this Sainte-Beuve cannot pretend, but what does
15   Lamartine retain of it now? It would still be absurd to place
Sainte-Beuve on a level with Molière or Milton; is it any
longer absurd to place him on a level with Lamartine, or even
above him? In other words, excellent work in a lower kind
counts in the long run above work which is short of excellence
20   in a higher; first-rate criticism has a permanent value greater
than that of any but first-rate works of poetry and art.

And Sainte-Beuve's criticism may be called first-rate. His
curiosity was unbounded, and he was born a *naturalist*, carrying
into letters, so often the mere domain of rhetoric and futile
25   amusement, the ideas and methods of scientific natural inquiry.
And this he did while keeping in perfection the ease of movement and charm of touch which belong to letters properly so
called, and which give them their unique power of universal
penetration and of propagandism. Man, as he is, and as his history
30   and the productions of his spirit show him, was the object of his
study and interest; he strove to find the real data with which,
in dealing with man and his affairs, we have to do. Beyond this
study he did not go,—to find the real data. But he was determined they should be the real data, and not fictitious and
35   conventional data, if he could help it. This is what, in our
judgment, distinguishes him, and makes his work of singular
use and instructiveness. Most of us think that we already possess the data required, and have only to proceed to deal with

human affairs in the light of them. This is, as is well known, a
thoroughly English persuasion. It is what makes us such keen
politicians; it is an honour to an Englishman, we say, to take
part in political strife. Solomon says, on the other hand, "It is
an honour to a man to cease from strife, but every fool will be   5
meddling;" and Sainte-Beuve held with Solomon. Many of us,
again, have principles and connections which are all in all to us,
and we arrange data to suit them;—a book, a character, a
period of history, we see from a point of view given by our
principles and connections, and to the requirements of this   10
point of view we make the book, the character, the period,
adjust themselves. Sainte-Beuve never did so, and criticised
with unfailing acuteness those who did. "*Tocqueville arrivait
avec son moule tout prêt; la réalité n'y répond pas, et les
choses ne se prêtent pas à y entrer.*"   15

M. de Tocqueville commands much more sympathy in England than his critic, and the very mention of him will awaken im-
pressions unfavourable to Sainte-Beuve; for the French Liberals honour Tocqueville and at heart dislike Sainte-Beuve; and
people in England always take their cue from the French Lib-   20
erals. For that very reason have we boldly selected for quotation this criticism on him, because the course criticised in
Tocqueville is precisely the course with which an Englishman
would sympathise, and which he would be apt to take himself;
while Sainte-Beuve, in criticising him, shows just the tendency   25
which is his characteristic, and by which he is of use to us.
Tocqueville, as is well known, finds in the ancient *régime* all
the germs of the centralisation which the French Revolution
developed and established. This centralisation is his bugbear, as
it is the bugbear of English Liberalism; and directly he finds it,   30
the system where it appears is judged. Disliking, therefore, the
French Revolution for its centralisation, and then finding centralisation in the ancient *régime* also, he at once sees in this
discovery, "*mille motifs nouveaux de haïr l'ancien régime.*"
How entirely does every Englishman abound here, as the   35
French say, in Tocqueville's sense; how faithfully have all
Englishmen repeated and re-echoed Tocqueville's book on the
ancient *régime* ever since it was published; how incapable are

they of supplying, or of imagining the need of supplying, any corrective to it! But hear Sainte-Beuve:—

"Dans son effroi de la centralisation, l'auteur en vient à méconnaître de grands bienfaits d'équité dus à Richelieu et à Louis XIV. Homme du peuple ou bourgeois, sous Louis XIII., ne valait-il pas mieux avoir affaire à un intendant, à l'homme du roi, qu'à un gouverneur de province, à quelque duc d'Epernon? Ne maudissons pas ceux à qui nous devons les commencements de l'égalité devant la loi, la première ébauche de l'ordre moderne qui nous a affranchis, nous et nos pères, et le tiers-état tout entier, de cette quantité de petits tyrans qui couvraient le sol, grands seigneurs ou hobereaux."

The point of view of Sainte-Beuve is as little that of a glowing Revolutionist as it is that of a chagrined Liberal; it is that of a man who seeks the *truth* about the ancient *régime* and its institutions, and who instinctively seeks to correct anything strained and *arranged* in the representation of them. "*Voyons les choses de l'histoire telles qu'elles se sont passées.*"

At the risk of offending the prejudices of English readers we have thus gone for an example of Sainte-Beuve's essential method to a sphere where his application of it makes a keen impression, and created for him, in his lifetime, warm enemies and detractors. In that sphere it is not easily permitted to a man to be a *naturalist*, but a naturalist Sainte-Beuve could not help being always. Accidentally, at the end of his life, he gave delight to the Liberal opinion of his own country and ours by his famous speech in the Senate on behalf of free thought. He did but follow his instinct, however, of opposing, in whatever medium he was, the current of that medium when it seemed excessive and tyrannous. The extraordinary social power of French Catholicism makes itself specially felt in an assembly like the Senate. An elderly Frenchman of the upper class is apt to be, not unfrequently, a man of pleasure, reformed or exhausted, and the deference of such a personage to repression and Cardinals is generally excessive. This was enough to rouse Sainte-Beuve's opposition; but he would have had the same tendency to oppose the heady current of a medium where mere Liberalism reigned, where it was Professor Fawcett, and not the Archbishop of Bordeaux, who took the bit in his teeth.

That Sainte-Beuve stopped short at curiosity, at the desire to know things as they really are, and did not press on with faith and ardour to the various and immense applications of this knowledge which suggest themselves, and of which the accomplishment is reserved for the future, was due in part to his character, but more to his date, his period, his circumstances. Let it be enough for a man to have served well one need of his age; and among politicians and rhetoricians to have been a naturalist, at a time when for any good and lasting work in government and literature our old conventional draught of the nature of things wanted in a thousand directions re-verifying and correcting.

Friendship's Garland

[Part II]

Letter VIII

Under a Playful Signature, My Friend Leo, of the "Daily Telegraph," Advocates an Important Liberal Measure, and, in so Doing, Gives News of Arminius

(A melancholy occasion brought Arminius and me together again in 1869; the sparkling pen of my friend Leo has luckily preserved the record of what then passed.)—ED.

ST. JAMES'S PLACE, June 8, 1869.

SIR,— 5

For the sake of my health it is my custom at this full-blooded time of the year to submit myself to a lowering course of medical treatment, which causes me for a few days to be voted below par for Fleet Street; so I have bethought myself of utilising my leisure, while universal humanity does not claim 10 me, and while my style is reduced nearer the pitch of the *Pall Mall Gazette*, by writing to you on a subject in which I am strongly interested, and on which your ideas are, I am sorry to see, far from sound. I mean that great subject of which a fragment will be brought under discussion to-night, by the 15 House of Commons going into Committee on Mr. Chambers's admirable bill for enabling a woman to marry her sister's husband.

My ideas on this subject have been stirred into lively activity by a visit I have just been making. I believe my name has been 20 once or twice mentioned in your columns in connection with the Bottles family near Reigate, and with a group of friends gathered round them. Poor Mrs. Bottles, I grieve to say, is not long for this world. She and her family showed an interest in me while I was rising to name and fame, and I trust I have never 25 forgotten it. She sate, as Curran says, by my cradle, and I

313

intend to follow her hearse. Meanwhile, with our Paris correspondent, who happens to be over here for a few days, I have
been down to Reigate to inquire after her. The accounts were
unhappily as bad as possible; but what I saw awakened a train
5   of ideas and suggestions which I am going to communicate to
you.

I found a good many people assembled, of whom several had
come on the same errand as I. There was that broken-down
acquaintance of my early youth, Mr. Matthew Arnold, who
10 has had many a dinner from Mrs. Bottles (for she was kind to
literature even in its humblest manifestations), snivelling and
crying in a corner. There was that offensive young Prussian of
his, who seems to have dropped him entirely, and to have
taken up with a much younger man than my poor old ac-
15 quaintance, and a much better-dressed man, with whom he is
pursuing researches concerning labour and capital, which are
hardly, as our Paris correspondent says, palpitating with actu-
ality. There was a Baptist minister who had been the shepherd
of the Bottles family in the old days when they were Dissent-
20 ers, and who has never quite lost his hold upon Mrs. Bottles.
There was her sister Hannah, just about the same age as poor
Sarah who married Bottles, and the very image of her. There
was Job Bottles, Bottles's brother, who is on the Stock Exchange; a man with black hair at the sides of his head, a bald
25 crown, dark eyes, and a fleshy nose, and a camellia in his
button-hole. Finally, there was that handsome niece of Mr.
and Mrs. Bottles, Mary Jane. *Mary Jane!* I never pronounce
the name without emotion; in season and out of season it keeps
rising to my lips.[1] But the life we live in Fleet Street is devour-
30 ing, and I have sacrificed to it all thought of marriage. Our
Paris correspondent comforts me by saying that, even with the
domestic affections suppressed, existence turns out to be a
much more tolerable affair than humdrum people fancy.

Presently the members of the family left the room, and as the
35 Baptist minister took the *Nonconformist* out of his pocket and

[1] Leo here alludes, I imagine, to what the world has doubtless noticed,
—the frequent introduction of *Mary Jane* into his articles for the *D.
T.*—ED.

began to read it, as the Prussian *savant* was quite absorbed with
his new young man, and as Mr. Matthew Arnold counts for
nothing, I was left to the conversation of our Paris correspondent, whom we call Nick because of the diabolical salt
which sparkles in his deliverances. "They say," I began, "that
if Mr. T. Chambers's excellent bill, which the Liberal party are
carrying with such decisive majorities, becomes law, the place
of poor Mrs. Bottles will be taken by her sister Hannah, whom
you have just seen. Nothing could be more proper; Mrs. Bottles wishes it, Miss Hannah wishes it, this reverend friend of
the family, who has himself made a marriage of the same kind,
wishes it, everybody wishes it." "Everybody but old Bottles
himself, I should think," retorted my friend: "don't envy him
at all!—shouldn't so much mind if it were the younger one,
though."

These light words of my friend, Sir, seemed to touch a spring
in me. Instantly I felt myself visited by a shower of ideas, full of
import for the Liberal party and for the future, and which
impel me to address to you the present letter. "And why not
the younger one, Nick?" said I, gently: "why not? Either as a
successor to Miss Hannah or in lieu of Miss Hannah, why not?
Let us apply John Bright's crucial tests. Is she his first cousin?
Could there be a more natural companion for Selina and the
other Bottles girls? Or,—to take the moral ground so touchingly and irresistibly chosen by our great popular tribune,—if
legislation on this subject were impeded by the party of bigotry, if they chose not to wait for it, if they got married
without it, and if you were to meet them on the boulevard at
Paris during their wedding tour, should you go up to Bottles
and say: Mr. Bottles, you are a profligate man?" "Oh dear,
no," said Nick; "I should never dream of it." "And if you met
them a year later on the same spot," I continued, "with a
Normandy nurse behind them carrying a baby, should you
cry out to the poor little thing: Bastard?" "Nothing of the
kind," he answered.

I noticed that my friend accompanied each of these assurances
with a slight rapid droop of one eyelid. "Let us have no flip-
pancy, Nick," I said. "You mean that you hardly feel yourself

in a position to take high moral ground of this kind." "Well," said he, "I suppose that even our great tribune, John Bright himself, does not very often address people as bastards and profligates, whatever he thinks of them. At least, I should im-
5 agine the offender must almost be a bishop or some other high-placed Anglican ecclesiastic to provoke him to do so." "A fig for your fine distinctions," cried I. "Secretly or openly, will any one dare call Bottles, if he contracts a marriage of this kind, a profligate man?"

10   Poor Mr. Matthew Arnold, upon this, emerged suddenly from his corner, and asked hesitatingly: "But will any one dare call him a man of delicacy?" The question was so utterly unpractical that I took no notice of it whatever, and should not have mentioned it if it had not led, by its extraordinary effect upon
15 our Paris correspondent, to the introduction and criticism of a literary star of the first magnitude. My friend Nick, who has all the sensitive temperament of genius, seemed inexplicably struck by this word delicacy, which he kept repeating to himself. "Delicacy," said he, "delicacy,—surely I have heard that
20 word before! Yes, in other days," he went on dreamily, "in my fresh, enthusiastic youth; before I knew Sala, before I wrote for that infernal paper, before I called Dixon's style lithe and sinewy—"

    "Collect yourself, my friend," said I, laying my hand on his
25 shoulder; "you are unmanned. But in mentioning Dixon you redouble my strength; for you bring to my mind the great sexual insurrection of the Anglo-Teutonic race, and the master-spirit which guides it. This illustrious man who has invented a new style—"

30   "He has, indeed," says Mr. Arminius the Prussian, turning towards us for the first time; "he has, indeed, and its right name is middle-class Macaulayese."

    Now, I detest this German lecturer and his oracles, but as I am, above everything, a man of letters myself, I never refuse to
35 listen to a remark upon style. "Explain yourself," said I; "why do you call Mr. Hepworth Dixon's style middle-class Macaulayese?" "I call it Macaulayese," says the pedant, "because it has the same internal and external characteristics as Macaulay's

style; the external characteristic being a hard metallic movement with nothing of the soft play of life, and the internal
characteristic being a perpetual semblance of hitting the right
nail on the head without the reality. And I call it middle-class
Macaulayese, because it has these faults without the compensation of great studies and of conversance with great affairs, by
which Macaulay partly redeemed them."

I turned away in pity. "Let us leave the envious," said I to
Nick, "to break their teeth on this magnificent file, the countless-
ness of whose editions has something analogous to the world-
wide circulation of the *Daily Telegraph*. Let us pursue his fine
regenerating idea of sexual insurrection. Let us deal with this
question as a whole. Why, after Mr. Chambers has succeeded
at his one single point to-night, are we to have to begin afresh
at other points to-morrow? We have established, I hope, that
no man may presume to call Bottles profligate for marrying
either his sister-in-law Hannah or his niece Mary Jane. But this
is not enough. A complication, like the complications of Greek
tragedy, suggests itself to my mind. You noticed Mr. Job Bottles. You must have seen his gaze resting on Mary Jane. But
what with his cigars, his claret, his camellias, and the state of
the money-market, Mr. Job Bottles is not a marrying man just
at this moment. His brother is; but his brother cannot last for
ever. Job, on the other hand, is full of vigour and vitality. We
have heard of the patience of Job; how natural, if his brother
marries Mary Jane now, that Job, with his habits tempered,
his view of life calmed, and the state of the money-market
different, may wish, when she is a widow some five years hence,
to marry her himself. And we have arrangements which make
this illegal! At such arrangements I hurl, with scorn and disgust, the burning words of our great leader:—Ecclesiastical rubbish!

'I thank thee, Friend! for teaching me that word.'

Why, I ask, is Mr. Job Bottles's liberty, his Christian liberty, as
my reverend friend yonder would say, to be abridged in this
manner? And why is Protestant Dissent to be diverted from its
great task of abolishing State Churches for the purpose of

removing obstacles to the sexual insurrection of our race?
Why are its more devoted ministers to be driven to contract,
in the interests of Christian liberty, illegal unions of this kind
themselves, *pour encourager les autres?* Why is the earnest
5   liberalism and nonconformity of Lancashire and Yorkshire to
be agitated on this question by hope deferred? Why is it to be
put incessantly to the inconvenience of going to be married in
Germany or in the United States, that greater and better
Britain

10   'Which gives us manners, freedom, virtue, power.'

Why must ideas on this topic have to be incubated for years in
that nest of spicery, as the divine Shakspeare says, the mind of
Mr. T. Chambers, before they can rule the world? For my part,
my resolve is formed. This great question shall henceforth be
15   seriously taken up in Fleet Street. As a sop to those toothless
old Cerberuses, the bishops, who impotently exhibit still the
passions, as Nick's French friends say, of another age, we will
accord the continuance of the prohibition which forbids a man
to marry his grandmother. But in other directions there shall
20   be freedom. Mr. Chambers's admirable bill for enabling a
woman to marry her sister's husband will doubtless pass triumphantly through Committee to-night, amidst the cheers of
the ladies' gallery. The Liberal party must supplement that bill
by two others: one enabling people to marry their brothers'
25   and sisters' children, the other enabling a man to marry his
brother's wife."

But this glorious prospect fills me with an *afflatus* which can
find its fit employment only in Fleet Street, and I am forced to
subscribe myself,

30   Yours in haste,

                                          A Young Lion.

                    _____

A Recantation and Apology

To the EDITOR *of the* PALL MALL GAZETTE.

SIR,—The glorious and successful issue of the Liberal operation for disestablishing and disendowing the Irish Church, the
chorus of mutual applause and congratulation which I hear all
round me, and I should add, perhaps, the universal disgust with   5
which my "Culture and Anarchy" speculations have been received, the severe but deserved chastisement which I have
brought on myself by giving way to a spirit of effeminacy and
cultivated inaction, have quite conquered me. My hour has
come for learning what the *Daily Telegraph* calls "the stern   10
lesson that we can guide the current of the time only by going
along with it." "A great act of justice and clemency has gone
forth," as the *Daily Telegraph* says, "to give peace and contentment to Ireland;" "A great and important principle of the
Nonconformists," says Mr. Miall, "has now received legislative   15
sanction." The House of Lords made a short stand against this
important principle, and were defeated; yet the House of
Lords—we have it on the very highest authority—"the House
of Lords have shown not merely ability in debate, but comprehensive sagacity and forethought, a power of realizing the   20
future and of preparing for it." Such a general testimony to
the triumph of goodness and wisdom overpowers me. I lay
down my arms and confess my errors; and I shall write by to-
morrow's post to Mr. T. Chambers, offering him, as some
expiation for my past faults, my humble but zealous help in a   25
future session towards the Liberal operation, of which he is the
soul, for enabling a man to marry his deceased wife's sister.
  But a young friend, who once shared with me the simple
dwelling from which I write, though he has since risen to great-

ness on the *Daily Telegraph*, suggests that my overtures to the Liberal party will be received with suspicion. I acknowledge that this would be but natural; yet I wish to plead how plausible were some of the appearances which led astray an untutored mind, not protected by a systematic philosophy; in the hope that the great Liberal party may in their justice remember mercy, and receive a convert whose errors had some excuse, and whose penitence is most sincere.

First, as to the House of Lords. I do confess that when I was noticing Mr. Carlyle's proposal to get help from this quarter for our difficulties, I said that these children of the established fact lacked the power, which is needed in an epoch of expansion like ours, of being penetrated and strongly moved by ideas. I said that they were like the Barbarians, people full of interesting and powerful gifts, but fitted for an earlier stage of society than ours; and that in our stage of society, with its lively movement of ideas, they were bewildered and helpless, and their action gave one a sense of futility and sterility. I know now that I was wrong, because their action, at the recent important juncture, gives even to their conquerors a sense not of futility and sterility, but of "comprehensive sagacity and forethought, a power of realizing the future, and of preparing for it." But even in the recent juncture how many appearances were there in their conduct to give an ordinary mind, before it was illumined by conversion as mine is now, a sense of futility and sterility! Their strongest impulse, as children of the established fact themselves, was to respect the established fact in Ireland and to do nothing. If no one else had stirred the question, an effort to abate Protestant ascendency in Ireland would never have come from the House of Lords; but the question was stirred, and something had to be done. The half a dozen children of light who are sown among the Barbarians, as a few children of light are sown in all classes, seized the opportunity for urging them to abate Protestant ascendency, since abated it must be, in the way most consonant to reason. The House of Lords had not, to prevent their doing this, that fetish-worship or stock notion of the Nonconformists, as in our days of darkness we used to call it, which proscribes establishments; on the contrary, they naturally like establishments. But even in this posture of things, with a necessity for acting, with a dislike of the particular way proposed for acting, with no prejudices to prevent their preferring a better, such (so one could naturally hardly help saying) is the clinging of the great class whom we call the Barbarians to the mere established fact, so faint is the power of ideas upon them, so bewildered are they in an epoch of expansion, that the House of Lords at first declined by a large majority to abate Protestant ascendency in the way most consonant to reason, and then at the last moment, when it was clear that abated it must be, they went round and decided for this way by a majority of but seven; the narrowness of the majority, coupled with their former adverse vote, furnishing alone an irresistible reason why their decision could not possibly have any effect. If ideas had had power enough on them to bring them to this decision any time within the last twenty years, it would have triumphed; if they had had power enough to bring them to it now in a commanding majority, it would have had great weight. It was reached by them at a time and in a fashion which deprived it of all weight whatever. This sort of proceeding is just what made us say of the Barbarians that in an epoch of expansion they give one a sense of sterility; and though I now see that this is not the sense which after they accept the Liberal programme they ought to give us, yet it will be admitted that there were appearances here which might well lead a simple mind into error, and that one who has so erred may be kindly treated when he repents.

Again, with respect to the Liberal party in the House of Commons, for whose earnest labours I once felt too little enthusiasm, and, indeed, proposed to improve them by bringing to bear on them a free play of consciousness. I was wrong, and a free play of consciousness was here, as we now see, out of the question. A great and important principle of the Nonconformists had, as Mr. Miall says, to receive legislative sanction. That is, the Irish Church had to be destroyed by the power of that stock notion or fetish of the Nonconformists, Scotch and English, which proscribes establishments. We desired, it must be

confessed, to bring a free play of consciousness to bear upon
this stock notion of the Nonconformists, because it seemed
that Protestant ascendency in Ireland might be abated in a way
more consonant to reason. We have at least one excuse for this
vain desire; and that is, that so many members of the Liberal
majority in Parliament seem to have desired the same thing.
But the Nonconformists had no notion of turning consciousness on in this fashion. They much prefer to affirm, if they
can, their ordinary selves and their stock notions; and they can
if they like. With the Barbarians stricken with sterility, the
clergy (this is in answer to the *Guardian,* which wants me to
find for its subscribers an independent place between the Barbarians and the Philistines) politically a mere appendage to the
Barbarians, and the Populace not yet ripe, the Nonconformists
are masters of the situation. Their organizations rule the boroughs, and the boroughs return the Liberal majority. To have
insisted upon a free play of consciousness under these circumstances would have broken up the Liberal party. "In all human
affairs," as Sir Roundell Palmer says, "there is a point at which
persons must accept an adverse decision and bow to the superior force and power of those with whom the practical control
of affairs rests." That point was reached when it became evident that the Nonconformists meant a great and important
principle of theirs to receive legislative sanction without any
interference from a free play of consciousness at all. It was
wrong, no doubt, to suggest such a play; but then the Liberal
majority in the House of Commons seem to have had a sort of
hankering after it too, and only to have renounced it because
they found with what power and tenacity the stock notion of
the Nonconformists is held. The same discovery has converted
me also; but I hope I shall be forgiven my fancy for letting
one's consciousness play freely around a stock notion or mental fetish, since so many Liberal members of the House of
Commons seem to have shared this same fancy. I now see
clearly when the fancy is to be abandoned—it is when the
stock notion is held with power and tenacity by those whose
organizations rule the borough elections. Sir Roundell Palmer's
crisis in human affairs has then been reached; and all we then

have to do is to make out in the best way we can that what
seemed, till its influence on the borough elections became manifest, a part of man's natural taste for the bathos, is in truth a
relish for the sublime.

To this I shall henceforth, Sir, as a proof of sincere repentance, 5
address myself. Yes, it is true, as that strong but sly Benthamite
contributor of yours says (he considers religion a morbid ex-
crescence upon the rational development of man, and would
sooner have Mr. Spurgeon and Mr. Ward Beecher than
Hooker or Butler to defend the nuisance against his inroads), 10
it is true that throughout the world there is a mounting wave
of feeling against all connection of religion with the State. We
English are famous for knowing things as they really are, and,
above all, things on the Continent; and we know that in the
most intelligent and prosperous countries of the Continent—in 15
France, Germany, Holland—the course of events tends, not so
much to separate the clergy from Rome, and every alien
power, and to connect them more closely with the State and
the public life of their own nation, as to sever rather their
whole connection with the State, to turn them all into volun- 20
taries, and to leave them free to form what extra-national at-
tachments they like. It makes for the good cause that we
should think this, and therefore let us say and believe it. Yes,
again, it is true that "the deep conviction and strong impulse
of justice" have been, as the *Daily News* says, the moving 25
power with the Nonconformists in the attack on the Irish
Church; and that "ecclesiastical preferences have had nothing
to do with the great end to which they have addressed themselves, but have at most vetoed some of the means!" Mr. Miall
may "rejoice that a great and important principle of the Non- 30
conformists has now received legislative sanction;" Mr. Spurgeon may say he would leave the Irish Establishment just as it
was sooner than give Papists a farthing of the money; still,
what is at the bottom of both these good men's hearts, and
what really moves both of them to action, is their deep convic- 35
tion and strong impulse of justice towards the Catholic people
of Ireland. And the people of Ireland have on their side, too, a
deep conviction that this is so, and are grateful accordingly. In

spite of the venerable Dr. Jobson's amenities about the man of
sin, or Mr. Spurgeon's about the Roman image, the Irish Catholics know what fine sentiments towards them British Puritanism really entertains, and their peace and contentment are now
5   assured. All this I am resolved steadfastly, like a good practical
Liberal, from henceforth to believe and preach; and instead of
idly going about any more to convince Philistinism of sin, I
shall make it my whole ambition, if my penitence is now fa-
vourably accepted by the Liberal party, to become one of
10 those people so beautifully described by the *Daily Telegraph:*
—"men of genial humanity, who put aside painfully enforced
instances, and enforce the higher wisdom of the heart."

Your humble servant,

Grub-street, Sunday night.   MATTHEW ARNOLD.

Melancholy if True

To the EDITOR *of the* PALL MALL GAZETTE.

SIR,—You have often amused yourself, if not your readers, by ridiculing my leaders in the *Daily Telegraph.* Envy of a style which you cannot imitate was obviously the well-spring of your affected laughter and your simulated contempt. If you hoped to suppress me you have made a grand mistake. You shall have the pleasure of learning authoritatively that you have led to my promotion. Look at the first leading article in the *Times* this morning (that which begins "The Tragedy of Spanish Republicanism is being rapidly played out"), and see if you do not recognize the hand: I flatter myself the style, the touch, is too distinctive and characteristic to be mistaken even by you. Mark my—"all the sea of blood which is being spilled in every district of the Peninsula." Or, "The modern Saguntum does not swear in vain. The volunteers of Saragossa had muskets; Prim's soldiers had cannon. The artillery, as we are told, 'played heavily upon the insurgents.' And now there is silence there, order in the Aragonese capital, order throughout that kingdom." But you will recognize the writer you endeavoured to destroy (in vain, you see) as much by his dexterity as his style. Beat them if you can. And let me add that I doubt very considerably whether a man is to be chaffed off the *Times* as easily as off the *D. T.*—Yours, &c.,

A YOUNG LION LATE OF FLEET-STREET.

Oct. 13, 1869.

P.S.—You have sneered at my philosophy. But the following passages from another leading article in to-day's *Times* ought to convince you that I can *think:*—"Homicidal negligence must be frowned down by society as well as homicidal anger. Railway companies are ordinarily equally guilty, as companies, when they pound to pieces their passengers in one train by the engine of another, as is a miserable madman of eighty-two

5   guilty as an individual when he resolves on avenging himself for being forbidden to maintain a nuisance by shooting his landlord."

Letter IX

Arminius, Starting for the Continent to Take Part in the War Between France and Prussia, Addresses a Disrespectful Farewell to Our People and Institutions

(After our meeting at Laburnum House,—have I ever mentioned that the mansion of Mr. Bottles at Reigate is called Laburnum House?—intercourse was renewed between Arminius and me, but alas! not the close intimacy of old days. Perhaps, had I foreseen his approaching end, I should have made more strenuous efforts to regain his confidence. But it was not to be; and the following letter will show the cruel injustice with which Arminius, misled, I am sure, by Mr. Frederic Harrison and the party with whom that gentleman generally acts, could bring himself to speak of the man who has done so much to popularise his name and ideas.) 10

CHEQUER ALLEY,[1] *August* 9, 1870.

SIR,—

I am off to-night for the Continent to join the Prussian army; if it had not been for an accidental circumstance with which I 15 need not trouble you,[2] I should have been off a fortnight ago. I have no love for the preaching old drill-sergeant who is called King of Prussia, or for the audacious conspirator who pulls his wires; this conspirator and his rival conspirator, Louis Bonaparte, stand in my affections pretty much on a par. Both 20 play their own game, and are obstacles to better things. I am a republican, I desire a republic for every country in Europe. I

[1] After our rupture, Arminius removed from my immediate neighbourhood in Grub Street and established himself in Chequer Alley. I love to think that pilgrims will one day seek out his lodging there!—ED. 25

[2] His debts, alas!—ED.

believe no country of Europe is so fitted to be a republic as
Germany; I believe her difficulties are from her Hohenzollerns
and Hapsburgs, and nothing else. I believe she will end by
getting rid of these gentry; and that till that time comes the
5   world will never know of what real greatness she is capable. But
the present war, though we are led by the old drill-sergeant and
his wire-puller, is a war of Germany against France. I must go
and take part in it.

Before I go, I am moved to send you a few farewell remarks
10   on your country and its position, about which you seem (and I
am sure I do not wonder at it) to be much concerned and
embarrassed just now. I have a great esteem for your nation,
its genius, and its past history; and your present stage of development has been a subject of constant study and thought with
15   me during the years I have lived here. Formerly I have more
than once communicated my ideas to you, as occasion arose,
through Mr. Matthew Arnold. But experience has shown me
that, though willing and inquisitive, he has hardly brain
enough for my purpose; besides, he has of late been plunged
20   over head and ears in some dispute of Greeks of the Lower
Empire with your foolish and impracticable Dissenters.[1]

Finding him unserviceable, therefore, I address you myself;
but I shall use some of the phrases with which he has familiar-
ised you, because they save circumlocution; and as he learnt
25   them all from me in the first instance, I see no reason why I
should not take back my own property when I want it.

You are horrified and astounded at this war; horrified and astounded at the projects for altering the face of Europe which
have been going on under your nose without your knowledge;
30   horrified and astounded at the coolness with which foreign
nations seem to leave you out of their account, or to estimate
the chances and character of your intervention. They put you
aside as if you were of no consequence; and this to you, who
won the last great European war, and made the treaties of

35   [1] I make no comment on the tone and spirit of this; but I cannot
forbear remarking that with the removal of Arminius and his influence
the main obstacle to my reconciliation with the Dissenters is withdrawn.
—ED.

Vienna! The time, you think, has clearly come when you must make a demonstration. Your popular veteran, Lord Russell, declares amid universal applause that "it is only the doubt that has long prevailed as to the course which England would take, which has encouraged and fostered all these projects of treaty, these combinations and intrigues." You have but to speak plainly, and all will be well. Your great organ, the *Times,* not satisfied with itself conveying to other Powers in the most magnificent manner (a duty, to say the truth, it always fulfils) "what England believes to be due from and to her," keeps exhorting your Government to do the same, to speak some brave words, and to speak them "with promptitude and energy."

I suppose your Government will do so. But forgive me if I tell you that to us disrespectful foreigners it makes very little difference in our estimate of you and of the future whether your Government does so or not. What gives the sense and significance to a Government's declarations is the power which is behind the Government. And what is the power which is behind the Government of England at the present epoch? The Philistines.

Simply and solely the Philistines, my dear friend, take my word for it! No, you will say, it is the nation. Pardon me, you have no nation. France is fused into one nation by the military spirit, and by her democracy, the great legacy of 1789, and subsisting even amidst her present corruption. Germany is fused into one nation by her idea of union and of the elevation of her whole people through culture. You are made up, as I have often told you through my poor disciple whom you so well know, of three distinct and unfused bodies,—Barbarians, Philistines, Populace. You call them aristocracy, middle, and lower class. One of these three must be predominant and lead. Your lower class counts as yet for little or nothing. There is among them a small body of workmen with modern ideas, ideas of organisation, who may be a nucleus for the future; there are more of them Philistines in a small way, Philistines in embryo; but most of them are mere populace, or, to use your own kindly term, *residuum.* Such a class does not lead. For-

merly your aristocracy led; it commanded the politics of the
country; it had an aristocracy's ideas,—limited enough, but the
idea of the country's grandeur and dignity was among them;—
it took your middle and lower class along with it, and used
5   them in its own way, and it made the great war which the
battle of Waterloo crowned. But countries must outgrow a
feudal organisation, and the political command of an aristocracy; your country has outgrown it. Your aristocracy tells
upon England socially; by all the power of example of a class
10 high-placed, rich, idle, self-indulgent, without mental life, it
teaches your Philistines how to live fast. But it no longer rules;
at most it but administers; the Philistines rule. That makes the
difference between Lord Grenville and Lord Granville. When
Lord Grenville had to speak to Europe in 1793, he had behind
15 him your aristocracy, not, indeed, fused with your middle and
lower class, but wielding them and using their force; and all the
world knew what your aristocracy meant, for they knew it
themselves. But Lord Granville has behind him, when he
speaks to Europe in 1870, your Philistines or middle class; and
20 how should the world know, or much care, what your middle
class mean? for they do not know it themselves.

You may be mortified, but such is the truth. To be consequent and powerful, men must be bottomed on some vital idea or
sentiment, which lends strength and certainty to their action.
25 Your aristocracy of seventy years ago had the sentiment of the
greatness of the old aristocratical England, and that sentiment
gave them force to endure labours, anxiety, danger, disappointment, loss, restrictions of liberty. Your ruling middle
class has no such foundation; hence its imbecility. It would tell
30 you it believes in industrial development and liberty. Examine
what it means by these, and you find it means getting rich and
not being meddled with. And these it imagines to be self-acting powers for good, and agents of greatness; so that if more
trade is done in England than anywhere else, if your personal
35 independence is without a check, and your newspaper publicity unbounded, your Philistines think they are by the nature
of things great, powerful, and admirable, and that their Eng-

land has only to speak "with promptitude and energy" in order to prevail.

My dear friend, do not hold your notions in this mechanical fashion, and do not be misled by that magnificent *Times* of yours; it is not the failing to speak "with promptitude and energy" which injures you, it is the having nothing wise or consistent to say. Your ruling middle class have no great, seriously and truly conceived end;—therefore no greatness of soul or mind;—therefore no steadfastness and power in great affairs. While you are thus, in great affairs you do and must fumble. You imagine that your words must have weight with us because you are very rich and have unbounded liberty and publicity; you will find yourselves mistaken, and you will be bewildered. Then you may get involved in war, and you imagine that you cannot but make war well by dint of being so very rich; that you will just add a penny or two to your income-tax, change none of your ways, have clap-trap everywhere, as at present, unrestricted independence, legions of newspaper correspondents, boundless publicity; and thus, at a grand high pressure of expenditure, bustle, and excitement, arrive at a happy and triumphant result. But authority and victory over people who are in earnest means being in earnest oneself, and your Philistines are not in earnest; they have no idea great enough to make them so. They want to be important and authoritative; they want to enforce peace and curb the ambitious; they want to drive a roaring trade; they want to know and criticise all that is being done; they want no restrictions on their personal liberty, no interference with their usual way of going on; they want all these incompatible things equally and at once, because they have no idea deep and strong enough to subordinate everything else to itself. A correspondent of your own *Times* wrote from Berlin the other day, "The complete control of this people by the State is most striking." How would your Philistines like that? Not at all. But it is by sacrifices of this kind that success in great affairs is achieved; and when your Philistines find this out, or find that a raised income-tax, torrents of clap-trap, everybody saying what he likes and doing what he likes, newspaper correspondents everywhere, and a generally animated state of the public mind, are not enough to command success, they will be still more bewildered.

5   And this is the power which Lord Granville has behind him, and which is to give the force and meaning to his words. Poor Lord Granville! I imagine he is under no illusions. He knows the British Philistine, with his likes and dislikes, his effusion and confusion, his hot and cold fits, his want of dignity and of

10   the steadfastness which comes from dignity, his want of ideas and of the steadfastness which comes from ideas;—he has seen him at work already. He has seen the Russian war and the Russian peace; a war and peace your aristocracy did not make and never would have made,—the British Philistine and his

15   newspapers have the whole merit of it. In your social gatherings I know you have the habit of assuring one another that in some mysterious way the Russian war did you good in the eyes of Europe. Undeceive yourselves; it did you nothing but harm, and Lord Granville is far too clever a man not to know

20   it. Then, in the Denmark quarrel, your Philistines did not make war, indeed, but they threatened it. Surely in the Denmark case there was no want of brave words; no failure to speak out "with promptitude and energy." And we all know what came of it. Unique British Philistine! Is he most to be

25   revered when he makes his wars or when he threatens them? And at the prompting of this great backer Lord Granville is now to speak! Probably he will have, as the French say, to execute himself; only do not suppose that we are under any delusion as to the sort of force he has behind him.

30   My dear friend, I think I am perhaps writing to you for the last time, and by the love I bear to the England of your past literature and history, I do exhort your Philistine middle class, which is now England, to get, as I say, "Geist;" to search and not rest till it sees things more as they really are, and how little

35   of a power over things as they really are is its money-making, or its unrestricted independence, or its newspaper publicity, or its Dissent, or any of the things with which it is now most taken; and how its newspapers deceive it when they tell it

night and day that, being what it is, and having the objects it has, it commands the envy and deference of the world, and is on the sure road to greatness and happiness, if indeed it be not already arrived there. My dear friend, I have told you our German programme,—*the elevation of a whole people through culture*. That need not be your English programme, but surely you may have some better programme than this your present one,—*the beatification of a whole people through clap-trap*.

And now, my dear friend, it is time for me to go, and to what fate I go I know not; but this I know, that your country, where I have lived so long and seen so much, is on its way either to a great transformation or to a great disaster.

Your sincere well-wisher,
Von Thunder-ten-Tronckh.

To the Editor *of the* Pall Mall Gazette.

Letter X

Arminius, Writing from the German Camp before Paris, Comments, in His Old Unappreciative Spirit, on the Attitude of Our Beloved Country in the Black Sea Question

BEFORE PARIS, *November* 21, 1870.

SIR,—

Another call "to speak with promptitude and energy!" We had all been full of the Russian note, and here is your magnifi-
5 cent *Times* to tell me what the great heart of my dear English friends is thinking of it. You have not forgotten, of course, that sentence of Mr. Lowe (a descendant of Pangloss, and a sort of hereditary connection of my family, though he took scant notice of me when I was in England): "The destiny of
10 England is in the great heart of England." So, having a sincere regard for you, I always listen when your great heart speaks, that I may see what sort of a destiny it is about to create for you. And I find that it is now speaking very loud indeed, even louder than when I wrote to you in August last, and that it is
15 bent on telling Russia "with promptitude and energy," in your own fine, full-mouthed fashion, "what England believes to be due from and to her." But even at such a crisis you do not forget to improve the occasion, and to indulge in the peculiar strain of moral reflection whence you get, your oracles tell us,
20 "that moral weight which your action, if conducted with tol-erable judgment, is sure to command" (see, in the last *Edin-burgh Review*, "Germany, France, and England," p. 591). It is not so much the matter of the Russian incident as its manner that pains you. "We protest," says your magnificent *Times*,
25 "that our sharpest feeling at the moment is pain at the apparent

334

faithlessness of the Czar, and at the rudeness with which he has denounced the treaty."

My dear friend, the weather is abominable, and the supply of tobacco, to me at any rate, short and bad; but I cannot resist sitting down without a pipe, in the mud, to write to you, when I see your great heart beating in this manner.

How like you,—how like the British Philistine in one of his hot fits, when he is moved to speak to Europe "with promptitude and energy!" Of history, the future, the inevitable drive of events, not an inkling! A moral criticism of Russia and a wounded self-consequence,—that is all you are full of. The British Philistine all over!

At your present stage of development, as I have often remarked to you, this beneficent being is the depositary of your force, the mover of your policy. Your Government is, in and by itself, nothing. You are a self-governing people, you are represented by your "strong middle part," your Philistine: and this is what your Government must watch; this is what it must take its cue from.

Here, then, is your situation, that your Government does not and cannot really govern, but at present is and must be the mouthpiece of your Philistines; and that foreign Governments know this very well, know it to their cost. Nothing the best of them would like better than to deal with England seriously and respectfully,—the England of their traditions, the England of history; nothing, even, they would like better than to deal with the English Government,—as at any time it may happen to stand, composed of a dozen men more or less eminent,—seriously and respectfully. But, good God! it is not with these dozen men in their natural state that a foreign Government finds it has to deal; it is with these dozen men sitting in devout expectation to see how the cat will jump,—and that cat the British Philistine!

What statesman can deal seriously and respectfully when he finds that he is not dealing mind to mind with an intelligent equal, but that he is dealing with a tumult of likes and dislikes, hopes, panics, intrigues, stock-jobbing, quidnuncs, newspapers, —dealing with *ignorance* in short, for that one word contains it

all,—behind his intelligent equal? Whatever he says to a British
Minister, however convincing he may be, a foreign statesman
knows that he has only half his hearer's attention, that only
one of the British Minister's eyes is turned his way; the other
eye is turned anxiously back on the home Philistines and the
home press, and according as these finally go the British Minister must go too. This sort of thing demoralises your Ministers
themselves in the end, even your able and honest ones, and
makes them impossible to deal with. God forgive me if I do
him wrong!—but I always suspect that your sly old Sir Hamilton Seymour, in his conversations with the Emperor Nicholas
before the Crimean war, had at last your Philistines and your
press, and their unmistakable bent, in his eye, and did not lead
the poor Czar quite straight. If ever there was a man who
respected England, and would have gone cordially and easily
with a capable British minister, that man was Nicholas. England, Russia, and Austria are the Powers with a real interest in
the Eastern question, and it ought to be settled fairly between
them. Nicholas wished nothing better. Even if you would not
thus settle the question, he would have forborne to any extent
sooner than go to war with you, if he could only have known
what you were really at. To be sure, as you did not know this
yourselves, you could not possibly tell *him*, poor man! Louis
Napoleon, meanwhile, had his prestige to make. France pulled
the wires right and left; your Philistines had a passion for that
old acrobat Lord Palmerston, who, clever as he was, had an
aristocrat's inaptitude for ideas, and believed in upholding and
renovating the Grand Turk; Lord Aberdeen knew better, but
his eye was nervously fixed on the British Philistine and the
British press. The British Philistine learnt that he was being
treated with rudeness and must make his voice heard "with
promptitude and energy." There was the usual explosion of
passions, prejudices, stock-jobbing, newspaper articles, chatter,
and general ignorance, and the Czar found he must either submit to have capital made out of him by French vanity and
Bonapartist necessities, or enter into the Crimean war. He entered into the Crimean war, and it broke his heart. France
came out of the Crimean war the first Power in Europe, with

French vanity and Bonapartist necessities fully served. You came out of it with the British Philistine's *rôle* in European affairs for the first time thoroughly recognised and appreciated.

Now for the "faithlessness" and "rudeness" of Russia's present proceeding. It has been known for the last half-dozen years in every chancery of Europe that Russia declared her position in the Black Sea to be intolerable, and was resolved to get it altered. France and Bonaparte, driven by the French *fat* as you are driven by the British Philistine,—and the French *fat* has proved a yet more fatal driver than yours, being debauched and immoral, as well as ignorant,—came to grief. I suppose Russia was not bound to wait till they were in a position to make capital out of her again. "But with us, at any rate," you will say, "she might have dealt seriously and respectfully, instead of being faithless and rude." Again, I believe Russia would have wished nothing better than to deal seriously with you, and to settle with you, not only the question of the Black Sea, but the whole Eastern question, which begins to press for settlement;—but it was impossible. It was impossible, because you offer nobody with whom a serious statesman can deal seriously. You offer a Government, with men in it eminent and able no doubt, but they do not make your policy; and their eye is always turning back to the power behind them which *does* make it. That power is the British Philistine. Was Russia, at a critical moment, to lose precious time waiting for the chance medley of accidents, intrigues, hot and cold fits, stock-jobbing, newspaper-articles, conversations on the railway, conversations on the omnibus, out of which grows the foreign policy of a self-governing people, when that self is the British Philistine? Russia thought not, and passed on to its object.

For my part, I cannot call this faithless, though I admit it may be called rude. But it was a rudeness which Governments with a serious object before them cannot well help committing when they are dealing with you. The question is: Will you at all better yourselves by having now one of your hot fits, speaking "with promptitude and energy," and, in fact, going to war with Russia for what she has done? Alas, my dear friend, this would be throwing the handle after the blade with a vengeance! Because your governing part, your Philistine middle class, is ignorant and impracticable, Russia has unceremoniously taken a step in the Eastern question without you. And what does your going to war with Russia in the present posture of affairs mean? It means backing up the Porte to show fight; going in, in Lord Palmerston's old line, for upholding and renovating the Grand Turk;—it means fighting against nature. This is how the ignorant and impracticable get punished; they are made to smart for being ignorant and impracticable, and they can only resent being made to smart by showing themselves more ignorant and impracticable still. Do not do so, my dear friend! Russia has no wish to quarrel with you; she had a serious object to gain, and, as time pressed, she did what she had to do without entering into an interminable and possibly fruitless conversation with your "young man from the country." But she does not mean more than her avowed object, which was really indispensable to her; she will try to make things now as pleasant as she can (consistently with getting her object) for your young man from the country; and the moment the young man has clear ideas she will ask nothing better than to deal with him seriously and respectfully.

All turns upon that, my dear friend!—the improving your young man and giving him clear ideas. At present he is vulgar, ignorant, and consequential; and because he is vulgar, he is ignoble; because he is ignorant, he is unstable; because he is consequential, he is on the look-out for affronts and apt to fly into a heat. With these qualities he cannot but bring mortifications upon you and himself, so long as he governs or tries to govern. All nations have their young man of this sort, but with you alone he governs, and hence the European importance of him and his failings. You know how I dislike the Junkerism and militarism of my own Prussian country and its government; all I say is, that the self-government of your Philistines is as bad, or even worse. There is nothing like it anywhere; for America, which in some respects resembles you, has not your necessary relations with Europe; and besides, her Philistines, if they govern, adminster also, and get the training which great affairs give. With you the Barbarians administer, the Philistines govern;

between them your policy is made. One class contributes its want of ideas, the other its want of dignity;—an unlucky mixture for you, my dear friend, it must be confessed.

The worst of it is, I do not see how things are to get better with you at present. The Philistines rule and rule abominably, but for the moment there is no remedy. Bismarck would say, "Muzzle them;" but I know well this cannot, nay, should not be. I say, "Improve them;" but for this time is needed. Your Government might, no doubt, do something to speed the improvement, if it cared a little more, in serving the Philistines, for what might do them good, and a little less for what might please them; but perhaps this is too much to expect from your Government. So you must needs have, my dear friend, I am afraid, what these poor wretched people here call a *mauvais quart d'heure*, in which you will be peculiarly liable to mistakes, mortifications, and troubles. While this period lasts, *your strength*, forgive me for saying so, *is to sit still*. What your friends (of whom I am one) must wish for you is that you may keep as quiet as possible; that the British Philistine may not be moved much to speak to Europe "with promptitude and energy;" that he may get out of his hot fits always as soon as possible. And perhaps you *are* getting out of your recent hot fit already; perhaps, even while I write, you have got into one of your cold fits, and are all for pacific solutions and moral suasion. I say, Heaven grant it! with all my heart.

And, meanwhile, how are my friends in England? I think I see Bottles by the Royal Exchange at this moment, holding forth, with the *Times* in his hand, on "the perfect unanimity of opinion among the mercantile community of the City of London!" I think I hear poor Mr. Matthew Arnold's platitudes about "the two great conquests of English energy,—*liberty and publicity!*" Liberty, my dear friend, to make fools of yourselves, and publicity to tell all the world you are doing so.

Forgive my *ur-deutsch* frankness, and believe me, your sincere friend,

VON THUNDER-TEN-TRONCKH.

To the EDITOR *of the* PALL MALL GAZETTE.

Letter XI

I Take Up the Cudgels for Our Beloved Country

GRUB STREET, *November* 25, 1870.

SIR,—

I know ·by experience how hard it is to get my bald, disjointed chat, as Arminius calls it, into the newspapers in these stirring times, and that was why I did not attempt to complain of that extraordinary effusion of his which you published in August last. He must have written that letter, with its unhandsome remarks at my expense, just after I had parted with him at his lodgings in Chequer Alley, with expressions of the tenderest concern, before he went off to the war. Since then, I have discovered that he had referred nearly all his tradespeople to me for payment; I am daily besieged in my garret by his tobacconist, and when I get out, the street is made quite intolerable to me by the violence of his washerwoman, though I am sure Arminius, like all foreigners, always gave his washerwoman as little trouble as possible. These things have nettled me a good deal; and now there comes this new letter of his from Paris, in which, besides totally uncalled-for sneers at Mr. Bottles and me, Arminius indulges in an outrageous attack on my country and her behaviour in this Russian business. I have kept silence for a few days to make sure of being perfectly cool; but now, Sir, I do hope you will give me space for a few lines in reply to him.

About the Russian note I disagree with Arminius *in toto*. I go thoroughly along with Lord Shaftesbury, whose admirable letter to the *Times* proves, what I have always thought, how unjust Arminius is in denying ideas to the British aristocracy. A treaty is a promise,—so I read Lord Shaftesbury's argument; men should keep their promises; if bad men will not, good men must compel them.

It is singular, Sir, but in my immediate neighbourhood here in Cripplegate we have lately had a case which exactly illustrates the Russian difficulty, and bears out Lord Shaftesbury's argument. We all do our marketing in Whitecross Street; and in Whitecross Street is a famous tripe-shop which I always visit before entertaining Arminius, who, like all North Germans, and like our own celebrated Dr. Johnson, is a very gross feeder. Two powerful labourers, who lodge like Arminius in Chequer Alley, and who never could abide one another, used to meet at this tripe-shop and quarrel till it became manifest that the shop could not stand two such customers together, and that one of the couple must give up going there. The fellows' names were Mike and Dennis; it was generally thought the chief blame in the quarrel lay with Mike, who was at any rate much the less plausible man of the two, besides being greatly the bigger. However that may be, the excellent City Missionary in this quarter, the Rev. *J-hn B-ll* (I forbear to write his name at length for fear of bringing a blush to his worthy cheek), took Dennis's part in the matter. He and Dennis set both together upon Mike, and got the best of him. It was Dennis who appeared to do the most in the set-to; at all events, he got the whole credit, although I have heard the Rev. *J-hn B-ll* (who was undoubtedly a formidable fellow in his old unregenerate days) describe at tea in the Mission Room how he got his stick between Mike's legs at all the critical moments; how he felt fresher and stronger when the fight ended than when it began; and how his behaviour had somehow the effect of leaving on the bystanders' minds an impression immensely to his advantage. What is quite certain is, that not only did our reverend friend take part in the engagement, but that also, before, during, and after the struggle, his exhortations and admonitions to Mike, Dennis, the bystanders, and himself, never ceased, and were most edifying. Mike finally, as I said, had to give in, and he was obliged to make a solemn promise to Dennis and the City Missionary that he would use the tripe-shop no more. On this condition a treaty was patched up, and peace reigned in Cripplegate.

And now, Sir, comes the startling point of resemblance to the present Russian difficulty. A great big hulking German, called Fritz, has been for some time taking a lead in our neighbourhood, and carrying his head a great deal higher in Whitecross Street Market than Dennis liked. At last Dennis could stand it 5 no longer; he picked a quarrel with Fritz, and they had a battle-royal to prove which was master. In this encounter our City Missionary took no part, though he bestowed, as usual, on both sides good advice and beautiful sentiments in abundance. Dennis had no luck this time; he got horribly belaboured, and 10 now lies confined to his bed at his lodgings, almost past praying for. But what do you think has been Mike's conduct at this juncture? Seeing Dennis disabled, he addressed to the City Missionary an indecent scrawl, couched in language with which I will not sully your pages, to the effect that the tripe-15 shop lay handy to his door (which is true enough); and that use it he needs must, and use it he would, in spite of all the Rev. *J-hn B-ll* might say or do to stop him.

The feelings, Sir, of the worthy Missionary at this communication may be easier imagined than described. He launched at 20 Mike the most indignant moral rebuke; the brute put his thumb to his nose. To get Mike out of the tripe-shop there is nothing left but physical force. Yet how is our estimable friend to proceed? Years of outpouring, since he has been engaged in mission-work, have somewhat damaged his wind; 25 the hospitalities of the more serious-minded citizens of Cripplegate to a man in his position have been, I hope, what they should be; there are apprehensions, if violent exercise is taken, of gout in the stomach. Dennis can do nothing; what is worse, Fritz has been seen to wink his eye at Mike in a way to beget 30 grave suspicion that the ruffians have a secret compact together. The general feeling in Cripplegate is that nothing much can be done, and that Mike must be allowed to resort again to the tripe-shop.

But I ask you, Sir, is this morally defensible? Is it right? Is it 35 honest? Has not Lord Shaftesbury's English heart (if it is not presumptuous in me to speak thus of a person in his lordship's position) guided him true in the precisely similar case of Russia? A treaty is a promise, and we have a moral right to de-

mand that promises shall be kept. If Mike wanted to use the
tripe-shop, he should have waited till Dennis was about again
and could talk things over with the City Missionary, and then,
perhaps, the two might have been found willing to absolve
Mike from his promise. His present conduct is inexcusable; the
only comfort is that the Rev. *J-hn B-ll* has a faithful press still
to back him, and that Mike is being subjected to a fearful daily
castigation in the columns of the *Band of Hope Review.*

Therefore, Sir, as to Russia, I emphatically think Arminius
wrong. His sneers at my zeal for the grand principles of liberty and publicity I have hardly left myself space to notice.
But, Sir, I do believe, with Mr. Bright, that the great function
committed by Providence to our English-speaking race is "the
assertion of personal liberty." If this be an error, I would
rather, I own, err with Mr. Bright than be right with Von
Thunder-ten-Tronckh. I know Von T. maintains that we so
intently pursue liberty and publicity as quite to neglect wisdom and virtue; for which alone, he says, liberty and publicity
are worth having. But I will ask him, Sir, have we ever given
liberty and publicity a full trial? Take liberty. The Lord
Chancellor has, indeed, provided for Mr. Beales, and it is whispered that Colonel Dickson will have a high command in the
approaching Russian war;—*but why is Mr. Bradlaugh not yet
a Dean?* These, Sir, are the omissions, these the failures to
carry into full effect our own great principles, which drive
earnest Liberals to despair!

Again, take the principle of publicity. Arminius (who, as an
observer of manners, attended the proceedings in the Mordaunt
case, and again in the Park and Boulton case, with unflagging
assiduity) has said to me scores of times: "By shooting all this
garbage on your public, you are preparing and assuring for
your English people an immorality as deep and wide as that
which destroys the Latin nations." What is my reply? That
we have never yet given publicity a fair trial. It is true, when a
member of Parliament wanted to abridge the publicity given
to the Mordaunt case, the Government earnestly reminded
him that it had been the solemn decision of the House of
Commons that all the proceedings of the Divorce Court should

be open as the day. It is true, when there was a suggestion to
hear the Boulton and Park case in private, the upright magistrate who was appealed to said firmly that he could never trifle
with the public mind in that manner. All this was as it should
5   be; so far, so good. But was the publicity thus secured for
these cases perfectly full and entire? Were there not some
places which the details did not reach? There were few, but
there were some. And this while the Government has an organ
of its own, the *London Gazette*, dull, high-priced, and of com-
10 paratively limited circulation. I say, make the price of the
London Gazette a halfpenny; change its name to the *London
Gazette and Divorce Intelligencer*; let it include, besides divorce news, all cases whatever that have an interest of the same
nature for the public mind; distribute it *gratis* to mechanics'
15 institutes, workmen's halls, seminaries for the young (these
latter more especially); and then you will be giving the principle of publicity a full trial. This is what I often say to Arminius; and, when he looks astounded, I reassure him with a sentence which, I know very well, the moment I make it public,
20 will be stolen by all the Liberal newspapers. But it is getting
near Christmas-time, and I do not mind making them a present
of it. It is this:—*The spear of freedom, like that of Achilles,
has the power to heal the wounds which itself makes!*
     This Arminius can never answer; and, badly as he has treated
25 me, my heart relents to think of the stupefied face I have often
seen him with at hearing it. Poor Arminius! I wonder what he
is doing now? If the Prussians keep sticking in the mud before
Paris, how will he continue to bear the wet weather, the winter nights, the exposure? And may not his prolonged requisi-
30 tions for tobacco and sausages (merciless I know they will
be!) prove too much at last for the patience of even some
down-trodden worm of a French *bourgeois?* Or, again, this is
the hour for a *sortie*, and Arminius is as brave as a lion. I go to
my garret-window; it is just midnight; how gloomy is Grub
35 Street at this hour! I look towards the familiar regions of
Whitecross Street Market and Chequer Alley; the venerable
pile of Cripplegate Church, which I could never get Arminius

to enter, rises darkly and sadly before me. Dismal presentiments begin to crowd upon my soul, and I sign myself,

Sir, your uneasy servant,

MATTHEW ARNOLD.

To the EDITOR *of the* PALL MALL GAZETTE. 5

Letter XII

"Life," as Mr. G. A. Sala Says, "a Dream!"

VERSAILLES, *November* 26, 1870.

MON CHER,—

An event has just happened which I confess frankly will afflict
others more than it does me, but which you ought to be in-
5   formed of.

Early this morning I was passing between Rueil and Bougival,
opposite Mont Valérien. How came I in that place at that hour?
Mon cher, forgive my folly! You have read *Romeo and Juliet*,
you have seen me at Cremorne, and though Mars has just now
10   this *belle France* in his gripe, yet you remember, I hope,
enough of your classics to know that, where Mars is, Venus is
never very far off. Early this morning, then, I was between
Rueil and Bougival, with Mont Valérien in grim proximity. On
a bank by a poplar-tree at the roadside I saw a knot of German
15   soldiers, gathered evidently round a wounded man. I approached and frankly tendered my help, in the name of British
humanity. What answer I may have got I do not know;
for, petrified with astonishment, I recognised in the wounded
man our familiar acquaintance, Arminius von Thunder-ten-
20   Tronckh. A Prussian helmet was stuck on his head, but there was
the old hassock of whity-brown hair,—there was the old square
face,—there was the old blue pilot coat! He was shot through
the chest, and evidently near his end. He had been on outpost
duty;—the night had been quiet, but a few random shots had
25   been fired. One of these had struck Arminius in the breast, and
gone right through his body. By this stray bullet, without
glory, without a battle, without even a foe in sight, had fallen
the last of the Von Thunder-ten-Tronckhs!

He knew me, and with a nod, "Ah," said he, "the rowdy Philis-

346

tine!" You know his turn, *outré* in my opinion, for flinging
nicknames right and left. The present, however, was not a
moment for resentment. The Germans saw that their comrade
was in friendly hands, and gladly left him with me. He had
evidently but a few minutes to live. I sate down on the bank   5
by him, and asked him if I could do anything to relieve him.
He shook his head. Any message to his friends in England? He
nodded. I ran over the most prominent names which occurred
to me of the old set. First, our Amphitryon, Mr. Bottles. "Say
to Bottles from me," said Arminius coldly, "that I hope he will   10
be comfortable with his dead wife's sister." Next, Mr. Frederic
Harrison. "Tell him," says Arminius, "to do more in literature,
—he has a talent for it; and to avoid Carlylese as he would the
devil." Then I mentioned a personage to whom Arminius had
taken a great fancy last spring, and of whose witty writings   15
some people had, absurdly enough, given Mr. Matthew Arnold
the credit,—Azamat-Batuk. Both writers are simple; but Aza-
mat's is the simplicity of shrewdness, the other's of helplessness. At hearing the clever Turk's name, "Tell him only,"
whispers Arminius, "when he writes about the sex, not to   20
show such a turn for sailing so very near the wind!" Lastly, I
mentioned Mr. Matthew Arnold. I hope I rate this poor soul's
feeble and rambling performances at their proper value; but I
am bound to say that at the mention of his name Arminius
showed signs of tenderness. "Poor fellow!" sighed he; "he had   25
a soft head, but I valued his heart. Tell him I leave him my
ideas,—the easier ones; and advise him from me," he added,
with a faint smile, "to let his Dissenters go to the devil their
own way!"

    At this instant there was a movement on the road at a little dis-   30
tance from where we were,—some of the Prussian Princes, I
believe, passing; at any rate, we heard the honest German
soldiers *Hoch-ing*, hurrahing, and God-blessing, in their true-
hearted but somewhat *rococo* manner. A flush passed over
Von Thunder-ten-Tronckh's face. "God bless *Germany*," he   35
murmured, "and confound all her kings and princelings!"
These were his last coherent words. His eyes closed and he
seemed to become unconscious. I stooped over him and in-

quired if he had any wishes about his interment. "Pangloss
—Mr. Lowe—mausoleum—Caterham," was all that, in broken
words, I could gather from him. His breath came with more
and more difficulty, his fingers felt instinctively for his to-
5 bacco-pouch, his lips twitched;—he was gone.

So died, *mon cher*, an arrant Republican, and, to speak my real
mind, a most unpleasant companion. His great name and line-
age imposed on the Bottles family, and authors who had never
succeeded with the British public took pleasure in his disparag-
10 ing criticisms on our free and noble country; but for my part I
always thought him an overrated man.

Meanwhile I was alone with his remains. His notion of their
being transported to Caterham was of course impracticable. Still,
I did not like to leave an old acquaintance to the crows, and I
15 looked round in perplexity. Fortune in the most unexpected
manner befriended me. The grounds of a handsome villa came
down to the road close to where I was; at the end of the
grounds and overhanging the road was a summer-house. Its
shutters had been closed when I first discovered Arminius; but
20 while I was occupied with him they had been opened, and a
gay trio was visible within the summer-house at breakfast. I
could scarcely believe my eyes for satisfaction. Three English
members of Parliament, celebrated for their ardent charity and
advanced Liberalism, were sitting before me adorned with a
25 red cross and eating a Strasburg pie! I approached them and
requested their aid to bury Arminius. My request seemed to
occasion them painful embarrassment; they muttered something about "a breach of the understanding," and went on
with their breakfast. I insisted, however; and at length, having
30 stipulated that what they were about to do should on no account be drawn into a precedent, they left their breakfast, and
together we buried Arminius under the poplar-tree. It was a
hurried business, for my friends had an engagement to lunch at
Versailles at noon. Poor Von Thunder-ten-Tronckh, the earth
35 lies light on him, indeed! I could see, as I left him, the blue of
his pilot coat and the whity-brown of his hair through the
mould we had scattered over him.

My benevolent helpers and I then made our way together to

Versailles. As I parted from them at the Hôtel des Réservoirs I met Sala. Little as I liked Arminius, the melancholy scene I had just gone through had shaken me, and I needed sympathy. I told Sala what had happened. "The old story," says Sala; "*life a dream!* Take a glass of brandy." He then inquired who my friends were. "Three admirable members of Parliament," I cried, "who, donning the cross of charity——" "I know," interrupted Sala; "the cleverest thing out!"

But the emotions of this agitating day were not yet over. While Sala was speaking, a group had formed before the hotel near us, and our attention was drawn to its central figure. Dr. Russell, of the *Times*, was preparing to mount his war-horse. You know the sort of thing,—he has described it himself over and over again. Bismarck at his horse's head, the Crown Prince holding his stirrup, and the old King of Prussia hoisting Russell into the saddle. When he was there, the distinguished public servant waved his hand in acknowledgment, and rode slowly down the street, accompanied by the *gamins* of Versailles, who even in their present dejection could not forbear a few involuntary cries of "*Quel homme!*" Always unassuming, he alighted at the lodgings of the Grand Duke of Oldenburg, a potentate of the second or even the third order, who had beckoned to him from the window.

The agitation of this scene for me, however (may I not add, *mon cher*, for you also, and for the whole British press?), lay in a suggestion which it called forth from Sala. "It is all very well," said Sala, "but old Russell's guns are getting a little honeycombed; anybody can perceive that. He will have to be pensioned off, and why should not you succeed him?" We passed the afternoon in talking the thing over, and I think I may assure you that a train has been laid of which you will see the effects shortly.

For my part, I can afford to wait till the pear is ripe; yet I cannot, without a thrill of excitement, think of inoculating the respectable but somewhat ponderous *Times* and its readers with the divine madness of our new style,—the style we have formed upon Sala. The world, *mon cher*, knows that man but imperfectly. I do not class him with the great masters of human thought and human literature,—Plato, Shakspeare, Confucius, Charles Dickens. Sala, like us his disciples, has studied in the book of the world even more than in the world of books. But his career and genius have given him somehow the secret of a literary mixture novel and fascinating in the last degree: he blends the airy epicureanism of the *salons* of Augustus with the full-bodied gaiety of our English Cider-cellar. With our people and country, *mon cher*, this mixture, you may rely upon it, is now the very thing to go down; there arises every day a larger public for it; and we, Sala's disciples, may be trusted not willingly to let it die.—*Tout à vous,*

A Young Lion.[1]

To the Editor *of the* Pall Mall Gazette.

[1] I am bound to say that in attempting to verify Leo's graphic description of Dr. Russell's mounting on horseback, from the latter's own excellent correspondence, to which Leo refers us, I have been unsuccessful. Repeatedly I have seemed to be on the trace of what my friend meant, but the particular description he alludes to I have never been lucky enough to light upon.

I may add that, in spite of what Leo says of the train he and Mr. Sala have laid, of Dr. Russell's approaching retirement, of Leo's prospect of succeeding him, of the charm of the leonine style, and of the disposition of the public mind to be fascinated by it,—I cannot myself believe that either the public, or the proprietors of the *Times,* are yet ripe for a change so revolutionary. But Leo was always sanguine.—Ed.

Dedicatory Letter

GRUB STREET, *Candlemas Day*, 1871.

MY DEAR LEO,—

Shall I ever forget the evening, at the end of last November, when your feeling letter describing the death of our friend first met my eyes? I was alone in my garret; it was just dark; my landlady opened the door and threw a paper on the table. Selfish creatures that we are! my first thought was: It is a communication from the Literary Fund! The straits to which I am reduced by my long warfare with the Philistines, have at last, I said to myself, become known; they have excited sympathy; this is no doubt a letter from Mr. Octavian Blewitt, enclosing half-a-crown, the promise of my dinner at Christmas, and the kind wishes of Lord Stanhope for my better success in authorship. Hastily I lighted my lamp, and saw the *Pall Mall Gazette*. You know, Leo, how, after vainly knocking at the door of the *Daily Telegraph*, I carried to Northumberland Street my records of the conversations of Arminius. I love to think that the success of the "Workhouse Casual" had disposed the Editor's heart to be friendly towards Pariahs; my communication was affably accepted, and from that day to this the *Pall Mall Gazette*, whenever there is any mention in it of Arminius, reaches me in Grub Street *gratis*. I took the paper, I opened it; your playful signature caught my eye. I read your letter through to the end, and then . . .

Suffer me, Leo, to draw a veil over those first days of grief. In the tumult of feeling plans were then formed to which I have not energy to give effect. I nourished the design of laying before the public a complete account of Arminius von Thunder-ten-Tronckh, and of the group which was gathered round him.

The history of his family has been written by the famous Voltaire in his *Candide;* but I doubt whether an honest man can in conscience send the British public to even the historical works of that dangerous author. Yet a singular fortune brought together in our set the descendants of a number of the personages of *Candide.* Von Thunder-ten-Tronckh is, perhaps, sufficiently made known by the following [i.e., preceding] letters; his curious delusion about the living representative of Pangloss is also fully noticed there. But not a glimpse, alas, do these records give of our poor friend Martin (de Mabille), who has just been shut up in Paris eating rats, the cynical descendant of that great foe of Pangloss's optimism, the Martin of *Candide.* Hardly a glimpse is given of the Marquis Pompeo Pococurante, little Pompey with the soft eyes and dark hair, whose acquaintance you made at Turin under the *portiques du Pô,* and whom you brought to London in the hope of curing, by the spectacle of the *Daily Telegraph,* his hereditary indifference and ennui. Of our English friends, too, the public would, doubtless, be glad to hear more. Mr. Bottles himself fills, in the following letters, by no means that space to which his importance entitles him; the excellent Baptist minister, for whom Mr. Bottles has so high a regard, the Rev. Josiah Jupp, appears far too unfrequently; your *Mary Jane,* Leo, is a name and nothing more; hardly more than names are my good and kind patroness, the late lamented Mrs. Bottles, and her sister and successor, Miss Hannah. It is a small matter, perhaps; but I should have liked, too, the public to know something of my faithful landlady here in Grub Street, Kitty Crone, on whom, after my vain conflict with the Philistines is ended, will probably devolve the pious duty of closing my eyes.

I had imagined a memorial of Arminius, in which all these would have found their place; but my spirits broke down in the attempt to execute my design. All, therefore, that I have done is to collect the stray records of Arminius which have already been published, to illustrate them with notes so far as appeared necessary, and to give myself the melancholy pleasure of dedicating to you, Leo, a collection which owes to your brilliant and facile pen some of its best ornaments.

Our friend had an odd way of showing it, but certainly Arminius had a love for this country. Do you remember, Leo, that conversation in the summer of last year, the last we spent together in his company? It was in the arbour of the garden of the "Bald-Faced Stag" at Finchley. We had all been to the gallery of the House of Commons to hear Mr. Vernon Harcourt develop a system of unsectarian religion from the Life of Mr. Pickwick; but from some obstacle or other the expected treat did not come off. We adjourned to Finchley, and there, you remember, Arminius began with a discourse on religious education. He exacted from me, as you know, the promise not, as he harshly phrased it, to "make a hash of his ideas" by reporting them to the public; and the promises of friendship are sacred. But afterwards the conversation became general. It then took a wider range; and I remember Mr. Frederic Harrison beginning to harangue, with his usual fiery eloquence, on the enervation of England, and on the malignancy of all the brute mass of us who are not Comtists. Arminius checked him. "Enervation!"—said he; "depend upon it, yours is still the most fighting people in the whole world. Malignancy!—the best character of the English people ever yet given, friendly as the character is, is still this of Burke's: 'The ancient and inbred integrity, piety, good nature, and good humour of the people of England.' Your nation is sound enough, if only it can be taught that being able to do what one likes, and say what one likes, is not sufficient for salvation. Its dangers are from a surfeit of clap-trap, due to the false notion that liberty and publicity are not only valuable for the use to be made of them, but are goods in themselves, nay, are the *summum bonum!*"

To the same effect he wrote to me from before Paris, a week or two before his death. "You know I do not join in the common dislike of your nation, or in the belief in its certain decay. But no nation can, without danger, go on stuffing its mind with such nonsense as is talked by the newspapers which you are stupid (*sic*) enough to quote with admiration. 'The Germans, forsooth,' says your precious *Telegraph*, 'cannot too soon begin the lesson, of which England has been the special teacher, that national greatness and wealth are to be prized only in so

far as they ensure the freedom of the individual citizen, and
the right of all to join in free debate. Without that liberty, a
German Empire will be only a gilded despotism, politically
weak in spite of its military power, barbaric in spite of its
schools and universities.' 'The fall, says your *Daily News*, 'of
the late Government of France is history's reassertion of the
principle of political liberty.' Do you not see that, if France,
without political liberty, has signally lost, and Germany, without political liberty, has signally won, it is absurd to make the
presence or absence of political liberty in themselves the
ground of the fall or success of nations? Of the fall or success
of nations, certain *virtues* are the ground; political, ay, and
social liberty, are, if you like, favourable to those virtues,
where a root of them already exists; therefore I am a Republican;—but they by no means ensure them. If you have not
these virtues, and imagine that your political liberty will pull
you through without them, you will be ruined in spite of your
political liberty. I admire England because she has such a root
in her of these virtues; not because they have given her, among
other good things, political liberty. Your fetish-worship of
mere liberty is, on the contrary, just now the gravest danger to
you. Your newspapers are every day solemnly saying that the
great lesson to be learned from the present war is so and so,
—always something which it is not. There are many lessons to be
learned from the present war; I will tell you what is for *you*
the great lesson to be learned from it:—*obedience*. That, instead of every man airing his self-consequence, thinking it bliss
to talk at random about things, and to put his finger in every
pie, you should seriously understand that there is a *right* way
of doing things, and that the bliss is, without thinking of one's
self-consequence, to do them in that way, or to forward their
being done,—this is the great lesson your British public, as you
call it, has to learn, and may learn, in some degree, from the
Germans in this war! Englishmen were once famous for the
power of holding their tongues and doing their business, and,
therefore, I admire your nation. The business now to be done
in the world is harder than ever, and needs far more than has
been ever yet needed of thought, study, and seriousness: mis-

carry you must, if you let your daily doses of clap-trap make you imagine that liberty and publicity can be any substitute for these."

I doubt whether this is sound, Leo, and, at any rate, the *D.T.* should have been more respectfully mentioned; but it shows that the feeling of Arminius towards this country was at bottom tender. My own patriotism, as you know, never wavered, even while I made myself, in a manner, the mouthpiece of Arminius, and submitted to the predominance which his intellect, I own, exercised over me. My affection for him remains as strong as ever, but now that his life is ended, and his predominance withdrawn, I feel that a new destiny is probably opening for me. My patriotic feelings will henceforth have free play; the iron hand of Arminius will no longer press them down. Your counsels, Leo, the study of our newspapers, the spectacle of our grandeur, will work with these my natural feelings; I shall earn the public approbation, I shall not be always an Ishmael. I shall ally myself to some of those great Liberal movements which,—however Arminius might choose to call them petty aimless activities, bustle without any *Ernst der ins Ganze geht,*—seem to me admirably suited to the genius of our national life, and highly productive of enjoyable excitement and honourable importance to their promoters.

We are now on the point of commencing what Arminius, with his fatally carping spirit, called our "Thyesteän banquet of clap-trap;"—we are on the eve of the meeting of Parliament. Mr. T. Chambers will again introduce that enfranchising measure, against which I have had some prejudices, but which you, Leo, have so eloquently upheld,—the bill for enabling a man to marry his deceased wife's sister. Mr. Miall, that Israelite indeed, will resume, on a more stupendous scale than ever, his labours for making all bitterness, and wrath, and anger, and clamour, and evil-speaking be put away from us, with all malice; and for our enjoyment of the pure milk of Christianity. The devoted adversaries of the Contagious Diseases Act will spread through the length and breadth of the land a salutary discussion of this equivocal measure and of all matters connected with it; and will thus, at the same time that they oppose im-

morality, enable the followers of even the very straitest sects
of Puritanism to see life. Some of these workers will doubtless
suffer me to put my hand to their plough. Like the tailor to
the poet Cowper, to some one or other of them I may be
allowed to make my modest appeal:—

> "Say, shall *my* little bark attendant sail,
>   Pursue the triumph, and partake the gale?"

If not on the hustings or the platform, at least I may do something in the closet, with the pen! My mind full of this new
thought, as I passed down Regent Street yesterday, and saw in a
shop window, in the frontispiece to one of Mr. Hepworth Dixon's numerous but well-merited editions, the manly and animated features of the author of the immortal *Guide to Mormonism*, I could not help exclaiming with pride: "I, too, am an author!"

And then, Leo, comes the reaction. I look up and see Arminius's vacant stool; I sniff, and my nostrils no longer catch the
scent of his tobacco. The dreams of excitement and ambition fly
away; I am left solitary with the remembrance of the past, and
with those consolations of piety and religion, which you, Leo,
have outgrown. Yet how can I do you such an injustice?
—when at this very moment my chief consolation, under our
heavy bereavement, is in repeating to myself that glorious passage you read to me the other day from one of your unpublished articles for the *D. T.*:—"*In the Garden of the Hesperi-
des, the inscrutable-eyed Sphinx whispers, with half-parted
lips, Mysteries more than Eleusinian of the Happy Dead!*"
                         Believe me, my dear Leo,
                                Your faithful admirer,
                                        MATTHEW ARNOLD.

To ADOLESCENS LEO, Esq.
       etc.   etc.   etc.

Critical and Explanatory Notes

References to Arnold's diary-notebooks are drawn from H. F. Lowry, K. Young, and W. H. Dunn, eds., *The Note-Books of Matthew Arnold* (London, 1952), supplemented by W. B. Guthrie, ed., *Matthew Arnold's Diaries: the Unpublished Items* (Ann Arbor, 1959). Most quotations from Arnold's letters to his publishers are drawn from W. E. Buckler, ed., *Matthew Arnold's Books* (Geneva, 1958); most quotations from his other letters are taken from the collection edited by G. W. E. Russell, where they can be found under their dates: the collection has been published in so many editions that page references are not helpful. A very few quotations are from unpublished letters. When the editor has consciously drawn information from the unpublished dissertations or notes mentioned in the Editor's Preface, by S. M. B. Coulling, Ian Gregor, J. P. Kirby, S. P. SenGupta, and Peter Smith, he has attached the writer's name (in parentheses) to the note.

[FRIENDSHIP'S GARLAND]

In May, 1868, as Arnold was drawing near the close of his articles on "Anarchy and Authority," he conceived the notion of gathering into a single volume his socio-political writings of the past two and a half years—"My Countrymen," the Arminius letters in the *Pall Mall Gazette*, "Culture and Its Enemies," and "Anarchy and Authority."—Buckler, *Matthew Arnold's Books*, p. 88. But *Culture and Anarchy* appeared without either "My Countrymen" or the Arminius letters, and after it was published early in 1869 the latter were resumed occasionally in the *Pall Mall Gazette*. When Arnold terminated the series on November 29, 1870, with Arminius' death before the fortifications of Paris, either he or his publisher George Smith conceived the notion of gathering the letters into a memorial volume, "edited" with notes and commentary by Arnold. Publisher and "editor" worked on the project with great speed and gusto. On January 6, 1871, Arnold apologized to Smith that "a dismal dose of 40 closely written grammar papers to look over," together with the rare and not-to-be-missed opportunity for skating, had "prevented me hitherto from turning to the literary remains of poor dear Arminius.... The grammar papers remain, but I am going through them fast, though they sicken me, in order to give next week to Arminius; and by Saturday the 14th I will send the MS. and preface. That will enable us to be out before Parliament meets."—Buckler, p. 94. On February 1 he sent back the first sheet of proofs. "You know how much there is in *look*, and from the way in which the letters and my comments are intermixed questions of *look* are constantly arising." Therefore he wanted Smith to give special thought to the design of the book. "I think it is more self-important and *bête* if I put *Ed.* after every note. It is rather fun making the notes." The notes, in fact, grew too numerous for Smith's taste. "The only thing to remember," Arnold told him on February 9, "is that though the public may not much like notes, it still less likes being puzzled and thrown out by allusions it does not know or has forgotten." But three days later, he wrote: "I am more & more coming to think you were right about the notes," and so he cut out all Smith had indicated for deletion. The printer originally placed Arnold's former university titles after his name, but these he struck out: "It would be carrying the joke too far." The book had already been advertised when Arnold read of Sala's successful suit for libel against the publishing firm of Hodder and Stoughton (see p. 482), and he hastened to ask Smith's opinion of the danger in his own references to Sala, but Smith must have been reassuring. It is not apparent who invented the title, which shows something of the influence of the literary annuals that were the fashion earlier in the century, *Friendship's Offering, Affection's Offering, The Garland, or Token of Friendship,* etc. The book was bound in white cloth with a black mourning border and a gold-stamped wreath above a ribbon bearing the motto from Vergil that was repeated on the title page. The endpapers were dark, and both Arnold and Smith were displeased with what Arnold called "the jar to the eye from the inside being darker than the outside.... Else the binding is a great success." Later copies were bound in reddish brown or in dark blue cloth, with the same ornaments. A second edition in November, 1897, followed the original page for page, and repeated the binding in white cloth. When Arnold's daughter published excerpts from his *Notebooks* in 1902, she used the same binding design, white cloth with black mourning border, but with a gold-stamped monogram in place of the wreath and ribbon. The first edition of *Friendship's Garland* was advertised in the *Times* on February 24, 1871, priced at 4 *s*. 6 *d*. The only other edition in Arnold's lifetime was printed in Edinburgh for publication in 1883 by Macmillan and Company in New York; it appeared appropriately in the same volume with *Culture and Anarchy*. An excellent modern edition was prepared as a doctoral dissertation by Professor John P. Kirby (Yale University, 1937), but it remains unpublished.

Professor Kirby points out the link between *Friendship's Garland* and Arnold's reading for his lecture on Heine in 1863: Heine's doctrine was Arminius' doctrine and his style was the model for Arnold's irony. Heine is prominent also in the treatment of *Friendship's Garland* and *Culture and Anarchy* in Walther Fischer's "Matthew Arnold und Deutschland," *Germanisch-romanische Monatsschrift* XXXV, 119–37 (April, 1954); Fischer comments too on the impact of Arnold's visit to Germany in 1865. Another literary kinship was pointed out by the *Saturday Review* on March 11, 1871— that with Carlyle's *Sartor Resartus*. But in the opinion of the *Saturday*, though Englishmen can benefit greatly from the self-criticism Arnold urges on them, he too often descends from his superb mastery of the rapier to breaking heads with his cudgel. If Teufelsdröckh was, like Arminius, tedious to his contemporaries, Count Zaehdarm's epitaph was more powerful than the satire on Lumpington. *Friendship's Garland* was not, in fact, warmly received by Arnold's contemporaries. As Arnold himself wrote of the *Saturday's* comment, "There is much that is conventional in our notion of what is amusing: and if a man tells the public that a thing is not amusing, the public, especially if a little affronted with the thing and its author, is very apt and glad to believe the assurance." The modern reader finds an even greater obstacle in the ephemeral matter of the book. Yet it is some of the wittiest writing of a very witty era.

In the book form, the Dedicatory Letter was of course at the beginning, "My Countrymen" and "A Courteous Explanation" were at the end, there was no division into Parts I and II, and "Stein Plus Hardenberg," "A Recantation and Apology," and "Melancholy If True" were not included. The present edition adopts the order in which the separate articles first appeared in the *Cornhill Magazine* and the *Pall Mall Gazette*.

The Epigraph (p. 2) is from the tribute to the dead Marcellus, Vergil *Aeneid* vi. 883.

[MY COUNTRYMEN]

When Fitzjames Stephen, in the *Saturday Review* for December 3, 1864, challenged Arnold's conclusions regarding the state of England in "The Functions of Criticism at the Present Time," he headed his article "Mr. Matthew Arnold and His Countrymen." Arnold wrote to his mother four days later, "From anything like a direct answer, or direct controversy, I shall religiously abstain; but here and there I shall take an opportunity of putting back this and that matter into its true light, if I think he has pulled them out of it; and I have the idea of a paper for the *Cornhill*, about March, to be called 'My Countrymen,' and in which I may be able to say a number of things I want to say, about the course of this Middle Class Education matter amongst others." On the same day he proposed the paper to George Smith, the *Cornhill*'s publisher, and on December 13 added by way of explanation: "The Saturday suggested a title to me: but I would not play you such a trick as to ask you to print my stupid controversies. I will give you leave to cut out every line you judge controversial: but there will be none such. You shall see however."—Buckler, *Matthew Arnold's Books*, p. 92. There exists a sheet of Athenaeum Club notepaper on which Arnold has copied quotations from the *Nonconformist* of November 30, the *Morning Star* and *Daily Telegraph* of December 2, and the *Daily News* of December 7, upon the subject of middle-class education, presumably for use in the article he described to his mother (Kirby).

All these quotations appeared in "My Countrymen" when he wrote the article more than a year later, but the early weeks of 1865 were devoted to writing a Preface to the collected *Essays in Criticism* (in which he made his first reply to Stephen's article), and most of the rest of the year went to his mission of investigating secondary schools and universities on the Continent. What he saw there gave quite a new focus to the essay he planned. "Heaven forbid that the English nation should become like this nation," he wrote from Paris on May 14, 1865, apropos of the platitudes of the English Liberals in the debates on Reform; "but Heaven forbid also that it should remain as it is. If it does, it will be beaten by America on its own line, and by the Continental nations on the European line. I see this as plain as I see the paper before me; but what good one can do, though one sees it, is another question. Time will decide." Again, after telling his sister Jane Forster of the political problems of Prussia, he added (July 17), "About this country, its classes, their relative power, their character, and their tendency, one might fill sheet after sheet, but I spare you. I will only say that all I see abroad makes me fonder of England, and yet more and more convinced of the general truth of the ideas about England and her progress, and what is needful for her, which have come to me almost by instinct, and which yet all I see keeps constantly confirming." "The present position of England in European esteem is indeed not a pleasant matter, and far too long to be begun upon at the end of a letter," he wrote to his brother-in-law, W. E. Forster, on September 30. The news of Palmerston's death, with its accompaniment of absurd panegyrics in the English newspapers, led him to reflect on October 24: "It may even be doubted whether, thanks to Bismarck's audacity, resolution, and success, Prussia, too, as well as France and the United States, does not come before England at present in general respect." And not long after he returned to London he wrote to his sister Frances: "I have a conviction that there is a real, an almost imminent danger of England losing immeasurably in all ways, declining into a sort of greater Holland, for want of what I must still call ideas, for want of perceiving how the world is going and must go, and preparing herself accordingly. This conviction haunts me, and at times even overwhelms me with depression; I would rather not live to see the change come to pass, for we shall all deteriorate under it. While there is time I will do all I can, and in every way, to prevent its coming to pass. Sometimes, no doubt, turning oneself one way after another, one must make unsuccessful and unwise hits, and one may fail after all; but try I must, and I know that it is only by facing in every direction that one can win the day." Thus by the time the essay on "My Countrymen" was published, nearly fourteen months after it was first projected, both the discussion of middle-class education and the reply to the *Saturday Review* had become subordinate to an examination of the place of England in the modern world—England, in the midst of the democratic agitations that preceded the Reform Law of 1867, as she appeared to her critics at home and abroad. "Will you keep a place in the February number of your Magazine for 'My Countrymen'?" Arnold asked George Smith early in January, 1866, and reported on the 8th that it was nearly written. But he begged for four more days to "give me more time to look over it, [as] the subject is ticklish. I think the paper will amuse you."—Buckler, pp. 92–93. It was published in the *Cornhill* for February and brought Arnold 25 gns.

Though two of his four lectures on Celtic literature remained to be written, Arnold had actually committed himself to a new career of political writing, for which he was much encouraged by the success of this first article. "Most of the ... weekly newspapers mention it as the event of the *Cornhill*, very witty and suggestive, and so on," he told his mother on February 3. "I think I told you of Carlyle's being so full of my article," he wrote to her again on the 23rd; "I hear that Bright is full of it also, but I have not yet heard any particulars of what Bright says. Carlyle almost wholly approves, I hear; I am going to see him. The country newspapers have had a great deal about it; two leading articles in the *Edinburgh Courant,* not by any means unfavourable, but trying to use it for their own Tory purposes. The Whig newspapers are almost all unfavourable, because it tells disagreeable truths to the class which furnishes the great body of what is called the Liberal interest." It was the more necessary that he send her the evidence of public awareness of the importance of his views, for (February 3), "I gather from Jane that you do not quite like it, but I am sure it was wanted, and will do good; and this, in spite of what the *Spectator* says, I really wish to do, and have my own ideas as to the best way of doing it. You see you belong to the *old* English time, of which the greatness and success was so immense and indisputable, that no one who flourished when it was at its height can ever lose the impression of it. Sir James Shuttleworth, who is a good judge, has just told me that without agreeing with every word, he entirely, on the whole, went along with the contents of the article, putting all questions of style and clever writing out of question, and that he thought the article timely and true. At the [Arthur] Stanleys' last night a good many people spoke to me about it, and with great amusement. I have received an indignant letter of expostulation from Lingen, however; but he thinks I want to exalt the actual aristocracy at the expense of the middle class, which is a total mistake, though I am obliged to proceed in a way which might lead a hasty and angry reader to think so. But there are certain things which it needs great dexterity to say in a receivable manner at all; and what I had to say I could only get said, to my thinking, in the manner I have said it." Arnold had found not only a subject, but a style for treating it.

3:22–4:22. "There is in England a school of philosophy which thoroughly understands, and on theoretical grounds deliberately rejects, the philosophical theory which Mr. Arnold accuses the English nation of neglecting, and . . . the practical efforts of the English people, especially their practical efforts in the way of literary criticism, are for the most part strictly in accordance with the principles of that philosophy. . . . Mr. Arnold's whole essay assumes the truth of the transcendental theory of philosophy. . . . Mr. Arnold surely cannot be ignorant of the fact that, from the days of Hobbes and Locke to those of Mr. Mill and Mr. Bain, the most influential of English thinkers have utterly denied the truth of transcendentalism, and have constantly affirmed that all knowledge is based upon experience and sensation. . . . Now the commonest acquaintance with this view of things will show that in principle, though of course not in detail, it justifies the common run of English criticism—that is, of the remarks which English people make on passing events for practical or literary purposes. . . . In fact, no nation in the world is so logical as the English nation. Once get it well convinced of the truth of a general principle—which is, as it ought to be, considering how hard it is to state general principles correctly, a very hard task—and it will do anything. For instance, the English nation believes in political economy, and the consequence is that it is the only nation in the world which has established free trade. . . . Bentham persuaded the English nation that the greatest happiness of the greatest number was the true rule for legislation, and every part of the law has been reformed by degrees by the application, more or less skilful and complete, of that abstract principle. . . . When abstract principles like these are embraced by and do influence the English people most deeply, is it just, or even decent, to talk about 'British Philistines' because we English do not choose to recognise as eternal truths a set of platitudes which may be proved to be false?"—[Fitzjames Stephen], "Mr. Matthew Arnold and His Countrymen," *Saturday Review* XVIII, 684 (December 3, 1864). Arnold amused himself with the charge of "transcendentalism" in the "Preface" to *Essays in Criticism* (*Prose Works*, ed. Super, III, 289) and the *Saturday Review* kept up the game by referring in an article on "Letters of Eugénie de Guérin" to "the transcendental critics who insist on the beauty of her example in a Benthamite age."—XIX, 317 (March 18, 1865).

4:19–20. See Arnold's expression, "that return of Burke upon himself," in "The Function of Criticism at the Present Time," *Prose Works*, ed. Super, III, 267. It is likely that Arnold inserted "as the

French say" because the *Saturday Review* had remarked that he had "taught himself to write a dialect as like French as pure English can be" (p. 683) and pointed to another part of the same passage about Burke. The French idiom is *revenir sur*, "to change" (one's opinion).

4:25. See p. 17:9–10.

4:26–27. The discussion was consequent upon the appointment of the Schools Inquiry Commission at the end of 1864.

4:29–5:1. Sir Thomas Bazley (1797–1885), one of the largest cotton manufacturers in England, represented Manchester in Parliament from 1858 to 1880. He was given a baronetcy by Gladstone in 1869. Arnold quotes a speech of November 29, 1864, reported in the *Times* two days later (p. 7, col. 6); Bazley referred to the forthcoming investigation of the Schools Inquiry Commission. On January 3, 1865, Arnold wrote to his sister Mrs. Forster: "Did you notice what Bazley said about the education of his own class at Manchester some weeks ago, and what Bright said yesterday, and the difference? I note all these things, however slight, with interest." Arnold jotted the *Times* quotation in his pocket diary early in December, 1864, and copied it into the back of his diary for 1865.— *Note-Books*, ed. Lowry, pp. 28, 32.

5:1–11. *Nonconformist* XXIV, 966 (November 30, 1864), leading article.

5:14–27. *Daily News*, December 7, 1864, p. 4, cols. 3–4 (leading article).

5:31–32. *Daily Telegraph*, December 2, 1864, p. 4, col. 5 (leading article). The *Telegraph* called the speech "broad" rather than "grand," and did not allude at all to Bazley's statement about education.

5:32–6:6. *Morning Star*, December 2, 1864, p. 4, col. 3. This leading article, like the preceding, is devoted to Bazley's principal subject of Reform, not to his remarks on education.

6:27–29. "Of the intellect of Europe in general, the main effort . . . has been a critical effort; the endeavour, in all branches of knowledge, . . . to see the object as in itself it really is. . . . How is criticism to show disinterestedness? By keeping aloof from practice."—Arnold, "The Function of Criticism at the Present Time," *Prose Works*, ed. Super, III, 258, 270 (532). The *Saturday Review* (XVIII, 685) retorted that Arnold "constantly object[ed] to practical measures on theoretical grounds."

6:33–36. See Arnold, *A French Eton, Prose Works*, ed. Super,

II, 297, and "The Literary Influence of Academies," *ibid.*, III, 257.

7:17–19. Arnold was in France, Italy, Germany, Austria, and Switzerland on a mission for the Schools Inquiry Commission from April 8 to the end of October, 1865.

7:20–21.

> O wad some Pow'r the giftie gie us
> To see oursels as ithers see us!
> It wad frae mony a blunder free us,
>   An' foolish notion.
> —Burns, "To a Louse," 43–46.

7:27. A commonplace. In a leading article on the death of Lord Palmerston the *Times* remarked that "it must awake a sort of envy" in France that England can be guided by "a perfect representative of the country, a thoroughly popular chief, a mean between all classes, without the surrender of our liberties or the formality of several revolutions."—October 24, 1865, p. 8, col. 3. And Kirby points out a leading article on Fenianism in the *Times* of December 13, 1865, p. 8, col. 5, in which the writer, after glancing at the alarmist views of England's unsettled social condition of the past thirty years, remarks: "Yet we have survived all these troubles—survived to find ourselves the most prosperous and most united nation in the world—objects, indeed, of so much envy as to create occasional ill will." Inconsistently enough, the article immediately before this one declared that French competition was threatening to best the English in both manufacturing and shipping.

8:3–15. Arnold's letters from Rolandseck, on the Rhine, in July, 1865, mention his reading the *Cologne Gazette* in his hotel there, and he jotted a memorandum of this article in his diary: "Militärische Briefe aus Norddeutschland: die kaiserlich französische Armee. II," *Kölnische Zeitung*, July 25, 1865, p. 3, col. 1. See Arnold, *Note-Books*, ed. Lowry, p. 31.

8:27. On October 23, 1865, the French government proposed an international commission to sit at Constantinople, which should investigate the causes and spread of cholera and suggest practical measures for confining the disease.

8:28–29. See Arnold's "Literary Influence of Academies," *Prose Works*, ed. Super, III, 250.

9:8–9. *Times*, October 25, 1865, p. 8, col. 4. Lord Palmerston died on October 18, 1865, and was buried in Westminster Abbey on the 27th. The *Times* had almost daily articles of eulogy during the interval.

9:15–18. Adolphe Thiers, *History of the Consulate and the Empire*, tr. D. Forbes Campbell (London, 1847), VI, 233 (one-third through Book XXIV). The younger Pitt died in January, 1806.

9:22–23. It must have been a Swiss city, perhaps Zurich.

9:38. The Latin may be Arnold's own.

10:17–19. "The precept which Aristotle laid down 2,000 years ago, in the words —'Happy and well governed those States where the middle part is strong and the extremes weak' (hear, hear.) ... well embodies the leading merit of our Constitution."—Robert Lowe, speaking to the Commons on the Borough Franchise Extension Bill, May 3, 1865; reported next day in the *Times*, p. 9, col. 6.

10:26–27. In 1864 Prussia and Austria invaded Schleswig-Holstein and defeated Denmark in a brief war. By the end of the year the duchies were severed from Denmark and two years later annexed to Prussia.

10:38. See pp. 338–39.

10:34–11:2. Leslie Stephen published a devastating analysis, made up for the most part of direct quotations, of *The "Times" on the American War* (London, 1865), with a view to showing how seriously the newspaper that was everywhere considered the voice of England had damaged the relations between the two countries by its vacillation and its persistent misrepresentation of the Northern cause and behavior. "I cannot see the force of a late piteous appeal of the *Times* 'to let bygones be bygones.' It is sufficiently impudent after abusing a man incessantly, and being mistaken in all you have said, to request him to forget all about it." The pamphlet was reprinted in 1915 by *The Magazine of History* (New York) X, Extra No. 37 (Kirby).

11:23–25. "We can pursue a policy of general non-interference without either disarming or losing our prestige," said one of Arnold's "political philosophers" (see p. 236:36–37), W. E. Baxter, *Hints to Thinkers* (London, 1860), p. 226.

12:11. John Orlando Parry (1810–79), musician and actor, joined Mr. and Mrs. Thomas German Reed in their production of "entertainments" at the Gallery of Illustration, 14, Regent Street, in 1860. "Here he delighted the public for nearly nine years by a series of droll impersonations and marvellous musical monologues. The comic song he treated as a comedy scene with musical illustrations. He invented his own entertainments, composed his own music, and played his own accompaniments."—*D.N.B.* The newspapers were advertising in December and January an entertainment at the Gallery called "A Peculiar Family." An admiring article on Parry in the *Spectator* XXXIX, 238–39 (March 3, 1866), throws no light on the one Arnold describes.

12:13. On January 22, 1863, a Polish revolutionary committee set in motion an insurrection against Russia that was carried on for nearly two years by partisan warfare. The Russians spurned England's offers of intervention. The suppression of the revolt marked the complete russification of the country, the end of all self-government and of its separate judicial system.

12:35–38. Arnold's foreign friends repeat Arnold's own views in *England and the Italian Question, Prose Works,* ed. Super, I, 85.

13:7. Arnold had said this in "The Literary Influence of Academies" and was to repeat it in *On the Study of Celtic Literature, Prose Works,* ed. Super, III, 237, 341.

13:21–23. These words form the preamble to the revolutionary decree of the Convention on December 15, 1792, instructing its generals to proclaim immediately, in all occupied territories, "the sovereignty of the people, the suppression of all the established authorities and of the existing imposts and taxes, the abolition of the tithe, of feudalism, ... and generally of all privileges."—F. M. Anderson, *The Constitutions and Other Select Documents Illustrative of the History of France, 1789–1901* (Minneapolis, 1904), p. 130.

14:8–10. From a letter addressed by Lord Grenville, foreign secretary under Pitt, to François de Chauvelin, French ambassador in London, dated December 31, 1792.—*Parliamentary History of England* (London: Hansard, 1817), XXX, 255.

14:18. Judges 5:20.

16:6. *Hamlet* III, ii, 16.

16:17–17:10. Lowe's speech in the Commons on the Borough Franchise Extension Bill, May 3, 1865; reported next day in the *Times,* pp. 8–9. The speech was separately published as a pamphlet, and Arnold used the pamphlet version. Lowe quoted "one the poetical charm of whose mind and style have perhaps a little overclouded his reputation as a political philosopher, ... Lord Macaulay." On May 14, 1865, Arnold wrote to his sister Frances from Paris: "I was much interested by Lowe's speech on Reform. I think I told you that what I saw of him in coming to Paris [on April 8] and going back to London [on April 14] struck me greatly. I found a side in him I did not know was there. I see by extracts from the *Telegraph,* etc., how furious he has made the vulgar Liberals, but he has necessitated a more searching treatment of the whole question of Reform, and the rank and file of English platform and House of Commons speakers, though, no doubt, they will still talk platitudes, will, at any rate, have to learn new ones. Heaven forbid that the English nation should become like this nation; but Heaven forbid also that it should remain as it is. If it does, it will be beaten by America on its own line, and by the Continental nations on the European line."

17:11–16. Speaking in the manufacturing city of Blackburn, Lancashire, on November 30, 1865, Bright said: "There is, and has been, no anarchy in Europe that could have matched the anarchy that must have existed in this country (Hear, hear) [if the Tory party for the last 40 years had been dominant in England]. The people would have been by millions and millions in a condition of poverty and abject degradation. If your Queen had been pure and just, as one of the angelic order, her Throne would not have been safe; . . . and, as for the members of the House of Lords, in all human probability they would long ago have been emptied into the Thames. (Loud laughter and cheers.)"—*Times*, December 1, 1865, p. 7, col. 5.

18:1–2. See note to p. 3:22.

19:20–25. In *A French Eton* Arnold summed up the interest of the middle class as "*Business and Bethels.*"—*Prose Works*, ed. Super, II, 317.

20:5. *Hamlet* IV, v, 84.

20:12. *Hamlet* I, v, 167.

20:34–35. See note to p. 3:22.

21:12–14. See pp. 57–64.

21:14–23. The Schools Inquiry Commission's study was principally directed at the nearly eight hundred schools in England supported wholly or in part by charitable endowments, and therefore opened the question as to whether these endowments—many of them set up under circumstances long past, or to satisfy certain crotchets of their donors—served the best interest of the nation. Arnold explained at length the conditions of charitable bequest in France in *Schools and Universities on the Continent, Prose Works*, ed. Super, IV, 53–55. "The age of endowments is gone," he had proclaimed in *A French Eton, ibid.*, II, 294.

21:28–29. The Mayor, Aldermen, and Common Council governed the City of London—the area within the old city walls; the vast areas of the metropolis outside the City were governed, after the Metropolis Management Act of 1855, by twenty-three popularly elected vestries and fifteen district boards that governed combinations of small parishes. Only certain functions, such as those performed by the Metropolitan Police and the Metropolitan Board of Works, were exercised on the basis of the entire metropolitan area. Other towns and chartered boroughs in England, which had grown up most variously in their traditions of government, were given a degree of uniformity by the Municipal Corporations Act of 1835 and its subsequent amendments.—John J. Clarke, *The Local Government of the United Kingdom* (15th ed.; London, 1955), pp. 34–43.

21:35–36. Islington is a metropolitan borough (formerly parish) of north-central London, east of King's Cross Station; Camberwell is a metropolitan borough (formerly parish) south of the Thames and of Southwark, east of Lambeth. Both were middle-class Nonconformist residential areas and (though Arnold can not have been alluding to the fact) Camberwell was the birthplace of Browning and the residence of Ruskin from the time he was four (1823) to 1871. The new Metropolitan (Underground) Railway was linked to the London, Chatham, and Dover Railway at Ludgate Hill, so that Arnold's traveler could go from King's Cross on the former to Camberwell on the latter.

21:37. Gladstone's Irish Church Bill was passed on July 23, 1869; see pp. 319–24. The Irish Land Act was passed in 1870.

22:22. The prefect was the executive at the head of each of France's eighty-nine *départements*, the largest units of local government. He was nominated by the national government. See Arnold, *Prose Works*, ed. Super, II, 33–34.

22:33–38. Isaac Barrow, "The Reward of Honouring God," *Theological Works* (Oxford, 1818), I, 81. Arnold owned this edition, and jotted the passage in his diary for October 15, 1870 (ed. Lowry, p. 137). For the Mordaunt trial and Lord Cole, see p. 343:28.

23:1–3. From Lowe's speech on Reform, *Times*, May 4, 1865, p. 9, col. 6.

23:8. Kirby points to a leading article in the *Daily Telegraph*, August 20, 1866, p. 4, cols. 3–4: "We certainly have done something in the way of inflicting our pet moral notions on foreigners. We have introduced, or at least popularized, soap and water in France and punctuality in Italy; we have taught Swiss landlords extortion, and have driven down the throats of German philosophers the conviction that Bass and Guinness are the drink of the future, well worth any quantity of bad Rüdesheimer or Liebfraumilch." (The

"German philosopher" alluded to is of course Arminius; see p. 48: 16–17, published August 7, 1866).

23:38. Count Pococurante was a Venetian nobleman in Voltaire's *Candide*, Chapter XXV, the epitome of *ennui*. Pompeo is more fully described in Arnold's "Dedicatory Letter," p. 352.

24:5–14. Arthur, vicomte de La Guéronnière, *L'Empereur Napoléon III. et l'Italie* (Paris, 1859), pp. 61–62. The *Times*, in "the belief that it was composed under the immediate inspiration of the Emperor, and that much of it is actually from his own hand," translated the entire pamphlet on February 5, 1859, pp. 9–10. This passage, from section XVI, is on p. 10, col. 2.

24:15–16. *Times*, February 4, 1859, p. 9, col. 2.

24:19–28. *Times*, February 7, 1859, p. 6, cols. 5, 4.

24:30–32. *Times*, January 28, 1859, p. 6, col. 3.

24:35–25:4. *Times*, January 19, 1859, p. 8, col. 3. Arnold's chronology is at fault.

25:5–16. *Times*, February 5, 1859, p. 8, cols. 3–4.

25:21–26. *Times*, October 11, 1860, p. 6, col. 3. It will be noted that this was the next year, not the same year as the preceding. Francis II was the last king of Naples, deposed by Garibaldi.

25:32–37. *Times*, October 16, 1860, p. 6, cols. 3–4.

26:12. The *Saturday Review*'s article on *England and the Italian Question* (August 13, 1859) disagreed with nearly every view Arnold expressed in his pamphlet.

27:2–8. See Arnold's letter to his sister Frances, November, 1865, quoted on p. 361.

27:11–12. Henry St. John, Viscount Bolingbroke, "The Idea of a Patriot King," *Letters on the Spirit of Patriotism and on the Idea of a Patriot King*, ed. A. Hassall (Oxford, 1917), p. 139. This essay was on Arnold's list of books to be read in 1866.—*Note-Books*, ed. Lowry, p. 580.

27:24–25. *Othello* V, ii, 244.

28:2–3. "What is the unsatisfactory element in Mr. Arnold as a writer? Why, with his great gifts, is he of little or no weight as a teacher? Why do his criticisms occasionally cause intense disgust? What is the defect in his powers of amusing which makes them soon annoying to minds of refinement and intelligence?" asked the reviewer of *Essays in Criticism*, with his eye fixed principally on the Preface. He concluded, "Misplaced jokes are dangerous things, and rash personalities are out of place, whether we are joking or in earnest."—*Guardian* (London), May 17, 1865, p. 502.

28:9. See p. 88:7.

28:16. The Spotted Dog, Thomas Wilson, prop., was a public house and booking office at 298 Strand.

28:18-22. The Marylebone Vestry, the Educational Home, railway management, and the Divorce Court had all been criticized elsewhere by Arnold; see *Prose Works*, ed. Super, I, 87 and III, 289; II, 281-82; II, 305; and III, 281, 534. The Crystal Palace, built to house the Great Exhibition of 1851, was moved to Sydenham in 1854 and thereafter housed a permanent exhibition of casts of sculpture, temporary exhibitions of various sorts, concert performances, and the like. It continued to be open "daily, except Sunday," until it was destroyed by fire in 1936.

28:25. *Hamlet* I, ii, 129.

28:36. A pennygaff was a low-class theater or music hall.

28:38. *Strathmore. A Romance*, by Ouida, was a "three-decker" published in June, 1865, at a guinea and a half. Kirby points out that the reviewer of the novel in the *Pall Mall Gazette* on May 4, 1866, cited this comment of Arnold's.

29:2. Belgravia is the part of London about Belgrave and Eaton Squares, south of Hyde Park. From the time it was built in the 1820's it was the most fashionable quarter of London. Arnold was living in Belgravia when he wrote this essay.

29:3. *Macbeth* II, iii, 22.

29:17-20. Heine, *Reisebilder* IV: "Die Stadt Lucca," end of Chapter XV.

29:37. Sir Charles Wentworth Dilke, *Greater Britain: a Record of Travel in English-speaking Countries during 1866 and 1867* (London, 1868).

30:6-19. In *A French Eton*; see *Prose Works*, ed. Super, II, 319.

30:9. "Buncombe" is claptrap. The word (now commonly spelled "bunkum" or merely "bunk") originated in America about 1827 and migrated to England about 1856.

30:35. The image of history as a series of waves is used most effectively in "Obermann Once More," a poem upon which Arnold was working at the time he wrote this essay.

31:3-4. Vergil *Aeneid* ii. 287.

31:5-14. Arnold, "Heine's Grave," lines 87-96. The poem was first published in Arnold's *New Poems*, 1867.

[NOTES TO CANCELLED PASSAGES]

488:31–37. Arnold had ridiculed A. W. Kinglake's description of Lord Stratford de Redcliffe's "thin, tight, merciless lips" (*Invasion of the Crimea*, 3rd ed., II, 33–34) in "The Literary Influence of Academies," *Prose Works*, ed. Super, III, 256. He made devastating use of the advertisements of "educational homes" from the *Times* in *A French Eton*, and in the same work spoke of the pleasure the middle class took in "being complimented on their self-reliance by Lord Fortescue": *Prose Works*, II, 281–82, 323. A pseudonymous letter to the *Pall Mall Gazette* on "The Mansion-House Meeting" on January 17, 1866 (at the very moment Arnold was reading the proofs of "My Countrymen") was not known as his by modern scholars until uncovered in 1937 by Professor Kirby; it is published in *Prose Works*, IV, 8–12. It may be added that Arnold much softened his criticism of Kinglake in the edition of *Essays in Criticism* published in 1869: early in February, 1867, he found himself next to Kinglake at a dinner party and despite Arnold's embarrassment, "we shook hands, and got very amiably along together."

489:2–5. Revelation 22:11. The *Saturday Review* was rather hard on Arnold for his use of what it ironically called "a beautiful and appropriate Scriptural quotation" which implied that "the unfortunate Philistines [were] unjust and filthy," and perhaps for this reason Arnold sensed that he had been too vehement in using it.— [Fitzjames Stephen?], "Mr. Arnold on the Middle Classes," *Saturday Review* XXI, 161 (February 10, 1866). The harsh quotation was also singled out by the *Spectator* a week earlier (XXXIX, 126).

[A COURTEOUS EXPLANATION]

Two letters headed "Your Countrymen," signed "Horace," and dated from Paris, appeared in the *Pall Mall Gazette* on March 14 and 17, 1866, pp. 4–5. Written from the point of view of the political liberals, they expressed the opinion that English freedom was far better than the tyranny of the French government under Napoleon III, whatever the advantages of the latter. One reference suggested at least some knowledge of Arnold's visit to Paris in 1865: "Mr. Arnold, I fear, has been smiting his Philistines with the jawbone of a Minister . . . [He] came to France on a Government mission connected with education, and naturally was thrown into official circles. I would venture to affirm, though I know nothing about it, that he has talked politics with the Minister [of Education] M. Duruy, and literature with the senator M. Ste. Beuve—two great authorities in their way, but very likely to mislead a foreigner as to the public mind of France." Arnold told his mother on March 17, "I am sure [the letter of March 14] is by a woman I know something of in Paris, a half Russian, half English woman who married a Frenchman. The first part is not good, and perhaps when the second part appears I shall write a short and light letter by way of reply." It is just as possible that "Horace" was an Englishman writing from London; the language is perhaps too idiomatic to have come from Paris, and the single gallicism—the word "assist" in the French sense—is precisely what an Englishman might use to color his disguise. Arnold's reply appeared under the title "An Explanation" on March 20; four days later he wrote to his mother: "I was glad to have an opportunity to disclaim that positive admiration of things foreign, and that indifference to English freedom, which have often been imputed to me, and to explain that I do not disparage freedom, but take it for granted as our condition, and go on to consider other things. All this I have said in the way which best, perhaps, enables these notions to penetrate, for penetrate they certainly do. People seem much taken with my answer, and now I can leave the matter." "Horace" replied to "An Explanation" with a third letter to the *Pall Mall Gazette* on March 29, pp. 3–4. Arnold received 3½ gns. for his letter.

32:3–7. In a letter to his mother on March 10, Arnold alluded to comments upon "My Countrymen" in the *Illustrated London News* of February 10 (p. 142) and the *Examiner* of February 17 (pp. 99–100). He certainly saw "Mr. Arnold on the Middle Classes" in the *Saturday Review* of February 10 (pp. 161–62) and probably "An Intellectual Angel" in the *Spectator* of February 3 (pp. 125–26). "The *Examiner* was very amusing.... Our morality is something, no doubt. Our being able to say what we like is, in my opinion, absolutely nothing to boast of or exult in, unless we are really made better by it, and more able to think and say such things as be rightful. We may like it and imagine it impossible to do without it; but it is, in itself, no *virtue*, it confers no excellence. I should be sorry to be a Frenchman, German, or American, or anything but an Englishman; but I know that this native instinct which other nations, too, have does not prove one's superiority, but that one has to achieve this by undeniable excellent performance." Mr. Peter

Smith has listed the following other journalistic comments upon "My Countrymen," some very brief: *The Edinburgh Evening Courant*, January 31, p. 4, February 2, p. 4, February 3, p. 6, and February 6, p. 11; *The Nonconformist*, February 7, p. 119; *The Court Circular*, February 10, p. 135; *The Illustrated Times*, February 10, p. 90; *The Sunday Times*, February 11, p. 2.

32:11. All four Gospels tell the story that when Pilate offered to release one prisoner at the Passover, the Jews clamored on behalf of the robber and assassin Barabbas rather than Jesus.

32:15. Grub Street was, according to Dr. Johnson's *Dictionary*, "much inhabited by writers of small histories, dictionaries, and temporary poems; whence any mean production is called grubstreet." By Arnold's day the name of the street had been changed to Milton Street. It is just to the east of the church of St. Giles, Cripplegate, where Milton is buried.

32:24–25. "Horace" remarked that "Mr. Arnold's foreign friends are sometimes *very* foreign indeed in their language," and referred to "the curious exotic language Mr. Arnold copies so prettily."— March 14, p. 4.

33:7. The "affair of the Duchies" was Prussia's violent settlement of the Schleswig-Holstein question.

33:10–11. The American Civil War cut off nearly the whole (some 85 percent) of England's cotton supply and threw out of employment most of the hands in her cloth manufacturing industry. The condition of the workers in the manufacturing cities was desperate, and there was a national voluntary movement for their relief.

33:18–20. "Those who are acquainted with the lower forms of provincial middle-class life here have some difficulty in picturing to themselves any less intellectual state of existence. A small French fundholder, retired from business and settled in a country town or village, is a mere human oyster.... He lives in a hideous house, built as near the road or street as possible, with its front perversely turned so as not to see the view should there happen to be one.... He does not shoot much, and scarcely walks, but he gardens a little, angles, and, when he can muster a friend or two, plays cards or dominoes in the middle of the day.... He assists at no lectures, be they on teetotalism, nunneries, or anything else, and has no bookclub, institute, or any kind of intellectual association.... Politics are excluded [from his newspaper], where he reads ... the doings of great people ... mixed up ... with indecent anecdote and scandal of the demi-monde."—March 17, p. 5.

34:4. In a description of a costume ball given by the French Emperor on February 7, 1866, the Paris correspondent of the *Daily Telegraph* wrote: "As for the female costumes, it is impossible to describe them.... The Angel Gabriel!—the angel of the flaming sword, which was wielded by so *mignonne* a hand—the angel whose tresses floated, 'in all the wildness of dishevelled charms,' over those white wings! 'Angel visits' are, I believe, rare; if many angels are like the Marquise de G——, it is a bore for humanity that it should be so."—Felix M. Whitehurst, *Court and Social Life in France under Napoleon the Third* (London, 1873), I, 169, reprinted from *Daily Telegraph*, February 10, 1866, p. 5, col. 5 (Kirby).

34:8–9. For the vestries, see note to p. 21:29. The St. Pancras Vestry was in the public eye because when its medical officer reported that sanitary conditions in the parish were not all that could be wished in view of the threat of cholera, one vestryman at a meeting of January 17, 1866, asserted that the report "bordered on impertinence" and moved a resolution demanding that the medical officer substantiate his statement that the Vestry had not been "prudent and energetic in caring for the health of the inhabitants." The motion passed unanimously. Then another vestryman remarked on the "coolness" (impertinence) of medical officers in general towards the vestries "by whom they were engaged and paid."—*Times*, January 27, 1866, p. 6, col. 5. The circumstance was made the subject of a scathing leading article two days later (pp. 8–9).

34:31. The Orleanists were supporters of the claim to the French throne of the Count of Paris, grandson of Louis Philippe, who was expelled by the revolution of 1848; they were a rather small group of cultivated liberals.

34:35–35:2. The *Morning Star* was perhaps singled out because of its comment on "My Countrymen": "It is very amusing, but we are not sure that it is likely to meet with the general sympathy of Mr. Arnold's countrymen."—February 5, 1866, p. 3, col. 4. Kirby cites as examples of the *Morning Star*'s doing its duty nobly, "Strong in the unbounded resources of a free people, we ought to bring our military expenditure to the level of the peaceful tendency of the times" (November 4, 1865, p. 4, col. 3) and "[Lord Elcho] is not worthy to sit in the ancient assembly of the Commons of free England" (December 7, 1865, p. 4, col. 2).

35:8. Arnold alludes to the Aesopic fable of "The Fox That Had Lost His Tail"—rather a favorite of his; see *Prose Works*, ed. Super, II, 257, and *Culture and Anarchy*, p. 240:14.

35:25. The Indian Mutiny, a revolt of the Bengal native troops against their English commanders, broke out in May, 1857, and was put down only with great difficulty after more than a year of fighting, in which the British seemed sometimes, even to their own press, less than humane.

35:26. In October, 1865, a riot broke out at Morant Bay, Jamaica, which threatened to lead to the expulsion of the British and the establishment of an independent Negro republic. Edward John Eyre, the governor, acted promptly and with great brutality to stamp out the rebellion. At the time Arnold wrote, a Royal Commission of Inquiry was sitting in Kingston. The Eyre case became a rather shameful political cause in the next few years and involved such literary figures as Mill, Huxley, and Herbert Spencer in a committee to prosecute Eyre, Carlyle, Ruskin, and Tennyson in a committee to defend him.

35:28. The Board of Guardians was the popularly elected local body for the administration of the Poor Laws under the Poor Law Amendment Act of 1834. The misconduct of the guardians in the metropolis was startlingly revealed by the articles of the "Amateur Casual" in the *Pall Mall Gazette* (see p. 351), and vestries and guardians together were condemned in the *Times*' leading article of January 29, 1866, pp. 8–9.

35:29–30. The *Daily Telegraph* had one or two panegyrics on Lord Palmerston almost every day from October 19 to October 28, 1865.

35:38. "The English Nobleman has still left in him . . . something considerable of chivalry and magnanimity: polite he is, in the finest form; politeness, modest, simple, veritable, ineradicable, dwells in him to the bone; I incline to call him the politest kind of nobleman or man (especially his wife the politest and gracefullest kind of woman) you will find in any country."—"Shooting Niagara: and After?" sect. V, *Macmillan's Magazine* XVI, 328 (August, 1867). See p. 124.

36:11. "We are unprofitable servants: we have done that which was our duty to do."—Luke 17:10. See Arnold, *Prose Works*, III, 76.

36:18. At the opening of the legislative session on February 14, 1853, Napoleon III said: "To those who regret that a larger part has not been assigned to liberty [in the Imperial constitution], I answer, Liberty has never aided in the foundation of any durable political edifice; it only crowns that which time has consolidated."

The expression of "crowning the edifice" was thereafter used again and again in the discussion of his tentative, hastily withdrawn steps in the direction of giving his subjects greater liberty.

36:22–23. On January 17, 1866, p. 9, the *Pall Mall Gazette* told its readers that it had "the honour of being scanned with a vigilance and seized with a frequency of which no other journal can boast—save the *Saturday Review* perhaps. Lately, we have never been able to pass through the post office at all, so desirous are his Majesty's police to enjoy the exclusive advantage of our observations" (Kirby).

36:27–36. The valedictory note loses some of its effectiveness by being printed here in the present edition, instead of at the close of the book as in Arnold's arrangement (where "My Countrymen" and "A Courteous Explanation" were placed last, instead of, as here, first).

36:33. For Sala see note to p. 316:21.

[NOTES TO CANCELLED PASSAGES]

490:30–31. Perhaps an allusion to Charles Kingsley's telling of the story of Epimetheus in *The Water-Babies:* "With the help of his wife Pandora . . . [he] understood so well which side his bread was buttered, and which way the cat jumped." The passage appeared on the page facing the beginning of Arnold's article on "Dr. Stanley's Lectures on the Jewish Church," *Macmillan's Magazine* VII, 326 (February, 1863). In an earlier chapter, Kingsley had praised Arnold's "Forsaken Merman."

490:31–37. *New York Times,* October 11, 1865, p. 1, col. 4. On October 10, 1865, President Andrew Johnson reviewed the First District of Columbia Colored Regiment at the Executive Mansion, then addressed to them *ex tempore* some rambling and rather simple-minded advice. It seems to have fallen into Arnold's hands at a happy moment; perhaps it was among the communications he mentioned to his sister in November as having arrived from America.

[LETTER I]

Four days after Arnold's reply to "Horace" appeared in the *Pall Mall Gazette*, he wrote to his mother that he was busy with his lectures on Celtic literature, "glad to deal in sheer disquisition sometimes, and to leave irony and the Philistines" (March 24, 1866). Leave them, that is, until he read in the *Daily News* of July 17 a letter by his friend Goldwin Smith on the part England should play in the European crisis of the Austro-Prussian war. (Arnold two years earlier introduced Goldwin Smith to Emerson as "one of our most powerful and distinguished men of the younger generation" and expressed his pleasure at "the opportunity for bringing two remarkable men together.") He immediately addressed a letter to the *Pall Mall Gazette* in reply, citing once more foreign opinion of England, then ironically using the authority of Goldwin Smith in rebuttal. At the same time he took the occasion to commend the book on European governments by his friend M. E. Grant Duff. The letter was published on July 21, and brought Arnold 3½ guineas.

Once again he reported to his mother his pleasure at the reception of the article (July 27, 1866): "[It] has been a great success, and I hear of it wherever I go. I understand what you feel about my graver and gayer manner, but there is a necessity in these things, and one cannot always work precisely as one would. To be able to work anyhow for what one wishes—always supposing one has real faith that what one wishes is good and needful—is a blessing to be thankfully accepted."

In attacking the *Daily Telegraph*, which he had referred to in a letter of May 15, 1865, as the organ of "the vulgar Liberals," Arnold was merely taking up with full sympathy the line of the newspaper to which he was contributing; as Professor Kirby points out, the *Pall Mall Gazette* often ridiculed the *Daily Telegraph* in its leading articles and "occasional notes," especially for its style. See also S. M. B. Coulling, "Matthew Arnold and the *Daily Telegraph*," *Review of English Studies* n.s. XII, 173–79 (May, 1961).

37:30. The Seven Weeks' War between Prussia and Austria broke out on June 15, 1866. The decisive victory at Sadowa was won by the Prussians on July 2 and the fighting ended on July 22.

38:12. Reigate is a pleasant town in Surrey twenty-four miles south of London, a suburban residence for many businessmen of the City.

38:20–24. A full-page political cartoon by Charles Keene in *Punch* LI, 7 (July 7, 1866).

38:27–30. The Danubian Principalities (Rumania), having united in 1859, forced the abdication of their reigning prince in February 1866 and were engaged in offering the throne to Prince Charles of Hohenzollern. They had a practical autonomy under the nominal suzerainty of Turkey, but there was an undercurrent wish for independence. Gladstone addressed a letter to Prince Ion Ghika, president of the council of regency, urging the advantages of peaceful settlement: "The progress on which the civilized world is now so intent should in all cases if possible be a peaceful progress.... Good commercial laws, well-understood relations, and consequent harmony between class and class, economical administration of the Government, liberal application of resources (made possible by such economy) to useful and reproductive works, and especially to the improvement of communications... [are] the best and most solid preparation for the contingencies of that, I trust, prosperous and distinguished future which Providence may have in store for your country."—*Times*, June 15, 1866, p. 5, col. 5.

39:8–9. "The Part of England in the European Crisis," *Daily News*, July 17, 1866, p. 5, col. 1. Goldwin Smith, a vigorous liberal, like Arnold was a member of the Athenaeum Club; they were personally on good terms, but they disagreed with each other often in print. Smith had been, however, the author of a long and favorable review of Arnold's *Empedocles on Etna and Other Poems* in the *Times* of November 4, 1853.

39:16–18. Humboldt, complaining to Varnhagen von Ense on April 3, 1843, of the motley crew that surrounded the court of the pietistic King Frederick William IV, described them as "Hofphilosophen, Missionsministerinnen, Hoftheologen und Überraschungsprediger."—*Briefe von Alexander von Humboldt an Varnhagen von Ense* (4th ed.; New York, 1860), pp. 79–80. M. E. Grant Duff picked up this phrase in 1866: "True it is that the brood of 'court theologians, missionary deaconesses,' and the like, who enraged Alexander von Humboldt, no longer flit about the palace. The king [of Prussia] is in the hands of a military clique—of the 'Ungeist in uniform' as the Berliners say."—*Studies in European Politics* (Edinburgh, 1866), pp. 246–47.

39:20. The needle gun was a breech-loading rifle invented in 1836 and gradually introduced into the Prussian service from 1841. It became famous as the weapon of the Prussian infantry in the wars of 1866 and 1870–71. Though inferior in range and accuracy to the muzzle-loading rifles that were used in other European armies, it was considered vastly superior in rapidity of loading and firing and was much talked of in the English journals.

39:20–23. "Many Englishmen, irritated by the conduct of Prussia in the Danish war, so far forgot themselves as to desire that France should avenge Denmark by seizing the Rhine. That there is, even amongst highly-intelligent and well-informed French politicians, an ardent desire for the frontier of the Rhine we know too well, but a wilder dream never entered into the imagination. Any attempt to realise it would bring about such a union of Germany as few have ever hoped for."—Grant Duff, *European Politics*, p. 250. Few prophets have seen their predictions so completely and quickly fulfilled.

39:25. "The Emperor Napoleon has been solemnly proclaimed by the most conservative statesmen and diplomatists in Europe, by Lord Stratford de Redcliffe only the other day, the 'Arbiter of Europe.' Who shall blame him if he takes these wise men at their word?"—*Daily News*, June 14, 1866, p. 4, cols. 3–4 (Kirby).

40:12–13. *European Politics*, chapters 3–5. Grant Duff was willing to believe that liberalism would prevail in Prussia, but was disappointed at the way in which Prussian military success seduced many liberals to Bismarck's side with dreams of aggrandizement.

40:31–33. "The thing most congenial to the Tories in Europe is the torpid despotism of Austria; but they also, with the sure instinct of a party, recognise the great patron of reaction in the Emperor of the French, with whom some of their chiefs appear to have formed intimate personal relations."—Goldwin Smith, *Daily News*, July 17, 1866, p. 5, col. 1.

41:3–5. The reply of Napoleon III to an address presented by the mayor of Auxerre, May 6, 1866; reported in the *Times*, May 8, p. 12, col. 2.

41:7. The Liberal ministry of Lord Russell resigned on June 26, 1866. There were "monster rallies" on behalf of Reform in Trafalgar Square on June 27 and July 2, the latter presided over by Edmond Beales, president of the Reform League, and said to have numbered 69,000 persons.

41:7–10. Had the equestrian statue of Charles I at Charing Cross turned his head to the left, he would have seen in large letters on the narrow building front of no. 3 the words "Coles's Truss Manufactory," with its shop on the street. The building was removed when Northumberland Avenue was put through in 1874. A photograph that shows the handsome edifice is in Peter Quennell's *Vic-*

torian Panorama (London, 1937), plate 34. Sir Robert Peel is said to have called Trafalgar Square "the finest site in Europe," and the phrase was repeated in most guide-book descriptions of the square.

41:10–11. In "The Function of Criticism at the Present Time," Arnold remarked that France was "the country in Europe where the *people* is most alive."—*Prose Works*, ed. Super, III, 265.

41:23–25. "A Liberal party, composed of the best of the land-owners and the best of the bourgeoisie, will have it all its own way in the end. It may be a question of one decade or two . . . ; but the 'Ungeist' in uniform, which rules the present king, no less than the 'Ungeist' in priestly garb, which ruled the late king, are both doomed to give way."—Grant Duff, *European Politics*, pp. 250–51. The Junkers were members of the landed aristocracy of Prussia, the squirearchy, whose families dominated both the military and the civil service; their leader and spokesman was Bismarck.

41:31–33. Arnold is repeating a joke from his "Literary Influence of Academies" upon the *Saturday Review*'s dislike of Napoleon III and passion for the Teutonic element in the English nation; see *Prose Works*, ed. Super, III, 250. Sedan was the scene of the defeat and surrender of the French armies and the capture of Napoleon III by the Germans on September 1, 1870.

42:9–10. "England will be compelled to speak at last, and the only question will be on which side her voice shall be raised. . . . The sympathies of Liberals . . . cannot be doubtful. The cause of Germany and Italy is ours."—Goldwin Smith, *Daily News*, July 17, 1866, p. 5, col. 1.

42:16–17. The day after the publication of this letter the Austrians capitulated, before any attack was made on Vienna.

[NOTES TO CANCELLED PASSAGES]

491:17–18. Goldwin Smith replied, "That France and Germany should 'tear each others' throats' is a wish which, I apprehend, nobody has either uttered or formed. A strong Germany is the best and the only guarantee for peace and good feeling between the two nations."—*Daily News*, July 25, 1866, p. 5, col. 2.

491:35–36. John Manners, Marquis of Granby (1721–70) was commander in chief of the British forces serving under Duke Ferdinand of Brunswick in the Seven Years' War; he was a popular hero in England for his bold and effective actions against the French.

[LETTERS II–IV]

As late as a week after the publication of the letter on "Geist," Arnold told George Smith (July 28, 1866): "Unless something special turns up, I don't think I shall pursue the 'Geist' subject just at present. The letter is having all the effect I could have wished, and a second might possibly do harm."—Buckler, p. 93. Yet in another week the *Pall Mall Gazette* published a letter headed "Democracy," over the signature "von Thunder-ten-Tronckh." Arnold had invented the character who was to be the central figure in this random series of political letters. The foreign commentators on England in "My Countrymen" had all been anonymous (though when the essay was republished as part of *Friendship's Garland* in 1871, some were given names); the Prussian among them who was brought forward to introduce the concept of "Geist" was referred to merely as a professor. Now, on August 4, a surname was borrowed from Voltaire's *Candide* and in a letter published in the *Pall Mall* on August 7 Arnold supplied the Christian name of Hermann, or Arminius. The fourth letter in the series followed on August 15. The three together brought Arnold 8 guineas.

Curiously enough, despite his admiration of the intellectual spirit of Prussian politics, Arnold was not fond of the Prussians. When he reached Vienna after his sojourn in North Germany in 1865, he wrote to his mother: "This is a different world from North Germany, and to me a far pleasanter one. It is also in agreement with all my notions that one unmixed element having it all its own way, as in North Germany, should not be such a success as a mixture and compromise between different elements such as one sees here. Although, to be sure, in one sense, in the vulgar sense, Prussia is much more of a success than Austria: but I mean that the Austrians are more what pleases and interests a good, central, human taste, and more what one with such a taste would wish his own nation to be. It is odd how one is struck with the analogy between Prussia and the United States, in both having the pretentiousness, jealousy, and irritability of a *parvenu* nation, whereas in Austria as in England and France, the national feeling seems to rest upon an indisputable, great past, and to be more dignified and serene in consequence.... And then, for the first time in Germany, one sees women with a charm about them: in North Germany one is inclined to wonder that they should ever, the whole sex, have been the occasion of the slightest romance."

43:6–7. Goldwin Smith replied to Arnold in the columns of the *Daily News* on July 25, p. 5. The *Spectator* had an article entitled "Get Geist" on July 28, pp. 828–29, and the *Illustrated Times* discussed Arnold's letter on the same day (pp. 49–50).

43:24. The Green Park Arch, which then faced the main entrance to Hyde Park and the Duke of Wellington's house, was designed to be surmounted (as it now is) by a figure in a quadriga. Instead of this figure, an equestrian statue of the Duke, paid for by public subscription of £36,000, designed by Matthew Cotes Wyatt, and cast in gun metal, was placed atop the arch in 1846. This "hideous equestrian monster," to quote a contemporary phrase, was removed to Aldershot in 1883.

43:25. Only a week before Arnold's letter was published, the *Saturday Review* asked, "Why is it that the fates conspire against our public buildings? ... Trafalgar Square; finest site in Europe; Wilkins's discreditable building; pepper-boxes; Carlton House Colonnade; national disgrace. The whole thing [has] taken the form of accepted commonplace."—"The National Gallery Site," XXII, 110 (July 28, 1866) (Kirby).

44:17–18. The sea-bear is a seal. For a description of a chemistry lecture, see p. 71.

44:26–27. Goethe, led by the rather naïve effrontery of a student who asked for the plan of the unfinished portion of *Faust* in order that he might complete it for the world, reflected upon the empty ambition of would-be artists. "Es ist ferner kein Ernst da, der ins Ganze geht, kein Sinn, dem Ganzen etwas zuliebe zu tun, sondern man trachtet nur, wie man sein eigenes Selbst bemerklich mache und es vor der Welt zu möglichster Evidenz bringe."—J. P. Eckermann, *Gespräche mit Goethe*, April 20, 1825.

44:32–33, 36–37. Goldwin Smith, *Daily News*, July 25, 1866, p. 5, col. 3. Arnold's remark on the slow progress in the construction of Trafalgar Square implied (at least in Goldwin Smith's eyes) a contrast with the rapid but costly reconstruction of Paris by Baron Haussmann (see p. 65:13).

45:2–4. "Get Geist," *Spectator*, July 28, 1866, p. 829.

45:9–11. John Bright, speaking on the borough franchise clause of the Liberal Reform Bill on June 18, 1866, quoted a northern manufacturer as saying that his workmen were more interested in American than English politics. "As a proof he expressed his belief that in his mill there were nearly as many American newspapers to be found as there were newspapers of this country."—*Times*, June 19, 1866, p. 10, col. 1.

45:14–16. P. J. Locke King, along with Arnold's friend J. D. Coleridge, moved a Real Estate Intestacy Bill which would give a widow and younger children a fixed share of real property possessed of a man who died intestate, instead of its passing entire to the nearest male heir. "Only the smallest estates would be affected," he assured the Commons on June 6, 1866, since the larger ones were all entailed and the upper classes were better informed of the need for wills and settlements. The present law, he assured the House, was the result of the Norman Feudal System, the object of which was to make the people poor. He himself wanted "to make the people rich, and give them a share in the responsibility of the Government." The bill was defeated.—*Times*, June 7, 1866, p. 6, cols. 2, 6. See *Culture and Anarchy*, pp. 200–205. Arnold, who had examined rather carefully the French law of bequests (see *Prose Works*, ed. Super, IV, 53–55n), wished for a far more thorough-going revision of English law than this weak proposal, which was scarcely even a gesture. On February 1, 1864, he wrote to Cobden, with reference to a speech of Bright's on the land question, "As for the law of succession of the French Code, that, or something like it, is, I am convinced, a mere question of time; it will inevitably make the tour of Europe. In the old feudal European countries so slight a measure as Mr. Bright, following the example of America, proposes, would I am certain prove quite inoperative. But we shall see."—W. H. G. Armytage, "Matthew Arnold and Richard Cobden in 1864," *Review of English Studies* XXV, 252 (July, 1949).

45:16–17. Church rates were taxes upon the assessed property in the parish, levied by the vestry for the maintenance of the church fabric and payable by all occupiers of property whether Anglicans or Dissenters. Their abolition became part of the Liberal party creed; after the Whigs failed in an attempt in 1834, Church-Rates Abolition Bills passed the Commons in 1858, 1860, and 1867, but were defeated by the Lords. Only in 1868 did Gladstone succeed in abolishing the compulsory aspect of the rate.

45:18–19. Gladstone's Irish Church Bill, disestablishing the Anglican Church in Ireland, was passed on July 23, 1869, after an appeal to the country by the dissolution of Parliament. See pp. 319–24.

45:19–20. See pp. 205–8, 313–18.

45:20–21. Gladstone's Reform Bill of 1866 proposed to give the franchise in the boroughs to any householder who paid £7 or more annual rent for his house.

45:24–26. The Reform League organized a monster meeting for

Hyde Park on July 23, 1866, despite a prohibition from the Commissioner of Police, Sir Richard Mayne, who acted on instructions from the Home Secretary, Spencer Walpole, and the new Conservative cabinet. The leaders of the League, Edmond Beales and Lt. Col. Lothian Sheffield Dickson, attempted to lead the throng to Trafalgar Square after being denied admittance to the park, but the greater part of the throng simply broke down the iron railings along Bayswater Road and Park Lane and held their meetings. At one point two companies of the Guards were called out, but the soldiers did not come into actual conflict with the people. Rioting was resumed the next day, and windows in the Athenaeum Club, of which Arnold was a member, were broken. Two days later, when a deputation from the Council of the Reform League waited upon Walpole at the Home Office, Walpole at one point in the proceedings "paused for some seconds, evidently being much affected," as the *Times* put it (July 26, p. 12, col. 5). In a "Great Ballad Concert" that *Punch* devised for the members of both parties, Walpole was put down to sing "Tears, Idle Tears"—a five-line parody of Tennyson (August 11, 1866, p. 60). "We have had a disturbed time," Arnold told his mother on July 27, "and both last night and Tuesday I was under the gallery of the House of Commons to hear what was said about the rioting. On the Monday night we were on our balcony, and saw the crowd break into our square, throw a few stones at Sir R. Mayne's windows opposite us, and then be dispersed by the police. The whole thing has been an exhibition of mismanagement, imprudence, and weakness almost incredible; but things being as they are in this country, perhaps the turn the matter has taken is not to be regretted. Even W[alpole]'s absurd behaviour and talking and shilly-shallying and crying have been of use in bringing about a state of good feeling in which the disturbance may gradually die away without either side getting a victory. Not that I do not think it, in itself, a bad thing that the principle of authority should be so weak here; but whereas in France, since the Revolution, a man feels that the power which represses him is the *State*, is *himself*, here a man feels that the power which represses him is the Tories, the upper class, the aristocracy, and so on; and with this feeling he can, of course, never without loss of self-respect accept a formal beating, and so the thing goes on smouldering. If ever there comes a more equal state of society in England, the power of the State for repression will be a thousand times stronger."

45:25. Three years earlier (November 5, 1863), Arnold wrote to his mother of the "Lord Palmerston scandal"—Timothy O'Kane cited Palmerston as co-respondent in a divorce case and claimed £20,000 damages for various adulteries, in what was clearly an extortion attempt—"which your charming newspaper, the *Star*—that true reflexion of the rancour of Protestant Dissent in alliance with all the vulgarity, meddlesomeness, and grossness of the British multitude—has done all it could to spread abroad. It was followed yesterday by the *Standard*, and is followed to-day by the *Telegraph*. Happy people, in spite of our bad climate and cross tempers, with our penny newspapers!" The first of the penny daily newspapers was the *Daily Telegraph* in its issue of September 17, 1855; its most important rival, the *Morning* (and *Evening*) *Star*, began publication on March 17, 1856, with the financial support of the Manchester school of Cobden and Bright. The *Evening Star* came to an end, and the *Morning Star* was absorbed by the *Daily News*, on October 13, 1869.

"Let us clearly understand the position," said the *Daily Telegraph* on July 24, 1866, pp. 4-5. "A Ministry which is only a few weeks old has already found time to array itself in opposition to the people, and to contest with them a right which is the dearest of their political privileges—that of public discussion.... All this lamentable state of feeling is induced because the Tories in their miserable obstinacy—for it is miserable both in its motives and its consequences—resist the just and temperate demands of the nation for Reform." After the meeting of the Reform League leaders with Walpole, it said: "A little more folly, a little more blind and bigoted dragooning of the people of England, and the tears which the Tory Minister shed at the interview of yesterday must have been dropped, if at all, for something which would have grown from a blunder to a crime. We do not speak of the Home Secretary's emotion otherwise than with respect and honour; ... it is a far more fortunate thing for the Tories than they can yet know, that, with an obsolete and detestable policy to pursue, they happened to possess for their agent a man simply incapable by natural goodness of making himself a callous oppressor of the common people, even to stifle the inconvenient cry for Reform."—July 26, p. 4, col. 3.

45:33-34. "The French Revolution was the close, not the commencement, of an era.... It brought into the world no new life, no new principles of action, because it brought no new religion. When great principles come upon the scene, they produce great men; the

French Revolution produced not a single great man, but a mere viper brood of canting egotists, who at last fell to murdering each other in the paroxysms of their selfishness and fear."—Goldwin Smith, *Daily News*, July 25, 1866, p. 5, col. 3.

45:35–46:1. "I have had very hard work, but I have seen a great many institutions," Arnold wrote to his wife from Naples about June 3, 1865. "On Wednesday [May 31, Edoardo] Fusco called for me at eight o'clock and took me to the great Lyceum here; it, and all such establishments are in fine buildings, because the Government gives them convents which it has suppressed."

46:1. Ticino, the only canton of Switzerland on the Italian side of the Alps, rebelled in 1798, with French encouragement, against the overlordship of the Confederation and the Swiss League, which had left it neglected and subject to vicious and mercenary bailiffs from the beginning of the sixteenth century. In 1803, under the direction of Bonaparte, Ticino became one of the nineteen cantons endowed with equal rights.

46:2. See Letter V.

46:6. Goldwin Smith was scornful of Arnold's suggestion that Napoleon III was "the representative of French Democracy"— "with four hundred thousand praetorians, a rapid creation of counts and dukes, a court blazing with gilded flunkeyism, a civil list of a million a year, and the leaders of the people at Cayenne! Abraham Lincoln would scarcely have known his brother."—*Daily News*, July 25, 1866, p. 5, col. 3. Cayenne, French Guiana, was the site of a prison for political exiles as well as criminals; the Tuileries was the official residence in Paris of Napoleon III.

46:28–31. "In the month of March last the idea occurred to one or two of the political friends and admirers of the late Richard Cobden that an appropriate way of perpetuating the memory of that earnest and consistent advocate of 'Peace, Retrenchment, and Reform,' and of doing honour to his principles, would be in the establishment of a club, which...should bear the name of the great Free-trader." And so about 150 men dined together as the Cobden Club, with Gladstone in the chair, at the Star and Garter Hotel, Richmond, on July 21, 1866.—*Morning Star*, July 23, p. 2, col. 1.

46:37. Edward Miall was leader of the Dissenters and John Stuart Mill of the nonsectarian freethinkers, the Utilitarians, the Philosophical Radicals.

[NOTES TO CANCELLED PASSAGES]

492:18-23. The National Convention was the governing assembly of revolutionary France from September 20, 1792, to October 26, 1795; it was the Convention that executed the king. The Fourth of August decrees (1789), three weeks after the fall of the Bastille, begin, "The National Assembly hereby completely abolishes the feudal system." There are nineteen articles, of which the eleventh reads: "All citizens, without distinction of birth, are eligible to any office or dignity, whether ecclesiastical, civil or military; and no profession shall imply any derogation."—Anderson, *Constitutions and Documents of France*, pp. 11-15. When published in the *Pall Mall Gazette* this passage on the French Revolution may have been intended to answer Goldwin Smith's remark, quoted in the note to p. 45:33-34.

492:30-31. Thrasybulus, an Athenian democrat, was banished by the Thirty Tyrants at the end of the Peloponnesian War, but set up headquarters at Phyle, just inside the frontier, from which place he led an expedition that defeated the Thirty and restored a moderate democratic government in Athens. Bright, an advocate of granting the franchise to householders, spoke on May 30, 1866, against a bill introduced by a Conservative member that would make franchise dependent on an educational test. "Those literary gentlemen outside who write for the London weekly papers, who are for what they call culture because they happen to have a smattering of two dead languages (laughter), talk of culture and say the great body of the working people of this country ought to be permanently excluded from the franchise. I have no sympathy with such a notion."—*Times*, May 31, 1866, p. 7, col. 2. When the Liberals were defeated on a question of Reform, Bright left the Parliament "with sadness and apprehension" and energetically devoted himself to addressing such huge mass meetings throughout industrial England as to arouse fears of revolution among his opponents.

———

48:4-5. Hermann was the German name of the national hero known to the Romans as Arminius, who destroyed the legions led by Varus in the Teutoburg Forest in 9 A.D.—the most devastating defeat suffered by the Romans in Augustus' long reign. Arnold introduced the notion of the "grand style" in his 1853 Preface and his lectures *On Translating Homer;* he continued to use it in his critical essays despite his amused awareness of the fun his critics were having with it. In the preceding letter Arnold first gave his Prussian a surname, taken from that of the baron with whom Candide was brought up in Voltaire's satire; here he first invents a given name for his friend.

48:10–11. Bismarck was reported to have been so angered by attacks on himself in the Frankfurt press that when the city fell to the Prussian army on July 16, 1866, he asked as a favor of his king that he might deal with Frankfurt as he wished, and thereupon exacted penalties of more than thirty million florins (two and a half million pounds), with the threat of bombardment and pillage if the demand were denied. The story was admittedly exaggerated; see leading article in the *Times*, July 26, 1866, p. 8, col. 4, and letter signed "A Frankforter," p. 10, col. 5.

48:16–17. Bass's pale ale and stout are still familiar in England. Gladstone in 1866 reported that the average annual consumption of the adult male in England was 600 quarts of beer. In his lectures *On the Study of Celtic Literature* Arnold referred to "the eternal beer, sausages, and bad tobacco, the blank commonness everywhere, pressing at last like a weight on the spirits of the traveler in Northern Germany."—*Prose Works*, ed. Super, III, 342.

48:17. "I have just had a magnificent present of a box of 400 Manilla cheroots; I do not smoke, but I am delighted with the present, as I shall so like to give it to dear old Tom [his brother] on his birthday: such a jolly present for him—creature comforts, and not books and head work, of which he has too much," Arnold wrote to his mother on November 8, 1867.

49:2–3. The French Revolution was, of course, a revolt against Catholicism as well as against feudalism and royalty, and Talleyrand, though he had been a priest and a bishop, married in 1803. Voltaire died in 1778, before the Revolution.

49:18–19. An echo of Arnold's essay on Democracy (1861); see *Prose Works*, ed. Super, II, 19, 28.

49:35–37. See pp. 16–17 and 23.

50:6–7. Francis Richard (1818–1914), eldest son of the ninth Earl of Wemyss, assumed the courtesy title of Lord Elcho when his father succeeded to the earldom. He was educated at Eton and Christ Church (Oxford), and sat in the Commons as a Conservative and independent almost continuously from 1841 to 1883, when he became tenth Earl of Wemyss. He was an opponent of the Franchise Bill of 1866, and the Hyde Park rioters hooted him and broke windows in his house on St. James's Place. Outside Parliament, he was active in military matters. When the organization of volunteer rifle corps was authorized in 1859, he formed and was lieutenant-colonel of the London Scottish regiment. He presided over the meeting that organized the National Rifle Association in 1859 and was its chairman, 1859–67 and 1869–70. The volunteers encamped annually on Wimbledon Common and competed for prizes in marksmanship under the direction of the Association. The meeting of 1866, held from July 9 to 21, was the most successful up to that time, and attracted an unusually large number of spectators. Professor Kirby points out that the *Illustrated London News* of July 30, 1864, p. 128, published a picture of Lord Elcho at Wimbledon.

50:12–13. St. Augustine *Confessions* viii. 2.

50:22–51:5. *Morning Star*, July 25, 1866, p. 5, cols. 3–4; Arnold uses the language of the article throughout. The Hon. Charles Clifford (1797–1870) was second son of the sixth Baron Clifford of Chudleigh. His eldest daughter was married to the twelfth Baron Petre.

50:28. Sir John Pakington, First Lord of the Admiralty in the new Derby government, was still remembered for his speech of 1840 against "the democratic spirit which had recently been making such strides." For Spencer Walpole, see note to p. 45:24.

50:33. John Hampden (1594–1643), a cousin of Cromwell's, touched off the revolt against Charles I by his resistance to the payment of ship money. Arnold's use perhaps derives from the "village Hampden" Gray envisioned in his "Elegy."

51:7–9. "Thus our democracy was, from an early period, the most aristocratic, and our aristocracy the most democratic in the world —a peculiarity which has lasted down to the present day, and which has produced many important moral and political effects."—Macaulay, *History of England*, Chapt. I (one-fourth through). Arnold makes his own opinion clear in *The Popular Education of France*, *Prose Works*, ed. Super, II, 13–16.

52:8–10. For example, "L'Anglais n'est pas mauvais, s'il mange; mais s'il ne mange pas, c'est un étrange dogue."—*Histoire de France au dix-huitième siècle* (Paris, 1864), XV, 30 (Kirby).

52:28. Candide's father was not allowed to marry the old baron's sister because he had only seventy-one quarterings (seventy-one ancestors who bore arms), and the young baron would not allow Candide to marry Cunegonde: "Would you have the impudence to marry my sister who has seventy-two quarterings!"

53:21–33. Commenting on Napoleon's demand for the rectification of the French frontier with Germany to that of 1814 (see notes to pp. 54:1 and 39:23), the *Pall Mall Gazette* said, in an article Arnold echoed: "The probabilities ... indicate that just as the intellectual Emperor was overmatched by an Italian statesman, he now finds himself outdone by a German statesman; a most intolerable thing for an intellectual Emperor.... Now, the map [of Europe] has been altered enormously to the profit of a great power; so what is the Emperor to do? Eat humble pie in the presence of his people, and *acknowledge* himself outwitted by Count Bismarck, just as he was overmatched by Count Cavour?"—"French Aggrandizement," August 10, 1866, p. 449 (Kirby).

53:34-35. The Constitutionalists in France were the supporters of the Republican Constitution of 1848, overthrown by the *coup d'état*.

53:38-54:1. The *Daily News* reported on August 10, 1866, p. 5, col. 2, that the French cabinet "made yesterday a further communication to the cabinet of Berlin, demanding the restoration of the French frontier as it existed in 1814." A leading article (p. 4, cols. 1-2) explained this as the frontier established by the allies on April 23, 1814; after Napoleon's return from Elba and final defeat in 1815, France lost further territory inhabited by nearly half a million people. The *Morning Star* commented on the demand of Napoleon III: "To the Prussian [people] the idea of surrendering territory to France has always been odious. Despite the assertions of Mr. Matthew Arnold's professorial believer in Geist, we are convinced that a distrust and dislike of France lies deep at the heart of Prussia."— August 11, 1866, p. 4, col. 3.

54:2. The Mark of Brandenburg is one of the largest provinces of Prussia; it includes Berlin.

54:10-11. Arnold may be alluding to Lord Stanley's address to his constituents at King's Lynn on July 11, 1866: "The justification of a policy of abstinence from warlike interference in Continental disputes lies deeper [than mere selfishness].... It lies partly in the just conviction which we entertain that example is worth more than precept, and that by simply existing, as we do, as a free, prosperous, and self-governed nation, we are doing more than could be done by a thousand despatches, or even by many campaigns, to protest in practice against both a policy of despotism and a policy of revolution."—*Times*, July 12, 1866, p. 6, col. 1 (Kirby). Stanley was foreign secretary under the new Conservative government.

54:27-36. Arnold wrote to his sister Mrs. Forster from Rolandseck on July 17, 1865, about plans for "the Abgeordneten Fest, or dinner to the Liberal Members to be given at Cologne and here on Saturday and Sunday. The Government have forbidden it, and the newspapers are filled every day with letters of notice to this and that person, from the Cologne police authorities warning them not to attend, and the answers. Yesterday the *Cologne Gazette*, the chief German paper, was seized, because it contained an advertisement to the effect that the dinner would still take place. It appears that the Government has no legal right to stop these dinners, and the police authorities at Cologne have no status or latitude of powers like those of a French prefect; and these worthy Germans have a trick, which they say is English and Teutonic, of stickling for the letter of the law, and objecting to the assumption by Government of arbitrary and undefined powers. English this trick is, but what is specially English, and what has made this trick successful in England, is that in England men have been ready to hazard person and fortune to maintain this view of theirs and to resist Government's setting it at nought; whereas our German cousins talk, and lament, and do nothing—have not, indeed, our genius for doing something, and just the something most likely to embarrass Government and to be successful. This Bismarck knows, and it is the secret of the contempt with which he treats the Liberals. It is, however, to be said that their position is hard, as the great English power of refusing the supplies is taken away from them by the clause in the Constitution which gives Government the power of continuing the old taxes till the new budget is voted. Also the King has always been so much in Prussia that there is all through the country a sense of his having the right to govern, of which we in England have no notion. I saw in Berlin a great deal of Lord Napier [the British ambassador], a very able man, or at least a man of a wonderfully active and open mind, and I could see that he thought Prussian constitutionalism a rather hollow affair, and that he even doubted whether its triumph over the King would be good for the country, which has formed its habits and is wonderfully prosperous." The constitutionalists were the advanced liberals, who protested against Bismarck's high-handed dealings with the lower house of the Parliament and pressed for constitutional guarantees of ministerial responsibility and legislative control of the budget.

55:21. Gotland, an island in the Baltic belonging to Sweden, would be far enough removed from the focus of any conflict between Prussia and France.

56:6–7. In the face of the most dire misfortunes Pangloss continued to maintain that this was "the best of all possible worlds." Lowe, in the Preface of his *Speeches and Letters on Reform* (London, 1867), p. 6, denied Arminius's implication: "I have been charged with optimism, but any one who reads my words will see that I have been exceedingly free in my criticism on the existing House of Commons, not dissembling its blemishes, but seeking to prove that such faults as it has will be aggravated rather than abated by any change in a democratic direction."

56:16–21. Lowe concluded his speech against the Representation of the People Bill on May 31, 1866, by urging postponement of action for another year. The bill was "parricide in the case of the Constitution, which is the life and soul of this great nation. If it is to perish, as all human things must perish, give it at any rate time to gather its robe about it, and to fall with decency and deliberation." He then concluded with the three lines adapted from Isabella's speech in *Measure for Measure* II. ii. 83–84, and "resumed his seat amid loud and long-continued cheering [and] clapping of hands."—*Times,* June 1, 1866, p. 8, col. 2. The other quotations are from his speech of May 3, 1865; see pp. 10, 16–17.

[NOTE TO CANCELLED PASSAGE]

493:30. Louis-Adolphe Thiers, liberal politician and historian, was exiled when Louis Napoleon became emperor, but soon was permitted to return to France and sat in the Chamber of Deputies in 1863. Eugène Forcade, likewise a firm liberal, was editor of the *Revue des Deux Mondes,* for which he wrote the semimonthly political commentary.

[LETTER V]

The two principal Irish problems that faced Parliament in the latter half of the nineteenth century appeared to be land tenure and church disestablishment. On March 31, 1865, Arnold was present to hear his brother-in-law W. E. Forster address the Commons on a motion to set up a select committee to investigate the conditions of landlordism and tenancy in Ireland, a committee of which Forster became a member. On July 17 he wrote to Forster's wife from Rolandseck, Rhenish Prussia: "Tell William that the effect on the people and property of Prussia of the land measures—called by the great proprietors Confiscation—of Stein, the great Prussian Minister, seems to me one of the most important things for a politician to study, with Irish tenant right a present question in England, and the land question undoubtedly coming on for the whole kingdom sooner or later." Bright's speech at Dublin on October 30, 1866, called public attention to the Prussian reforms and Arnold offered to write an explanation of them for the readers of the *Pall Mall Gazette:* "I have to go to Sudbury and the letter is not quite finished, but I will send it by this night's post to the P.M.G. office, in time for tomorrow's paper," he told George Smith on November 7. "Do not put it in if you are not quite satisfied with it; I am *abgestumpft,* as the Germans say, by all this report writing; and cannot hit my more natural style again to my own satisfaction. I have been half inclined to throw what I have done into the fire, only I was afraid of your reproaching me with perfidy."—Buckler, p. 93. The letter was published on November 8, and brought Arnold 3½ guineas.

57:9. The *Daily Telegraph* used Arnold's letter to Hugh Owen on the Eisteddfod (see *Prose Works,* ed. Super, III, 540) as a point from which to attack his doctrine of *Geist,* his remarks on his countrymen, and his admiration of the French and Germans. He was an "elegant Jeremiah" and "the high-priest of the kid-gloved persuasion"—September 8, 1866, pp. 4–5. On July 14, 1870, the young journalist James Macdonell sent his bride-to-be a copy of Arnold's *St. Paul and Protestantism* with this comment: "You will be much amused, I think, by the high-and-mighty airs which Arnold puts on when he speaks of Dissent. In a savage article, written by way of retort to Arnold's fling at 'the magnificent roaring of the young lions of the *Daily Telegraph*' (N.B.—I myself am a dull lion, and don't roar), I called him 'an elegant Jeremiah.' He didn't like the phrase; but it's true for all that, and he was never more emphatically an elegant Jeremiah than in the present volume. Still, Arnold is the most delicate of living English critics; he writes from a French elevation of criticism; and his style, if it lacks masculine strength, is, at any rate, full of beauty."—W. R. Nicoll, *James Macdonell, Journalist* (London, 1890), p. 199.

57:20–25. For Arnold's statement, see p. 21:13–14. Speaking at a banquet in Dublin on October 30, 1866, Bright alluded to the Prussian reform of the land problem at the beginning of the century. Thereupon a correspondent who signed himself "A." asserted that the Prussian law had been "simply the conversion of serf tenures into produce rents," the commutation of the serf's (*Leibeigener's*) liability to labor in his lord's field into a fixed portion of the produce. "It is neither more nor less than a compulsory commutation such as the English tithe-owner was required to accept a quarter of a century ago."—*Times*, November 3, 1866, p. 5, col. 6. Meanwhile the *Times* had condemned Bright roundly in a leading article: "The free right to contract lies at the bottom of all individual and national prosperity,"—this of course was the present relation of landlord and tenant in Ireland—"and the man who invades this may be a leveller, but is not a Liberal."—November 2, p. 8, col. 3. A few days after Arnold's letter first appeared, an Irish land-owner who signed himself "I." supported Bright's proposal and "our amusing instructor, Mr. Matthew Arnold ... (I was as much puzzled as he by the cool audacity of the *Times*)."—*Daily News*, November 13, 1866, p. 3, col. 1.

58:2. For Arnold's serious use of the "square Teutonic head" in May, 1866, see *On the Study of Celtic Literature*, *Prose Works*, ed. Super, III, 340.

58:5. A pilot coat is a pea jacket, "a stout short overcoat of coarse woollen cloth, now commonly worn by sailors."—*N.E.D.*

58:22–23. See p. 56:6–7.

58:24. "in well-rounded phrase"—Horace *Ars Poetica* 323.

59:15–32. Arnold simplifies the provisions of the German agrarian reform and compresses into a single work of Stein what was not in fact completed until 1850, when the government Rent-Banks were established. The tenant paid to these $4\frac{1}{2}$ percent or 5 percent of the value of the land he was acquiring; the banks paid the landlord 4 percent as interest and devoted the remainder to paying off the principal over some fifty-six or forty-one years. The peasant who did not wish to redeem his land through the government bank might do it on his own account by paying the landlord eighteen times the annual rental. See G. S. Ford, *Stein and the Era of Reform in Prussia* (Princeton, 1922), pp. 218–19, and H. D. Hutton, *The Prussian Land-Tenure Reforms and a Farmer-Proprietary for Ireland* (Dublin, 1867), pp. 15–19.

59:33. That is, in terms of the doctrine of the classical school of free trade, the Utilitarian economists, Adam Smith, Ricardo, Mill, etc.

59:34–36. Leading article, November 6, 1866, p. 6, col. 6.

59:36–38. "[The conditions of Irish land tenure] are the result of unrestricted personal liberty, of acquisitions by the provident and of alienations by the reckless. . . . The tendency of liberty is towards inequality. . . . Legislation restrictive of individual liberty, though powerless to arrest, is very potent to increase the calamities of nations."—*Times*, November 2, 1866, p. 8, col. 3.

60:3–5. On July 17, 1866, the Marquis of Clanricarde, one of the largest landowners in Ireland, referred to the Commons' bill on Irish land tenure as the sort of confiscation that might have followed the success of Wolfe Tone's rebellion or a French invasion of Ireland.—*Times*, July 18, 1866, p. 6, col. 1.

60:11–15. Prussian edicts of 1749 and after forbade the nobility to absorb the peasant holdings into their own land, even where they had the right to dispossess one tenant in favor of another.—Ford, *Stein*, p. 179.

60:16–17. Small proprietors are "improved off the face of the earth" by the practice of dispossessing them to convert arable land to pasture, just as earlier in the century they lost their rights to common land through enclosure.

60:34. "Settled estates" were those bound by entail; for the magistracy and the game laws, see pp. 66–74.

60:36–38. On July 11, 1860, Edward Baines moved to strike out the new question of "religious profession" from the subjects of inquiry under the census. The Home Secretary, Sir George Cornewall Lewis, who sponsored the census bill, defended the question on the ground that if the government was to act on matters in which religion was involved—such as education—it was imperative that the facts be known. But Baines insisted, "with what seemed to be an instinctive feeling in the minds of Englishmen," that religious inquiry was "beyond the legitimate scope of civil interference"; the government "had no right to intrude into the domain of conscience." The Government yielded, as Palmerston said, to the strength of Nonconformist opposition: "We defer to their feelings, but we cannot assent to their reasoning"—and in fact there was little point in retaining the question if large bodies of the population refused, as groups, to answer it.

61:1–3. A Churchman is a member of the Church of England. The Particular Baptists were Calvinist in origin and sprang from the Independents; they were not united with the Arminian sect of General Baptists until 1891. The Muggletonians, by the late nineteenth century an almost extinct sect, were followers of the 17th-century visionary tailor Lodowicke Muggleton, who in 1651 began to have divine revelations.

61:4-7. Arnold developed this idea at greater length in "Democracy" and *A French Eton, Prose Works,* ed. Super, II, 19-20, 302-8.

61:9-10. "And Herod with his men of war set [Jesus] at nought, and mocked him, and arrayed him in a gorgeous robe, and sent him again to Pilate. And the same day Pilate and Herod were made friends together: for before they were at enmity between themselves."—Luke 23:11-12.

[STEIN PLUS HARDENBERG]

"The letter [on Prussian Tenant Right], about which you write so kindly, went better as I got on with it, and it seems to have given satisfaction—or dissatisfaction, which does equally well. I have it in my mind to write another to finish with the subject, but I am too *report-laden* at present to undertake anything, and I am sure these letters take all the better for coming seldom," Arnold wrote to George Smith on November 13, 1866.—Buckler, pp. 93-94. On that very evening the *Pall Mall Gazette* published a gay letter signed by "An Irish Squire," raising certain questions about the Prussian land laws which Arnold had not answered. Arnold's reply was published in the *Pall Mall* on Monday, November 19; his diaries record no payment for it, and he omitted the letter from the collection in *Friendship's Garland.* Its existence was noted in the dissertations of Professor Kirby and Mr. Peter Smith, and it was published, with the letter of the "Irish Squire," in Fraser Neiman, *Essays, Letters, and Reviews by Matthew Arnold* (Cambridge, Massachusetts, 1960), pp. 114-17.

62:24-28. *Erb-pächter* were tenants with hereditary rights to the land, *Zeitpächter* were tenants at will, or for a fixed term of years, or for life. By the law of September 14, 1811, the former surrendered a third of their holdings to their landlord as indemnity for the relief from manorial duties and the latter surrendered half their holdings. The landlord was also relieved thereafter of his obligations to the tenant. The hereditary leaseholders might in addition commute their services into rent charges in cases where the new law still left them obliged to perform services (as in return for grazing on the lord's estate).

62:27. Vergil *Aeneid* ix. 641. The second half of the same line is quoted in Letter VI (p. 68:23).

63:1. Bickers and Son were booksellers at No. 1, Leicester Square. At the date of Arnold's letter R. J. Bush was separately established in bookselling, bookbinding, and publishing at 32 Charing Cross.

64:7–8. The "Irish Squire" asserted that he "still [held] by the tenure of presenting the King with a lighted turf to light his pipe when he hunts in the Bogs of Allen." These bogs were wasteland to the west of Dublin, at the meeting of Counties Meath, Kildare, and Offaly.

64:25–29. A. F. d'Allonville and others, *Mémoires tirés des papiers d'un homme d'état* (Paris, 1836), XI, 122–23. These anonymous memoirs falsely pretended to be Hardenberg's.

[LETTERS VI–VII]

When the *Pall Mall Gazette* on November 8, 1866, came out against compulsory education, a correspondent named John Oakley wrote (November 10): "The evidence is conflicting as to the working of compulsory education abroad, and we want some light on the method of its enforcement. I wish Mr. Arnold would ask his friend 'Arminius' about it." Whether in response to this suggestion or not, Arnold wrote to his mother on February 10, 1867: "I have ... in my head a letter to the *Pall Mall* on Compulsory Education, in which, through the mouth of '*Arminius*,' I shall manage to say a number of things I want to say; but this ... must wait till the Report [on Continental education] is done." By April 8 his last Appendix to that work was completed. His two letters were published in the *Gazette* on April 20 and 22, 1867, and brought him 8 guineas. But the actual working of compulsory education on the Continent was more fully described in the Preface to *Schools and Universities on the Continent*.

65:7–10. Snow fell at a rate unprecedented for London for six hours on the morning of Wednesday, January 2, 1867, to an average depth of six to eight inches, and brought metropolitan traffic to a standstill. The vestries, on whom the responsibility for snow removal fell, were powerless to provide either vehicles or labor. The few cabdrivers available charged exorbitant fares, and so did the conductors of the few omnibuses still operating. Temperatures remained below freezing until the 6th, when a heavy rain reduced all to an impassable slush. The storm and cold threw many laborers out of work at the same time there was no means to use them in snow removal, and the homeless, for whom the Guardians made little enough provision, suffered desperately. "What weather!" Arnold wrote to his mother on January 5 (misdated 11th by Russell).

"I have been on the Serpentine to-day, where the ice is excellent. . . . The state of London and its helplessness this last day or two have been extraordinary. On Wednesday evening, the first day of it, I was engaged to dine without Flu at the Prices', to play whist. When my cab came to the door at seven to take me the man said his fare would be 6s, the right fare being 1s. Upon this I said I would walk, and walk I did, the frost being so hard that the snow was frozen and I got neither wet nor dirty, only was a little late for dinner. . . . Yesterday evening my thermometer was seventeen, and this morning twenty, not so low as you have had it, but wonderfully low for London, and my jug in my dressing-room, which is exposed and the coldest room of the house, was full of ice, and the sponge frozen to the marble of the washhandstand."

"A Tradesman," writing to the *Daily Telegraph*, January 5, 1867, p. 3, col. 2, asked: "Is it not a most extraordinary thing, that while so many thousands of poor men at the East-end of London are out of work, who would willingly do anything to earn a few shillings, and while bands of labourers parade our streets singing doleful ditties to obtain a penny, our roads should be suffered to remain in the condition they are at the present moment?" On the same day a leading article (p. 5, col. 2) commented: "The state of the thoroughfares is, we grant, a serious evil; but we shall have to face worse before long. The 'interruption' which is only an annoyance to the rich means something very like starvation to the poor and, unless the weather breaks swiftly, the streets will be full of people out of work." Two days later (p. 3, col. 2) it remarked: "It has, indeed, been a practical satire on the complaint of a deficiency of hands to clear the streets, that gangs of sturdy fellows in the garb of navvies should actually have perambulated those very streets, bawling their distress of mind and body, at the want of work to do." (Kirby)

65:13. "London herself seems helpless and resigned; or else growls pettishly for M. Haussmann, a terribly 'thorough' practitioner."— *Daily Telegraph*, January 5, 1867, p. 5, col. 2. Georges-Eugène Haussmann (1809–91), prefect of the Seine from 1853 to 1870, gave central Paris its modern appearance, but was severely criticized for his ruthless demolition of the tenements of the poor to replace them with elegant buildings and broad boulevards. "The Budget has again attracted the public attention to the Haussmannisation of Paris," wrote the Paris correspondent of the *Daily Telegraph* on June 4, 1865. " 'If they pull down any more streets,' said the poor mother of a family yesterday, 'we shall have to live in tents; and I do so hate a roving life.'" On January 7, 1867, the same correspondent compared Paris to London during the cold spell: "Of course, '*duce* Haussmann,' things are very different here from what they are with you. Snow disappears, and dirt is only annoying, not dangerous."— Whitehurst, *Court and Social Life* I, 85, 231, reprinted from the *Daily Telegraph*, June 6, 1865, p. 5, col. 6, and January 9, 1867, p. 5, col. 4 (Kirby).

65:28–29. Kirby points to a leading article in the *Daily Telegraph*, February 24, 1865, p. 5, col. 1: "Bit by bit reform is a principle to which Englishmen are, perhaps, addicted beyond measure. We dislike wholesale innovations and radical changes of every kind. Apart from all political considerations, the Napoleonic system of demolition and reconstruction, which has renovated the face of Paris, would have found but few partisans if applied to our own metropolis."

66:18. "The Prussians [are] the bureaucratic people, as is believed, *par excellence*," remarked Walter Bagehot in "The English Constitution," *Fortnightly Review* VI, 522 (October 15, 1866).

66:25. Not long after its incorporation of the *Morning Chronicle* in 1860 the *Daily Telegraph* took to printing in every issue the boast, "Largest circulation in the world."

66:26. "Westward the course of empire takes its way."—George Berkeley, "On the Prospect of Planting Arts and Learning in America," st. 6. The young lion composed Letter VIII in his lodgings in St. James's Place (p. 313).

66:38. Horace *Odes* III. xxx. 6.

67:12–13. "His style is boisterous and rough-hewn; his rhyme incorrigibly lewd, and his numbers perpetually harsh and ill-sounding."—"Preface to Notes and Observations on *The Empress of Morocco*," *Works*, ed. W. Scott and G. Saintsbury (London, 1892), XV, 399.

68:23. Vergil *Aeneid* ix. 641.

69:2. "Then shall ye bring down my gray hairs with sorrow to the grave."—Genesis 42:38.

69:16. The *Pall Mall Gazette* of July 27, 1867, p. 2239, described the establishment of a newspaper, the *Day*, by Lords Grosvenor, Elcho, and Lichfield, as organ of their "Constitutional Liberal" party, and its failure in about six weeks at a loss to them of more than £5600 (Kirby). These three aristocratic members or former members of the Commons, along with Robert Lowe, split from the

Radical element of the Liberal party on the issue of Reform: they believed in general that the Constitution reached perfection with the Reform Law of 1832 and opposed further extension of the franchise.

69:18. The Manchester school was devoted to the principles of free trade and *laissez-faire;* the Radicals were Benthamites or Utilitarians.

69:20–23. A voluntary was one who believed that education should be financed entirely by voluntary support, without help from the state; he similarly insisted that the Church be deprived of state support. In 1843, Sir James Graham, Conservative Home Secretary, introduced a factory bill that both limited the hours of employment for children and required the provision of schools for them. But because they viewed these schools as merely a device to strengthen the power of the Church of England, the Dissenters and Roman Catholics flooded the table of the House of Commons with petitions against the bill and Graham withdrew it. The next year, when he re-introduced his bill, the education clauses had disappeared. But now a new battle raged over the fixing of a maximum work-day: the reformers regarded ten hours as long enough, the Liberals favored twelve. The act was passed with no provision for limiting the working day. Not until 1847 was the House able to overcome the resistance of the manufacturers and pass a factory act that contained a ten hours' clause.—Spencer Walpole, *A History of England from . . . 1815* (London, 1912), V, 72–79.

69:24. The Dissenters were able to defeat the proposal to impose a church rate in certain parishes where they were strong; when the churchwardens in Braintree in 1837 collected the rate despite the refusal of the Dissent-dominated vestry to impose it, protracted litigation began which only ended when the House of Lords in 1853 declared the rate illegal under these conditions. Thereupon, over 1500 parishes followed the example of Braintree and declined to rate themselves.—*Ibid.,* V, 267.

69:26–27. Grant Duff, speaking to his constituents at Elgin on October 10, 1866, defended, while he regretted, Lowe's opposition to his own party's attempts at parliamentary reform. "Table the whole Liberal creed and you will find few politicians who accept so many of its articles as Mr. Lowe."—*Times,* October 12, 1866, p. 9, col. 1.

69:32. A scholar "on the foundation" was educated at the expense of the endowment of the school; others were educated at the expense of their parents. It will be observed that need was not the criterion for the granting of scholarships.

70:3–4. In the form "Charite schuld begyne at hemself," this proverb is recorded as early as Wyclif, about 1380.—*Oxford Dictionary of English Proverbs.*

70:8–9. "Longs and shorts" were Latin verses, composed in this case upon a subject set from classical mythology. On February 8, 1867, F. W. Farrar, a master at Harrow School, delivered a lecture at the Royal Institution (later published) to attack the dominant mode of educating public school boys exclusively—and badly—in the classics. "Year after year I see boys of eighteen and nineteen who have been working for ten years or more at Latin verses under conscientious and able teachers, and who at the end of that time are unable to produce one single line that is not flagrantly incorrect and intolerably odious to every reasonable mind, . . . poor boys ploughing barren poetic fields in the shape of verse-books with a grammar and a dictionary 'unequally yoked together like ox and ass.' "—*On Some Defects in Public School Education* (London, 1867), pp. 29–30. Farrar appealed to "knowledge, ideas, and *Geist*" (p. 23) to effect a remedy. Arnold alluded to this lecture in the Conclusion to *Schools and Universities on the Continent, Prose Works*, ed. Super, IV, 298.

70:17. The Bullingdon Club is one of Oxford's oldest and best-known social clubs, whose members are traditionally devoted to riding and field sports.

70:21. "Fast" means extravagant, devoted to pleasure, dissipated.

70:29. Lycurgus, after whom the Academy was named, was the legendary Spartan lawgiver. Peckham is in South London, adjacent to Camberwell.

70:35. The Ph.D. was a German degree, unknown in the older English universities (to which Silverpump, as a Dissenter, would not in any case have been admitted before 1854), and held in rather low esteem.

[NOTE TO CANCELLED PASSAGE]

495:11–17. James Fraser was an assistant commissioner to both the Newcastle Commission and the Schools Inquiry Commission. His series of long letters on national education appeared in the *Times* on April 16, 17, 18, 20, and 26, 1867, and indeed were heralded by two letters of his on February 28 and March 6. Arnold commented on them in the Preface to *Schools and Universities on the Continent, Prose Works*, ed. Super, IV, 22–23. Fraser became bishop of Manchester in 1870.

73:11–15. Justices of the peace were appointed by the lord chancellor on recommendation of the lord lieutenant of the county, an aristocratic functionary whose duties were largely decorative. "There are families in every county whose heads at least, and generally one other of their members, have a prescriptive right to a place in the Commission [i.e., to be justices of the peace]. The man who inherits, or even acquires, a certain position in the county walks into his place on the bench almost as naturally as he walks into his family mansion. . . . In short, the class who find their way into the Commission are what may be roughly called the local aristocracy. . . . The Crown cannot promote him in his own line, nor can it visit him with any punishment save removal from the Commission—a punishment most unlikely now-a-days to be resorted to, except in cases of extreme misconduct. . . . He is neither elected by the people nor responsible to the people; but, except in the solitary case of the game-laws, he has no interests contrary to those of the people."—"The English Justice of the Peace," *Saturday Review* XVIII, 804–5 (December 31, 1864). Kirby points out also a leading article in the *Daily News*, January 30, 1865, p. 4, col. 4: "The theory is (a very comprehensive and well-worn theory) that much of the vitality and freedom of our public life and society in England is owing to this local administration of justice by unpaid, unprofessional, and incompetent gentlemen. . . . Many, if not most, of our county magistrates are simply persons who have made money and bought land, and . . . have acquired all the prejudices and privileges of a caste as rapidly as they have acquired wealth." A "living" is a benefice, a church office endowed with funds for its performance (such as the rectory or vicarage of a parish); the right of making the appointment resided in the patron (in this case Lord Lumpington).

73:17–23. The laying of the Atlantic cable was completed by the steamship *Great Eastern* at Trinity Bay, Newfoundland, on July 27, 1866. On that day the *Times* proclaimed that "the genius and enterprise of this country have completed a work which transcends not only experience, but fancy. . . . It needed men of talent and courage to conceive it as a practical enterprise, and to enter energetically on the work. . . . The two most active and energetic nations of the globe are placed in hourly communication. . . . To the mercantile interests of both countries the gain must be immense."—p. 9, cols. 1–2. "We are in great haste to construct a magnetic telegraph from Maine to Texas; but Maine and Texas, it may be, have nothing important to communicate. . . . We are eager to tunnel under the Atlantic and bring the old world some weeks nearer to the new; but perchance the first news that will leak through into the broad, flapping American ear will be that Princess Adelaide has the whooping cough."—Thoreau, *Walden* (1854), Chap. I.

73:31–34. See Arnold's description of the Prussian system in *Schools and Universities on the Continent, Prose Works*, ed. Super, IV, 210–14. Robert Lowe had been vice-president of the Committee of Council on Education; George Grote was one of the founders of the University of London and its vice-chancellor from 1862.

74:29. The Lippe flows from the Teutoburg Forest (note to p. 48:4) westward to the Rhine.

75:24. See the essay on "Joubert," *Prose Works*, ed. Super, III, 187–88.

75:34. Precise definition of the qualification for franchise was the stumbling point of the reform bills brought in during the sixties. As even Bright said in the debate on the bill of 1867, on March 26, "At this moment I do not believe there is a majority in this House who are in favour of household suffrage pure and simple"—i.e., of giving the vote to every householder, however poor. The Conservative bill before the House provided for giving the franchise to all who were personally rated under the Poor Law, but in cases where a house was rented and the rent included an agreement that the landlord pay the rates (for which the tenant "compounded" with the landlord, sometimes at a figure lower than the full rate), so that the householder did not appear on the rate books, he would be barred unless the rent was as high as £10. The Liberal bill of the preceding year, which used the annual rental rather than the annual ratable value as the criterion, of course avoided this difficulty. But the "compound householder" (p. 76:14) became a well-known figure in the parliamentary debate.

76:3–4. Frederic Harrison's essay, "Our Venetian Constitution," began and ended with quotations from Comte; it belittled the debate on Reform and insisted that what was important was not franchise but power, that sooner or later both the governing classes and the working classes would be aware that a revolution was at hand— "another orderly, bloodless, more truly 'glorious' revolution, let us trust." Hence Arnold's suggestion that Harrison was a Jacobin. It was in the same essay that Harrison attacked the "man of culture" (see p. 87).—*Fortnightly Review* VII (March, 1867), 261–83. The story is told that Arnold somewhere in these letters wrote that Harrison "always looked as if his coat had come home from the tailor the day before and as if the rest of his dress had just been taken out of a bandbox." When Smith, the publisher, said that the description was perfectly accurate, but hardly worthy of Arnold's pen, Arnold replied, "Good heavens, you don't mean to say he is like that! I have never seen him." The passage is not now in the letters.—J. W. Robertson Scott, *The Story of the Pall Mall Gazette* (London, 1950), pp. 152–53. Harrison was nearly nine years younger than Arnold.

76:5–6. Arnold seems to have anticipated a famous remark of Robert Lowe in the House of Commons on July 15, 1867, with respect to the passing of the Reform Bill: "I believe it will be absolutely necessary that you should prevail on our future masters to learn their letters"—a remark popularized into "We must educate our masters." In his speech of May 3, 1865, Lowe remarked that he feared the "swamping aspect" of the Reform Bill—its doubling or trebling the constituencies in the larger towns, so that the present constituency might as well be abolished altogether.

76:25–32. See note to p. 116:1.

76:34. G. W. F. Hegel, *Phänomenologie des Geistes;* Arnold is pretending that this is the great source book for the gospel of *Geist*.

[THEODORE PARKER]

When the *Pall Mall Gazette* was founded in February, 1865, its proprietor, George Smith, naturally turned to Arnold for contributions and extracted the promise of two short articles. Theodore Parker seems to have proposed himself to Arnold's mind as a subject immediately, and Joseph Milsand, whose book Arnold had received from the hand of Robert Browning, seemed possible as a second subject.—*Note-Books*, ed. Lowry, p. 577. But Arnold viewed his commission without enthusiasm: "I am pestered with applications to write for new periodicals, and I shall be glad to get abroad to escape them," he told his mother late in March, on the eve of his mission to visit Continental schools. From Paris on May 8 he assured Smith that he had his two articles for the *Pall Mall* in his mind, "and...I think I shall really be able to write [them] down before long." But the article on Parker was not written for more

than two years and was far from Arnold's first contribution to his
friend's newspaper. It was published anonymously on August 24,
1867, and brought Arnold 3½ guineas. Fraser Neiman, who was the
first to attribute the article to Arnold, published it in his *Essays,
Letters, and Reviews, by Matthew Arnold* (Cambridge, Massachusetts, 1960), pp. 118–23.

78:2–8. Less than half a column, in fact: *Nouvelle biographie
générale* (Paris: Firmin Didot Frères, 1862), XXXIX, col. 225.

78:9. Moncure Daniel Conway (1832–1907), Unitarian preacher,
went to England in 1863 to lecture on behalf of the Northern side in
the Civil War. Early in 1864 he was made minister of the South
Place Chapel, Finsbury (London), and· remained there for twenty
years. Arnold knew him personally. He was a frequent contributor
to the *Fortnightly Review.*

78:13–23. "Theodore Parker," *Fortnightly Review* VIII, 143–52
(August, 1867). Arnold quotes from pp. 146, 152 (the concluding
sentence of the article).

79:1–3. Theodore Parker, *Lessons from the World of Matter and
the World of Man,* selected from notes of unpublished sermons by
Rufus Leighton, ed. Frances Power Cobbe (London, 1865). The
title on the spine was *Selections from Theod. Parker's Unpublished
Sermons.* Frances Power Cobbe (1822–1904), feminist and philan-
thropist, had already attracted Arnold's attention by her attempts to
lay the basis for modern religious thinking; see "The Function of
Criticism at the Present Time," *Prose Works,* ed. Super, III, 278–80.

79:32–38. *Lessons,* p. 227.

80:4. Wordsworth, "Tintern Abbey," line 39.

80:6–22. *Lessons,* pp. 167, 169.

80:30. Arnold attributes to Bacon the expression "drench . . . in
matter"; see *On Translating Homer, Prose Works,* ed. Super, I, 179.

80:34–81:8. *Lessons,* pp. 212–13 (with omissions). James M.
Mason (1798–1871), senator from Virginia, drafted the Fugitive
Slave Law of 1850. Parker, an ardent abolitionist, vigorously op-
posed the enforcement of this law in Massachusetts.

81:23. The earliest edition of Whitman in England was the volume of selections edited by W. M. Rossetti in 1868. But Conway
had published an article on him in the *Fortnightly Review* VI, 538–
48 (October 15, 1866), and there had been other articles on his
work. W. D. O'Connor proclaimed at the end of his vindication of
Whitman, *The Good Gray Poet* (New York, 1866)—a pamphlet

written with Whitman's assistance—"I send this letter to Victor Hugo, for its passport through Europe; I send it to John Stuart Mill, to Newman, and Matthew Arnold, for England." On September 16, 1866, Arnold acknowledged the gift of two books from O'Connor, and added: "I do not contest Mr. Walt Whitman's powers and originality.... As to the general question of [his] poetical achievements, you will think it savours of our decrepit old Europe when I add that while you think it his highest merit that he is so unlike any one else, to me this seems to be his demerit: no one can afford, in literature, to trade merely on his own bottom and to take no account of what other ages and nations have acquired; a great original literature America will never get in this way, and her intellect must inevitably consent to come, in a considerable measure, into the European movement. That she may do this and yet be an independent intellectual power, not merely, as you say an intellectual colony of Europe, I cannot doubt; and it is on her doing this, and not on her displaying an eccentric and violent originality that wise Americans should, in my opinion, set their desires." Arnold's references to Whitman in the article on Theodore Parker must be added to the data assembled by Harold Blodgett, *Walt Whitman in England* (Ithaca, N.Y., 1934), pp. 166–69.

82:3–16. *Lessons*, pp. 19, 43, 51, 150.

82:22–40. *Ibid.*, pp. 276, 278, 296–97 (with omission), 303 (with omissions), 321, 327–28 (with omissions).

83:10. The phrase *"tendance à l'ordre"* comes from Senancour, *Oberman*, ed. A. Monglond (Paris, 1947), I, 217 (Letter 44). Arnold quoted the passage again on p. 297:10 and used it later at the head of *Literature and Dogma*.

83:14. *Lessons*, pp. 276, 271.

83:21–25. A letter of Whitman's to a newspaper, July 22, 1863, quoted by John Burroughs, *Notes on Walt Whitman* (New York, 1867), p. 92. Late in 1867 Burroughs wrote to a friend: "I hear from Conway occasionally. He says my book irritates and interests Matthew Arnold, who has written Conway a letter about it."—Clara Barrus, *Life and Letters of John Burroughs* (Boston, 1925), I, 126.

83:26–29. *Lessons*, p. x (Miss Cobbe's Preface).

83:30. "... jeglicher das Beste, was er kennt,/ Er Gott, ja seinen Gott benennt."—"Gott, Gemüth, und Welt," lines 23–24.

83:39–84:1. For example, *Lessons*, p. 306.

[CULTURE AND ANARCHY]

After giving the fourth of his lectures on "The Study of Celtic Literature" on May 26, 1866, Arnold might have been expected to deliver three more discourses from the chair of Poetry before the expiration of his term as professor in June, 1867. Two subjects had been on his mind for several years, Alexandre Vinet and Propertius; his diary shows him at work on the latter almost daily throughout the first quarter of 1866, while he was also composing his final Celtic lectures. But he was so deeply engaged in writing the report on his Continental mission for the Schools Inquiry Commission that an official notice at Oxford on November 15 announced merely that "The Lecture of the Professor of Poetry is postponed," and his niece's husband after Arnold's death was able to refer with some regret to the "lecture, on Propertius, he often announced but never delivered." Curiously enough, there is not a single quotation from Propertius in Arnold's *Note-Books*.

Meanwhile, he had conceived an article on "Culture and Its Enemies" for the *Cornhill*. On December 28, 1866, he wrote to George Smith, the publisher, that he hoped to have it "ready for the February magazine; but, if you do not have it or hear of it by the 12th of Jany. conclude that I am still in bondage [to the foreign schools report]."—Buckler, p. 85. He was indeed so overwhelmed with work that by February 10, 1867, he had decided that he could deliver only one final lecture at Oxford, and he had probably already determined that "Culture and Its Enemies" must serve that purpose; he wrote to his mother, "My last lecture for Oxford is forming itself in my mind, but I shall not write a word of it till my Report is fairly done with." At first he thought of giving it early in the summer term. A week after he finished the report on Continental schools he told her (April 15) that the date had been fixed for May 4, but not a word had been written. On May 17, however, he remarked that along with a great deal of other literary work, he still had to write his last lecture for Oxford. "This too, as I know pretty well what I have to say, will not be disagreeable. I more and more have the satisfaction of seeing that what I do produces its effect, and this inspirits me to try and keep myself at my best, in good temper and clear spirits, and in that variety of activity which is, in my opinion, necessary for producing a fruitful effect in a country like this." He had just completed the Introduction to his book *On the Study of Celtic Literature,* an essay which has a decided kinship with his final Oxford lecture and which he was quite pleased with. The lecture was first announced for June 1, then June 4, and was finally completed between three and six in the morning of June 7 and given at two o'clock that afternoon to a very crowded audience that applauded vigorously at the end. "Flu [Arnold's wife] will have told you how well I was received, and that the lecture went off satisfactorily," he wrote to his mother about the 10th. "I tried to make this last lecture one in which I could keep to ground where I am in sympathy with Oxford, having often enough startled them with heresies and novelties; and I succeeded. The boys [his sons Tom and Dick] will have a pleasant remembrance of the one lecture of mine at which they were present. I now nearly speak my lecture, though it is all written, but the attention of my audience animates me to speak rather than read what I have written." He was much pleased a week later when a fellow guest at Oxford's term-end festivities told him "she could hardly express her pleasure at the turn I had given to this final lecture, after all my liberties with Oxford and old Oxford notions in former lectures."

It was while he was at Oxford on June 16 that he corrected the proofs for the *Cornhill,* to which he had sent the manuscript a week earlier. "I have several times profited by your judgment as to my articles in the Magazine and I want you to give it me now," he wrote to Smith. "The lecture was my *last,* and having often trod on the toes of Oxford and yet having a sincere affection for her, I wanted to make my last lecture as pleasing to my audience and as *Oxfordesque* as I could. I succeeded, and finished my career amidst a most gratifying display of feeling. But I find on looking it over that the lecture remains incurably Oxfordesque, though I had left points of transition by which I thought I could make it pass into a magazine article. That, however, will be a bungling business. I think it had better either appear in the Magazine with a note, saying what it is—a last lecture and therefore printed as such for the sake of the peculiar circumstances &c—or not appear there at all. I dislike printing a single lecture as a pamphlet, but I suppose I must print this one if it does not appear in the Magazine. I want you to decide —shall it appear in the Magazine as it stands, with a note? shall I patch it and adapt it? shall it not appear in the Magazine at all? I am perfectly in your hands: only it must not come later than July."—Buckler, pp. 85–86. Smith's decision was for publication as a lecture, unchanged, and Arnold combined a few of his paragraphs to make room on the proofs for his explanatory note (which he gave Smith leave to alter in any way he wished).

The lecture, however, did not say all Arnold had in his mind upon his subject. At the very moment he returned the proofs of it, on June 16, 1867, he told Smith that he would "like to follow this, in the August number, with a paper to be called 'Anarchy and Authority'—to say several things which need to be said in accompaniment to what has been said here."—Buckler, p. 86. He even thought of accepting an invitation to address the Eisteddfod at Carmarthen—a consequence of the publication of his book on Celtic literature—in order to speak upon "Progress through Puritanism and Progress through Culture, with reference to Welsh dissent, the Liberation Society's workings there, etc., in connexion with these Eisteddfods and their popularity," but, he told his mother, "my desire is always for keeping quiet, and I took advantage of the possibility that my appearance at Carmarthen might be ascribed to popularity-hunting, and the attacks upon me do harm to the Eisteddfod, to refuse to go," much as he would have enjoyed a few summer days in Wales. The response of the daily and weekly press to "Culture and Its Enemies" was such, however, as to make him suggest to Smith that "Anarchy and Authority" might "wait a little, so as to be able to gather up all the murmurings into one and see what they come to"—until the October or November number, perhaps.

Replies and murmurings there were in sufficient number, anonymous or signed; two of the latter were by young men of brilliant promise, Henry Sidgwick (then only twenty-nine) and Frederic Harrison, who was still in his mid-thirties. The latter's "Culture: a Dialogue" in the November number of the *Fortnightly* at last set Arnold in motion; he conceived still only a single paper for the Christmas (January) *Cornhill*, "a sort of pendant to *Culture and Its Enemies*" : "It will amuse me to do it, as I have many things to say; and Harrison, Sidgwick, and others, who have replied to my first paper, have given me golden opportunities," he told his mother on November 16. He finished the paper on December 2 and 3, "while battering about in the cold ... in Northamptonshire" on a tour of school inspecting. The matter grew in his hands; Smith agreed to a sequel in the February number, only to be told on December 18 that "matter is so abundant that it will very likely run into a third —but the third will certainly end it." The death of his infant son

Basil on January 4 found most of the paper written, and he declined Smith's offer to let him defer the work until a later issue: "I think it should come this next month, that I may finish with the subject in March."—Buckler, p. 87. The manuscript was delivered to the magazine office on January 16, 1868. As the deadline for the third installment approached, Arnold wrote on February 9 to defer it a month, and then again on April 14 to postpone it until the June number. By this time he was at work on it, but it was still unfinished on May 8, and the manuscript did not reach the office until the 16th. Already a fourth installment was in prospect; and "Do not you think a timely and pleasing little volume might be made of these Anarchy and Authority essays, the Culture one, My Countrymen, and the Arminius letters?" he asked Smith on May 8.—Buckler, p. 88. The fourth installment went to the printer on June 13 for the July number, and since the matter was still growing in his hands, there was a final installment which he brought close to completion on July 17 for publication in the August number, and to the proofs of which he added about a page of conclusion two days later. "Culture and Its Enemies" and the five succeeding articles brought him £25 apiece. "These are the payments that do one good," Arnold told his mother on June 2, 1868, "—for I feel that I have earned them, and have not written in order to get them but have got them because I have written." The reader of *Culture and Anarchy* may be made slightly uncomfortable if he is not aware of this piecemeal composition and publication extending over thirteen months: one chapter may allude to printed criticisms of a preceding chapter; the course of political events moved on, and revision into a book still did not make the separate articles a perfectly coherent whole. An excellent study of the growth of the work out of contemporary controversies is S. M. B. Coulling's "The Evolution of *Culture and Anarchy*," *Studies in Philology* LX, 637–68 (October, 1963); a more limited aspect of the question gets illuminating treatment from Martha Salmon Vogeler, "Matthew Arnold and Frederic Harrison: the Prophet of Culture and the Prophet of Positivism," *Studies in English Literature* II, 441–62 (Autumn, 1962).

  The notion of bringing the articles together in one volume, and perhaps of including also "My Countrymen" and such of the Arminius letters as had already been published, was first broached, as has already been mentioned, on May 8, 1868. On July 25 Arnold told his mother the series of papers then being concluded would be published as a book. On October 1 he asked Smith, "How about reprinting *Anarchy and Authority?*" When a fortnight later he wrote to him, "I find I have all the parts of *Anarchy & Authority*, but will you send me the number which contains *Culture & Its Enemies*, as I may have to use that," he was probably expressing doubt, not whether to include the latter essay in his book, but whether he could find a copy of it without Smith's assistance. He also indicated then that he would provide an Introduction of some dozen or fifteen pages.—Buckler, p. 90. His oldest boy, always an invalid, died on November 23, but on December 5 he told Smith he "must on every account get back now to regular work again" and therefore wished to see the proofs of the new book. "[The essays] will be published under the title of *Culture & Anarchy*," he told his mother on December 16, "and in going through them I have much improved their arrangement and expression, and think them, now, a well-looking and useful body of doctrine. I have got to write the preface, all of which is well in my head and can be written in a week; I began to write it the Sunday [November 22] which was darling Tommy's last day of his life. I wrote the finishing part of what I wrote, sitting in his room after luncheon while he was dozing, that mild, rainy, dim afternoon; I remember turning round from the table where I was writing to look at him dozing. . . . I have not touched the preface since—there was some persiflage in what I had written and I could not go on in that strain; now I must see how the thing is to be turned." Proofreading on the text was completed about Christmas, and the manuscript of the second half of the Preface went to Smith on January 6: "It is longer than I meant it to be, but I got interested as I went on, and though I thought I had no heart to chaff any one any more I have been led, here and there, to chaff my enemies."—Buckler, p. 91. The book was published on Monday, January 25, 1869 (according to the advertisement in the *Times*), at 10 *s*. 6 *d*. Its title was a felicitous conflation of the titles of its elements, "Culture and Its Enemies" and "Anarchy and Authority"; it is linked to Arnold's previous Oxford lectures by its subtitle, "an essay in political and social criticism."

The first edition had no chapter headings, but the numbered divisions differed slightly from the original division into articles and were preserved as chapters when headings were supplied for the second edition in 1875. From the beginning, Arnold had feared that the handsome format of the first edition would make the book expensive, when such a book should rather be inexpensive. (He assured his mother, however, in response to a question, that "No one buys a book the less because he has read it in the magazines; that is the publishers' experience.") The sale (to "an undiscerning public," as he humorously remarked) was a good deal less rapid than he had hoped. By the summer of 1875, however, a second edition was needed; for this he provided chapter headings "supplied by the phrases in the book which have become famous: 'Sweetness & Light,' 'Hebraism & Hellenism,' &c."—Buckler, p. 91. Another significant revision was the omission of many of the personal names, perhaps because some of them had lost their significance with the passage of time, perhaps because Arnold learned that their use was offensive to his readers. His "kind monitor," the *Guardian*, rebuked him for his personalities in its reviews of both the *Essays in Criticism* and *Culture and Anarchy*, and he revised his Preface to the former at the end of 1868 to remove what he called "too much of mere temporary matter," including a good many personal names.* The second edition of *Culture and Anarchy* was advertised in the *Athenaeum* on October 9, 1875, and was priced at 7 shillings. A third edition, advertised as ready on October 7, 1882, was priced also at 7 shillings. In the summer of 1883 the book was combined with *Friendship's Garland* as a volume in the edition of Arnold's works printed in Edinburgh for publication by Macmillan and Company of New York. An earlier American edition of "Anarchy and Culture" announced by James R. Osgood and Company of Boston in 1875 as "in the press" was not published.

Culture and Anarchy grew directly out of the political restlessness of England in the mid-nineteenth century, a restlessness that came in part from the rapid industrialization of the country with its consequent depression of the lower classes, and that brought the country, as many people believed, to the brink of revolution. "I, who do not believe that the essential now to be done is to be done

---

* Only nineteen names were omitted, and for some of these omissions one can find individual reasons: the dean of Canterbury, Alford, died in 1871; Mrs. Lincoln's mental aberrations, once they became known for what they were, did not well illustrate American vulgarity nor was it gallant to mention them; Oscar Browning had been unjustly dismissed from Eton and Dr. William Smith of the *Quarterly* had proved himself an ally, not an enemy; the Rev. W. Cattle had not uttered the words which made him the symbol of middle-class bigotry—they had been spoken by Murphy, whose name Arnold sometimes substituted for Cattle's in his revision. The elimination of some further personal allusions in the 1875 edition of *Essays in Criticism* sprang from Arnold's "desire ...to die at peace with all men."—Buckler, p. 72.

through this external machinery of Reform bills and extension of the franchise, yet look upon the outward movement as a necessary part of the far more vital inward one, and think it important accordingly," Arnold wrote to his mother on November 25, 1865. "But I wish I could be sure that the inward one will be effected as I am that the outward one will." The word "anarchy" was common in discussion; at almost the same time Arnold was incorporating it into the title of his series of essays, Carlyle was violently harping upon it in his article "Shooting Niagara: and After?" in *Macmillan's Magazine* for August, 1867. Arnold was always well aware of Carlyle's impact on his thinking; if he spoke slightingly of Carlyle's lack of balance, he was merely saying what is clearly enough perceived today: Arnold has survived while Carlyle is unread. A thoroughly interesting study of their intellectual kinship in the decade of the sixties is D. J. DeLaura's "Arnold and Carlyle," *PMLA* LXXIX, 104–29 (March, 1964), though its author might have spared turning Arnold's clear-sighted awareness of the difference between Carlyle and himself into a "fixed need to depreciate Carlyle, combined with something very close to concealment of his influence."

Arnold knew so well that his mother disliked his tone of "persiflage" that he was at some pains to explain to her not only that the ideas of his Preface were indeed his father's ideas but that his tone was what was most needed to achieve the ends at which he aimed. "For my part," he wrote on December 5, 1867, "I see more and more what an effective weapon, in a confused, loud-talking, claptrappy country like this, where every writer and speaker to the public tends to say rather more than he means, is *irony*, or according to the strict meaning of the original Greek word, the saying rather less than one means. The main effect I have had on the mass of noisy claptrap and inert prejudice which chokes us has been, I can see, by the use of this weapon; and now, when people's minds are getting widely disturbed and they are beginning to ask themselves whether they have not a great deal that is new to learn, to increase this feeling in them is more useful than ever." Arnold, who delighted to ridicule the Liberal catchwords, was nevertheless expert at providing catchwords of his own; the swiftness with which "Geist" was taken up after he used the term in a letter to the *Pall Mall Gazette* was quickly overshadowed by the impact of such terms as "sweetness and light," "Hebraism and Hellenism," and "Philistines." "I think [the expression] *Barbarian* will stick," he told his mother on February 5, 1868, and his later letters to her are filled with pleased accounts of hearing on various occasions and under various circumstances the widespread use of the terms he had coined. When on August 14, 1867, the *Daily Telegraph* alluded to "sweetness and light" in a leading article on the new Reform Law and on August 15 spoke of "Philistinism" in a leading article on lower middle-class education, Arnold wrote to his mother, "Hardly a day passes without the Telegraph having some fling at me—but generally in a way that is not at all vicious." "The merit of terms of this sort is that they fix in people's minds the *things* to which they refer," he remarked to her on April 5, 1869, and some two months later, "The chapters on Hellenism and Hebraism are in the main, I am convinced, so true that they will form a kind of centre for English thought and speculation on the matters treated in them." When he was given the honorary degree of D.C.L. at Oxford on June 21, 1870, the Chancellor, Lord Salisbury, said privately that he should have addressed Arnold as "*Vir dulcissime et lucidissime.*" The most illuminating analysis of Arnold's rhetoric is a chapter in John Holloway's *The Victorian Sage* (London, 1953), a worthy companion to his splendid critique of the *Essays in Criticism* in *The Charted Mirror* (London, 1960).

Arnold's position with respect to certain Liberal proposals in Parliament has sometimes been misunderstood. He ridiculed his friend John Duke Coleridge's Real Estate Intestacy Bill not because he had a fine conservative devotion to primogeniture, but because the bill was such a trifling patch upon the law of bequests, which (as he made clear in a long footnote to *Schools and Universities on the Continent*) needed renovation from the ground up. The Deceased Wife's Sister Bill was in his view merely a way of currying favor with the Nonconformists; a just and rational settlement of the Irish Church question was made impossible by the attempt of the Gladstone ministry to win popularity in that same quarter. As he himself put it in a letter to his mother on December 5, 1867 (and the example he named was his own brother-in-law, for whom he had a high regard): "With time a conviction will spread that a man has no business to deal with matters of public concern without having seriously studied them; and if they do not take care, even men like William Forster, who entirely give up real study and think they are or can keep qualified for public affairs by mother-wit, going into Bradford, reading the newspapers, going to the House, going to the Cosmopolitan, will be left behind. I can see signs of this change of things in the impatience with which I hear the House of Commons treatment of things like education, or the feverish effort of members to grab that and other questions for their own honour and glory, begin to be spoken of. People at last are wanting these matters really weighed, and have not the least disposition to see them serve for capital to ambitious politicians. But I must not run on about this, only you may depend upon it that whoever lives ten years will see great changes, not only in other respects, but in our very centre of movement, which has long been the H. of Commons, and bids fair to be so no longer, but the real mind of the nation."

Culture and Anarchy did not attract such great immediate attention as *Literature and Dogma* was to receive, but it has continued to hold interest in a way Arnold's religious writings have not, and is probably his best-known work today. Its terminology and ideas are usually taken as central to his thinking, so that an account of criticisms of this book is almost a history of criticism of Arnold in general, and for such a history the present is not the place. Some of the most thoughtful critics, while always aware of Arnold's lively mind and graceful style, have been in the end discontent with his analysis of the problems and his solutions; J. M. Robertson's chapter in *Modern Humanists* (London, 1891) is in this respect a predecessor of Geoffrey Carnall's recent essay, "Arnold's 'Great Critical Effort,'" *Essays in Criticism* VIII, (July, 1958) 256–68: Arnold, Carnall concludes after a close analysis, betrays too much of the gladiator, "cheerful,...no doubt, but at heart...weary,...and therefore unscrupulous." Paradoxically, though he "attacked the complacency of others,...one of the main things which his method teaches is how to keep complacency intact." Patrick J. McCarthy's *Matthew Arnold and the Three Classes* (New York: Columbia University Press, 1964) is a bold undertaking for an American—especially for one who is easily confused by such matters as British titles of nobility—but despite a rather large number of factual errors it is a very interesting and useful attempt to show the social background from which Arnold sprang and to indicate his personal relationships with members of the three great classes of English society for which he invented names in *Culture and Anarchy*. Walter J. Hipple's "Matthew Arnold, Dialectician," *University of Toronto Quarterly* XXXII, 1–26 (October, 1962) takes its start from Arnold's mock disclaimer of a systematic philosophy in *Culture and*

Anarchy; it is an excellent discussion of the consistency that links all Arnold's work. Like the *Saturday Review* in Arnold's day, Hipple discovers him to be fundamentally a transcendentalist or Platonist. Professor J. Dover Wilson's edition, with its useful introduction and notes (Cambridge: at the University Press, 1932), is well known; its text is eclectic, but on the whole follows the first edition of 1869, and it does not list textual variants.

P. 86. Epigraph: "Be ye therefore perfect."—Matthew 5:48 (Vulgate version).

87:1–9. "Those literary gentlemen outside who write for the London weekly papers, who are for what they call culture because they happen to have a smattering of two dead languages, talk of culture and say the great body of the working people of this country ought to be permanently excluded from the franchise.... If ... a man scientifically or classically educated knows nothing of politics, which is very often the case, how shall he be more competent to decide who shall sit in this House, or, if he sit here himself, how shall he be more competent to decide what laws shall be passed than men in the humbler classes of society?"—John Bright in the parliamentary debate on the Elective Franchise Bill, May 30, 1866; see p. 117:18. The bill proposed an education test for the franchise.

87:10–88:2. Frederic Harrison, a graduate of the University and former fellow of Wadham College (where under the influence of Richard Congreve he became a Comtist), in "Our Venetian Constitution," *Fortnightly Review* VII, 276–77 (March, 1867); see note to p. 76:3–4. The essay was entitled "Parliament before Reform" in Harrison's *Order and Progress* (London, 1875), and to this passage Harrison appended the footnote (p. 150): "It seems necessary to say that these words were not directed against mental cultivation or literary grace, much less against a poet and writer whom to speak of these qualities is to name. My complaint was of a *political* faction, who brought to a great national struggle nothing but the bitterest reaction and trivial criticisms of the academic sort."

88:4–7. The proverbs "Know thyself" and "Avoid extremes" were inscribed on the temple of Apollo at Delphi. The former was ascribed by Diogenes Laertius (I, 40) to Thales. They were discussed by Socrates in Plato's *Charmides* 164D–167A and *Protagoras* 343B. See p. 28:5–10.

88:10–13. See note to p. 57:9.

88:36. J. Dover Wilson suggests that Arnold has his eye on "peace, retrenchment, and reform," which Earl Grey proclaimed as the motto of the Whig government in 1830; see p. 46:30–31.

90:14–16. In "The Function of Criticism at the Present Time," *Prose Works,* ed. Super, III, 268.

90:21–22. "M. Sainte-Beuve," *Quarterly Review,* American edition, CXIX, 42–57 (January, 1866); according to Professor W. E. Houghton of the Wellesley Periodical Index, the author was F. T. Marzials. The word "curiosity" played less part in the article than Arnold remembered, but the reviewer did insist that Sainte-Beuve "has only performed half his work. He has indeed *understood*— that is the critic's first duty—but he has not *judged,* which is a duty equally imperative," and he pointed to Mill's essay on Coleridge as an example of the more complete method. "This, however, is a view which would very possibly call for an earnest protest from a writer whose graceful but perfectly unsatisfactory essays have latterly been attracting considerable attention,... Mr. Matthew Arnold.... In many things [Arnold] may even be called [Sainte-Beuve's] disciple; and indeed it would form the object of a very interesting process of critical dissection to determine to what extent he is mentally indebted to M. Sainte-Beuve" (pp. 54–55). The reviewer set up in opposition to Arnold the criticisms of E. S. Dallas in *The Gay Science.*

91:5–6. For "seeing things as they are," see Arnold, *On Translating Homer* and "The Function of Criticism at the Present Time," *Prose Works,* ed. Super, I, 140 and III, 258.

91:11–14. "Le premier, c'est la satisfaction intérieure que l'on ressent lorsque l'on voit augmenter l'excellence de son être, et que l'on rend plus intelligent un être intelligent."—"Discours sur les motifs qui doivent nous encourager aux sciences," *Oeuvres complètes,* ed. Edouard Laboulaye (Paris, 1879), VII, 78.

91:37–38. Thomas Wilson, "Sacra Privata," *Works* (London, 1796), II, 303; see Arnold, *Note-Books,* ed. Lowry, p. 48 (diary for February 3, 1867).

94:1–2. Luke 17:21.

94:8–12. In *A French Eton, Prose Works,* ed. Super, II, 318.

94:29–30. Wilson, "Sacra Privata," *Works,* II, 176; see Arnold, *Note-Books,* ed. Lowry, pp. 48, 50 (diary for February 4 and March 1, 1867).

96:11–12. See p. 156:33–38 and "The Function of Criticism at the Present Time," *Prose Works,* ed. Super, III, 272.

96:23–26. Ten weeks after Arnold published this, the Paris correspondent of the *Times* quoted *Figaro* as saying, "Now-a-days, when one remarks in the orchestra stalls a soft dirty hat and a red flannel shirt, one may, without fear of mistake, exclaim 'It is an Englishman.' . . . The English . . . travel abroad to wear out their old clothes." The correspondent then remarked: "There is a large class of Englishmen who in their own country, perhaps, are neat and careful enough in externals, who no sooner cross the Channel than they cast away all regard for them, and appear in the most crowded and fashionable Continental resorts accoutred in all sorts of slovenly 'slang' habiliments, unfitted to the place, and arguing, as foreigners not unnaturally assume, contempt for the people among whom they find themselves . . . —dressed as if they were going to a prize fight, and had tried to adapt their appearance to that of the company they were likely to meet there."—September 18, 1867, p. 7, cols. 3–4 (Gregor).

96:32–36. In April, 1865, the young economist William Stanley Jevons published *The Coal Question: an Enquiry Concerning the Progress of the Nation and the Probable Exhaustion of Our Coal Mines.* The next year J. S. Mill argued in the Commons (April 17) for the systematic reduction of the national debt on the ground set forth exhaustively and unanswerably by Jevons; a fortnight later (May 3), Gladstone advanced a scheme for such reduction, citing Jevons and appropriating his argument on the prospective decline in the material prosperity of the country.—*D.N.B.*

98:12–13. "When Marriages are many and Deaths are few it is certain that the people are doing well," was the comment of the *Times* upon the Registrar-General's last quarterly report for 1865. "The Marriages were remarkably numerous, and the Births beyond all precedent."—February 3, 1866, p. 9, col. 1.

98:32–34. I Timothy 4:8.

98:35–37. The first of the "Rules of Health and Long Life" at the end of *Poor Richard, An Almanack* for 1742. Arnold recorded this maxim in his pocket diary for June 30, 1867; *Note-Books,* ed. Lowry, p. 56. Both read "as the constitution of thy body allows of."

99:4–11. Epictetus *Encheiridion* xli, somewhat modified by Arnold.

99:15–18. Aesop, in Swift's "Battle of the Books," moralizes thus on the bee's quarrel with the spider: "Instead of dirt and poison, we [the Ancients] have rather chosen to fill our hives with honey and wax, thus furnishing mankind with the two noblest of things, which are sweetness and light."—ed. Temple Scott (London, 1899), I, 172.

100:36. James 4:7; I John 2:13, 14.

101:18–23. The Independents were Calvinists who in church government insisted on the autonomy of each congregation; they were an important force in the Puritan revolt against Charles I. By Arnold's day they were more generally known as Congregationalists. The motto of *The Nonconformist* (edited by Edward Miall) comes from Burke's speech *On Conciliation with the Colonies*, one-fourth through.

101:28. I Peter 3:8.

103:33. "Ye are all the children of God by faith in Christ Jesus." —Galatians 3:26.

104:1–2. Sallust *Catilina* lii. 22. Arnold used a parallel expression in *A French Eton, Prose Works*, ed. Super, II, 271. He jotted the Latin in his pocket diary for April 16, 1867.—*Note-Books*, ed. Lowry, p. 53.

104:5–7. See note to p. 45:25.

104:16–17. The term "muscular Christianity" was applied to the doctrine of Charles Kingsley and his followers, defined by the *Edinburgh Review* in terms of "his deep sense of the sacredness of all the ordinary relations and all the common duties of life, and the vigour with which he contends...for the great importance and value of animal spirits, physical strength, and a hearty enjoyment of all the pursuits and accomplishments which are connected with them."—CVII, 190 (January, 1858). This was the review of *Tom Brown's School Days* that Arnold attributed to Fitzjames Stephen and the offensiveness of which led him to write "Rugby Chapel." Kingsley was not fond of the term, but could never shake it off.

105:4–8. "Prosperity to energetic labour, and peace to men of good intent—this is the object at which we aim. The secret of finance is very simple. The general riches which have accumulated are the basis of every prosperous condition, and the lever which raises that condition is liberty."—Gladstone at the dinner of the Society of Political Economy in Paris, January 31, 1867; *Times*, February 1, p. 10, col. 1.

105:36. Edmond Beales (1803–81) was president of the Reform League during its short and prosperous life (1865–69) and organizer of the monster rallies on behalf of reform in July, 1866 (see p. 45: 24). Charles Bradlaugh (1833–91) was the member of the League most energetic in persisting to hold the Hyde Park meeting despite the prohibition of the police. He was a vigorous platform orator, "the popular leader of an extreme party in the country, chiefly composed of working men, which combined freethought in religion and republicanism in politics."—*D.N.B.* He was proprietor of the weekly *National Reformer*.

105:38–106:18. On July 23, 1867, Arnold wrote to his brother Edward: "Perhaps none but Oxford men can know how much truth there really is in the praise I have given to Oxford for her sentiment. I find I am generally thought to have *buttered her up* to excess for the sake of parting good friends; but this is not so, though I certainly kept her best side in sight, and not her worst."

106:20–22. Note A of Newman's *Apologia* explains at length what, in his view, Liberalism was and how his movement reacted to it.—ed. C. F. Harrold (New York, 1947), pp. 259–69 and Index.

106:27. Vergil *Aeneid* i. 460.

107:4–6. See pp. 16–17.

108:21–30. The first phrase is from a leading article, the rest from the report of Bright's speech the preceding afternoon at Leeds, in the *Morning Star*, October 9, 1866, p. 4, col. 2, and p. 2, col. 5. Arnold jotted both in his pocket diary for October 12.—*Note-Books*, ed. Lowry, pp. 36–37. Bright's speech is also printed in the *Times*, October 9, p. 7, cols. 3–5.

108:36. An allusion to Spurgeon's huge Metropolitan Tabernacle.

109:5–6. See Matthew 22:11–14.

109:10–11. [Thomas Wright], *Some Habits and Customs of the Working Classes*. By the Journeyman Engineer (London, 1867).

109:26. Richard Congreve (1818–99) was a contemporary of Clough's at Rugby, then a scholar and fellow of Wadham College, Oxford. He was converted to positivism by a meeting with Auguste Comte in Paris in 1848 and while he was embarking on its study was tutor to Frederic Harrison at Wadham. They were thereafter closely associated for nearly thirty years.

109:36. Arnold's "current" here represents what he elsewhere refers to as the *Zeitgeist*.

110:7–14. Ludwig Preller, *Römische Mythologie* (3rd ed.; Berlin, 1881), I, 21–23, 147. The book was on Arnold's reading list for 1866 and 1867; see *Note-Books*, ed. Lowry, pp. 579, 582.

110:28–37. "Bagatelles," *Works*, ed. Jared Sparks (Boston, 1840), II, 167. As Paul Shorey first pointed out in the *Nation* XLVI, 486 (June 14, 1888), Franklin's version was intended to be comic, not serious; perhaps Arnold read the passage out of context. In his pocket diary for January 6, 1867, Arnold wrote: "Read Franklin once a week."—*Note-Books*, ed. Lowry, p. 47.

111:5–10. Jeremy Bentham, *Deontology; or, the Science of Morality*, arranged and edited by John Bowring (London, 1834), I, 39–40. Bentham reads "was writing history, and Euclid giving instruction in geometry."

111:16. Henry Thomas Buckle (1821–62) wrote the *History of Civilisation in England* (1857, 1861) on empirical principles, and achieved great contemporary reputation as popularizer of the application of scientific treatment to historical problems.

111:18. Matthew 23:8.

111:33–112:1. See p. 87.

112:7–8. James 3:16.

112:22–28. This was the thesis of Arnold's inaugural lecture from the chair of Poetry, "On the Modern Element in Literature"; see especially *Prose Works*, ed. Super, I, 23–29.

113:32–114:5. *Confessions* xiii. 18.

115:11–19. The *Saturday Review* seems first to have indicated that Arnold's "culture" was a kind of religion, and to have spoken of "the apostles of culture."—"Mr. Matthew Arnold on Culture," XXIV, 78–79 (July 20, 1867). Then, comparing Harrison and Arnold as representative of two temperaments, after the appearance of Harrison's dialogue on "Culture," the *Saturday* called Arnold's doctrine a "religion" that Harrison's Arminius "somewhat rudely pronounces to be a sort of parmaceti," and added that Arnold "may, roughly speaking, be said to represent the . . . spirit of cultivated inaction"; such a spirit "will not lend a hand to the humble operation of uprooting [certain definite evils to be eradicated]," and "produces philosophers and critics full of antipathies against the rougher and coarser movements they see on all sides of them." It thus summed up the view of Harrison's Arminius: "It briefly amounts to this, that culture, as expounded by Mr. Arnold, is all moonshine."—"Culture and Action," XXIV, 591–93 (November 9, 1867). The *Saturday Review* can claim also to have originated the parallel between Arnold and the delicate lord who approached Hotspur immediately after the heat of battle in *1 Henry IV*, I. iii. 30–64: "With all his ability, [Arnold] sometimes gives himself the airs of the distinguished courtier who shone so bright and smelt so sweet when he had occasion to talk with Hotspur about the prisoners. He is always using a moral smelling-bottle."—"Mr. Matthew Arnold and His Countrymen," XVIII, 685 (December 3, 1864). The figure was taken up by the *Daily Telegraph* on July 2, 1867, then used by Henry Sidgwick at the close of "The Prophet of Culture," *Macmillan's Magazine* XVI, 280 (August, 1867), and again by Frederic Harrison in "Culture: a Dialogue," *Fortnightly Review* VIII, 610 (November, 1867). Harrison placed two lines from the passage of Shakespeare at the head of his article: "The sovereign'st thing on earth/ Was parmaceti for an inward bruise."

115:20–22. The *Morning Star*, Bright's newspaper, assailed Arnold's "absurd misconception" of Bright's words about culture: "Has Mr. Arnold lived so much out of the world of political literature that he does not know what culture means when the word is used as the slang phrase of those who have lately made it odious and contemptible to all intelligent ears? ... To be a man of culture ... in the modern and slangy sense—we explain for Mr. Arnold's instruction—is to be a small, pedantic Tory prig who, knowing very little Latin and less Greek, is proud of declaring that he knows and wants to know nothing else."—June 28, 1867, p. 4, col. 4 (Coulling). "Both the *Star* and *Telegraph* I shall continue gently to touch up on occasion," Arnold promised his mother on November 8, 1867 (SenGupta). Alcibiades was a brilliant but irresponsible leader of the Athenians in the Peloponnesian War, suspected of attempting to overthrow the State. Dover Wilson comments: "The comparison of the narrow-minded and smug puritan editor ... with the type of all that was luxurious, cosmopolitan, brilliant, accomplished, fascinating and unprincipled in the Athens of Socrates is a good example of Arnold's irony."—*Culture and Anarchy*, p. 224.

115:22–26. "He employs a keen faculty for finding fault in criticising every one who, more earnest than himself, descends into the rather dusty arena of political life, and, by pen or by tongue, helps on true culture—not the schooling of the cloister, but the widest culture, and the greatest possibility of 'light and sweetness' for all. Then when, like Hotspur, just after the battle, one is somewhat heated with 'rage and extreme toil,' this elegant creature, 'neat, trimly dressed,' enters, and expresses surprise at our want of coolness, and thinks that our utterance is at least a semi-tone too high." —*Daily Telegraph*, July 2, 1867, p. 6, col. 6. See Matthew 20:12.

115:27–29. [E. L. Godkin,] "Sweetness and Light," *Nation* V, 212–13 (September 12, 1867).

116:1–8. Harrison's "Culture: a Dialogue" is a fancied conversation between the author and Arminius von Thunder-ten-dronck, the author in the role of an admirer of the new Gospel of Culture and Arminius the hard-headed rationalist waxing more and more indignant as the philosophical shortcomings of Arnold's doctrine become apparent in the loving account of his new disciple. "[Mr. Harrison's dialogue] is scarcely the least vicious, and in parts so amusing that I laughed till I cried," Arnold wrote to Lady de Rothschild on October 30, 1867. This, then, was the beginning of Arnold's fiction in *Friendship's Garland* that Arminius had broken off correspondence with himself and taken up with Frederic Harrison (see pp. 76–77, 314). " 'How do you describe the basis of your social philosophy?' [Arminius demanded of the new disciple.] 'Remember, my friend,' I rejoined, with a confident smile, 'culture knows nothing so finite as a system.' 'No!' he answered; 'not any system, but you have principles? These principles are of course coherent; they are interdependent, subordinate, and derivative, I presume?' I was still silent, and smiled as blandly as was courteous. 'They are derived,' he went on, 'through some definite logical process surely, either from history, or from consciousness, or from experiment, or the like? They agree in part or in whole, or they disagree, with the stated principles of known moralists and thinkers? They can be harmonised with other branches of philosophy as a whole, they can be grasped by the student and imparted to the disciple. Your principles are of this sort, I suppose?' said he, puzzled by my continued silence. 'My friend,' I replied, laughing aloud, though, I trust, always within the limits of the courteous and the graceful, 'has Dagon stricken thee, too? ... Learn how culture—with that flexibility which sweetness and light give, with that exquisite sensibility to truth which is its note—has no need of these leading-strings and finger–posts.... It is eternally passing onwards and seeking—seeking and passing onwards eternally. Where the bee sucks, there suck I,' I murmured cheerily, as I observed the increasing bewilderment of my philosophical friend.... 'Soul of my namesake!' he burst forth with sad, sad vehemence of manner, 'must I hear more? Here are we, in this generation, face to face with the passions of fierce men; parties, sects, races glare in each other's eyes before they spring; death, sin, cruelty stalk amongst us, filling their maws with innocence and youth; humanity passes onwards shuddering through the raging crowd of foul and hungry monsters, bearing the destiny of the race like a close-veiled babe in her arms, and over all sits Culture high aloft with a pouncet-box to spare her senses aught unpleasant, holding no form of creed, but contemplating all with infinite serenity, sweetly chanting snatches from graceful sages and ecstatic monks, crying out the most pretty shame upon the vulgarity, the provinciality, the impropriety of it all!' "—*Fortnightly Review* VIII, 608, 610 (November, 1867).

The *Daily News* commented in a leading article on this chapter of "Anarchy and Authority" that "Mr. Frederic Harrison, to whose wit and logic his antagonist [Arnold] pays a graceful tribute, is likely to add to his conquest of Arminius the conquest of the creator and inspirer of Arminius," for though Arnold "is largely occupied in attacking the school of Comte, he has adopted unconsciously their views of the functions of the State."—December 30, 1867, p. 4, col. 3.

"A Mr. Robarts...asked me to dine with him at the Star and Garter, that I might meet Frederic Harrison," Arnold told his mother on June 29, 1868; but Arnold was not free on that evening.

116:13. Arnold took the phrase "drive at practice" from Jeremy Collier's translation of Marcus Aurelius; see *Prose Works,* ed. Super, III, 138:13.

117:15–16. The eighth section of Walter Bagehot's *The English Constitution* was called "Its Supposed Checks and Balances."—*Fortnightly Review* VI, 807–26 (December, 1866).

117:18–22. In his speech on the Elective Franchise Bill (see p. 87), Bright repeatedly said, "I am unwilling to depart from the ancient practice of the Constitution of this country," "I am for standing on the old line of the Constitution of this country," "the ancient line on which our forefathers always travelled, and on which we have hitherto travelled." On one of the back pages of his pocket diary for 1867 Arnold wrote, without making any attribution, "The assertion of *personal liberty.*"—*Note-Books,* ed. Lowry, p. 66.

117:29–30. This definition of the State, which Arnold uses some sixteen times in his essays, depends on Burke, though the language is not precisely his. See Arnold, *Prose Works,* ed. Super, II, 377; III, 78:5.

117:35–36. "[A man] is the person most interested in his own well-being: ... In each person's own concerns, his individual spontaneity is entitled to free exercise. Considerations to aid his judgment, exhortations to strengthen his will, may be offered to him, ... but he himself is the final judge."—Mill, *On Liberty,* Chapter IV.

118:2–3. The sheriff and lord-lieutenant are county officers appointed by the crown; their offices are of great antiquity, but are now largely ceremonial. The lord-lieutenant recommends to the lord chancellor persons qualified for appointment as justices of the peace. See note to p. 73:11–15.

118:8–9. See pp. 21, 34, 35.

118:17–20. In *The Popular Education of France, Prose Works*, ed. Super, II, 162.

118:30. Clay Cross is a colliery town 4½ miles south of Chesterfield, the center of a large coal and iron district.

118:37. Mr. Gregor calls attention to Bagehot's description of the English people: "We are ... a deferential nation, but we are deferential by imagination, not by reason.... Our ignorant classes ... are impressed by the great spectacle of English society, and they bow down as a whole and willingly, but they do not reckon their idols, they do not rationalise their religion.... They now defer involuntarily, unconsciously, and happily, but they would not defer argumentatively.... The middle classes rule under the shadow of the higher classes.... The mass of the English lower classes defer to the English higher class, but the nominal electors are a sort of accidental intermediaries, who were not chosen for their own merits and do not choose out of their own number."—"The English Constitution. IX," *Fortnightly Review* VII, 91–92 (January, 1867).

119:9–11, 18–19, 33–34. Allusions to the Hyde Park riots; see note to p. 45:24.

119:34. When some Fenians killed a police sergeant in rescuing two prisoners in Manchester and were sentenced to death a disorderly mob of English sympathizers on November 18, 1867, forced their way into the outer office of the Home Secretary to demand a pardon.

119:37–120:24. On Sunday, June 16, 1867, William Murphy, "agent of the London Protestant Electoral Union," commenced a series of anti-Catholic lectures in a wooden "tabernacle" erected for the purpose in the center of Birmingham. Riots threatened, the police were reenforced and the hussars were held in readiness. The lectures continued and the disturbances increased in magnitude, but Murphy insisted upon his right of free speech; the passage quoted by Arnold (lines 7–11) appears in the *Times* on June 19, p. 12, col. 2. On June 18, with the Rev. William Cattle, Wesleyan minister from Walsall in the chair, Murphy (not Cattle) delivered himself of the remarks Arnold quotes on p. 131 (the *Times* account, June 20, p. 7, col. 6, could easily be misread to imply the remarks were Cattle's, whose name the *Times* spelled "Cassel"; see Textual Note to p. 180:15). By this time the rioting had subsided. On June 19 Murphy, after attacking the institution of nunneries, proclaimed that "his object was to protect their wives and daughters. If Mayors and magistrates did not care for their wives and daughters, he did. He cared for his wife, and therefore she should not go to the confessional."—*Times*, June 21, p. 12, col. 4. Meanwhile in the House of Commons, G. H. Whalley, who spoke from the same platform as Murphy on June 17, asked the Home Secretary, Gathorne Hardy (who had replaced Spencer Walpole after a second Reform League meeting in Hyde Park), for assurance that Murphy's rights would be protected, and received the reply Arnold quotes.—*Times*, July 21, p. 6, col. 4.

120:29–121:1. "The existing owner, although he is confined to the limits of twenty-one years after lives in being, with regard to any power over property to be exercised on behalf of his family, is allowed to appropriate the same property for ever to any public purpose (consistent with law, religion, and morality) that his imagination may devise. . . . One testator, not long since, bequeathed 300 *l.* a year to be for ever applied as a pension to some person who had been *unsuccessful* in literature, and whose duty it should be to support and diffuse by his writings the testator's own views as enforced in the testator's publications. An inquiry was directed as to whether the testator's publications contained anything contrary to religion or morals, and this being answered in the negative, the so-called charity was established."—Vice-Chancellor Sir William Page Wood, "Charitable Trusts," *Transactions of the National Association for the Promotion of Social Science* (1859), pp. 187–88. James Kay Shuttleworth quoted this passage in a paper read before the same association on October 5, 1866, printed in the *Transactions* for that year (p. 345) and reprinted as *A Scheme for General and Local Administration of Endowments* (London, 1866). Arnold took the story from Shuttleworth's pamphlet (p. 16). The testator in question (Mr. Gregor points out) was probably Simon Gray, whose will in this matter was upheld by the vice-chancellor (not Wood at that date) on August 7, 1844; the bequest was £50 per annum, not £300.—*Times*, August 8, 1844, p. 7, col. 6 ("Thomson *v.* Thomson").

121:16. The Fenians were an Irish-American revolutionary society whose terrorizing tactics had England and Ireland in a state of alarm, especially in 1867, when two of their number were released from police custody in Manchester on September 18 by a violent attack upon a police van and when the attempt to release two others by dynamiting the walls of Clerkenwell prison in London on December 13 caused the death of twelve persons and injury to more than a hundred others.

121:36–37. See note to p. 41:7–8.

122:8–14. Sir Daniel Gooch (1816–89) resigned his post as locomotive superintendent of the Great Western Railway in 1864 to conduct the laying of the Atlantic cable; upon the success of the enterprise he was made a baronet in 1866. He became chairman of the board of directors of the Great Western Railway in 1865, rescued it from imminent bankruptcy, and held the post until his death. He sat in Parliament from 1865 to 1885. Swindon, Wiltshire, is the site of the Great Western locomotive and carriage works. Gooch tells the same story in his *Diaries* (London, 1892), pp. 25–26: "My dear mother gave me much good advice, which has been of use to me through life. I remember well her telling me always to keep my thoughts fixed on obtaining for myself a good position in life, never to be satisfied to stand still; and although I was going to the Vulcan [Foundry of Robert Stephenson] as a boy and a pupil, to strive to one day become the manager. I have often in after life thought over my mother's words, and seen the wisdom of them."

122:10. Arnold used the Latin version of this text (Matthew 5: 48) as Epigraph for *Culture and Anarchy* (p. 86).

122:34–35. I.e., making the streets impassable with a procession to a monster rally.

124:10–11. F. Harrison, "Our Venetian Constitution," *Fortnightly Review* VII, 277 (March, 1867).

124:19–22. See note to p. 35:38.

124:35. John 12:31.

125:6–12. For example, in the essay on "Democracy," *Prose Works,* ed. Super, II, 13–14.

125:25–27. For example, *ibid.,* II, 23–26.

125:28. *Dives* is the Vulgate word for the "certain rich man" of Luke 16:19, "which was clothed in purple and fine linen, and fared sumptuously every day," while the beggar Lazarus desired the crumbs from his table.

126:28–29. See note to p. 116:1.

126:33. Oxford "in the bad old times" was the university before the reforms, internal and legislative, of the middle of the century, symbolized externally by the Oxford University Act of 1854.

126:35-36. Lowe spoke at Edinburgh on November 1, 1867, on the necessity of reforming higher education, breaking down the ascendancy of Greek and Latin, and giving a fair stage for English history, law and letters, the modern languages, and the physical sciences. He lightened a well-reasoned speech by remarking, "The advantage of knowing French would be that when [an Englishman] goes to Paris he would be able to order his dinner at the café, and to squabble over his bill without making himself a laughingstock to every one present. . . . If the object [of education] be to make [mankind] fit for the business of life, I submit . . . that we have too much Latin and Greek, and that if we are to have it, it ought to be taught on a very different system."—*Times*, November 4, 1867, p. 8, col. 5. Lowe modified this passage when he published a revised version of the speech as a pamphlet, *Primary and Classical Education* (Edinburgh, 1867).

127:1-2. Aristotle *Nicomachean Ethics* II. vi. 15-16.

127:2-24. See Textual Notes. The date must have been June 4, 1866—the only occasion when Lord Elcho and Sir Thomas Bateson both spoke on the Reform Bill. Bateson's was indeed an ill-tempered speech, deliberately sailing close to the wind in his personal remarks about the leaders of the Government (see p. 151). Lord Elcho's speech that evening was very brief, but reasonable and good-tempered. Though Arnold had already used Lord Elcho as the type of the governing class (p. 50), he may owe something here to the account of Elcho in the *Pall Mall Gazette*, February 2, 1867, pp. 393-94 (Kirby). For Carlyle on aristocratic virtues, see p. 124 and note to p. 35:38.

127:24-26. See, for example, "The Literary Influence of Academies" and *On the Study of Celtic Literature, Prose Works*, ed. Super, III, 237, 341, and "My Countrymen," V, 13:5-7.

128:1-4. See pp. 10, 16-17.

128:22-27. See p. 69.

128:31. *Hamlet* I.ii.85.

128:32. A Free Church was a disestablished church.

128:34-35. Harrison, Congreve, and other Comtists founded a chapel for their new religion of Positivism, with religious services to honor a faith, not in the supernatural, but in "our common humanity."

128:35-37. *Maxims of Piety and of Christianity*, ed. Frederic Relton (London, 1898), p. 151.

129:3–9. E. L. Godkin in the *Nation* V, 213 (September 12, 1867); see p. 115:27–29.

129:9–17. "A Plea for the Uncultivated," signed "A Philistine," *Nation* V, 215 (September 12, 1867).

130:20–24. Sir Thomas Bazley's speech at Manchester, November 29, 1864; see pp. 4–5.

131:4–23. See note to p. 119:37.

131:31–132:12. On Monday, June 3, 1867, the City of London Militia, some 600 strong, marched with their regimental band from their barracks in Finsbury past the Mansion House and into the West End. The parade attracted large gangs of roughs, who attacked and robbed spectators all along the line of march. Questions were asked of the Home Secretary in the House of Commons on June 6, and the plea was made that the police were undermanned and had not been warned that the march was in prospect. When the Court of Aldermen met on June 18, the colonel of the regiment, Alderman Samuel Wilson, a man of seventy-five who had led the march, defended himself and his troops for not intervening to put down the roughs, using the language Arnold quotes (*Times*, June 19, p. 10, col. 2). Despite Arnold's sweet reasonableness, the matter was one for the police and the intervention of the military in cases of civil commotion is jealously circumscribed by English (and American) law. A previous editor of *Culture and Anarchy*, Professor J. Dover Wilson, was surprised to recognize in Arnold's alderman-colonel a kinsman of his.

132:24–26. Beales fancied that in the conference between his delegation and Walpole after the Hyde Park riots, the Home Secretary had given permission to the Reform League to hold one meeting in Hyde Park on July 30, and to keep back the police and the military on the League's guarantee that order would be kept. The misunderstanding was instantly removed; no such permission had been given. "It is, indeed, difficult to understand how any man of education could have persuaded himself that a Home Secretary—a Minister responsible to the Crown and Parliament—could have handed over Hyde Park upon the faith of the personal guarantee of Mr. Beales that order should be maintained in it."—*Times*, July 27, 1866, p. 8, col. 6.

132:32–133:4. See notes to pp. 87:10, 124:10.

133:13. See notes to pp. 45:24, 105:36, and 343:21–22.

133:20. George Odger (1820–77), secretary of the London Trades Council from 1862 to 1872, one of the most influential of trade-union officials, believed in the necessity of combining trade unionism with vigorous political activity and therefore became a member of the National Reform League and persuaded the Trades Council to take a leading part in agitation for extension of the franchise in 1866 and subsequent years. He was five times unsuccessful in attempts to secure election to Parliament between 1868 and 1874.—*D.N.B.*

133:27. See pp. 105:36 and 343:23.

133:31–32. *Maxims* (1898), p. 157.

135:24–25. *Ibid.*, p. 61, with an echo of Matthew 6:23 and Luke 11:35.

135:37–136:1. In the debate on the Reform Bill of 1832, the Duke of Wellington said (April 10) that "this Bill . . . had a revolutionary tendency, and he thought it had a tendency so strong in that way that it must lead to revolution. . . . A revolution might be effected by law as well as by violence."

137:7–8. Note that Arnold used the same device of showing the mean, excess, and defect in the lectures *On the Study of Celtic Literature, Prose Works*, ed. Super, III, 351.

138:9. "Urbanity" is an ideal Arnold proposed for English writers in "The Literary Influence of Academies."

138:20–23. "It is because Mr. Arnold will not lend a hand to the humble operation of uprooting [certain definite evils], that [the believers in action] grow impatient with him, and want to know what he means by all his contemplation."—"Culture and Action," *Saturday Review* XXIV, 593 (November 9, 1867).

138:37–38. "The Friend of Humanity and the Knife-Grinder," by George Canning and John Hookham Frere, in the *Anti-Jacobin*, November 27, 1797.

139:4–5. See p. 66.

139:16–17. See p. 5:16–17.

139:23. His fullest explanation is in "Heinrich Heine," *Prose Works*, ed. Super, III, 111–14.

139:33–34. In "Shooting Niagara: and After?"

140:31. Arnold earlier used this term in the Preface to *Essays in Criticism, Prose Works*, ed. Super, III, 290:4.

142:5–7. See note to p. 35:38.

142:20–23. See p. 108:20–30.

142:35. The trades unions were much before the public eye; on February 12, 1867, the Queen named a royal commission to inquire into their organization and rules—a commission that included, of persons familiar to readers of this book, Lord Elcho, Sir Daniel Gooch, J. A. Roebuck, and Frederic Harrison.

143:7–8. Perhaps *Apology* 36 C: "Where I could do the greatest good privately to every one of you, thither I went, and sought to persuade every man among you that he must look to himself, and seek virtue and wisdom before he looks to his private interests, and look to the state before he looks to the interests of the state; and that this should be the order which he observes in all his actions." (Jowett's translation)

144:8–9. Swinburne, with an eye to Dr. Arnold, referred to Matthew Arnold as "David, the son of Goliath."—"Mr. Arnold's New Poems," *Fortnightly Review* VIII, 425 (October, 1867). Arnold addressed an amiable note or two to Swinburne regarding the review (only one, of October 10, has survived, in the Ashley Library of the British Museum), and then met Swinburne at dinner at the Frederick Lockers' on November 18; he "turned out very well behaved and interesting," Arnold told his mother. See Edmund Gosse, "Matthew Arnold and Swinburne," *Times Literary Supplement*, August 12, 1920, p. 517.

144:15–16. As Arnold's friends well knew, he was seldom happier than when he had a gun or a fishing-rod in his hands. See p. 75:10–12.

145:17. Rattening is "the act or practice of abstracting tools, destroying machinery or appliances, etc., as a means of enforcing compliance with the rules of a trade-union, or of venting spite."— *N.E.D.* The Trades Union Commission in the summer of 1867 discovered that this extra-legal practice was widespread in Sheffield.

147:13–16. Pope, Arbuthnot, and Swift, "Martinus Scriblerus *Peri Bathous:* or the Art of Sinking in Poetry," beginning of Chapter II.

147:21–32. In "The Literary Influence of Academies" and "The Function of Criticism at the Present Time," *Prose Works*, ed. Super, III, 243–44, 270, 249–50.

148:1–2. The *British Banner*, a weekly newspaper of the Evangelical Nonconformists, and more especially of the English Congregationalists, came to an end with its final number for 1858. Its intellectual caliber was low and its appeal to the families of "the middle classes of Society" was through a curious combination of piety, scandal, and horror.

148:28–32; 149:1–3, 7–12. William Hepworth Dixon, *New America* (3rd ed.; Philadelphia, 1867), pp. 168, 351, 358, 353–54. The first passage refers to the Mormons, the last three to the Spiritualists,

whose third annual convention was held in Pratt's Hall, Broad
Street, Providence, Rhode Island, in August, 1866.

149:22–24. *Ibid.*, p. 307. For Elderess Polly and Elderess Antoinette, see p. 304.

150:28–29. Proverbs 28:26.

150:30–32. *Maxims* (1898), p. 23.

150:37–151:3. *The Princess*, Conclusion, lines 85, 54–56, 65–66.

151:5–14. See pp. 5–6, 124:10–11.

151:26–27. "When the aristocracy of this country is emasculated
—the Chancellor of the Exchequer [Gladstone] laughs at that—no
doubt the right hon. Gentleman thinks the emasculation of the aristocracy a very pleasant amusement. When, I say, the aristocracy
of the country is emasculated—[*Laughter*]—oh, that is no laughing
matter, I can assure you—when the House of Lords has been
emasculated—in spite of that laugh and in spite of that sneer from
the right hon. Gentleman opposite—I say when the House of Lords
has been emasculated by the abolition of the law of primogeniture
and of entail, what, I ask, will then happen? Is it not probable
that when the Constitution of Old England has been Americanized
that an attack upon the monarchy of this country will very soon
follow?"—Sir Thomas Bateson in the debate on the Reform Bill,
House of Commons, June 4, 1866 (a debate Arnold heard; see
p. 127:2).

151:31. When Lowe won the election at Kidderminster in the
spring of 1857, the mob, angered at his failure to provide the cus-
tomary beer and bribes, assailed him and his friends with stones
and brickbats; Lowe was struck and suffered a fracture of the skull.
In the debate on the Reform Bill, therefore, on March 13, 1866,
he said: "I have had such unhappy experiences, and many of us
have—let any Gentleman consider the constituencies he has had the
honour to be concerned with. If you want venality, if you want
ignorance, if you want drunkenness, and facility for being intimi-
dated; or if, on the other hand, you want impulsive, unreflecting,
and violent people, where do you look for them in the constituencies? Do you go to the top or to the bottom?" Bright and his
friends immediately seized upon these words as Lowe's characterization of the working classes and it was vain for Lowe to protest
that he was quoted out of context. Gladstone in Parliament referred
to the epigrammatic "ignorant, drunken, venal, violent," and Bright
urged that the words be printed and hung up "in every factory,

workshop, and clubhouse, and in every place where working men are accustomed to assemble."—A. P. Martin, *Life and Letters of . . . Robert Lowe, Viscount Sherbrooke* (London, 1893), II, 153–55, 273–74.

152:11–13. Simonides of Ceos, fragment 58 (Bergk), 65 (Edmonds) or 37 (Diehl), based on Hesiod *Works and Days* 289–91.

152:21. An aside of Don Bazile's (not Figaro's), in Beaumarchais' *Le Barbier de Séville*, III, xi.

153:12–17. See p. 69:23. The words were those of Thomas Milner Gibson, M.P. for Manchester, in the debate of June 19, 1843.—Hansard's *Parliamentary Debates,* Third Series, LXX, col. 95. Arnold's much admired friend Kay-Shuttleworth had been largely responsible for the insertion of the education clauses into the bill, but he had provided guarantees for the Dissenters which the Church party refused to accept when the bill was framed.

153:20–23. "Our Venetian Constitution," *Fortnightly Review* VII, 271, 277 (March, 1867).

154:7–18, 30–32. See *Schools and Universities on the Continent, Prose Works,* ed. Super, IV, 197–98, 200.

155:2–8. Dover Wilson suggests that Arnold was alluding obliquely to the opening by the Prince of Wales of the Warehousemen and Clerks' Schools at Russell Hill, near Caterham Junction, on June 18, 1866. "Such a consummation, when we reflect on the numerous classes of the great commercial community of our country whose interests it promotes, cannot but be gratifying to every one present, and will induce us all gratefully to invoke the Divine blessing on the ultimate success of this undertaking," said the Prince. —*Times,* June 19, p. 14, col. 4. Lord Russell, still prime minister (though his Government was overthrown that very day in the Commons) spoke as president of the charity. There was in fact, however, a Licensed Victuallers' School, set up by the Incorporated Licensed Victuallers' Society, and a Commercial Travellers' School at Pinner, founded in 1845 for the education of needy children of commercial travellers. (Licensed victuallers are public house or tavern keepers.)

156:25–33. A leading article on a published appeal from the American Fenians to English and Irish "brothers" to overthrow aristocratic tyranny and establish a republic.—*Times,* January 3, 1868, p. 7, col. 2 (Coulling).

156:33–38. From a speech at Sheffield, August 18, 1864; quoted by Arnold earlier in this work (p. 96) and in "The Function of

Criticism at the Present Time," *Prose Works*, ed. Super, III, 272.

157:10–18, 25–30. *Times*, December 2, 1867, p. 9, col. 1 (Coulling, Gregor).

157:37–159:3. A leading article on Arnold's first paper on "Anarchy and Authority," *Daily News*, December 30, 1867, p. 4, cols. 1–3 (Coulling).

159:29–31. Aristotle *Nicomachean Ethics* II.i.4–8, ii.9, iv.1–6.

160:1–2. See note to p. 157:37.

160:35–161:2. "Dangers of Democracy" (an article on Carlyle's *Shooting Niagara: and After?* and W. von Humboldt's *The Sphere and Duties of Government*), *Westminster Review*, American edition, LXXXIX, 1–17 (January, 1868).

160:9–10. In "The Literary Influence of Academies," *Prose Works*, ed. Super, III, 237.

161:2–19. Arnold may be drawing, for this analysis, on P. Challemel-Lacour, *La Philosophie individualiste: étude sur Guillaume de Humboldt* (Paris, 1864), pp. 77–78, 37–38. The former passage is a summary of *The Sphere and Duties of Government*, chapter II; the latter is a statement of Humboldt's aim as minister of education: "Si l'on observe l'esprit de ces mesures et avec quel soin Humboldt se tient éloigné aussi bien de l'utilitarisme que d'une religiosité servile, on reconnaît qu'il vise à former une aristocratie, aussi nombreuse que possible, de caractères vigoureux, force et honneur unique des nations."

161:20–27. See Arnold, *Schools and Universities on the Continent*, *Prose Works*, ed. Super, IV, 198–99, 209, 218–19, 307.

162:7–12. "L'Instruction supérieure en France," *Questions contemporaines* (Paris, 1868), p. 73.

163:11–12. See "The Literary Influence of Academies" and *On the Study of Celtic Literature*, *Prose Works*, ed. Super, III, 237, 341.

163:28. Arnold took the contrast between "Hebraism" and "Hellenism," as he drew the term "Philistine," from Heine; see *Prose Works*, ed. Super, III, 127–28. Arnold also knew Heine's *Ludwig Börne. Eine Denkschrift* (1840): "Beide Ausdrücke ['jüdisch' und 'christlich'] für mich synonym sind und von mir nicht gebraucht werden, um einen Glauben, sondern um ein Naturell zu bezeichnen. 'Juden' und 'Christen' sind für mich ganz sinnverwandte Worte, im Gegensatz zu 'Hellenen,' mit welchem Namen ich ebenfalls kein bestimmtes Volk, sondern eine sowohl angeborene als angebildete Geistesrichtung und Anschauungsweise bezeichne. In dieser Be-

ziehung möchte ich sagen: alle Menschen sind entweder Juden
oder Hellenen, Menschen mit asketischen, bildfeinlichen, vergeisti-
gungssüchtigen Trieben oder Menschen von lebensheiterem, ent-
faltungsstolzem und realistischem Wesen."—Book I, one-third
through.

164:16. II Peter 1:4.

164:25–29. F. W. Robertson, "Notes of Advent Lectures. No. 1,
The Greek," *Sermons on Christian Doctrine* (London, 1906), II,
283–92 (preached December 6, 1849). On November 18, 1865, Arnold wrote to his mother: "I took up by accident the other day
at the club this new life of Frederick Robertson [by Stopford
Brooke] which has just come out, and after I had read a page or
two I could not stop till I had gone through the two volumes. It is
a most interesting, remarkable life. I had once seen him, heard him
preach, but he did not please me, and I did him no justice. Now I
shall read his sermons which, from the impression I took, I had
abstained from reading, and, very likely, I shall make him the
subject of a lecture at Oxford. It is a mistake to put him with papa
as the *Spectator* does: papa's greatness consists in his bringing such
a torrent of freshness into English religion by placing history and
politics in connexion with it; Robertson's is a mere religious biography, but as a religious biography it is deeply interesting. And as
the English do not really like being forced to widen their view,
and to place history, politics, and other things in connexion with
religion, I daresay Robertson's life will be all the more popular for
its being so eminently and intensely a religious biography. The bits
about papa are an account of his first lecture at Oxford, and an
occasional mention here and there: Robertson had imbibed so much
of him that there must be more about him somewhere in what he
has left, one imagines, and one wants to know how and when the
influence came."

165:7–9. Proverbs 29:18; Psalms 112:1 (reading "the Lord" for
"the Eternal").

165:16, 21. Frederick the Great, quoted by Sainte-Beuve, *Causeries du lundi*, 3rd ed., VII, 459, and jotted down by Arnold in his
pocket diary for January 20, 1867.—*Note-Books*, ed. Lowry, p. 48
(Coulling).

165:16–20. Romans 12:9; Psalms 1:2 (Prayer-Book version); I
Corinthians 15:31; Revelation 7:9.

166:13. Romans 3:31.

166:21–22. Zechariah 9:13.

166:31–32. Proverbs 16:22.

166:33–34. For example, Luke 2:32; John 8:32.

166:35–38. Aristotle *Nicomachean Ethics* II.iv.3. The *Ethics* were on Arnold's reading lists for 1867 and 1868; see *Note-Books*, ed. Lowry, pp. 581, 583.

167:1–2. James 1:22.

167:2–5. Epictetus *Encheiridion* 35, 52.

167:5–7. Plato *Phaedo* 64A.

167:9–11. See I Kings 3:11–14 and Proverbs 3:13, 17.

167:11–15. Philippians 4:7; John 8:32; Galatians 5:24; Romans 3:31.

167:16–18. *Nicomachean Ethics* X.viii.

167:23. The idea can be traced in *Phaedo* 82D–83E and *Republic*, end of Book V.

167:38–168:4. Xenophon *Memorabilia* IV.viii.6.

168:6–11. "The Divine Plato [not Socrates] is . . . undoubtedly a rare and opulent human genius, and most lofty Athenian Gentleman; but dreadfully *'at his ease* in Zion,' which is reckoned a fault in some epochs!"—Carlyle to John Llewelyn Davies, April 27, 1852, acknowledging his translation of Plato's *Republic;* C. L. Davies, ed., *From a Victorian Post-Bag* (London, 1926), p. 10. Professor Kathleen Tillotson, whose sharp eye discovered this passage, points out that, though the letter had not been published when Arnold wrote, Arnold was himself then a correspondent of Davies and Davies was a dinner guest of the Arnolds on March 30, 1867.—"Arnold and Carlyle," *Notes and Queries* CC, 126 (March, 1955). "Woe to them that are at ease in Zion."—Amos 6:1.

168:28. Edward Bouverie Pusey (1800–1882), regius professor of Hebrew at Oxford, was a supporter of the Oxford movement but did not, like his friend Newman, go over to the Roman Catholic Church. He remained the leader of the high-church party of Anglicans, an aggressive and vigorous assailant of all moves to reduce the authority or tamper with the orthodoxy of that church.

169:6–7. Romans 8:26, 7:24.

169:20–22. Zechariah 8:23.

169:33.   "Thy Saviour sentenc'd joy,
        And in the flesh condemn'd it as unfit."
            —"The Size," lines 25–26.

Herbert's poems were on Arnold's reading list for 1867.—*Note-Books*, ed. Lowry, p. 581.

169.34. Lucretius invoked *Alma Venus* to inspire his book: *De rerum natura* I.2.

169:37–170:1. Ephesians 5:6.

170:4. Romans 6:3.

170:24. Romans 3:2.

172:6. Since the present edition does not note variant spellings, it might be pointed out that in all Arnold's works before this date (June, 1868) he spelled the word "Renaissance," and he retained that spelling in the 1869 edition of *Essays in Criticism*, but that in the 1875 edition he altered it to "Renascence" and retained that form thereafter. The single occurrence of the word in *On the Study of Celtic Literature* remained "Renaissance" in the American edition of 1883 (printed in Britain).

172:27–28. I.e., dialectic; see *Republic* VII. 532.

173:4. Numbers 22:28–30.

173:11. I Timothy 1:7.

173:29. The "science," that is, of ethnology. See F. E. Faverty, *Matthew Arnold the Ethnologist* (Evanston, Illinois: Northwestern University Press, 1951) for a full discussion of Arnold's use of this learning.

176. Chapter V, Title. "But one thing is needful."—Luke 10:42 (Vulgate version). "I think with great pleasure of the Nonconformists reading in this [next] month's Cornhill my discussion of their favourite text with them," Arnold wrote to the publisher George Smith on June 28, 1868.—Buckler, *Matthew Arnold's Books*, p. 89.

178:1–2. I Corinthians 1:21.

178:12–13. See note to p. 172:27.

178:35–179:1. Henry Sidgwick, "The Prophet of Culture," *Macmillan's Magazine* XVI, 274 (August, 1867). Sidgwick, a friend of Oscar Browning's, wrote of Arnold's "Culture and Its Enemies" in generally approving terms to his mother at the moment he was writing his rather flippant article.—Arthur and E. M. Sidgwick, *Henry Sidgwick, A Memoir* (London, 1906), p. 166. Professor Coulling takes the chapter on "Hebraism and Hellenism" to be Arnold's reply to Sidgwick's contention that his conception of religion was shallow, his view of its relationship to culture was distorted, and "that a man ought not to touch cursorily upon such a question, much less to dogmatize placidly upon it, without showing us that he has mastered the elements of the problem" (p. 275). Sidgwick was an Old Rugbeian.

179:9. See note to p. 111:16.

179:13–14. Presumably a deliberate allusion to the end of Keats's "Ode on a Grecian Urn."

181:35–36. Romans 11:34.

181:38–182:3. See p. 171.

183:23–24. The Collect for Easter Even: "Grant, O Lord, that as we are baptized into the death of thy blessed Son our Saviour Jesus Christ, so by continual mortifying our corrupt affections we may be buried with him; and that through the grave, and gate of death, we may pass to our joyful resurrection; for his merits, who died, and was buried, and rose again for us, thy Son Jesus Christ our Lord."

184:30–31. *Hamlet* I.ii.85.

184:36. Michael Faraday (1791–1867), the great English physicist of his day, was the son of a Yorkshire smith who, like Faraday's mother and most of his relatives, was a follower of John Glas and John Sandeman, secessionists from the Scottish Presbyterians. The sect, which spread to England and America, retained its rigid Calvinism, but was opposed to state establishment and central government of the church, and it preserved many customs which seemed authorized by the New Testament picture of the primitive Church. Faraday was long an elder and continued a member of the sect until his death, only ten months before Arnold published this essay.

185:26–27. *Symposium* 197B (Shelley's paraphrase of Plato's simple "the loving of beautiful things").

185:32–34. Romans 12:11; Ecclesiastes 9:10 (without the word "all").

186:14–17. On February 29, 1868, Frederick G. Smith, sixty-six-year-old secretary to the London Board of the Scottish Union Fire and Life Insurance Company, walked out of his office, bought a six-barreled revolver, returned to his office and shot himself in the head. Arnold quotes from the testimony at the coroner's inquest. —*Times*, March 4, p. 10, col. 3; see also March 3, p. 7, col. 2.

188:7–13. Romans 2:21–22 (for the first "sayest," read "preachest").

190:17–20. Gymnastics and music (including literature) were the two disciplines in the program of elementary education described by Socrates in Plato *Republic* II.376E–III.412B; see especially 403C–412B.

191:27–28. "Canst thou not minister to a mind diseased?"— *Macbeth* V.iii.40.

192:19–20. "Disbelief in the established ideas in which they all have been educated appears, in the case of some men, to lead to a species of delicate conservative scepticism, . . . [a] spirit of cultivated inaction."—"Culture and Action," *Saturday Review* XXIV, 592 (November 9, 1867).

193:20–21. See *The Popular Education of France, Prose Works*, ed. Super, II, 198.

194:1. "Political philosophers like Mr. Baxter and Mr. Charles Buxton" (first edition). William Edward Baxter (1825–90), Liberal M.P. from Scotland, 1855–85, addressing his constituents of the Montrose burghs on October 3, 1867, said: "The separation between [church and state] in every instance is a mere question of time. The example of the United States, the history of the religious endowments in our own colonies, the munificent liberality of the Free Church of Scotland, of the great dissenting bodies, and of the church of England itself in the towns and elsewhere, seems gradually converting our statesmen, and even our ecclesiastical dignitaries, to the opinion . . . that national establishments of religion have seen their day, and must now give place to free churches supported by voluntary contributions. Yet . . . the time has not yet arrived for bringing [the question] in all its bearings to a practical solution. Such, however, is not the case with the Irish Church, whose hour, I hope and believe, has come. . . . Disestablish it at once and appropriate its revenues to secular purposes. As for the proposal to endow the Roman catholic priesthood out of its revenues, let me tell Lord Russell that there are voluntaries enough in the House of Commons to defeat any such measure. . . . The statesman who does not see that the age of indiscriminate endowments is past had better let his mantle fall on younger men."—*Daily News*, October 5, 1867, p. 3, col. 5.

Charles Buxton (1823–71) was an independent liberal M.P. from 1857 until his death. Eight years after this passage was first published, Arnold, commending the candidacy of Sydney Buxton for the London School Board, wrote to F. W. Farrar: "[He is] a son of Charles Buxton . . . [and] would be a very good member; he has the philanthropy of his family, and a long and painful lameness has given him a serious reflective side to his character in advance of his years."

194:10. John 18:36. See note to line 35.

194:27–29. Gladstone concluded one phase of the debate on Irish Church Establishment on April 3, 1868, by saying: "The intention and desire of the [Conservative] Government . . . is to set up along-side of the Establishment other Established Churches—Presbyterians and Roman Catholics, and lesser bodies, all endowed out of the Consolidated Fund. . . . I ask, Is the country prepared for such a policy? . . . It was earnestly desired by the Liberal politicians of . . . a generation ago. . . . [But now it] cannot and will not be adopted by the people of this country. It is detested by Scotland; it is not desired by England; it is repelled and rejected by Ireland."

194:35–195:2. On April 22, 1868, John Bright presided at a meeting in support of Gladstone's resolutions looking toward disestablishment of the Irish Church. C. H. Spurgeon, in whose Metropolitan Tabernacle the more than 7000 persons assembled, was kept from the meeting by an attack of rheumatic gout in the leg, but addressed a letter to Bright in which he said: "Our Lord's Kingdom is not of this world. This truth is the corner-stone of our dissent. . . . The one point about which the Dissenters of England have any fear is . . . lest any share of the Church property should be given to the Papists. To a man we should deprecate this. Bad as the present evil is, we would sooner see it let alone than see Popery endowed with the national property. . . . We are not agitated by the dead horse of 'No Popery,' . . . but we are very determined that it shall never be said that, under guise of removing the grievances of Ireland, we made an exchange of endowed Churches, and put down the Anglican to set up the Roman image."—*Times*, April 23, p. 5, col. 2 (Gregor).

196:28. The Society for the Liberation of Religion from State Patronage and Control, founded in 1853 by Edward Miall in succession to his British Anti-State Church Association (founded 1844).

197:6–7. In "The Function of Criticism at the Present Time," *Prose Works*, ed. Super, III, 278–80.

197:19–29. Joseph Joubert, *Pensées*, ed. P. de Raynal (7th ed.; Paris, 1877), II, 29, 28, 24 (i, 107, 102, 76).

198:2–3. Bright, speaking on behalf of the disestablishment of the Irish Church in Spurgeon's Metropolitan Tabernacle, said: "Why, if we want a proof of what [voluntaryism] can do and a monument of what it has done, let us look around us. (Loud cheers.) I would not undertake to say that the voluntary efforts of the whole of the Protestant Episcopal congregations in Ireland have done so much for Protestantism, for a generation past, as has been done by that grand congregation which assembles from week to week in this building. (Renewed cheers.)"—*Times*, April 23, 1868, p. 5, col. 1.

200:4–6. Arnold had a "really effeminate horror of simple, practical, common-sense reforms, aiming at the removal of some particular abuse, and rigidly restricted to that object," said the *Illustrated London News* of the first essay on "Anarchy and Authority."—LII, 10 (January 4, 1868) (SenGupta, Coulling).

200:8–11. Bright spoke at the debate on the second reading of the Real Estate Intestacy Bill on June 6, 1866 (see p. 45:14–15).

202:23. See note to p. 200:4.

202:38–203:1. *Maxims* (1898), p. 131.

203:32–33. Proverbs 26:8 (reading "that bindeth" for "who putteth").

203:38–204:1, 5. See pp. 185:26–27 and 147:13–16.

205:15–16. See p. 151:31.

205:25–27. Thomas Chambers, M.P. for Marylebone, on May 2, 1866, moved the second reading of his bill to permit a man to marry his deceased wife's sister. "All [the supporters of the bill] desired was that the law be put in such a state that a man's freedom of action should not be limited according to other men's consciences." No speaker is recorded as having said that "Liberty is the law of human life." The bill was defeated. See pp. 45:19–20; 313–18; 319:24–27.

206:11. J. W. Colenso, Bishop of Natal, was much applauded by the liberals for his demonstrations of arithmetical inconsistencies in the Pentateuch, but was ridiculed by Arnold for his naïveté in "The Bishop and the Philosopher," *Prose Works*, ed. Super, III, 40–55.

206:14–24. Dixon, *New America*, pp. 154–55, 179, 184, 213 (of the Mormons); 387 (of John Humphrey Noyes at the Oneida Community).

206:32–33. The final chapter of Dixon's *Spiritual Wives* (1868) is called "The Gothic Revival." "All the Teutonic seers and scribes have had more or less of this mystic sense of a higher sexual affinity than that of ordinary wedlock.... In all our Gothic capitals from Stockholm to London, from Berlin to New York—we see a rapid slackening and unwinding of the old-fashioned nuptial ties.... Perhaps we have hardly come as yet, to see how much these strange beginnings of a new life are due to a sudden quickening of the Gothic blood.... Never, perhaps, since our fathers came out of their pine forests, and threw themselves into the front of history, has the Gothic family shown more stress and storm of noble passion than in this present day." The *Pall Mall Gazette* on January 30, pp.

410–11, reviewed the book most severely and suggested that on the basis of style "Mr. Dixon would have made the most of himself as the 'special correspondent' of a daily newspaper." A few years later when a writer in the *Pall Mall Gazette* said that Dixon was "best known as a writer of indecent literature," Dixon sued and on November 29, 1872, won damages to the amount of a farthing.— George Smith, "Lawful Pleasures," *Cornhill Magazine* X n.s., 194–95 (February, 1901).

206:33–37. A leading article calls the style of Dixon's *Spiritual Wives* "brilliant" and speaks of "the artistic arrangement of his facts and . . . the lively and sparkling language of which he is an acknowledged master." "He shows us the nature and extent of what may be called the sexual insurrection in the three chief Anglo-Teutonic countries—Germany, England, and America."—*Daily Telegraph*, January 30, 1868, p. 7, col. 2. But Arnold had been reading the lavish advertisements for the book, which quoted the panegyrics of the press, and in one of them, immediately below a quotation from the *Daily Telegraph*, there appeared this sentence from the *London Review:* "A lithe and sinewy style, and a picturesque knowledge of the most attractive literary forms, enable Mr. Dixon to make his subject at once interesting and instructive."

207:12–13. Carlyle, drawing from Goethe's *Wilhelm Meister*, made this proposition the thesis of "The Everlasting Yea" in *Sartor Resartus*. Both he and Arnold doubtless also remembered Faust's "Entbehren sollst du! sollst entbehren" (Part I, "Studirzimmer ii").

207:13–14. "O God, . . . whose service is perfect freedom."— Second Collect, for Peace, in the Order for Morning Prayer, *Book of Common Prayer*.

208:13–17. *Maxims* (1898), p. 19.

208:34–35. See I Kings 11:3.

209:7–17. For example, in the speech of Bright's that Arnold quotes on p. 241: "In all public discussions in which I have been engaged during the last 25 years I have always argued that the ignorance of the people was the most deplorable feature in our national character. I argued that if food could be cheaper, and trade more free, and industry more regular, and wages higher, the result would be to raise the mental condition of our population. I believe it has been raised, and is being raised. . . . [I must] ask those who think I am slow and conservative (laughter) to make such allowances for me as they can. I am sure, whatever is offered to the public and to Parliament that appears to me to be likely in the smallest degree to add to the intellectual and moral elevation of our population, I shall never be found unwilling to give it my cordial and hearty support."—*Times*, February 6, 1868, p. 10, col. 3.

211:8. This proverbial expression was defined as early as 1670 as "To spend more than one's allowance or income."—*Oxford Dictionary of English Proverbs*.

211:18–25. Leading article, *Times*, July 7, 1868, p. 9, cols. 4–5, the phrases very much rearranged but the sense fairly represented (Gregor).

212:25–26. Frédéric Bastiat (1801–50) was a French economist and propagandist for free trade whose widest influence lay in his distinction between usefulness and value.

213:13. From a note on "Pauperism," *Times*, July 10, 1868, p. 10, col. 5. The figure was for January 1, 1868 (Gregor).

213:33–214:5. On December 11, 1867, p. 8, cols. 5–6, the *Times* forecast earlier and heavier appeals than usual from the East End of London, and suggested that charitable response to these appeals was in fact not a benefit but an evil, for it encouraged people to remain where the market for labor was poor. "With more energy and versatility, numbers of those for whom help will be solicited might now be employed at good wages far from the East End of London." Essentially, the distress was caused by the shift in demand from wooden ships to metal ships and the less expensive construction of the latter in the northern English and Scottish shipyards. The unions in London refused to accept any reduction in wages and the workers remained idle. The disaster struck; in January numerous emergency committees sprang up to distribute aid to the poor in Poplar and Bethnal Green and gave rise to such meetings as that presided over by the bishop of London on January 29, 1868, to coordinate the effort. Again the *Times* deplored the reluctance of the shipwrights to move or to accept competitive wages and held that the universal concern for the miseries of the unemployed led only to harmful overlapping of charities and misplaced generosity. But the precise expressions Arnold quotes do not appear in these articles.

214:19–32, 215:6. Robert Buchanan, *David Gray, and Other Essays, Chiefly on Poetry* (London, 1868), pp. 198–99, ii. The prose passage is from an essay on "The Student and His Vocation"—a passage really directed against Arnold—; the line of verse comes, not "presently after" the prose, but in a passage on poetic aspiration used as epigraph to the book. In yet another essay, "On My Own Tentatives," Buchanan discussed the relation of contemporary poets to modern life: "Mr. Arnold no sooner touches the solid ground of contemporary thought, than all his grace forsakes him, and his utterance becomes the merest prose," inferior far to Mrs. Browning, who "alone, of all the recent poets, reached the deep significance of her century" (pp. 296–97). When the reviewer in the *Spectator* XLI, 165 (February 8, 1868) disagreed with this evaluation of Arnold, Buchanan attacked Arnold's poetry and tone at some length in the two succeeding issues of that journal (February 15, 22).

In early September, 1866, while Arnold was guest of the Grant Duffs in Scotland, his hostess read him some of Buchanan's poetry. He wrote to Buchanan—a letter of advice that Professor Coulling is certainly right in saying is the one Buchanan quotes in *David Gray*, p. 291—and had "a very good letter" in reply, as he told Grant Duff on October 13. But almost at the moment of the visit Buchanan published in the *Spectator* XXXIX, 1028 (September 15, 1866) over the signature of "Caliban" a satiric poem called "The Session of the Poets," with a humorous characterization of Arnold among others. When *David Gray* was savagely reviewed in the *Pall Mall Gazette* (February 21, 1868, pp. 11–12), Arnold told his mother that the "onslaught" was "very well as showing that there are people ready to take up one's defence without one's having to do it oneself; still, I had rather it was not done, as these bitter answers increase and perpetuate hatreds which I detest. Buchanan probably credits me with some of the severe reviews which have appeared of his verses, as doctrines of mine appear up and down in them. I am very sorry for this, and wish it could be known I never write anonymous criticisms." (The last statement requires a certain amount of modification.) "You see how Mr. Robert Buchanan dislikes me," he wrote to his mother again on March 2, 1868, "and I am told he has a long article in the strain of what he has already vented, to appear as soon as he can find an editor to take it. I hear also, though, that he is going off his centre, poor fellow: about which I must try and learn the truth."

That Arnold was trying in his reference to Buchanan to turn away wrath is clear enough. The purpose of his whole discussion of the poor of East London, however, is to reply to the statement of the *Spectator* XLI, 170 (February 8, 1868) that he had "an intellectual scorn for unintellectual persons," a statement Buchanan seized upon in his reply to the criticisms of himself; he focussed his attack on Arnold's lack of charity. "The *Spectator* does me a very bad service by talking of my contempt for un-intellectual people," Arnold wrote to his mother on February 22; "it is not at all true, and it sets people against one. You will laugh, but fiery hatred and malice are what I detest, and would always allay or avoid, if I could."

Buchanan achieved his greatest notoriety for his treatment of Rossetti, Swinburne, and their group as "The Fleshly School of Poetry," *Contemporary Review* XVIII, 334–50 (October, 1871)— an essay in which the poets of the day were cast in parts for *Hamlet*, with Arnold as Horatio to Tennyson's prince.

215:31–32. I Corinthians 12:12–27.

215:35. Wisdom 6:26.

215:37–216:3. *Maxims* (1898), pp. 13, 94; cited in Arnold, *Note-Books*, ed. Lowry, pp. 64, 517 (diary for October 12, 1867, and a "General" notebook).

216:4–7. *De Imitatione Christi* iii. 18.

216:33. See note to p. 341:17.

217:3, 5–6, 8. Genesis 1:28, 8:17 and *passim*; Psalms 127:3–5; Deuteronomy 15:11.

217:19–28. Mr. Gregor suggests that Arnold alludes to the Rev. William Tyler (1812–90), pastor of the Congregational Church in Hanbury Street, Spitalfields, to whom Arnold also referred in the sonnet "East London," first published in 1867. See C. B. Tinker and H. F. Lowry, *The Poetry of Matthew Arnold. A Commentary* (London, 1940), pp. 141–42.

220:18. See p. 192:19–20.

224:38. See p. 178:38.

225:17–24. *Nicomachean Ethics* X.ix.3–5.

226:11–12. See p. 135:37.

227:7–9. "The Prophet of Culture," *Macmillan's Magazine* XVI, 280 (August, 1867).

227:14–15. "Handeln ist leicht, Denken schwer; nach dem Gedanken handeln unbequem."—*Wilhelm Meister's Lehrjahre*, Book VII, Chapter ix, "Lehrbrief." Arnold used the same quotation in "The Function of Criticism at the Present Time," *Prose Works*, ed. Super, III, 276.

228:10. Bradlaugh did, Odger did not, achieve election to Parliament.

228:29–35. *Symposium* 215–16.

229:11. Disraeli, speaking at Edinburgh on October 29, 1867, said: "I had to prepare the mind of the country and to educate— if it be not arrogant to use such a phrase—to educate our party ...

on this question of Reform."—*Times*, October 30, p. 5, col. 3 (Gregor).

231:8-9. T. H. Huxley. On February 19, 1869, Arnold was Huxley's guest at the annual dinner of the Geological Society. In one of his presidential speeches, "Huxley brought in my *Culture and Anarchy*, and my having made game of him in the Preface," Arnold told his mother the next day (Coulling). This interchange gives point to a note Huxley sent to Arnold on July 8, 1869, after dining at Arnold's home in Harrow: "My dear Arnold,—Look at Bishop Wilson on the sin of covetousness and then inspect your umbrella stand. You will there see a beautiful brown smooth-handled umbrella which is *not* your property. Think of what the excellent prelate would have advised and bring it with you next time you come to the Club. The porter will take care of it for me.—Ever yours faithfully, T. H. Huxley."—Leonard Huxley, *Life and Letters of Thomas Henry Huxley* (New York, 1900), I, 335.

231:11-14. On November 19, 1868, the Court of Common Pleas determined (in "Baxter *v.* Langley") that the "Sunday evenings for the people," conducted in St. Martin's Hall, Longacre, by an association that called themselves "Recreative Religionists," did not constitute a violation of an eighteenth-century statute designed to prevent public entertainments or amusements, or public debates, on the Lord's Day. The meetings consisted of discourses on social subjects or on science, with a view to instructing the audience and making science the handmaid of religion; sacred music was performed by professional artists, but there was no public worship of the deity.—*Times*, November 20, p. 11, col. 3 (Gregor).

The Alhambra, a huge structure of pseudo-oriental design with central dome and minarets, was erected on the east side of Leicester Square in 1851-53 as the "Panopticon of Science and Art," a rival to Professor Pepper's Polytechnic Institution. It was sold in May, 1857, was renamed the Alhambra, and thereafter housed circuses, musical performances, etc. In the latter part of 1868, it was advertising 400 performers, a band of sixty, acrobats, pantomimists, and ballet stars in the "largest and most magnificent theatre in the world," "open nightly all the year round."

231:22-29. The British Museum has a copy of an edition of 1832 published by the Society for Promoting Christian Knowledge, and one of 1870 published by Parker in Oxford. Mr. Gregor was unable to learn from the S.P.C.K. of a new printing after the first publication of *Culture and Anarchy*, but he was informed that the book was still in print, according to their records, as late as 1876. Professor Dover Wilson points out that an article on Keble's *Life of Wilson* in the *Quarterly Review* for July, 1866, aroused Arnold's interest in Bishop Wilson. He discovered a copy of what he called Wilson's *Manual* (presumably the *Maxims*) in his father's study the following autumn, and told his mother on November 3: "The book..., which I have now nearly got through reading, re-reading, and re-rereading, is delightful to me and just the sort of book I like. So its peaceful slumbers in the study have not been disturbed for nothing." In 1867-68 he jotted seventy-four quotations from the *Sacra Privata* and the *Maxims* in his pocket diary.

232:8. *Sacra Privata. The Private Meditations and Prayers of... Thomas Wilson, D.D., Lord Bishop of Sodor and Man* were "accommodated to general use" in an edition distributed by the Society for Promoting Christian Knowledge in 1792.

232:22-23. *Pensées*, II, 351 (xxiv, § ii, 6); see Arnold, *Prose Works*, ed. Super, III, 203.

232:29-31. In describing the English character with reference to the treatment of Joan of Arc, Michelet says: "Nulle nation n'est plus loin de la grâce. C'est le seul peuple qui n'ait pu revendiquer l'*Imitation* de Jésus; un Français pouvait écrire ce livre, un Allemand, un Italien, jamais un Anglais."—*Histoire de France* (Paris, 1893?), V, 140 (Book X, chapter iv, three-quarters through).

232:37-233:4. This is more nearly what Arnold said of St. Francis' *Hymn* in "Pagan and Mediaeval Religious Sentiment" than of the *Imitation* in "Marcus Aurelius."—*Prose Works*, ed. Super, III, 226, 133.

234:9-27. Arnold alludes to his essay on "The Literary Influence of Academies," *Prose Works*, ed. Super, III, 232-57. He makes the same protest that he has been misread in "My Countrymen," p. 6.

234:20. The expression comes from II Chronicles 32:8.

234:32-34. Philip, fifth Earl Stanhope (1805-75) sponsored the Copyright Act of 1842 and the act that established the National Portrait Gallery in 1856; he was one of the founders of the Historical Manuscripts Commission in 1869 and was President of the Royal Literary Fund (see p. 351) from 1863 to his death.

Henry Hart Milman (1791-1868) was dean of St. Paul's from 1849 until his death. His name did not appear in Arnold's Preface until the edition of 1875.

Samuel Wilberforce (1805-73) was bishop of Oxford from 1845 to 1869, of Winchester from 1869 until his death.

Arthur Penrhyn Stanley (1815–81) was dean of Westminster from 1864 until his death. He was a close friend of the Arnold family and biographer of Dr. Thomas Arnold.

James Anthony Froude (1818–94) edited *Fraser's Magazine* when some of Arnold's early essays were published in it, was a member of the Athenaeum Club, and was author of a long *History of England from the Fall of Wolsey to the Defeat of the Spanish Armada* (1856–70).

Henry Reeve (1813–95) guided the foreign policy of the *Times* from 1840 to 1855 and was editor of the *Edinburgh Review* from July, 1855, until his death.

234:37. See p. 316:21.

235:18–19. The Liberals were restored to power in December, 1868, on the issue of disestablishing the Anglican church in Ireland, and proceeded forthwith to bring in a disestablishment measure.

236:7–8. See p. 135:24–25.

236:36–38. The first edition gives as examples of the "philosophical politicians" W. E. Baxter and Charles Buxton (see note to p. 194:1), of the "philosophical divines" Henry Alford (1810–71), dean of Canterbury, whose article on "The Church of the Future," *Contemporary Review* IX, 161–78 (October, 1868), takes the line Arnold indicates.

237:20. White, a friend of Dean Stanley's, was minister of St. Paul's Chapel, Hawley Road. Arnold forwarded to his mother a letter from White about *Culture and Anarchy* (February 27, 1869) but the pamphlet Arnold quotes has not been identified.

237:32. Isaac Watts (1674–1748) is perhaps the best known of English hymn writers, author of "When I survey the wondrous Cross," "Jesus shall reign where'er the sun," and "O' God, Our Help in Ages Past."

237:34. Richard Hooker (1554–1600), Isaac Barrow (1630–77), and Joseph Butler, bishop of Durham (1692–1752) were among the most important of Anglican preachers and theologians.

Richard Baxter (1615–91) was ordained in the Church of England but, holding strong Presbyterian convictions, withdrew from it on the passing of the Act of Uniformity in 1662. John Wesley (1703–91), founder of Methodism, never gave up his Anglican orders.

239:19–20. Goethe, advising Eckermann on September 18, 1823, about the writing of poetry, said: "Besonders warne ich vor *eigenen* grossen Erfindungen."—J. P. Eckermann, *Gespräche mit Goethe.*

240:14–16. See p. 35:8.

240:30–32. August 12, 1868, p. 6, col. 6.

241:2–6, 12–17. John Bright at a breakfast in Birmingham on February 5, 1868, for certain delegates from the Society of Arts to the Paris Exhibition, reported in the *Times*, February 6, p. 10, col. 2. In Thorold Rogers' edition of Bright's *Public Addresses* (London, 1879), p. 62, the speech credits America with "more valuable inventions" rather than "more valuable information"—a more likely reading, in the context, than the *Times* version Arnold necessarily used. See M. M. Bevington, "Matthew Arnold and John Bright," *PMLA* LXX, 543–48 (June, 1955).

241:18–24. *Questions contemporaines* (2nd ed.; Paris, 1868), p. vii (Preface).

241:29–32. On November 9, 1868; reported in the *Times*, November 11, p. 12, col. 1. Arnold had been reading the reports of a good many of Bright's speeches in the late autumn of 1868 and alludes specifically also to one at Edinburgh on November 5, reported in the *Times* next day, p. 5, col. 1: "I once advised the Financial Reform Association of Liverpool, who are against all indirect taxation, to hoist a flag with the motto, 'A free breakfast-table'— that, as the bread was no longer taxed, some effort should be made to untax the tea, the coffee, and the sugar."

243:31. Edward Payson Hammond (1831–1910), American Presbyterian evangelist, in November, 1868, conducted a series of revival meetings for children in Spurgeon's tabernacle that stirred up a good deal of opposition on grounds of taste (Gregor).

244:11–12. "Auferre trucidare rapere falsis nominibus imperium, atque ubi solitudinem faciunt pacem appellant."—Tacitus *Agricola* xxx.

244:35. For Arnold's opinion of Henry Ward Beecher, the American preacher, see *A French Eton, Prose Works,* ed. Super, II, 319. John Humphrey Noyes (1811–86) was founder of the Oneida Community, promulgator of a doctrine of free love, and one of the heroes of Hepworth Dixon's *Spiritual Wives* (see p. 206).

244:37. Cornell University was founded by act of legislature signed by the governor of New York on April 27, 1865: "The leading object ... shall be to teach such branches of learning as are related to agriculture and the mechanic arts, including military tactics, in order to promote the liberal and practical education of the industrial classes in the several pursuits and professions of life. But such other branches of science and knowledge may be embraced in the plan of instruction and investigation pertaining to the university as the trustees may deem useful and proper."—Morris Bishop, *A History of Cornell* (Ithaca, N.Y., 1962), p. 68. The university opened its doors in October, 1868.

245:32–246:3. Stanley, a pupil of Dr. Arnold's at Rugby, became Dean of Westminster in January, 1864. "To obtain recognition for the comprehensiveness which was, in his opinion, secured to the church by its union with the state, and, within the limits of the law, to widen its borders so that it might more worthily fulfil its mission as a national church, were the objects to which he devoted himself.... The sacrifices which he was prepared to make for the attainment of his ideal repelled numbers of the best men in his own church, whether their views were high or low.... He opposed every effort to loosen the tie between church and state, to resist or evade the existing law, or to contract the freedom which the widest interpretation of the formularies of the church would permit."— R. E. Prothero in *D.N.B.* In 1870 Stanley collected his *Essays, Chiefly on Questions of Church and State, from 1850 to 1870.*

246:23–25. Richard Hooker, *Works ... with an Account of His Life and Death by Isaac Walton,* ed. John Keble (3rd ed.; Oxford, 1845), II, 3.

247:4–30. *Ibid.,* I, 51–52, 27–29 (the latter passage not Walton's, but an addition by John Strype in 1705).

247:34. Thomas Binney (1798–1874) was by the date of Arnold's Preface the most widely respected of Congregationalist ministers, with a reputation that extended to America and the colonies. He was twice chairman of the Congregational Union of England and Wales.—*D.N.B.*

248:14–27. Henry St. John, Lord Bolingbroke, *Works* (Philadelphia, 1841), I, 400 ("Remarks on the History of England," Letter XVIII).

248:29–32. Edward, Earl of Clarendon, *History of the Rebellion* (Oxford, 1849), I, 125 (Book i, ¶186). Clarendon says not that Andrewes would have reconciled the separatists, but that "the infection [of Geneva] would easily have been kept out [of the church], which could not afterwards be so easily expelled."

249:10–16. Hooker, *Works,* ed. Keble, I, 36.

250:38. Constantine by his Edict of Milan in 313 granted toleration to the Christians and by his convocation of the Council of Nicaea in 325 gave the Church a new unity and force within the

Roman state. "Arthur Stanley moved his chair round to me after dinner [last night at the Geological Society], and told me of his delight with my Preface, and how entirely the ideas of it—particularly those of a passage about Constantine—were exactly what papa would have approved," Arnold wrote to his mother on February 20, 1869.

251:37–38. *On the Study of Celtic Literature, Prose Works,* ed. Super, III, 364.

252:4–7. "Auslegung des eilften Capitels Daniels," commentary on verse 38.

253:2. Hosea 8:9.

254:31. The first Parliament elected under the Reform Law of 1867 was that returned in the autumn of 1868 on the specific issue of Irish Church disestablishment. Gladstone's new Liberals had a great majority.

254:37. Joel 3:1–14.

255:6. Ecclesiasticus 37:25.

255:28–29. Hebrews 11:1.

255:35–36. John 13:17.

256:1–3. "Ihm [Goethe] ist die *Bibel* ein ewig wirksames Buch, nicht nur ein Volksbuch, sondern das Buch der Völker."—F. W. Riemer, *Mittheilungen über Goethe* (Berlin, 1841), I, 123, with a reference to Goethe, *Nachgelassene Werke* (Stuttgart, 1833), XIII, 79.

256:6–8. Baruch 4:37.

[NOTES TO CANCELLED PASSAGES]

504:1–13, 31–35. See p. 404. In his mock dialogue with Arminius, Frederic Harrison posing as Culture's convert found himself somewhat embarrassed when Arminius in a conciliatory mood sought some ground for praising Culture's great apostle. " 'I hear he has done a knight's service in consigning to public odium a sect of bloodthirsty fanatics who were striving to undermine society in your country, and has crushed the sour French pedant by whose writings their crimes were inspired.' I felt that this question was a little perplexing, for it partly concerned some youthful indiscretion of my own, and indeed was a phase of Culture which I was hardly prepared to defend.

" 'A French sciolist was it not,' he asked, 'who invented some random formulae from the prejudices current in his clique?' "

" 'I suppose they said the same of Bacon and Leibnitz,' I replied, wishing to escape the subject.

" 'A man, I think it was said, full of furious indignation with the past,' he went on.

" 'Well,' I answered, 'he is usually charged with preposterous veneration for it; but that, like everything else, is a matter of taste.'

" 'Who proposed a wholesale system of violent renovation, I believe?' he went on.

" 'No! pardon me,' said I: 'as I read him, it was just the reverse.'

" 'Who hated all thorough cultivation of the human faculties?' he said.

" 'I had strangely supposed him its principal apostle,' I rejoined.

" 'With no spark of any moral or social passion?' he asked.

" 'Well,' I replied; 'I used to think that he had something of the sort.'

" 'And your Jacobins,' said he; 'have the police secured them?'

" 'Oh, it is not so bad as that yet,' I answered.

" 'Well, but I thought,' he rejoined, 'that one of them had been caught oiling a guillotine in some highly suspicious costume?' [see p. 76]

" 'Oh!' I said, with a smile, 'that was only, I believe, what is called a sweet and light practical joke. The truth is, to be frank, my friend,' for I felt the necessity of saying something, 'I must admit that Culture made some trifling blunder in the matter. Jacobinism, as you say, denounces the past, seeks violent revolutions, and disdains all complex cultivation. The school you speak of, on the contrary, love and take counsel of the past, discard all violent for moral agencies of progress, and preach universal and perfect education. You see that believing in infinite, though peaceful and gradual, progress, to be gained by spiritual methods alone, they exactly contrast with Jacobinism, which imposes its crude type by tyrannical force. They occupy, in a word, the opposite pole of modern politics, except as both dream of an infinite change.'

" 'Why,' cried Arminius, whom I had long seen swelling with a new storm, 'this was rank misrepresentation, then, on the part of Culture!'

" 'My friend, my friend,' I urged, pained at this indelicate plainness, 'inadequate illumination, partial observation, misapprehension, hastiness, or rather, say fleetness—anything you please but that; let us say airiness.'

" 'You mean that Culture had not adequately studied the great French thinker whom it travestied?' said Arminius.

" 'Perhaps it was so,' I replied; 'but reflect—the bee touches not the root of any tree. His to suck the floweret; ours to sip his honey.'

" 'And yet,' he mused, 'there seems very much in which the higher Culture may be said to coincide with this philosopher, just as you say it coincides with religion.'

" 'Oh!' said I figuratively, 'of the mighty river of Egypt whole tribes drink and are refreshed, not knowing whence those living waters come, and many cast their bread upon them, and find it after many days.' "—"Culture: a Dialogue," *Fortnightly Review* VIII, 612–13 (November, 1867).

504:19–28. Harrison, "Our Venetian Constitution," *Fortnightly Review* VII, 271, 270, 268, 277 (March, 1867).

505:1–4. Auguste Comte, *The Catechism of Positive Religion*, translated from the French by Richard Congreve (London, 1858), p. 305, at the conclusion of Comte's description of the hierarchy of his Religion of Humanity.

505:25–506:1. Comte, *Catechism*, p. 43 and Table D; Table A; pp. 300–305.

506:12–13. For Mount Gerezim, see Deuteronomy 27:12, Joshua 8:33; for Mount Moriah, see II Chronicles 3:1.

506:14. Auguste Comte lived at No. 10 Rue Monsieur-le-Prince (near the Odéon and the School of Medicine) from 1841 to his death in 1857. His will provided that his apartment there should be preserved just as it was, as the first seat of the Religion of Humanity; it is still so preserved.

506:22. See p. 28:21–22.

506:23–24. See Arnold, "The Bishop and the Philosopher," "Dr. Stanley's Lectures on the Jewish Church," and "The Function of Criticism at the Present Time," *Prose Works*, ed. Super, III, 48, 74, 277.

507:34–35. The *Daily Telegraph* on October 17, 1867, p. 3, cols. 1–2, gave a long and pathetic account of Mrs. Lincoln's attempts to eke out her inadequate income of $1,700 a year by selling through a commission-broker in New York, W. H. Brady, some personal effects, including shawls, capes, and diamond rings; her wants, she said, were urgent. She registered in various hotels under assumed names while she carried on this transaction, but Brady turned over the whole of her correspondence, it appears, to the *New York*

World. Her letters were filled with reproaches against the Republican leaders, who owed everything to her husband (and in a few instances to her own good will), yet now declined to assist her.

508:16. Jacob Bright (1821–99), younger brother of John Bright, sat in Parliament for Manchester almost continuously from 1867 to 1895.

514:13–14. Ecclesiasticus 23:37.

514:26–27. Romans 1:18.

521:33. See Arnold, "The Function of Criticism at the Present Time," *Prose Works*, ed. Super, III, 279–80: "Like the British College of Health [in the New Road]; the grand name without the grand thing."

521:39. George Anthony Denison (1805–96), archdeacon of Taunton, was militant leader of the High Church party in most of its notorious causes in mid-century, such as the censure by the Convocation of Canterbury of Bishop Colenso and of *Essays and Reviews.* He was editor of the *Church and State Review* for its brief life, 1862–65. See Arnold, *Prose Works*, ed. Super, III, 479–80.

525:20. Parliament adjourned on July 31, 1868, with the understanding that there would be an election before it reconvened.

525:24. Sir Henry Ainslie Hoare, Bart., sat for the new constituency of Chelsea in the Parliament that met December 10, 1868.

526:2–11. "I shall like to know what you think of [the final 'Anarchy and Authority' paper]," Arnold wrote to his mother on July 25, 1868. "In the passage quoted from Papa, [Arthur Penrhyn] Stanley's impression is that Papa's words were 'Crucify the slaves' instead of 'Flog the rank & file'—but as the latter expression is the milder, and I have certainly got it in my memory as what he said, I have retained it. Do you remember which the words were, and in what letter they occur? Stanley remembers the whole passage perfectly, and the moment I began it to him he finished it, with the difference as to the words I have mentioned; but he cannot recollect to whom the letter (which he has himself read) containing them, was addressed. I send you a characteristic note addressed to me by Stanley, who was of course much pleased with my remarks on the Irish Church proceedings."

527:36–39. Samuel Morley and Edward Baines, both staunch voluntaryists in principle, were nevertheless compelled by events to recommend to the Congregational Union on October 11, 1867, that that body now accept government grants in aid of its schools. See Arnold, *Prose Works*, ed. Super, IV, 16, 354.

530:18. "There is a vicious article in the new *Quarterly* on my school book [*Schools and Universities on the Continent*] by one of the Eton undermasters, who, like Demetrius the silversmith, seems alarmed for the gains of his occupation," Arnold wrote to Lady de Rothschild on October 24, 1868. "I am in full work inspecting Schools, and have not even time to bless in prose my Scholastic enemies like the Eton master in the new number of the Quarterly," he told E. S. Dallas six days later as he begged off a request for some verses. The reviewer, Oscar Browning (1837–1923), was a popular assistant master at Eton and head of a boarding house for forty boys, with an income from his post of £3000 a year. Of his brother William, fifteen years his senior, who had been his own teacher, Browning himself later wrote: "Before he died he made for himself a distinguished name as a schoolmaster. I doubt whether any preparatory school [i.e., school that prepared boys for Eton and other secondary schools] in England of the same size has turned out so many distinguished scholars as the school which he conducted for so many years at Thorpe Mandeville."—Browning, *Memories of Sixty Years* (London, 1910), pp. 12–13. While the second edition of *Culture and Anarchy* was in the press, Oscar Browning was dismissed from his post at Eton under circumstances that aroused a great deal of sympathy for him.

531:9–12. Dr. William Smith (1813–93), editor of the *Quarterly Review* from 1867 to his death, was compiler of classical grammars and exercise books and school editions of classical authors; his large *Dictionary of Greek and Roman Antiquities* is still useful. He was educated for the most part privately. "[Smith] came up to me a day or two ago with his hand held out, saying he forgave me all I had said about him and the *Quarterly*—which, he added, was a great deal—for the sake of the truth and usefulness of what I had said about the Nonconformists. He said he was born a Nonconformist, was brought up with them, and had seen them all his life, so he was a good judge," Arnold wrote to his mother on February 20, 1869.

531:15–19. James Macpherson, "The War of Inis-thona" *Poems of Ossian*, ed. W. Sharp (Edinburgh, 1896), pp. 389–90. This is Arnold's summary of Browning's position, not a passage Browning has quoted.

534:1–10. William Rathbone Greg (1809–81), a mill owner who resided for some years at Ambleside near the Arnold home at Fox

How, sent Arnold a copy of his anonymous article on "The Bishop and the Philosopher" in the *Westminster Review*, American edition, LXXIX, 265–72 (April, 1863). The article, "Truth *versus* Edification," civil but still critical of Arnold's thesis, was reprinted in 1868 as part of Greg's *Literary and Social Judgments* and in 1869 as a separate pamphlet.

534:12. Arnold coins the term from the name of Edward Miall, leading spokesman of the Nonconformists and proprietor of their weekly newspaper, *The Nonconformist*.

534:24–26. Izaac Walton, "Life of Wotton," two-thirds through.

534:27. Thomas Jackson (1783–1873), Methodist minister, biographer of Charles Wesley and editor of John Wesley's works.

535:39. See note to p. 194:35.

537:26–27. Hebrews 12:14.

[A NEW HISTORY OF GREECE]

On October 3, 1868, Arnold wrote to his mother: "I have written for the Pall Mall a long notice of that history of Greece, translated by Adolphus Ward, I was reading at Fox How; the book deserved it well, though I was also glad to do the translator a good turn. Doing it has done me the service of fixing in my head the contents of the book and its answers to the main questions in early Greek history. In this, as so often, I have been reminded of Papa, and of the lively interest he took in these questions, and would have taken in such a book." In the same letter he told her, "More and more I begin to see my way to making a natural and useful book about Greek poetry, and I expect it will give me, if other things go well, a pleasant year." It was about ten months earlier that Macmillan had advanced him £150 for this book, which was presumably to have contained a large portion of his own translations from the Greek, as well as critical essays. Only a few weeks after *Culture and Anarchy* appeared as a book, he wrote (March 6, 1869): "I am glad to be now engaged in a line which takes me quite away from all the questions in which I have had so much controversy, and on which it would be easy to say too much and go on too long. Yet this Greek poetry book will in its way be the best of answers to those who say that I praise culture and tell them to get it, but do not tell them how it is to be got." It was to prepare the way for this book that he published his eleven-year-old inaugural lecture "On the Modern Element in Literature" in *Macmillan's Magazine* for

February, 1869 (a lecture printed in the first volume of the present
edition of Arnold's prose). Controversy, however, called him back
to the arena against the Nonconformists with "St. Paul and Protestantism," and despite diligent work on his Greek poetry book in
the early months of 1869 he gradually abandoned his plans for it
and in due course returned the publisher's advance with interest;
see W. E. Buckler, "Studies in Three Arnold Problems," *PMLA*
LXXIII, 264–68 (June, 1958). The articles on successive volumes of
Ward's translation of Curtius are the only survivors of this impulse
to return to a classical subject. The first was published in the *Pall
Mall Gazette* for October 12, 1868, and brought Arnold 5 gns.; the
second on April 28, 1871 (5 gns.); the third and fourth on June 4
and July 22, 1872 (6 gns. and 4 gns.), and the fifth on March 25,
1876 (5 gns.). The articles, which appeared anonymously, were first
identified as Arnold's by Fraser Neiman and were published in his
Essays, Letters, and Reviews by Matthew Arnold (Cambridge,
Massachusetts, 1960), pp. 124–52.

257:1. On February 15, 1824, Goethe remarked to Eckermann:
"Deutschland selbst steht in allen Fächern so hoch, dass wir kaum
alles übersehen können," and on April 3, 1829, he remarked that
French writers like Cousin, Villemain and Guizot had "eine
Gelehrsamkeit, wie man sie früher nur bei Deutschen fand."

257:27. Theodor Mommsen (1817–1903) published in 1854–56
his monumental *Roman History*, still a standard work, based on an
unparalleled knowledge of inscriptions and Roman law. Its hero
was Julius Caesar, with whose dictatorship the work came to an end.

Ernst Curtius (1814–96), an archeologist as well as historian,
wrote in an admirable style and with admirable good sense, but
without Mommsen's vast learning.

258:4–5. The parliamentary session ended July 31, 1868, with the
understanding that there would be a new election. Writs were
issued about November 11.

On August 20, 1868, the Irish Limited Mail from London through
Chester to Holyhead collided near Abergele with some goods
wagons that had run away from a shunting engine ahead of it; bar-
rels of petroleum in one of these were ignited and burned three
first-class carriages of the Mail. Thirty-three persons were killed,
and their remains so completely destroyed that identification of
most of them was impossible. The accident occupied the columns
of the *Times* for fifteen consecutive issues.

All Saints' Church, Lambeth, became the focus of the Ritualistic movement in the Church of England by a series of services beginning September 7, 1868, the eve of the nativity of the Blessed Virgin Mary. About the same time a Harvest Home service of the Ritualists at Haydock, Lancashire, attracted the ridicule of the *Times* leader-writer (September 12, p. 7, cols. 3–4). The readers of the *Times* kept up a lively correspondence on these matters. There was, in addition, a trial and conviction of the vicar of St. Alban's, Holborn, on charges of practicing rituals contrary to the statutes and the Book of Common Prayer. Other leading articles, sternly hostile to Ritualism, appeared in the *Times* of July 10 (p. 7, col. 4), July 16 (p. 9, col. 1), and July 21 (p. 9, col. 3).

258:6–8. Connop Thirlwall (1797–1875), after translating Niebuhr's *History of Rome*, embarked on a *History of Greece* (1835–47) that was almost immediately overshadowed in the public mind by the much larger *History of Greece* (1846–56) of his friend George Grote (1794–1871). Grote's was essentially a political history that reflected his enthusiasm for the forces of Greek democracy, and was handicapped (in comparison with Curtius') by his lack of familiarity with the country.

258:12. The Wesleyan Conference at Liverpool (July 30 to August 14, 1868) was the subject of daily reports in the *Times* and of leading articles on August 17 and 22 (on Pusey's correspondence with the Conference regarding the abolition of religious tests at the universities) and on August 18 (when the Conference was held up to the assemblies of the Church of England as a model of efficiency).

258:13. On August 20–21, 1868, Sarah Rachel Leverson (or Levison), who under the name of Madame Rachel advertised exotic and expensive treatments at her establishment in New Bond Street for "giving the appearance of youth and beauty to persons however far advanced in years," was tried for defrauding one of her clients of large sums of money under pretense of arranging a marriage between her and an allegedly love-stricken nobleman. The jury could not reach a verdict, but the *Times* leader-writer was of opinion that acquittal had been warranted by the evidence (August 22, p. 6, cols. 4–5). A second trial, September 21–25, brought conviction and sentence of five years penal servitude. The *Times* found the judge's summing-up astonishing (September 26, p. 6, cols. 4–5). Arnold complained to his mother about a week later that his son Budge had "no interest, really, in any literature except such literature as that of Madame Rachel's trial."

259:10–11. Jean Charles Léonard de Sismondi (1773–1842), best known for his *Histoire des républiques italiennes du moyen âge* (1807–17), embarked in 1818 on an *Histoire des Français* on a grand scale, and completed twenty-nine volumes of it before his death. Despite his fresh insight into economic matters, the latter work is not highly regarded.

259:34–38. Ernst Curtius' *Griechische Geschichte* was published in three volumes (Berlin, 1857–67), and in a revised edition, three volumes, 1868–74. The five volumes of Ward's translation appeared in 1868, 1869, 1870, 1872, and 1873. Adolphus William Ward (1837–1924) was the son of an English foreign service officer and his schooling began at Leipzig. His grandmother was Dr. Arnold's sister, and he was briefly examiner at the Education Office. The translation was his first work after appointment to the professorship of history at Owens College, Manchester. At the beginning of the present century he was one of the editors, first of the *Cambridge Modern History*, then of the *Cambridge History of English Literature*, an undertaking conceived by himself.

260:23–24. Henry Fynes Clinton, *Fasti Hellenici* (Oxford, 1824–34), 3 vols. The first volume (the third to be published, however) attempts a chronology of Greek history up to 559 B.C.

260:32–261:24. Curtius, *History*, I, 39–42 (with omissions).

261:34–262:22. *Ibid.*, I, 43–47 (with omissions).

262:31–32. *Ibid.*, I, 49.

262:38–263:12. *Ibid.*, I, 31–32 (with omissions).

263:15–17. *Ibid.*, I, 66.

263:23–25. *Ibid.*, I, 88.

263:28–34. *Ibid.*, I, 93–94.

264:4–22. *Ibid.*, I, 113, 117–18, 161–62 (with omissions and transposition).

265:22–23. "Die feindliche Seemacht war nichts weniger als vernichtet" is the reading of the German; in context, it means "was far from annihilated."

265:25–266:1. *History*, II, 118 ("die den Lydern befreundete Dynastie"), 312 ("Auch ist Herodot weder gegen die anerkennungswerthen Seiten der Feinde blind, noch gegen die Schwächen seiner Landsleute"), 531.

266:20–34. *Ibid.*, II, 170–71.

267:3–16. *Ibid.*, II, 253–54.

267:20–25. *Ibid.*, II, 255.

267:28–30. The London School Board, established under the Education Act of 1870, in the process of determining what permanent officers it would need to carry on its business, discussed the qualifications and remuneration of a secretary. Huxley moved a salary of £1000. B. Lucraft, a workingman member of the Board from Finsbury, said he "believed [they] would get just as good a man for £500 as for £1000.... He asked them to consider the ratepayers in the matter.... He was a ratepayer himself, and he admitted that he had something to do to make both ends meet."—*Times*, December 22, 1870, p. 10, cols. 4–5.

267:32–38. *History*, II, 445.

268:5–6. Hugh Grosvenor, Marquess and later Duke of Westminster, was one of the wealthiest men in England. He owned the whole of Belgravia, a fashionable section of London which his grandfather developed and in which Arnold had resided until recently. He and Arnold had been undergraduates together at Balliol.

268:10–20. *History*, II, 205.

270:20–22. *Ibid.*, II, 10.

271:19–21. *Ibid.*, II, 83.

271:28–30. *Rhetoric* 1390b. 30–31.

272:12–15. *History*, II, 502.

273:9–11. *Ibid.*, II, 315 (with transposition).

273:14–24. *Ibid.*, III, 535 (with omissions).

273:25. *Hamlet*, III.iv.53.

273:34–274:9. *History*, II, 263 (with omissions).

274:15. Arnold was fond of this term; see pp. 271:26, 281:13, 283:22, and *Prose Works*, ed. Super, III, 16:35.

274:20–29. *History*, II, 418.

274:37–275:6. *Ibid.*, II, 440 (with omissions).

275:13–26. *Ibid.*, II, 442, 444.

275:28–31. *Ibid.*, II, 447–48.

275:32–276:2. *Ibid.*, II, 443–48 (summary, not quotation).

276:4–19. *Ibid.*, II, 444.

276:20–25. *Ibid.*, II, 453, 455.

276:26. Frankenstein, in Mary Shelley's novel (1818) the name of the student who created the monster, as early as about 1840 was commonly used for the monster itself, or for any machinery which was uncontrollable by its creator.

276:29–33. *History*, II, 441.

277:4–8, 13–19. *Ibid.*, II, 459.

277:20–23, 30–36; 278:1–6. *Ibid.*, II, 442, 441.

278:14–21. *Ibid.*, III, 81.

278:34–279:28. *Ibid.*, III, 84–85.

279:31–280:4. *Ibid.*, III, 316 (with omission).

280:6. Georgius Gemistus Pletho (c. 1355–1450), Neoplatonic scholar at Constantinople and Mistra, is credited with the introduction of Plato to the Western world on the occasion of his visit to the Florence of Cosimo de' Medici in 1439.

280:24–30. *History*, III, 518–19.

281:2–4. At a meeting of the Manchester Athenaeum on December 27, 1850, Cobden said: "I take it that, as a rule, grown-up men, in these busy times, read very little else but newspapers; ... and I doubt if a man with limited time could read anything else that would be much more useful to him. I believe it has been said that one copy of the *Times* contains more useful information than the whole of the historical books of Thucydides—(laughter);—and I am very much inclined to think that to an Englishman or an American of the present day that is strictly true." Cobden's biographer commented that the statement was "a standing joke against him. ... Too much was made of [it] by journalists and collegians who knew little more about Thucydides than did Cobden himself, but who now wrote as if that rather troublesome author were the favourite companion of their leisure hours."—John Morley, *Life of Richard Cobden* (London, 1896), II, 428–29n.

281:4. Parliament's Whitsuntide recess was May 14–26, 1872.

281:22–27. *History*, III, 80 (with omission).

282:31. Perhaps the ἀνάρχετος βίος of *Eumenides* 526.

283:33–284:12. *History*, IV, 115–16.

284:15–24. *Ibid.*, IV, 285 (with omissions).

284:26–34. *Ibid.*, IV, 294–95.

284:37–285:3. *Ibid.*, IV, 374. Ward reads: "herself was not what she had been" and "lasting ardour for war."

285:8–10. *Ibid.*, IV, 415–16.

285:20–24. *Ibid.*, IV, 490.

286:1–3, 7–12. *Ibid.*, IV, 466, 467.

286:15–21. *Ibid.*, IV, 491, 492.

286:25–27. *Ibid.*, IV, 488.

286:34–38. *Ibid.*, IV, 455. Leuctra was the battle in which the Thebans under Epaminondas defeated the Spartans, 371 B.C.; Mantinea was the battle in which, though his forces were again victorious over Sparta, Epaminondas was fatally wounded, 362 B.C.

287:4–7. See note to p. 88:7.

287:24–35. *History*, IV, 90, 84, 91.

287:37–288:12. *Ibid.*, IV, 98, 97.

289:30–290:12. *Ibid.*, V, 21–22. Ward reads: "waters have contrived to stop up."

290:19–291:3. *Ibid.*, V, 58–59. Ward reads: "reputation of regal power" and "country, in a more limited."

291:6–13. *Ibid.*, V, 78. Ward reads: "that its efforts had no endurance."

291:14–21. *Ibid.*, V, 212. Ward reads: "allow its comfortable ease."

291:27–35. *Ibid.*, V, 139, 138. Ward reads: "of Attic democracy" and "germs of the pernicious contained."

292:11–20. This proposition Arnold was to develop at greater length in his essay on "Numbers" (1883).

292:32–293:4. *History*, V, 164.

293:7–10. *Ibid.*, V, 225.

293:13–24. *Ibid.*, V, 229, 230.

293:27–294:5. *Ibid.*, V, 231–32. Ward reads: "sentiments which dominated over the citizens" and "most thorough way possible."

[OBERMANN]

In 1869 Charles E. Appleton founded a new monthly critical journal, *The Academy*, with the aim of achieving the ideal Arnold had stated in "The Literary Influence of Academies" and "The Function of Criticism at the Present Time." Associated with him was Arnold's friend Mark Pattison, rector of Lincoln College, Oxford, and Arnold himself gave approval to the general plan of the new journal. The first pages of the first number (October 9, 1869) contained a signed article by Arnold on *Obermann*, a subject to which he had been giving attention lately with the publication of "Obermann Once More" in his *New Poems* (1867). His article, indeed, made use of the note on Senancour he had composed for the second edition of *New Poems* in 1868. The financial accounts in his diary-notebooks make no mention of payment for the article.

291:1–5. The catalogue of the Bibliothèque Nationale lists the first edition of 1804, a second edition with preface by Sainte-Beuve in 1833, and editions with preface by George Sand in 1840, 1844, 1847, 1852, and 1863. The catalogue of the British Museum lists an edition of 1865 with the same pagination as that of 1863.

295:15–296:8. Arnold here repeats the substance of a note he appended, first to "Obermann Once More" in the second edition of

New Poems (1868), then to "Stanzas in Memory of the Author of 'Obermann'" in his collected *Poems* of 1869 and thereafter.

296:3–4. Arnold owed his knowledge of the epitaph to a letter from Sainte-Beuve dated November 6, 1854.—Arnold Whitridge, ed., *Unpublished Letters of Matthew Arnold* (New Haven, 1923), p. 68 (misdated). The words come from Senancour's *Libres méditations d'un solitaire inconnu* (Paris, 1819), p. 410 (Soirée XXVIII).

296:9–10. "Tourmenté par le problème de la vie, il se demandait souvent: 'Bernard, qu'es-tu venu faire ici-bas?' (*Bernarde, ad quid venisti?*)."—Henri Martin, *Histoire de France* (4th ed.; Paris, 1855), III, 324. Arnold wrote the Latin words in his pocket diary for April 23, 1867.—*Note-Books*, ed. Lowry, p. 54.

297:10–17, 22–23. Senancour, *Oberman*, ed. A. Monglond (Paris, 1947), I, 217, 216, 219 (Letter 44).

297:30–298:10. *Ibid.*, I, 220–21 (Letter 44). Between "worship" and "The principle" Arnold omits: "Les grandes conceptions étaient avilies."

298:11–12. "Then Paul stood in the midst of Mars' hill, and said, Ye men of Athens, I perceive that in all things ye are too superstitious. For as I passed by, and beheld your devotions, I found an altar with this inscription, *To the Unknown God.*"—Acts 17:22–23.

298:14–35. *Oberman*, I, 221–22 (Letter 44).

298:36–37. The first Vatican Council, summoned by Pius IX, met from December 8, 1869, to July 18, 1870. It promulgated the infallibility of the Pope when he spoke *ex cathedrâ* on matters of doctrine concerning faith or morals.

299:1–10. *Oberman*, I, 220, 215 (Letter 44).

299:20–29, 34–38. *Ibid.*, I, 216, 211 (Letter 44).

300:1–4. *Ibid.*, I, 50 (Letter 7).

300:5–12. *Ibid.*, I, 230 (Letter 45).

300:13–14. *Hamlet* I. v. 189–90.

300:16–26. *Oberman*, I, 183 (Letter 41).

300:32–33. *Ibid.*, I, 100 (Letter 22).

300:34–301:5. *Ibid.*, I, 65 (Letter 11).

301:11–20. *Ibid.*, II, 25 (Letter 48).

301:27–302:40. *Ibid.*, I, 23–25 (Letter 4).

303:2–10. Sainte-Beuve wrote of Senancour's funeral: "Un seul ami, prévenu à temps, accompagna sa dépouille mortelle. Aucun journal n'entonna l'hymne funèbre, et je ne sais même s'il en est un seul qui daigna annoncer sa mort. Ceux qui ne se règlent dans leur jugements ni sur le renom, ni sur la fortune, et qui, après avoir suivi la foule, savent aussi s'en séparer, mettront tout bas en balance cette fin silencieuse et cette sépulture ignorée avec les pompes reten- tissantes du rocher de Saint-Malo; ils se demanderont si c'est là toute la justice. Mais ils ne s'en étonneront point; car, après tout, pour être regretté des hommes, il ne suffit ni de les avoir aimés ni de les avoir voulu éclairer, il faut les avoir éblouis, amusés, occupés long- temps, insultés quelquefois et fustigés ou flattés, et presque toujours égarés dans bien des voies."—*Chateaubriand et son groupe littéraire* (new ed.; Paris, 1889), I, 358.

[SAINTE-BEUVE]

"Sainte-Beuve is dead, and I am asked to write a few pages on him, which I do not like to refuse, but for which I do not feel inclined," Arnold told his mother on October 16, 1869, in a letter which en- closed his article on *Obermann* from *The Academy*. "But I have learnt a great deal from him, and the news of his death struck me as if it had been that of some one very near to me. When George Sand and Newman go, there will be no writers left living from whom I have received a strong influence: they will all have de- parted." Arnold's signed article on Sainte-Beuve appeared in the second number of *The Academy* on November 13, again on the front page. His financial accounts do not record payment for the article. It seems unlikely that he was asked to give his services with- out charge to the struggling young journal, but in any case the *Academy*'s normal rate of payment, one pound per page, was too low to attract Arnold, and though in 1873 he spoke of Appleton's terms as "handsome" in declining a proposal that he contribute again, he appeared only once in *The Academy* after the first two numbers.—Diderik Roll-Hansen, "Matthew Arnold and the *Acad- emy*," *PMLA* LXVIII, 384–96 (June, 1953). F. J. W. Harding, *Mat- thew Arnold the Critic and France* (Geneva: Droz, 1964) is the most thorough discussion of Arnold's writings upon French literature.

304:3–4. Sainte-Beuve died October 13, 1869.

304:19–22. The first edition of *Portraits contemporains*, 3 vols., was published in 1846; it contained essays dating from 1831 to 1846, and an appendix written as early as 1826. A second edition in three volumes appeared in 1854. The revised and enlarged edition ap- peared on July 17, 1869 (vols. 1–2) and in 1871 (vols. 3–5, post- humously).—J. Bonnerot, *Bibliographie de l'oeuvre de Sainte-Beuve* (Paris, 1952), III, part i.

304:25–305:8. *Portraits contemporains* (new ed.; Paris, 1881), I, 517.

305:20–21. These six, with Senancour, make up the first volume of the revised *Portraits contemporains*. "Title-page" is obviously a slip of the pen for "Table of Contents."

305:27. *Les Consolations* (1830) was a volume of verse and *Volupté* (1834) was a novel by Sainte-Beuve, both published anonymously.

305:31–306:21. Arnold said much the same thing at the beginning of "The Function of Criticism at the Present Time" (1864).—*Prose Works*, ed. Super, III, 259–61.

307:4–7. Proverbs 20:3, which reads "honour for a man."

307:13–15. "M. de Tocqueville," *Causeries du lundi* (Paris, 1862), XV, 116.

307:34; 308:3–11. *Ibid.*, XV, 97.

308:25–26. Sainte-Beuve addressed the Senate on the freedom of the press on May 7, 1868, and on freedom of instruction twelve days later. Cardinal Donnet, archbishop of Bordeaux, interrupted the latter to make clear the Catholic view of toleration. Both speeches are reprinted (with the interruptions) in *Premiers lundis* (Paris, 1875), III, 243–326.

308:37. Henry Fawcett (1833–88), first professor of political economy at Cambridge, though blind, was elected to Parliament in 1865 and was one of the most outspoken members of the radical wing of the Liberal party. He was an important leader in the passing of the Reform Law of 1867 and a vigorous opponent of religious tests at the universities.

309:1. For Arnold's discussion of the sense of the word "curiosity" as it applied to Sainte-Beuve, see pp. 90–91.

[FRIENDSHIP'S GARLAND: LETTER VIII]

After a lapse of more than two years, Arminius von Thunder-ten-Tronckh made his appearance once more as witness of the touching scene at Mrs. Bottles' death bed. There is nothing to indicate that Arnold had any intention of continuing the series beyond the present letter, which was published in the *Pall Mall Gazette* on June 8, 1869, and brought Arnold 5 gns.

313:4. St. James's Place, then a fashionable residential street, extends from St. James's Street westward to the Green Park. Lord Elcho's house was in St. James's Place. See note to p. 50:6. The *Pall Mall Gazette* version of the letter had no place or date.

313:9. The *Daily Telegraph* was published at No. 135, Fleet Street.

313:16–18. Chambers again brought in his bill to legalize marriage with a deceased wife's sister (see p. 205) on February 25, 1869. It passed its second reading on April 21. Though it was due to be considered by the House in committee on June 8, as Leo indicates, other business that evening took so much time that the debate was deferred first until June 22, and then again, for the same reason, until July 1, then until July 20, when once more the hour was so late that nothing could be accomplished. The bill was quietly withdrawn on August 2. Marriage with a deceased wife's sister was not legalized until 1907, with a deceased brother's widow not until 1921.

313:26–314:1. John Philpot Curran (1750–1817), Irish barrister, member of the parliament in Dublin, and later judge, though a Protestant, was a vigorous supporter of Catholic emancipation and an energetic defender at the bar of those who sought, even by violent means, the independence of Ireland. Shortly before his death, he appeared at the ceremonial that opened a Roman Catholic cemetery in Dublin, and remarked to the assembled dignitaries, "Having rocked you in your cradle, I was anxious to see you stepping forth into manhood."—Leslie Hale, *John Philpot Curran* (London, 1958), p. 258. Nevertheless the precise source of Arnold's allusion has not been found, and Kirby, pointing to the fact that the words "as Curran says" were added in 1871, suggests that Arnold may be merely parodying the *Daily Telegraph*'s fondness for quoting Curran. Speaking at a banquet of the Jewish Free School in London on May 21, 1884, no doubt extemporaneously, Arnold used the same expression and attributed it to Grattan; see *Prose Works*, ed. Super, vol. X, 245.

314:14–16. The young man was Frederic Harrison. In the first section of "Anarchy and Authority" (January, 1868) Arnold spoke of Harrison's "having apparently achieved such a conquest of my young Prussian friend, Arminius" (see p. 116). The note on pp. 76–77 describing their relationship was added in 1871. Harrison in 1867–69 was a member of the Royal Commission appointed to inquire into the organization and rules of the trade unions, and he had written such essays as "The Iron-Masters' Trade Union," "The Limits of Political Economy," "The Good and Evil of Trade-Unionism," and "Industrial Co-operation," *Fortnightly Review* I, 96–116, 356–76 (May 15, June 15, 1865); III, 33–54, 477–503 (November 15, 1865; January 1, 1866).

314:17. The Paris correspondent of the *Daily Telegraph* was Felix M. Whitehurst, many of whose articles were collected, after his death, as *Court and Social Life in France under Napoleon the Third* (London, 1873).

314:36–38. When Ruskin wrote a letter to the *Daily Telegraph* on the servant problem, the *Telegraph* replied with a leading article (September 6, 1865, pp. 4–5) in which the hypothetical female domestic was called "Mary Jane." Five days later another leading article discussed "Mary Jane," and there was for some weeks thereafter a lively correspondence on the subject (Kirby).

315:11. See p. 318:2–4 and note.

315:17. Presumably an allusion to the shower of gold which fell on Danaë and begat Perseus.

315:23. The reason for Arnold's changing the name of Bottles' daughter from Jemima to Selina (see Textual Notes) is not now apparent; E. K. Brown's suggestion that the former was perhaps offensive to Arnold's friend, Wordsworth's granddaughter Jemima Quillinan, is at best not convincing.—*Studies in the Text of Matthew Arnold's Prose Works* (Paris, 1935), pp. 43–44. But one can guess that what first suggested "Jemima" was the publisher George Smith's remark in February, 1867, that *On the Study of Celtic Literature* was "hardly the sort of book a British parent buys at a railway bookstall for his Jemima."

315:24–35. Professor Kirby points out that Arnold deliberately echoes Bright's speech in the debate of April 21, 1869: "The Church of England permitted the marriage of first cousins.... Was there any man of common-sense who would not say that on every natural ground the marriage of first cousins was more objectionable than the marriage of a man with his deceased wife's sister? ... [He had always thought the consideration of the position of children by these marriages one of immense importance.... It was notorious beyond dispute that there were many cases ... in which the dying mother hoped that her sister might become in a closer sense than that of aunt the protector of her children.] He appealed to ... all ... opponents of the Bill, as to whether they themselves deemed the man who married his deceased wife's sister a profligate man? ("No.") ... Was there any man that regarded a woman married to her deceased sister's husband as an immoral person who was not to be admitted to his house, and who he thought would be likely to taint the society of his wife and daughters? (Hear, hear.) No such feeling existed. (Hear, hear.) And if there were children of those marriages, there was no man in that House or out of it cruel enough—he had nearly used a harsher word—to point to those children by the almost odious name of bastard. (Cheers.)"—*Times*, April 22, p. 6, col. 5.

316:12. Arnold's fondness for the word "delicacy" was seized on by his critics: a writer on "The Politics of Young England," speaking of "the causes which persistently set culture against popular struggles," alluded to "the delicacy of mental organisation which we note on going to that higher place in the intellectual scale of Young England over which Mr. Matthew Arnold keeps watch and ward," and later alluded to Arnold's "delicate ear."—*Fraser's Magazine* LXXVII, 349, 351 (March, 1868), signed "M." (James Macdonell)

316:21. George Augustus Sala (1828–96), after a varied career in journalism, became a contributor to the *Daily Telegraph* in 1857 and was considered by such critics as the *Saturday Review* to have set its tone of tawdry, turgid, inflated writing. He was its special foreign correspondent in America (1863–64) and elsewhere and was in Paris at the beginning of the Franco-German war in 1870.— *D.N.B.* Arnold was moved to this comment, and to his later allusions to Sala (pp. 349–50), by a rather unpleasant reference to himself in Sala's recently published *Rome and Venice* (London, 1869), pp. 23–24: "As to being a Philistine, I scarcely know what the term, intellectually used, means, or how it applies. The shallow and conceited sciolist who devised the sneer, in order to insult writers whose minds and views were broader than his, may plume himself mightily on his device; but twenty years hence, I fancy, we shall trouble ourselves no more about what a literary Philistine may have been, than we trouble ourselves now about . . . that 'Satanic' school about which poor Southey made such a pother." See Sidney M. B. Coulling, "Matthew Arnold and the *Daily Telegraph*," *Review of English Studies* XII n.s., 177–78 (May, 1961).

316:24–28. See p. 206:33 and note. *The New America* was published on January 17, 1867, and reached a sixth edition by mid-March, a seventh by early June; *Spiritual Wives* was published on January 15, 1868, and reached a fourth edition before March 28. The latter carried the author's portrait as frontispiece.

316:32. The *Daily Telegraph* devoted a leading article to the "picturesque" style of its correspondents—a term it preferred to "sensational"—on June 22, 1868, p. 7, cols. 1–2. "A new journalistic profession has arisen for gentlemen who combine great powers of observation with physical energy and a happy use of descriptive language." And "have we any right to attack [this tendency of our age]? Is there anything essentially debased in picturesque, as com-

pared with purely statistical writing? Did Macaulay pander to a
low taste when he painted for us the great scene in Westminster
Hall [at the trial of Warren Hastings]?" See also pp. 206:33-35
and 332:1-2 (Kirby).

317:21-22. In the spring of 1869 there was a scarcity of money
available for investment in England, and the Bank of England dis-
count rate was raised from 3 percent in the week ending March 27
to 4½ percent in the week ending May 8—the highest since 1866
—in the hope of increasing its reserve.

317:29-30. On the very evening Leo's letter made this protest,
Thomas Collins moved that the House in committee be empowered
also to make provision for a woman to marry her deceased husband's brother.

317:31-32. Bright concluded his remarks on April 21, 1869, by
urging his colleagues not to "treat this as a question to joke about,
or merely to talk ecclesiastical rubbish about."—*Times*, April 22,
p. 6, col. 5.

317:33. *Merchant of Venice*, IV, i, 341. Bright was a Quaker,
hence the substitution of "Friend" (capitalized) for Shakespeare's
"Jew."

317:36-318:9. A royal commission to investigate the effect of the
laws of marriage with respect to the prohibited degrees was appointed in 1847 and reported a year later. Testimony before the
commission showed that such marriages were still contracted in
England in apparent defiance of the laws or through falsification,
and that in some instances the laws were circumvented by taking
temporary residence abroad and having the ceremony performed
there—in America, Denmark, or Germany. The great bulk of the
marriages was among the middle classes—merchants, manufacturers,
professional men, tradesmen. The Nonconformists generally approved marriage with a deceased wife's sister, and a number of
Baptist ministers were cited as favoring it or even practicing it
themselves.

318:4. The reason given for the execution of Admiral Byng in
Chapter XXIII of Voltaire's *Candide*.

318:8-9. An allusion to C. W. Dilke's *Greater Britain;* see p.
29:37.

318:10. Wordsworth, "London, 1802," line 8. Wordsworth reads
"virtue, freedom."

318:12. *Richard III*, IV, iv, 424.

318:23. Four years earlier the *Daily Telegraph* referred to "the gilded bird-cage over the Speaker's head, where we gallantly enclose [the ladies]."—June 17, 1865, p. 4, col. 4 (Kirby).

318:31. The expression "young lion" occurs more than a dozen times in the King James Version of the Old Testament; Arnold's latinization of it into "Adolescens Leo" is humorous, however, and not the Vulgate form. "Like as the lion and the young lion roaring on his prey, when a multitude of shepherds is called forth against him, he will not be afraid of their voice, nor abase himself for the noise of them."—Isaiah 31:4. Arnold first used the expression "the magnificent roaring of the young lions of the *Daily Telegraph*" in the Preface to *Essays in Criticism*, 1865 (*Prose Works*, ed. Super, III, 287), and (as Professor Kirby points out) the term was caught up in an article by Théodore Karcher on "La Presse anglaise," *Revue moderne* XXXVII, 119 (April 1, 1866): "Naguère on les a qualifiés de 'jeunes lions hurleurs,' quoiqu'ils rappellent plutôt à l'esprit l'animal braillard que la fable bien connue associe au roi des forêts."

[A RECANTATION AND APOLOGY]

Although the article was signed with his name, Arnold's ironic "Recantation and Apology" has hitherto been buried in the files of the *Pall Mall Gazette*. Its existence was noted by Professor Kirby in his unpublished dissertation on *Friendship's Garland* and the present editor's independent discovery of the article was announced in *Modern Language Quarterly* XXII, 308 (September, 1961). It appeared in the *Pall Mall* on August 2, 1869, and brought Arnold 4 gns.

319:2–3. The Liberals were returned in a considerable majority in December, 1868, after an appeal to the country on the issue of disestablishing and disendowing the (Anglican) Irish Church. Gladstone's Irish Church Bill was passed on July 23, 1869, and received the royal assent three days later. For a study of the whole question, see Anna L. Evans, *The Disestablishment of the Church of Ireland in 1869* (Lancaster, Penna., 1929).

319:5–7. For example by the *Daily News*, whose leading article on February 10, 1869, p. 4, cols. 5–6, handled the book with "more acerbity than I expected," as Arnold wrote to his mother on February 27. The *London Review*, after an "outrageous" and bitter attack on "Culture and Its Enemies" on July 13, 1867, likewise attacked *Culture and Anarchy* on February 13, 1869.

319:12–14. "The sooner that the finishing touches are given to this measure of clemency and justice, the better will it be for both the great political parties in England, and for the peace and contentment of Ireland," said the *Daily Telegraph* on the eve of the final passing of the Irish Church Bill.—July 23, 1869, p. 4, col. 4; partly copied by Arnold at the back of his diary for 1869 (ed. Lowry, p. 116, misprinting "D.N." for "D.T.").

319:14–16. Edward Miall in the Commons, July 23, 1869; reported in the *Times*, July 24, p. 7, col. 1.

319:18–21. Gladstone in the Commons, July 23, 1869, as summarized in a leading article in the *Times*, July 24, p. 9, col. 4.

319:24–27. See pp. 205–6, 313–18.

320:9–18. See pp. 124–26.

320:32–321:13. The Commons had provided that none of the surplus of the property of the Irish Church remaining after provision had been made for its necessary support—and this surplus would be about half the value—should go to the maintenance of any church or clergy or for the teaching of religion, but should be used mainly for the relief of unavoidable calamity and suffering among the Irish people. The Lords looked in the direction of using Irish Church property for the concurrent support of all religions in Ireland, rather than for secular purposes. On July 12, 1869, the final night of debate over the third reading of the Irish Church Bill in the House of Lords, Earl Stanhope moved to provide residences and glebe lands for Roman Catholic and Presbyterian clergy as well as Anglican clergy out of the surplus funds. Earl Granville, the Liberal leader, warned that the constituencies in the last election were unalterably opposed to any sort of concurrent endowment and begged the Lords not to insist upon it, but Stanhope's amendment was passed by a majority of seven, headed by the archbishop of Canterbury, A. C. Tait. The Commons rudely rejected the Lords' proposal, and the upper house was obliged to yield.

322:11–13. The *Guardian* reviewed *Culture and Anarchy* on April 14, 1869, pp. 418–19: "Does [Mr. Arnold] think this description [of the *Philistine*] applies to our professional classes? ... How are we to regard our physicians and barristers? What is to be said of most readers of the *Guardian?* Have they the tastes of Mr. Arnold's *Philistine?*"

322:18–22. In the final debate on the Irish Church Bill in the Commons, July 23, 1869; reported in the *Times*, July 24, p. 6, col. 4.

323:6–12. Perhaps the author of the leading article, "Disestablishment as a Precedent," in the *Pall Mall Gazette* of July 28, 1869, p. 1: "There is indeed one sentiment on the subject which would undoubtedly have received a considerable shock from the disestablishment of the Irish Church if it had still existed. We are thinking of the sort of theories which Dr. Arnold, Mr. Gladstone, and a variety of other writers from Hooker downwards, have tried to frame as to the true nature of the Church of England; but any one who is at all acquainted with the course of speculation upon these subjects ought to know that such theories have had their day, and have been decisively refuted by the only test which can refute such theories, the general course of events." Arnold, of course, placed a wide gulf between the intellectual attainment of Hooker and Bishop Butler, developed within the establishment, and of popular preachers like the English Baptist C. H. Spurgeon and the American Congregationalist Henry Ward Beecher, working outside it.

323:24–29. *Daily News*, July 16, 1869, p. 4, col. 7 (leading article).

323:31–33. See pp. 194–95.

324:1–2. On July 29, 1869, Dr. Frederick James Jobson (1812–81) was elected president of the Wesleyan Conference in its session at Hull. Accepting the presidency, he said: "[We are] resolved to continue firm in [our] adherence to Scriptural Protestantism, united in Christ with all evangelical churches, but never consenting to any alliance with the 'Man of Sin.' Men might 'level up' or 'level down,' but with those who advocate concurrent endowment or indiscriminate endowment, or who, though bound by oath to 'drive away damnable heresy,' could Judas-like betray the truth for pieces of silver, [we can] have no sympathy."—*Daily News*, July 30, p. 3, col. 5; reported also in the *Times*, p. 5, col. 4. A few months later Arnold quoted more fully from Jobson's speech in "Puritanism and the Church of England"; see *Prose Works*, ed. Super, VI, 101.

324:4–5. "Now that the Irish Church cease[s] to be a political body, the Nonconformists [will] be ready to afford it any assistance in promoting its views, and placing it in a strong position.... [I trust] that the result [will] be the commencement of an era of peace and prosperity for Ireland."—Miall in the Commons, July 23, 1869.

324:11–12. Copied near the end of Arnold's diary for 1869, but the original passage has not been found.—*Note-Books*, ed. Lowry, p. 116 (where "D.N." should read "D.T.," for *Daily Telegraph*).

[MELANCHOLY IF TRUE]

Though Arnold coined the expression "the young lions of the *Daily Telegraph*" early in 1865, he did not use it again until he signed his letter in the *Pall Mall Gazette* of June 8, 1869, "A Young Lion." Professor Kirby discovered another letter with this signature in the *Gazette* of October 14, 1869, and attributed it, with considerable probability, to Arnold. Confirmatory evidence is still lacking: the letter was not reprinted by Arnold, it is not mentioned in any of his correspondence as yet uncovered, and there is no indication in his diaries that he received payment for it. Moreover, it appeared in the *Gazette* on the very evening of the day in which the *Times* articles it ridiculed were published: if Arnold wrote it, he was very prompt in delivering it to the *Gazette* office; this was, however, only a few minutes' walk from the Athenaeum Club. It is perhaps not likely, though it is possible, that another writer should use the pseudonym of "A Young Lion" in the *Gazette* only four months after Arnold used it there. A year later, in his final letter of *Friendship's Garland* (p. 349), Arnold repeated the joke of the Young Lion's moving to the *Times*, though Leo then spoke of it as still in the future.

325:13–19, 28–326:7. The quotations are from two leading articles in the *Times* of October 13 (p. 6, col. 6, and p. 7, col. 4). The first dealt with the Spanish Revolution of 1868–69. In the second, the editor reflected upon an account of a senile murderer and upon the news of a fatal rear-end collision of four trains that were deliberately dispatched in too close succession, and made the rather subtle point that only a more punctilious reverence for human life could reduce the number of murders, and that such reverence clearly was not felt by the coroner's jury that exonerated everyone from blame in the case of the railway accident.

[FRIENDSHIP'S GARLAND: LETTERS IX–XII]

The outbreak of the Franco-German War on July 14, 1870, led Arnold to plan a resumption of his Arminius letters, and the first of them had already been dispatched to the *Pall Mall Gazette* when he learned of the French disaster at Weissenburg on August 4. His letter appeared on August 9, somewhat to his surprise; he told the editor he had supposed "that events were too great and too earnest for anything *ironical* like my letters.... As to the two other letters, do you not *really* think that events are too great and rushing just now to make these letters suitable; ironical, and, to a certain extent, *chaffy*, they must be, if they come at all. You shall be judge—if you really wish for them, I will write them; only weigh well what I say before deciding." The letters Arnold here alluded to were not published, but the outcry against Russia's reopening of the Black Sea question at the end of October drew from him two more Arminius letters that appeared in the *Gazette* on November 21 and 25. Arminius, however, was doomed; before the imminent fall of Paris should turn the comedy of his comments into something altogether too serious, Arnold killed him off in a letter that (as Professor Kirby points out in his dissertation) parodies the style of the *Daily Telegraph*. It was published on November 29. The first of these four letters brought Arnold 4 gns; the last three, with an article on charitable endowments (to appear in volume VI of this edition) and (presumably) one or two other articles that have not been identified, brought him 20 gns.

327:12. A Chequer Alley ran east from Dowgate Hill (opposite the Dyers' Hall) to Bush Lane. By the time Arnold wrote it had been obliterated by the erection of the new Cannon Street station. —Walter Besant, *London City* (London, 1910), p. 237. The language of Letter XI, however, suggests an alley closer to St. Giles Cripplegate.

327:14. On July 14, 1870, Napoleon III declared war on Prussia and on August 2, the first military encounter took place with the French occupation of Saarbrücken. The direction of movement was quickly reversed, however, by the defeat of the French at Weissenburg on August 4 and at Spichern and Wörth on August 6. By September 2, the Emperor and his most important army were prisoners of war. Meanwhile, Bismarck maneuvered the publication in the *Times* on July 25 of a draft proposal made by Count Benedetti, French ambassador to Prussia, in 1866 for the annexation of Belgium by France in return for French consent to a unified Germany under the Prussian crown. That this should have been proposed by one of the guarantors of the neutrality of Belgium to another, with no regard for the other three signatories of the treaty of 1839 (England, Russia, and Austria) aroused a storm of British indignation.

327:17–19. William I and Bismarck.

328:19–21. In "Puritanism and the Church of England," February, 1870; see *Prose Works*, ed. Super, VI, 96–99.

329:2–13. Leading article in the *Times* discussing, and in part quoting, the previous night's debate in the House of Lords between Lord Russell and Lord Granville, the latter speaking for the Government.—August 3, 1870, pp. 8–9. Russell's words were greeted in the House with cheers (p. 5, col. 6).

329:38. "Residuum" was the word Bright used in the debate on parliamentary reform (March 26, 1867) to embrace those of "almost hopeless poverty and dependence" whom he was willing to see still excluded from the franchise. The *Guardian* (April 14, 1869, p. 419), rather than the *Pall Mall Gazette*, equated the term with Arnold's "Populace."

330:13–19. For Lord Grenville, foreign secretary under Pitt, see p. 14. Lord Granville, foreign secretary under Gladstone, was obliged to speak out because of the threat of Belgium's neutrality from the Franco-German War, and in the light of the Benedetti draft. On the night before Arnold's letter was published, he reported to the Lords that his Government had notified the belligerents that "if the armies of either ... violate the neutrality of Belgium, Great Britain will co-operate with the other in defending that neutrality, but does not engage to take part in the general operations of the present war between them," and was inviting a corresponding declaration from other guarantors of Belgian neutrality by the treaty of 1839. His aim, he said, was to avoid "menace," or doing "anything offensive to the two belligerents." His report was received by the Lords with gratification that "we shall be enabled to remain in a state of perfect neutrality, at the same time maintaining inviolate the honour of this country." Meanwhile, Gladstone was explaining to the Commons that his Government had been anxious to take a course which would avoid the danger of a forthright declaration as regards Belgium.—*Times*, August 9, p. 4, cols. 1–2; p. 5, col. 1.

331:31–33. The correspondent continued: "Not only do they march off unmurmuringly from all men value in this world, but they submit to the loss of their professional prospects, and private careers of all kinds with ... resignation.... This warlike submissive German is a creation or a manufacture of the Government.... He has given up his life and merged his individuality in the great national current, which is directed by the will of a few men, who can guide its forces as they list."—*Times*, August 2, 1870, p. 8, col. 1.

332:12–13. The Crimean War of 1854 and its conclusion in the Treaty of Paris of 1856.

332:28. "S'exécuter" means "fork out," "pay up."

[NOTE TO CANCELLED PASSAGE]

541:25–26. "There's Crispinus again"—Crispinus being a writer ridiculed in Horace's *Satires*.

334:4. The Treaty of Paris in 1856 prohibited Russia and Turkey from keeping warships or arsenals in the Black Sea and neutralized its waters. On October 31, 1870, the Russian chancellor, Prince Alexander Gortschakoff, taking advantage of the preoccupation of the Prussians and the French, notified the signatory powers that Russia no longer proposed to be bound by that provision of the treaty. Action was deferred until a conference of the signatory powers was held, and by mid-March, 1871, the Russians having repudiated their right to abrogate the treaty by themselves, their demands with respect to the Black Sea were met.

334:9–10. See p. 17:9–10.

334:20–22. This final article in the number (anonymous, as always) was later acknowledged by Gladstone himself, then prime minister, and was republished in his *Gleanings of Past Years* (London, 1879), IV, 197–257 (Kirby). Attribution of the article to Gladstone was general only a few days after it appeared.

334:24–335:2. *Times*, November 16, 1870, p. 8, col. 6.

335:17. See p. 10:18–19.

336:10–14. In January, 1853, Czar Nicholas I had several conversations with British Ambassador Sir George Hamilton Seymour, in which he pointed out that Turkey was a "very sick man" and suggested that some agreement be reached before the patient's inevitable demise. The British Government declined the proposal. Two days before Arnold's letter was published, J. A. Froude wrote in the *Times:* "I was one of those who deplored the Crimean War itself as a mistake, if it was nothing worse.... I believed that the overtures of the Emperor Nicholas to Sir Hamilton Seymour ought to have been met in a less jealous spirit; that England should rather have accepted Russia's hand, and have preferred conciliation and co-operation to distrust and hostility."—November 19, p. 5. col. 5. The *Times* itself in a leading article (p. 9, col. 2) endorsed this part of Froude's statement (Kirby).

336:28–30. Lord Aberdeen, who had been party some years earlier to conversations with the Czar on the Turkish question and whom the Czar regarded as friendly to his aims, became prime minister of a Coalition Government of Whigs and Peelites in 1852. In order to check his belligerent colleague, he gave Palmerston the

Home Office instead of the Foreign Office, which went first to
Lord Russell and then to Lord Clarendon. None the less, Palmerston carried the cabinet into the Crimean War, with Aberdeen re-
luctant and helpless. The incompetence of the conduct of the
war led to the fall of the coalition and a Whig Ministry under Palmerston early in 1855. For a study of the effect of public opinion in
England upon the events that led to the war, see B. Kingsley Martin,
The Triumph of Palmerston (London, 1924).

336:36–37. Nicholas I, broken in spirit by the Crimean War, ignored the warning of his doctor and reviewed a regiment of guards
in freezing weather despite a serious attack of influenza. He seemed
almost to court the death that came on March 2, 1855.

337:8. A *fat* is a fop.

338:15–16. See p. 12.

339:7. Bismarck became chief minister of Prussia in September,
1862. In May, 1863, the lower house of the legislature, with its Liberal majority, was prorogued and at the beginning of June ordi-
nances were issued in restraint of the liberty of the press. A new
parliament met in November, 1863, and was prorogued within three
months. In 1865 the Supreme Court in Berlin pronounced certain
limitations upon the freedom of speech guaranteed by the constitution to all members of the legislature.—Grant Duff, *European Politics*, pp. 234–41.

339:17. Isaiah 30:7. See Arnold, *Prose Works*, ed. Super, II, 240.

339:28–30. "While there is perfect unanimity of opinion among
the mercantile community of the City of London that the course
adopted by Russia is such as could not for an instant be acquiesced
in by any civilized State, it may be added that up to this time the
growth of a most friendly feeling toward Russia had been steadily
observable among our financial and mercantile classes, and that
even the re-opening of the Treaty of 1856 had been regarded as
a matter which, in view of her own dignity and interests, she was
fully entitled to bring forward with the expectation of satisfactory
results."—*Times*, November 19, 1870, p. 6, col. 1 (Kirby).

340:15–16. See p. 23:8.

340:25–30. *Times*, November 22, 1870, p. 3, col. 5.

341:2, 4. The Church of St. Giles Cripplegate (where Milton is
buried) is on Fore Street, facing the southern end of Whitecross
Street. Grub Street (now Milton Street) runs parallel to Whitecross Street, one square to the east.

341:7–8. In Macaulay's language: "Being often very hungry when he sat down to his meals, [Johnson] contracted a habit of eating with ravenous greediness. Even to the end of his life, and even at the tables of the great, the sight of food affected him as it affects wild beasts and birds of prey. His taste in cookery, formed in subterranean ordinaries and alamode-beef shops, was far from delicate. Whenever he was so fortunate as to have near him a hare that had been kept too long, or a meat pie made of rancid butter, he gorged himself with such violence that his veins swelled and the moisture broke out on his forehead."—*Encyclopaedia Britannica*, 8th edition. Arnold alluded to this alleged racial characteristic of the Germans in *On the Study of Celtic Literature, Prose Works,* ed. Super, III, 343.

341:17. The London City Mission was an unsectarian charitable society that worked in connection with the established and dissenting churches in the poorer parts of London; of nearly 500 missionaries in 1865, some 200 were employed by the former. The missionaries visited the poor, distributed scriptures and tracts, reclaimed drunkards and prostitutes, sent children to school, urged Sunday closing of shops, and held weekly or more frequent public religious services in some 488 rooms—halls, schoolrooms, mission rooms, and rooms in private houses and cottages. The income of the society in 1865 was about £40,000, the great part coming from evangelicals in the Church of England.—*Nonconformist* XXV, 997 (December 13, 1865). The missionaries were not usually ordained ministers.

342:19–20. Lord Granville's reply to the Gortschakoff Circular is printed in the *Times,* November 17, 1870, p. 9, col. 5.

343:8. The Band of Hope Union, founded in 1855, was a temperance organization that worked to improve the condition of children in the slums and to provide wholesome recreation for them. The *Band of Hope Review* was a monthly (not daily) leaflet of four folio pages that provided poems, stories, and pictures as moral provender for the children.

343:13–14. See p. 117:21–22.

343:14–15. "Errare mehercule malo cum Platone...quam cum istis vera sentire."—Cicero *Tusculan Disputations* I.xvii.39.

343:20–24. Edmond Beales, who as president of the Reform League arranged the march which led to the Hyde Park riots of 1866, was appointed judge of the county court circuit of Cambridgeshire and Huntingdonshire by Lord Chancellor Hatherley in September, 1870. For Col. Dickson, see note to p. 45:24. Charles Bradlaugh, their associate in the Reform League, an advocate of free thought, was prosecuted by the government in 1868 for failing to give securities against the publication of blasphemy and sedition in his weekly periodical, the *National Reformer*.

343:28–29. The case of Mordaunt *v.* Mordaunt, Cole, and Johnstone in February, 1870, was one of the longest and most sensational in the short history of the Divorce Court. Sir Charles Mordaunt charged his lady with specific adulteries with Viscount Cole and Sir Frederick Johnstone, and the Prince of Wales himself volunteered to take the stand to deny that there had been any improper familiarity between himself and Lady Mordaunt. On April 28, 1870, Ernest Boulton, twenty-two, and Frederick William Park, twenty-three, were arrested as they left the Strand Theatre, which they had attended in female costume, and were charged with intent to commit felony. The hearing in Bow Street Police Court consumed eight days from April 29 to May 30 and attracted great crowds, "including many persons of rank, besides many literary and theatrical celebrities."

343:34–344:1. On March 1, 1870, a Member asked whether it might not "be expedient in the interest of public morality, to impose some check upon the publication of the proceedings in the Divorce Court?" The Home Secretary, H. A. Bruce, replied that when the Divorce Court was set up in 1859, the Lords inserted a provision that the judge might hear cases with closed doors, but the Commons rejected the provision on the ground "that publicity was necessary for the pure and impartial administration of justice, and that, admitting that much misery and occasional mischief might result from the publication of those proceedings, yet, on the whole, public morality rather gained than lost by it."

344:1–4. The testimony in the Boulton and Park case was so lurid that on May 21 the *Times* pointed out that a preceding magistrate had cleared the court of all except reporters and those immediately concerned, in cases of similar character, "for the sake of public decency." At the beginning of the seventh session, when an agent of the Society for the Suppression of Vice somewhat belatedly urged that the case be heard behind closed doors, the magistrate replied that he might have done so if the direction of the case had been foreseeable at its beginning. "There was a strong feeling against secret inquiries in the present age, and it was only in very rare instances—and this might certainly have been one of them— that such a course would be tolerated in England."—*Times*, May 30, 1870, p. 13, col. 1.

344:9. The *London Gazette*, which has been in existence continuously since 1666, is now the official (semiweekly) organ for announcements by the government. "It contains all proclamations, orders of council, promotions and appointments to commissions in the army and navy, all appointments to offices of state, and such other orders, rules and regulations as are directed by act of Parliament to be published therein. It also contains notices of proceedings in bankruptcy, dissolutions of partnership, etc."—*Encyclopaedia Britannica*.

344:22–23. Telephus, son of Herakles, was wounded in battle by Achilles (according to a post-Homeric legend) and the wound remained incurable until rubbed with rust from the spear that caused it. Professor Kirby points out that Arnold in this epigram has polished his straight-forward statement of p. 119:16.

344:33. The correspondent to the *Times* from the crown prince's headquarters wrote on November 21: "A month ago the Army of Paris made its first great sortie. Is it to be its last? I think not.... Deserters from Paris say that the troops have received six days' rations, and that a sortie may be expected at any moment."—November 24, p. 7, col. 6 (Kirby).

346:1. Versailles was the headquarters of the Prussian army besieging Paris.

346:6–7. Bougival is west of Paris, some four miles north of Versailles. Rueil is another two miles northeast (Malmaison lies between them). Mont Valérien, the largest of the forts around Paris, lies a mile and a half east of Rueil. These places were all familiar to readers of the *Times* from the large maps of the seat of war that appeared frequently on its pages (e.g., on November 16, p. 13).

346:9. Cremorne Gardens were on the north bank of the Thames, in Chelsea, west of Battersea Bridge. Opened in 1845 as a pleasure garden, with dancing, fireworks, ballet, etc., they were frequented by a rabble that became such a nuisance in the neighborhood (the gardens remained open until three in the morning) that they were closed in 1877. Baedeker's French edition of his London guide, 1873, indicates that they were "surtout fréquenté pendant la belle saison (le soir par le demi-monde)."

346:29–347:1. See p. 58:19–20.

347:9. Amphitryon married his niece Alcmene. After the comedy of Plautus, his name could not be taken quite seriously.

347:11–14. On March 20, 1871, John Morley wrote to Harrison: "Arnold has done good work, but I can't see the fun or sense of the

last. It is clumsy, very, though *you* are handsomely enough dealt
with. Why kill Arminius again? You had run the creature through
with your dialogue three years since." Ten months later Morley
wrote again to him (January 12, 1872): "This is the true waste—to
hide your talent in the ground. The dying Arminius was a wise
monitor to you."—F. W. Hirst, *Early Life and Letters of John
Morley* (London, 1927), I, 182, 210.

347:17. Nicolas Leon Thieblin contributed a series of letters to
the *Pall Mall Gazette,* beginning June 29, 1869, over the pseudonym
"Azamat-Batuk." They were reprinted in 1870 as *A Little Book
about Great Britain.*

348:2. In 1856 Lowe purchased a country house near the village of
Warlingham, Surrey, overlooking the Caterham Valley. Arminius
fancies that this descendant of Pangloss will give him resting place
in a mausoleum there.

348:25. The British National Society for Aid to the Sick and
Wounded in War was very active in carrying assistance to both
sides during the siege of Paris. Its chairman on October 27, 1870,
published a letter in the *Times* protesting that "there are many
persons wearing the red cross who have nothing to do with any
society, and some who wear the red cross and share the privileges
accorded to it by the Geneva Convention, who have no right whatever to do so."—P. 4, col. 4. The correspondent of the *Daily Telegraph* remarked, respecting the use of the red-cross arm band:
"Unfortunately, it is liable to abuse, and is worn by many who
have no part in the work—not among Englishmen, so far as I have
seen, but very largely by Belgians, who use it to protect them in a
tour and to gratify a meddlesome curiosity, and, to some extent,
by merely idle Dutch tourists."—September 21, 1870, p. 5, col. 2
(Kirby).

349:1. The Hôtel des Réservoirs was the billet of the greater part
of the crown prince of Prussia's staff. In his letter dated November
22, W. H. Russell spoke of its proprietors as "the cruel persecutors
of the Reservoirs" for their poor accommodation.—*Times,* November 26, p. 10, col. 1.

349:4-5. Sala had been imprisoned and mistreated under suspicion
of being a spy in Paris early in September, 1870. By the end of that
month he was back in London, and then was sent by the *Daily
Telegraph* into Italy, so that he was not in fact in Versailles when
Arminius died. Arnold's allusion to the glass of brandy caused an
anxious moment when, just on the eve of the publication of the col-

lected letters as *Friendship's Garland,* Sala was awarded damages of £500 against the firm of Hodder and Stoughton for their publication of James Hain Friswell's *Modern Men of Letters Honestly Criticised,* in which one of the libels was that Sala was "often drunk, always in debt, sometimes in prison and ... totally disreputable." "The horrid thought struck me," Arnold wrote his publisher George Smith when he read the account of the case in the morning papers of February 18, 1871: "Do we give them any *possible* handle for legal proceedings?—Remember that the scandal and discussion of a law court is mere play to them, seared as by this time they are: and is keen pleasure, if anything is to be got by it. Nothing would compensate me for being mixed up, and having my name mixed up, in serious legal encounter with such a crew: not if I beat them a thousand times over. ... Consider, too, whether mentioning Hepworth Dixon as *the author of the immortal guide to Mormonism* [p. 356:13–14] could possibly warrant that worthy in dragging us into the law courts."—S. M. B. Coulling, "Matthew Arnold and the *Daily Telegraph,*" *Review of English Studies* XII n.s., 178 (May, 1961).

349:12. William Howard Russell, the *Times* correspondent at the crown prince of Prussia's headquarters, had managed to get on familiar terms with a good many of the most important figures there, and his letters to the *Times* did not underplay this intimacy. Professor Kirby suggests that Arnold may be ridiculing especially the adulatory tone with which he described the banquet in honor of the crown princess's birthday at the Prefecture in Versailles on November 21 (*Times,* November 26, pp. 9–10). The guests included a considerable number of reigning German princes or their heirs, among them (rather far down on Russell's list of precedence) the Grand Duke of Oldenburg. On November 15 Arnold wrote to his mother: "The *Times* generally has been poor [on the French war], and old Russell twaddling. It has been a great thing for the *Daily News,* which has increased its circulation immensely, and I am glad of it, for I like the paper."

350:2. Sala early in his journalistic career was a contributor to Dickens' *Household Words.*

350:11. Milton said of himself, "By labour and intent study, ... joined with the strong propensity of nature, I might perhaps leave something so written to after times as they should not willingly let it die."—*Reason of Church Government,* Book II, Introduction.

[DEDICATORY LETTER]

351:1. February 2, the feast of the Purification of the Blessed Virgin Mary.

351:8, 11, 13. The Royal Literary Fund was founded in 1790 with the purpose of assisting "Authors of genius and learning, who may be reduced to distress by unavoidable calamities, or deprived, by enfeebled faculties or declining life, of the power of literary execution."—Report for 1866. Octavian Blewitt was its secretary from 1839 to 1884 and Philip, Earl Stanhope its president from 1863 to 1875. In 1865 it made fifty-two grants, most of them for twenty or thirty pounds. It celebrated its anniversary with annual dinners, presided over by men of the very highest distinction in affairs of church or state. An article on the Literary Fund dinner of 1869 in the *Pall Mall Gazette* condemned the Fund as tending "to foster the merest mediocrities" and asked, "in all seriousness," if it was "not time to reform a declining usage altogether."—May 11, p. 1,614 (Kirby).

351:15–16. The *Pall Mall Gazette* started publication at 14 Salisbury Street, Strand. On December 26, 1866, it moved its offices to 2 Northumberland Street, Strand.

351:18. In January, 1866, less than a year after the *Gazette* began, the editor's brother James Greenwood and a friend disguised themselves as paupers and applied for a night's lodging at the Lambeth workhouse. Their account of the miserable accommodation and the wretched condition of their fellow inmates, headed "A Night in a Workhouse," appeared on January 12, 13, and 15, and caused a sensation in London. The circulation of the *Gazette* was materially increased and its reputation grew higher and higher from this time. —J. W. Robertson Scott, *The Story of the Pall Mall Gazette* (London, 1950), pp. 166–69.

352:10–13. Martin, in Voltaire's *Candide*, was the cynical but loyal friend of the hero in the latter half of the book, whose comments served to rectify the optimism of Pangloss and the naïveté of Candide. The Jardin Mabille was the most luxurious of the public dance halls in Paris, best remembered because there the *can-can* was invented. The rigors of the siege of Paris (September 19, 1870 to January 28, 1871) were said to have driven the inhabitants of the city to eat rats in order to fend off starvation.

352:15–16. Presumably the colonnade along the Via del Po in

Turin. Arnold is ridiculing the affectation with which Sala
sprinkled his reports with foreign phrases, though when he wrote
to the *Telegraph* from Turin on June 12, 1866, he did not in fact
use this expression.—*Daily Telegraph*, June 16, p. 7, col. 4.

353:5. The Bald-Faced Stag, George Orpwood, prop., was a tavern on the Common in Finchley (north of London), at the beginning of the Great Northern Road.

353:6–8. William Vernon Harcourt (1827–1904) was elected to
Parliament in 1868, an independent liberal. One of the most important acts of the 1870 session was the Elementary Education Act, introduced by Arnold's brother-in-law W. E. Forster on February 17
and passed, after many sessions of debate, early in August. Throughout, Harcourt was much concerned to insist that all elementary
education be unsectarian and undenominational (see his letter to the
Times, June 10, 1870, p. 4, cols. 4–5). Challenged to define the terms
he replied: "These words came from somewhere, they were used
by some people, and people who used them imagined that some
sense attached to them." He then quoted several paragraphs from
Newman's *Grammar of Assent* to describe what he meant by unsectarian religion; perhaps Arnold meant to suggest, however, that
he had in fact defined his term in the Pickwickian sense.—*Times*,
June 22, p. 7, cols. 1–2.

353:22–24. "Letter to a Noble Lord" (1796), three-fifths through;
recorded by Arnold in his pocket diary for July 17, 1869.—*Note-
Books*, ed. Lowry, p. 105.

353:35–354:5. Leading article, *Daily Telegraph*, December 23,
1870, p. 4, col. 5—actually nearly a month after Arminius' death
(Kirby).

354:5–7. Leading article, *Daily News*, September 5, 1870, p. 5, col.
1 (Kirby).

355:15–23. "The Liberal party, which seems to Mr. Arnold so
raw and so vulgar in its earnest claim for political rights, has long
fought for the education of the masses, and until lately Oxford and
Cambridge have been the centres of resistance to the demand....
It is very easy to ... be merely a spectator of the fight. Even in a
literary point of view Mr. Arnold surely might do better than
criticise critics. He once gave the world a poem of some promise,
which we shall all forget unless he follows it up with something
better than essays on Arminius and [the *Daily Telegraph*]. Nor,
though he strains every nerve to do the scholastic traditions of his
father full justice, can we quite forgive him for not reproducing

more of the parental example. Dr. Arnold was a fearless worker
in many a good cause; and we are sure that he taught his son practical liberalism as well as the taste for teaching.... Why be content
with clever little barkings at the heels of the men who advance,
when he has the scholarship and the ability to be himself a valued
combatant in the same good cause?"—*Daily Telegraph*, July 2, 1867,
pp. 6–7 (leading article on "Culture and Its Enemies"). See p.
115:22–26.

355:20–21. See p. 44:26.

355:25–26. See p. 227:32–33.

355:27–30. Parliament met on February 9, 1871; the next day
Thomas Chambers again brought in his bill to permit a man to
marry his deceased wife's sister, and in this session carried it through
the Commons. It was defeated at the second reading by the Lords.

355:30. In a final comment on the Elementary Education Act,
Miall told the Commons that in his opinion the Dissenters had received far too little compensation for the support they had given
the Liberals in the election of 1868.—*Times*, July 23, 1870, p. 6,
col. 4. Miall was an Israelite, presumably not because he Hebraized,
but because he demanded usurious repayment.

355:32–34. Ephesians 4:31.

355:35–356:2. The Contagious Diseases Acts of 1866–69 were essentially acts to compel the physical examination of women suspected of prostitution at places where the armed forces were based
and to provide for their cures if found diseased. The acts were
attacked by the Puritans as condoning immorality, and in the session
of 1870 a move to repeal them was unsuccessfully launched. The
debates were closed to reporters, but public discussion was very
lively. The attempt to secure their repeal was not renewed in 1871.

356:3–7. "A Welsh attorney sends me his verses to revise," wrote
Cowper to Walter Bagot on January 3, 1787, "and obliging asks, ..."
There follow the two lines quoted from Pope's *Essay on Man*, IV,
385–86 (Kirby).

356:13–14. See pp. 148, 206–7, 316:22.

Textual Notes

[FRIENDSHIP'S GARLAND]

71.* Friendship's Garland: | Being the | Conversations, Letters, and Opinions | of the Late | Arminius, | Baron von Thunder-ten-Tronckh. | Collected and Edited, | with a Dedicatory Letter to Adolescens Leo, Esq., | of "The Daily Telegraph," | By Matthew Arnold. | .... *manibus date lilia plenis.* | London: | Smith, Elder and Co., 15, Waterloo Place. | 1871. | [All Rights Reserved.]

80. Passages from | the Prose Writings | of | Matthew Arnold | London | Smith, Elder, & Co., 15 Waterloo Place | 1880 | [*All rights reserved*]

    Also issued with the imprint: New York | Macmillan and Co., | 1880

83c. Culture & Anarchy | an Essay in | Political and Social Criticism | and | Friendship's Garland | Being the Conversations, Letters, and Opinions | of the Late | Arminius, Baron von Thunder-ten-Tronckh. | Collected and Edited, | with a Dedicatory Letter to Adolescens Leo, Esq., | of "The Daily Telegraph" | By Matthew Arnold | New York | Macmillan and Co. | 1883

97. Friendship's Garland: | Being the | Conversations, Letters, and Opinions | of the Late | Arminius, | Baron von Thunder-ten-Tronckh. | Collected and Edited, | with a Dedicatory Letter to Adolescens Leo, Esq., | of "The Daily Telegraph," | By Matthew Arnold. | .... *manibus date lilia plenis.* | Second Edition. | London: | Smith, Elder, & Co., 15 Waterloo Place. | 1897. | [All Rights Reserved.]

    This edition, a page for page re-setting of the first, has no textual authority and is not collated.

03. Friendship's Garland | Being the | Conversations, Letters, and

* For 71 read 1871, etc.

487

Opinions | of the Late | Arminius | Baron von Thunder-ten-
Tronckh | Collected and Edited | with a Dedicatory Letter
to Adolescens Leo, Esq. | of "The Daily Telegraph" | By
Matthew Arnold | ... *manibus date lilia plenis* | *Popular Edi-
tion* | London | Smith, Elder, & Co., 15 Waterloo Place |
1903 | [All rights reserved.]

This edition has no textual authority and is not collated.

[MY COUNTRYMEN]

Cornh.   *Cornhill Magazine* XIII, 153–72 (February, 1866).
Ev.Sat.   *Every Saturday* I, 240–48 (March 3, 1866). Reprinted from
           Cornh.; not collated.
Lit.   *Littell's Living Age* LXXXVIII, 784–96 (March 17, 1866).
           Reprinted from *Cornh.;* not collated.
Reprinted 71, 83c, 97 (not collated), 03 (not collated).

The following passages appear in 80: 10:12–11:16 (pp. 135–36,
headed "Middle Class Foreign Policy"); 11:36–12:23 (pp. 137–38,
headed "The Young Man from the Country"); 13:11–14:15 (pp.
138–39, headed "The Great War with France"); 15:30–36 (p. 125,
headed "Arminius on the Middle-Class Era"); 27:36–28:26 (pp.
107–8, headed "The Spotted Dog"); 28:27–29:28 (pp. 151–53, headed
"Reasons for Hope").

3:1–21. *not in Cornh.*
4:37–38. *not in Cornh.*
5:35–38. *not in Cornh.*
6:25–30. mistake. I had been breaking one of my own cardinal
25   rules: the rule to keep aloof from practice, and to confine my-
        self to the slow and obscure work of trying to understand things,
        to see them as they are. So I   *Cornh.*
6:36. difference. I had been meddling with practice, proposing this
        and that, saying how it might be if we had established this or
30   that. I saw   *Cornh.*
6:38. no more. Henceforward let Mr. Kinglake belabour the French
        as he will, let him describe as many tight merciless lips as he
        likes; henceforward let Educational Homes stretch themselves
        out in *The Times* to the crack of doom, let Lord Fortescue be-
35   witch the middle class with ever new blandishments, let any num-
        ber of Mansion House meetings propound any number of patch-
        work schemes to avoid facing the real difficulty; I am dumb. I

let reforming and instituting alone; I meddle with my neighbour's practice no more. *He that is unjust, let him be unjust still,
and he which is filthy, let him be filthy still, and he that is righteous, let him be righteous still, and he that is holy, let him be
holy still.* Cornh.   5

8:35, 37–38. *not in Cornh.*
9:38. *not in Cornh.*
10:12. foreigners are   80
10:13. England. They   80
10:28. so far as   *Cornh.*, 71, 80
10:38. *not in Cornh.*, 80
11:4. respect. Very   80
12:3. say that the   80
13:12–13. day,' said Arminius to me, 'that instead   80
15:30–31. over,' said Arminius; 'nations   80
16:32–33. himself says: *Cornh.*
16:35–36. prosperity,—what . . . more?' *Cornh.*, 71, 83c; *corrected by
Ed.*
17:27. doubt your   *Cornh.*
21:37–38. *not in Cornh.*
22:6. to go from   *Cornh.*, 71
22:32–39. *not in Cornh.*
23:38. *not in Cornh.*
25:30. language of the rhetorician!'   *Cornh.*
26:38. *not in Cornh.*
27:37–38. *not in Cornh.*
28:1. seems   80
28:9. how blank   *Cornh.*; how black   71, 80, 83c
28:19–20. Home, or our Divorce   80
28:35. to a more   80
28:37. life. It   80
29:4. ideallessness   80
29:9. the boon   *Cornh.*
29:37–38. *not in Cornh.*
31:1. on the top   *Cornh.*
31:15–28. *not in Cornh.*

[A COURTEOUS EXPLANATION]

PMG "An Explanation," *Pall Mall Gazette*, March 20, 1866, pp. 3–4.
Reprinted 71, 83c, 97 (not collated), 03 (not collated).

The following passage appears in 80: 33:36–34:16 (pp. 128–29, headed "Paris and London").

Title: An Explanation. *PMG*

32:1. *not in PMG*

32:2. *To the* EDITOR *of the* PALL MALL GAZETTE. | SIR,— *PMG*

33:14. present. ¶There is no real difference between "Horace" and me about the Italians. He will observe, if he looks back to my report of the conversation, that my Italian friend (who was good enough to describe himself to me as *molto furbo, molto astuto*) never denied that he felt small gratitude to the French, or that he reckoned unhesitatingly on English good-will and sympathy. What he said was that the intellect of France had great influence on the Continent, and that little gratitude was excited by English good-will, because this seemed a chance feeling, wholly undirected by any perception of the real bearings of the matter in hand. *PMG*

33:36. ¶ What makes   80

33:38. not of the same kind as ours,   80

34:1. not of the same kind as ours,   80

34:2–3. envy my Orleanist critic, 'Horace,' his   80

34:29–30. Emperor, and to make it useless for them.   *PMG*

34:35. so long as   *PMG*

35:6. I spoil his   *PMG*

35:22. if our economy   *PMG*

35:28. stand in St. Pancras—   *PMG*

35:38. *not in PMG*

36:20. in that letter   *PMG*

36:25. March 19, 1866. MATTHEW ARNOLD | ¶P.S.—It was not from Monsieur Duruy I got that idea about watching to see how the world is going, or, as a classical friend of mine phrases it, how the cat jumps; it was from President Johnson. "I do not assume or pretend that I am stronger than the laws of nature, or that I am wiser than Providence itself. It is our duty to try and discover what those great laws are which are at the foundation of all things, and, having discovered what they are, conform our actions and our conduct to them." He said that to a negro regiment last October. *PMG*

36:26. *not in PMG*

36:27–36. *not in PMG*

[LETTER I]

PMG ' "Geist," ' *Pall Mall Gazette,* July 21, 1866, p. 5.
Ev.Sat. "Geist," *Every Saturday* II, 175–77 (August 18, 1866). Reprinted from *PMG;* not collated.
    Reprinted 71, 83c, 97 (not collated), 03 (not collated).

Title: "Geist." *PMG*
37:1–24. *not in PMG*
37:25. *To the* EDITOR *of the* PALL MALL GAZETTE. | SIR,— *PMG*
38:2–3. though, as a seeker of truth, I value his frankness, as an Englishman *PMG*
38:14. way, I think), a *PMG*
38:17–18. first bloodshed in Germany. *PMG*
38:27. Gladstone's advice *PMG*
39:5. going all through *PMG*
39:6. make the envy and vindictiveness in what *PMG*
39:7. incredible. *PMG*   15
39:14. are then to *PMG*
40:1–2. let us. But why are France and Germany to tear one another to pieces? Why are England and Germany to unite against *PMG*
40:4. actual Germany, what the ground of antipathy between actual Germany and actual France?" *PMG*   20
40:26–27. sympathy with that firm believer in democracy, the Emperor of the French. We have no *PMG*
40:37–38. Europe hate the Emperor *PMG*
40:38–41:2. envy his strength, . . . his principles; they hate the Sovereign who *PMG*   25
41:10. making the people *PMG*
41:11. in them, and by making good and rational administration do all it can for them. We *PMG*
41:22–23. won the battle for *PMG*   30
41:28. none. Prussia and France will neither of them, for your benefit, go counter to the current of forces which is driving the world. The French Emperor will not, to keep an isolated superiority which does him no real good, tie himself to a corpse to fight a living Germany. Germany will not, to revive the Marquis 35
of Granby, alienate or put to straits the representative of French democracy. There will be a great France and a great Germany;

they will be good friends, and they will have the pleasure of admiring together the happiness of Ireland, the effectiveness of your
administration, and the insight of such people as your friend of
the bottles. *PMG*

41:31–39. *not in PMG*

42:24. *not in PMG, which has date here:* July 19, 1866.

[LETTER II]

PMG "Democracy," *Pall Mall Gazette*, August 4, 1866, pp. 4–5.
   Reprinted 71, 83c, 97 (not collated), 03 (not collated).

Title: Democracy. *PMG*

43:1. *not in PMG*

43:2. *To the* EDITOR *of the* PALL MALL GAZETTE. | SIR,— *PMG*

43:15. begins to cry, *PMG*

43:21. running through with *PMG*

43:28–29. *not in PMG*

44:5. is told of *PMG*

44:9. what then, I ask, *PMG*

44:26. here; you have "kein *PMG*

45:31–32. about. "Nature and reason!" cried the Convention orator,
   "these are my gods;" and these madmen, if you like, sat about
20   remodelling society on the principles of nature and reason. If
   you want to know how they went to work, read the records of
   the National Assembly for one single sitting—the sitting of the
   4th of August, 1789. In that revolution was an "Ernst der ins
   ganze geht," which makes the masses, who have felt it, into a
25   people, and into a power in the world for ever after. They were
   unripe for their task, and yet by the strength *PMG*

45:36–38. *not in PMG*

46:7. above it corrupt; because *PMG*

46:18–19. German way, by every man *PMG*

30   46:21–22. to clap-trap, by culture. I see your Thrasybulus, Mr.
   Bright, before he retired to his Phyle, declared against culture;
   he is for the spiritual *PMG*

46:35–38. *not in PMG*

47:11. *not in PMG, which has date here:* Berlin, July 31, 1866.

[LETTER III]

PMG "An Aggrieved Friend," *Pall Mall Gazette*, August 7, 1866,
   p. 3. Reprinted 71, 83c, 97 (not collated), 03 (not collated).

Title: An Aggrieved Friend. *PMG*
48:1. *not in PMG*
48:2. *To the* EDITOR *of the* PALL MALL GAZETTE. | SIR,— *PMG*
48:13. I don't in *PMG*
49:32–39. *not in PMG*
50:21. him my copy *PMG*
50:23. was that most *PMG*, 71
50:36–38. *not in PMG*
51:10–11. incident, and so I wrote him word. Would *PMG*
51:25. *not in PMG, which has date here: August 6, 1866.*

[LETTER IV]

PMG ' "Ce Dogue," ' *Pall Mall Gazette*, August 15, 1866, p. 3.
Reprinted 71, 83c, 97 (not collated), 03 (not collated).

Title: "Ce Dogue." *PMG*
52:1. *not in PMG*
52:2. *To the* EDITOR *of the* PALL MALL GAZETTE. | SIR,— *PMG*
53:4. so that vulgar dog, Bottles's father, in *PMG*
53:18. for an encounter. *PMG*
53:26–27. most intolerable thing *PMG*
53:27–28. The Emperor distinctly *PMG*
53:29. he must interpose. *PMG*
53:30. profit of a great Power, so *PMG*
53:31. the Emperor to *PMG*
54:19. people too have *PMG*
54:26–28. with ours. Constitutionalism all the world over believes
in mechanical expedients rather than in vital force for giving na- 25
tions strength. Thus, your constitutionalism believes in a ten-
pound franchise or an exemption from church rates. Democracy
believes more in vital force, and with French democracy we can
much easier find ourselves in sympathy and come to an understanding than with M. Thiers or M. Forcade; and as to our consti- 30
tutionalism at home, I have not yet quite faith enough in that to
wish to leave it all our work to do *PMG*
54:34–35. kick to his applicant, who then *PMG*
54:37. of a liberal spirit *PMG*
55:8. wise, and seeing *PMG*
55:13. be moderate enough to give it him. *PMG*
55:27, 30–37. *not in PMG*
56:14. discontent with it was *PMG*

56:26. *PMG dated at end: Berlin, August* 11, 1866.
56:27–32. *not in PMG*

[LETTER V]

PMG "Prussian Tenant-Right," *Pall Mall Gazette*, November 8,
    1866, p. 3.
    Reprinted 71, 83c, 97 (not collated), 03 (not collated).

Title: Prussian Tenant-Right.   *PMG*
57:1. *not in PMG*
57:2. *To the* EDITOR *of the* PALL MALL GAZETTE. | SIR,—   *PMG*
57:27–29. *not in PMG*
58:4. a white moustache   *PMG*
58:25. sound, no faltering,   *PMG*
58:26. excite misgivings in his oracle; like   *PMG*
58:30–31. admit, if it can help it, that   *PMG*
59:36–37. the power of government   *PMG*
60:36–37. late Sir George Lewis   *PMG;* late Sir George Cornwall
    Lewis   71, 83c
61:20. *not in PMG, which has date here: Grub-street, Wednesday
    night,* 11:30 P.M.

[STEIN PLUS HARDENBERG]

PMG "Stein Plus Hardenberg," *Pall Mall Gazette*, November 19,
    1866, p. 3. Not reprinted by Arnold.

[LETTERS VI–VII]

PMG "Von Thunder-ten-Tronckh on Compulsory Education,"
    Pall Mall Gazette, April 20, 1867, pp. 5–6 and April 22, p. 3.
    Reprinted 71, 83c, 97 (not collated), 03 (not collated).

Title: Von Thunder-ten-Tronckh on Compulsory Education.—I
    [II].   *PMG*
65:1. *not in PMG*
65:2. *To the* EDITOR *of the* PALL MALL GAZETTE. | SIR,—   *PMG*
65:13. Hausmannized   *PMG;* Hausmannised   71, 83c; *corrected by
    Ed.*
65:16. this many   *PMG*

65:28. now at breakfast. *PMG*

66:30. his five thousandth. *PMG*

66:36–38. *not in PMG*

67:35. a fit occasion *PMG*

68:2. sighed Arminius. *PMG*

69:21–22. opposition which threw out the education *PMG*

69:23. Act, and paid *PMG*

69:25. he has married his deceased *PMG*

70:33. to the teaching, *PMG*

71:16. peculiarly English *PMG*

71:23–25. ¶Sir, there is an esteemed friend of mine, the Rev. James Fraser, who has convinced himself, after much meditation, that it is the will of God that in England no poor man's child shall stay at school after he is ten years old. And about the education of this poor little shrimp under ten he writes four colossal letters to the *Times*. Positively four bites does my reverend friend take at this very small cherry of his; so, as the midnight oil is beginning to run low, I hope you will not mind if at my much bigger cherry of compulsory education I take a second bite to-morrow. And meanwhile, *PMG*

71:29. *not in PMG, which has date here: Grub-street, Thursday night.*

72:1. *not in PMG*

72:2. *To the* Editor *of the* Pall Mall Gazette. | Sir,— *PMG*

72:5. left it on Thursday night. *PMG*

72:6. continued he, *PMG*

72:19. about its callings. *PMG*

72:23. as magistrates and judging." *PMG*

72:25. a public school and university; Bottles *PMG*

73:7. and something which *PMG*

73:15. British energy *PMG*

73:17. English qualities *PMG*

74:24. eye *PMG*, 71, 83c; *corrected by Ed.*

75:3. thinks of *PMG*, 71; thinks on 83c

75:11–12. this year than last, eh?" *PMG*

76:3. Mr. Frederick Harrison, *PMG*

76:20. *not in PMG, which has date here: Grub-street, Saturday.*

76:21–77:15. *not in PMG*

76:35. *not in PMG*

77:15. the world. A melancholy 71, 83c (*see p.* 313:1)

[THEODORE PARKER]

PMG "Theodore Parker," *Pall Mall Gazette*, August 24, 1867, pp.
11–12. Anonymous. Not reprinted by Arnold.

79:34. first moored *PMG; corrected from Parker*
80:20. loudly entreated *PMG; corrected from Parker*
80:21. whole country *PMG; corrected from Parker*
82:22. all change *PMG; corrected from Parker*

[CULTURE AND ANARCHY]

Cornh.   "Culture and Its Enemies," *Cornhill Magazine* XVI, 36–53
(July, 1867) [pp. 87–114 in this edition]; "Anarchy and
Authority," *Cornhill Magazine* XVII, 30–47 (January,
1868) [pp. 115–36]; XVII, 239–56 (February, 1868) [pp.
137–62]; XVII, 745–60 (June, 1868) [pp. 163–184:9];
XVIII, 91–107 (July, 1868) [pp. 184:10–205:16, 220:16–
221:14]; XVIII, 239–56 (August, 1868) [pp. 205:17–220:16,
221:14–229].

Ev. Sat.   "Culture and Its Enemies," *Every Saturday* IV, 97–105
(July 27, 1867); "Anarchy and Authority," *Every Saturday*
V, 131–39 (February 1, 1868), 262–71 (February 29, 1868),
801–8 (June 27, 1868); VI, 139–47 (August 1, 1868), 257–
64 (August 29, 1868). Reprinted from *Cornh.;* not collated.

69.*   Culture and Anarchy: | an Essay | in | Political and Social
Criticism. | By | Matthew Arnold. | *London:* | *Smith, Elder
and Co.*, 15, *Waterloo Place.* | *1869.* | [*The right of Trans-
lation is reserved.*]
         The earliest appearance of the Preface.

75.   Culture and Anarchy | an Essay | in | Political and Social
Criticism | By | Matthew Arnold | Formerly Professor of
Poetry in the University of Oxford | and Fellow of Oriel
College | *Second Edition* | London | Smith, Elder, & Co., 15
Waterloo Place | 1875 | [*The right of translation is reserved*]

80.   Passages from | the Prose Writings | of | Matthew Arnold |
London | Smith, Elder, & Co., 15 Waterloo Place | 1880 |
[*All rights reserved*]

* For 69 read 1869, etc.

Also issued with the imprint: New York | Macmillan and Co., | 1880

82. Culture and Anarchy | an Essay | in | Political and Social Criticism | By | Matthew Arnold | *Third Edition* | London | Smith, Elder, & Co., 15 Waterloo Place | 1882 | [*All rights reserved*]

Also issued with the imprint: New York | Macmillan and Co. | 1882

83c. Culture & Anarchy | an Essay in | Political and Social Criticism | and | Friendship's Garland | Being the Conversations, Letters, and Opinions | of the Late | Arminius, Baron von Thunder-ten-Tronckh. | Collected and Edited, | with a Dedicatory Letter to Adolescens Leo, Esq., | of "The Daily Telegraph" | By Matthew Arnold | New York | Macmillan and Co. | 1883

89. Culture and Anarchy | an Essay | in | Political and Social Criticism | By | Matthew Arnold | Popular Edition | London | Smith, Elder, & Co., 15 Waterloo Place | 1889 | [*All rights reserved*]

This edition has no textual authority and is not collated.

The following passages appear in 80: 96:31–97:14 (pp. 99–100, headed "Our Coal"); 99:11–27 (p. 101, headed "Sweetness and Light"); 102:10–103:9 (pp. 94–96, headed "The Pilgrim Fathers"); 105:38–107:31 (pp. 71–73, headed "The Oxford Movement"); 112: 13–113:10 (pp. 111–13, headed "The Social Idea"); 122:24–123:12 (pp. 92–94, headed "The Rough"); 124:31–126:3 (pp. 119–21, headed "Aristocracies in Epochs of Expansion"); 131:37–132:22 (pp. 91–92, headed "The Alderman-Colonel"); 135:36–136:29 (pp. 159–60, headed "Revolution by Due Course of Law"); 139:15–142:15 (pp. 84–89, headed "Barbarians, Philistines, Populace"); 145:20–146:21 (pp. 109–10, headed "Humane Individuals"); 153:34–155:12 (pp. 82–84, headed "The Licensed Victuallers"); 163:14–165:35 (pp. 169–72, headed "Hebraism and Hellenism"); 167:30–168:6 (p. 174, headed "Hellenism"); 168:34–170:11 (pp. 174–76, headed "Hebraism"); 174:15–175:32 (pp. 177–79, headed "Hebraism of the English"); 186:14–36 (pp. 98–99, headed "Mr. Smith"); 199:17–22 (pp. 214–15, headed "False Hebraisers"); 216:8–28 (pp. 100–101, headed "Free Trade"); 224:9–33 (pp. 165–66, headed "Anti-Anarchy"); 224:36–225:13 (p. 103, headed "Fire and

Strength"); 226:16–227:6, 227:23–228:3, 228:16–26, 229:9–26 (pp. 104–7, headed "Anti-Politics"); 232:4–233:12 (pp. 317–19, headed "Bishop Wilson's 'Maxims'"); 234:9–235:7 (pp. 17–19, headed "An English Academy"); 239:8–34 (pp. 195–97, headed "Church and Sect"); 243:6–33 (pp. 89–90, headed "America"); 254:23–255:5 (pp. 108–9, headed "Young Liberals"); 255:24–256:4 (pp. 180–81, headed "Future of Hebraism").

P.86, Epigraph. *not in Cornh.*, 69

P.87, Title. Culture and Its Enemies.* [*footnote:*] * What follows was delivered as Mr. Arnold's last lecture in the Poetry Chair at Oxford, and took, in many places, a special form from the occasion. Instead of changing the form to that of an essay to adapt it to this Magazine, it has been thought advisable, under the circumstances, to print it as it was delivered. *Cornh.;   no heading* 69

87:1–2. speeches last year, or the year before last, that famous liberal, *Cornh.;* speeches a year or two ago, 69

87:12. truth which the earlier liberals merely touched the outside of, *Cornh.;* truth of which the earlier Liberals merely touched the outside, 69

87:13. of this university, *Cornh.*

87:19. a possessor of *Cornh.*, 69, 75, 82, 83c; *corrected from MS, 112:1, 133:3, and from Harrison*

88:3. no ¶ *Cornh.*

88:23–25. culture; I have striven to make my whole passage in this chair serve the interests of culture; I take culture *Cornh.*

88:25. culture; I 69

88:37–38. Therefore, as this is the last time that I shall have an opportunity of speaking from this place, I propose to take the occasion for inquiring, in the simple *Cornh.*

89:3. shall try to *Cornh.*

90, Title. *not in Cornh., which marks no division here;* [Part] I. 69

90:10. differing estimate *Cornh.*, 69, 75, 82

90:14. *no* ¶ *Cornh.*, 69; that in English we do not *Cornh.*, 69

90:16. sense: with *Cornh.;* sense; with 69

90:17. sense; a liberal *Cornh.*, 69

90:23. was; its inadequacy consisting chiefly *Cornh.*

91:1. why it is really worthy *Cornh.*

91:4. desire for the *Cornh.*

91:11. ¶Montesquieu *Cornh.*

91:17. ground, though   *Cornh.*
91:19. *no* ¶   *Cornh.*
91:22. of it; a view in which   *Cornh.*
91:24. for stopping human error,   *Cornh.*, 69
91:25. diminishing the sum of human misery,   *Cornh.*, 69
91:28. main and primary part.   *Cornh.*
92:1. *no* ¶   *Cornh.*, 69
92:5–6. conceptions, proceeding from . . . and sharing in   *Cornh.*
92:9. it has worthy   *Cornh.*, 69
92:11. for them; and that, knowing   *Cornh.*, 69
92:12. which are not   *Cornh.*, 69, 75, 82
92:18–19. than the other,   *Cornh.*
92:34. yielded; the danger   *Cornh.*, 69
93:3. prevail in it.   *Cornh.*
93:15. not as the endeavour to merely *see*   *Cornh.*
93:18. learn it for   *Cornh.*, 69
93:20. way for it,   *Cornh.*
93:23. degeneration; but   *Cornh.*
93:34. which culture—seeking   *Cornh.*, 69, 75
93:35. through all [*rom.*] the   *Cornh.*, 69, 75
93:36. upon it, art,   *Cornh.*, 69
93:37. as well as religion,   *Cornh.*, 69
94:3. an internal [*rom.*] condition,   *Cornh.*
94:4–5. animality, in the ever-increasing efficaciousness and in the general   *Cornh.*, 69
94:16. *no* ¶   *Cornh.*, 69
94:22–23. isolated: the individual is obliged, under   *Cornh.*, 69
94:27. thitherward; and . . . it lays   *Cornh.*, 69
94:28–31. as religion. Finally, perfection—as   *Cornh.*
94:31. [*no* ¶] Finally,   69
94:36. Here it goes   *Cornh.*, 69
95:6. liberals suppose, has   *Cornh.*
95:18. an inward [*rom.*]   *Cornh.*
95:21. a general [*rom.*]   *Cornh.*
95:24. himself." The idea   *Cornh.*, 69
95:25. an harmonious [*rom.*]   *Cornh.*; an *harmonious*   69
95:29. to do in   *Cornh.*
95:30. country; and its preachers   *Cornh.*, 69
95:34. persevere; and meanwhile,   *Cornh.*, 69
95:36–37. against, may be made quite clear to any one who will

look at   *Cornh.;* should be made quite clear to every one who
may be   69

96:7. what are religious   *Cornh.,* 69

96:11. have once before noticed   *Cornh.,* 69

96:31. ¶In the same   *Cornh.;* [*no* ¶] And in the same   69

96:31–32. ¶Every one   80

96:33. failure   *Cornh.,* 69, 75, 80, 82; failures   83c

97:3. which, a hundred   *Cornh.*

97:12–13. are and on fixing   *Cornh.*

97:32. call the Philistines.   *Cornh.,* 69

98:11. I have heard   *Cornh.,* 69

98:14. of large families   *Cornh.,* 69

98:20. [*no* ¶] Bodily   *Cornh.;* [*no* ¶] But bodily   69

99:2. assign   *Cornh.,* 69, 75, 82

99:9. *by the way:* [*ital.*]   *Cornh.,* 69

99:11. ¶The Greek   80

99:11–12. words ἀφυΐα, εὐφυΐα, a finely tempered nature, a coarsely
tempered nature, give   *Cornh.,* 69

99:13–14. conceive of it: a perfection in which   *Cornh.,* 69

99:19. εὐφυής, I say, is   80

99:20. ἀφυής is precisely our Philistine.   *Cornh.,* 69

99:28. ¶It is by thus making   *Cornh.,* 69

99:29. perfection, that culture   *Cornh.,* 69

99:30–32. Far . . . us.   *not in Cornh.,* 69

99:32. a more   *Cornh.,* 69

100:5. *no* ¶   *Cornh.,* 69

100:16. paramount; it   *Cornh.,* 69

100:28–29. of the most obvious   *Cornh.*

100:33. perfection. And no   *Cornh.*

100:35. has; for   *Cornh.,* 69

101:3. nothing is more   *Cornh.*

101:6. use concerning   *Cornh.,* 69

101:10–12. itself supplies in abundance this grand language which
is really the severest criticism of   *Cornh.;* itself, I need hardly
say, supplies in abundance this grand language, which is really
the severest criticism of   69

101:17. Puritanism; nowhere   *Cornh.,* 69

101:20. ability, which serves as their organ. The motto   *Cornh.*

101:27–28. judge it: "Finally,   *Cornh.,* 69

101:34. the first faults   *Cornh.*

102:10. ¶Men of   80

102:12. stage to perfection, *Cornh.*, 69
102:13. of the religious   80
102:15. fail: they have often had neither the virtues nor   *Cornh.*;
     fail: they have often been without the virtues as   69
102:19. expense; they   *Cornh.*, 69
102:20. indispensable; they have   *Cornh.*, 69
102:23. beauty and sweetness and   *Cornh.*, 69
102:26. abundantly rewarded.   *Cornh.*
102:35. all round   *Cornh.*
103:11–12. was, a few days ago, giving   *Cornh.*
103:19–20. unattractive, so narrow,   *Cornh.*, 69
103:22. image it,   *Cornh.*, 69, 75
103:30. how many years.... enrolled in some   *Cornh.*
103:35. speak?   *Cornh.*
103:36–37. our *city*, is London!   *Cornh.*
103:38. and its internal   *Cornh.*
104:3. word which   *Cornh.*
104:18. and is wholesomely   *Cornh.*
104:20–21. a more complete perfection.   *Cornh.*, 69
104:36. necessary, and as   *Cornh.*
105:4. *no* ¶   *Cornh.*, 69
105:13. sins. Culture   *Cornh.*
105:25. men are sacrificed.   *Cornh.*
105:26. was necessary   *Cornh.*, 69
105:32. is necessary   *Cornh.*, 69
105:35. is necessary   *Cornh.*, 69
105:38–106:2. *not in Cornh.*
106:2–4. ¶We in Oxford, brought up amidst beauty and sweetness,
     have not failed to seize the truth that beauty   *Cornh.*
106:6. on this truth,   *Cornh.*
106:14–15. advance; but we have told   *Cornh.*
106:15–16. upon literature and upon the mind   80
106:19. shook this place   *Cornh.*
106:28. And what was this liberalism,   *Cornh.*
107:4–5. Lowe or Mr. Bright with   80
107:5. he is so   *Cornh.*
107:5–6. and of whose rule they cry: *Esto perpetua!*   80
107:9. has made its appearance,   80
107:21. movement,   *Cornh.*, 69; movements,   *mispr.* 75, 80, 82, 83c
107:27. under the self-confident   *Cornh.*, 69, 75, 80, 82; under self-
     confident   83c

107:30. may it long   *Cornh.*

107:36. form: we   *Cornh.*

108:6–8. that it is an inward...increased sympathy. [*rom.*] *Cornh.*

108:31. the style   *Cornh.*

108:32. debauch..., and make   *Cornh.*, 69, 75, 82

108:36. Tabernacle   *MS*, 69

109:9. the excellent account   *Cornh.*

109:16. of their own   *Cornh.*, 69

109:27. old acquaintance of   *Cornh.*, 69, 75

109:34–36. Culture...like.   *not in Cornh.* (*see textual note to p. 110:14*)

110:7. no ¶   *Cornh.*, 69

110:10. reconciliation, observes that   *Cornh.*, 69

110:14–20. ideas. In a similar way, culture is always assigning to the system-maker and the system a smaller share in the bent of human destiny than their friends like. ¶Culture feels even a pleasure, a sense   *Cornh.*

110:15–16. the current in human affairs,   69

110:21. by so doing   *Cornh.*

110:22. no ¶   *Cornh.*, 69

111:1. behind Franklin's   *Cornh.*

111:7. of talking wisdom   *Cornh.*, 69, 75, 82, 83c; *corrected from Bentham*

111:12. longer, I   *Cornh.*;   longer; I   69

111:13. for being the rule   *Cornh.*, 69

111:14. no ¶   *Cornh.*, 69

111:14–15. system, with disciples,   *Cornh.*

111:16–17. Mill. It remembers   *Cornh.*

111:20–21. and unreached   *Cornh.*

111:30–33. away with culture, culture with its inexhaustible indulgence, its consideration...its severe...its merciful   *Cornh.*, 69

112:9–10. ¶On this the last time that I am to speak from this place, I have permitted myself, in justifying culture and in enforcing the reasons for it, to keep chiefly on ground where I am at one with the central instinct and sympathy of Oxford. The pursuit of perfection is the pursuit of sweetness and light. Oxford has worked with all the bent of her nature for sweetness, for beauty; and I have allowed myself to-day chiefly to insist on sweetness, on beauty, as necessary characters of perfection. Light, too, is a necessary character of perfection; Oxford must not suffer herself

to forget that! At other times, during my passage in this chair, I
have not failed to remind her, so far as my feeble voice availed,
that light is a necessary character of perfection. I shall never
cease, so long as anywhere my voice finds any utterance, to insist
on the need of light as well as of sweetness. To-day I have spoken   5
most of that which Oxford has loved most. But he who works for
sweetness works in the end for light also; he who works for light
works in the end for sweetness also. He who works for sweetness
and light works to make   *Cornh.*

112:10. sweetness works in the end for light also; he who works   10
for light works in the end for sweetness also. But he who works
for sweetness and light united, works to make   69

112:14–15. has but one great . . . light. Yes, it has one yet greater
—   *Cornh.,* 69

112:22–23. I have again and again insisted   *Cornh.*

112:30–31. the masses an intellectual   *Cornh.*

112:36–38. The religious organizations give an example of this way
of working on the masses. I disparage neither; but   *Cornh.*

113:4. watchwords; but it seeks   *Cornh.*

113:4. with classes and sects;   80

113:4–6. with classes, to make all live in an   *Cornh.,* 69

113:7. light, and use ideas, as   *Cornh.,* 69

113:8. to be nourished   *Cornh.,* 69

113:9. *no* ¶   *Cornh.*

113:19. Ages; and thence   *Cornh.*

113:22–23. were inestimably   *Cornh.*

113:26. yet their names will fill   *Cornh.*

113:28. awaken. Because   *Cornh.,* 69

115:1. [Part] II.   69

115:1. I spoke lately of Culture, and tried to show that it was, or
ought   *Cornh.*

115:4–5. were the main characters. But from special reasons spring-
ing out of the occasion on which I spoke, I insisted chiefly
Cornh.

115:8. perfection; and this I had always the intention, at some convenient time, to do.   *Cornh.*

115:9. [*no* ¶] Meanwhile, both here and   *Cornh.*

115:10. have been raised   *Cornh.*

115:19. critics more familiarly   *Cornh.,* 69

115:29–116:1. it; while   *Cornh.*

116:2. witty rejoinder,   *Cornh.*

116:16. ¶But just one word, first, of self-defence to Mr. Frederic
Harrison and the Comtist body generally, as to my alleged misrepresentations of their revered master. A distinction is to be
drawn, in what I said about the Comtist doctrine and Jacobinism,
5   between what applies to the Rabbi, as I called him, or master, and
what applies to his English disciples. This distinction the disciples
will have no difficulty at all in drawing for themselves, if they
will turn again to what I have said, and will read my words without changing them. For instance, I never said that Comte was
10   "full of furious indignation with the past;" and his followers are
welcome to say, if they like, that Comte "loves and takes counsel
of the past, discards all violent for moral agencies of progress,
and thus exactly contrasts with Jacobinism." But when I talked
of "violent indignation with the past" and the "ways of Jaco-
15   binism," I was speaking of the English disciples of Comte, of some
of their recent manifestoes, and of their way of preaching the
gospel of their master. For example, in that very same powerful
manifesto in which Mr. Frederic Harrison criticized culture, he
spoke of "every hopeful movement being met with the shriek
20   of superstition;" he spoke of the "bigotry of priests and sectaries;"
he spoke of the "ancient iniquities unabated;" he spoke of the
"men who care for public good wearied out or hunted down;"
he spoke of "the 658 well-bred gentlemen of the House of Commons duping the people, degrading their political tone, stifling
25   public activity, zealous for little but their personal ambitions
and class privileges." And then he turned to the working-class
and said:—"Here are the brightest powers of sympathy and the
readiest powers of action!" Now no one admires this vigorous
language, as language, more than I do; but I think it breathes
30   "violent indignation with the past." I cannot admit that it is the
language of one "loving and taking counsel of the past, discard-
ing all violent for moral agencies of progress;" or that it "exactly
contrasts with Jacobinism." On the contrary, it seems to me to be
exactly Jacobinical language, as I called it. Granted that Comte
35   himself had even a "preposterous veneration for the past," then
the English Comtist should be grateful to me for recalling him to
the benevolent ways of his master.

And, perhaps, if I am to be driven to confess it, it was my very
regard for Mr. Frederic Harrison's talents, and my solicitude for
40   his future career, which made me give the English Comtists this
sort of caution. No one knows better than he does that in the

book of the master (Congreve's translation, authorized version),
it is written:—"Every servile or seditious priest who aims at
temporal power by flattering the patriciate or the proletariate
will be absolutely banished from the priesthood." Why am I to
be compelled to publish my own good feelings, and to avow that   5
when I read Mr. Frederic Harrison's strictures on *Our Venetian
Constitution*, the idea rushed into my mind of some enemy, or
rival, bringing up against him this text from the sacred volume,
and charging him with flattering, not certainly the patriciate, but
the proletariate? I figured to myself the odious accusation suc-   10
cessful, the youthful Religion of Humanity robbed of one of its
choicest ministers, and Mr. Frederic Harrison deprived of that
promotion in the Comtist hierarchy to which, I am sure, his zeal
and his abilities abundantly entitle him.

So far as to the English disciples of Comte; now as to Comte   15
himself. What I said about violence applied to the English Comtists and their recent language—language which they themselves,
as they grow in the doctrine of their good master, will no doubt
learn to deplore. But where I touched upon the doctrine itself,
and on Comte, was in speaking of "abstract systems of renovation   20
applied wholesale—a new doctrine drawn up in black and white,
for elaborating down to the very smallest details a rational society for the future." Not a word here as to *violence* or *violent*
revolutions; only a charge of system-mongering and machinery-
mongering on an excessive scale. What I had in my mind was   25
such things as Comte dating a preface the 15th of Dante, 66th year
of the Comtian era, instead of the 30th of July, 1854; dating an appendix the 22nd of Moses, a circular the 27th of Aristotle. It was
such things as his "System of Sociolatry, embracing in a series of
eighty-one annual Festivals the Worship of Humanity under all   30
its aspects," in which the 1st of January that we are now approaching—for old-fashioned Christians the Circumcision, and for
the multitude New Year's Day—becomes the "Synthetical Festival of the Great Being." It was such things as the hierarchy
declared in the sacred volume by the Priest in answer to that im- 35
portant appeal of the Woman:—"This leads me naturally, my
father, to ask you to end this general survey by pointing out the
actual constitution of the Positive Priesthood;"—the philosophical
presbyteries then announced by the Priest, the four national su-
periors for the Italian, the Spanish, the English, and the German 40
Churches, and the High Priest of Humanity, "whose natural res-

idence will be Paris, as the Metropolis of the Regenerated West."
This, and a multitude of other things like this, was present to
my mind when I talked of "abstract systems of renovation, and of
elaborating down to the very smallest details a rational society for
the future." Granted that Comte did not, like the Jacobins, "seek
violent revolutions," still this "Synthetical Festival of the Great
Being," these reformed months and years, are so much in their
style, that I cannot allow that he "exactly contrasts with Jacobinism"; and I should even be inclined, regarding him on this side,
to call him Jacobinical. So much machinery is not to my taste,
who am, as I have said, plain and unsystematic, and who am not
inclined to have given up worshipping on Mount Gerezim or
Mount Moriah, merely to find myself worshipping in the Rue
Monsieur le Prince and the Metropolis of the Regenerated West
instead. And to my countrymen, with their fatal weakness for
machinery, their bent for attaching themselves to this, and losing
all sense, while they so attach themselves, of the spirit and truth
of things, everything excessive in the way of machinery, all that
gives them a chance of forgetting the principal in the accessory,
the end in the means, is particularly dangerous. As they have
been capable of thinking that vital religion was concerned with
keeping the Crystal Palace shut on Sunday, or of thinking that it
was concerned in exploding (through the instrumentality, hu-
manly speaking, of Dr. Colenso) the fallacy of the 88 pigeons, so
they are capable of setting an exaggerated value upon what, in
the Comtist faith, is formal and ceremonial. Over such a result
of "the systematization of ideas conducting" (to use the language
of the master) "to the systematization of sentiments" a people of
our peculiar temperament, every good Comtist would grieve; so
that, here again, the votaries of the new religion have not only
no ground for complaining of my misrepresentations, but have in
truth, if they will consider the thing dispassionately, more reason
to be pleased with me than to be annoyed.

And now, having quite, I hope, cleared away all shadow of misunderstanding between me and the young and powerful school
of Comte's disciples in this country, I pass to my proper subject.
I want to investigate the function of culture in giving us light,
and in doing so to find, as far as possible, a practical side to this
function.

It is said that   *Cornh.*
116:36. and danger to   *Cornh.*, 69
117:3. ¶When last I spoke of culture,   *Cornh.*

118:37–38. upon this class. *Cornh.*

119:17. classes are in *Cornh.*

119:25–26. condition; and *Cornh.*, 69

119:27. less and less trifles, *Cornh.*

119:29. and that somehow or *Cornh.*

119:34. Park *Cornh.*, 69, 75

120:1. says Mr. Hardy, *Cornh.*, 69

120:29–30. affairs, Sir William Page Wood relates *Cornh.*

120:35–36. publications. This bequest was appealed *Cornh.*, 69

121:6. we have thought *Cornh.*

122:3. *no* ¶ *Cornh.*, 69

122:14. this fruitful maxim *Cornh.*, 69, 75, 82; this truthful maxim 83c

122:19. like theirs to rule, and *Cornh.*; theirs. Meanwhile *Cornh.*, 69

122:23. mouths; the rioter has *Cornh.*, 69

122:24. The rough is just 80

122:26. Exactly as the 80

122:33. and if he *Cornh.*

122:35. he cries out that he 80

122:36. is embarrassing, *Cornh.*

123:1. submissive to *Cornh.*

123:2. when he comes, he *Cornh.*

123:16. time; however, *Cornh.*, 69

123:19. may take *Cornh.*

123:25. all, is beginning *Cornh.*, 69

124:10. working class, with its "brightest *Cornh.*, 69

124:11–13. Now, culture, simply trying *Cornh.*

124:15–17. thinking, these three candidates *Cornh.*

124:29–30. must be wanting *Cornh.*

124:31. great requisite, helpless. *Cornh.*

124:33. concentration; in *Cornh.*

125:10. hideousness in the type *Cornh.*

125:12. colours. From such an ignoble spectacle as that of poor Mrs. Lincoln—a spectacle to vulgarize a whole nation—aristocracies 35 undoubtedly preserve us. But *Cornh.*, 69

125:22. [*no* ¶] I have often *Cornh.*; [*no* ¶] One has often 69

125:27–28. Why, you will hear *Cornh.*

125:36. he manages *Cornh.*

126:4. all this while *Cornh.*

126:27–28. to be sadly to seek, as Mr. Frederic Harrison says, in *Cornh.*

126:35. ourselves,—as *Cornh.,* 69

126:36. Lowe's recent great speech we *Cornh.*

126:37. of life with the German waiters, my *Cornh.,* 69

127:5. them Lord Elcho and Sir Thomas Bateson, I *Cornh.,* 69

127:7. that Lord Elcho was *Cornh.,* 69

127:9. Sir Thomas Bateson the excess; and *Cornh.,* 69

127:13–14. hand, in Lord Elcho, showing *Cornh.,* 69

127:19. hand, Sir Thomas Bateson, in *Cornh.,* 69

127:26. honesty; and *Cornh.,* 69

127:27–29. perturbed social state gave me *Cornh.,* 69

127:33. boon culture confers *Cornh.,* 69

128:28. ¶I know, when *Cornh.*

128:29. has now grown *Cornh.*

129:3. *no* ¶ *Cornh.,* 69

15 129:18. *no* ¶ *Cornh.,* 69

130:7–9. man. Mr. Bright's brother, Mr. Jacob Bright, would, perhaps, be more to the purpose; he seems to sum up very well in himself, *Cornh.,* 69

130:12–14. them. Now it is clear, from what has been already said,
20 that there has been at least an apparent want of light in the force and spirit through which these great works have been done, and that the works have worn in consequence too much a look of machinery. But this will be clearer still if we take, as the happy mean of the middle class, not Mr. Jacob Bright, but his colleague
25 in the representation of Manchester, Mr. Bazley. Mr. Bazley sums up for us, in general, the middle-class, its spirit and its works, at least as well as Mr. Jacob Bright; and he has given us, moreover, a famous sentence, *Cornh.,* 69

130:19. education, Mr. Bazley, as the *Cornh.,* 69

130:25. of Mr. Bazley with *Cornh.,* 69

130:26–27. and enhances his claim (if that were necessary) to stand *Cornh.,* 69

131:4. than the Rev. W. Cassel [Cattle 69], a Dissenting *Cornh.,* 69

131:8. Catholics, the Rev. W. Cassel [Cattle 69] exclaimed:— *Cornh.,* 69

131:22–23. handed him down from his pulpit, and kicked him out [of church 69]. *Cornh.,* 69

131:23–24. case of Sir Thomas Bateson, *Cornh.,* 69

131:29. —of kindling a fire which neither *Cornh.*

131:30. easily quench. *Cornh.*

131:32–33. man, Alderman Wilson, Alderman of *Cornh.,* 69

131:37. remembers the virtuous   80
131:38. who had to lead   80
133:12. *no* ¶   *Cornh.*, 69
133:12-13. take, of course, Colonel   *Cornh.*, 69
133:24. Mr. Odger, as in Lord Elcho, there is   *Cornh.*, 69
133:32-33. like Sir Thomas Bateson and the Rev. W. Cassel [Cattle 69], *Cornh.*, 69
134:17-18. wishes of Sir Thomas Bateson;   *Cornh.*, 69
134:19-20. those of the Rev. W. Cassel [Cattle   69];   *Cornh.*, 69
134:21. those of Mr. Bradlaugh.   *Cornh.*, 69
134:28. selves we are   *Cornh.*
134:37-38. culture seeks to develope   *Cornh.*
135:28. manfully, the Rev. W. Cassel [Cattle   69] and the rest of us, according   *Cornh.*, 69
136:12-13. enjoins us to prohibit.   *Cornh.*   15
136:19-21. enable Sir Thomas Bateson to affirm himself as against Mr. Bradlaugh, or the Rev. W. Cassel [Cattle   69] to affirm *Cornh.*, 69; our Tory aristocrat to affirm himself as against our Radical working man,   80
136:21. stablishing   *Cornh.*, 69, 75, 80; establishing   [*in this sentence*   20 *only*]   82, 83c
136:23. reason; and   *Cornh.*, 69
136:26-28. with Sir Thomas Bateson's Protestant ascendancy, or with the Rev. W. Cassel's [Cattle's   69] sorry education of his children, as it deals with Mr. Bradlaugh's street-processions.   25 *Cornh.*, 69; with our Tory aristocrat's prejudices, or with the fanaticism of our middle-class Dissenter, as it deals with our Radical working man's street-processions.   80;
   ¶ But I know that in these humble speculations of mine I am watched by redoubtable adversaries; and—not having the safe-   30 guard of a philosophy with principles coherent, interdependent, subordinate, and derivative—it behoves me to walk with great caution. So I must take a little more time to show in somewhat fuller detail the different ways in which light, that new principle of authority which culture supplies to us, may have a real prac-   35 tical operation upon our national life and society.   *Cornh.*
137:1. [Part] III.   69
137:2. may confess, without   *Cornh.*
137:5-6. I failed to complete   *Cornh.*
137:6-7. analysis which I was attempting, and did not show in *Cornh.*
137:9. matters; still   *Cornh.*, 69

137:16. *no* ¶   *Cornh.*

137:18–19. found in Lord Elcho's chivalrous style, and its excess in
Sir Thomas Bateson's turn for   *Cornh.*, 69

137:24–25. speeches of Mr. Bazley, and   *Cornh.*, 69

137:26. force and that   *Cornh.*, 69

137:27. speeches of the Rev. W. Cassel [Cattle   69],   *Cornh.*, 69

138:3. *no* ¶   *Cornh.*, 69

138:6–7. taking Lord Elcho and Mr. Bazley, the Rev. W. Cassel
[Cattle   69] and Sir Thomas Bateson, to exemplify,   *Cornh.*, 69

138:29. utter defect   *Cornh.*

139:12–13. also to make my nomenclature for them a little fuller,
with a view to making it thereby more clear and manageable.
Cornh., 69

139:17–20. departments,' we have a   80

139:18. as chiefly moving   *Cornh.*, 69

139:19–20. points of Mr. Bazley and the Rev. W. Cassel [Cattle
69], but inclining, in the mass, rather towards the latter than the
former,—for   *Cornh.*, 69

139:24–26. aristocratic class we have   80

139:25–26. points of Lord Elcho and Sir Thomas Bateson, but as a
whole nearer to the latter than the former, we   *Cornh.*, 69

139:32. *no* ¶   *Cornh.*, 69

140:12–13. and the children of light,   80

140:14–15. who prefer   *Cornh.*, 69

140:16. Mr. Murphy and the Rev. W. Cassel [Cattle   69], which
Cornh., 69

140:22. is seduced from   *Cornh.*, 69, 75

140:26. but they are   *Cornh.*, 69, 75, 80

140:28. what is natural.   *Cornh.*, 69

140:30–31. fancy of putting side by side with the idea of our aristocratic class, the idea of *the Barbarians*. The Barbarians   *Cornh.*, 69

141:13. bright complexion   *Cornh.*

141:16–17. fine manners,   *Cornh.*

141:17–18. beautiful commencement   *Cornh.*, 69

141:19. noble one would   *Cornh.*

141:21. of Lord Elcho.   *Cornh.*, 69

141:22. mainly: it   *Cornh.*, 69

141:24. prowess; the   *Cornh.*, 69

141:27. spirit, self-reliance.   *Cornh.*

141:32. thing in our   *Cornh.*

142:3. class, Lord Elcho, was   *Cornh.*, 69

142:6–7. aristocratic class, the one   *Cornh.*, 69
142:12. *Barbarians; and   Cornh.; Barbarians:* and   69
142:18–19. with Mr. Bazley and other   *Cornh.*, 69
143:1. lively and interesting part   *Cornh.*, 69
143:9. real State. That   *Cornh.*
143:29. exists,   *Cornh.*, 69, 75, 82, 83c; *corrected by Ed.*
143:38. entirely Barbarian   *Cornh.*
144:1. the Philistines,   *Cornh.*
144:4. *no* ¶ *Cornh.*, 69
144:9. Philistine—and though,   *Cornh.*, 69
144:13–14. brought any nearer   *Cornh.*
144:29–30. spirit of Lord Elcho, or the eminent power of resistance of Sir Thomas Bateson, but,   *Cornh.*, 69
145:5. untameably?   *Cornh.*, 69
145:15. likes business and   *Cornh.*, 69
145:17. likes trades' unions;   *Cornh.*, 69
145:20. ¶In   80
145:25. make them prevail; for   *Cornh.*
145:37. true characters   80
146:2. tends, as I have said, to   *Cornh.*, 69
146:5. a bad time   *Cornh.*
147:9. people; but   *Cornh.*, 69
147:13. The immortal Martinus   *Cornh.*
147:21. *no* ¶ *Cornh.*, 69
147:22. this; each   *Cornh.*, 69
147:31. to a great number of   *Cornh.*, 69
148:14. none; it   *Cornh.*, 69
148:18. reading last year,   *Cornh.*
148:23–24. it is enough   *Cornh.*
148:26. rifles; that   *Cornh.*
149:11–12. Rolt's Hall   *Cornh.*, 69, 75, 82, 83c; *corrected from Dixon*
149:13–14. the teaching of Plato or St. Paul, Mr.   *Cornh.*, 69; the doctrine of Plato or the following St. Paul, Mr.   *mispr.* 75
149:24. Now as far as   *Cornh.*, 69, 75, 82
149:26. scientific thought of   *Cornh.*, 69
149:32. one of the most significant factors.   *Cornh.*, 69
149:36. which the Rev. W. Cassel exercises   *Cornh.*
150:1–2. treating the Rev. W. Cassel as   *Cornh.*
150:11–12. sphere with which we are at present specially concerning ourselves—the sphere of   *Cornh.*

150:33. *no* ¶   *Cornh.*, 69
151:15. *no* ¶   *Cornh.*, 69
151:22. tyrannical aristocracy,   *Cornh.*
151:25–26. when Sir Thomas Bateson describes   *Cornh.*, 69
151:27. hideous passion for   *Cornh.*
151:37. *no* ¶   *Cornh.*, 69
152:33–34. wants to represent his brother Philistines,   *Cornh.*, 69
153:3. *no* ¶   *Cornh.*, 69
153:6. self-reliance, continually striking out new paths of industry
   and subduing the forces of nature, knows   *Cornh.*
153:14–15. parliamentary representatives,   *Cornh.*, 69
153:34. ¶Every thing   80
154:2. van, to give   *Cornh.*, 69
154:5. *no* ¶   *Cornh.*, 69
154:24. *no* ¶   *Cornh.*, 69
154:29. with the natural . . . bathos uncured;   *Cornh.*
155:9. they are doing   *Cornh.*, 69
155:17. is nothing of the   *Cornh.*
156:2. pretty equal   *Cornh.*, 69
156:7. *no* ¶   *Cornh.*, 69
156:12. come in time   *Cornh.*
156:14. *no* ¶   *Cornh.*, 69
156:22. and beauty of   *Cornh.*
156:24. this sad doctrine   *Cornh.*
157:5. inconvenient now that   *Cornh.*
157:7. *no* ¶   *Cornh.*, 69
157:10–11. here," says *The Times*,   *Cornh.*
157:32–33. reason! Sir Thomas Bateson here, the Rev. W. Cassel
   [Cattle   69] on this side, Mr. Bradlaugh on that! pull   *Cornh.*, 69
157:33. baker! presented   *Cornh.*
158:8–10. honesty, that no class, if it exercise power, having only
   the ideas . . . effect to, shall treat its ordinary   *Cornh.*, 69
158:12–13. others—the Rev. W. Cassel [Cattle   69], for instance, in
   his Papist-baiting, and Mr. Bradlaugh in his Hyde   *Cornh.*, 69
158:23. "You may make   *Cornh.*, 69; "You make 75, 82, 83c
158:35. are inclined to be   *Cornh.*
159:1–3. action, because, as the explorers multiply, the true track is
   more likely to be discovered. The common reason of society can
   check the aberrations of individual eccentricity only by acting on
40   the individual reason; and it will do so in the main sufficiently, if
   left to this natural operation."   *Cornh.*, 69

159:8. individual reason, *Cornh.*, 69
159:19–20. explorers; even in this short paper I have *Cornh.*, 69
159:22. Noyes, the Rev. W. Cassel [Cattle 69], the Licensed
  Cornh., 69
159:23–24. the numbers of this *Cornh.*, 69; the members of the
  75, 82, 83c
159:28. main sufficiently" *Cornh.*, 69
159:33. the Rev. W. Cassel [Cattle 69] comes *Cornh.*, 69
160:2. mind and its inertness, *Cornh.*, 69
160:6. for this charge *Cornh.*, 69
160:7. without full grounds, *Cornh.*, 69
160:11–12. of the Rev. W. Cassel [Cattle 69] or Mr. Bradlaugh
  with *Cornh.*, 69
160:14–15. we have *Cornh.*, 69
160:34. is far better *Cornh.*
160:34–35. In the last number *Cornh.*
161:5. beautiful and perfect *Cornh.*, 69
161:19–20. necessary; and *Cornh.*, 69
161:25. State, the obligatory State-examination for schools, the
  obligatory State-examination for schoolmasters, *Cornh.*, 69
161:28. word of; perhaps he did not know it, it is possible he would
  not have understood it if he had known it. But *Cornh.*
162:2. feel to enable *Cornh.*, 69
162:4. of the keenest of *Cornh.*
162:14. some such public *Cornh.*
162:15–20. reason, as culture leads us to try and embody in the
  State. We see, too, the many inconveniences which come from
  its non-recognition, and the almost fanatical zeal which opposes
  itself to its recognition. These inconveniences and that zeal the
  lover of perfection must make himself thoroughly acquainted   30
  with, in order to see how they may be most fitly dealt with; and
  as we have not yet exhausted the rich varieties of their development, or the lessons they have to teach us, we must return to the
  subject once more before concluding. *Cornh.*
163:1. [Part] IV. 69   35
163:1–2. ¶I come now to the last of those obstacles which our national character and habits seem to oppose to the extrication and
  elevation of that best self, or paramount right reason, which we
  have been led to look for as our true guardian against anarchy,
  and only sound centre of authority at the present time. This   40
  last, and perhaps greatest, obstacle is our preference of doing to

thinking. Now this preference goes very deep, and as   *Cornh.*
163:5. to what I have already quoted from Bishop Wilson:—
   Cornh., 69
163:7. I said we show,   *Cornh.*, 69
163:14–16. the energy ... the paramount ... the earnestness   80
163:17–18. force; and this intelligence driving at the ideas   *Cornh.*
163:19. this ardent   *Cornh.*
163:21. this indomitable   *Cornh.*
164:18. ¶When   80
164:32. of his turn,   *Cornh.*
164:36. misrepresentation; the   *Cornh.*
165:4. difference; the   *Cornh.*, 69
165:7–9. is he;" "There is nothing sweeter than to take heed unto
   the commandments of the Lord;" that is the   *Cornh.*, 69
15   165:16–17. when they turn from their iniquities?—   *Cornh.*
165:18. no; when they lose their life to save it?—   *Cornh.*
165:24–25. God; but   *Cornh.*
165:25. seizes on   *Cornh.*
165:27. to the study   *Cornh.*
165:37–38. Self-conquest, the following   *Cornh.*
166:8–9. by Christ;   *Cornh.*, 69
166:29. They are borne   *Cornh.*
166:32. it;" and   *Cornh.*
166:33. again, Christ   *Cornh.*, 69
167:2. *word, Cornh.; work, mispr.* 69, 75, 82, 83c
167:15–16. law. To St. Paul, it appears possible to "hold the truth
   in unrighteousness," which is just what Socrates judged impossible. The moral   *Cornh.*, 69
167:22. vision; he   *Cornh.*, 69
30   167:33. nature. From   80
168:10. saying runs,   *Cornh.*
168:13. a severe sense   *Cornh.*
168:21. *no* ¶   *Cornh.*, 69; is sin [*rom.*];   *Cornh.*
169:16. bring them   *Cornh.*
169:17. to it. The bright   *Cornh.*
169:20. of all languages of the nations   *Cornh.*, 69, *and Zechariah;*
   of all languages and nations   75, 80, 82, 83c
169:23. and led a   *Cornh.*
169:26–27. Hebraism; Hebraism aiming   *Cornh.*
170:2. For age after   *Cornh.; Throughout age after   69
170:19. braces man's   *Cornh.*, 69

170:29. these great forces *Cornh.*
170:31. all, at *Cornh.*
170:34. no ¶ *Cornh.*
170:38. *not in* 80
171:4–5. showing themselves *Cornh.*
171:15–16. forces which move it, *Cornh.*
171:18. ¶Perhaps this may be made clearer by an *Cornh.*
171:22. idea of the immortality of the soul, as *Cornh.*, 69
171:24–25. satisfying, than the forms by which . . . famous chapter of *Cornh.*
171:27. it. Who does not feel, that *Cornh.*
171:29. is confused and *Cornh.*
171:35–36. And . . . also. *not in Cornh.*
171:37. ¶Meanwhile, *Cornh.*
171:37–38. of man's *Cornh.*, 69
172:6. Renaissance (but why should we not give to this foreign word, destined to become of more common use amongst us, a more English form, and say Renascence?) was *Cornh.*
172:25. written; it *Cornh.*, 69
172:29. Whatever superiority, *Cornh.*
172:33. conscience; its *Cornh.*, 69
172:35–38. *not in Cornh.*
173:12–14. In . . . purged. *not in Cornh.*
173:14. I do not think it has been enough *Cornh.*
173:17. great awakening *Cornh.*
173:38. another; and *Cornh.*, 69
174:4. and of our *Cornh.*, 69
174:27. fruits; undoubtedly *Cornh.*, 69
174:35. no ¶ *Cornh.*
175:3. Hebraism; primitive *Cornh.*, 69
175:24–32. In . . . life. *not in Cornh.*
175:25. habitual courses *MS, Cornh.*, 69, 75, 80; habitual causes 82, 83c
175:27. ourselves; everywhere 69
176:1. *no division Cornh.;* [Part] V. 69
176:4. our present discussion. *Cornh.*
176:7–8. us, to be doing, and to *Cornh.*
176:22–23. important obedience was owed to a power not of this world, and that this power was interested in *Cornh.*
176:22. with their obedience 69; with obedience 75, 82, 83c
176:26–28. strictness of conscience, . . . spontaneity of consciousness, [*rom.*] *Cornh.*

176:29. They think they have in   *Cornh.*

177:11. no ¶   *Cornh.*, 69

177:12. only, or eminently, a   *Cornh.*

177:14. and no less eminently, an   *Cornh.*

177:23. moral side,   *mispr. Cornh.*, 69, 75

177:30–31. state of struggle and confusion is the result.   *Cornh.*

178:4. say (what is   *Cornh.*

178:13. the true, firm, the intelligible law   *Cornh.*; the love of light,
    MS, *Cornh.*, 69

178:22. inasmuch as both rest   *Cornh.*

178:34. no ¶   *Cornh.*

179:7. it; a   *Cornh.*

179:16. show, and arrived—   *Cornh.*, 69

180:1. no ¶   *Cornh.*

180:5. for powerful generalisation?   *Cornh.*, 69

180:11. light; but   *Cornh.*

180:15. lecturer, or that the Rev. W. Cattle (for so, I am told, we
    ought to call him, and not Cassel), and his friends,   *Cornh.*;
    lecturer, and the Rev. W. Cattle and his friends,   69

180:18. needful, remains satisfied   *Cornh.*

180:26. need conquering,   *Cornh.*

180:37–38. points, and the real *unum necessarium* is to come there.
    Cornh.

181:12–13. for the Rev. W. Cattle at   *Cornh.*, 69

181:22–23. mechanical, and unlike   *Cornh.*, 69

181:29. give it what it deemed canons   *Cornh.*

181:33. do; and indeed,   *Cornh.*

181:37. entirety—shows that   *Cornh.*, *redundantly*

181:38. in an Epistle of   *Cornh.*

182:1–2. of the immortality of the soul—transcending and spreading
    beyond, so to   *Cornh.*; of the immortality of the soul,—tran-
    scending and overlapping, so to   69

182:4. no ¶   *Cornh.*, 69

182:19. and passing way   *Cornh.*

183:10, 12. of self-conquest and   *Cornh.*

183:25–26. future; but almost as signal as is the   *Cornh.*, 69

184:9. Bible." ¶Having undertaken to recommend culture, the en-
    deavour to follow those instincts which carry us towards know-
    ing things as they really are, towards a full harmonious develop-
40   ment of our human nature, and finding this recommendation
    questioned and spoken against, I have been obliged to show, at

more length than I wished or intended, what are the instincts which seem to make us rather disregard seeing things as they are, and to carry us towards a partial, though powerful, development of our human nature. I have tried to point out that many of us have long followed this second set of instincts too exclusively, 5 and how the time is come to give a more free play to the other set. The test of the insufficiency of the second set by themselves is the number of points in which, professing generally to pursue perfection, they have, after a long ascendancy, left our nature imperfect, and the faulty action, and faulty conception of our 10 rule of action, in which, professing to regard action as all in all, and to have a sure rule of action, they have landed us. In all directions our habitual courses of action seem to be losing efficaciousness, credit, and control, both with others and even with ourselves; we see threatenings of confusion, and we want a clue to 15 some firm order and authority. This we can only get by going back upon the actual instincts and forces which rule our life, getting behind them, seeing them as they really are, connecting them with other instincts and forces, and enlarging our whole view and rule of life. Once more, and for the last time, I must return 20 to the subject, to try and show, in conclusion, how we are to do this.

MATTHEW ARNOLD.

ANARCHY AND AUTHORITY.
(Continued.)

It was all very well to say that we English wrongly imagine happiness to consist in asserting one's personal liberty, doing what one's ordinary self likes, and that all our habits are such as to 25 prevent us from coming at the idea of a high best self, a paramount authority of right reason, and tend to keep strong and unimpaired in us that inborn taste for the bathos which nature herself has implanted in every man's soul. It was not hard to show that in this way we had at last come to a state of things in which 30 the ordinary self, or class spirit, of all the important bodies of men amongst us, and the action in which this ordinary self expressed itself, neither quite satisfied them themselves nor any one else; and how, in this manner, with little belief anywhere in a paramount best self or right reason, and with the principal or- 35 ganisations which embodied, up to this time, our ordinary self, losing their inherited or acquired authority, society was left to every man's mere unorganised impulse to do as he likes, and signs of anarchy and confusion were beginning to make their appearance. But to get at the causes of this mistaken imagination of ours about happiness, and to know how to cure the false habits and the embarrassment which it has created, it was necessary to look at the main impulses which move human nature, and we found that these impulses gathered themselves naturally into two great groups—a group producing a force which may bear the name of Hebraism, and another group producing a force which may bear the name of Hellenism. Then we took notice how exclusively we had been swayed by the force we call Hebraism, and how its unbalanced preponderance had made us cut our being in two, leave one part of it very much unused, and use the other part of it in a blind and extravagant manner.

Now the force   *Cornh.*

184:11. moral force and   *Cornh.*, 69, 75

184:14. to this notion…two, attributing   *Cornh.*

184:19–20. chance; because the characteristic   *Cornh.*, 69

184:21–24. things, and there is no intelligible law of things, things cannot really appear intelligible, unless they are also beautiful. The body is not intelligible, is not seen in its true nature and as it really is, unless it is seen as beautiful; behaviour   *Cornh.*, 69

184:26. beautiful; the same   *Cornh.*

184:27. worship, the same with all the modes in which   *Cornh.*, 69

184:28–29. when one shows what is mean,   *Cornh.*, 69

184:33. Murphy's and the Rev. W. Cattle's, or poetry   *Cornh.*, 69

185:1. *no* ¶   *Cornh.*, 69

185:4. granted; the   *Cornh.*, 69

185:12–13. Hellenism; and have we   *Cornh.*, 69

186:3. circumstances; we   *Cornh.*, 69

186:11. the subordination   *Cornh.*

186:15. company or other,   80

186:36. the one of their two master-   *Cornh.*

186:38–187:1. another master-concern as the second becomes *Cornh.*

187:3. as the first.   *Cornh.*

187:4. *no* ¶   *Cornh.*, 69

187:7. is), and the concern   *Cornh.*, 69

187:15–16. this nobler master-concern, making it stand,   *Cornh.*, 69

187:18. play in amusement, or business,   *Cornh.*, 69

187:24. consciousness, the letting *Cornh.*, 69, 75, 82

188:1. going back upon a fixed *Cornh.*, 69

188:7. Hebraism? And as St. *Cornh.*, 69

188:16-17. of it—even so, when we *Cornh.*, 69

188:33. he exhausted, *Cornh.*, 69

188:37. at all points— *Cornh.*, 69

188:38. activity, and only by *Cornh.*, 69; can rightly *Cornh.*

189:19. *no* ¶ *Cornh.*, 69

189:21-22. success; not *Cornh.*, 69

189:29. *no* ¶ *Cornh.*, 69

189:35. perfection? and this makes our pursuit *Cornh.*, 69; perfection; and this makes the pursuit 75, 82, 83c

189:38. fetish; British *Cornh.*

190:11. *no* ¶ *Cornh.*, 69

190:31. seeking skilfully the *Cornh.*, 69

190:38. authority; we *Cornh.*, 69

191:9. fosters. Proceeding from this idea of the harmonious perfection of our humanity, and seeking to help itself up towards this perfection by knowing and spreading the best which has been reached in the world—an object not to be gained without books 20 and reading—culture has got its name touched, in the fancies of men, with a sort of air of bookishness and pedantry, cast upon it from the follies of the many bookmen who forget the end in the means, and use their books with no real aim at perfection. We *Cornh.*, 69 25

191:18-20. ourselves, whether by reading, observing, or thinking, to come as near *Cornh.*, 69

191:35-36. countrymen to let *Cornh.*

192:1. *no division Cornh.*; [Part] VI. 69

192:3. generalities, but he must *Cornh.*, 69

192:6-10. Therefore I am bound to take [, before concluding, 69] some of the practical operations in which my friends and countrymen are at this moment engaged, and to make these, if I can, *Cornh.*, 69

192:12. *no* ¶ *Cornh.*, 69

192:12-13. of my inexpertness *Cornh.*

192:22. us just at *Cornh.*, 69

192:28. *not in Cornh.*, 69; 1869 [*bis*] 75, 82, 83c; *corrected by Ed.*

193:3. *no division Cornh.*, 69

193:10-11. forms, with due *Cornh.*, 69

193:14-15. characteristics; and overlooking *Cornh.*, 69

193:25. religion; but   *Cornh.*, 69
193:26–27. religion, and our statesmen   *Cornh.*, 69
193:31. in England the   *Cornh.*
194:1. philosophers, like Mr. Baxter and Mr. Charles Buxton, to   *Cornh.*, 69
194:4. English national   *Cornh.*
194:6. *no* ¶   *Cornh.*, 69
194:7–8. English Nonconformists   *Cornh.*
194:9–10. by Christ when   *Cornh.*, 69
194:25. of the English Nonconformists'   *Cornh.*
194:27. *no* ¶   *Cornh.*, 69
194:31–32. on the English Nonconformists. . . . the English Nonconformists   *Cornh.*
195:6. the English Nonconformists   *Cornh.*
195:29. understanding; nay,   *Cornh.*, 69
195:35. *bulwarks*   *Cornh.*, 69
196:3. it; for   *Cornh.*, 69
196:21. because Christ said: *Cornh.*, 69
196:27. much machinery   *Cornh.*, 69
196:35. that Christ's words   *Cornh.*, 69
197:9. devotion; Christ certainly   *Cornh.*; devotion. Christ certainly   69
197:21. its way *MS,Cornh.*,69;its sway *others; Joubert wrote* insinuée
197:34. *no* ¶   *Cornh.*, 69
197:34–35. to Christ's   *Cornh.*, 69
198:7–8. when, very soon after   *Cornh.*, 69
198:13. that Christ's command   *Cornh.*, 69
198:16. *no* ¶   *Cornh.*
198:22. a true play   *Cornh.*, 69
198:24. Church; thinking   *Cornh.*, 69
198:30. has; it has   *Cornh.*, 69
198:34. *no* ¶   *Cornh.*, 69
198:36. *world;* because,   *Cornh.*, 69
198:37. soul, and   *Cornh.*;   soul; and   69
199:4. satisfies much worse   *Cornh.*, 69
199:8. than Nonconformity.   *Cornh.*
199:26. be not unreasonable   *Cornh.*, 69
200:1. *no division*   *Cornh.*, 69
200:11. fine speaker,   *Cornh.*;   Bright; so   *Cornh.*, 69
200:16. *no* ¶   *Cornh.*, 69
201:1. *no* ¶   *Cornh.*, 69

201:5. about the right   *Cornh.*, 69
201:8. it; or   *Cornh.*
201:36. live; with   *Cornh.*
202:4. *no* ¶   *Cornh.*, 69
202:19. *no* ¶   *Cornh.*
202:20. do [*rom.*]   *Cornh.*, 69
202:23. a really effeminate   *Cornh.*, 69
202:33. real welfare ... real welfare   *Cornh.*, 69
203:4. labours and   *Cornh.*
203:5. it; these   *Cornh.*, 69
203:16. the youth of   *Cornh.*
203:18. struck; how   *Cornh.*, 69
203:25. to their actual effect   *Cornh.*, 69
203:26. can this be   *Cornh.*, 69
203:34. *no* ¶   *Cornh.*, 69
204:3. this desire   *Cornh.*, 69
204:25–26. observation, carries us,   *Cornh.*, 69
205:13–14. strength tear them passionately off it, because it applauded   *Cornh.*, 69
205:16. venal. ¶Here again, then, we seem entitled to conclude that   20
the believers in action are really balked by their practice of
Hebraising too much, and that they ought to be content to let
us Hellenise, and even themselves should try, at the present
moment, to Hellenise too. And it is clear ... [*passage transferred
to p. 220:16–221:6 in 69 etc.*] ... complete human perfection.   25
Thus we shall perhaps praise [¶Thus we may often, perhaps,
praise   69] much that a so-called Liberal thinks himself forbidden
to praise, and yet blame much that a so-called Conservative
thinks himself forbidden to blame, because these are both of
them partisans, and no partisan can afford to be thus disinterested.   30
But we who are not partisans can afford it; and after [and so,
after   69] we have seen what Nonconformists lose by being
locked up in their New Road forms of religious institution, we
can let ourselves see, on the other hand, how their ministers, in
a time of movement of ideas like our present time, are apt to be   35
more exempt than the ministers of a great Church establishment
from that self-confidence and sense of superiority to such a
movement which are natural to a powerful hierarchy, and which
in Archdeacon Denison, for instance, seem almost carried to such
a pitch that they may become, one cannot but fear, his spiritual   40
ruin. But seeing this does not dispose us, therefore, to lock up all

the nation in forms of worship of the New Road type; but it
points us to the new [quite new 69] ideal of combining grand
and national forms of worship with an openness and movement
of mind not yet found in any hierarchy. So, again, if we see what
is called ritualism making conquests in our Puritan middle class,
we may rejoice that portions of this class should have become
alive to the æsthetical weakness of their position, even although
they have not yet become alive to the intellectual weakness of
it. In Puritanism, on the other hand, we can respect that idea of
dealing sincerely with oneself, which is at once the great force
of Puritanism, Puritanism's great superiority over all products,
like ritualism, of our Catholicising tendencies, and also an idea
rich in the latent seeds of intellectual promise. But we do this,
without on that account hiding from ourselves that Puritanism
has by Hebraising misapplied that idea, has as yet developed
none or hardly one of those seeds, and that its triumph at its
present stage of development would be baneful.

Everything, in short, ... [*transferred to p. 221:7–14 in 69 etc.*]
... time grow. I had fully hoped to bring now to an end all I
have to urge in behalf of this doctrine upon the believers in
action, but, on reflecting, I perceive that one or two of their
choicest practical reforms have escaped my notice; and as, between the high-stepping political writers who deal with the reality
of our stock ways of thinking and acting, and the enchanting
imaginative writers who represent these stock ways of thinking
and acting to us in fiction, there seems by common consent to
be left for the friends of culture a humble place as purveyors of
what is called padding for the magazines, I shall without difficulty, I hope, be allowed to make one more appearance here with
a supply of this modest and unpretending article. | MATTHEW
ARNOLD. *Cornh. The passage "Thus we shall ... would be baneful" was transferred with the rest in 69, omitted thereafter*

205:17. *no division* 69; ¶When once *Cornh.*
205:21. operation of this kind—the *Cornh.*, 69
205:25. *no* ¶ *Cornh.*, 69; Chambers, I think, *Cornh.*, 69
206:17. as a fixed, *Cornh.*, 69
206:29. *no* ¶ *Cornh.*, 69
207:32. feeling, this delicate *Cornh.*, 69
207:38. *no* ¶ *Cornh.*
208:21–22. voice of the divine and *Cornh.*

209:1. *no division Cornh.,* 69;   we seem to minister *Cornh.,* 69
209:11. kind of solemnity; it *Cornh.,* 69
209:11–12. on their lead in *Cornh.*
209:20. *no* ¶ *Cornh.,* 69
209:25. rate, instead *mispr. Cornh.*
210:1. establishments and endowments, *Cornh.,* 69
210:30. the untaxing *Cornh.,* 69, 75, 82; the taxing *mispr.* 83c
211:2. creates such *Cornh.*
211:26. only a day or two ago. *Cornh.*
211:28–213:1. for years. We fix upon *two paras. om. Cornh.*
211:38. *not in Cornh.,* 69;   in 1869. 75, 82, 83c; *corrected by Ed.*
212:5. is just, perhaps, 69
212:20. *no* ¶ 69
212:23. in much greater 69
212:38. *no* ¶ 69
213:18. here comes in our *Cornh.,* 69
213:19. object, and *Cornh.,* 69
213:24. of trade business, *mispr. Cornh.*
213:38. *not in Cornh.,* 69;   in 1869. 75, 82, 83c; *corrected by Ed.*
214:5. ¶We *Cornh.*
214:37. and the beautiful *Cornh.*
215:21–22. our Liberal free-trading friends, *Cornh.*
215:23. of small houses *Cornh.,* 69
215:27. spoken, that culture *Cornh.*
215:29. as real *Cornh.;* general [*rom.*] *Cornh.*
215:33. it; individual *Cornh.,* 69
216:8. ¶All 80
216:24–25. people—one pauper, at the present moment, for every nineteen of us—to the *Cornh.,* 69
216:25. are, I repeat, absolutely 80
216:29. ¶And though Hebraism, following its best and highest instinct, identical, as we have seen, with that of Hellenism in its final aim, the aim of perfection, teaches us this very clearly; and though from Hebraising counsellors—the Bible, Bishop Wilson, the author of the *Imitation*—I have preferred (as well I may, for   35 from this rock of Hebraism we are all hewn!) to draw the texts which we use to bring home to our minds this teaching; yet Hebraism seems powerless, *Cornh.,* 69
216:35. inevitable; but *Cornh.,* 69
217:6–8. happy. Thus *Cornh.*

217:12. paupers; only,   *Cornh.*

217:19. *no ¶   Cornh.*, 69; I remember that the other day a good
Cornh.

218:3. right or   *Cornh.*

218:20. the greater the scale on   *Cornh.*; the larger the scale on
69; the larger scale on   75, 82, 83c

218:20–21. reason's laws   *Cornh.*, 69

218:33. *no ¶   Cornh.*

218:35. can we put it   *Cornh.*

219:3–4. another sort keeps   *Cornh.*, 69

219:14. imprudent and unlucky,   *Cornh.*, 69

219:23. *no ¶   Cornh.*, 69

219:28. humanity; and that for every   *Cornh.*

219:29. and every   *Cornh.*

220:1. when allowed   *Cornh.*

220:3. concerning it; and firmly   *Cornh.*

220:5. condition and to diminish our formidable rate of one pauper
to every nineteen of us than is the Hebraising and mechanical
Cornh., 69

220:7. *no division   Cornh.*, 69

220:16–221:14. And . . . grow.   *follows 205:16 in Cornh.*

220:17. regards this particular operation of theirs last canvassed,
Cornh.

220:18. conservative scepticism; for here   *Cornh.*; Conservative
scepticism; for often   69

220:27. float [*rom.*]   *Cornh.*

221:6. *For passage printed here in Cornh., 69, omitted 75, 82, 83c,
see Textual Note to p. 205:16.*

221:11–12. create a frame   *Cornh.*

221:13. which really fruitful   *Cornh.*, 69

221:15. their impatience . . . reproaches of   *Cornh.*

221:16. and still   *Cornh.*

221:26–27. our commendable interest, but not else. For example,
our [example. Our   69] Liberal friends assure us at the very top
35   of their voices that their present actual operation for the disestablishment of the Irish Church is fruitful and solid. But what if,
on testing it, the truth appears to be that the statesmen and
reasonable people of both parties wished for much the same
thing—the fair apportionment of the church property of Ireland
40   among the principal religious bodies there—but that behind the
statesmen and reasonable people there was, on one side, a mass of

Tory prejudice, and on the other, a mass of Nonconformist prejudice, to which such an arrangement was unpalatable? that the
[Well, the 69] natural way [, one thinks, 69] would have
been for the statesmen and reasonable people of both sides to
have united, and to have allayed and dissipated, so far as they   5
could, the resistance of their respective extremes, and where
they could not, [to 69] have confronted it in concert; but that,
[But we see that, 69] instead of this, Liberal statesmen waited
to trip up their rivals, if they proposed the arrangement which
both knew to be reasonable, by means of the prejudice of their   10
own Nonconformist extreme; and then, themselves proposing an
arrangement to flatter this prejudice, made the [other 69] arrangement, which they themselves knew to be reasonable, out
of the question, and drove their rivals in their turn to blow up
with all their might, in the hope of baffling them, a great fire   15
among their own Tory extreme of fierce prejudice and religious
bigotry, a fire which once kindled may always very easily spread
further? If, I say, on testing the present operation of our Liberal
friends for the disestablishment of the Irish Church, the truth
about it appears to be very much this, then, I think, even on the   20
eve of an election [—even with a triumphant Liberal majority,
69] and with our Liberal friends making impassioned appeals to
us to take a commendable interest in their operation and them,
and to rally round what Sir Henry Hoare (who may be de-
scribed, perhaps, as a Barbarian converted to Philistinism, as I, on   25
the other hand, seem to be a Philistine converted to culture)
finely calls the conscientiousness of a Gladstone and the intellect
of a Bright, it is rather our duty to abstain, and, instead of lending a hand to the operation of our Liberal friends, to do what we
can to abate and dissolve the mass of prejudice, Tory or Non-   30
conformist, which makes so doubtfully begotten and equivocal
an operation as the present, producible and possible. *Cornh.,* 69

222:1. *no division Cornh.; no heading* 69
222:1-5. And ... safety. *not in Cornh.*
222:5. ¶Thus resolutely *Cornh.*
222:13. to make, amidst the stormy agitations and confusions which
seem threatening and thickening around us, the actual *Cornh.*
222:16. *no* ¶ *Cornh.,* 69
222:16-17. much of these agitations is due *Cornh.*
222:22. they long ruled *Cornh.*
223:2. from the tenure *Cornh.,* 69

223:3. administer society, we   *Cornh.*

223:7. With me, indeed, this rule of conduct is hereditary. I remember my father, in one of his unpublished letters, written more
than forty years ago, when the political and social state of the
5   country was gloomy and troubled and there were riots in many
places, goes on, after strongly insisting on the badness and foolishness of the government, and on the harm and dangerousness of
our feudal and aristocratical constitution of society, and ends
thus: "As for rioting, the old Roman way of dealing with that
10   [*that*   69] is always the right one; flog the rank and file, and
fling the ringleaders from the Tarpeian Rock!" And this opinion
we can   *Cornh.*, 69

223:11. hand, and may   *Cornh.*

223:14. and to abstain   *Cornh.*

224:9. *no* ¶   *Cornh.*, 69; ¶Even for the sake of the actual present,
but   80

224:13. makes them   *Cornh.*

224:16. self, and   *Cornh.*;   self; and   69

224:19. and so our   *Cornh.*, 69, 75, 80, 82; and as our   *mispr.* 83c

224:20. Barbarian governors let the Park palings be   *Cornh.*

224:28. Barbarian governors and   *Cornh.*

224:31. Park palings,   *Cornh.*

224:36. ¶It is not   80

225:2. afterwards. How much   80

225:2-3. present difficulties and   *Cornh.*

225:3-4. notion has caused already, and is tending still to perpetuate!   80

225:4. perpetuate; and the true   *Cornh.*

225:7. men to allow their thought and consciousness to play on
their stock notions and habits disinterestedly and freely, and try,
[freely; to get men to try,   69] in preference   *Cornh.*, 69

225:11. with us, and may   *Cornh.*

225:18. for whom ideas   *Cornh.*, 69

225:19. can have   *Cornh.*, 69

225:23. their [*rom.*]   *Cornh.*

225:29. admit the desponding   *Cornh.*

226:1. light, and thus   *Cornh.*;   light; and thus   69

226:2. should no longer   *Cornh.*, 69

226:3. but should be   *Cornh.*, 69

226:4. towards perfection?   *Cornh.*, 69

226:6. *no* ¶   *Cornh.*, 69

226:9. change; but *Cornh.*
226:13. offering us. *Cornh.*, 69
226:16. action permitted *Cornh.*
226:16-17. ¶It is our business, 80
226:23. the Barbarian *Cornh.*
226:24. the Nonconformist *Cornh.*
226:25. of church-rates would *Cornh.*, 69
226:26. ideas than churchmen have of God *Cornh.*, 69
226:34. Alderman-Colonel can say that we 80
227:2. that place, *Cornh.*
227:4. we can content ourselves with it and find *Cornh.*, 69
227:5. not making it *Cornh.*
227:6. us place, *Cornh.*
227:7. And though Mr. Sedgwick *Cornh.*
227:11. but to find the intelligible *Cornh.*, 69
227:18. details, we *Cornh.*
227:22. suppose. And even in education, where our Liberal friends
are now, with much zeal, bringing out their train of practical
operations and inviting all men to lend them a hand, and where,
since education is the road to culture, we might gladly lend them
a hand with their practical operations if we could lend them one
anywhere, yet, if we see that a foreign [that any German or
Swiss or French 69] law for education rests on very clear ideas
about the citizen's claim, in this matter, upon the State, and the
State's duty towards the citizen, but has its mechanical details
comparatively few and simple, while an English law for the same
concern is ruled by no clear ideas [idea 69] about the citizen's
claim and the State's duty, but has, in compensation, a mass of
minute mechanical details about the number of members on a
school-committee, and how many shall be a quorum, and how
they shall be summoned, and how often they shall meet. Then
[meet,—then 69] we must conclude that our nation stands in
more need of clear ideas on the main matter than of laboured
details about the accessories of the matter, and that we do more
service by trying to help it to the ideas than by lending it a hand
with the details. So while Mr. Samuel Morley and his friends
talk of changing their policy on education, not for the sake of
modelling it on more sound ideas, but "for fear the management
of education should be taken out of their hands," we shall not
much care for taking the management out of their hands and
getting it into ours, but rather we shall try and make them per-

ceive that to model education on sound ideas is of more importance than to have the management of it in one's own hands ever
so fully. ¶At this exciting   *Cornh.*, 69
227:27. a sage lover   *Cornh.*
227:28. is the fitting place.   80
227:30. lawyers in search of a post,   80
227:34. been. So   *Cornh.*, 80;   been. Because, so   69, 75
227:37. Parliament; where the   *Cornh.*
228:3. Philistines. Conservatism will   *Cornh.*
228:3–16. Philistines. [*12 lines om.*] But through   80
228:4–5. and Liberalism, that   *Cornh.*
228:9. are the heirs, ... of all that great   *Cornh.*
228:13. no ¶   *Cornh.*, 69
228:15. transformation of all of   *Cornh.*
228:18. their transformation,   80
228:19. grows; in   *Cornh.*
228:20. inevitably, as I have already urged, be   80
228:20–22. strongest, and it may   *Cornh.*
228:22–23. that at present the centre   *Cornh.*
228:29–30. eloquence. Yet Alcibiades declares that   *Cornh.*
228:33. talk, with   *Cornh.*
228:35. Socrates is poisoned and dead;   *Cornh.*, 69, 75
228:36. breast every man carries about   *Cornh.*
229:10. taking; Mr.   *Cornh.*
229:13. ourselves; but   *Cornh.*
229:15. things, that the detaching   *Cornh.*
229:17. a desire for   *Cornh.*
229:18–19. -impulse now   *Cornh.*, 69
229:20. for this moment,   *Cornh.*, 69
229:20–21. decisively for the   *Cornh.*, 69
229:23. no ¶   *Cornh.*, 69, 80
229:24. will, they are going   *Cornh.*, 69
229:27–28. the same fortune,   *Cornh.*, 69; they would have   *Cornh.*
229:30. ours; but   *Cornh.*
229:30–31. way the world is going,   *Cornh.*, 69
231, title.   *date not in* 69
231:6. familiar; but   69
231:21. In old times   69
231:22. *Christianity;* the   69
231:28–29. *not in* 69

232:4. ¶Bishop Wilson's 'Maxims of Piety and Christianity' deserve
    80
232:6. this sort of designation, 80
232:16. *Privata;* still 69
232:19. speaks only as 80
232:28. of direct religious 80
232:29. doubts 80
232:36–37. done such great 69
233:11. life, and has so faithfully striven to do its allotted 80
233:13. [*no* ¶] But with ardour 69
233:19. impossible; his 69
233:21. charity; his 69
233:29. or out of 69
233:31. To pass now to 69
233:31–32, 234:4. following essay. 69, 75, 82, 83c
234:4–6. essay. I say again here, what I have said in the pages which
    follow, that from the faults and weaknesses of bookmen a notion
    of something bookish, pedantic, and futile has got itself more or
    less connected with the word culture, and that it is a pity we
    cannot use a word more perfectly free from all shadow of re-   20
    proach. And yet, futile as are many bookmen, and helpless as
    books and reading often prove for bringing nearer to perfection
    those who use them, one must, I think, be struck more and more,
    the longer one lives, to find how much, in our present society,
    a man's life of each day depends for its solidity and value on   25
    whether he reads during that day, and, far more still, on what he
    reads during it. More and more he who examines himself will find
    the difference it makes to him, at the end of any given day,
    whether or no he has pursued his avocations throughout it with-
    out reading at all; and whether or no, having read something, he   30
    has read the newspapers only. This, however, is a matter for each
    man's private conscience and experience. If a man without books
    or reading, or reading nothing but his letters and the newspapers,
    gets nevertheless a fresh and free play of the best thoughts upon
    his stock notions and habits, he has got culture. He has got that   35
    for which we prize and recommend culture; he has got that
    which at the present moment we seek culture that it may give
    us. This inward operation is the very life and essence of culture,
    as we conceive it.
        Nevertheless, it is not easy so to frame one's discourse concern-   40

ing the operation of culture, as to avoid giving frequent occasion
to a misunderstanding whereby the essential inwardness of the
operation is lost sight of. We are supposed, when   69

234:9. because I have   69; ¶Because I have   80

234:13. I want   69, 80

234:14. I have ... that I   69, 80

234:15. thing. But let me   80

234:18. would make us seize,   80

234:19. prevent   80

234:28–29. life, knows   80

234:29. following pages,   69, 75, 82, 83c

234:31. it was already   69

234:32. Stanhope, the Bishop   69; Stanhope,[1] [*footnote*][1] The late
Lord Stanhope.   80

234:38. *not in* 69

235:7–8. faults, shows us this   69

235:8. as truly. ¶It is by a like sort of misunderstanding, again, that
Mr. Oscar Browning, one of the assistant-masters at Eton, takes
up in the *Quarterly Review* the cudgels for Eton, as if I had
attacked Eton, because I have said, in a book about foreign
schools, that a man may well prefer to teach his three or four
hours a day without keeping a boarding-house; and that there
are great dangers in cramming little boys of eight or ten and
making them compete for an object of great value to their parents; and, again, that the manufacture and supply of school-
books, in England, much needs regulation by some competent
authority. Mr. Oscar Browning gives us to understand that at
Eton he and others, with perfect satisfaction to themselves and
the public, combine the functions of teaching and of keeping a
boarding-house; that he knows excellent men (and, indeed, well
he may, for a brother of his own, I am told, is one of the best of
them,) engaged in preparing little boys for competitive examinations, and that the result, as tested at Eton, gives perfect satisfaction. And as to school-books he adds, finally, that Dr. William
Smith, the learned and distinguished editor of the *Quarterly Review*, is, as we all know, the compiler of school-books meritorious
and many. This is what Mr. Oscar Browning gives us to understand in the *Quarterly Review*, and it is impossible not to read
with pleasure what he says. For what can give a finer example
of that frankness and manly self-confidence which our great public schools, and none of them so much as Eton, are supposed to

inspire, of that buoyant ease in holding up one's head, speaking
out what is in one's mind, and flinging off all sheepishness and
awkwardness, than to see an Eton assistant-master offering in fact
himself as evidence that to combine boarding-house-keeping with
teaching is a good thing, and his brother as evidence that to train   5
and race little boys for competitive examinations is a good thing?
Nay, and one sees that this frank-hearted Eton self-confidence is
contagious; for has not Mr. Oscar Browning managed to fire Dr.
William Smith (himself, no doubt, the modestest man alive, and
never trained at Eton) with the same spirit, and made him insert   10
in his own *Review* a puff, so to speak, of his own school-books,
declaring that they are (as they are) meritorious and many?
Nevertheless, Mr. Oscar Browning is wrong in thinking that I
wished to run down Eton; and his repetition on behalf of Eton,
with this idea in his head, of the strains of his heroic ancestor,   15
Malvina's Oscar, as they are recorded by the family poet, Ossian,
is unnecessary. "The wild boar rushes over their tombs, but he
does not disturb their repose. They still love the sport of their
youth, and mount the wind with joy." All I meant to say was,
that there were unpleasantnesses in uniting the keeping a board-   20
ing-house with teaching, and dangers in cramming and racing
little boys for competitive examinations, and charlatanism and
extravagance in the manufacture and supply of our school-books.
But when Mr. Oscar Browning tells us that all these have been
happily got rid of in his case, and his brother's case, and Dr.   25
William Smith's case, then I say that this is just what I wish, and
I hope other people will follow their good example. All I seek
is that such blemishes should not through any negligence, self-
love, or want of due self-examination, be suffered to continue.
¶Natural, as   69   30
235:16. than either of the two we have mentioned, the   69
235:22. establishments, we are charged with being dreamers of
    dreams, which the national will has rudely shattered, for endow-
    ing the religious sects all round; or we are called   69
235:23-24. Establishment. More than   69
235:30. perfection. Culture,   69
235:31-32. following pages   69, 75, 82, 83c
236:4. all that, in   69;   follows, is   69, 75, 82, 83c
236:19. and develope their   69
236:20. perfectly; and to seek   69
236:22. come across the present operation   69

236:37. stream, like Mr. Baxter or Mr. Charles Buxton, and 69
236:38. turn, like the Dean of Canterbury, seeking 69
237:5–6. way to help Mr. Baxter, and Mr. Charles Buxton, and the Dean of Canterbury, in their labours at once philosophical and popular. 69
237:15. and a full, 69
237:20. has lately written 69
238:9. which seems to 69
238:10. national establishments, 69
238:18. Nonconformists, a provincialism which has two main types, —a bitter type and a smug type,—but which in both its types is vulgarising, and thwarts the full perfection of our humanity? Men of 69
238:28–29. following essay 69, 75, 82, 83c
238:33. them; but 69
239:9. of an Establishment is 69
239:37. with the national Establishment, to 69
240:23–24. For the Rev. Edward White says 69
240:29. *no* ¶ 69
240:32. irritating of responsibilities." 69
241:8. us all in culture and totality; and these are the cure for provincialism. 69
241:12. Bright affirms that, 69
241:20–24. *rom.* 69
241:25. friends of culture 69
241:26. have in his eye 69
241:36. leur faute 69, 75, 82, 83c; *corrected from Renan*
242:22. what manner, 69, 75; what matter, *mispr.* 82, 83c
242:26. following essay 69, 75, 82, 83c
242:27. operating of ours, pursued 69
242:28. as we pursue 69
242:29–30. or, in our own words, a reference of all our operation to a firm intelligible law of things was just 69
242:34. do; and when he says 69
242:37. and that, in culture and 69
243:5. following essay 69, 75, 82, 83c
243:6. ¶Our 80
243:22. in a man 69
243:34. *no* ¶ 69
244:9. mind, his 69
244:18. said, that seemed 69

244:31–32. become secondary matters; and the   69
244:38–245:1. on a provincial misconception   69
245:4. the Rev. Edward White   69
245:15. that culture, and sweetness,   69
245:28. which culture, as I have said, teaches   69
245:35. others would give   69
246:2. and they would   69
246:7. attach itself to   69
246:8. the Rev. Edward White   69
246:10–11. is, as we have seen, devoid   69
246:17. *no* ¶   69
247:2–3. by not one-half of those   69
247:5–6. had just been   69
247:11. successor, the society … to him, and   69
247:12–13. After Hooker's appointment to the Mastership,   69
247:21. all; he   69
247:32. time; but   69
247:37. *not in* 69
249:23. has such strength   69
249:31. by making Churchmen   69
249:33–34. formerly found in … still found in   69
249:38. Presbyterian or Congregational   69
250:1. congregation's power in   69
250:7. a Congregational Church   69
250:10. Then,—through   69
250:17. jurisdiction; and   69
250:26. convictions, while their latitudinarian friends make light of
 it. Not   69
251:1. *no* ¶   69
251:2. climbing towards   69
251:12–13. life. Christianity might have lost herself, if it had not
 been for some such change as that of the fourth century, in a   69
251:23. *no* ¶   69
251:29. Christianity. Even   69
251:30. through the last   69
252:12. ¶All this is true; and yet culture, as we have seen, has more
 tenderness for scruples of the Nonconformists than have their
 Broad Church friends. That is because culture, disinterestedly
 trying, in its aim   69
252:13. sees how worthy   69

252:15–16. of man. And when Mr. Greg, who differs from us about
edification, (and certainly we do not seem likely to agree with
him as to what edifies), finding himself moved by some extra-
neous considerations or other to take a Church's part against its
enemies, calls taking a Church's part *returning to base uses*, culture teaches us how out of place is this language, and that to use
it shows an inadequate conception of human nature, and that no
Church will thank a man for taking its part in this fashion, but
will leave him with indifference to the tender mercies of his Benthamite friends. But avoiding Benthamism, or an inadequate conception of the religious side in man, culture makes us also avoid
Mialism, or an inadequate   69

252:19–20. totality. True, the order and liturgy of the Church of
England one may be well contented to live and to die with, and
they are such as to inspire an affectionate and revering attachment. True, the reproaches of Nonconformists against this order
for "retaining badges of Antichristian recognisance;" and for
"corrupting the right form of Church polity with manifold
Popish rites and ceremonies;" true, their assertion of the essentialness of their own supposed Scriptural order, and their belief in
its eternal fitness, are founded on illusion. True, the whole attitude of horror and holy superiority assumed by Puritanism towards the Church of Rome, is wrong and false, and well merits Sir
Henry Wotton's rebuke:—"Take heed of thinking that the farther you go from the Church of Rome, the nearer you are to
God." True, one of the best wishes one could form for Mr. Spurgeon or Father Jackson is, that they might be permitted to learn
on this side the grave (for if they do not, a considerable surprise
is certainly reserved for them on the other) that Whitfield and
Wesley were not at all better than St. Francis, and that they
themselves are not at all better than Lacordaire. Yet, in spite of
all this, so noble and divine a thing is religion, so respectable is
that earnestness which desires a prayer-book with one strain of
doctrine, so attaching is the order and discipline by which we
are used to have our religion conveyed, so many claims on our
regard has that popular form of church government for which
Nonconformists contend, so perfectly compatible is it with all
progress towards perfection, that culture would make us shy even
to propose to Nonconformists the acceptance of the Anglican
prayer-book and the episcopal order; and would be forward to

wish them a prayer-book of their own approving, and the church discipline to which they are attached and accustomed.

Only not at the price of Mialism; that is, of a doctrine which leaves the Nonconformists in holes and corners, out of contact with the main current of national life. One can lay one's finger, indeed, on the line by which this doctrine has grown up, and see how the essential part of Nonconformity is a popular church-discipline analogous to that of the other reformed churches, and how its voluntaryism is an accident. It contended for the estab-lishment of its own church-discipline as the only true one; and beaten in this contention, and seeing its rival established, it came down to the more plausible proposal "to place all good men alike in a condition of religious equality;" and this plan of proceeding, originally taken as a mere second-best, became, by long sticking to it and preaching it up, first fair, then righteous, then the only righteous, then at last necessary to salvation. This is the plan for remedying the Nonconformists' divorce from contact with the national life by divorcing churchmen too from contact with it; that is, as we have familiarly before put it, the tailless foxes are for cutting off tails all round. But this the other foxes could not wisely grant, unless it were proved that tails are of no value. And so, too, unless it is proved that contact   69

252:24-25. possible, admit Mialism.   69

252:26-27. ¶But now, as we have shown the disinterestedness which culture enjoins, and its obedience not to likings or dislikings, but to the aim of perfection, let us show its flexibility,—its independ-ence of machinery. That other and greater prophet of intelligence, and reason, and the simple natural truth of things,—Mr. Bright, —means by these, as we have seen, a certain set of measures which suit the special ends of Liberal and Nonconformist parti-sans. For instance, reason and justice towards Ireland mean the abolishment of the iniquitous Protestant ascendency in such a particular way as to suit the Nonconformists' antipathy to estab-lishments. Reason and justice pursued in a different way, by dis-tributing among the three main Churches of Ireland,—the Ro-man Catholic, the Anglican, and the Presbyterian,—the church property of Ireland, would immediately cease, for Mr. Bright and the Nonconformists, to be reason and justice at all, and would become, as Mr. Spurgeon says, "a setting up of the Roman image." Thus we see that the sort of intelligence reached by culture is

more disinterested than the sort of intelligence reached by belonging to the Liberal party in the great towns, and taking a
commendable interest in politics. But still more striking is the
difference between the two views of intelligence, when we see
5   that culture not only makes a quite disinterested choice of the
machinery proper to carry us towards sweetness and light, and
to make reason and the will of God prevail, but by even this machinery does not hold stiffly and blindly, and easily passes on
beyond it to that for the sake of which it chose it.

10   For instance: culture leads us to think that the ends   69
252:29. life,—in Ireland the Roman   69
252:30–31.' Anglican Church; and, in England, a Presbyterian or
Congregational Church of like rank and *status* with our Episcopalian one. It leads us to think that we should really,   69
252:33–34. citizens, and Nonconformists,—nay, and Churchmen
along with them,—larger-minded and   69
252:35. men. But undoubtedly   69
252:37–253:5. adopted. It is a . . . like the present. The Churchman
must . . . favour it; and . . . wish still to remain, . . . himself." The
centre of   69
253:5. our instrumental statesmen   69
253:6. temptation, as is shown more at large in the following essay,
in the first place, to "relieve themselves," as *The Times* says,
["] of troublesome and irritating responsibilities"; in the second
place, when they must   69
253:9. possible, with impulsiveness.   69
253:11. thinkers like Mr. Baxter, Mr. Charles Buxton, and the Dean
of Canterbury, to swim with the stream, but to swim with it
philosophically; to call the   69
253:14. expression. A generous statesman may honestly, therefore,
soon unlearn any disposition to put his tongue in his cheek in
advocating these desires, and may advocate them with fervour
and impulsiveness. Therefore a   69
253:19. ¶But to tell us that our fond dreams are on that account
35   shattered is inexact, and is the sort of language which ought to
be addressed to the promoters of intelligence through public
meetings and a commendable interest in politics, when they fail
in their designs, and not to us. For we are fond   69
253:20. own; and we have no doubt that perfection   69
253:23. statesmen. But it can never   69
253:25–26. that culture sticks fondly. It insists   69

253:28. sublime; and   69

253:29. or through a generous impulsiveness, tell them their natural
69

253:31. need for culture to tell   69

253:32. *no* ¶   69

253:36–37. believe, with our pauperism increasing more rapidly than
our population, that they   69

253:37. an heroic,   69

254:11. one pure and Christ-ordained way   69

254:22. to be pliant and easy about   69

254:23. ¶Because   80

254:23–24. machinery is the bane of politics, and an inward   69

254:32–33. reared in Hebraising, could   69

254:33. anything better than a   69

254:34. —for would   69

254:37. before their final   69

254:38. come; but for this conversion   69

255:2. them; no, we must   80

255:3–6. inwardly and cure them of Hebraising. ¶Yet *the days*   69

255:3. Expelled they   75

255:4. Expelled they do not desire   75

255:15. assign them   69, 75; being ready   69

255:16. restore them to the   69

255:16–18. to-morrow. To walk   69

255:24. Hebraism. Sophocles and Plato knew as well as the author   25
of the Epistle to the Hebrews that "without holiness no man shall
see God," and their notion of what goes to make up holiness was
larger than his. But the intense   69

255:24. ¶Hebraism has its faults and dangers; still, the intense   80

255:26–27. his ideal, and which   69   30

255:28. *the substantiation of*   80

255:30. faith in its ideal   69

255:31. idea of holiness enlarges, and our scope of perfection widens
69

255:32–33. shall come   69

[A NEW HISTORY OF GREECE]

PMG "A New History of Greece," *Pall Mall Gazette*, October 12,
1868, pp. 9–10.
    "Curtius's 'History of Greece,'" *Pall Mall Gazette*, April 28,

1871, pp. 10–11; June 4, 1872, pp. 11–12; July 22, 1872, pp. 11–12; March 25, 1876, p. 12.
Anonymous. Not reprinted by Arnold.

264:11. wandering forth of   *PMG; corrected from Curtius*
267:14. graduated off   *PMG; corrected from Curtius*
268:13–14. but what manner   *PMG; corrected from Curtius*
270:20–21. out, to every state of   *PMG; corrected from Curtius*
276:31, 277:34. to govern itself   *PMG; corrected from Curtius*
284:34. purpose of   *PMG; corrected from Curtius*
285:23. were men   *PMG; corrected from Curtius*
286:16. their own faults;   *PMG; corrected from Curtius*
289:38. give it   *PMG; corrected from Curtius*

[OBERMANN]

Acad. [Review of Senancour's *Obermann*], *The Academy* I, 1–3 (October 9, 1869). Not reprinted by Arnold.

[SAINTE-BEUVE]

Acad. "Sainte-Beuve," *The Academy* I, 31–32 (November 13, 1869). Not reprinted by Arnold.

305:19. title-page of   *Acad.; corrected by Ed.*

[FRIENDSHIP'S GARLAND, PART II]

For list of editions see p. 487

[LETTER VIII]

PMG "The Deceased Wife's Sister," *Pall Mall Gazette*, June 8, 1869, pp. 3–4.
Reprinted 71, 83c, 97 (not collated), 03 (not collated)
The following passage appears in 80: 316:37–317:7 (pp. 65–66, headed "Middle-class Macaulayese").

Title. The Deceased Wife's Sister.   *PMG*
313:1–3. *not in PMG; in 71, 83c follows p. 77:15 without break*
313:4. *not in PMG*
313:5. *To the* EDITOR *of the* PALL MALL GAZETTE. | SIR,—   *PMG*
313:7–8. course of treatment,   *PMG*

313:10. does not want *PMG*
313:11. reduced more towards the *PMG*
313:15. which a corner is brought into discussion *PMG*
313:19. been put into *PMG*
313:20. by an event...been witnessing. I think my *PMG*
313:26. sate by my *PMG*
314:3-4. were as bad as possible; *PMG*
314:10. who had had *PMG*
314:10-11. she loved literature even in its humblest *PMG*
314:16. researches about labour *PMG*
314:20. had never *PMG*
314:24. the side of *PMG*
314:27. Bottles, Mary Jane; I never *PMG*
314:28. emotion; and in *PMG*
314:31. fortifies me by remarking that, *PMG*
314:32. affections thus suppressed, *PMG*
314:33. than people might fancy. *PMG*
314:36-38. *not in PMG*
315:7. decisive firmness, *PMG*
315:17. permeated with a shower *PMG*
315:21. in lieu to *PMG*
315:22. apply the usual tests. *PMG*
315:23-24. for Jemima and the other girls? Finally, to take the
    PMG
315:25-27. tribune, John Bright,—if Mr. Chambers's bill were not
    to become law, if they chose *PMG*
315:36. of his assurances *PMG*
315:37. with a rapid *PMG*
316:2. suppose that almost divine man, John *PMG*
316:4-5. I should think *PMG*
316:5-6. or a high-placed *PMG*
316:10. emerged from *PMG*
316:12. so absurdly unpractical *PMG*
316:15-16. introduction of a great name. My friend, who *PMG*
316:21. my imaginative youth; *PMG*
316:26. redouble my forces; *PMG*
316:26-27. the sexual *PMG*
316:28. This great man, *PMG*
316:33-34. am a man of *PMG*
316:35. ¶"Explain *PMG*
316:37. ¶"I call...," said *PMG;* 'You ask me,' said Arminius, 'why

I call Mr. Hepworth Dixon's style middle-class Macaulayese. I
call it Macaulayese because   80

317:10–11. to the circulation   *PMG*

317:11–12. his regenerating idea   *PMG*

317:12–15. insurrection. We have established that   *PMG*

317:19. presents itself to   *PMG*

317:33. thee, friend,   *PMG*

317:36. manner? Why   *PMG*

318:2. are their more   *PMG*

318:7–8. put to the inconvenience of making journeys to Germany,
or to the United   *PMG*

318:11. How long must ideas on this subject be left to be incubated
in   *PMG*

318:14–15. shall be   *PMG*

318:16–17. impotently reflect, as Nick's French friends say, the passions of another   *PMG*

318:19–20. directions we will have freedom.   *PMG*

318:23. We will supplement   *PMG*

[A RECANTATION AND APOLOGY]

PMG "A Recantation and Apology," *Pall Mall Gazette*, August 2,
1869, p. 3. Not reprinted by Arnold.

[MELANCHOLY IF TRUE]

PMG "Melancholy If True," *Pall Mall Gazette*, October 13, 1869,
p. 3. Signed "A Young Lion." Not reprinted by Arnold.

[LETTER IX]

PMG "England's Position," *Pall Mall Gazette*, August 9, 1870, p. 10.
Reprinted 71, 83c, 97 (not collated), 03 (not collated)
The following passage appears in 80: 329:7–331:2, 332:5–
29 (pp. 140–44, headed "Lords Grenville and Granville").

Title. England's Position.   *PMG*

327:1–13, 23–26. *not in PMG*

329:5. that has   *PMG*

329:7 ¶'Your great... "Times,"' said Arminius another day, 'not
80

329:9. duty, to do it justice, it *PMG*
329:11. same, and to *PMG*
329:38. residuum [*rom.*] *PMG*
331:3–4. friend, do not be misled *PMG*
331:6–7. you, it is the holding your notions in this mechanical fashion. Your ruling *PMG*
331:14. you get *PMG*
331:17–18. ways, have unrestricted independence, *PMG*
331:31–32. A newspaper correspondent of your own wrote from *PMG*
331:37–332:1. income-tax, newspaper correspondents *PMG*
332:7. illusions, he *PMG*
332:17. much good *PMG*
332:30. am writing *PMG*
333:16. *not in PMG, which has date here:* Chequer-alley, Monday Afternoon.

[LETTER X]

PMG "The Great Heart of England," *Pall Mall Gazette*, November 21, 1870, p. 4.
　　Reprinted 71, 83c, 97 (not collated), 03 (not collated)
　　The following passage appears in 80: 335:16–337:3 (pp. 144–46, headed "The British Philistine and Continental Governments").

Title: The Great Heart of England. *PMG*
334:1. *not in PMG*
334:2–4. *To the* Editor *of the* Pall Mall Gazette. | Sir,—*Ecce iterum Crispinus!* We had all *PMG*　25
334:6. thinks of it. *PMG*
334:12. to make for *PMG*
335:13. no ¶ *PMG*
335:15–16. Government is nothing; you *PMG*; 'You are … people,' Arminius went on, 'you are represented 80　30
335:34. respectfully with you, when 80
335:38. ignorance [*rom.*] *PMG*
336:10. always think that *PMG*
336:18. it should be *PMG*
336:23. him [*rom.*], poor man. *PMG*
336:24. Napoleon had *PMG*

336:30–31. was treated   *PMG*

336:33–34. articles, and general   *PMG*

338:12. be so,   *PMG*

339:5. and rule admirably,   *PMG*

339:7. "Coerce them," but   *PMG*

339:8–13. Your Government...from your Government.   *not in PMG*

339:16–18. lasts, what your friends must   *PMG*

339:38. *not in PMG, which has date here: Before Paris, Nov. 18.*

[LETTER XI]

PMG "Audi Alteram Partem," *Pall Mall Gazette*, November 25, 1870, p. 4.

Reprinted 71, 83c, 97 (not collated), 03 (not collated)

The following passage appears in 80: 341:1–343:8 (pp. 146–50, headed "The Black Sea Question Illustrated").

Title. Audi Alteram Partem.   *PMG*

340:1. *not in PMG*

340:2. *To the* Editor *of the* Pall Mall Gazette. | Sir,—   *PMG*

340:4. Arminius von Thunder-ten-Tronckh calls   *PMG*

340:12. am nearly besieged   *PMG*

341:1. ¶In my immediate   80

341:3–4. the present difficulty with Russia as to her use of the Black Sea. We all   80

341:4. all market in   *PMG*

341:6–7. Germans, is a gross   *PMG*

341:13. Dennis. It   80

341:17, 23. Rev. J—— B——   *PMG*

341:30–31. but before, during,   *PMG*

341:38. And now comes   80

342:15. enough), that use   *PMG*

342:17. Rev. J—— B——   *PMG*

342:18. *no* ¶   *PMG;* feelings of   80

342:34. But I ask, is   80

342:38. Russia? As Lord Shaftesbury says, a treaty   80

343:6. Rev. J—— B——   *PMG*

343:8. excoriation in   *PMG*

343:24. are the failures   *PMG*

343:25. our great   *PMG*

344:13. have interest   *PMG*
344:18. looks alarmed,   *PMG*
344:31. be) be too much   *PMG*
345:5. *not in PMG, which is dated here: Grub-street, Thursday Night.*

[LETTER XII]

PMG "A Sad Story," *Pall Mall Gazette*, November 29, 1870, p. 3.
  Reprinted 71, 83c, 97 (not collated), 03 (not collated)

Title. A Sad Story.   *PMG*
346:1. *not in PMG*
346:2. *To the* EDITOR *of the* PALL MALL GAZETTE. | MON CHER,—
 PMG
346:21. hair. There was   *PMG*
346:25. these struck   *PMG*
346:25–26. and had gone   *PMG*
347:6. anything for him.   *PMG*
347:10. whispered Arminius, "that   *PMG*
347:20. says Arminius,   *PMG*
347:25. said he;   *PMG*
347:35. Germany [*rom.*],"   *PMG*
348:15. round me in   *PMG*
350:13. *not in PMG, which has date here: Versailles, Saturday Evening, Nov. 26*
350:14–25. *not in PMG*

[DEDICATORY LETTER]

Printed 71, 83c, 97 (not collated), 03 (not collated)
The following passage appears in 80: 354:22–355:3 (pp. 150–51,
headed "A German Lesson").

352:7–8. following letters;   71, 83c
354:22. The last tirade of Arminius to me, before he went off to
 the wars, was this:—'Your newspapers   80
354:23. war between France and Germany is   80

Index

A reference to a page of text should be taken to include the notes to that page.